Popular Mechanics
COMPLETE CAR CARE MANUAL

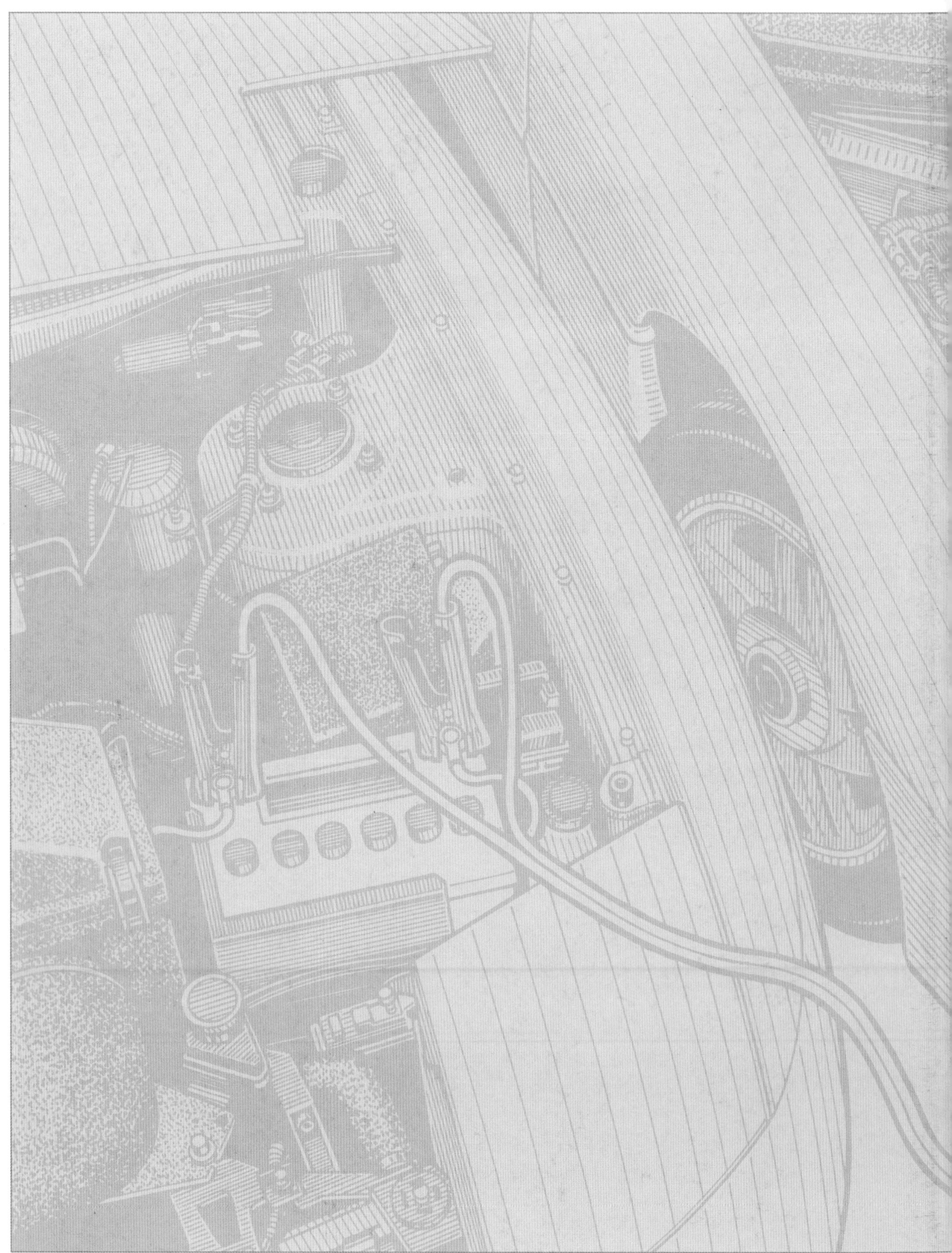

Popular Mechanics COMPLETE CAR CARE MANUAL

Illustrations by
RUSSELL J. VON SAUERS,
RON CARBONE,
AND DON MANNES

HEARST BOOKS
A Division of Sterling Publishing Co., Inc.
NEW YORK

COMPLETE CAR CARE MANUAL

Every effort has been made to ensure that all the information in this book is accurate. However, due to differing conditions, tools, and individual skills, the publisher cannot be responsible for any injuries, losses, and/or other damages that may result from the use of the information in this book.

Produced by Bishop Books
611 Broadway, Suite 308
New York, New York 10012

Library of Congress Cataloging-in-Publication Data
Popular mechanics complete car care manual /
illustrations by Russel J. Von Sauers,
Ron Carbone, and Don Mannes.
p. cm.
ISBN 1-58816-260-5
1. Automobiles--Mainenance and repair--
Amateurs' manuals. I. Popular mechanics.
TL152.P625 2003
629.28'72--dc21 2003050841

10 9 8 7 6 5 4 3 2 1

Published by Hearst Books
A Division of Sterling Publishing Co., Inc.
387 Park Avenue South, New York, NY 10016

www.popularmechanics.com

Distributed in Canada by Sterling Publishing
c/o Canadian Manda Group, One Atlantic Avenue,
Suite 105
Toronto, Ontario, Canada M6K 3E7

Distributed in Australia by Capricorn Link (Australia)
Pty. Ltd.
P.O. Box 704, Windsor, NSW 2756 Australia

Manufactured in China

ISBN 1-58816-260-5

Contents

Foreword

For almost 100 years, the editors of *Popular Mechanics* have made car care and maintenance a central component of the magazine. From the very beginning, we understood just how passionate readers were about their cars, and just how far they would go to protect, repair, and maintain their beloved vehicles. How else to explain an executive trading in his workday suit for a pair of overalls and spending his Saturday afternoons hunkered down under the hood of his car? For some of our readers, saving money is no doubt a major motivation. But for most, working on their cars is a labor of love, pure and simple. That, and they want to make sure the repair is done right. The cars may have changed over the years, but the dedication of readers has been a constant. And *Popular Mechanics* has been a partner all the way, delivering the hands-on information car enthusiasts need to get the job done right.

We understand that the key to any successful piece of advice is clarity. So we strive to make sure our instructions and our illustrations are legible and to the point. We hope you'll find those qualities in evidence in the pages that follow. You'll find chapters on all the basic car components—engine, chassis, electrical system, drivetrain, and interior/exterior—as well as an opening chapter on the essential maintenance information that every owner should know. Each project is labeled "easy," "moderate," or "difficult" to allow you to make your own decision as to whether you have the requisite expertise, not to mention the time and energy, to undertake a given procedure. So, whether you're breaking out the brand-new wrenches from your first tool set, or sliding under a car on your creeper for the umpteenth time, you'll find this book to be an indispensable reference source, packed with easy-to-follow, step-by-step instructions that take the mystery out of auto maintenance and save you money. And, should you decide that a given repair is a bit too tricky for you, the book will arm you with the knowledge necessary to discuss the work intelligently with your professional mechanic.

Our goal is a simple one: We want to provide you with the information you need to keep that treasured car of yours in peak condition regardless of its make, model, or age. We know how much you love your car and how dedicated you are to maintaining it. We're hoping our book provides you with a way to put that dedication into action.

Joe Oldham
EDITOR-IN CHIEF
Popular Mechanics

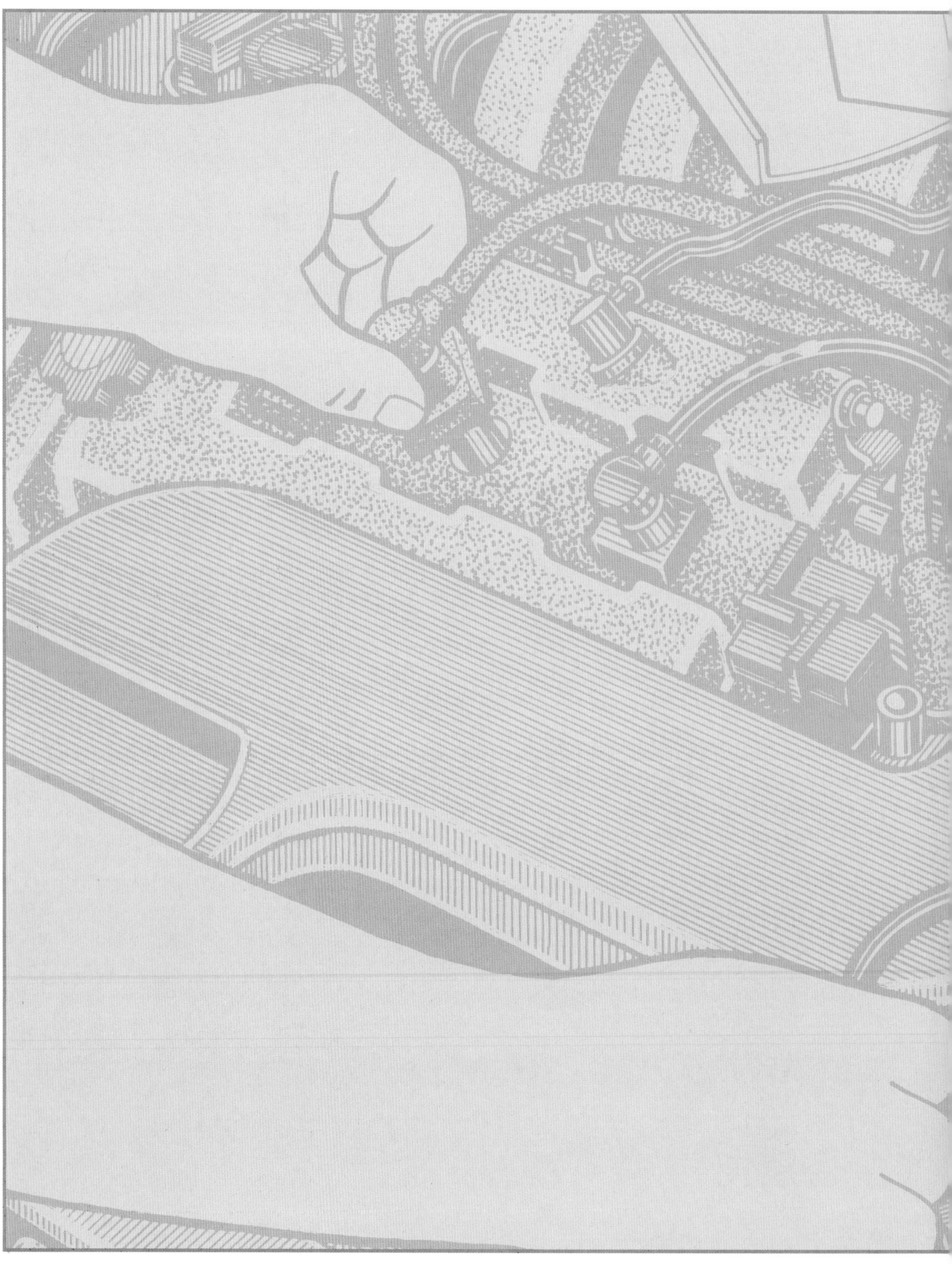

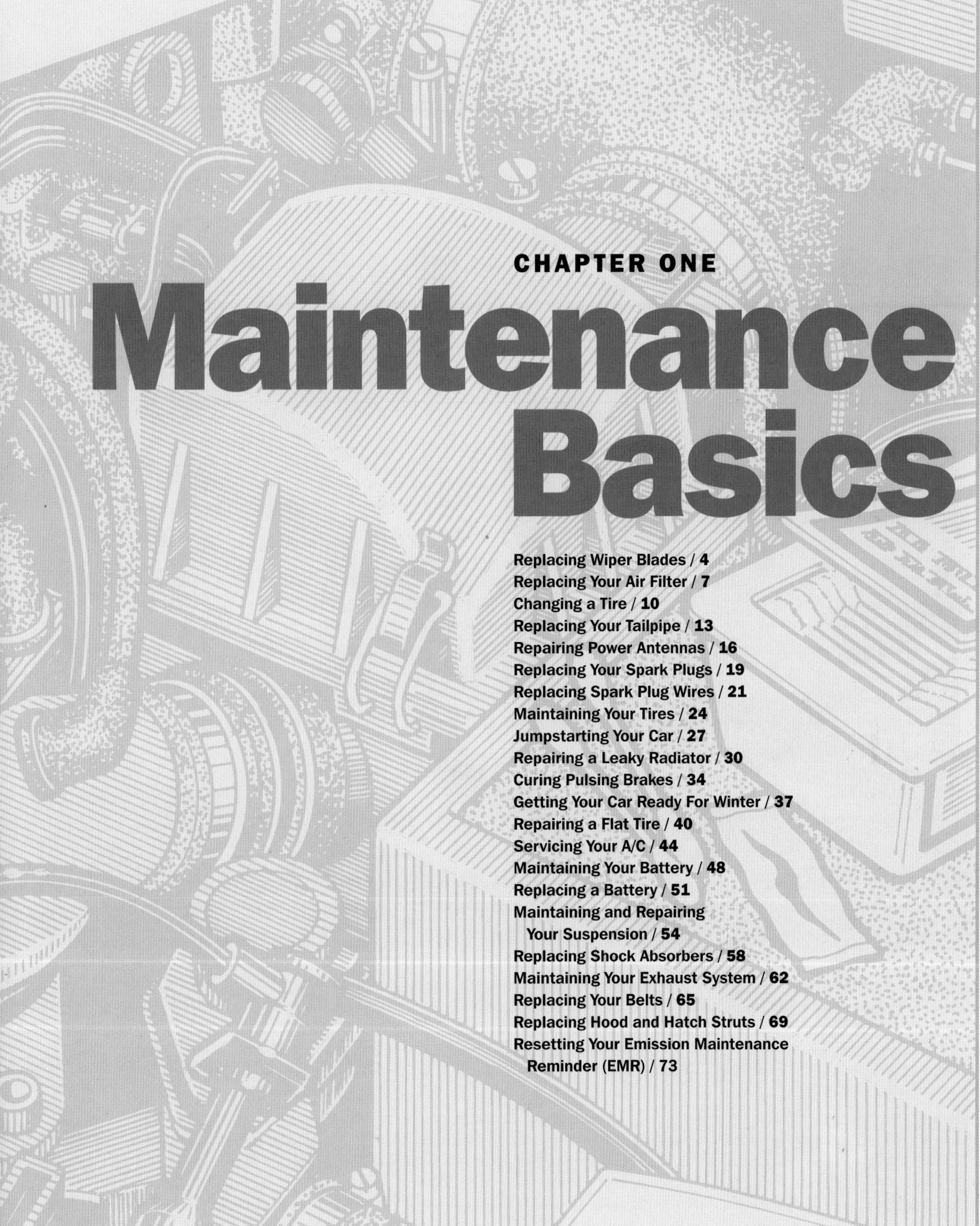

CHAPTER ONE

Maintenance Basics

EASY

Replacing Wiper Blades

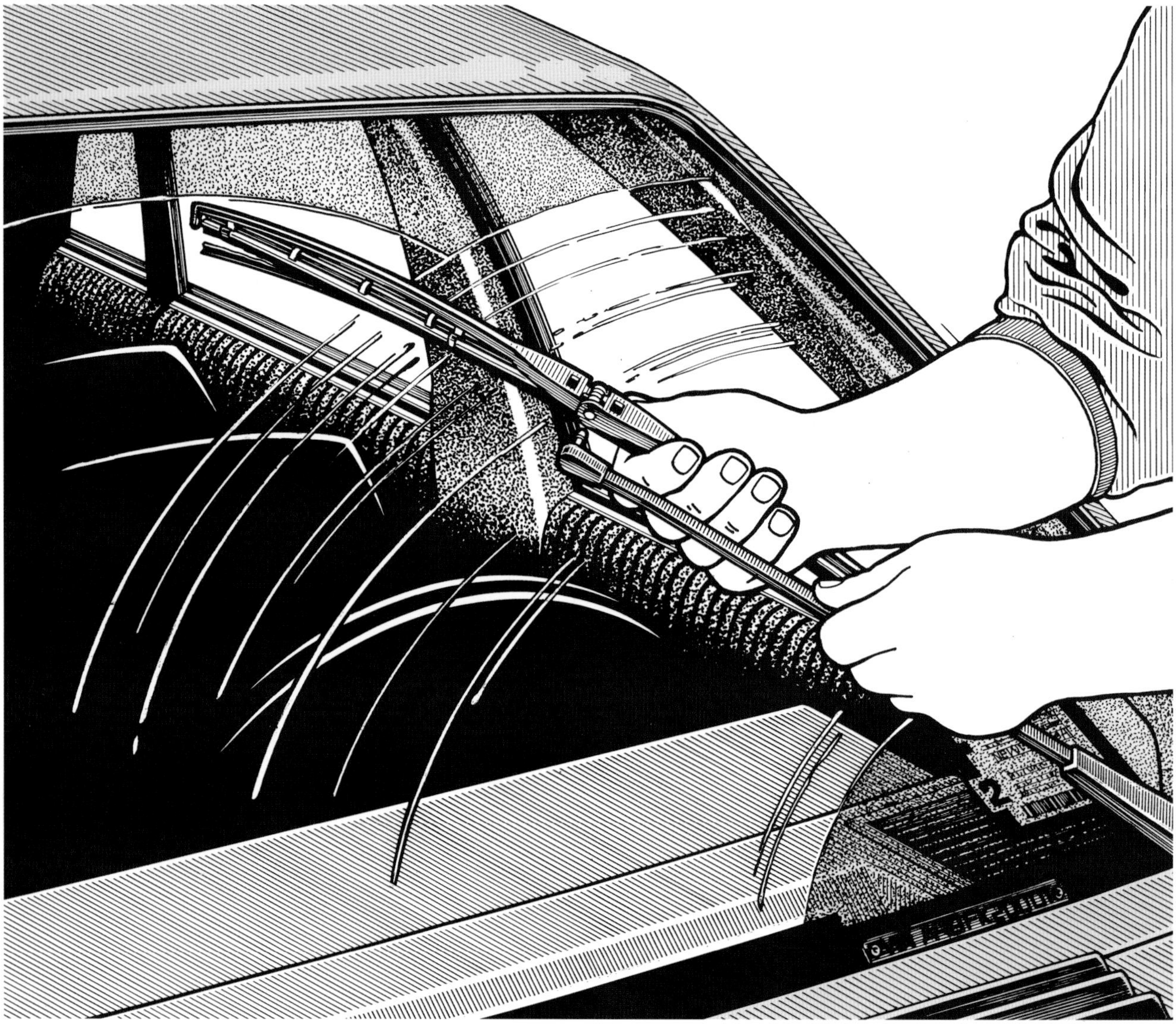

(Fig. 1) In 10 minutes, you can replace your streaky view of the world through a windshield with fresh wiper blades.

Through the monsoonlike rain, you see some sort of flashing lights ahead of you. But despite the best efforts of your windshield wipers, all you can see are blurry blobs of yellow, amber and red. Slowing to half speed, you continue to press forward through the deluge. Suddenly you realize that those flashing blobs are the warning lights of a stopped school bus, and children are running across the road in front of you. Fortunately, your brakes work infinitely better than your windshield wipers.

Once it's dry and sunny again, grab a tape measure and head for the garage. Lift one of the wiper arms (it's usually easier to grab the driver's-side arm) off the windshield against its spring tension and keep lifting until the pivot point locks the arm upright **(Fig. 1)**.

Look for contaminated rubber inserts, which can be caused by road film or car-wash chemical adhesion. Inspect the wiping edges for "park set rubber," the term used to describe hardened finely-cracked inserts that have been exposed to the sun too long in a parked position. This will cause chattering and skipping. Check for a rubber insert that has been partially torn away from its metal support. It will slap the windshield with each wiping pass.

Plain old dried out, cracked rubber inserts mean they've seen better days. You also may find rubber inserts that are abrasion-worn from winter conditions, infrequent car washes and/or a

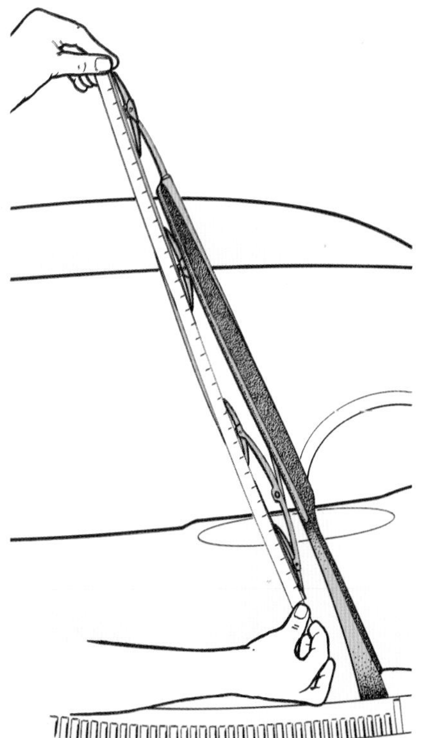

(Fig. 2) Measure your old blades before heading down to the parts store.

lack of preventive maintenance. And rear-window wiper blades are subjected to a lot more road grit than front blades. In the rear, you get aerodynamic backwash, with the rear tires kicking up all sorts of debris. And don't rule out an improperly installed refill. Maybe someone else had tried to replace the inserts before you got to them. Buy a pair of full-blade assemblies to get a factory fit. Also check the wiper arms. If they're okay, proceed to replace the blades.

Blade Runner

But first, measure the length of the wiper blade to the nearest inch (**Fig. 2**). Most vehicles today use blades anywhere from about 16 to 21 in. in length. However, some cars or minivans with very large windshields may exceed that by a few inches.

Parts catalogs, even those for simple items like wiper blades, are full of all sorts of extraneous information. You may find three different types of refills and three different types of blades for almost every vehicle listed.

HOW IT WORKS

Windshield Wipers

As the rubber insert of a wiper blade sweeps across your wet windshield, a wedge of water builds up in front of the rubber—a squeegee effect—and the wiper displaces that water elsewhere. What's left is clean, clear glass that allows you to continue on your way safely. That's the way it's supposed to work. The illustrations to the right show some of the reasons why it may not.

Other reasons may involve components that work behind the scenes—actually, behind the cowl or dashboard of your car. They include the splined shafts that the wiper arms pivot on, the mechanism that creates the back-and-forth pivoting motion and the electric wiper motor that drives the whole system.

A small nut under a cosmetic plastic cover jams the wiper arm onto the splines of its shaft. The splines keep the shaft from slipping in the arm as it turns in one direction and then the other, over and over and over. This reciprocating motion is created by a metal crank-type linkage assembly that's attached to each wiper arm's splined shaft, and to the wiper motor with another splined shaft. Picture the chugging action of a steam locomotive's piston and drivewheels and you'll get the idea.

Rear wipers—found on minivans, SUVs and some sport coupes—work the same way, except the reciprocating mechanism is much smaller and built into the motor.

Wiper speed depends on the amount of voltage that's sent to the motor from the wiper switch—low voltage equals low speed, high voltage equals high speed. Intermittent wiper action is created by a separate electronic module wired between the switch on your dashboard or steering column stalk and the motor. Some cars even have electronically controlled road-speed-sensitive wipers that wipe faster the quicker you go.

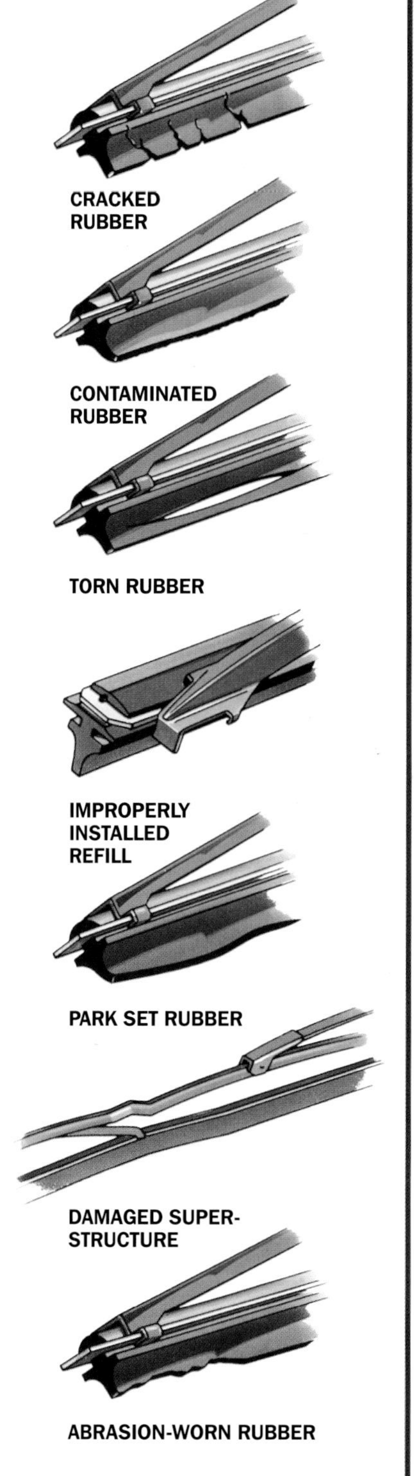

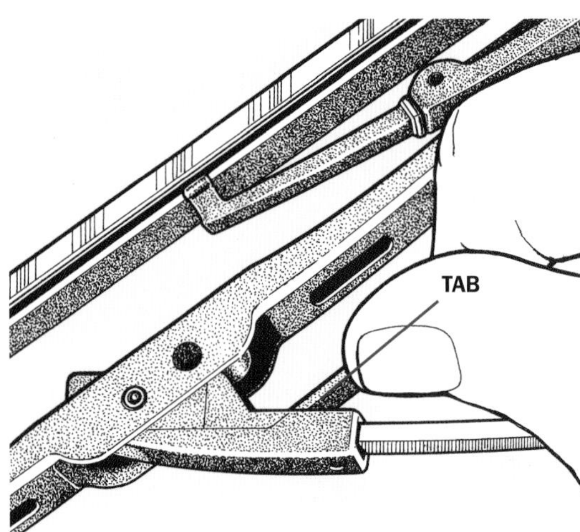

(Fig. 3) Release the tab to disengage the blade from the straightened arm.

If you don't know what brand of blade your car has, don't buy rubber insert refills. The refills may not fit the blades properly, and you'll get lousy wiper performance.

If you do know what brand of blade is currently on the car, refills are okay as long as you buy the same brand and type. Experience has shown that mixing blade and refill brands doesn't lead to optimum wiper performance. But realistically, you're still better off just buying a pair of blade assemblies no matter what the brand. The few extra bucks get you new, matched components that mount quickly and easily.

Fresh Rubber

Now that you've got new blades in hand, it's time to determine what method to use to mount the wiper blade to the wiper arm. There are many variations: hook-slot connector, pin-type arm, wide-straight end, narrow-straight end, side saddle, pin-type blade, narrow-dead locker, flat hook and rock to lock.

At the very least, you'll need a small screwdriver to gently pry the blade off the arm or to unlock a tab of some sort. Sometimes a pair of needle-nose pliers helps too, but the pliers tend to mar the wiper-arm finish more than a screwdriver.

Bear in mind that most wipers will stay raised in an upright position away from the windshield so you can work on them. Others will not. So if this is the case, you'll have to hold the blade off the glass while you work. If your car has wipers that park behind a cowl or the lip of the hood, turn on the ignition, turn on the wipers and then shut off the ignition when the wipers are in midstroke so you can have access to them.

Always remember to lay a clean rag on top of the windshield to protect the glass in case the bare-metal wiper arm suddenly snaps down on the windshield's glass.

For the hook-slot connector, you generally need to raise the arm off the windshield to a working height. Then, swing the blade perpendicular to the arm so that you have more light on the connector. You'll find some sort of tab at the connector that either needs to be lifted or pushed to release the lock that holds the blade pivot in the hook slot. Once the tab is released, a firm shove toward the base of the arm will slide the blade right out of the hook slot (**Fig. 3**). Then, simply line up the new blade's mount (there may be an adapter in the box to create this mount) with the hook slot and slide it in until it clicks. This means it's locked in place.

For the pin-type arm, raise the arm to a working height and take a close look at the type of locking tab that holds the blade onto the pin. You'll either have to push the tab up from underneath the blade or lift the tab from the top with a screwdriver (**Fig. 4**). Once the tab "uncollars" the pin, pull the blade assembly with a sideways motion away from the arm. (Try to imagine pulling the blade up the windshield, to picture the motion.) Depending on the blade manufacturer, the new unit may simply lock onto the pin. Sometimes, the box will contain an adapter that locks into the blade opening and accepts pins in different sizes.

The straight-end connector can be tricky. Sometimes you need to lift a tab on top of the existing blade with a screwdriver to clear the locking nub on the arm. You may also need to cock the old blade a few degrees out-of-parallel with the arm to slide it off the arm's end.

Once the old blade is off, applying a little antiseize compound to the arm's end couldn't hurt. The new blade may come with an adapter to fit the arm's end or it may just slide on. Again, give a firm shove until the blade clicks into place.

If you're replacing a rubber insert, just grab it with needle-nose pliers at the open end. The other end generally has some sort of deadstop that prevents the insert from sliding out. You may need to unlock a tab or squeeze together the locking tangs of the insert before you can begin pulling. Then, just hold the blade firmly while you pull the insert out like a piece of spaghetti. Grab the new insert—make sure that you've got the right end if they're different—line it up with the first set of guides on the blade, then feed it in carefully. Make sure to engage each set of guides as you go. Sometimes there are as many as eight guides. Once the insert is all the way in, make sure it is locked in place.

(Fig. 4) With pin-type wiper blades, push down on the pin lock to release the wiper blade from the wiper arm with a sideways motion.

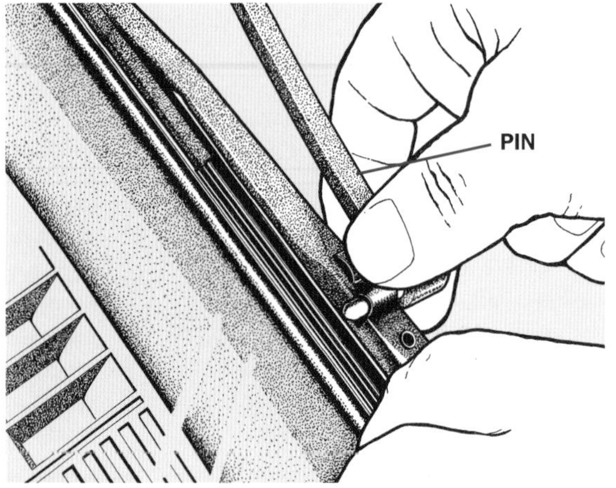

Replacing Your Air Filter

(Fig. 1) **Check your old filter element for dirt, oil or moisture, cracks and proper sealing at the gasket.**

Your mileage has been dropping steadily for months. A tuneup is in order, so a fine Saturday morning finds you on a deserted stretch of road. You figure a few miles of spirited driving should blow out the cobwebs and restore that ponycar performance. But what happens instead is a lot of noise and not much performance at all. Time to check the air cleaner—which is plugged with dirt, bugs and leaves.

Every engine has an air filter, and although there have been many types of air-filtering materials tried over the years—including oil-wetted plastic foams and wire mesh—dry, pleated "paper" (actually resin-impregnated, heat-cured fiber) continues to be the material of choice for filter elements in everything from cars to heavy-duty trucks and off-road equipment.

Housing Project

Check your air filter at least once a year. All air-filter housings are somewhere under the hood (**Fig. 1**). The housing cover may be held by wingnuts or spring clips—pretty straightforward stuff. Separate the cover from the housing and you can lift the filter out for inspection. Many filters, particularly the narrow cylinders used on older rear-drive cars and even on many of today's trucks, can be rotated. If there's a dirty area near the air intake, tap the filter against a table to remove loose dirt, then turn it 180° and expose a fresh surface to

(Fig. 2) **If a conical filter has a dirt buildup on only half the circumference, it can be rotated 180° to equalize dirt pickup, extending service life. Clean the housing's interior before assembly.**

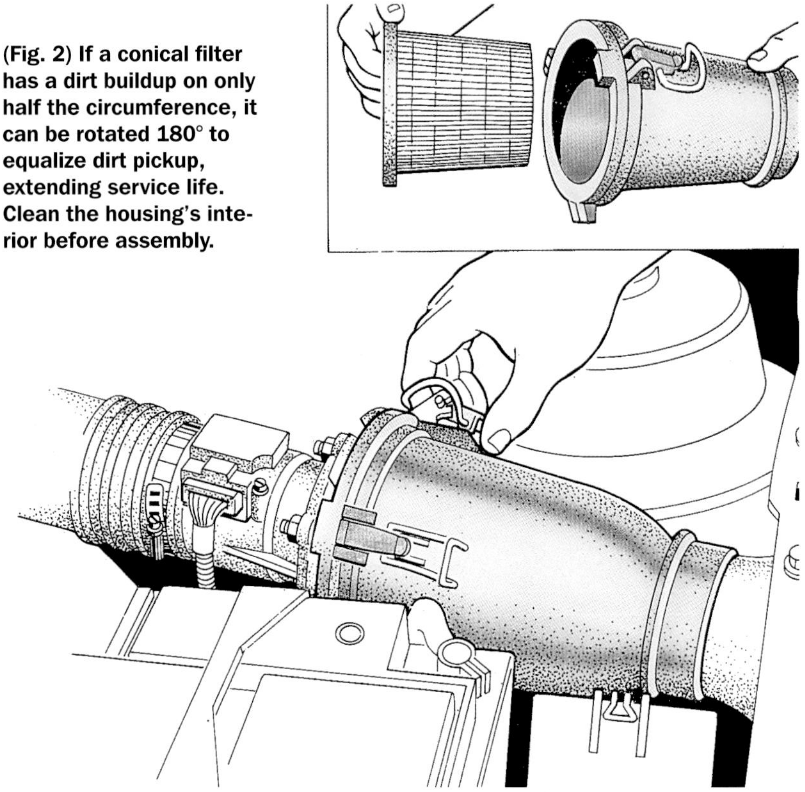

the air intake (**Fig. 2**). Some conical filters also can be rotated, but others can't. Never try to clean a "paper" automotive filter in detergent and water. Some heavy-duty filters are designed to be cleaned several times, but automotive filters are not.

Before you reuse a filter, however, inspect it for cracked pleats. The best way is to hold the dirty side of the filter in front of your eyes with good lighting on the opposite side (with a cylindrical filter, hold a trouble light in the middle of the opening). Of course, you should see some translucence (if you don't, the filter is plugged). But if you see even a single line of light, which indicates a hairline crack, discard the filter. A lot of unfiltered air can get through a crack, and it's the abrasive dust in the air that wears engines. Sure, that wear takes place over time, but if you're in a dusty area that time can be a lot shorter than you'd like.

Buy a quality replacement filter. The top brands are different from the no-name cheapies you may see. There are many grades of filter "paper" and the more expensive ones used by the top brands have more consistent pores, so they do a better job of trapping dirt. In addition, their pleats are more precisely spaced so the filter has the maximum surface area for the size of the housing.

Metering the Air

Just downstream of the filter housing, perhaps connected by a duct, will be the engine's airflow meter, or sensor. (Some engines have no airflow meter. Instead, their computer calculates air intake using rpm, intake vacuum and barometric pressure.) Contamination of the airflow meter will give your engine's computer inaccurate information about the amount (mass) of air the engine is burning. That could mean poor driveability, poor mileage and hard starting.

Don't, however, try to clean the airflow sensor, save for blowing loose dirt and cobwebs with your breath. The calibration of these instruments is fragile, and you stand a good chance of mucking your sensor up irreparably.

Duct Hunting

Before you install the new filter, inspect the duct from the throttle body to the filter housing. Spread the flutes of the duct, looking for cracks. If the duct is cracked, it may be closed at idle but spread on acceleration, when the engine torques. That not only brings in unfiltered air, but on today's engines with mass airflow sensors, the dirty air also is "unmeasured." The amount of fuel sprayed by the injectors is determined by how much air is flowing in, so if some of that airflow isn't measured by the sensor, not enough fuel will be injected. The engine will run lean and hesitate and/or stumble. The same thing can occur if the duct isn't properly fitted and clamped at each end.

Find a crack? Well, it's a duct, so you can repair it with duct tape (**Fig. 3**). That's a move that no professional would make, because in time the tape will lose its grip in the heat of the engine compartment, as the duct flexes. But it's your car, and if you are willing to recheck periodically and retape as necessary, you can save the cost of the new part, or at least postpone the expense.

Fit Is Important

Carefully check the fit between the lips of the housing and the rubber gasket rimming the filter. This gasket not only seals the filter housing's two halves together, but also provides an airtight and dirt-tight seal between the filter and the clean side of the housing. Look carefully at the old filter's gasket. It should show a smooth, clean line 360° around at the sealing face on both sides. The rim of the filter housing will have compressed the rubber gasket if everything is correct. If not, a little detective work is in order. Is the filter the correct part? If not, is your replacement filter the correct part? Don't rely on just a visual comparison—look up the correct part number and cross-reference. Ad it's possible another brand will fit better.

Are all of the spring clamps properly latched? Some air cleaners use screws to hold them shut, while others use a large wingnut. All of the fasteners need to be tight, even that one

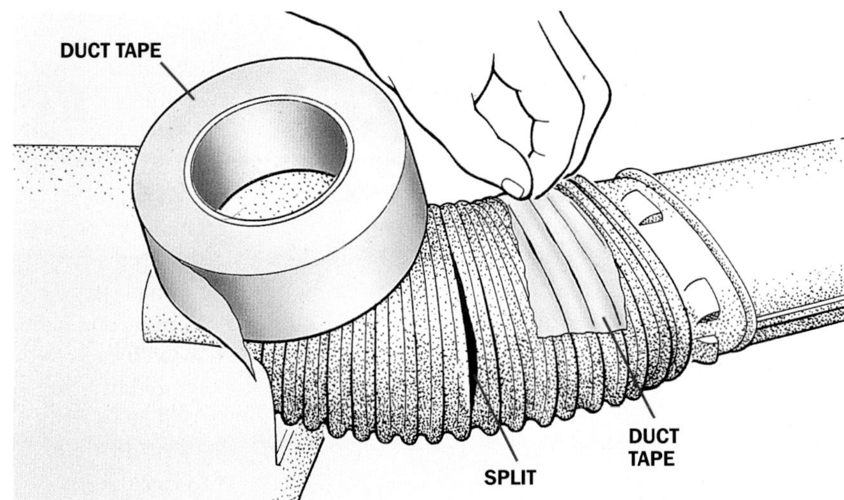

(Fig. 3) Check the air cleaner's ductwork for leaks and splits, especially if you're having driveability problems. Temporary repairs can be made with ordinary duct tape.

you can hardly see or reach next to the battery. On a few vehicles, the housing is attached by a bolt or spring clamp that can be removed to allow the housing to be displaced an inch or two, permitting big hands to fit into a narrow space.

Ready to install the filter element? Clean out the housing first, wiping the inner surface with a cloth lightly moistened with solvent. Insert the element so it seats properly. A filter has a specific side up or toward the throttle body, and you have to install it correctly so the end seal lines up with the shape of the housing or its cover. If it doesn't, you won't get a good end seal, and incoming air may bypass the filter and allow dirt into the engine.

Buttoning Up

It's time to finish up. Install the cover or the halves of the filter housing. In addition to the spring clips and wingnuts that hold the parts together, there also may be alignment tabs in areas you can't reach with your fingers. Be sure the tabs are engaged as you fit the halves together, so the two parts of the housing form an airtight joint when you turn the wingnuts or engage the spring clips.

Be sure that both ends of any ductwork are properly sealed to both the air cleaner body and the airflow meter or throttle body, including hose clamps or retaining clips.

HOW IT WORKS

Your Air Filter

The resin-impregnated, heat-cured "paper" element looks like a pleated sheet, and most of the dirt particles are stopped at the outside surface. A light coating of dirt actually improves the filtering ability of the paper. But soon the dirt builds up and even starts filling the bottoms of the pleats, restricting airflow. The paper also has multiple layers, and if you looked at it under a microscope, it would look like a forest with an irregular criss-cross of vines and limbs—the fiber strands of the "paper."

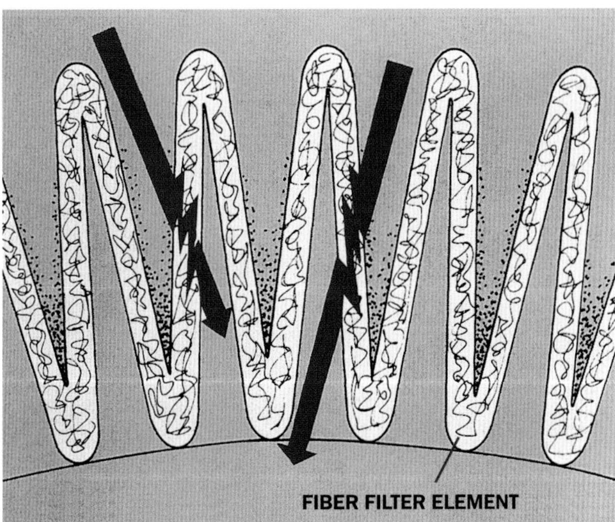

It all looks random, but the premium-priced filter "papers" are more consistent in the sizes of the pores than it seems, and a quality material is a mathematically predictable barrier to dirt particles. In actuality, the layers of fibers form a maze and some of the dirt also is trapped within the layers of the paper. The inrushing air produces some static electricity, which also causes some smaller dirt particles to adhere to the surfaces of the paper fibers.

A point comes when not enough voids remain to pass the air needed to supply your engine. The result is inadequate oxygen to burn the fuel at wide-open throttle. With carbureted engines, this used to mean rich running. Modern fuel-injected engines meter the air admitted to the intake and add appropriate fuel—making for a clean-running engine that eventually won't get out of its own way. At least carbureted cars coughed and sputtered to let you know that you had a problem.

But with today's engines, a filter has to be really bad to restrict acceleration. A bigger hazard is an overloaded filter rupturing and dumping 20 miles of bad road into your engine.

EASY

Changing a Tire

Flat tires are never a fun thing—but this one takes the cake. It's late, of course, and in the middle of a frog-choking rain. You're stuck in the ankle-deep mud on the shoulder of a deserted road. How deserted? Out-of-cell-phone-coverage deserted, or you'd be sitting in the cab of a service truck while somebody else gets drenched. That's how deserted.

Yes, you could drive along the shoulder on the rim for a few miles to civilization, but insurance won't cover the damage to your expensive alloy rim. It's time to knuckle down and put on the spare.

A pressure can of flat-fix foam can get you home if the problem is a simple puncture, and that may be a viable option, especially for smaller individuals or the elderly who would have a tough time changing a tire. Just remember two things: This stuff is a temporary solution, and the flat will need to be attended to by a tire technician at the earliest opportunity. Be sure to warn the technician that you've used this stuff. The propellant is flammable, and unless he's warned, he stands the chance of causing a nasty explosion. Aerosol flat-fix, however, is no help if the problem is a tire unseated from the wheel rim after an encounter with a pothole.

Be Prepared

First of all, remember to check the pressure in your neglected spare tire (Fig. 1) whenever you check the pressure in the other four, which you do faithfully every month or so, right? A flat spare is no help. And if you're like most people who save a plugged or nearly worn tire for the spare, it's likely that the spare has a slow leak, which would leave you stranded.

(Fig. 1) Be sure to check the air pressure in your spare tire periodically.

Furthermore, you'll never be able to change a tire if you don't have the basics—a jack and a lug wrench (Fig. 2). Go back into their hidy-hole and confirm their existence (Fig. 3). While you're there and you have enough light to read the owner's manual, figure out how to unship them and make sure the jack isn't rusted into immobility. Check the manual and find the vehicle's jacking points. You'll probably need to lie on the ground to find them, but this will be a lot more palatable now in your driveway than later on the shoulder of some mud bog.

Grunting Helps

The most common difficulty in changing a tire is lugs that are tightened far too tightly. A casual rattle with a mechanic's air wrench can deliver a tightening torque that only a pro wrestler could remove with the stock lug wrench. Wheel lugs need to be tightened to no more than the manufacturer's recommended torque to ensure they won't loosen. Check your

(Fig. 2) Loosening lug nuts calls for a lot of upper-body strength. An inexpensive 4-way lug wrench can substantially increase your leverage and break loose overly tightened lugs.

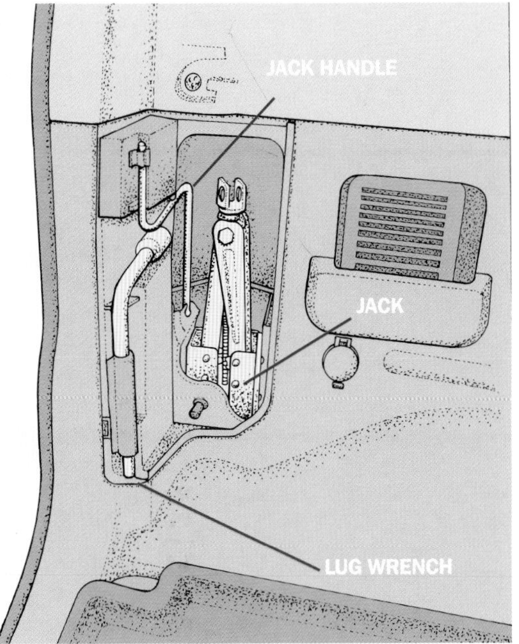

(Fig. 3) Locate the jack and other tire tools and make sure you know how to use them.

(Fig. 4) A cheater bar helps loosen lugs. Never use it to tighten them.

owner's manual, but the figure will be 75 to 100 ft.-lb. of torque. Do the math—that means a 200-pound adult should be able to tighten the lugs by placing all his weight on top of the wrench only 6 in. away from the fastener. A few drops of engine oil or grease on the threads and the lug chamfer (where the lug touches the wheel, not the threads) will prevent galling and seizing.

When removing a wheel, first loosen all of the lugs in a crisscross pattern a half-turn or so. It may be necessary to use the mechanic's favorite cheater bar (Fig. 4)—a piece of water pipe or thick wall pipe about 4 ft. long—to add enough leverage to break the lugs loose. Remove them one at a time and lube them if they squeak. Retighten them in three stages, again in a crisscross pattern.

Black And Round

Many carmakers, in an attempt to reduce vibration by making sure the wheels are more concentric with the hub, use a protruding lip that mates closely with the centerhole on the rim. This works well for a couple of years, but eventually corrosion from road grime can make it impossible to budge the wheels, even after you've loosened all the lugs. Correct this now, and you won't need to try it in the field. Jack up the corner of the car to take the load off the wheel and kick the wheel, alternating sides until it pops loose. No joy, and now your feet hurt? Be sure the lugs are only a single turn from tight, lower the car and move it a foot forward and back, rapping the brakes smartly to break the wheel loose. A shot of penetrating oil may help in an hour or two. Clean up the corrosion with emery paper (Fig. 5) and coat all the surfaces lightly with wheel bearing grease, Vaseline or, best of all, antiseize compound.

You'll need a few things besides the on-board tools for your emergency tire change. Pack a flashlight with good batteries or, better yet, a cigarette-lighter-powered trouble light, an emergency triangle, a couple of road flares, some gloves and a poncho or ground cloth. Toss in three pieces of scrap 2 x 4 as well, each about a foot long, and a piece of thick plywood 2 x 2 feet.

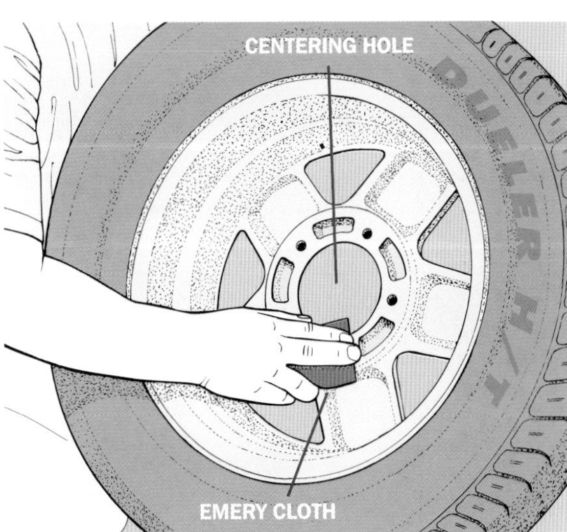

(Fig. 5) Remove corrosion from the centering hole with emery cloth or a wire brush.

That Fateful Day

When changing a tire the first, and most important, thing to do is to get the vehicle to a safe area, far enough from the road to save you from becoming road pizza—particularly if the flat is on the left side and your back side will be poking out into traffic while you work. Set your triangle or flares 100 ft. or so upstream.

Leave the vehicle in Park and set the handbrake. Block the wheel diagonally opposite the flat with two pieces of wood (Fig. 6). Loosen all the lugs on the flat a full turn. Take the spare out of the trunk and put it halfway under the car near the jack. In the unlikely event the car falls off the jack, it will only fall onto the spare—not your foot or head—and will leave you a fighting chance of raising the car and continuing. If the car falls to the ground, you'll have no way to raise it.

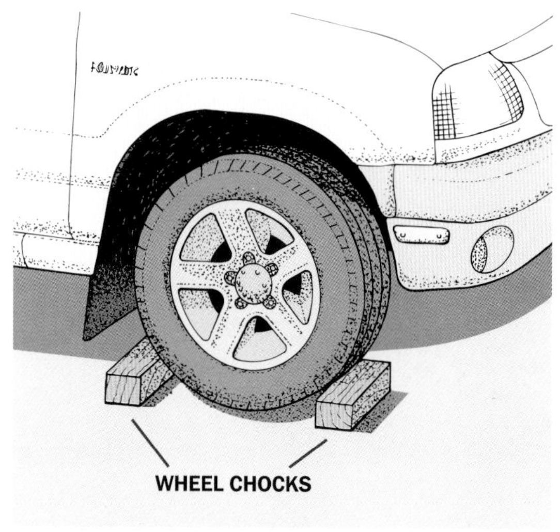

(Fig. 6) Block the opposite corner of the car to keep it from rolling off the jack.

Raise the jack from its stowed position to nearly high enough to contact the bottom of the car. If you've got a different style of jack than the one pictured here (Fig. 7), check your owner's manual for specifics.

If the ground isn't firm, put the 2 x 2 piece of plywood under the jack point, and the jack on top of the wood. Be sure everything is level. Jack the car up until the flat clears the ground by several inches, because the spare isn't flat and will need more clearance.

Remove the lug nuts, and put them inside the hubcap or in some other place where they won't get lost in the dark, or accidentally scattered into the weeds by your feet.

Pull the flat off and put it halfway under the car. Hang the spare on the studs. No studs? You've got lug bolts (common on many European cars) and you'll need to juggle the wheel while you get the top one started. The easy way is to sit down on the ground facing the hub and balance the spare on your legs while you start the first lug bolt. If you begin with the top bolt, the wheel will hang gracefully from it and you can start the rest. Finger-tighten all the lugs and then lightly tighten them with the lug wrench, again in a crisscross pattern.

Be sure you don't have anything (like a stone or mud) trapped between the rim and hub, or the rim will wobble. In fact, if the mud compresses later, the lugs could lose their torque and the wheel could fly off. If you need to, remove the wheel again in the morning to remove the debris, corrosion and rust from all the mating faces and between the wheel and hub, and then lightly lube. This will have the added benefit of making the wheel easier to remove the next time. Hint: There should be some grease to be found on the jackscrew of your jack, and there's probably enough to put a smidgen on the lugs with your finger. Be sure to get it on the mating chamfer as well as on the threads.

Lower the vehicle and pull the jack out. Now you can tighten the lugs to their correct torque. Check the owner's manual for the torque specification. Measure carefully. If the lug is dry and unlubricated, it may take a lot more force to tighten the lugs.

The only accurate way to torque the lugs is to use a mechanic's torque wrench. These can be purchased for 20 bucks or so. If you have expensive alloy wheels, you may want to buy one and keep it in the trunk.

As you're putting away your tools and jack, be sure you haven't left them covered with mud or moisture, which might cause them to rust while stored. If they're a mess, clean them and relubricate at your earliest opportunity. Don't forget to pick up your safety triangle.

Next Morning

Take your flat to a competent tire technician for repair ("Repairing A Flat Tire," page 40). And don't let him overtighten your lugs with his fancy-dan air wrench.

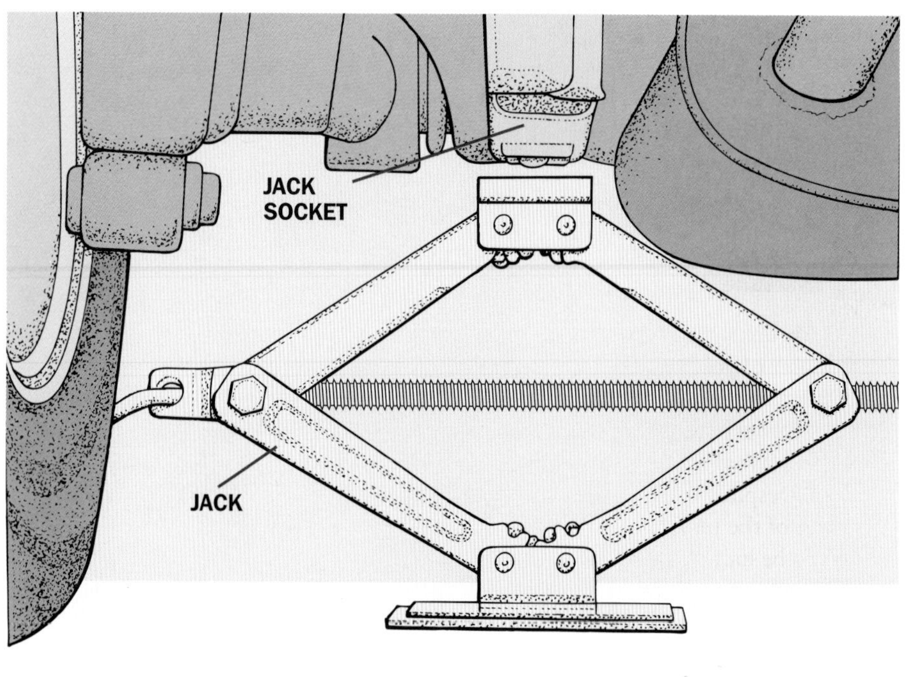

(Fig. 7) The correct jack point on the frame of your vehicle may be difficult to reach.

EASY

Replacing Your Tailpipe

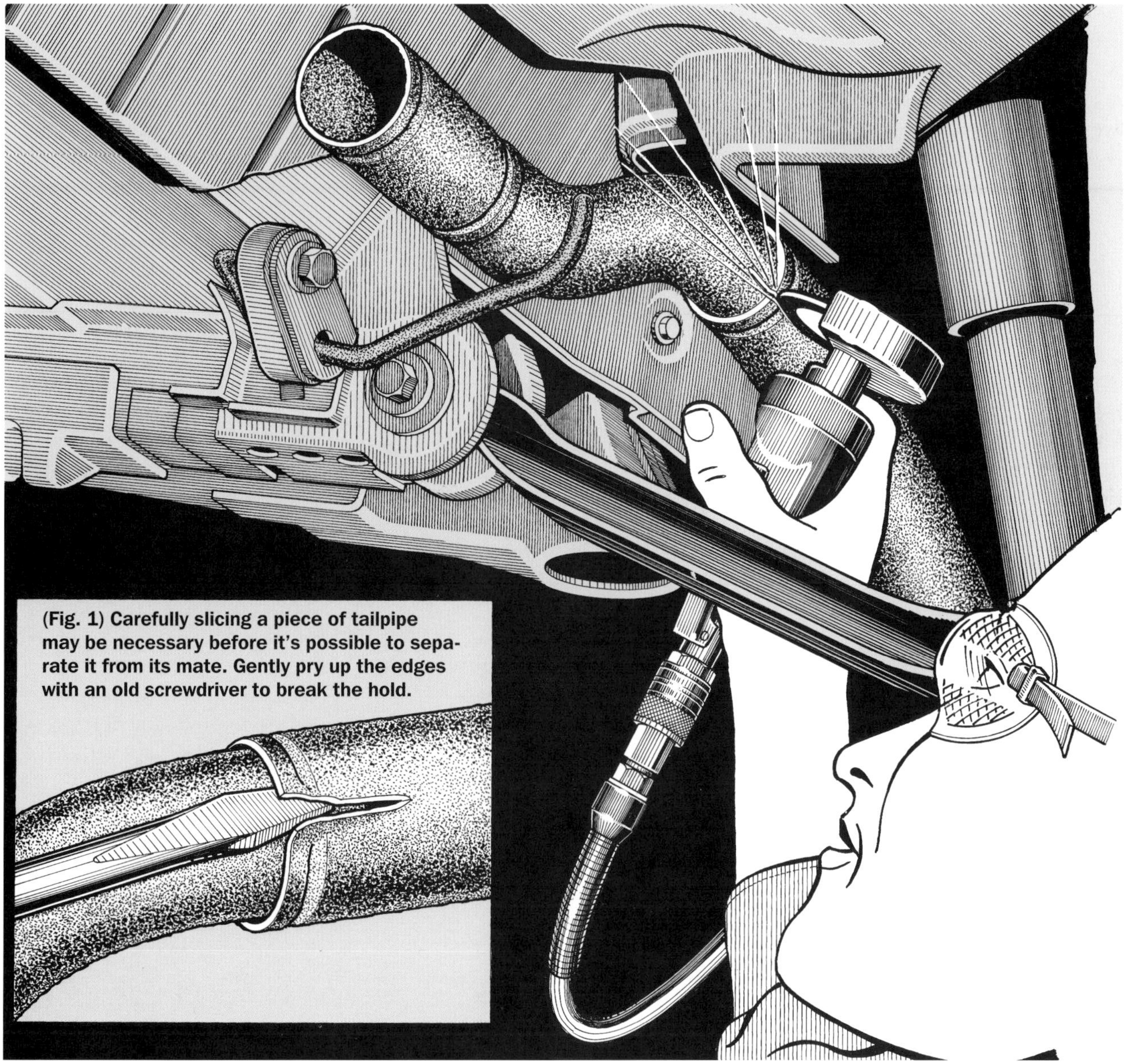

(Fig. 1) Carefully slicing a piece of tailpipe may be necessary before it's possible to separate it from its mate. Gently pry up the edges with an old screwdriver to break the hold.

Brakelights flicker suddenly in front of you, followed rapidly by the screeching of tires. Cars before you swerve to the left and right as you slow as safely and rapidly as practical. Despite your best efforts, the source of the pandemonium, what appears to be half of a cement block, disappears directly under your front bumper at a high speed. Thump. And as it exits from your rear bumper, you follow it in your rearview mirror for a few seconds. It has company. Your muffler—or at least most of your muffler—has apparently developed a lasting relationship with the aforementioned cement block. They're eloping at high speed toward the curb, inextricably intertwined.

The next thing you notice is the sound of what seems to be a B-29 landing in the next lane as you press back down on the gas. Actually, it's your engine—minus its muffler—waking up again as you try to negotiate through the traffic, back home to safety, family and something tall and cold that will make your hands stop shaking.

To add insult to injury, you replaced your exhaust system from the catalytic converter back only last spring. Inspection of the underside of your car reveals good, solid pipe most of the length of the vehicle, terminating in shards of muffler. Here's your chance to replace a few feet of pipe and the missing muffler yourself.

Now That You're Home

Actually, it may not be road debris that removes your muffler and tailpipe. Rust never sleeps, and cars in short-trip service may rust out the farthest, coolest portions of the exhaust system in as little as 18 months.

The following scenario is typical of vehicles that have had part of their exhaust system replaced at least once. The saga begins with a section of the original exhaust plumbing behind the catalytic converter rusting out and making a ruckus. Because the original exhaust pipes are welded together, however, all the pipes from the cat back need to be replaced. There's no practical way to remove just the rotted section because of all the welds.

If you had the wherewithal, you could probably cut out just the rusted portion and have a pipe custom-fitted. But that would be extremely labor-intensive and not particularly economical over the long haul. Also, exhaust work just isn't done that way. So, generally, two or three aftermarket pipes and the muffler are clamped together behind the converter to repair the exhaust.

Then you drive around for another year or two in peace and quiet—unaware that the replacement pipes hanging under you tend to rust at different rates. Sometimes, the middle pipe of the three you installed goes first. Other times, the muffler at the end falls off before the other two. Still other times, the flanged pipe bolted to the cat is the first to go bad. In all cases, though, you want to replace only the bad pipe. Problem is, the pipes it's connected to at both ends have been crimped by clamps. How do you remove the Swiss-cheese pipe without ruining the other two? By using a power cutting wheel and a very steady hand **(Fig. 1)**. The preferred tool is an air-powered die grinder with a cutoff wheel, but a high-speed electric drill will work, albeit more slowly.

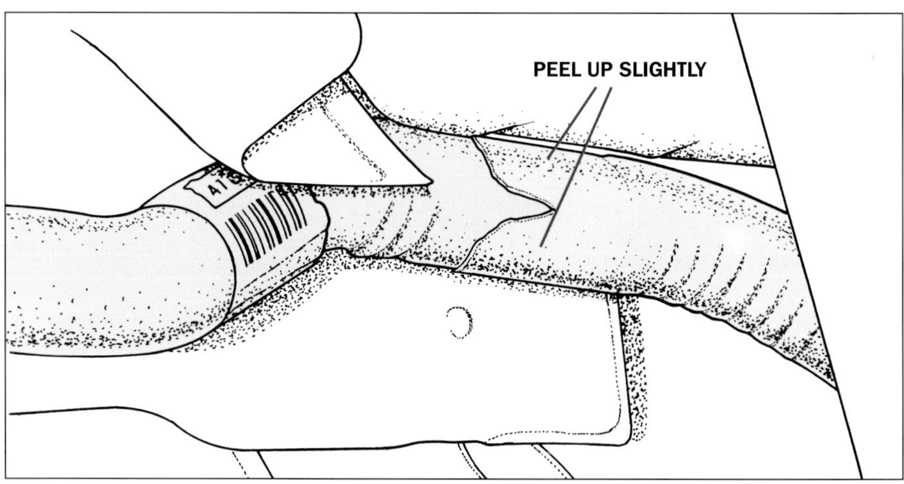

(Fig. 2) Peel up the corners of the old pipe to slide in the new piece.

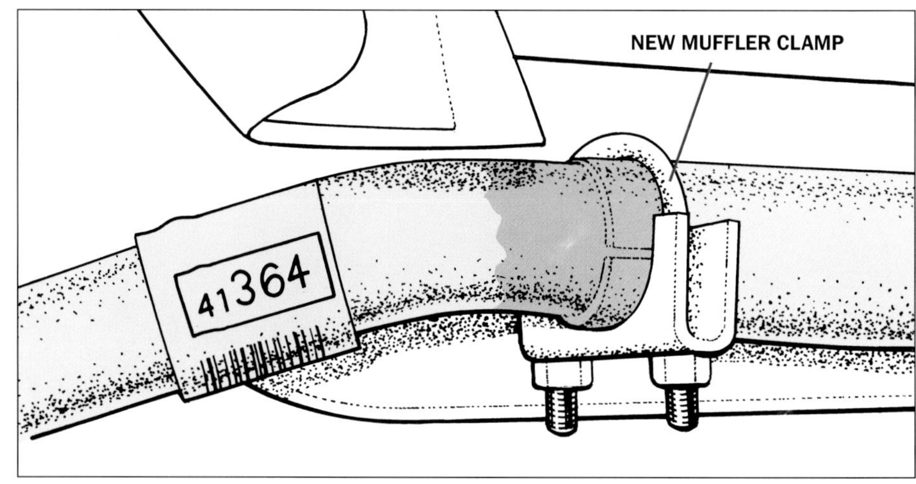

(Fig. 3) After installing all the parts, adjust for fit and tighten the clamps.

Sizing It Up

Get the back of the car up on jackstands, with chocks securing the front wheels. Be sure to wear safety goggles, as exhaust systems tend to drop razor-sharp flakes of rust that are seemingly attracted to your eyes.

Get under the vehicle to see what kind of couplings you're dealing with. The flanged type is easy. Just spray the rusty bolts with penetrant oil, so you can get them out, pry the flange from its rusty partner and secure the new flange with a new gasket and fresh bolts. Use antiseize compound on everything to ease removal the next time.

The other type of coupling is made up of a larger pipe slipped over a smaller one or a smaller pipe slipped into a larger one, depending on which way the coupling is facing. Both may be present in the same exhaust system. The important thing to remember is that you may need to save the inner pipe, so use a gentle touch with the cutting wheel. If the outer pipe needs to be saved, there's nothing you can do to keep from cutting it. But that's why you're going to use a cutting wheel instead of an impact chisel. It makes for a neater, smoother cut.

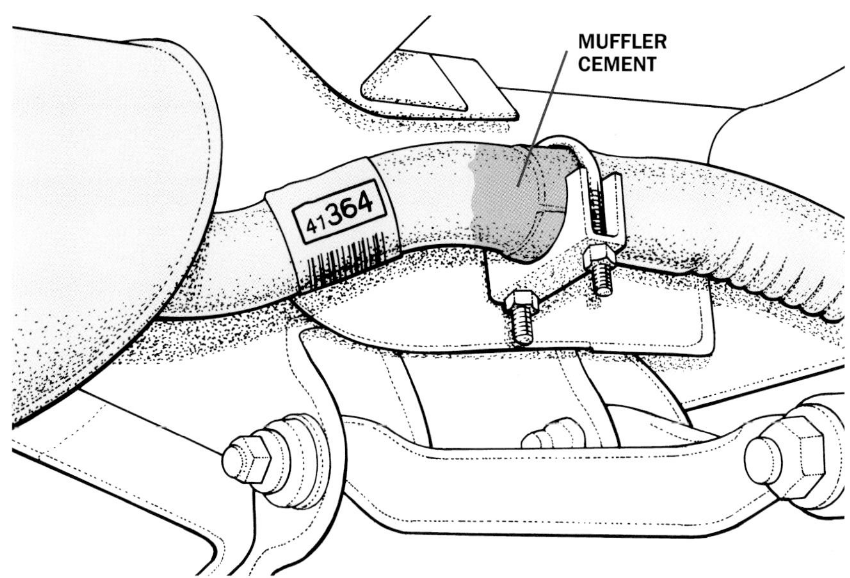

(Fig. 4) Smear muffler cement over the joint after you install the clamp.

Slice, Don't Dice

To begin, remove the bad pipe's clamps. Then, make a lengthwise mark 1 to 2 in. long where you want to slice open the outer pipe. Put on a pair of goggles, get a good double-handed grip on the cutter tool and start it up. Slowly raise the spinning wheel to the mark on the pipe. With gentle pressure, score the mark.

If you're saving the inner pipe, repeat this step until you're through the outer pipe. It's okay for the inner pipe to get a little score groove in it—just as long as you don't cut it all the way through. If you're saving the outer pipe, the second cut can take you all the way through the inner pipe.

With the cut made, use a screwdriver or a chisel to pry open the outer pipe like a tin can. That will give you enough play at the crimped area to wiggle the pipes apart.

Spread 'em

Fitting a new pipe over an old one is no problem. Fitting a new pipe into an old one sometimes is, because of the crimp from the old clamp. If you're having trouble, use an exhaust-pipe expander to gain some extra clearance. Then, simply fit the pipes together as if they were both new after smearing a little muffler cement on the joint.

If you saved the outer pipe, it now has a 1- to 2-in. slice at the end. Make sure to slide the inner pipe in past the end of the cut, so there's no hole between the pipes (Fig. 2). Install a new muffler clamp, but don't tighten it until the rest of the system is hung from the hangers and aligned properly (Fig. 3).

Once everything is back together and clamped down tight, a little muffler cement strategically applied with your thumb over the cut will take care of any tiny residual gaps (Fig. 4). Lower your car and enjoy the silence.

MODERATE

Repairing Power Antennas

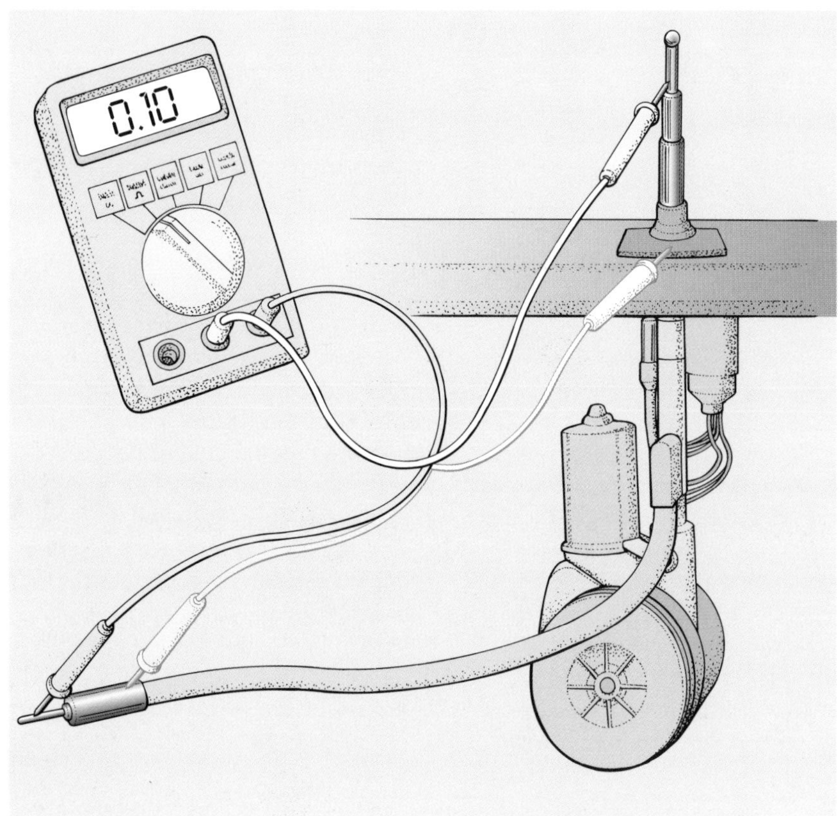

(Fig. 1) Scratchy radio reception might be caused by poor ground or antenna connections. Use an ohmmeter to chase high resistance points.

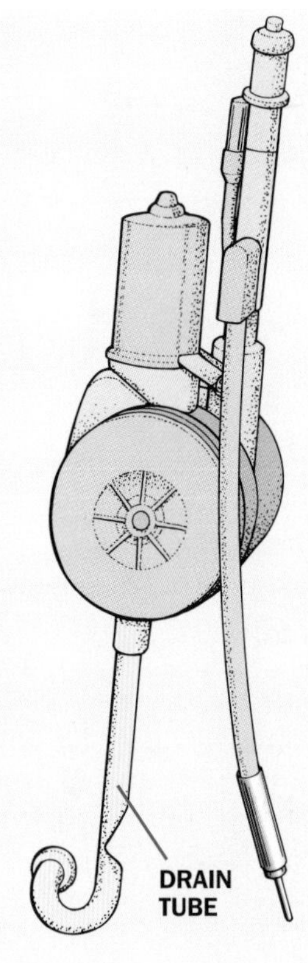

(Fig. 2) If water that leaks down the mast can't escape, the mechanism may freeze up.

It's time to kick out some jams, so you reach into the console for your favorite MC5 CD. Popping open the jewel box, you reach for the CD, only to find out that Junior has liberally lubricated it with peanut butter and jelly. After making a mental note to give Junior a good talking-to, you decide to surf the airwaves for some good oldtime rock-and-roll. Punching the FM button, you hope that at least one of the radio presets has some Bob Seger tunes hiding behind it. But no, there's nothing to be heard on any channel except a great rushing noise, not even so much as CONELRAD. Time to come back to this millennium and find out what's wrong with your antenna.

Manual Or Power?

Fixed antennas have only a couple of failure modes, and generally they involve mechanical damage to the antenna mast or the cable. If part of the mast is still there, you'll generally get some sort of signal. A poor connection between the antenna base and the fender also could be a problem. Unscrew the antenna mounting nut and check for corrosion. A cleanup with a wire brush and reassembly might re-establish a good ground.

Power antennas are more coy. If they're too shy to come out of the fender, you're listening to static.

No-Show

The issue could be either electrical or purely mechanical. Go back to your antenna and try to pull the mast out with your fingers. If it moves out readily, pull it out all the way, and then cycle the radio power with the key on. If the mast moves even the slightest amount, or you can hear the motor running at all, the problem is mechanical.

If the motor seems deceased, go back to basics—check the fuse. Determining which fuse protects the antenna motor may require some detective work. It may be the radio fuse, or it may be a separate fuse, perhaps shared with the rear-window defroster grid or a trunk-mounted CD changer. (Finding something else that doesn't work often is a good clue.)

Fuse is okay? Check the antenna's mounting, as described previously, for

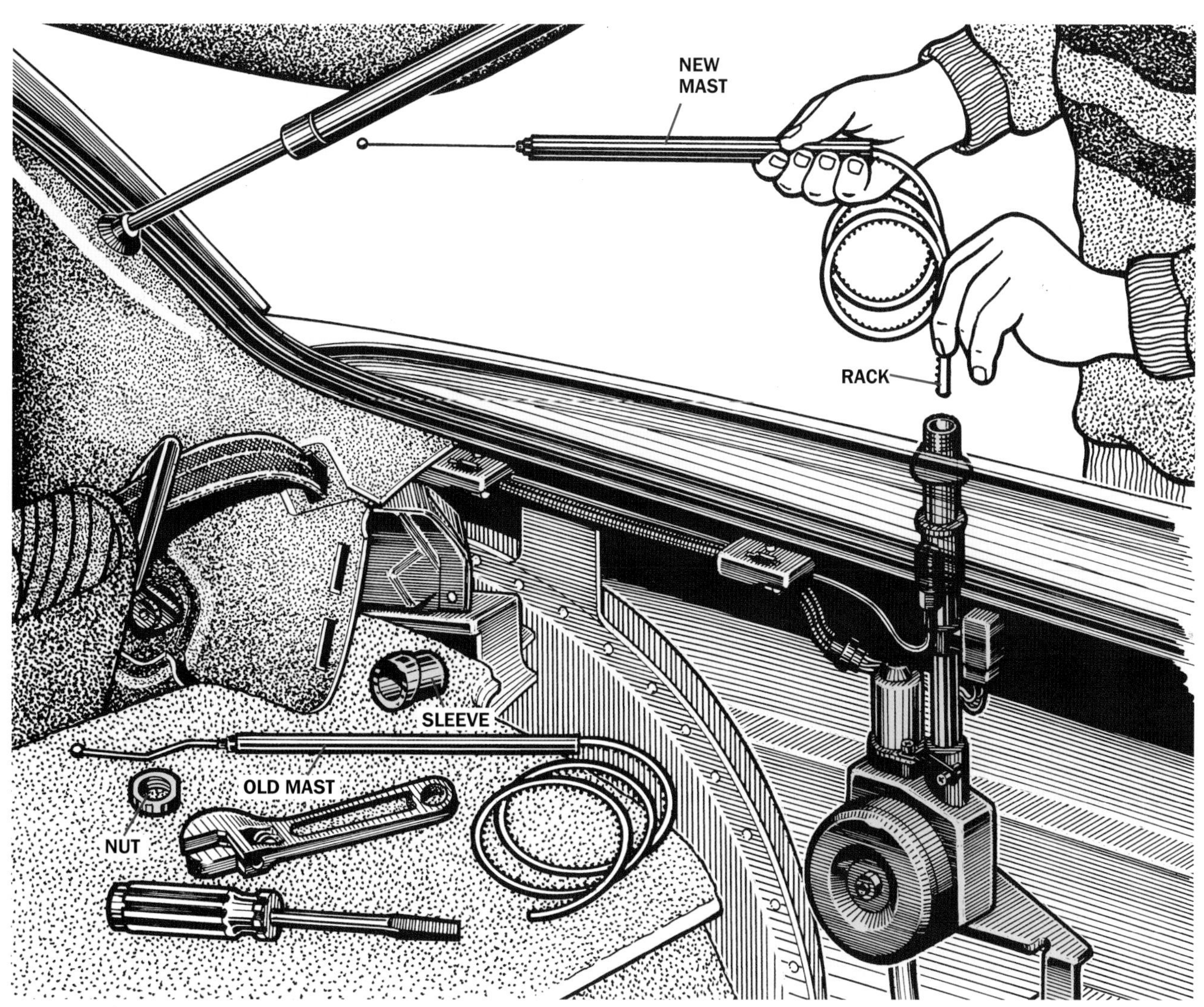

(Fig. 3) A sticky or damaged antenna mast can often be replaced without accessing or disassembling the mechanism. As we show here, this can be done without removing the interior trim.

a good ground pathway, although there may be a separate ground wire to a specific chassis ground point. You may want to use an ohmmeter (**Fig. 1**) to hunt for resistance. Incidentally, if you try to measure the resistance of the antenna cable's RF lead between the mast and the radio connector, it may check out as infinite. Some antenna assemblies use a capacitor in series with the RF lead, some don't. The ground shell of the antenna cable should have a low resistance to chassis ground, normally 5 ohms or less.

You'll need to find a schematic of the antenna wiring to troubleshoot any deeper. But with the radio and key on, the harness to the antenna assembly should have one hot wire on, and a different wire hot when the key or radio is off. Good hunting.

Stubborn

Does the antenna motor run briefly but not actually move the mast up and down? Or does it move a few inches and then grind to a halt? One problem we've seen is a kinked or pinched drain tube. (**Fig. 2**) The mechanism can fill with water, which then freezes solid in cold weather, or corrodes the works and causes a jam. Check the tube, especially if you can pull the mast out manually and it's wet. If the tube is compromised and the works are full of water, you may need to disassemble the thing, dry it out, and put it back together with fresh lubricant.

Can you help the mast along in and out? If so, the sliding sections of the mast may be corroded or bent. Careful bending by hand may restore movement, and polishing with 600-grit sandpaper or rubbing compound can smooth the action. At the very least, run the mast completely out and clean it thoroughly with a soft cloth, relubricating with a sparse amount of silicone grease or paste wax.

What's That Funny Noise?

Modern power antennas use a simple, flexible rack-and-pinion mechanism. It's pretty reliable, but abuse and the ravages of time and weather can literally strip the gears. So if you hear noises that sound like interrupted gear meshing, there's probably some section of the rack or pinion that's in need of dental work. It's possible to fix this without replacing the antenna assembly outright (**Fig. 3**). (You may not even have to access the mechanism.)

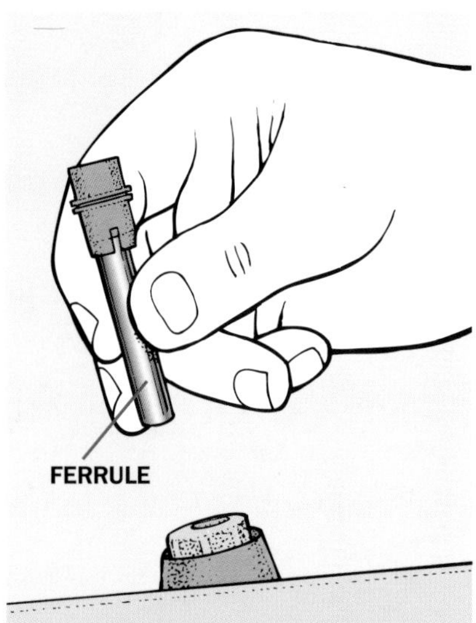

(Fig. 4) Remove the outer nut and collar as a first step to removing or replacing the mast.

Visit your dealership's parts department. GM, for one, offers a repair kit for power antennas. This consists of a new mast and rack assembly, ready to install. You may need to order it, as the two dealers we tried didn't have it in stock. There are aftermarket antenna parts to be had, but finding the right part is going to be difficult unless you have better luck than we did interrogating the staff behind the parts counter at the local warehouse distributor.

Here's how the system works: The limit switches that stop the motor at both ends of the antenna mast's travel are built into the mechanism, and you can consider them unserviceable. The limit switches rely on the antenna bottoming out or topping out to rotate a switch drum, at which point the current to the motor turns off.

At the top of the antenna mechanism is a large nut that holds the whole works onto the fender. Remove this nut. This isn't as easy as it sounds if it doesn't have flats that you can turn with a wrench. You may need to use a spanner with pins—although a pair of snap ring pliers may work if the nut isn't wickedly tight. At the potential expense of the chrome finish, you may need to fall back on the mechanic's friend, locking pliers. Under the nut and perhaps a plastic spacer or two there will be a ferrule (Fig. 4), which is the stepped sleeve that the mast actually bumps into at the end of its travel upward. Pull out this ferrule. Now have someone else turn on the radio. The mast should elevate itself completely out and flop over, so you have to be there to catch it. Carefully notice which way the teeth of the rack point as the mast clears the fender. Note the state of the teeth. Missing teeth probably mean you should disassemble the housing and clear all the bits out, but teeth that are simply worn should be okay.

The new mast's rack has been curled up like a pig's tail in the package, and it will be difficult getting it to mesh with the gears. With your fingers or pliers, bend the bottom 2 or 3 in. backward to remove the curl. The end should be straight now. After making sure that the radio is turned off, take a look at the last tooth—you may need to remove a small amount of casting flash. A pocketknife does that job well.

Take the new mast, with the teeth of its rack appropriately oriented, and insert it into the hole until it bottoms. Rotate the mast a little to the left and right to get the teeth to mesh with the pinion gear (Fig. 5). Have your helper turn the radio on and off while you push the new mast firmly down. This will cause the limit switch to cycle inside the mechanism. Now have your helper turn the radio on, and if all is well, the mast will suck itself very neatly in until it bottoms out. All you need to do now is reinstall the ferrule, spacers and nut. Lightly lube the mast sections with silicone grease or paste wax.

Outer Limits

If the limit switch mechanism stops working, you may be able to disassemble it, clean up any foreign matter or corrosion, and get it running again. The switch consists of a plastic drum with wiper fingers and electrical traces, so it's vulnerable to moisture and dried-out lubricant. If you can't fix it, or the motor itself is toasted, you'll need to replace the whole shootin' match. An aftermarket antenna will set you back about $60 to $75 at the local auto parts store, or more than a hundred at the dealer—maybe more for a luxury import. The OEM parts will, of course, drop in. Aftermarket pieces may require a certain amount of adaptation to mount properly, and perhaps even some creative wiring to make them work properly. Don't forget to check for used parts at the local scrapyard or auto recycler.

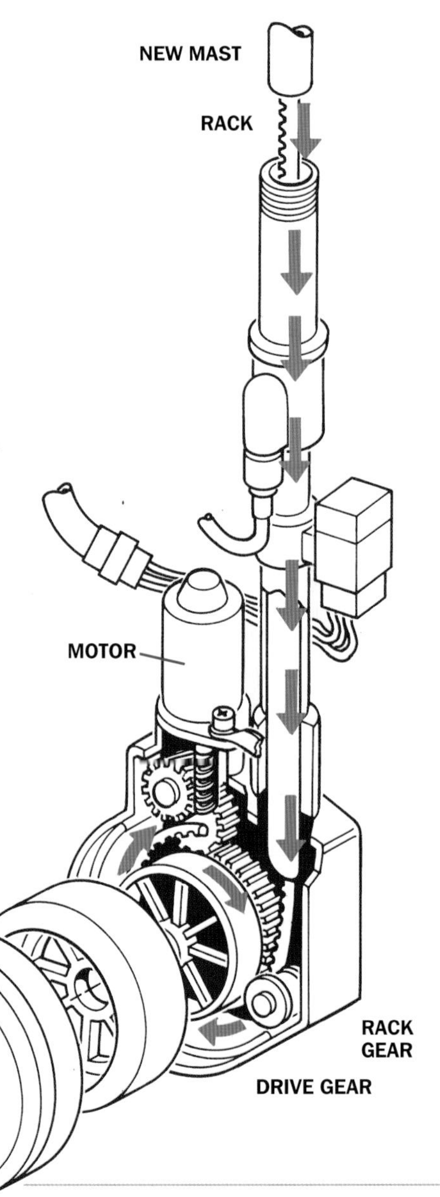

(Fig. 5) It may take a little fumbling to get the rack to mesh with the drive pinion, but when it does the mast will run completely home by itself.

EASY

Replacing Your Spark Plugs

Despite the heavy traffic—periods of slow-go interspersed with longer periods of no-go—things are okay. You've got that new Yanni disc in the player and your java is still piping hot. However, as your drive wears on, the CD starts skipping and the coffee in your cup starts spilling over the top. Suddenly you realize that your engine is no longer idling with its accustomed silky smoothness. In fact, it's getting as lumpy as cold oatmeal. The engine's developed a bad misfire.

As you sit and jiggle along in the rough-running car, you figure that it can't be the spark plugs. After all, with today's unleaded gasoline they can last twice as long as they used to. And the engine's high-output electronic ignition system produces enough voltage to fire even a worn plug.

Well, think again.

CHANGING PLUGS IS EASY on this overhead-cam engine, but might call for just the right combination of swivels and sockets for your ratchet on V-engines. Always check a new plug's gap with a wire-style gap gauge before installing.

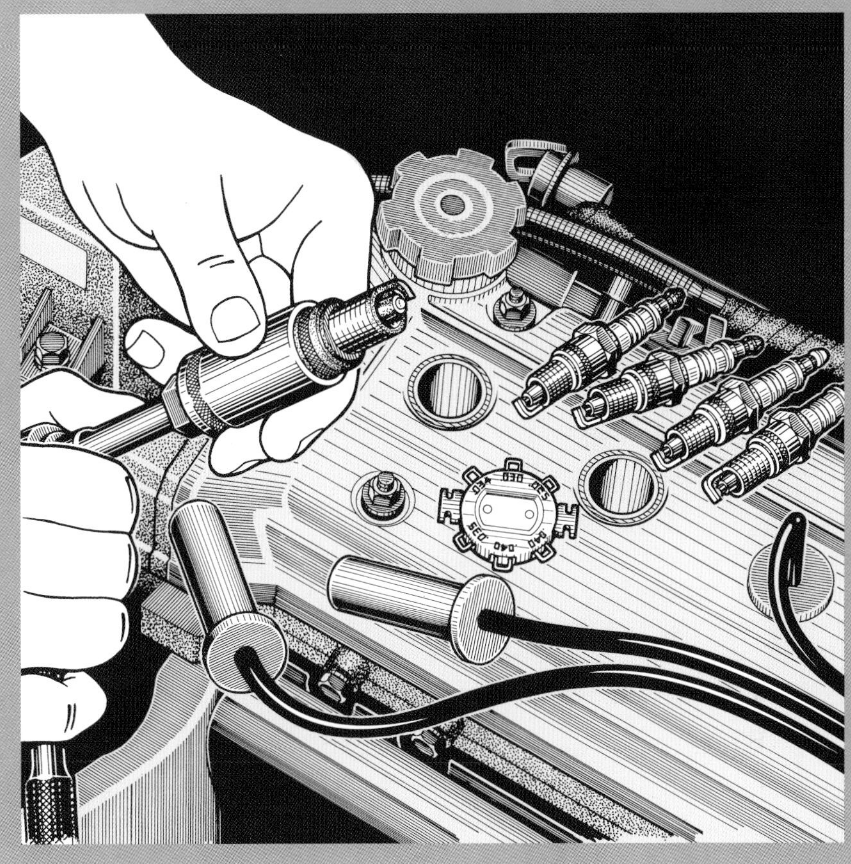

Fair is foul

Although plugs won't lead-foul with today's unleaded gasoline, they can oil-foul, carbon-foul or even be fouled by some fuel additives. So if you've got a misfire, there's a fair chance a plug is the cause. In fact, it's more likely a plug than the fuel injector. So, back home, it's time to take the plugs out. Look for oily-black or sooty carbon-black deposits. The former usually are from defective intake valve stem seals, the latter from an overly rich fuel mixture, or a lazy or defective oxygen (O_2) sensor. The oxygen sensor is what signals the computer to adjust the fuel mixture.

It can be tough to hear a misfire, which is one reason why emissions-control standards require the engine computer's on-board diagnostics (OBD) to log trouble codes for each of the cylinders. However, the first cars equipped with that setup (called OBD II) weren't produced until 1994, and most cars didn't have it until 1996.

Even with an earlier model, you should check for trouble codes indicating a problem with the engine, particularly those involving the oxygen sensor. But if engine performance is down and you're not seeing trouble codes, and the plugs have gone a couple of years or about 30,000 miles, it's worth pulling them for a look. But not so fast—this may not be as easy as in your last car.

First, it may be harder to disconnect the plug wires. If they're recessed, you can't just pull on the wire. Worse, most of the simple spark plug pullers we've tried won't work on a stuck boot. You need pliers that grip the end of the boot and give you something solid to hold. These pullers cost $20 or so. In any case, twisting the boot to break the heat seal often is necessary, even with pliers. Never try to pull on the plug wire itself, or you'll probably cause a separation in the resistance wire.

A second thing to watch for is whether your spark-plug socket really fits. To meet the latest standard of the Society of Automotive Engineers, many new plugs are about ⅛-in. longer than you're probably used to. An older, marginal socket may not fit the hex properly and could slip off and break the plug. It also helps to use a socket with a rubber insert to securely hold the plug.

Finally, the elbow grease

Start with a warm engine. Clean the plug hole recesses with compressed air, crack all the plugs loose one-quarter turn, and let the engine cool. Removing plugs from a hot cylinder head can damage the threads.

Once you have the plugs out, check them carefully before you decide they've got a lot of life left. Use a magnifying glass and feeler gauge to be sure. If the gap is worn .005 in. over the specs, and you can see rounding off of the center electrode and wear on the side electrode, install new plugs. Forget trying to file the plugs.

If you're reinstalling the old plugs, smear a film of antiseize on the threads near the tip. New plugs have a coating that will lubricate the threads on the way in and prevent the plug from seizing on their next removal, but it's only good for one stab.

If any spark plugs are dry-soot black, that's from carbon—a rich-fuel mixture problem. If there's a trouble code indicating the oxygen sensor is incorrectly signaling lean, the sensor could be responsible. If it's correctly indicating a rich mixture, then you have to look for a cause, such as leaking fuel injectors or engine misfire, perhaps caused by defective plug wires. It would seem that misfire would throw a lot of raw gas into the exhaust, which it does. But it also throws in a lot of oxygen, and that's what the sensor sees, and in this case it just tells the computer to add more fuel.

Not sure or no code? Then check the oxygen sensor, which resembles a spark plug threaded into the exhaust manifold. If there's an O_2 trouble code and no apparent other cause, you could just replace the sensor. Or, before you invest in a new one, test the sensor you've got. You can do this using one of the inexpensive testers made for Saturday mechanics. With a warmed-up engine (necessary to get the O_2 sensor working) and the throttle cracked open (so the engine is running at about 2000 rpm), the tester's indicator lights typically will flash on and off (or will both glow steadily) if the O_2 sensor is working properly.

If you don't get the lights, or as an extra check, let the engine cool. Remove the sensor with a tight-fitting wrench and bench-test it. The typical sensor has a closed but slotted end and is a heat battery of sorts. If you envelop the sensor end with the flame of a propane torch (so it gets hot but not cherry red), it should produce over 0.4v with a high-impedance digital voltmeter hooked up, or turn on the tester lights. If the sensor is good, the voltage should drop or the lights go out within 3 seconds after you pull away the flame.

Occasionally a vehicle has a different type of sensor, and in some designs it has an open tip. This is a varying-resistance device that doesn't respond to these voltage-generating tests, so you'll have to rely on the on-board diagnostic system for openers, and a shop manual checkout procedure to find out if it's bad. This type (widely used on new cars) also was used on 1987-90 Jeeps, an occasional Toyota in the late 1980s and a lot of Nissans. These days you should have access to factory service information (or a good aftermarket equivalent) for your car, so refer to it.

Whether you install a new sensor or refit the one you've got, coat the threads of the O_2 sensor with antiseize compound.

HOW IT WORKS

The Right Plug

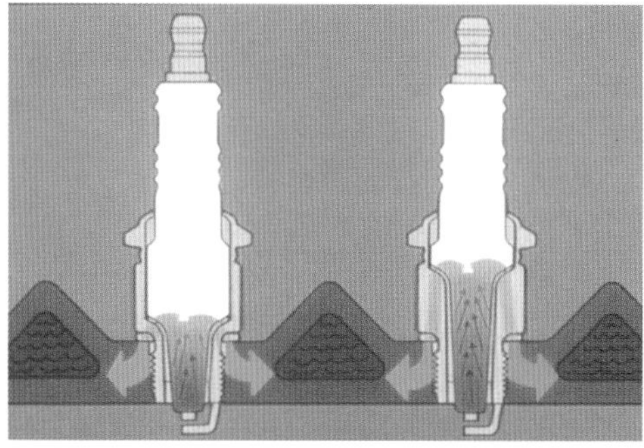

The correct plug for your engine is, of course, the exact part number that the manufacturer installed at the factory. When it's time to retire them, you'll be forced to choose from several manufacturers' offerings, and they're all pretty much alike, right? Wrong. There are subtle differences in a plug's ability to dissipate heat that belie what would otherwise be an exact physical match. A "hot" plug has a long path through the ceramic to the (relatively) cool cylinder head. A "cold" plug has a shorter heat-conduction path and tends to run cooler.

Plug manufacturers cross-reference their product lines to other manufacturers' lines, and you should be able to find a plug to fit almost anything in the cross-reference chart. More important than heat range are things like thread diameter and length, and the type of tip.

Installing the wrong plug can ruin your engine instantly if the plug is too long and whacks the top of the piston, especially in today's aluminum heads.

Too short a plug not only won't fire, carbon will quickly fill the threads on the cylinder's head, preventing you from installing the correct plug.

Replacing Spark Plug Wires

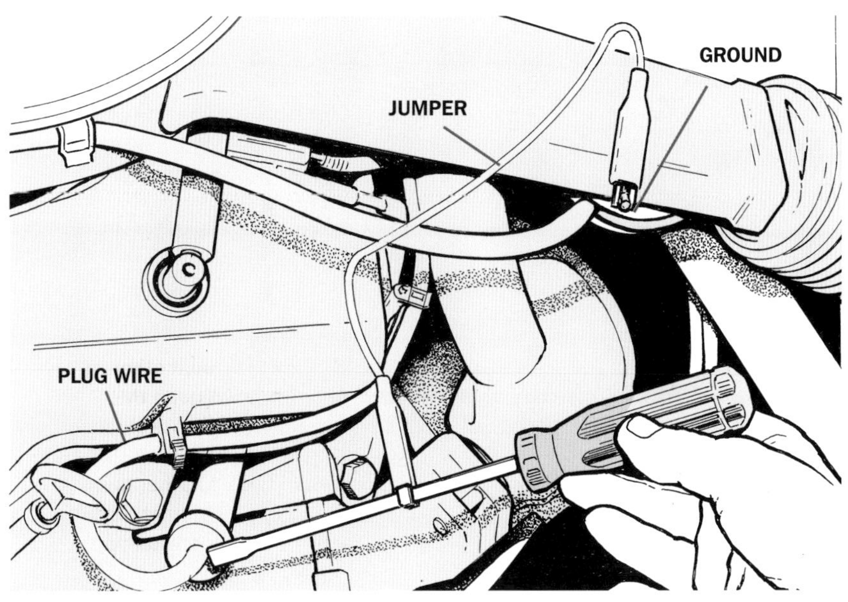

(Fig. 1) Dampen the wires with a spray bottle and clear water, and look for arcs with a grounded, insulated screwdriver.

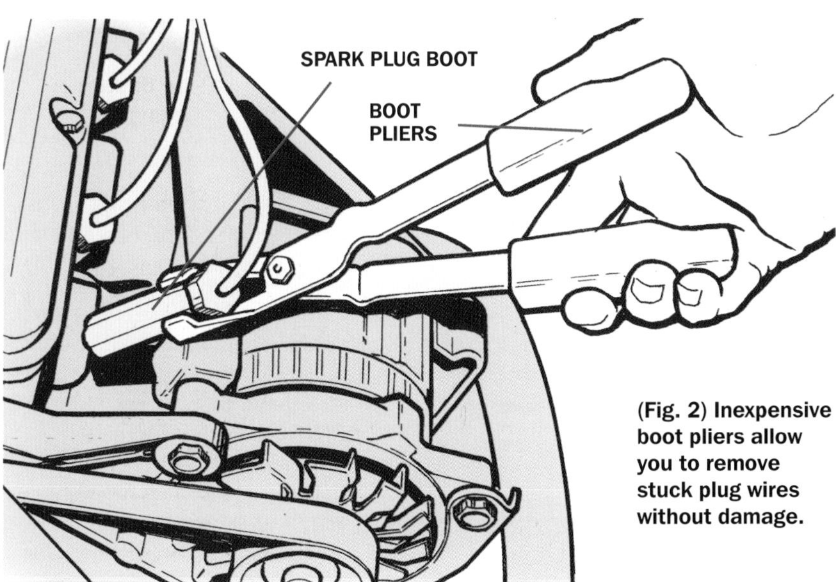

(Fig. 2) Inexpensive boot pliers allow you to remove stuck plug wires without damage.

Before easing out of the fast-food's parking lot, you grab a sip of the hot coffee you picked up at the drive-thru. You take your time as you place the cup in its holder in the center console. No hurry. The approaching traffic may be moving fast, but it's far enough away for you to accelerate up to cruising speed. Good thing, because at about half-throttle you feel the engine misfire. The closing traffic has time to back off and let you sputter up to road speed. But now your engine sputters like a Harley idling at the curb, even at normal traffic speeds. And there's coffee all over the console from the vibration.

What's Up?

A brief underhood inspection confirms that all the vacuum hoses are on and that none of them have been burned open by leaning against the exhaust manifold. You've touched every sensor connection to see if it's on tight, you've even checked for trouble codes.

However, not everything calls for high-tech diagnostics and the latest scan tester. Engine misfire often is caused by leaking spark plug wires, so visual inspection could reveal what's wrong. The jackets may be damaged from the outside by abrasion caused by engine vibration (particularly at the plug-end boots), a hot engine compartment, spilled fluids or battery acid, multiple disconnections and reconnections for other service, or even a family of nesting rodents.

Run the engine in near darkness, and then look and listen. If you see little electrical arcs, or hear a snap-crack, there is high-voltage electrical leakage. Of course, running the engine at idle doesn't exercise the ignition system very hard, so you can add something to the test by spraying the plug wire ends with clean water from a household spray bottle.

Another test: With a jumper wire, ground the metal shank of a screwdriver that has a well-insulated handle. Then, run the tip of the screwdriver along the length of each wire and all around at the coil and plug boots. This will often produce an arc from the wire to the screwdriver (Fig. 1).

Now look at the wires under good lighting. If they are damaged by abrasion, oil-soaked, cut, burned from contact with the exhaust, or have a dried-out look with heat cracks, it definitely shouldn't be a surprise if you see arcs in the dark under some conditions. However, if they look bad but there are no arcs, do a resistance check.

A conventional plug wire has a resistance of 10,000 to 15,000 ohms per foot of length—if it's measurably higher, the wire probably is bad. An absolutely failed wire will have a hairline break somewhere, and the resistance will be infinity.

Out With The Old, In With The New

Once you've found a bad wire, the solution should be simple: Replace the plug wires.

First, you have to decide whether you want to buy from a car dealer at list price or get a quality aftermarket brand, if you have that choice. Prices for 1980s models may be under $35 for a popular make at the parts store. For a late-model V8, be prepared to pay the dealer up to $200 or more, even for a popular car.

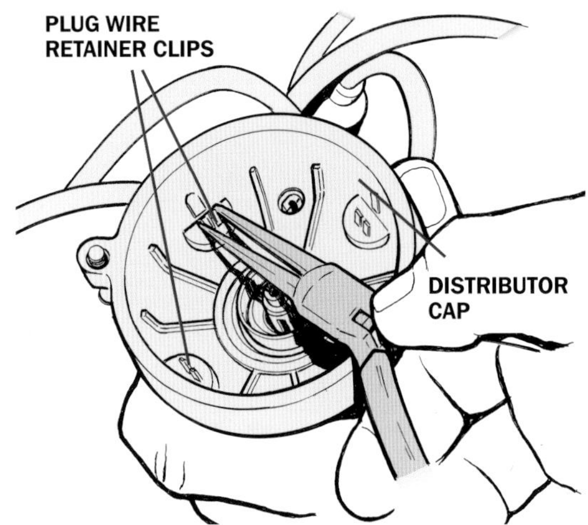

(Fig. 3) Some wires are secured inside the cap by spring clips. Use needle-nose pliers here.

A word of caution: You may not want "high-performance" wires, even if they fit your car (and they may be cheaper than a conventional type). Some high-performance wires are not the resistance type, and although they may do well on racing cars, they can affect the operation of underhood electronics by not containing radio waves.

The actual method of removing the old wire is not always "just pull it off." Pulling on the wire itself is sure to cause an internal separation (see p. 19). Of course, if you're replacing a bad wire, it may not matter, but if any one of the old wires is still good, it's best to keep it as a spare.

Grasp the plug wire by the boot at the plug end. If it's in a recess or is difficult to access for some other reason, use a spark plug wire tool. There are special pliers of all sorts designed to reach in and grasp the boot (Fig. 2). They're not expensive, and having them could prove useful if you ever have to disconnect wires for other underhood service. Twist the boot if necessary to break the heat seal to the plug, then pull. As you do this

HOW IT WORKS

Spark Plug Wires

The spark plug wire has a seemingly simple job: Carry the high-voltage electricity produced by the ignition coil to the terminal of the spark plug. Once at the plug, the electricity travels to the other end of the plug, and jumps a gap between electrodes to produce the "spark" that ignites the fuel mixture. Because high-voltage electricity looks for an easier path to jump across than a pair of electrodes in a spark plug, containing the electricity within the wire takes a thick jacket of insulation, and some wires have an outer jacket to resist cuts, high underhood temperatures, etc. If that outer jacket is damaged, the electricity may leak out to follow the easier path. In addition, high-voltage electricity produces radio waves, which can cause interference with all types of on-car electronic devices, from sensors and computers to radios and other entertainment systems. So, a simple length of solid wire can create problems.

The electrical conductor typically has a carbon-impregnated core of a suitable fiber, and everything from nylon to Kevlar has been used by different makers. That conductor (often covered by a second layer of a nonconductive material such as synthetic rubber) has enough electrical resistance to suppress radio interference without unduly weakening the spark. Some premium wires may have copper or stainless steel wire wound around the carbon core to reduce resistance. In some special applications in which minimum resistance is needed for engine performance, a solid metal wire has been used as a conductor, but over the inner layer of insulation is a layer of wound wire as a shield. On other types of wires, the outer jacket of the wire may have a metallic shield to prevent interference.

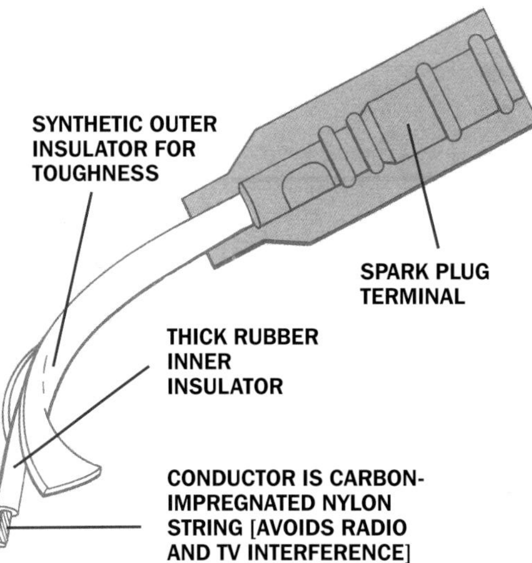

(Fig. 4) Replace plug wires one at a time to maintain the exact same routing as original. Use silicone grease on the boots to allow easy removal in the future.

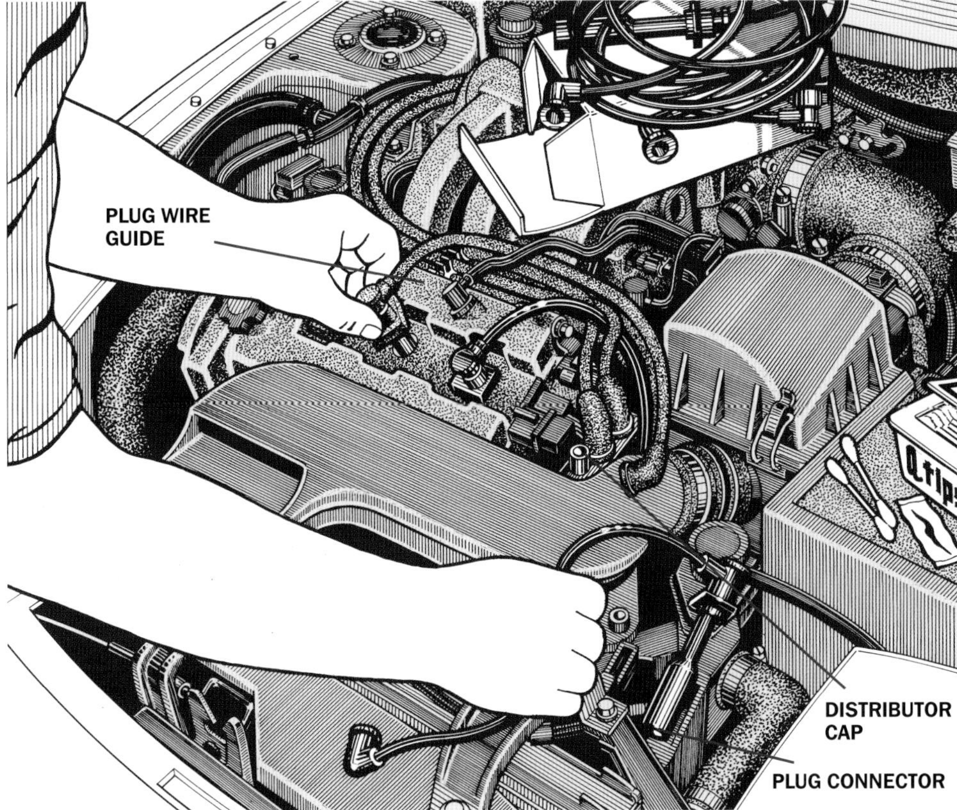

take note if you feel some looseness at the connection (it may have been caused by engine vibration).

The plug wire usually is more accessible at the coil end, but it may not be a simple push-on. Since the early 1980s, Chrysler plug wires on engines with distributors have been held in the cap by spring clips. Compress the tangs of the clip with pliers and push out to disengage the wire (Fig. 3). Some Japanese makes have thread-in "boots."

Follow the routing of a spark plug wire as if it were the road to success, because when it comes to engine operation, it really is. Every manufacturer includes little plastic guides, and although they may cost pennies to make and install, they're used to locate each wire so it doesn't cause crossfire (a transfer of high-voltage electricity from one cylinder's wire to the one that's next in the firing order) (Fig. 4). If you see one wire crossing over or under another at nearly right angles, that's an example of the routing strategy used to avoid crossfire.

Of course, on some engines with coil-on-plug ignition (COP), there is no wire and the boot is out of sight, out of mind. Although this type is immune to hungry rodents, a boot may suffer internal damage from high-voltage electricity or cracking from engine heat. It's even possible for spilled oil to flow under the cover and get down onto the boots on some cars, so have a rag handy when you're adding engine oil. It's impractical to check these boots with the engine running, so you've got to remove the ignition cover and lift the COP modules to make a physical inspection. There are some "hybrid" designs, with one coil on one plug to serve two cylinders (Fig. 5). The coil directly feeds a plug in a boot underneath, and there's a plug wire (replaceable) to a second plug.

The COP boots alone are usually under $25 a set, and are strictly a dealer part. Just pull the coil/electronics module off the plug and then pull the boot off the module. If the boot is integral to the electronics the price could be $100 each.

There's no maintenance you can perform to extend the life of plug wires. However, before you install the boot on the plug, coat the inside with boot release lube (a silicone grease) to make it easier to remove next time. And whenever you work under the hood, avoid nicking the wires, spilling solvent on them, or mishandling if you have to set them aside while you work on something else. And if you see a wire dangling very close to the exhaust manifold, reposition it in its guide to gain some clearance. A penny of prevention can be worth a couple of hundred dollars of cure.

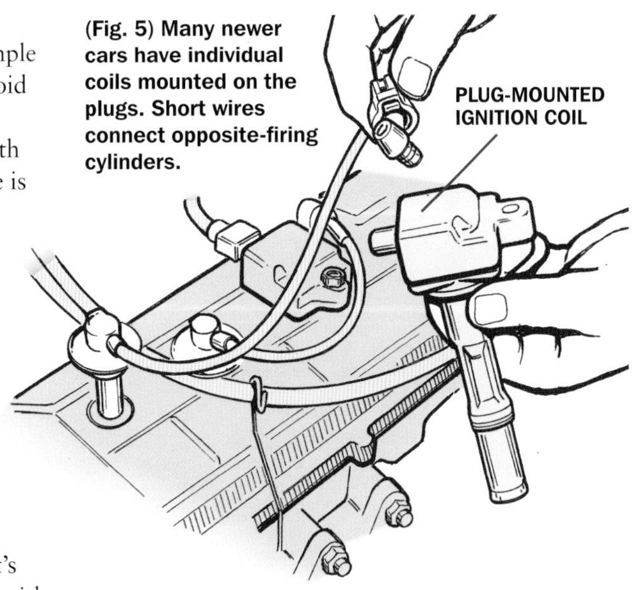

(Fig. 5) Many newer cars have individual coils mounted on the plugs. Short wires connect opposite-firing cylinders.

EASY

Maintaining Your Tires

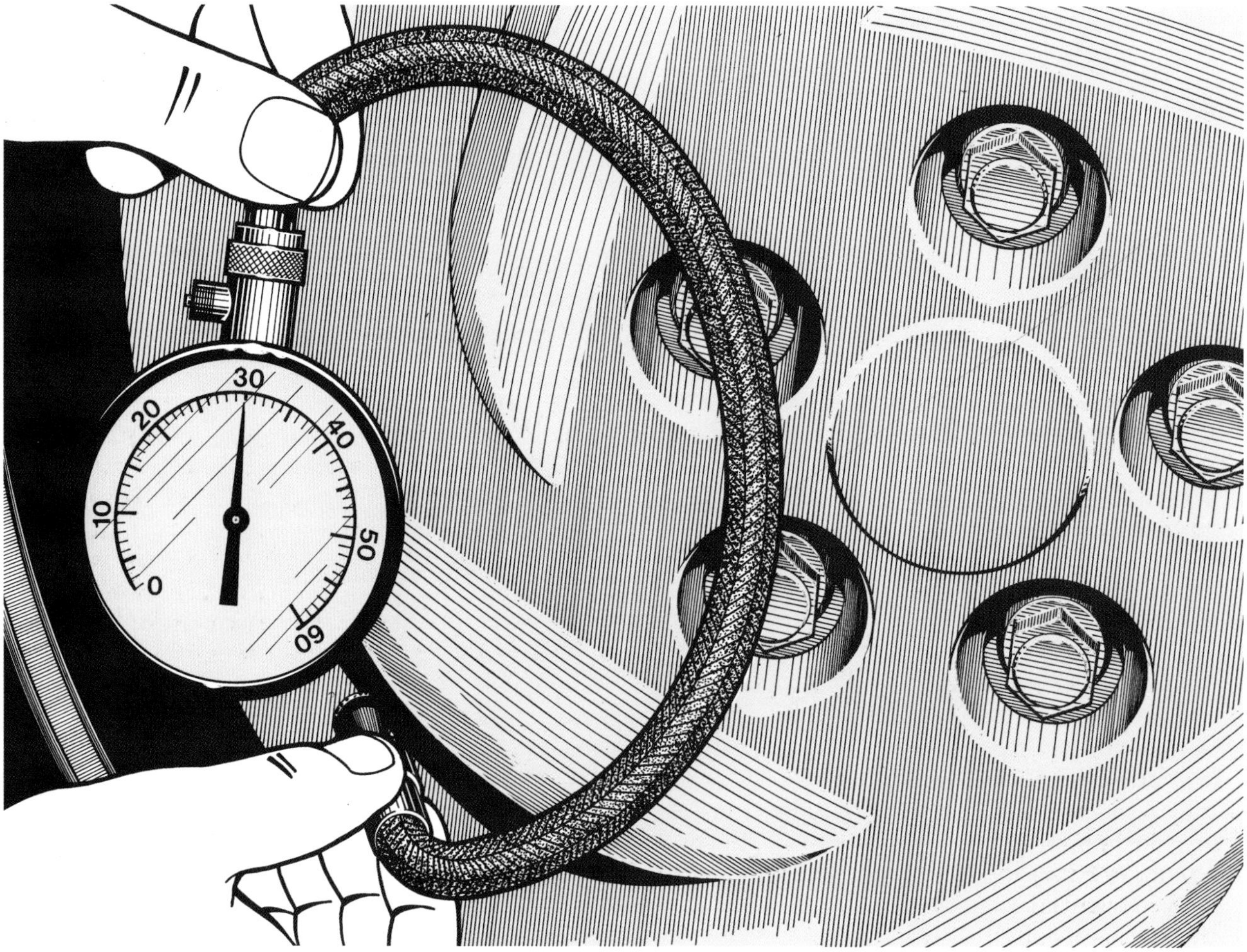

Any kind of tire failure—even a simple flat—is a huge hassle. But this can be avoided with careful tire maintenance. If the recent tire recalls and reports of tread separation have alerted you to the importance of regular tire inspection and care, you're ready to go beyond just a quick look to make sure the tires aren't flat. Most failures are caused by underinflation, overloading your vehicle, or damage from debris, curbs and potholes. These are things you can check yourself.

Preflight Inspection

At least once a month, check your tire pressures—in your driveway, preferably when the tires are overnight cold, or when it has been at least 6 hours since the vehicle was driven (Fig. 1). Don't try to "eyeball"a tire for normal inflation. You can't tell the difference between a properly inflated tire and one that's even 10 psi under. Some tires always look underinflated. Some have stiff sidewalls and always look normally inflated.

Read the tire specification label, which usually is on the driver's front doorjamb or the matching surface on the pillar (Fig. 2). These pressure specs usually are lower than the maximum pressure allowed on the tire's sidewall, but they're based on each particular vehicle and its rated load, not what the tires are physically capable of withstanding.

(Fig. 1) Always check your tires cold. Driving even a few miles will heat them up and change the internal pressure, possibly masking underinflation.

Although tire pressure specifications usually peak at 32 to 36 psi, buy a tire pressure gauge that reads to at least 60 psi. That's a typical pressure specification for a compact spare. If the vehicle manufacturer specifies a pressure range, such as a minimum and a maximum, always use the maximum. The higher the pressure, the greater the load-carrying capacity of the tire, the more stable the vehicle's

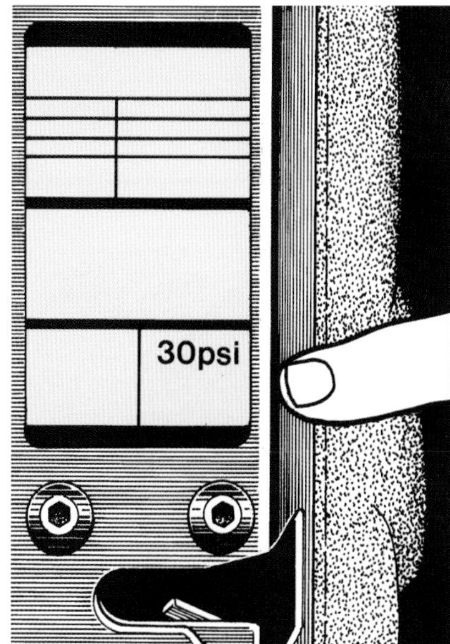

(Fig. 2) Appropriate tire pressures are listed on a sticker on the doorframe or the matching door pillar.

handling will be, and the cooler the tire will run at speed. All tires leak air pressure over time. The closer the tires are to the recommended maximum pressure, the greater the safety margin for all operating parameters. A normal tire leaks about .5 to 1 psi per month.

In addition, as ambient temperatures drop with the changes of seasons, so do the tires' air pressure—one psi per 10°F. It might seem that the temperature-related drop is matched by lower operating temperatures of the tires in cold weather. But the key to tire safety is adequate pressure to carry your vehicle's load. Although higher tire pressures stiffen the ride somewhat, it's a small price to pay for the extra safety and the ability of the vehicle to accommodate greater loads. Maintaining proper tire pressure also improves fuel economy, although not by much. Caution: Overinflation increases center tread wear.

Don't forget the spare. And note our earlier warning about the higher specified pressure for a compact spare. If your spare is carried in the underbody, as it is on many minivans, you'll need to crawl underneath with a pressure gauge and air hose.

Inspecting Tires

If you hit a road hazard such as a sharp rock, of course you're going to look as soon as possible for damage. But remember, even if the exterior looks fine, the tire may be damaged inside. Although it may not slow-leak, it could fail suddenly. You'd be wise to get the car to a tire shop so the tire can be demounted and given an internal inspection. The few dollars is a great investment in peace of mind, and if there is internal damage, forget about a patch. Invest in new rubber.

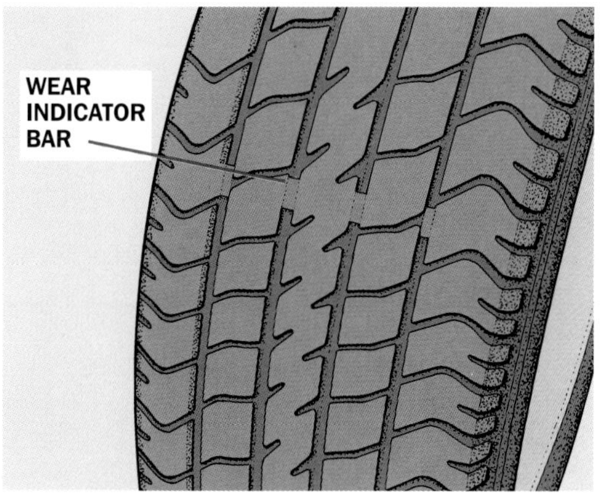

(Fig.3) Check the tread for cuts, foreign objects and abnormal wear. The wear bars will indicate when the tire is worn out.

Wheel alignment also plays an important role in tire performance. If the wheels are misaligned, they don't roll true down the road. The side slippage produces friction, which raises tire temperatures and not only increases tread wear but causes the wear to be uneven.

So inspect the tire treads. As you do, pry out pebbles from the grooves. They reduce traction and can damage the tread area.

The treads should be deepest at midpoint—at least ⅛ in. thick. That's $\frac{1}{16}$ in. above the tread bars that are the official "replace them" indicators (**Fig. 3**). However, you need tread above those bars or the tire will do a poor job of shedding any water and slush it runs into on the road. The wear pattern should be relatively even at each side, although it might be somewhat greater in the middle. Tread wear that is "feathered"—worn to a sharp edge at one or both sides—or much greater on one side is a sign of misalignment.

If you see cuplike wear in the treads, typically along one side, the possible causes are wheels that are out of balance, worn-out shocks or struts, and loose suspension components. The classic sign of unbalanced wheels is high-speed (50 mph and up) vibration, and it usually surfaces before the cuplike wear becomes noticeable. Suspension problems usually produce shake at lower speeds.

Look for any cuts on the surface of the tire that expose the steel belt or fabric cord. This is grounds for immediate replacement.

Tires with unevenly worn treads should be replaced, unless the problem is caught early and there's plenty of tread depth left. In that case, they could provide a moderate amount of life on the rear wheels, particularly on a front-drive car. However, if you have an all-wheel drive that you push pretty hard, invest in an entire set of new tires.

Wheel Balancing

Most shops have off-car electronic balancers that allow the wheels to be rotated to any position without affecting their balance. The disadvantage is, if there's any unbalance in the wheel hub, it won't be corrected. If this doesn't cure the vibration, it's worth finding a shop with on-car equipment before you try something else. In addition, make sure the shop has weights designed for your wheels. It takes at least a half-dozen differently shaped weights to fit properly on the rims of all the popular wheels. There are several so-called "universal" weights, but they may not fit your rim, and could pop off or cause rim damage.

If the wheels are balanced and you have wheel shake at medium speeds on up, or the tires have cup wear, check the shocks and struts.

HOW IT WORKS

Reading A Passenger Tire Sidewall

A "P" or "LT" stands for passenger car or light truck tire. The 3-digit number (215 on this diagram) is the tire cross-section width in millimeters. The 2-digit number that follows (65) is the aspect ratio—the height of the sidewall relative to the cross-section. A lower number indicates a wide tread area relative to the sidewall—today's sporty look. The letter "R" means radial tire construction. The next 2-digit number (15) is the wheel rim diameter in inches. A 2-digit number following the size information is a load-versus-pressure rating. A letter that follows that 2-digit rating is a speed rating. Example: "S" is for a tire rated for speeds up to 112 mph. You'll also find maximum pressure (in psi and kilopascals), and maximum load (in kilograms and pounds). In addition, there are numerical or letter grades for relative tread life, traction and temperature (UTQG). The layout of the information may vary according to make.

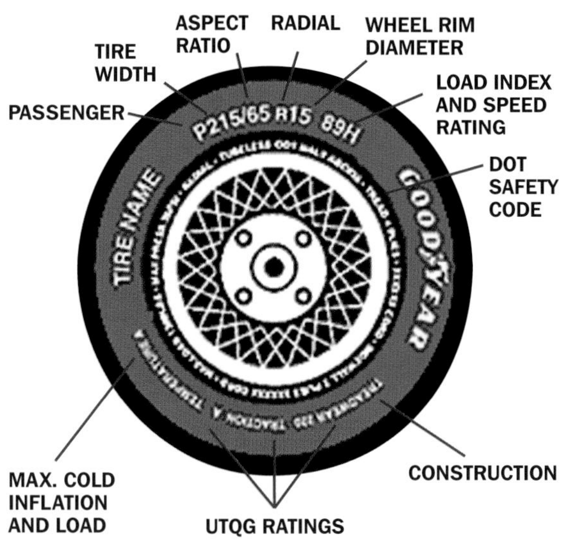

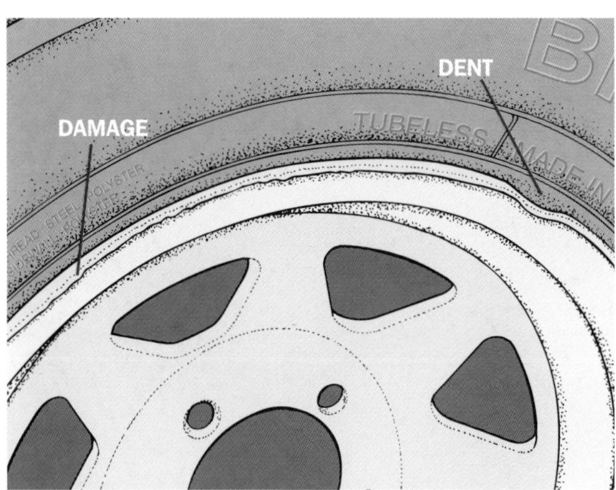

(Fig. 4) Minor scraping on the rim's lip is okay, but a bent bead surface may cause a leak or vibration.

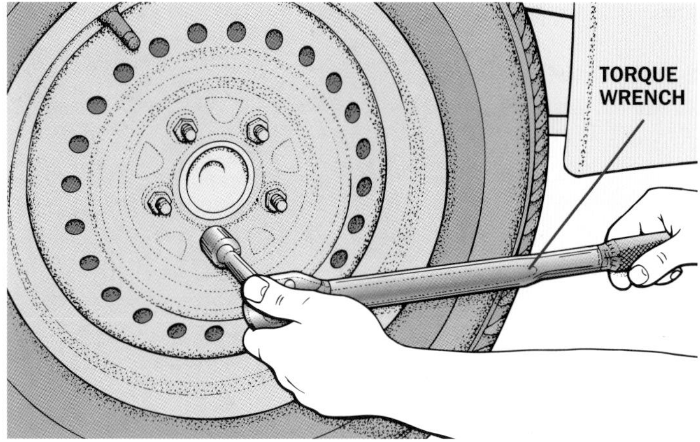

(Fig. 5) To avoid warping brake discs, tighten the lugs in a crisscross pattern with a torque wrench.

Sidewall Check

Using a tire and wheel cleaning product will give you a clear look at both the tires and wheels. You should be able to find cracks in the wheel, damage beyond surface nicks to the tire sidewalls, and damage to the bead area that could be responsible for pressure leakage (Fig. 4).

Tire Rotation

Every owner's manual has a tire rotation diagram, and tire rotation may seem like motherhood and apple pie—always good. However, this subject is not so simple. Cost of rotation versus longer tire life is not a precise equation. It depends on the tires, the driving, wheel alignment and suspension condition. Further, professional service is not always expertly done. Unless the lug nuts are tightened to specifications in three even stages, using a crisscross pattern (Fig. 5), the rotors may become warped, which adds to maintenance costs. If you let the mileage stretch out a bit, such as to 10,000 miles or more, tires may develop almost imperceptible wear patterns that will affect ride when they're moved to a new position on the car. If you can't rotate the tires often, you may be better off leaving them in place and accepting the somewhat shorter tread life.

Some tire treads are directional. They should rotate in only one direction and should not be rotated except by a professional who can demount them.

How can you tell if you have this type of tire? Look for a directional arrow on the sidewall.

EASY

Jumpstarting Your Car

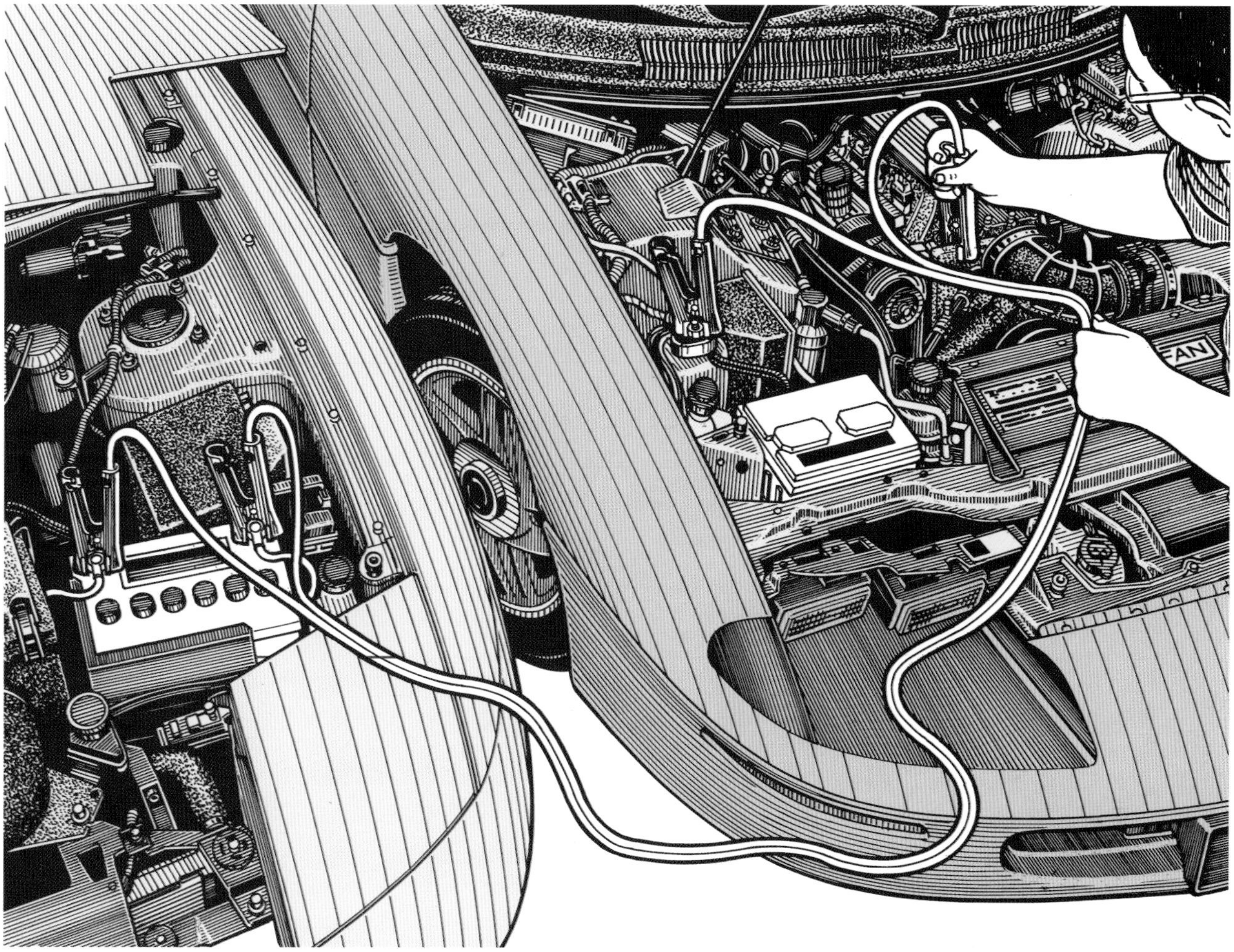

It hits you like an electrical shock just as the airliner door slams and the flight attendant oh-so-politely instructs you to turn off your cellphone. Less than an hour ago, you parked your car in the middle of a 10-acre airport parking lot, expecting the vehicle to take you home when you return in five days. Except you realize that you forgot to turn off the headlights after your predawn departure from home and the warning buzzer hasn't worked for eons, if your car has one. And if it doesn't, there's no surprise—you've done this before. Great. Now when you get home you'll have to call the airport-approved towing service and drop close to a hundred bucks for a jump.

Neglect Is Abuse

Lead-acid automotive batteries are actually remarkable at delivering extremely high current for the few seconds it takes to start your engine, even in extremes of heat and cold. What they are not good at is being able to recover after delivering more modest amounts of current for a long time. Irreversible chemical changes take place. Specifically, sulphate needles that bridge the separator between the positive and negative plates form when a battery is deeply discharged. These needles not only internally short the plates, causing a high self-discharge rate, they also coat the plates and interfere with the normal lead/sulfuric acid reaction that makes electricity to spin your starter motor and run your fuel injection and ignition long enough to coax your engine into life.

(Fig. 1) Make the last connection to a ground point not on the battery to prevent creating a spark near any venting, explosive hydrogen gas.

Before you do anything else, check to see that the dead battery isn't frozen. While a fully charged battery is almost freeze-proof, a highly discharged battery can freeze when temps hit the low 20s. If the battery has them, remove the filler caps and look for ice crystals in the electrolyte. Don't try to charge a frozen battery. It won't

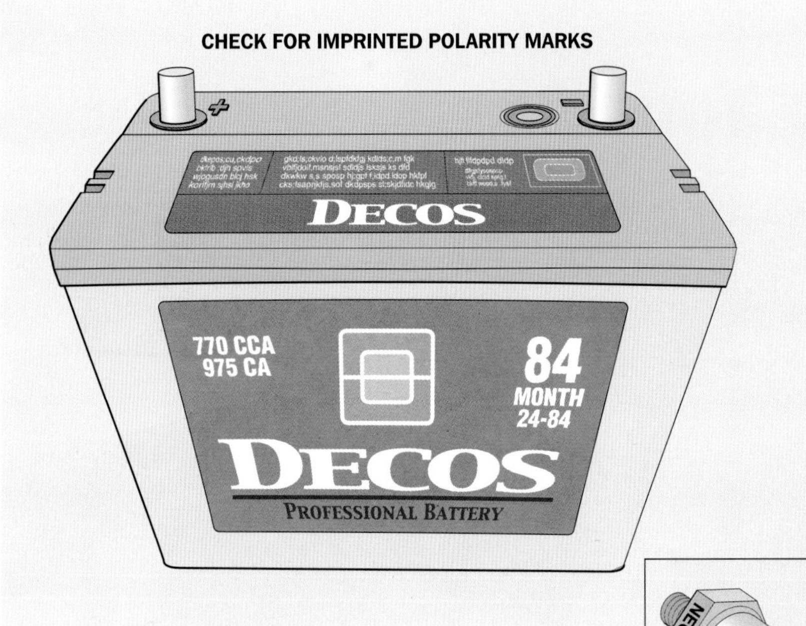

(Fig. 2) Make absolutely sure you've got the polarity correct whenever you work on a battery. If your battery has side terminals, use these adapter bolts (right) when jumping it or use jumper cables with clips shaped for side terminals.

HOW IT WORKS

Deeply Discharged Batteries

A lead-acid car battery, like any battery, has an internal resistance, normally a few tenths of an ohm. This means that a charging voltage only a little higher than the battery's normal 12.6 volts will provide enough current to actually charge the battery at some decent rate, say, 10 to 12 amps. But as the battery discharges, its internal resistance goes up. And the curve is steep. When the battery is almost totally discharged, internal resistance can be high enough to prevent the 13.5 to 14 volts your alternator puts out from doing any significant charging. Charging current in this instance can be as little as only a few hundred milliamps until the battery's resistance goes down—and that might take many hours, or even days of charging at normal voltages.

The answer is a high-voltage, high-rate professional charger that can supply as much as 25 to 30 volts for a brief period to give the battery a kick in the pants. This will generate a lot of heat, enough to cook a battery within a few minutes. Leave this business to a professional, and follow up with a normal 6- to 10-amp charge.

work, and will damage the battery further. If you need a boost start to get home, well . . . life's like that.

Safety First

Your first task is to get jumper cables. Preferably nice fat ones with a quality, heavy-duty set of clamps. This is more than just tool envy—there's a lot of current passing along those wires, more than an arc welder, at least for a few seconds. Resistive losses in the cable can reduce the voltage available to your stalled car's electrical system to the point at which it will still be difficult to start, even with a healthy donor battery and alternator adding their all to the mix. It's important to use fat cables and to have good electrical connections to reduce these losses to a minimum.

A set of 6-ft. cables won't do you much good if you're parked nose-in to a parking space—unless you feel up to pushing a 3-ton SUV back a truck length to make the engine compartment available. Twelve or 15 ft. is better, which makes using heavy-duty cables more important because resistance losses are proportional to the length of the cable.

Keep your cables clean and dry to prevent corrosion from becoming a high-resistance factor.

Doing The Deed

It's nitty-gritty time. You've got cables, you've got a healthy donor car available. Open the hoods and position the donor car nearby, so that your cables will reach.

Some cars, like the one illustrated on the previous page (**Fig. 1**), have a remote positive terminal someplace in the engine compartment. The battery is mounted in an inaccessible area or with its terminals inaccessible even in the engine compartment. As for where to attach the jumper cable, this junction will be clearly marked and covered in a red plastic sheath. If in doubt, consult your owner's manual.

Wear eye protection, even if it's only a pair of sunglasses. Once in a blue moon, a battery will explode

(Fig. 3) If your car or RV is in storage and chronically needs help starting, a trickle charger will keep it ready and improve your battery life as well.

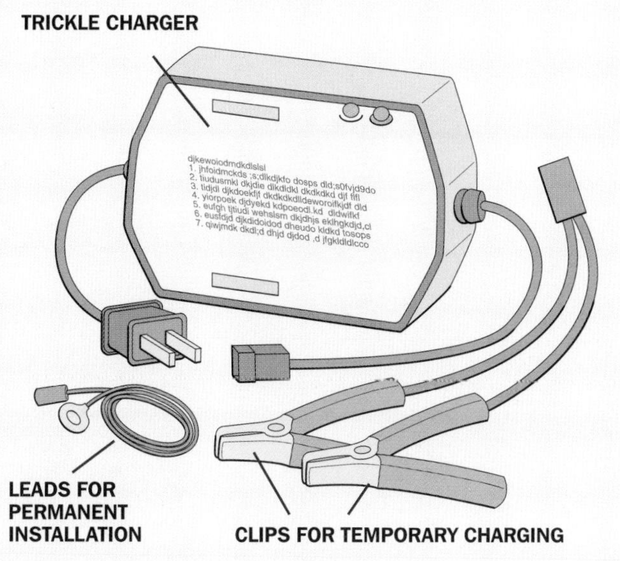

when you try to jump it. Explode? Yes, explode. It's caused by hydrogen gas, which is normally vented by a battery that's being charged or discharged at a high rate, say, when you're trying to start a car, the battery runs down and you need a jumpstart. Hydrogen is explosive, and a spark from making a connection can ignite it. It won't be a big explosion, but it can certainly blow the top of the plastic battery case off and spray acid into your eyes.

Connect the red clamp on one end of the jumpers to the positive terminal on the dead car. Verify the polarity of the terminals by the plus symbol molded into the battery case (**Fig. 2**). Don't just use the red terminal—someone may have installed an incorrect, red-colored terminal onto the negative pole of the battery. Do the same on the positive terminal of the donor car. Start the donor car and let it idle. Lights, heaters, stereos and rear-window defrosters—all electrical drains—should be off.

If possible, cover the dead battery with a shop towel or a sheet of cardboard. Any acid that manages to bubble out of the vents will wind up on the cloth instead of on your clothes or the paint on the fender.

Connect to the negative terminal of the donor car's battery with the black clamp. Verify the polarity. Now connect the remaining black clamp to the dead car's engine block, an accessory mounting bracket or a protruding ear on a manifold. Use the battery's negative terminal as a last resort. This procedure will generate any sparks far from any hydrogen gas venting from the battery and reduce the risk of explosion.

Now wait. This will let the dead battery recharge slightly. It will charge more when the dead car starts, but it will help the donor car's battery start your engine a little if you give it a quick shot of charge. If the dead car's battery had enough charge left to make the solenoid click and run the interior and instrument lights, then a minute or so is enough. If the battery was dead, dead, dead, give it 5 minutes or so.

Crank, Zoom

Now you can actually try to start your dead car. When the car starts, let it run at fast idle for another few minutes still connected to the donor car to continue charging by both alternators. Idling provides only a modest charge rate, so after a few minutes the best thing is to drive the car at normal speeds for 30 to 60 minutes.

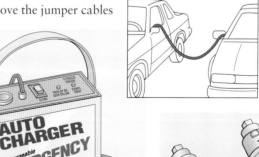

Remove the jumper cables in the reverse order. Wash your hands if possible to prevent any battery acid from bleaching your clothes or getting into your eyes.

Options

If your RV or second car is in storage for extended periods of time, the battery will self-discharge. The simplest solution is to use a trickle, or maintenance, charger (**Fig. 3**). These chargers will automatically adjust their charge rate to a safe level, low enough to keep the battery at 100 percent charge without cooking it. They're not recommended for charging dead batteries—just maintaining them.

If you're not in a crashing hurry, you might find cigar-lighter cables will get you started (**Fig. 4**). These gadgets just plug into the two vehicles' lighter plugs, providing a modest level of charging, but not carrying enough current to start a car with a truly flat battery. But if the engine will almost start, a 10- or 20-minute charge will get you on your way, out of the weather and with clean hands. Remember that the lighter socket on the dead car must be electrically hot with the key off, or you'll need to turn on the key in the dead car to complete the circuit.

(Fig. 4) Minor cases of won't-quite-start will answer to simple-to-use lighter-plug starters and jumper cables.

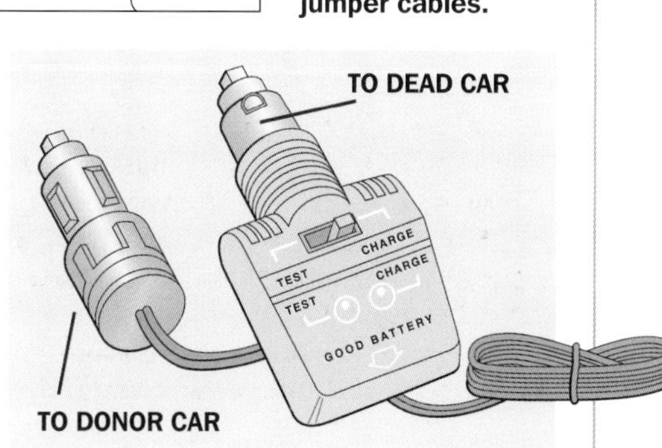

Repairing a Leaky Radiator

Your radiator is leaking. Well, it happens. If you haven't changed the coolant on a reasonable schedule, it can become corrosive and eat through the radiator. Even normal shaking and vibration will eventually cause separations between the parts that are connected by solder, epoxy or mechanical crimps. Thermal forces from engines heating up and cooling down can cause cracks in stressed areas. Sealing gaskets can compress and allow leakage. And if you have a rear-drive car with a mechanical fan and weak engine mounts, the engine can lurch forward under braking far enough for the engine-mounted fan to "kiss" the radiator. Or it could be just plain bad luck—a rock gets thrown up and punches a hole in a tube.

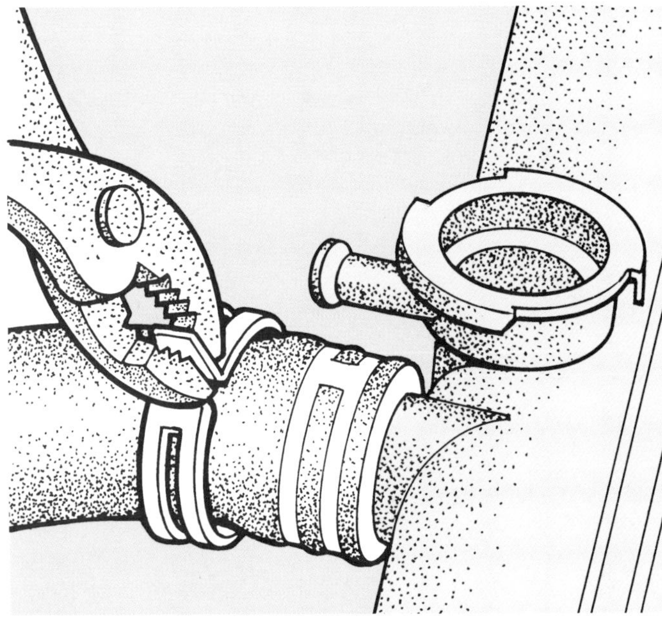

(Fig. 1) Loosen and slide the hose clamps on the hoses clear of the radiator necks. Then, disconnect the hoses.

Whatever its root cause, a leak is generally obvious. But what to do about the radiator? Replace it? After all, today's radiators are supposed to be unrepairable. This is not true at all, and the best thing you can do is take out the radiator and bring it to a radiator shop for a free consultation. If it can be repaired, you'll not only save money, but the repaired original-equipment (OE) radiator probably will be a lot better than a new discount part. It's no different from any rebuilt automobile component, except that the radiator has no moving parts.

Everything starts with removing the leaking radiator. Although doing so takes some care, it's a straightforward job. In the easier cases, you can lift it out with shroud and fans attached, then complete the strip-down on the garage floor. And even in a really tight engine compartment you can usually get it out without touching the a/c lines, or at worst you would only have to unbolt the radiator from the same module that holds the a/c condenser.

Begin by disconnecting the battery ground strap (even if the car has belt-driven, rather than electrical, fans). The next step normally is to drain the radiator, but before you do, inspect both radiator tanks carefully. If you find a heater hose connection, as on a few cars, pinch off the hose just a few inches from the neck, using locking pliers. (If necessary, use a pair of tongue depressors or popsicle sticks between the jaws to get a good squeeze.) With the heater hose pinched, you won't lose coolant from the heater during the drain. It can be tough to get coolant to completely fill the heater on some cars, so unless you're prepared to do a complete drain-and-refill, this preliminary step can help prevent trapping a lot of air in the system. Air bubbles lead to engine hot spots and ping in summer operation, and poor heater output in the winter.

If there's an underbody plastic cover at the front, remove it, even if it's not necessary to do so to drain the coolant. With the cover off, you'll surely be able to collect the draining coolant with less splash. You'll also be able to get to the lower radiator hose more easily, and you can inspect the lower end of the radiator as well. You might see a bolt-on connection to the condenser or the support member that you wouldn't otherwise notice. And with most Japanese cars, which have downflow radiators (tanks at the top

(Fig. 2) f you have an electrical cooling fan, you'll need to disconnect the wiring to it.

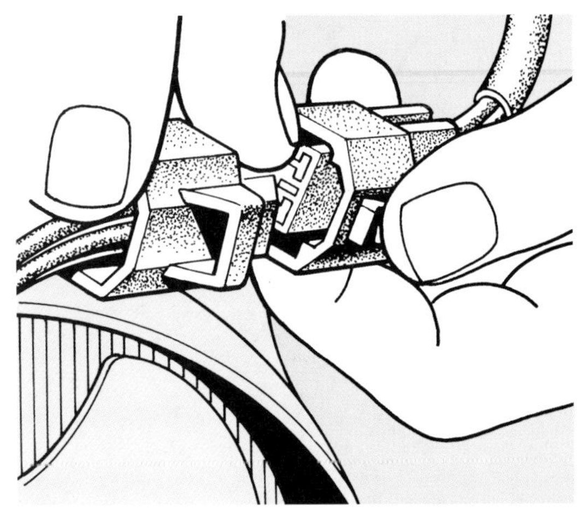

and bottom), you'll be able to reach any hoses or wires that you must disconnect from the bottom tank.

Ready? Now remove the pressure cap, even if it's on a separate tank or on the engine. Remove the radiator drain plug (or open the drain cock) and let the radiator drain. Move the clamps off the necks toward the midpoints of the radiator hoses **(Fig. 1)**, then disconnect the hoses—including the heater hose if there's a connection at the radiator. If the hoses are heat-sealed to the radiator necks but in good condition, slip a thin screwdriver between the hose and neck, and work it around to free the hose, then twist the hose and work it off. Don't pry with a large screwdriver or you could distort a metal neck or even crack a plastic one. You may find it necessary to carefully slit the hose with a sharp knife to get it to let go. Don't scratch the neck, or it'll leak in the future.

As you disconnect the lower hose, a fair amount of engine coolant is likely to flow out, so make sure you have a large catch pan underneath.

Evaluate the radiator installation and begin the wrench work to free it up. A typical approach is to remove the upper mount/retainer on each side, or the single support member across the front. If there's enough clearance for the radiator to come up and out with its shroud and electric fans intact, just unplug the electrical connectors for each fan **(Fig. 2)**. If not, you'll often be able to just unbolt the shroud and fans from the radiator and tilt them back to provide clearance to lift out the radiator.

PULLING OUT THE RADIATOR is easy once it has been drained. You may need to disconnect or remove the fan shroud.

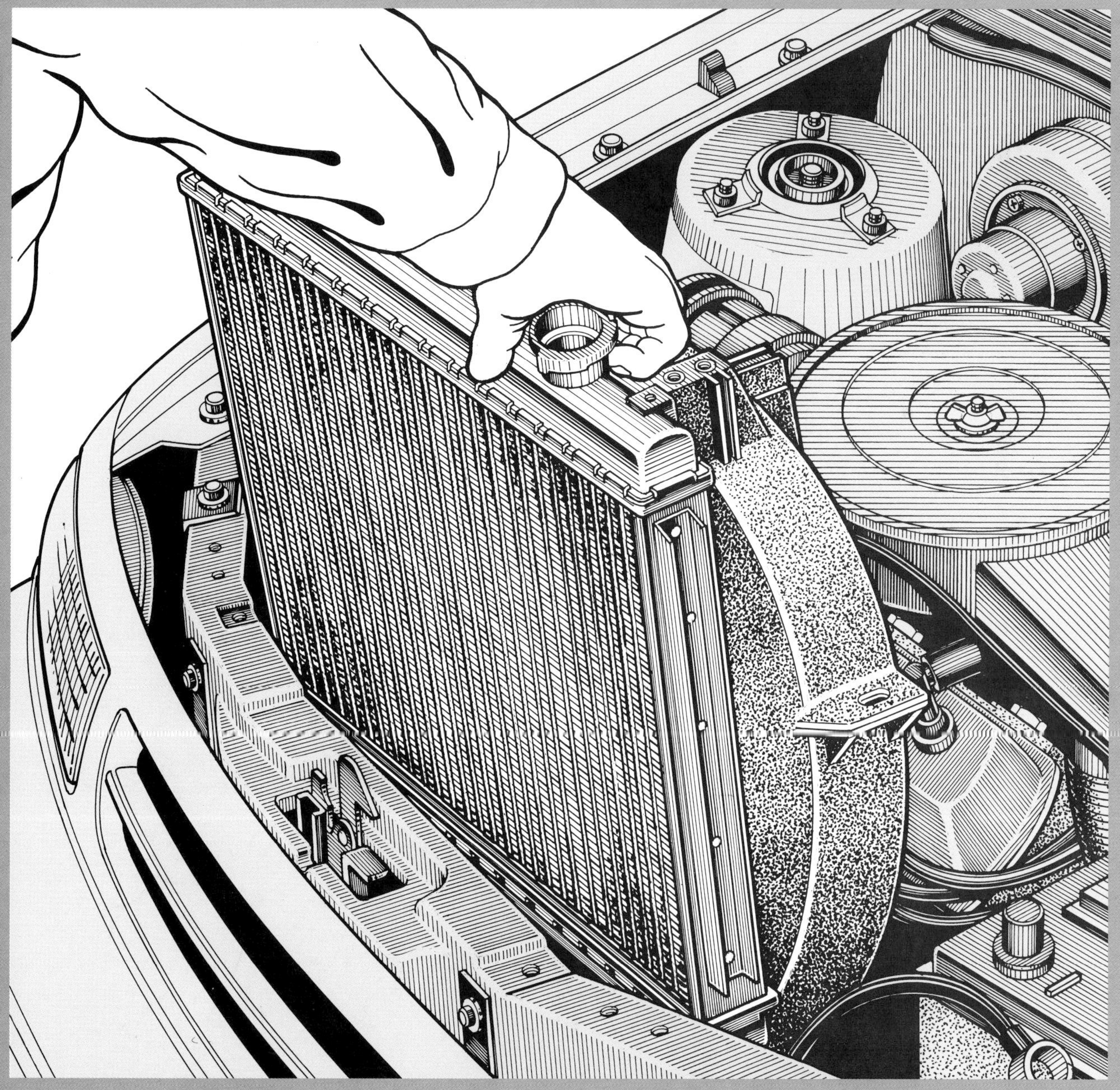

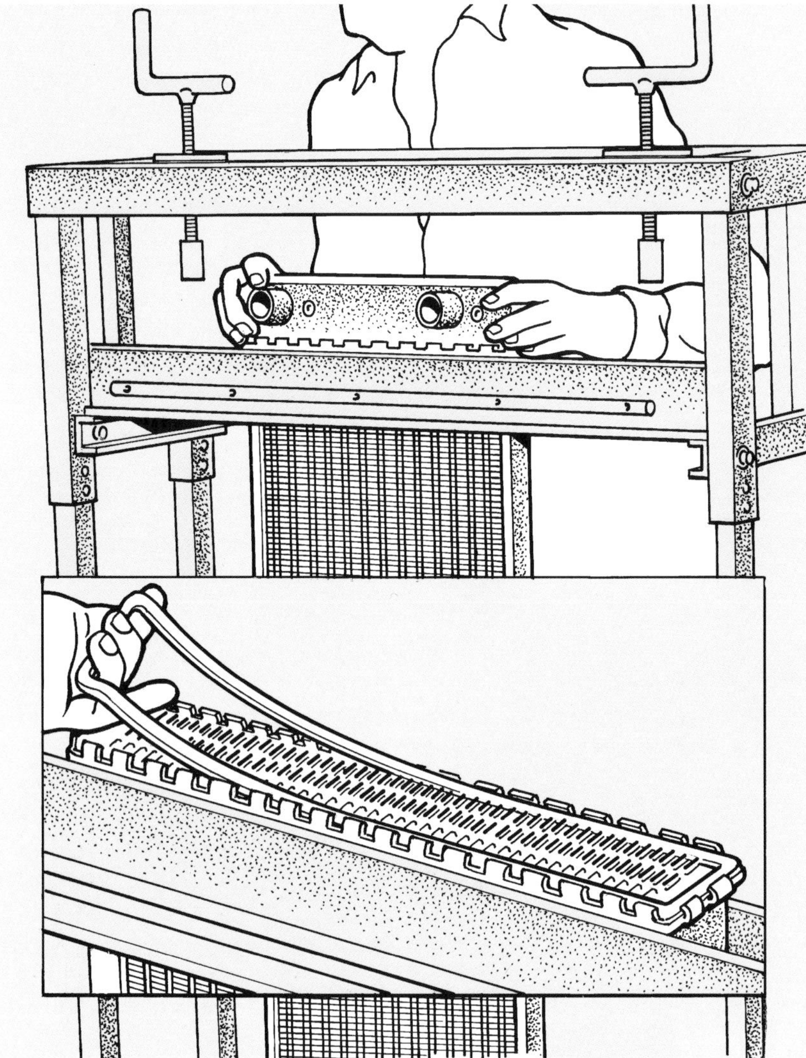

(Fig. 3) A radiator shop can replace a leaky O-ring seal, one or both end tanks or the core relatively inexpensively.

Disconnect the overflow hose and if the reservoir is in the way, take it out. This can give you your first close look at the reservoir. Many reservoirs develop hairline cracks that allow hard-to-trace leaks, so if you have a leak here, you just may have saved a bundle. If not, keep working.

If you have an automatic transmission, the radiator usually contains an automatic transmission cooler. Disconnect the cooler lines, a job that isn't always a simple wrench operation. In the easiest cases, there's a hose connection and a clamp. In the most difficult, there's a quick-disconnect fitting that requires a special (but inexpensive) tool to separate. If you have a quick-disconnect, as on most Ford products, and you can't get the tool, you'll find that the radiator end of the quick-disconnect has fittings that thread into the cooler. So a fitting can be unscrewed, but be careful. Use a tight-fitting wrench and unthread slowly, so you don't damage the quick-disconnect coupling.

Whatever type the cooler connections are, be prepared to plug them. Yes, you want to avoid transmission-fluid leakage. But more critically, if any amount of coolant gets into the cooler or its lines, it can be sayonara for the automatic transmission. You can plug a hose end with a bolt. Plug a fitting with a rubber eraser, vacuum hose plug or some other clean, soft, flexible material that will stay in place (but also come out easily when you're ready to reinstall the radiator).

All clear? Lift out the radiator and strip off any parts you were able to leave in place. Virtually all late-model vehicles have radiators with plastic tanks crimped onto the core. Your next step is to take the radiator to a radiator shop that actually repairs plastic-tank radiators. The National Automotive Radiator Service Association (NARSA) has been giving its members intensive training in the repair of these radiators, whether with copper/brass or aluminum cores, for several years (215/541-4500). So a radiator shop should know how to fix it, and not simply try to unbox a cheap new radiator and sell it to you. The cheap radiators just don't transfer heat as well, and unless you can get a spectacular price on a well-made replacement, you're usually better off with a repair.

Can it be repaired?

Almost all car, light-truck and sport/ute radiators have plastic tanks, either with aluminum or copper/brass core sections. They're precisely engineered to cool. And given today's tiny grille openings or no-grille underbody breathers, a cheap radiator is a bad gamble. It may look shiny new, but it could corrode and fail a lot faster than a properly repaired unit.

When a radiator leaks, the most common causes usually are readily repairable at far less than the cost of a new quality radiator. It certainly has been true with the copper/brass radiators largely out of use. It's even more likely with today's designs, particularly aluminum-core radiators, which can run $200 to $400 for a first-rate replacement. Here are some repair examples:

- Leaking gasket between plastic tank and core: The shop uncrimps the tank, installs a new gasket and recrimps the tank (**Fig. 3**). It should cost less than $75.
- Damaged tube (perhaps from a stone): These can be fixed for an extremely modest labor charge with special epoxy or solder. Even aluminum radiator tubes can be soldered.

• Cracked plastic tank (perhaps from thermal stresses): A new tank today is relatively inexpensive for most makes, so the job should cost less than $150.

• Leaking header: The headers are the metal plates at each end of the tubes. The radiator tanks attach to the headers, either by crimping a gasket joint or by soldering. Older Ford radiators have epoxy sealing between the headers and the tubes. If leaks occur from cracked epoxy, a radiator shop can remove the old epoxy and install a new sealing film using specially shaped guns and other tools. The cost is typically about $175 to $200 for both ends of the radiator, about half the price of a new Ford radiator.

• Fan "kiss" or corroded radiator: the core is smashed in or leaking from corrosion pinholes. If the tanks are good, the shop can install a new core—perhaps even an OE one—and reuse the old tanks, saving about 25 to 30% on the cost of a new radiator. And the result should be equal to a new OE radiator. If the OE radiator is an inexpensive design, then there won't be much of a difference (perhaps less than $75), and you might as well buy new if it's in stock. However, one core fits many different sets of tanks, so stocking cores is simpler for a shop. Result: The choice may come down to a new core that's available now versus waiting for a new radiator and having to spend up to $100 more besides.

Putting It All Together

When you're ready to install, inspect the rubber support bushings for the radiator. Many of today's radiators are held by mounting systems that allow them to shake at a frequency that absorbs engine vibration. Replace heat-cracked or oil-soaked bushings. Otherwise, engine idle will be rough and the radiator may shake itself into a leak. Clean the threads of oil-cooler quick-disconnect fittings and apply Teflon pipe sealer before reinstallation.

If your drained coolant was relatively fresh, it's okay to put it back in if it's not contaminated with dirt, oil or transmission fluid. Otherwise, use a 50/50 coolant/water mix. If you've taken this opportunity to flush the system with water, then add half the system's capacity of pure coolant and top off with water.

Always check the carmaker's instructions for filling a radiator—and then go beyond that and add a little more. Today's cooling systems are notorious for convoluted passages that balance heat transfer if the system is full, but trap air bubbles if not completely filled. If there are air bleeds, they must be open during the fill-up. Jack up the front of the car to raise the pressure-cap fill neck before you pour in coolant. Even if the fill neck isn't on the radiator itself, the higher it is, the better the system will burp air as you pour in coolant. Make sure the reservoir level is correct and that the air-sealing gasket in the pressure cap is in good condition, so the system won't draw in air as the coolant cools.

And "thermocycle" the system, which simply means to warm it up, then let it cool down. Check the radiator coolant level when the system is cool, and top it off if necessary.

Once is not enough. Keep checking every day or so for a few weeks. Some air purging will continue, and the system should draw in additional coolant from the reservoir. The reservoir level drops modestly? Hey, that's the way it's supposed to work. Top it off when necessary and you can conclude that all has gone well.

Curing Pulsing Brakes

The driver in the left lane suddenly realizes he's about to miss his exit, so he cuts in front of you. You mash the brake pedal, and it vibrates like a running chain saw as the antilock braking system (ABS) keeps you out of a skid. Thankfully, you don't rear-end the jerk's car, as he also brakes to slow down. He's on the off ramp and gone, so you don't get the chance to pull alongside and express your feelings with universal sign language. But that's probably a good thing.

While it can be reassuring to feel that ABS-connected brake pedal pulsating beneath your firmly planted foot, it's reason to suspect a problem if you get the same pedal pulsation with a light to medium braking application.

ABS-esque

If the brake feels like the ABS is cycling, but you know that it's not, check the individual axle trigger wheels in front (and on some cars also in back) and the adjacent wheel speed sensors. If you see a damaged wiring connector, bent sensor mounting bracket or stone-damaged trigger wheel, that's a likely cause. But on almost all cars, the cause normally is something in the service brake itself, and the primary problems are ones you usually can check and correct yourself.

Before you check even the most likely problems on a late model, make absolutely sure there isn't a factory problem with a specific fix. Sure, this is low on the "likely" list, but it's a lot easier to look for a bulletin than to pull wheels, etc. One possibility: the AllData Web site, a leading supplier of information for professional mechanics (www.alldata.com). If you work your way through its consumer information section and technical service bulletins (TSBs), you can check the titles of all bulletins for your specific make and model car.

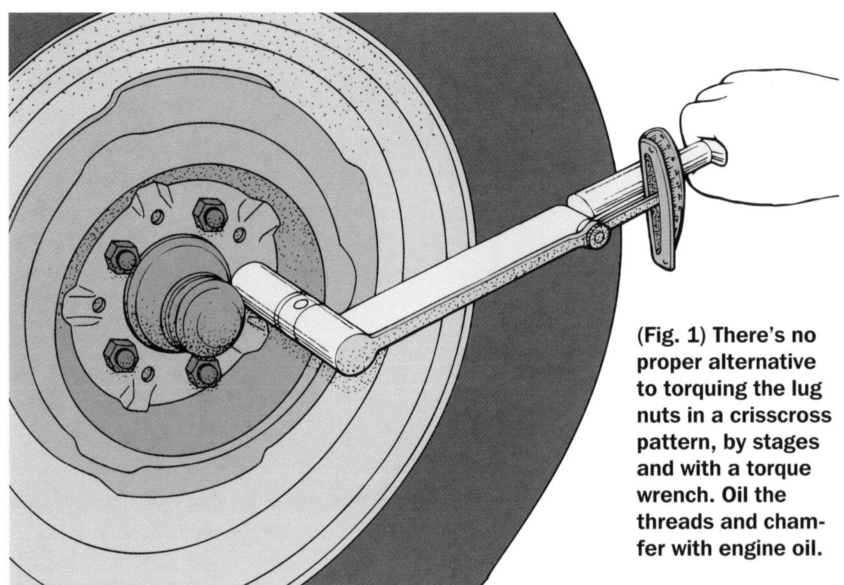
(Fig. 1) There's no proper alternative to torquing the lug nuts in a crisscross pattern, by stages and with a torque wrench. Oil the threads and chamfer with engine oil.

Lug Nut Torque

The No. 1 cause of brake pedal pulsation is uneven lug nut torque. The usual reason is that some mechanic overtightened the wheel lug nuts with an impact wrench, distorting the brake disc.

How do you know if your torque wrench is accurate? Well, if it's by a name-brand tool company and hasn't been thrown around or had a cement block dropped on it, it should be okay. Check the torque at each wheel and compare the reading with manufacturer's specifications. If there's a difference of 20% between any two lug nuts, that's too much. Try loosening all the lug nuts, cleaning the stud threads with

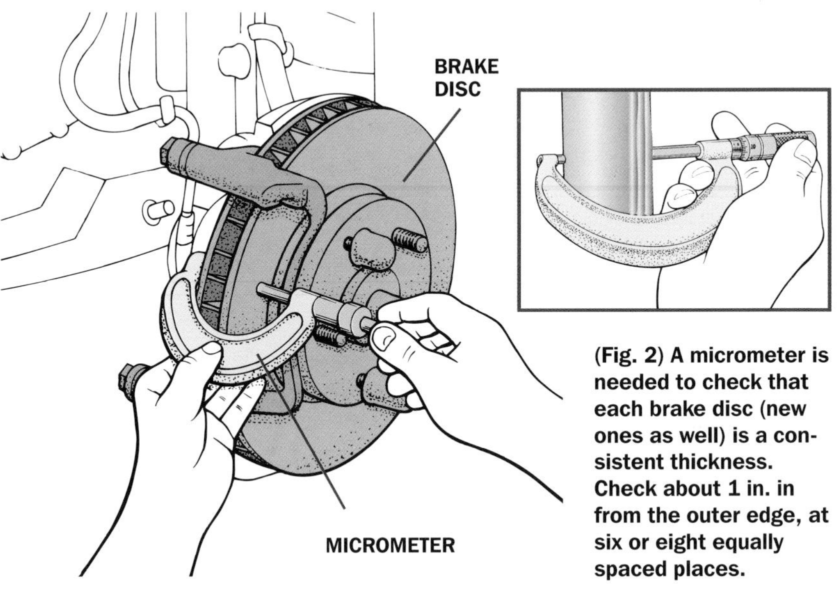

(Fig. 2) A micrometer is needed to check that each brake disc (new ones as well) is a consistent thickness. Check about 1 in. in from the outer edge, at six or eight equally spaced places.

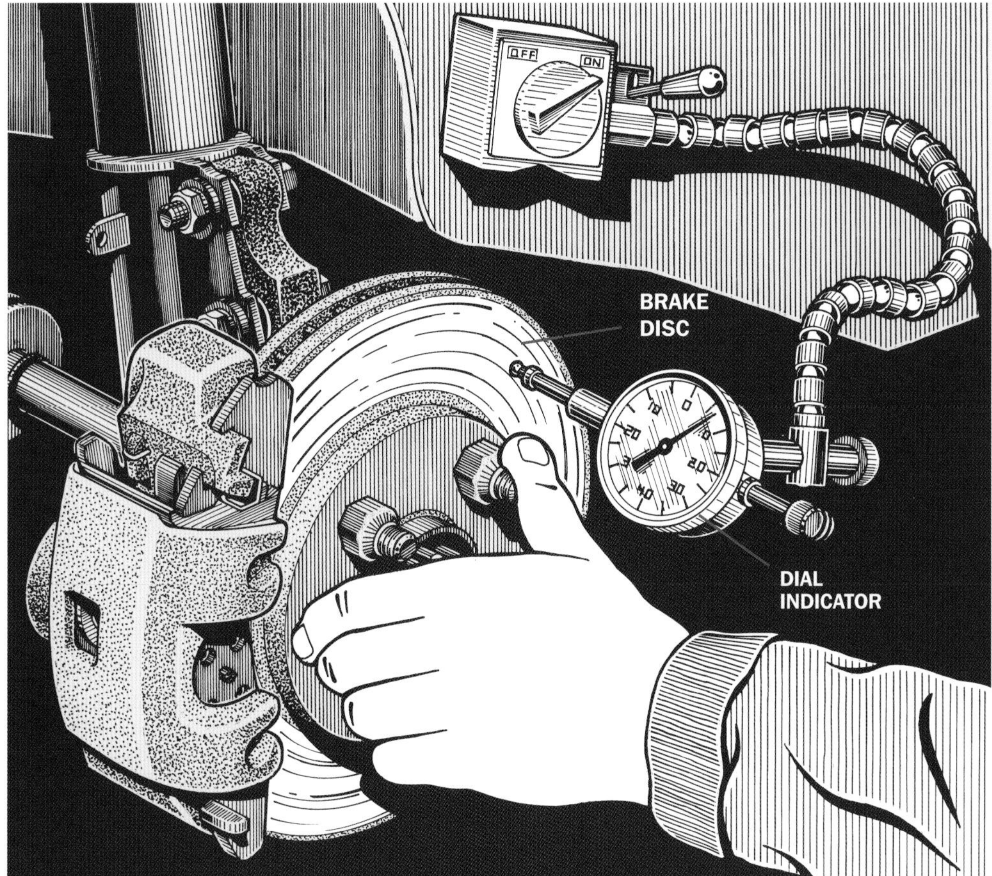

(Fig. 3) Borrow or rent a dial indicator to measure brake disc runout. Even a scant thousandth of an inch of wobble will make your right foot dance on the pedal.

a wire brush, lightly coating them and the nut chamfer with clean engine oil, and then reinstalling the nuts fingertight.

Next, using a crisscross pattern, (Fig. 1) tighten all of them to about one-third the specified reading, then to two-thirds and finally to the specified torque.

Basic Diagnosis

If simple retightening doesn't fix the problem, particularly if all wheels were off torque specs, you'll have to pull the wheels for a closer inspection. First, isolate the problem to the front or rear wheels. Try driving the car and then slowing or stopping with the parking brake lever lightly pulled up and your finger on the ratchet's release button. If the car has a pedal parking brake, try applying that lightly, but be sure to pick a safe, deserted parking lot with smooth pavement. If the car slows down smoothly to a stop, the brake problem is in the front wheels. If the car decelerates in surges, one or more of the rear brakes may be out-of-true.

Full Inspection

Actually inspecting the wheel and brake is the next step. Make alignment marks for the wheel and a lug stud before removal so you're able to index the rim to the same stud. With the wheel off, inspect the mating surfaces of the wheel and disc hub surface. If they're packed with dirt or badly rusted, clean them thoroughly (use 100-grit sandpaper or emery cloth). Remove sanding residue with a cloth and brake solvent. Lube sparingly with antiseize.

Look closely at both sides of the brake lining contact surfaces of the disc. Moderate scores (too small to snag your fingernail on) are not normally a concern, but rust or other materials are (typically brake lining transfer). Rust often occurs on cars that sit for extended periods in damp climates with not-so-clean air. Use a finer abrasive (200 grit) on the disc contact surfaces.

'Miking' A Disc

Check the disc for uneven thickness, using a micrometer (Fig. 2) at six to eight evenly spaced locations on the disc, and compare the readings with manufacturer's specs. As little as .0005 in. (that's five ten-thousandths!) is the maximum, and you can believe that you'll feel a lot of disc pulsation at .0008 in. Should you get the disc machined? A lot of evidence says unless a shop does a good job of maintaining its brake lathe, the results often are poor. And if the disc is cut too thin, it will warp easily in service. A brand-new disc is the best choice, but even that should be checked for even thickness.

Measuring Disc Runout

Measure lateral runout with a dial indicator (Fig. 3) on the lining contact surfaces, on both sides, with the lug nuts reinstalled and tightened to approximately 30 ft.-lb. The maximum amount of runout should be .003 in. If it's more, index-mark the caliper to the hub, and remove the caliper and then the disc. Inspect the mating surfaces of the disc and hub and if there's rust, remove it with gentle use of 200-grit paper. Also remove any debris and clean the surfaces with brake solvent.

Rotate the disc clockwise one stud, reinstall, tighten the lug nuts and recheck. Do this a couple of times to see if you can bring runout down to an acceptable level (the problem may have been produced by

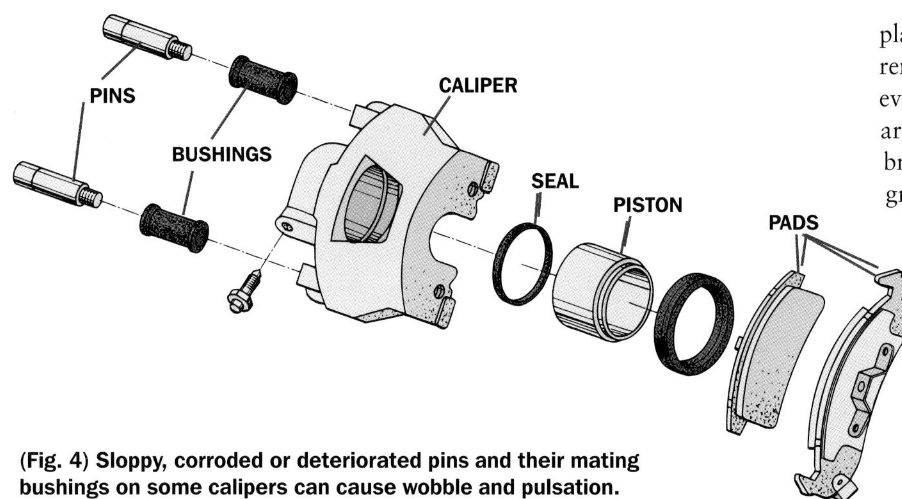

(Fig. 4) Sloppy, corroded or deteriorated pins and their mating bushings on some calipers can cause wobble and pulsation.

failure to make and follow alignment marks after some earlier service procedure).

If you can't bring runout down enough, check the hub for runout—.002 in. is the maximum. The thought of replacing the hub may not be appealing, but unless runout is far beyond reason and pulsation is intolerable, keep it in mind if nothing else surfaces as a possibility. A professional shop with an on-car lathe may (we repeat, may) be able to machine a disc so that it's referenced to the hub, to compensate for a small amount of excessive hub runout.

Brakes Not Releasing

When there's an uneven thickness problem on the discs at relatively low mileage (under 50,000), accompanied by short lining life, it's possible the brakes aren't releasing fully, allowing the shoes to stay in contact with the discs. A defective caliper piston (sticking when you try to push it back), a bad piston seal (not retracting the piston) and a sticking caliper are all possibilities.

When the caliper doesn't slide smoothly back and forth, that's trouble, and short lining life from failure to retract the shoes completely is just one consequence. The brake shoes may also slap unevenly against the disc, another cause of pulsation.

Most calipers slide along guide bolts or pins, through bushings with plastic or metal sleeves. When you remove the caliper (**Fig. 4**), inspect everything. If the guide bolts or pins are corroded, replace them with brand-new ones, lubed with silicone grease (don't try cleaning them). Ditto (including silicone lube) for the sleeves if they're corroded or cracked, and the bushings if they are deteriorated.

Rear Drum Brakes

The rear drums are not as frequent a cause of pulsation as rear discs, but if they're warped, or if the linings are not making good contact, they certainly can be responsible. Unless a drum contact surface is badly grooved (grooves here are not as acceptable as on a disc), you'll need a drum gauge to check for taper or out-of-round. Or ask a machine shop to measure it for you, as the typical shop will do it for free or a nominal charge. Linings that are worn very unevenly are a tip-off to a drum that should be measured. Also check for broken springs, or springs that show obvious signs of weakness by allowing shoes to move easily.

Invest in a good torque wrench, keep it in the trunk and use it to tighten the lug nuts instead of the lug wrench when you have a flat. You should enjoy smooth moderate stops for the life of the car.

HOW IT WORKS

Tire Imbalance

Tire imbalance, per se, shouldn't cause a pulsating brake pedal. Brake pedal vibrations are almost always caused by an out-of-true condition somewhere in the braking system. But on rare occasions it can happen. Normally, each tire has to be balanced statically first—i.e., so no part of the tire is heavier and always sinks to the bottom. Then they all need to be balanced dynamically, so the rim doesn't wobble at higher speeds. Any imbalances from either of these conditions normally will manifest themselves as steering-wheel vibration, not brake pedal vibration. Even a tire with a high or low spot will normally be felt through the wheel.

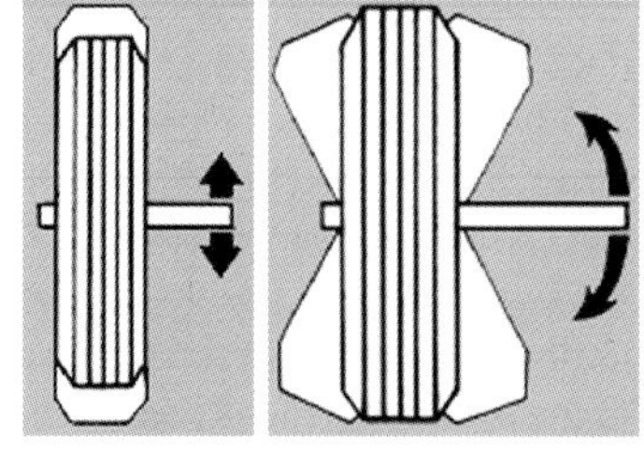

But once in a great while you'll find a tire that has inconsistent stiffness. Some parts of the tire's sidewall will be more or less easy to deflect under load than others. This won't show up on the wheel balancer, but will make a brake pedal pulsate at a rate proportional to your road speed. The diagnosis is to swap for a different tire and see if the problem goes away.

Getting Your Car Ready For Winter

Snow covers your car. After 10 minutes of shoveling snow and ice from the roof and windows (not to mention 30 minutes of shoveling the driveway), you're ready to go to work. Twisting the key languidly brings the engine to life, much to your relief. But ... the windshield wipers leave streaks, the washers drizzle fluid inches short of the glass, the battery light flickers and the heater fan blows little air of any temperature. Not a particularly good day for even a late-model car that's been neglected.

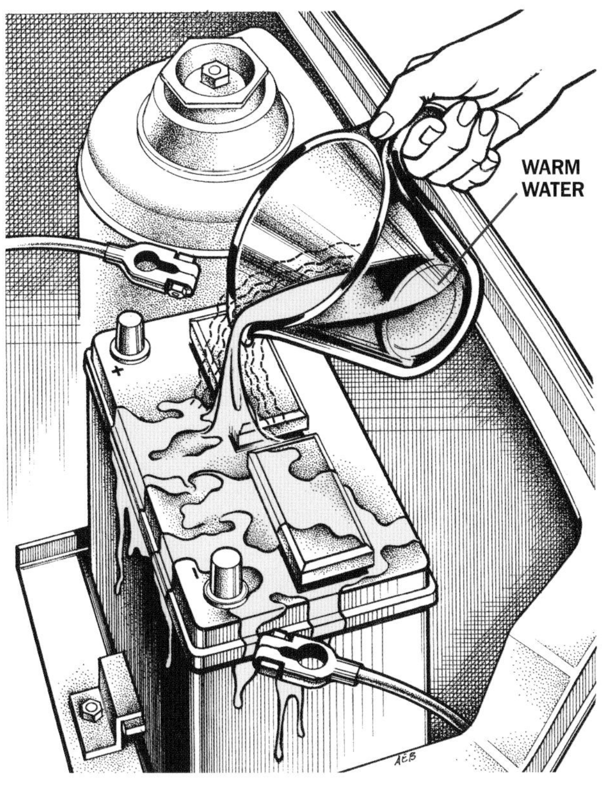

(Fig. 1) Use warm water to clean the battery posts and clamps. Use baking soda for stubborn sulfate deposits.

Winter Takes Its Toll

The traditional tuneup is gone. Newer cars are largely self-tuning, and don't have ignition points or carburetors to tweak. Factory-fill radiator coolant in some new cars is rated for five years or far longer than many people keep a car in this age of low-monthly-payment leases.

Cars are still imperfect, mechanical contrivances, however. Although many maintenance requirements are reduced, there's still plenty of stuff that can break or fall off. An afternoon of preventive maintenance will greatly reduce the possibility of bad things happening. It's autumn—the leaves are falling, but the weather is still relatively warm. A couple of hours of maintenance will be a lot easier to take now than a couple of hours of repairs when you have to shovel your way an extra 50 ft. to work in an unheated garage.

The Easy Stuff

Clean. Clean out the interior and the trunk. Shampoo the carpets and the seats, because a winter of slush and melted snow will infiltrate dirt deep into the fibers, there to remain forever. Dump the ashtray. Clean the wheel well arches and undercarriage of mud and road dirt, so that salty slush doesn't soak into them, providing a perfect environment for rust.

Electrical

While you're cleaning, clean the battery with warm water. Remove the terminals and wirebrush them and the battery posts with warm water and baking soda (**Fig. 1**). Reattach the terminals and coat all exposed metal with petroleum jelly. You're not done yet—using some sort of household cleaner, clean all traces of dirt and oil from the battery's top and sides, particularly near the terminals. Traces of dirt can trap moisture, especially during damp winter days. This moisture acts as a conductor along a path that normally doesn't conduct electricity at all, and can leak enough current between the battery posts to prematurely drain your battery. In fact, consider replacing your battery if it's more than 4 years old. Newer cars tend to use smaller batteries to reduce weight and improve mileage, and, combined with high underhood temperatures, that spells an earlier demise than you may have gotten 10 to 15 years ago.

While you're at it, check all the electrical connections for looseness and corrosion. That may mean getting underneath the car to see the ground strap and solenoid/starter motor connections.

Check all light bulbs and replace any that aren't working. The days are short during the winter, and you'll depend on these bulbs for visibility a much larger proportion of the day.

Underhood in General

Still in an electrical mode, check the alternator connections and mounts for looseness and evidence of overheating. High electrical demands for lights, heater fans and rear-window defrosters, as well as recharging a battery abused by coaxing a reluctant engine to life, can make a marginal connection overheat.

Check accessory belt condition and tension, because that extra electrical

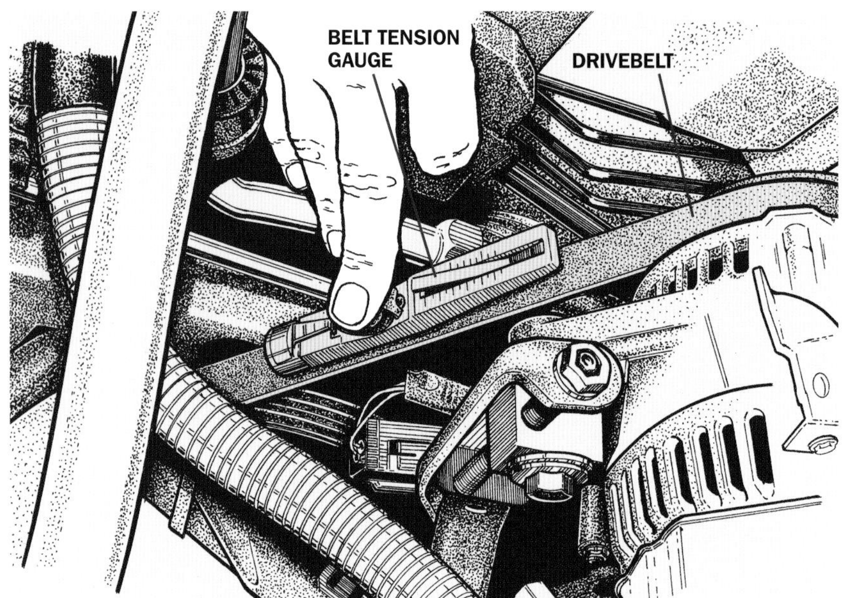

(Fig. 2) Check belts for proper tension using a tension gauge. Serpentine belts can also be checked with a gauge, although they aren't as likely to be loose.

demand will strain a marginal belt (**Fig. 2**). Many modern cars have a single serpentine, automatically tensioned belt, but it still can fray and come off.

Check all rubber hoses. Five years, in these times of air pollution and high underhood temperatures, is a legitimate life span for a radiator hose. If one seems squishy, brittle or just suspect, now would be a good time to replace them all. Check the date on the coolant. (Remember many new cars have extended drain intervals—but not permanent coolant. Read the owner's manual.) If it's due to be replaced, use a 50-50 mix of fresh coolant and water (**Fig. 3**).

Consider changing your transmission fluid, differential lubricant and brake fluid if your car is more than 3 years old. Lubricants break down, and brake fluid attracts moisture and deteriorates. At any rate, check the levels, and don't forget the power steering reservoir.

Fill the windshield washer tank with washer fluid. Check the pump and nozzles for a healthy, well-aimed spray pattern. Many nozzles can be re-aimed by inserting a pin into the nozzle to use as a handle.

Windshield wipers are essential for winter driving, and after a summer of sunshine, the rubber squeegees are probably in sorry shape. Play it safe and replace them. Be sure the wiper arms and springs are in good shape,

HOW IT WORKS

Oil Viscosity

Fall is a good time to change oil and filters. Check your owner's manual for the rating and viscosity, but most cars nowadays use an SL-service rated oil. This rating is some measure of the oil's longevity and resistance to oxidation and evaporation. SL oil is fine for older engines that specify an SG-, SH-, or SJ-rated oil, because the rating always improves when a new one is introduced. The SAE viscosity rating is a measure of how thick the oil is. All modern cars should use a multigrade oil, probably a 5W-30 or 10W-30. The W in these ratings stands for a winter viscosity. A multigrade oil will be as thin as the thinner (5W- or 10W- rating) when the engine is first started. This will allow oil to flow more rapidly and lubricate parts that have had all the oil drain off of them overnight. A thicker oil might not be pumped to remote parts of the engine rapidly enough. On the other hand, a thicker oil (the second number in the rating) will resist becoming too thin when the engine reaches operating temperature. The American Petroleum Institute is an industry watchdog and oils bearing the API emblem can be expected to meet their specifications.

In spite of what your brother-in-law the shade-tree mechanic tells you, don't use a heavier grade of oil just because you used to in your older car. Modern cars were engineered to use 5W-20, 5W-30 or 10W-30 oil year-round. Check the owner's manual to be sure. The lighter oils are also better on fuel consumption and can significantly improve mileage.

When buying engine oil, check for API certification and SAE rating.

and that the blade is held square to the windshield surface. You may need to bend it slightly to keep everything square.

Check the air cleaner, and consider replacing it and the fuel filter (if your vehicle has a replacement type, not the permanent one in the gas tank). The fuel filter will tend to trap water, and once it traps enough, it will fail and may dump some accumulated dirt into your fuel injection system. And winter, of course, is when you tend to find the most water in gasoline at the pump.

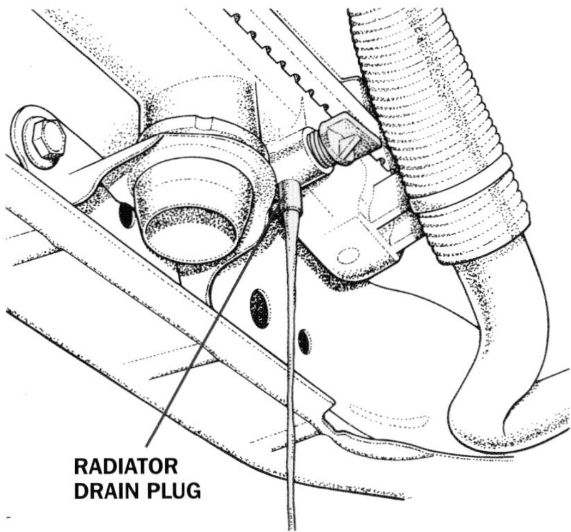

(Fig. 3) In spite of long-life coolant in many new cars, eventually you'll need to drain and refill with fresh coolant mix.

Where The Rubber Meets The Road

Driving in snow demands good tires. Be sure you have adequate tread depth, and consider changing to snow tires if you live in a heavy snow area. Go ahead and pick up a set of inexpensive steel wheels at the local salvage yard for your snows instead of having your tires remounted and balanced every fall and spring. And while the car is up on the safety stands, inspect the suspension bushings, control arms, ball joints and tie rods, and the brakes. Now would be a good time to replace the brake pads if they are more than 60 percent worn. Even if they are not, check carefully for corrosion around the calipers and sliding pins. While the wheel is off, pull the pads out of the calipers and be sure everything is sliding freely. Wirebrush sliding-key ways and pins that let the pads pull back from the disc when you remove your foot from the brake. Exercise the pistons by pushing them back into the calipers and then pressing on the brake pedal once or twice to break up corrosion between the piston and the caliper.

Again, it's a lot easier to look at this stuff on a crisp autumn day than it is to try to fix it some subzero morning when all of your wrenches stick to your fingers like the proverbial dared 6-year-old's tongue sticks to a frigid flagpole.

Rust Never Sleeps

Before the salt trucks come out is a good time to get out the touchup paint. Use it to cover all the bare metal at the bottom of any stone chips and parking lot dings. Clean the chipped area thoroughly, and use a toothpick or a match to apply a touch of zinc-rich primer to the bare metal. Allow this to dry, and chase any overlap back to the lip of the scratch with lacquer thinner. Then carefully fill the chip with touchup paint. It'll shrink, so you may need several applications to build up the level of paint to flush.

On the Road

Even a perfectly running car may wind up stuck in a snowbank. So put together a kit of essentials for your trunk. This should include flares, a flashlight, jumper cables (if only to help some unfortunate soul whose car wasn't winterized like yours), a folding camp shovel, kitty litter for traction, a can of gasoline anti-freeze, and tire chains if they're legal in your state. If you ever travel outside of urban areas, a couple of blankets and a cellphone or CB radio ought to be on board as well.

EASY

Repairing a Flat Tire

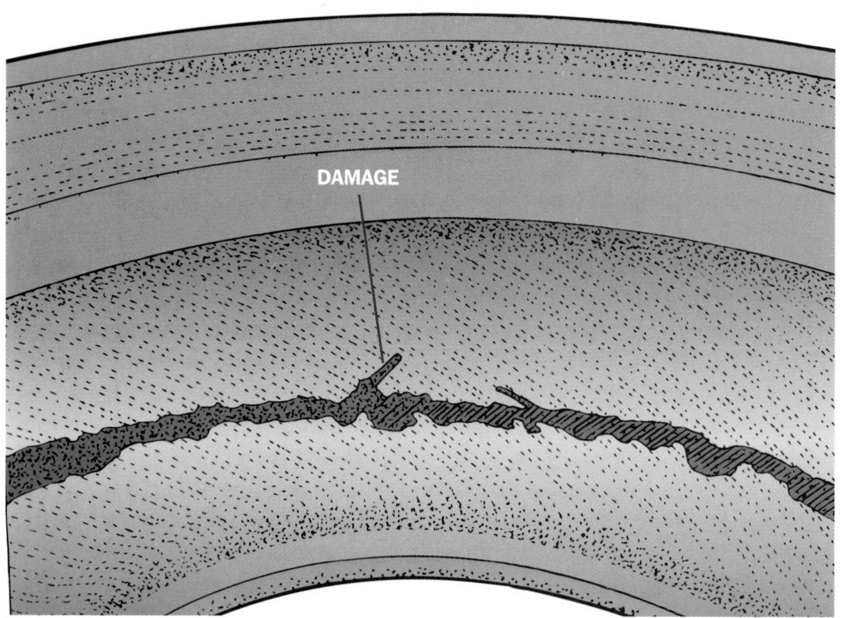

(Fig. 1) This damaged area inside the sidewall was caused by driving the tire when it was flat.

There's rarely a more welcome sight than the inside of a warm garage late at night, as your door rolls open to welcome you and your family home after a trip out of town. Particularly tonight, because you're far later than expected. Flat tires are generally no more than a nuisance—but this time you found your spare tire to be as flat as yesterday's beer. Fortunately, a nice young gentleman working in a gas station only a half mile up the road managed to plug your tire within a few minutes. You watch the inflation pressure of the tire for a week or so, and everything seems fine.

Until a few weeks later. Then the same tire disintegrates suddenly on the interstate in heavy traffic. You manage to maintain control of your SUV by lifting partway off the throttle and gingerly steering over to the shoulder, ignoring the cacophony of the failed tire as it flaps violently in the wheel well, shedding parts as it tears into pieces. It's not just flat, it's a smoking ruin, and there's substantial damage to your wheel well's sheetmetal to boot. Obviously, there was more damage to your tire than met the eye—and the nice fellow who repaired it for you didn't necessarily do you any favors.

The Right Way—And The Wrong Way

The tire industry has a rule about externally plugging a tire with a worm. Don't. It's a qualified exclusion, and we agree with it, for good reasons. An externally applied worm might be an acceptable emergency get-home-tonight quick fix, but a properly trained tire technician must later complete the repair by removing the tire from the rim and doing a complete inspection of the tire for additional punctures and damage. Damage can come from not only the nail or whatever caused the air loss, but also from running the tire at low pressure or flat. Driving more than a few feet with the tire at zero inflation pressure may cause the rim to gouge the inner liner, damaging the body cord. Driving at more than a walk with the tire at very low pressure may build up enough heat to damage the sidewall beyond serviceability **(Fig. 1)**. The portion of the nail or wire that entered the tire's interior may have flailed around and ripped the inner liner or plies **(Fig. 2)**. After inspecting the tire, the technician may apply a proper patch, remount the tire and reinflate it.

Here's How

Okay, we doubt many readers will ever repair a flat themselves because it involves some pretty expensive tools. However, we've done it with nothing more than hand tools and a 12-volt portable compressor, and more than once, too. Once, it was late at night and we didn't want to wait for the tire shop to open. Another time, it was because we were in a very remote area, and a trip to town was nearly a two-day hike.

Busted

Wheel/tire assembly off the car? (We've done it with the rim still bolted to the axle of a trailer but it's tough work.) Start by inflating the tire and submerging it in water to look for bubbles. Now roll the tire along the ground in a good light to look for the puncture. Chalk any suspicious holes in the tread, even if there was no stream of tiny little bubbles associated with it. You'd be amazed at how many times tires are taken in for repair with multiple punctures. Make a chalkmark on the tire sidewall next to the valve stem, because the tire should be reinstalled in the same index. Now you can remove the valve core to completely

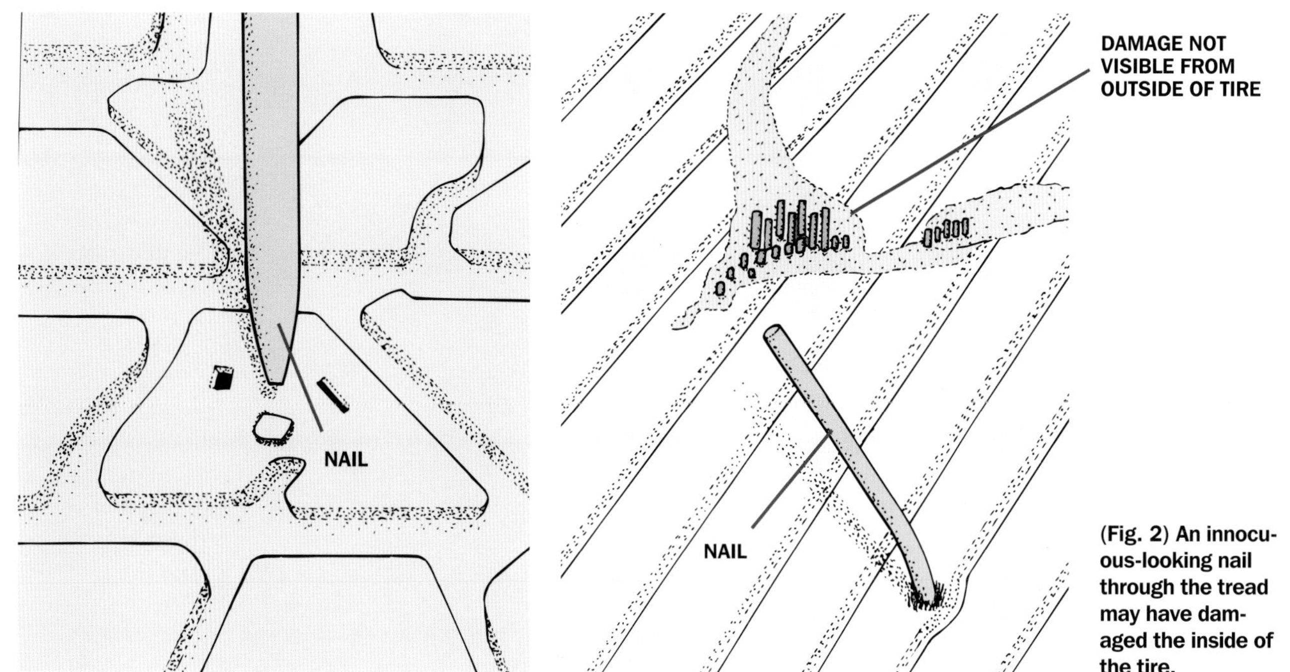

(Fig. 2) An innocuous-looking nail through the tread may have damaged the inside of the tire.

deflate the tire and demount it. Next, with a bright light, carefully inspect every square inch of the inner liner. Pay particular attention to the areas inboard of the chalkmarks you've made. Look for damage caused by the foreign object. Such a hole may be patched if the object hasn't damaged any cord, although any exposed cord usually means the tire should be scrapped.

Also look for peripheral damage caused by the tire being pinched between the rim and the pavement. Any damage to the inner liner that came about as a result of friction by being pinched and then driven makes the tire a likely candidate for immediate replacement.

Any puncture through the sidewall of the tire automatically means the tire needs to be scrapped.

Remove any foreign objects in the tread by grasping them with pliers and yanking them out. Make note of the angle the object made to the surface of the tread. In fact, you should take a thin probe, like an awl, and probe the hole straight through into the inside of the tire. Look for evidence of cut cords or separated plies, because they'll be sticking out of the hole.

HOW IT WORKS

Run-Flat Tire

A few late-model cars come equipped with tires that can be run without any air at all, at least far enough to get to a place where they can be repaired. These tires, available from several different manufacturers, can be retrofitted to any car that uses an appropriate size tire. The sidewalls of these tires have an extra piece of molded rubber near the bead. This reinforcement is stiff enough to keep the rim from contacting the inside of the tire, even under cornering and braking. The tire and auto manufacturers specify an upper limit on speed—usually 50 or so miles per hour—and a maximum range—often 50 or 100 miles—when the tire is deflated. Because the performance of these tires with zero air pressure is so good, tire manufacturers require any car fitted with them to have a tire-pressure monitoring system that will alert the driver to the fact that he's driving on a flat.

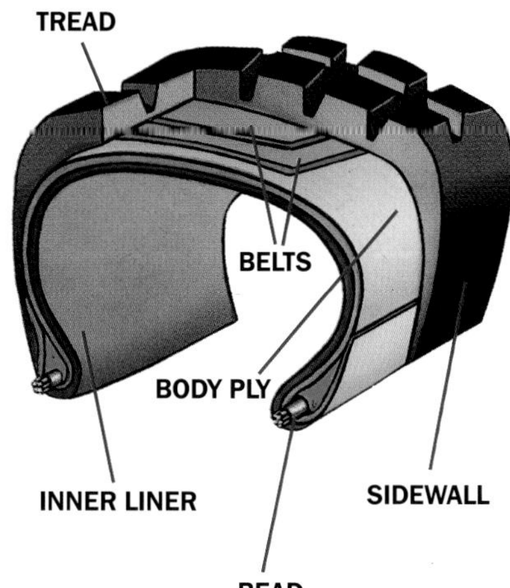

Run-flat tires' bead reinforcement provides stiffness to keep the bead seated on the rim and prevent sidewall damage.

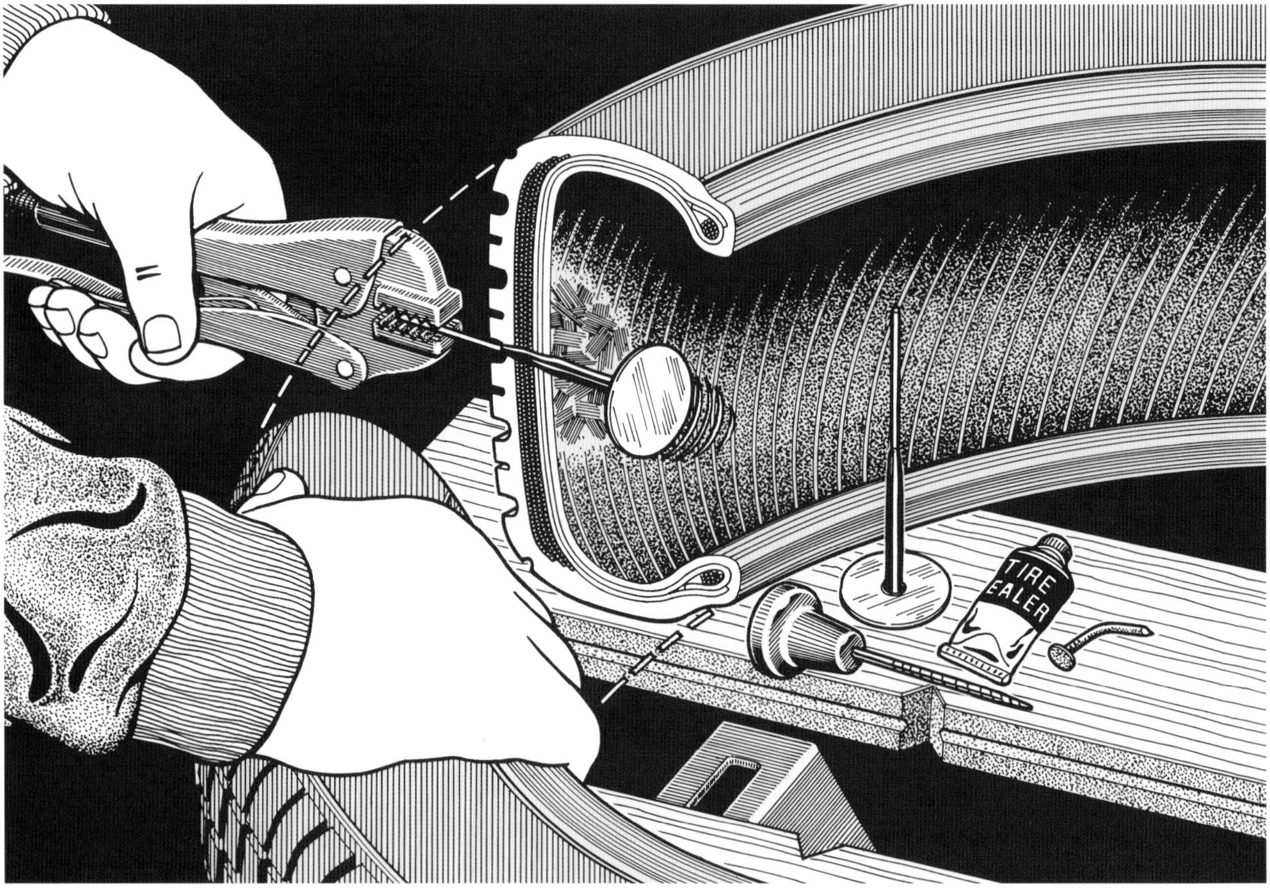

(Fig. 3) A tubeless tire puncture can be properly repaired only by breaking the tire off the rim and pulling a stem-type patch through the tread from the inside.

Straight Holes

If the hole makes a 25° or smaller angle to the tread, the correct patch to use is a "mushroom" patch **(Fig. 3)**. The head of the mushroom provides a good adhesive seal to the tire's inner liner for proper air retention. The stem of the patch serves several purposes. It plugs the hole to anchor the patch and, in concert with the chemical vulcanizing cement, prevents water from entering the hole and working its way into the tire's tread.

Using a proper tire reamer, clean out the hole from the inside out **(Fig. 4)**. Again, look carefully for evidence of wire or tire cord. The reamer will remove any road dirt or oil and any damaged rubber from the hole, leaving a fresh rubber surface for bonding the cement.

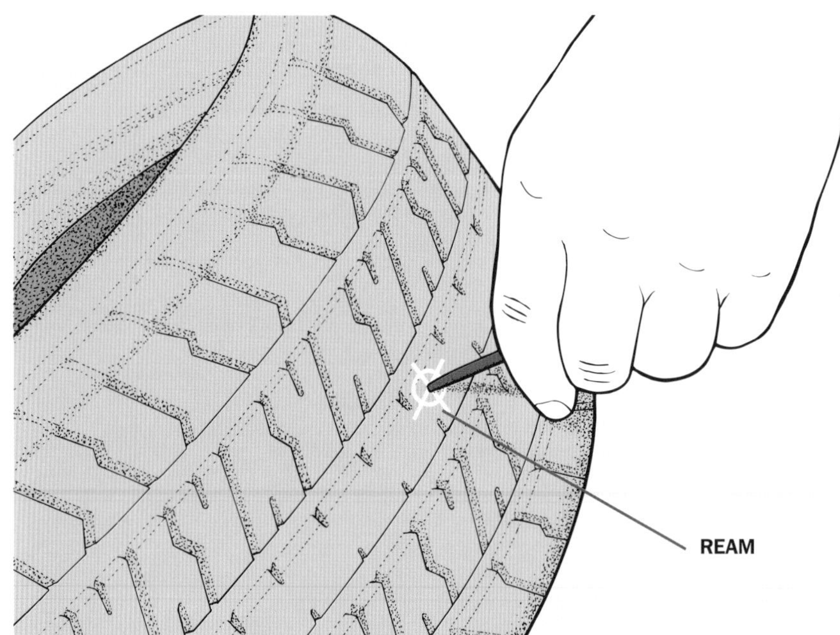

(Fig. 4) Thoroughly ream the puncture to clean the rubber and provide a good bond.

Center the patch over the hole inside the tire, and mark a half-inch around its periphery with chalk. Use a tire buffing tool to remove the surface of the rubber and leave a smooth texture. A power buffing tool is best, but a hand scraper will work. Don't buff through the liner into the ply rubber or the cord. Brush, blow or vacuum the rubber dust away from the buffed area. Don't touch this area with your fingers or a rag.

Coat your awl liberally with cement and run it in and out of the hole several times to carry the cement throughout the hole. Leave the awl in the hole until just before installing the patch so the cement stays liquid. Remove the peel-off tab from the patch, and put a single coat of vulcanizing cement on the head of the patch and the buffed area. Allow this to dry thoroughly, and don't touch the cemented areas because the moisture and oil in your fingerprints will prevent good adhesion.

Lightly coat the stem of the patch with cement. Pull out the awl, and pull the stem of the patch through the hole. Stitch the patch (using a tire patch stitching tool) to the tire from the middle out to prevent any air bubbles from being trapped under the patch. Now cut the protruding stem off nearly flush with the surface of tread rubber.

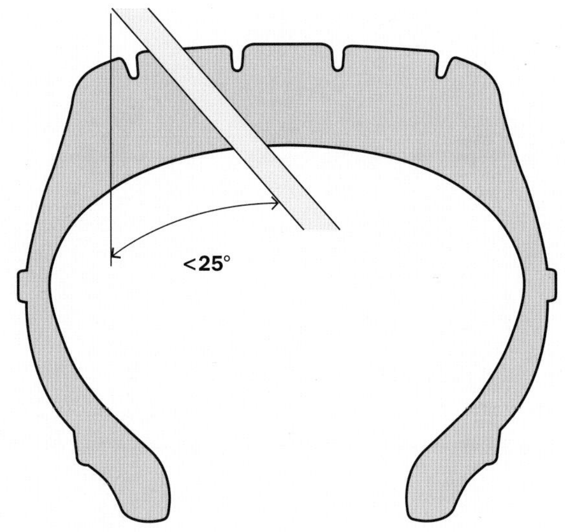

(Fig. 5) Oblique punctures require a different plug.

Oblique Holes

If the hole isn't within 25° of vertical **(Fig. 5)**, you'll need to use a two-piece patch. This involves reaming the hole and installing a rubber stem with cement. The stem is then trimmed flush with the inner liner, the area buffed and a patch is cemented over the top of the stem.

Back On The Road

Before remounting the tire on the rim (a job for a professional with special equipment), take a hard look at the rubber valve stem. If it's weather-beaten, damaged or just more than about 5 years old, pop it out and pull in a new one. Use the correct diameter and length, and a valve core that matches. Valve stem caps aren't there to simply backstop the valve core's air retention—they keep moisture and dirt out of the stem and out of your tire.

Reinflate the tire. Use soapy water to check the beads, valve stem and the repair for leaks. And keep a close eye on your tire for a few weeks, both by monitoring the air pressure and looking for evidence of delamination or a belt failure. A failed belt usually will cause an out-of-round condition and the ride will often indicate it.

Can you adequately repair speed-rated tires? Some tire manufacturers disagree, but at least one (Goodyear) says you can. They do specify that there can be only a single repair, less than one-quarter inch in diameter, per tire.

MODERATE

Servicing Your A/C

It's hot, so hot your car's interior shimmers. Getting into the car is clearly out of the question, at least until the air conditioning hauls out a few million BTUs. You lean in and twist the key, being careful not to raise blisters by touching the steering wheel. The engine fires and idles smoothly, then you punch the max cold button on the dash—nothing happens.

Great, you think, at least in the old days, ordinary folks used to be able to purchase R-12 refrigerant to punch up a tepid air conditioner. Not anymore. And it won't be too long before R-12 is off the market completely—a victim of federal regulations that restrict the manufacture of ozone-depleting chlorofluorocarbons.

Fortunately, it's still possible for the average Saturday mechanic to fix some of what ails his air conditioner without having to open up the system. To keep you in the service picture, let's consider just a few of the common causes of poor—or zero—cooling that you can diagnose and cure. Start by acquiring the a/c service manual and electrical schematic for your vehicle. You'll also need a 12-volt test light. A volt-ohmmeter comes in handy as well.

No Cooling

If the compressor doesn't engage, there will be zero cooling. An electromagnetic clutch should lock the drive hub/plate on the compressor **(Fig. 1)**, with the belt-driven pulley to spin the compressor shaft.

The clutch circuit is fused, so check the fuse. The fuse is good? With the engine and the a/c on, check to see if juice is getting to the clutch by probing its wiring connector with a 12-volt test light **(Fig. 2)**. If the light doesn't go on, there's a break in the circuit. If it does go on brightly, attach a jumper wire to the ground side of the clutch circuit. If the clutch still won't engage, it's bad.

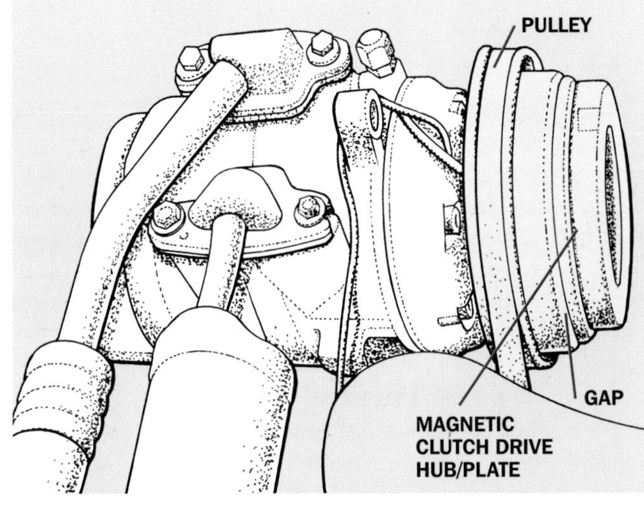

(Fig. 1) Gap between hub/plate and pulley should close when a/c is turned on.

It takes special tools to change a compressor clutch. Unless you can rent them, leave this job to a pro.

If the clutch engages when you jump it, there's a problem with the ground circuit, which may be wired through to the engine computer. Both circuit problems require straight electrical diagnosis and a good wiring diagram.

However, the refrigeration system may also be involved. There's a low-pressure switch in the current-feed circuit that is designed to keep the compressor from engaging when pressure is low.

See if there's enough refrigerant pressure to close that switch, which requires pressure gauges, and hoses that attach to your system. When the system is running, one half operates at low pressure and the other at high. However, after the system has been shut off for a few minutes, pressures equalize, so you can check pressure at both of the service valve ports (one low-pressure, one high-pressure). They should be the same—roughly equal to the ambient temperature.

If pressure is less, the refrigeration system is low on refrigerant, and that could account for the failure of the compressor to engage. Have a professional trace the leak and then recharge the system with refrigerant. Incidentally, if the service valve caps are missing, they could be the cause of your loss, as they provide the real seal, not the valve itself. Warning: Do not try to seal leaks witha/c sealer products—period.

Important: Use only R-12 in an R-12 system, R-134a in an R-134a system; never mix the two! Right now, there's still some R-12 around, so you might want to keep the system on R-12. However, if you ever have a compressor failure, the replacement will likely be compatible with R-134a, which would make changing over to the new refrigerant simpler. But this is not do-it-yourself work. It takes special equipment.

The a/c pressure is normal? Apparently, the problem is purely electrical. And in this case the first step is to check for a computer trouble code. The engine computer? You bet. On most American cars and some imports, turning on the air conditioning at the dashboard is just a request to the engine computer to provide the electrical ground to complete the compressor clutch circuit. If the engine computer sees a reason not to, the a/c won't come on. Possible reasons, in

addition to low refrigerant, include warning signals from certain engine sensors. The coolant-temperature sensor may be signaling a very high coolant temperature, and allowing the a/c to come on could cause overheating. Or a power-steering switch may be signaling high pressure (as in a parking maneuver), and allowing the a/c to come on could add to the engine load from the belt-driven accessories and stall the engine. Of course, some of these signals may be wrong, and you'll need to investigate the solution to these engine problems to get the a/c online again.

No computer trouble codes? Check for a bad a/c clutch relay. Also, note that some of the computer sensors are not covered by trouble codes—the power-steering switch is a common example. If your car has one, bypass it for testing. If the compressor now comes on, replace the switch.

No clues in the computer circuit? Refer to an a/c circuit diagram to see what additional switches or relays are in the compressor-clutch circuit. On many cars of all makes (particularly R-12 systems), there's a switch that cycles the compressor clutch on and off to control performance. You can find out if the switch is bad by unplugging it and attaching a jumper wire across its connector. If the compressor now comes on, the switch apparently isn't closing. Confirm this with an ohmmeter across the switch terminals. On GM and Ford vehicles, the switch usually is on a large cylindrical can called the accumulator. On many Chrysler products, it's in a block at the firewall.

(Fig. 2) Use a 12-volt test light to probe the a/c compressor's clutch wiring. If the clutch isn't pulling in, there's no cooling.

Bad switch? On late-models, the switch is mounted on a Schrader valve. As you unthread the switch, the valve closes so you won't lose any refrigerant. Grease the new O-ring with mineral oil, gently position it on the port and then thread the new switch into place. If the switch has a plastic body, a firm hand-tightening is enough. With metal, a gentle nudge with a wrench does it, because the O-ring makes the seal.

Note: Your circuit diagram may show other pressure switches. The variety is almost endless, depending on the type of vehicle, so without a diagram, you're in Guess City. Among the most common variety are a high-pressure cutout and a dedicated low-pressure cutout (often in addition to the cycling clutch switch). If the basic pressure check showed nothing awry, unplug and bypass these switches for testing. In most cases, the bypass is achieved with a jumper wire across the wiring connector terminals—but read the wiring diagram details, as some switches are normally closed and open up as a signal. If so, simply unplug these to bypass. Double-check each switch with an ohmmeter.

USE A TEST LIGHT to check for voltage at the low-pressure switch. Back up that reading by checking the switch with an ohmmeter.

Many cars—particularly Japanese models and many late-model Chrysler products—use a temperature sensor on the evaporator (the in-car heat exchanger that cools the interior air) in conjunction with an electronic module to cycle the clutch. The shop manual should provide specifications for a resistance check of the temperature sensor and where to connect a voltmeter to test for an output signal to operate the clutch. Make these checks under the dashboard.

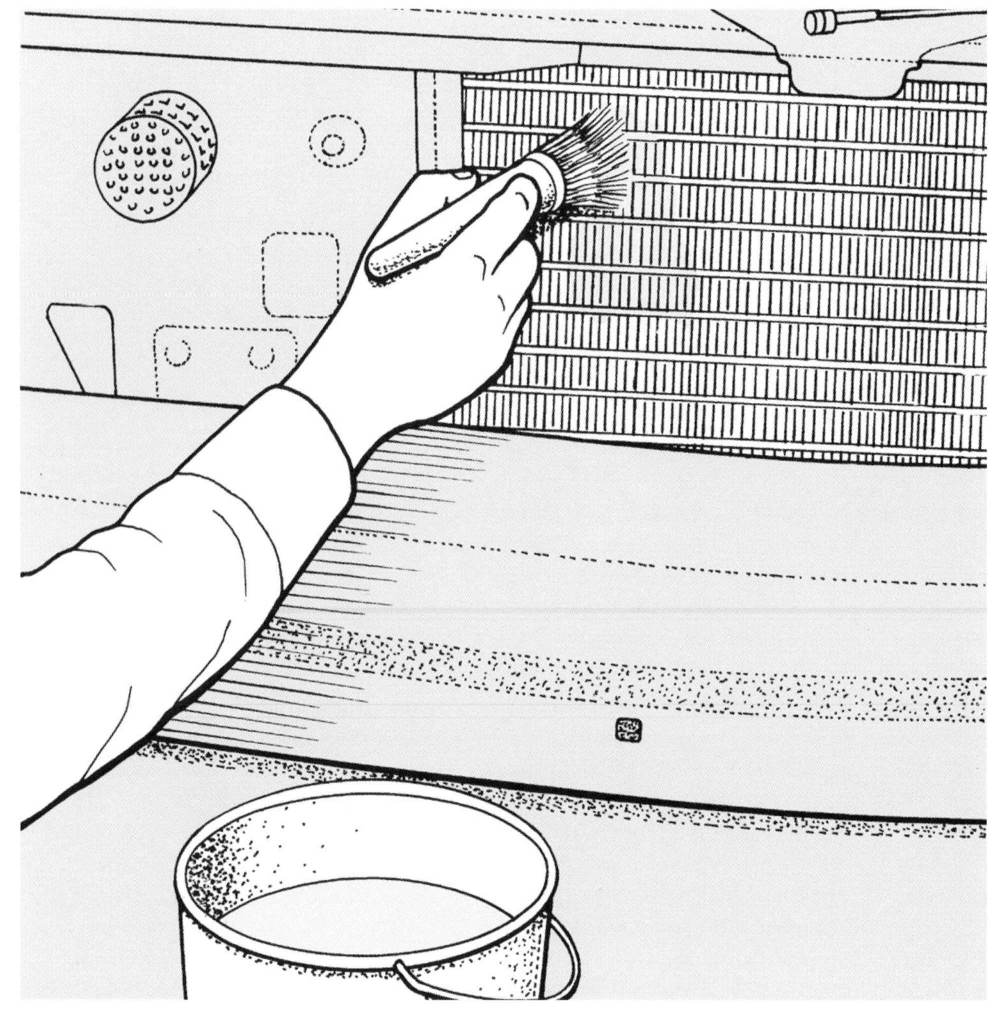

Poor Cooling

The temperature of the air coming out of the registers will not necessarily be very low on a humid, hot day. The a/c may expend all its effort just wringing humidity out of the air, and the air blowing out of the registers easily could be as high as 60° to 65°F. If there is some cooling, but clearly not a normal amount, make this simple check: Is the front of the condenser (the heat exchanger in front of, or alongside, the radiator) free of bugs, leaves, road film and other debris? If it isn't, airflow is restricted. Clean the condenser with a soft brush and a detergent-and-water solution (**Fig. 3**).

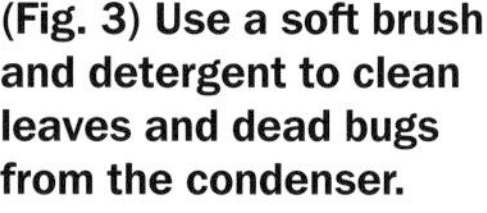

(Fig. 3) Use a soft brush and detergent to clean leaves and dead bugs from the condenser.

If you've got a car that has either no grille or a tiny one, you've got an "underbody breather." Inspect any underbody airdams and covers. If they're damaged or missing, they could be responsible for reduced airflow and poor cooling. And on almost all cars, when the air conditioning is turned on, a radiator/condenser electric fan should also come on. If it doesn't, that also reduces airflow and a/c performance, particularly in slow-driving conditions.

Of course, if the airflow is normal, you'll want to make sure a partial loss of coolant is not responsible for a drop in performance. Some older Japanese-made and some Chrysler systems (with R-12 refrigerant) have a sight glass—a tiny window into the refrigeration circuit. Check it to see if there are any bubbles when the clutch is engaged (bubbling when it's disengaged or in the first few seconds after engagement is normal). Bubbles with the clutch engaged may—repeat, may—indicate a low charge **(Fig. 4)**. Also, check operating pressures with a pressure gauge and compare them with factory specifications. You must use the specs because pressures vary widely with ambient temperatures.

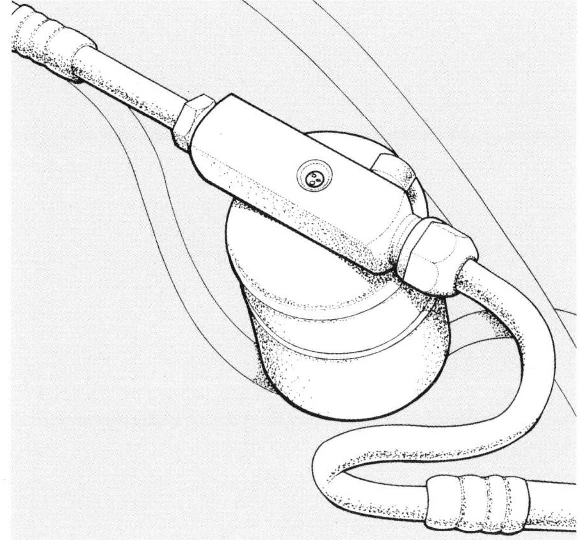

(Fig. 4) Bubbles in the sight glass may mean the air conditioner is undercharged. Have a professional (using special equipment) recharge.

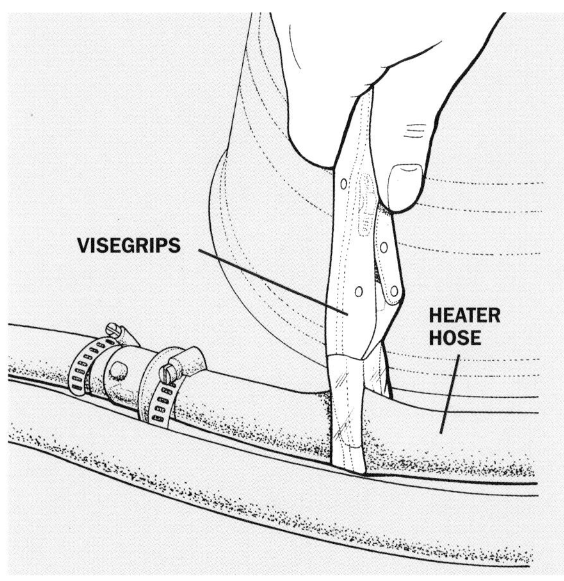

(Fig. 5) Clamp off the heater hose with padded Vise-Grip pliers to check for a leaky flap.

As explained earlier, a power-steering switch may misbehave, signaling "high pressure" with just a slight rise in pressure, thus killing the a/c. If your system runs fine with the car parked, but stops as soon as you pull away, either a bad power-steering switch or a misbehaving throttle-position sensor (TPS) is possible. The TPS is supposed to signal "kill the a/c" on full throttle to provide improved passing performance, but the sensor may come in with this signal when you're just barely touching the gas pedal. Or if the air-conditioning system has an evaporator-temperature sensor, take a careful ohmmeter reading and convert it to degrees by consulting the table in the manual. You may find that the sensor thinks it's cold when it's really not.

If the air blowing in your face is cool, but there isn't enough air blowing, operate the blower switch and see if the airflow picks up. A non-running blower fan and a slow-running blower motor are purely electrical problems, and are as likely to be responsible for poor system performance as anything. If the blower simply won't reach high speed, check the circuit diagram for a high-speed blower relay. You might be able to fix a bad connection by simply plugging in the wiring connector properly. Or you may find a broken wire by probing the wiring connector with a test light.

Another common cause of poor performance: the heater core's high temperature is bleeding into what should be purely chilled air from the evaporator. Some heat transfer is normal if you move the temperature lever or turn the knob from the max cold position. However, at max cold, there should be no hot-air bleed.

Clamp off a heater hose to block the hot-coolant flow **(Fig. 5)**. If a/c performance improves considerably, one of the following could be occurring:

- A heater coolant-flow valve (used on many but not all vehicles) is stuck in the open position.
- The flap door that's supposed to regulate the airflow through the heater or evaporator isn't operating properly. If it's a manual, cable-controlled type with a lever, try slamming the lever against the max cold stop. If you don't hear a flap door hit a stop inside the underdash case, the cable may need adjustment. With an electric motor-driven design, check the case for a bad wiring connection at the motor.

And, of course, there may be cold air, but in the wrong place. If the cold air is going to your feet or out of the defrost ducts—but not to your face—that's an air-distribution problem. Air distribution is controlled by operating flap doors inside the heater/air-conditioning case, and it's done either by vacuum or electricity. If it's vacuum-operated, look for a leak.

EASY

Maintaining Your Battery

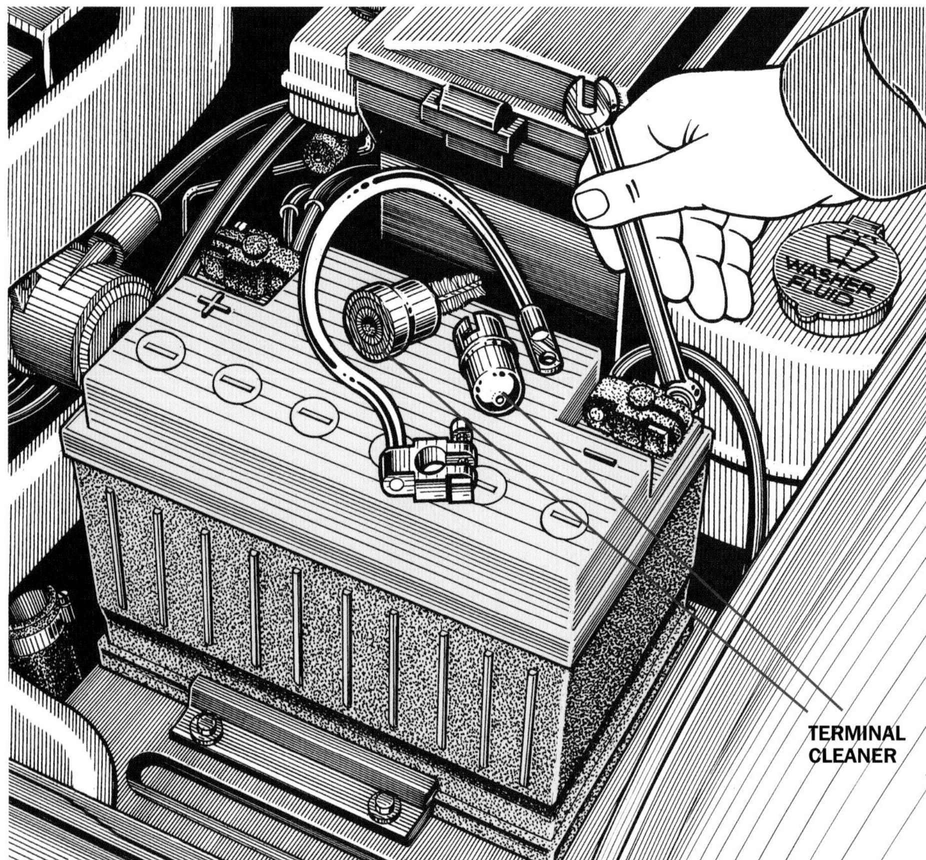

(Fig. 1) Always remove the negative connection from a battery first and reconnect it last to prevent shorting the wrench out on nearby metal objects.

It's the second time this week that you've had to jumpstart your car. Bad enough first thing in the morning, when you can use the battery in your RV to give you a start—but standing in a rainy Wal-Mart parking lot with your hood open and jumper cables in your dripping hands is just plain humiliating, not to mention uncomfortable and inconvenient.

The standard solution: Install a new battery—which means coughing up enough money to buy a new one and have it installed.

A few minutes of attention once or twice a year can perhaps double the life of your battery, saving you cold, hard cash. And, just as importantly, keep rain from running down your neck in shopping mall parking lots on stormy nights.

Would You Like Fries With That, Sir?

First, you need to determine if your battery is indeed fried or not. Other reasons for a no-start or barely start condition include, for openers, a marginal starter motor and high-resistance wiring in the primary (starter motor) circuit.

Open the hood. If your top-post battery terminals are covered with green fur that looks like it belongs in a bad sci-fi movie, you'll need to clean that up. Start by pouring some warm water over the terminals to dissolve the sulfation. This accretion is normal, but it can prevent good contact between the battery posts and the clamp, which in turn keeps your battery from providing enough voltage to start or prevents it from charging properly. Remove the terminals, and brighten up all the metal with a wire brush-style battery post terminal cleaner and a baking soda paste. Don't splash liquid around the engine compartment or onto the paint, and rinse everything off thoroughly. Side-terminal batteries rarely look worse than dull, but that's enough to cause hard starting. Wire-brush the contact surfaces to brighten them. (See page 80.)

Dirt on the top and sides of the battery, even greasy dirt, can hold enough moisture to create a current leak from the positive terminal directly to the negative terminal, making your battery self-discharge more rapidly. Leave the battery clean and dry.

Now take a close look at the terminal clamps on the cables. If they're eroded too badly to provide good mechanical contact, replace them.

Warning: Whenever you work on a car battery, always disconnect the negative terminal first—not the positive (**Fig. 1**). Why, you may ask? Simple: If you accidentally brush up against the fenderwell or any other grounded metal part of the car while you're unhooking the ground side, nothing will happen. But if the ground is still connected, and you're wrenching on the positive side and happen to touch any metal, you'll be holding onto a wrench that's suddenly conducting several hundred amperes. That's as much current as

HOW IT WORKS

Maintenance-Free Batteries

Like many things in life, the term "maintenance-free" is only partially true. Lead-acid batteries normally consume some of the water in their dilute sulfuric acid electrolyte during a normal charge-discharge cycle. It actually electrolyzes into hydrogen and oxygen and escapes as gas. So adding water periodically is necessary to keep the plates flooded, although it can't be done on some batteries. (See page 50) Maintenance-free batteries use a calcium alloy of lead instead of an antimony alloy, which reduces the amount of electrolysis. In addition, the amount of free-standing electrolyte above the plates is designed to be much higher in a new maintenance-free battery. This means that there's enough electrolyte to keep the plates covered even after a few seasons of normal use. So, during the battery's normal service life there should be no need to add water.

Any abnormal electrical system condition or high ambient temperatures may boil off more than the normal amount of water, however. Adding water where possible may extend the service life of these supposedly maintenance-free batteries.

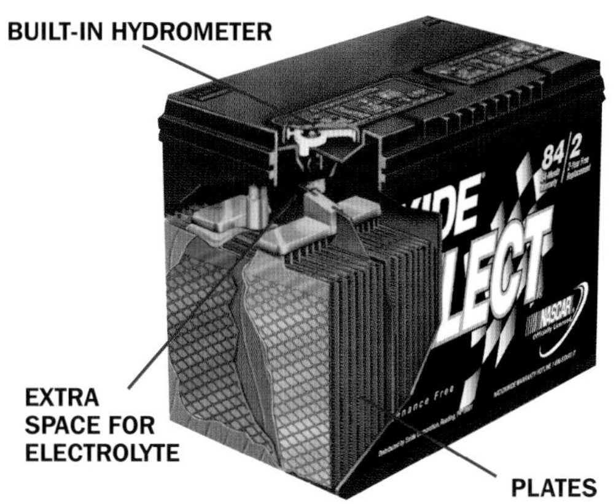

Maintenance-free batteries often can have their lives extended by proper attention to electrolyte level and good connections.

an arc welder—which means a large spark, lots of heat and enough energy released to turn your wrench cherry red within a few seconds.

Avoid quickie aftermarket universal clamps that simply let you saw off the old clamp and clamp on the new one. While these have their uses (keep one in your on-car toolbox as a get-home-tonight expedient) they'll develop corrosion between the clamp and the cable in a few months and leave you stranded, again. If you feel up to it and have a soldering iron (probably propane-fired) capable of generating enough heat, you can solder a new clamp onto the existing cable. Use rosin-core electrical solder, not plumbing solder.

Don't have the Great Mother of All Soldering Irons? The simple way out is to replace the entire cable. If you're lucky, you can pick up an appropriate cable at the auto parts counter. Generally, all they stock are simple one-lead cables, in positive and ground. Yes, there is a significant difference between the terminals on the battery, and you really ought to use a black-insulated cable on the ground and a red-insulated cable on the positive or the post will fit the clamp poorly, which is how you got into this mess in the first place.

Unfortunately, it's not always that simple. Some battery clamps, both positive and negative, are soldered to more than a single wire. You have a choice here. The best solution is to go to the dealer and get the correct piece. That may be inconvenient, and will certainly be expensive. Also (see page 89), you may be able to get (at an auto parts store) a "cable repair section" (terminal attached to a section of cable). It's designed to attach to cable ends from which the battery connections and extra wires have been amputated. Or you can solder lugs of the appropriate size and gauge to the extra wires, and then attach the lugs to the clamp either by means of the clamp bolt or a large sheetmetal screw into the clamp body. Look for a clamp with an extra terminal if this is necessary, although if you've got side-terminal batteries this might be impossible. As a last resort, splice and solder the cables together ahead of the terminal. Be sure to use shrink tubing to cover the splice, especially if you're splicing the positive side.

When you reinstall the clamps, cover all exposed metal with petroleum jelly, white grease or my own personal favorite, Cop-Graf or Nevr-Seez brand antiseize compound. This will delay the inevitable growth of sulfur salts on the terminals by keeping moisture from collecting on the bare metal.

All Hooked Up

You've eliminated battery cables and clamps as the cause of your no-start or almost-start problem. And you figure

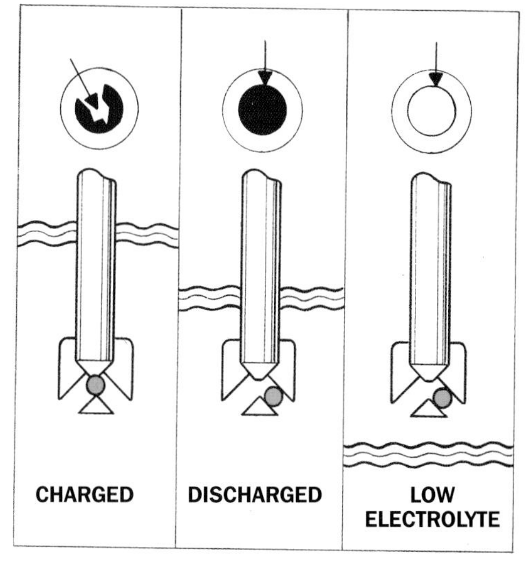

(Fig. 2) A built-in hydrometer eye is a good check, but won't necessarily find a bad battery.

it's not a problem with the starter motor, because a jumpstart instantly brings the engine whirring to life. So far, so good. Maybe it really is the battery.

Does the battery have a built-in hydrometer eye (**Fig. 2**)? This eye has a small plastic ball suspended at the bottom of a clear plastic window. The ball floats when the battery is charged, turning the window green. When the battery is discharged, the ball sinks and turns the window yellow. If the level of electrolyte is below the hydrometer, then the battery is past its useful life.

(Fig. 3) A proper battery hydrometer can detect an undercharged battery, as well as pinpoint a single bad cell.

One danger of these built-in hydrometers: They check only one of the six cells. If you've got a bad cell (the normal failure mode for batteries), there's only one chance in six you'll know it from the hydrometer.

A better check is to use a handheld hydrometer (**Fig. 3**). First you'll need to remove the filler caps. Battery clean? Cover the battery with a rag and pry the caps up. Warning! Battery acid will remove paint, corrode electrical connections and potentially destroy your eyesight. Wear eye protection.

First hitch: no battery caps to remove, it's a sealed, maintenance-free battery. Maybe so, but there's access to the individual cells, perhaps disguised under a label (**Fig. 4**).

Open it up and look inside. The electrolyte should come up to the bottom of the filler cap, or at least near it. If the level is down, especially if the plates are exposed, add water. Always use distilled water in a battery. There is never any need to add additional electrolyte. Batteries will normally consume water, but the sulfuric acid component of the electrolyte remains behind and never needs to be replenished.

Before you add any water, suck enough electrolyte out of one cell into the hydrometer to float the bulb. Write down the reading. Squirt the liquid back and repeat with the next cell. All six cells should have readings that agree within 0.050, or you've got a bad cell. These readings are temperature sensitive, so if it's very cold or hot out, you may need to correct the readings. The hydrometer scale equates the specific gravity of the electrolyte with the state of charge of the battery. If all the readings agree, and the gravity is low, the battery needs to be charged.

Charge

An alternative to the hydrometer test (and one used by professionals): With the battery charged, open circuit voltage should be 12.6 to 12.8 volts with the engine off and all loads off. With the car running and all loads off, the voltage should be between 13.6 and 14.5 volts.

Disable the engine by pulling the fuel pump fuse. Measure the battery voltage while cranking the engine. It should read at least 9.5 to 10 volts while cranking.

If the charging voltage is low, suspect some charging system problem. But if the charging voltage is correct and the cranking voltage is low, then the battery is suspect, as you've already troubleshot the wiring from the battery to the starter and ground.

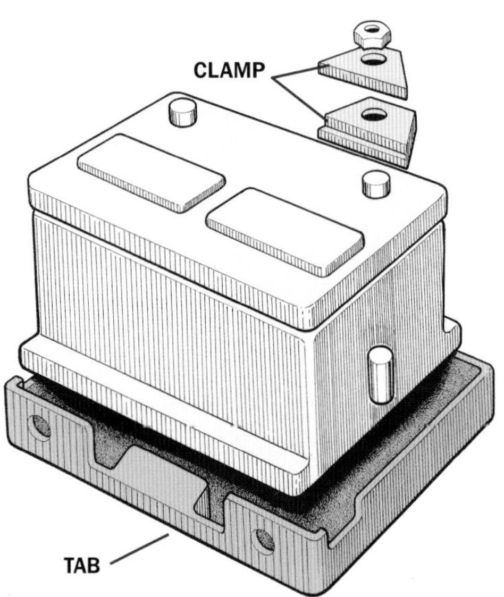

(Fig. 5) Battery hold-down clamps are essential to prevent a battery from becoming ballistic.

Strapping In

Replacing the battery is straightforward. It's vital that the hold-down clamps be reinstalled properly (**Fig. 5**). Some batteries use a wedge/lip arrangement at the bottom of the battery, while others (usually in older cars) use a pair of long bolts and a frame or lip to hold the battery down to the tray. A battery is perfectly capable of holing a radiator or smashing expensive fuel-injection components if it doesn't stay put.

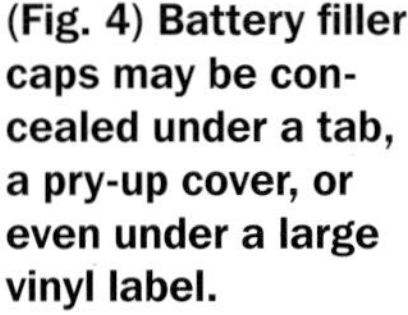

(Fig. 4) Battery filler caps may be concealed under a tab, a pry-up cover, or even under a large vinyl label.

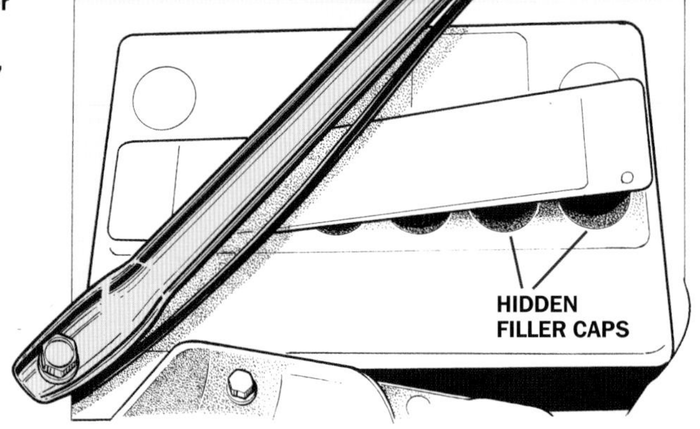

EASY

Replacing a Battery

"Honey! There's a woodpecker in the car!" she says. It's too early in the morning for this, and far too cold for woodpeckers anyway. You politely suggest to your wife that she do two things immediately: Let you go back to sleep, and let the woodpecker fly away in his own good time. No luck, the kids have to go to hockey practice—now.

As you stumble outside, you realize the absurdity of it all. Now, you know that there is no woodpecker in your car, or anywhere nearby. The pecking sound your significant other has identified as avian in origin is really just your starter solenoid clacking away merrily as she tries to start the car. Sleepily, you jumpstart the recalcitrant conveyance, and then try to grab another 40 winks. After hockey practice, you'll have to find out why your night's rest was suddenly abbreviated.

Time Is On Our Side

The useful life span of an average automotive battery is four to seven years. With the auto companies' eternal quest to make cars and trucks more efficient, two things have conspired to shorten this life span: smaller batteries and higher underhood temperatures. Higher temperatures are so damaging that many cars have insulating blankets for the battery, or the battery is mounted in the trunk.

A single instance of deep-discharging a battery can reduce its life span by half, so avoid running a battery into deep discharge. If you do, then charge it properly as soon as possible before the plates inside build up a layer of sulfates. A properly charged battery won't freeze, but a discharged battery will freeze at temperatures well above zero. Any battery that's been frozen is finished.

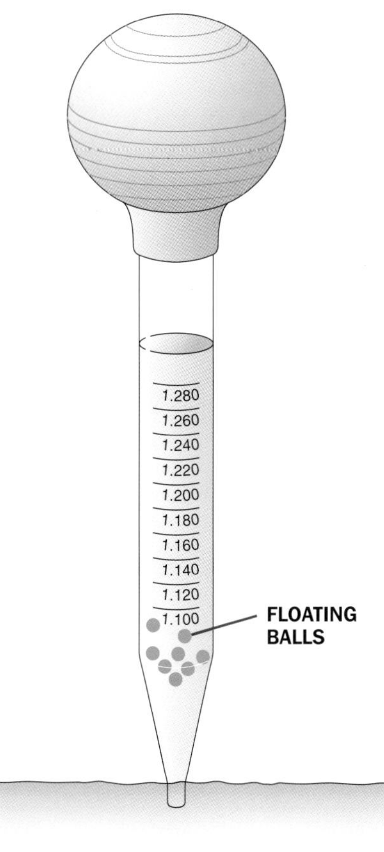

(Fig. 1) This battery hydrometer shows a fully discharged cell.

How Can You Tell?

Is one cell of the battery visibly different than the others? Look through the side of a translucent-cased battery. If one cell has substantially less electrolyte than the rest, or if one cell's lead plates are much lighter in color, then that cell has gone bad and the battery is junk. Charge the battery for an appropriate time (depending on how powerful your battery charger is) and then use a hydrometer (**Fig 1**) to measure the specific gravity of the electrolyte. The more charge on the battery, the more sulfuric acid there is in the electrolyte and the higher the hydrometer float will be on the scale. A battery that shows a low state of charge on the hydrometer after a long charge is dead. Don't rush to judgment, however, because a deeply discharged battery will take a charge very slowly at first.

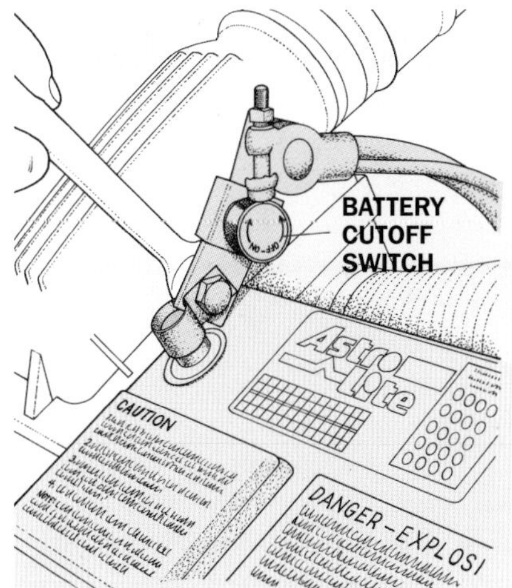

(Fig 2) Use a battery cutoff switch to diagnose parasitic current drains.

Is there some parasitic drain in your vehicle that's discharging your battery? An easy way to check is to temporarily install a battery cutoff switch (**Fig 2**) in the ground side. With everything in the car shut off, put an ammeter across the switch, turn the switch off, wait at least one hour, and measure the current drain. Up to 40 milliamperes (ma) is normal to keep the vehicle computers, radio presets and clock alive. Anything more than 200 ma will run your battery down in a few days.

Transplant

Once you've determined the battery is bad and the charging system and the rest of the electrical system is good, it's time to install a new battery. Start by rinsing the bad battery and the surrounding area with plenty of water. This will wash away any splattered battery acid, which otherwise would eat through sheetmetal, electrical wiring and the seat of your britches. Try not to splash it around.

Next, disconnect the battery's negative terminal. If you accidentally touch your wrench to anything nearby, no big deal. Then, you can unhook the positive side. If you try to unhook the positive side first, any random contact with nearby metal, such as the inner fender, will result in a welder-like shower of sparks and heat. Removing the ground side first breaks the circuit and prevents this.

Side-terminal battery hardware is notorious for not wanting to turn. Try tapping lightly with a hammer, and rotating the wire terminal slightly as you turn the wrench. Top-post battery terminals are sometimes very difficult to release. Light tapping may help, but you stand the chance of breaking the post off if you apply any substantial force. You may need to use a battery post tool to elevate the clamp loose from the post.

Nurse! Clamp!

Now's the time to seriously evaluate all of the wiring and clamps. This hardware carries substantial amounts of current—hundreds of amps for short periods when starting the car, and dozens for longer periods when the engine is running. It's imperative that it all be in good shape. The clamps should not be deformed. Light corrosion can be wire-brushed off, and a paste of baking soda will help neutralize any acid. Rinse thoroughly. If the attachment point of the wire to the metal clamp is good, fine. If the clamp or the connection is nasty-looking, you should replace the cable. Reserve the clamp-on, universal cable-end terminals for emergencies—they won't last as long as a proper connection and may contribute to yet another premature battery failure. Remember that the positive and negative posts on top-post batteries are physically, as well as electrically, different. Don't interchange. You may be able to rehabilitate an otherwise good terminal clamp by replacing the bolt—but be sure to use a lead-plated battery terminal bolt, not just something left over from installing your screen door.

How Dry I Am

Most conventional batteries are shipped without any electrolyte in them. If you have a good auto parts store, they'll keep a supply of ready-to-use batteries in assorted sizes on hand. If not, you'll have to have one filled and charged. Here's the procedure: Fill the dry battery with electrolyte of the correct specific gravity. Any place that can sell you a battery will have this. Fill to the bottom of the filler neck, no higher. Now wait several hours while the electrolyte seeps into the spongy lead plates. The level will go down, but as long as it covers all of the plates inside you can proceed to charging the battery. At this point the battery probably will start the car—but it's important

(Fig 3) A proper battery holddown is necessary for safety and long battery life.

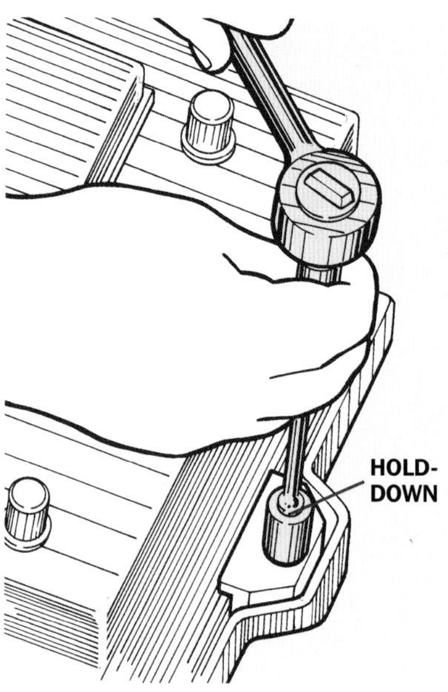

HOW IT WORKS

Built-In Battery Test Windows

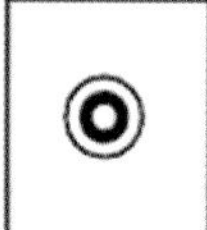

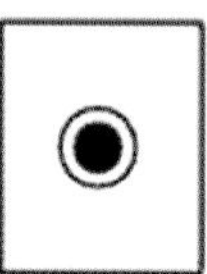

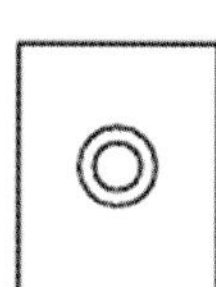

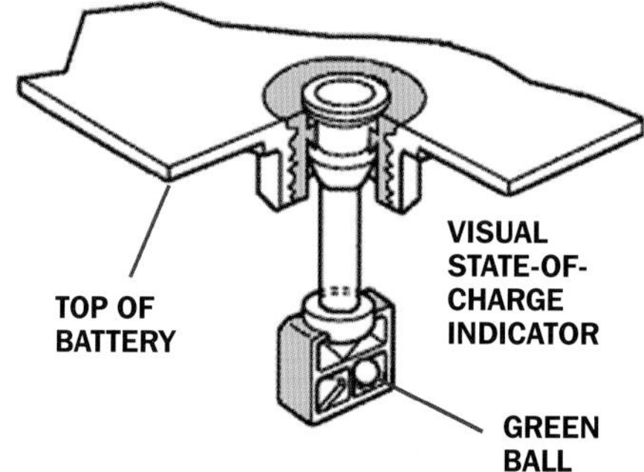

Many maintenance-free batteries have no access to the electrolyte to check the level or state of charge. But many of them have a built-in tester. This is a Plexiglas wand that sticks down into the battery just below the normal level of the electrolyte. At the bottom of this is a small chamber containing a loose plastic ball that floats in the dense electrolyte when the battery is charged. When it's floating, you can see the green ball at the top window through the Plexiglas. When the battery is discharged, the ball sinks and all you can see is the dark electrolyte. But when the electrolyte is too low, the plastic wand's bottom isn't submerged in it, and you'll notice a light color through the window. This means it's time to replace the battery. Remember, this tester sees into only one cell—there are five others, any one of which could be faulty.

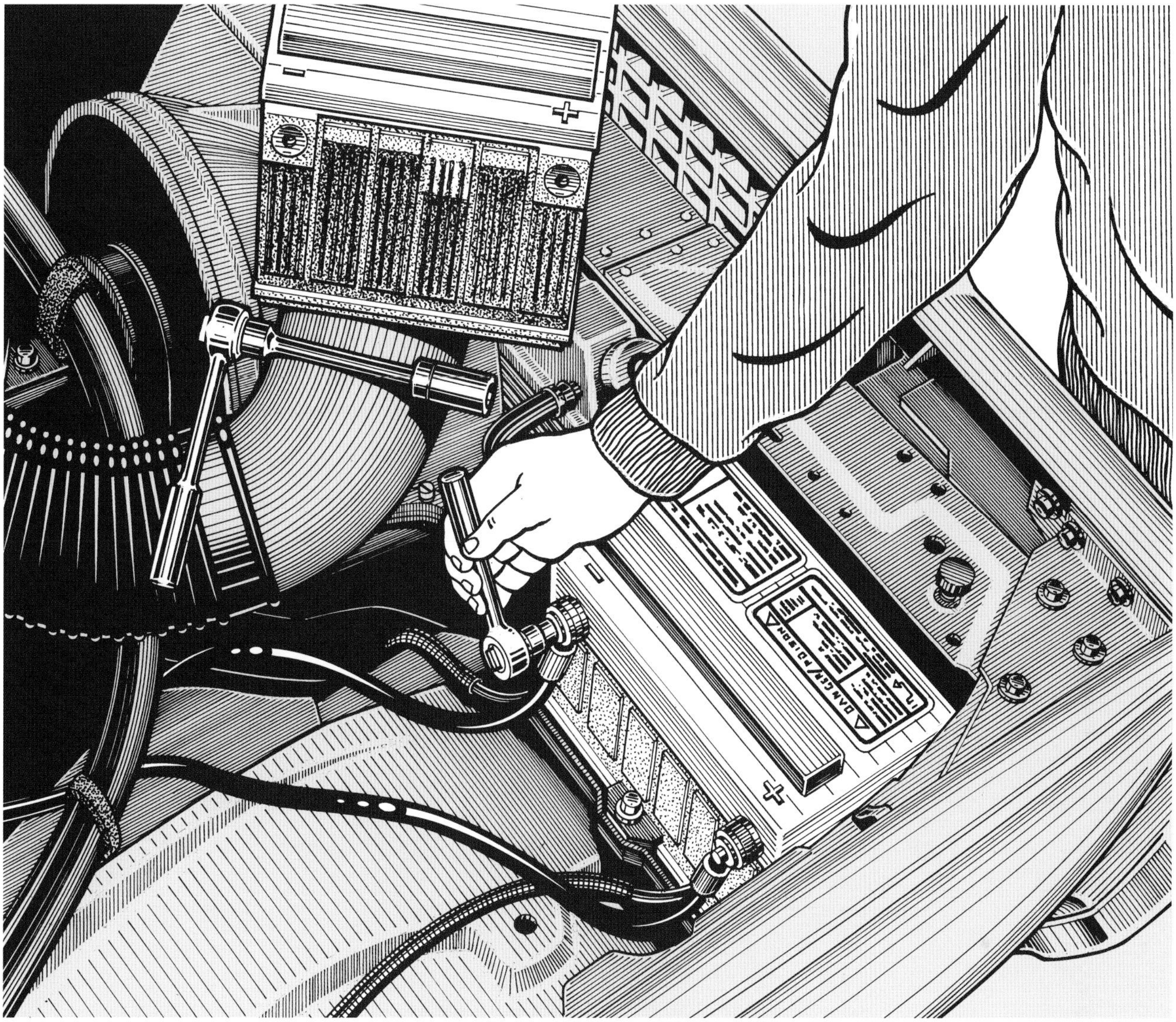

(Fig 4) Always reattach the battery's negative (–) terminal last.

that it be fast-charged for an hour or so. This means being charged at a higher current than your 4-amp household charger can muster, so it must be done with at least 1½ hours of super highway cruising, or by a shop with a fast charger capable of putting out 20 amps or so. Failing to do so will shorten the battery's life span and reduce its capacity. Now top up the electrolyte, and rinse well.

Dropping It In

You've got the correct battery, right? Check that the positive and negative terminals are on the proper sides, and that the holddown clamp is the correct style. You may as well fasten the holddown first (Fig 3). Use some anti-seize compound on the hardware in case you ever need to remove the battery in the future. Don't skip this step because vibration will shorten the battery's life by cracking the delicate lead plates away from the internal bus bars. The worst case would be the battery shooting out of the tray as you bottom out in some pothole.

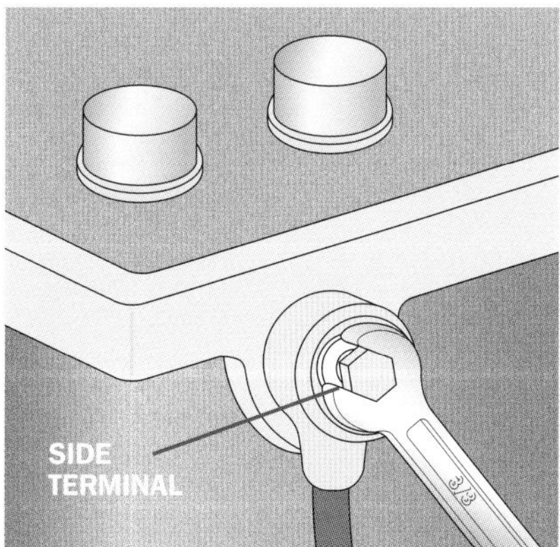

(Fig 5) Side-terminal battery posts are easy to overtighten—be careful.

Now hook up the positive terminal. When it's tight, put on the red rubber cover. Now hook up the negative (ground) side (Fig 4). Side-terminal batteries (Fig 5) have a very small bolt head for a reason. It's to keep overenthusiastic mechanics from overtightening them and stripping the threads out of the soft lead terminal. Use a short wrench to keep torque down.

Now cover the terminals with petroleum jelly. This will substantially slow down the buildup of corrosion on the terminals. Finally, be sure to replace the battery heat insulator if there was one installed.

Maintaining and Repairing Your Suspension

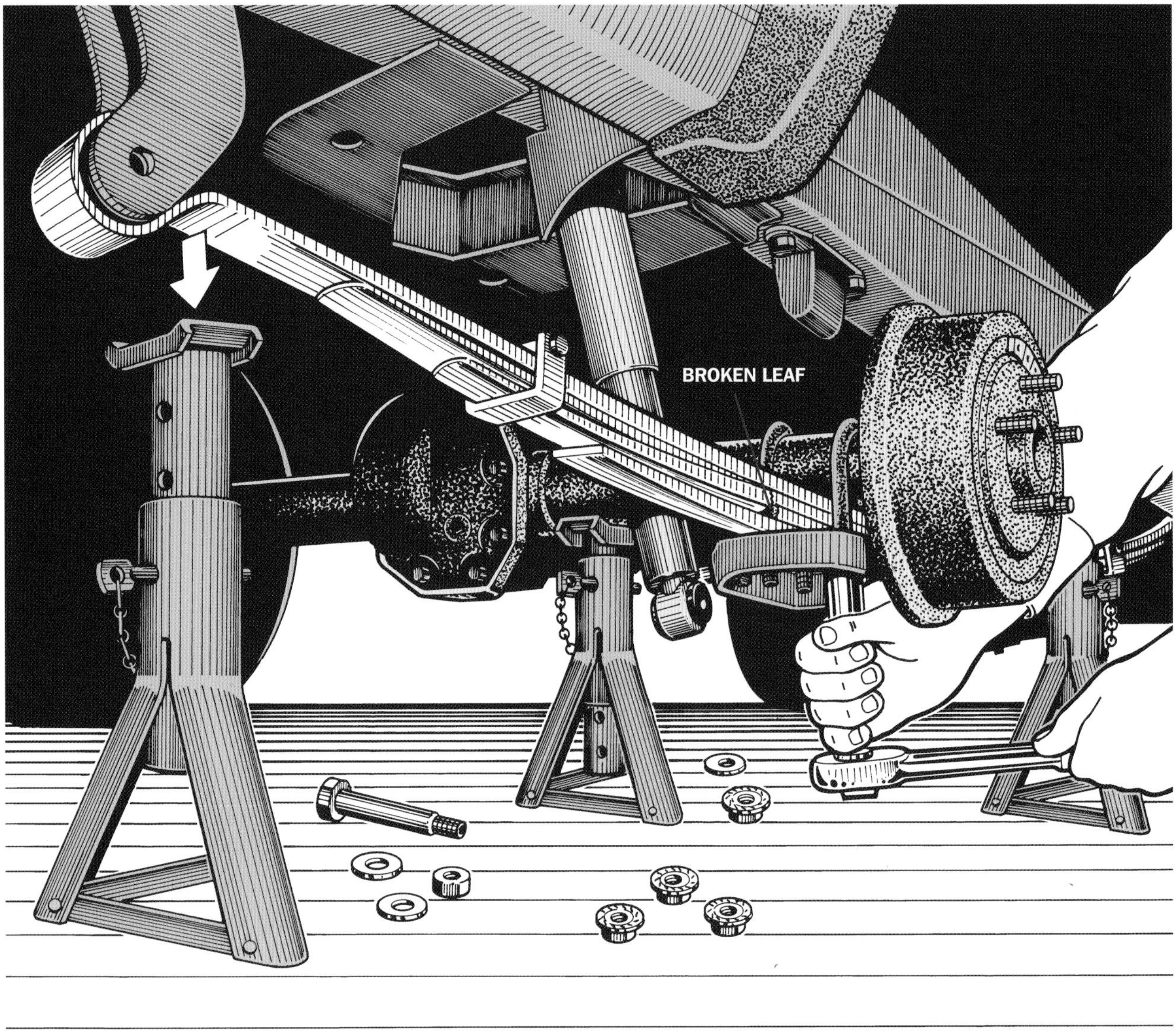

(Fig. 1) Raise the vehicle on safety stands. Then support the axle itself to get the tension off the spring. Remove the center U-bolt nuts, washers, plate and then the U-bolts.

"It feels like driving a truck," complains your significant other. Okay, she was the inspiration for "The Princess and the Pea," and you point out, "Well, it is a truck." But you know the truth: It used to ride and drive a lot more like a car, and that's why you bought it.

The carlike feel of today's pickups and sport utility vehicles is there when they're new. But most pickups and some SUVs have solid axles (at the rear and even the front of some four-wheel-drive models), and rear suspensions with leaf springs. The tuning is carefully balanced between an acceptable ride at no load (besides passengers) and something tolerable when the pickup bed is stacked high with 2 x 4s, paneling and decorative brick.

So it doesn't take a lot of deterioration to make the ride/drive experience something that even you have to admit is somewhat harsh.

You can get all kinds of assist springs for the rear axle, including auxiliary leaves—even air assists that you can deflate or inflate. But the object of these is to increase the load-carrying capacity of the vehicle.

What you want to do is restore the ride/handling of everyday or weekend trips after 20,000 to 30,000 miles or so have precipitated a harsher ride and vaguer handling. There are aftermarket shock absorbers made for pickups and SUVs used primarily as transportation, and they will help. If you want more, there are additional steps you can take to further restore the ride and handling.

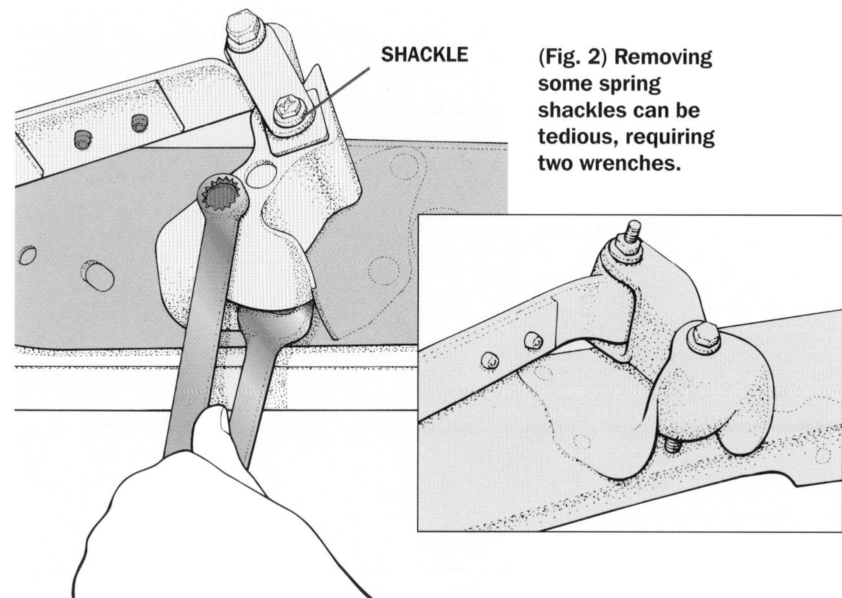

(Fig. 2) Removing some spring shackles can be tedious, requiring two wrenches.

Springs and Shackles

Look at the leaf springs—at the rear on each side, even at the front if your vehicle also has them there. Loose center U-bolts are an occasional problem, and retightening with a torque wrench could be helpful. But when the ride quality is down significantly, look closely for a cracked leaf (**Fig. 1**), and if you find one, change the spring, plus the mounting bushings and shackle in back. In fact, even with the leaves intact, there can be enough deterioration in the rear shackles to justify replacing both for a real ride improvement.

Take out the bolts that hold the spring assembly at front and rear, which can be easier said than done in many cases. Turning the bolts while holding the nuts with a second wrench is straightforward stuff (**Fig. 2**), but the rear bolts can almost "mate" with the rubber bushings inside the shackle, and getting them out can be a tedious job if that happens. You may have to slowly unthread the bolt, while at the same time prying under the bolt head to keep outward pressure on the bolt. Or you may be able to tap it out with a hammer and punch. Just keep clear of the top of the end of the leaf spring, which could snap up (against the frame) if there's still some tension on the spring.

On some trucks, the shackle's upper

HOW IT WORKS

The Leaf Spring Suspension

The leaf spring suspension is a popular choice for the rear of trucks and some sport utility vehicles. It has been used for some heavy-duty truck front suspensions and the rear of passenger cars, but the leading application is the truck/SUV with the nonindependent rear axle. The leaf spring has several leaves—simply adding leaves increases the load-carrying ability of the suspension. The top leaf typically is the longest and each end of that leaf is formed into an eye, into which a rubber bushing is installed. The spring eyes are bolted to the chassis in front and attached at the rear through a hinge joint called a shackle. The shackle permits the spring to effectively change its length as it flexes to absorb impacts. The leaf spring also attaches (through U-bolts) to the solid rear axle, so it locates the axle without the use of arms, an important function. This permits a simple suspension design with obvious packaging benefits. However, these advantages are offset in passenger cars and some SUVs by the superior ride qualities of the coil spring, which merely supports the vehicle and simply compresses and expands as it absorbs the impacts.

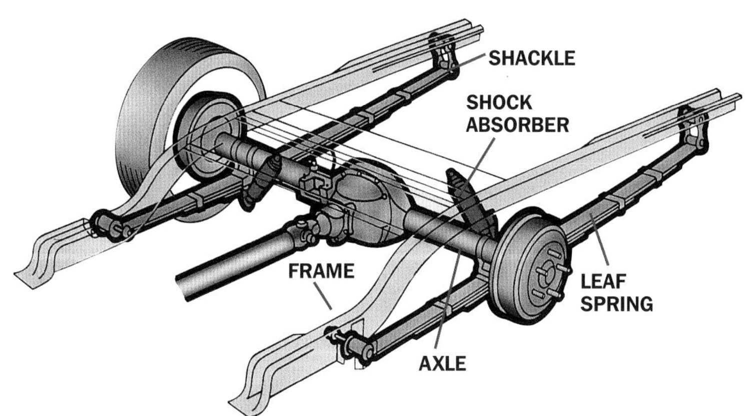

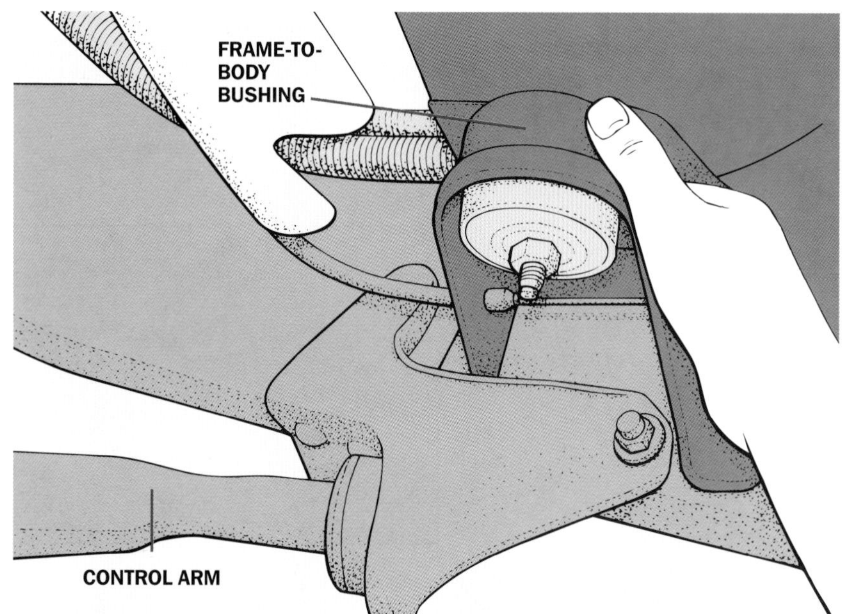

(Fig. 3) Check frame-to-body and suspension bushings. Look for cracks or overly brittle rubber as well as missing chunks.

bolt is installed on the inboard side and it won't clear the frame to come out. Jack up the rear of the vehicle until the shackle end of the leaf spring comes down far enough below the frame.

The original equipment bushings with those metal shackles are part of the reason for loss of ride quality. To get a long-term smoother ride, install aftermarket shackles that include small rubber springs with two metal sleeve inserts and metal arms—almost a reverse of the original equipment design. The Dana Velvet-Ride series that we installed is an example. You attach the metal arms to one metal sleeve of the rubber shackle, insert and tighten the through bolt and nut, and then install the new shackle in place of the original. The metal arms connect to the chassis and the rubber spring, and the rubber spring is bolted (through its second metal sleeve) to the leaf spring.

Inspect the underbody frame-to-body bushings (**Fig. 3**) and the radius rod bushings, and apply rubber lubricant as routine maintenance. If they're badly cracked, perhaps missing chunks of rubber, installing replacements will help eliminate body shake. Occasionally, the metal floor pan of the vehicle is the problem—it's rusted and weak. A piece of galvanized flat sheetmetal, thick enough for support, should be welded in place.

Even if you just have to replace bad bushings, don't simply loosen the bolts and pry to get clearance to install replacements, or you could cause damage you won't see. This work normally requires loosening radiator mounts, the steering gear and column, and other parts, so check and follow the factory-prescribed procedure for your vehicle. Or better still, lube periodically and the bushings will be fine.

Steering Stabilizers

Is a lot of vibration coming through the steering wheel? The problem could be wheel balance or alignment, even the steering gear's free play adjustment. But if it's a low-speed problem on secondary roads, look for something worn out.

If your operation has pounded the tightness out of steering parts, you can feel the looseness when you grab

(Fig. 4) Shimmy can be caused by a worn or loose steering stabilizer. Check the mounts, and check the damper for a bent rod or leakage.

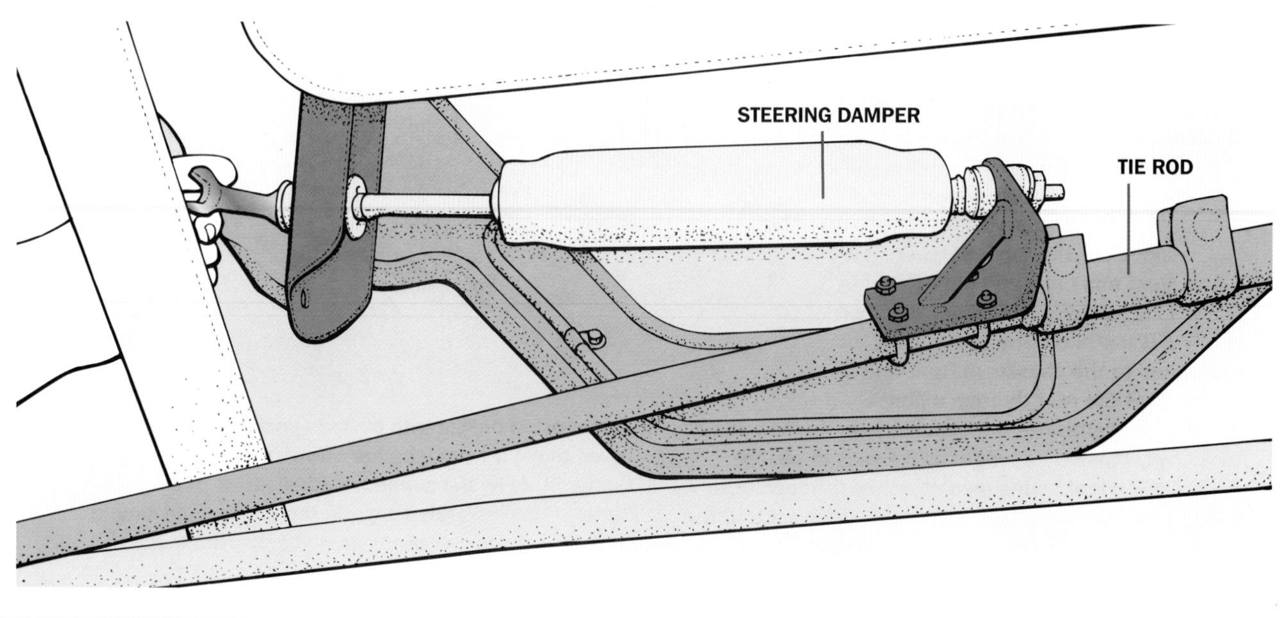

the tie rod and idler arms and find you can flex them too easily. If you want to replace them just this once, get heavy-duty parts specifically designed for pickups and SUVs. They'll not only be labeled for heavy-duty use, but they'll have grease fittings, which the original equipment may not.

Many vehicles have steering stabilizers. If the vehicle is suffering from vibration and shimmy, look for worn-out stabilizers, basically one or two horizontally installed "dampers" (shock absorbers) that connect the steering linkage to the frame or axle (**Fig. 4**).

The dampers mount to the steering linkage with a bracket (held by U-bolts) and to the frame or front axle with another bracket, and there are washers and rubber bushings at each end. If they're loose but the bushings look good, a simple tightening may remedy the problem. When they have significant mileage on them, replace the dampers along with mounting hardware and bushings.

If you don't have stabilizers, but use the vehicle on bad roads a lot and want to get rid of the shimmy, there are kits you can install, complete with frame brackets and U-bolts. These kits have been a factory fix for otherwise unfixable shimmy for years, and aftermarket kits for trucks and SUVs are available.

CHECK SHOCK MOUNTS and bushings before condemning any shock absorbers.

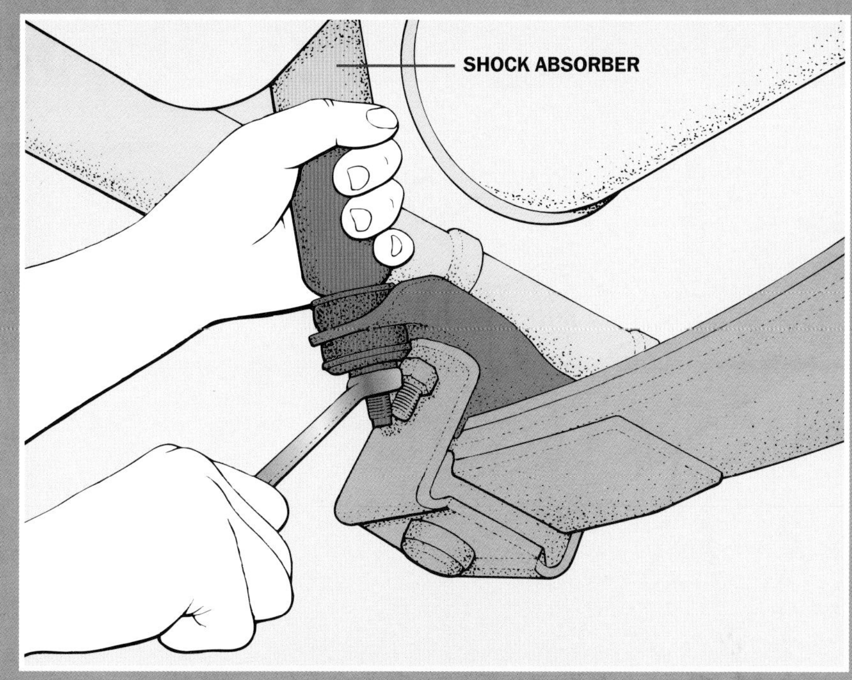

Jounce Bumpers

Have the rear axle jounce bumpers been taking a beating? If they have, you may see that the ends are scuffed. However, you probably know without even looking whether or not the vehicle has been bottoming. If you get stiffer shocks, your normal ride will suffer. A better approach is to replace the jounce bumpers with ones that really are small rubber assist springs, such as Monroe's Muscle LSE. They look like a short stack of thick pancakes, and when you're driving on bad roads they make contact with the jounce pad on the axle and prevent bottoming out. You could perceive this as causing a slight stiffening of the ride, but the bottoms of the "short stacks" have a couple of inches of clearance to the pads, so they're only in the picture on bumps. And because they're springs, they absorb impact so the overall ride quality should be better.

On many trucks, you can just unbolt the bracket that holds the original jounce bumper, bolt on a universal bracket (with elongated holes) and attach the "short stack." If the jounce bumper bracket is riveted to the frame, use a chisel or hand grinder to cut it loose.

After installing the bracket and rubber spring, tighten the bracket bolts lightly, then lower the vehicle to the ground, adjust the bracket height to the recommended clearance with a normal load in the truck bed, and do a final tightening.

Replacing Shock Absorbers

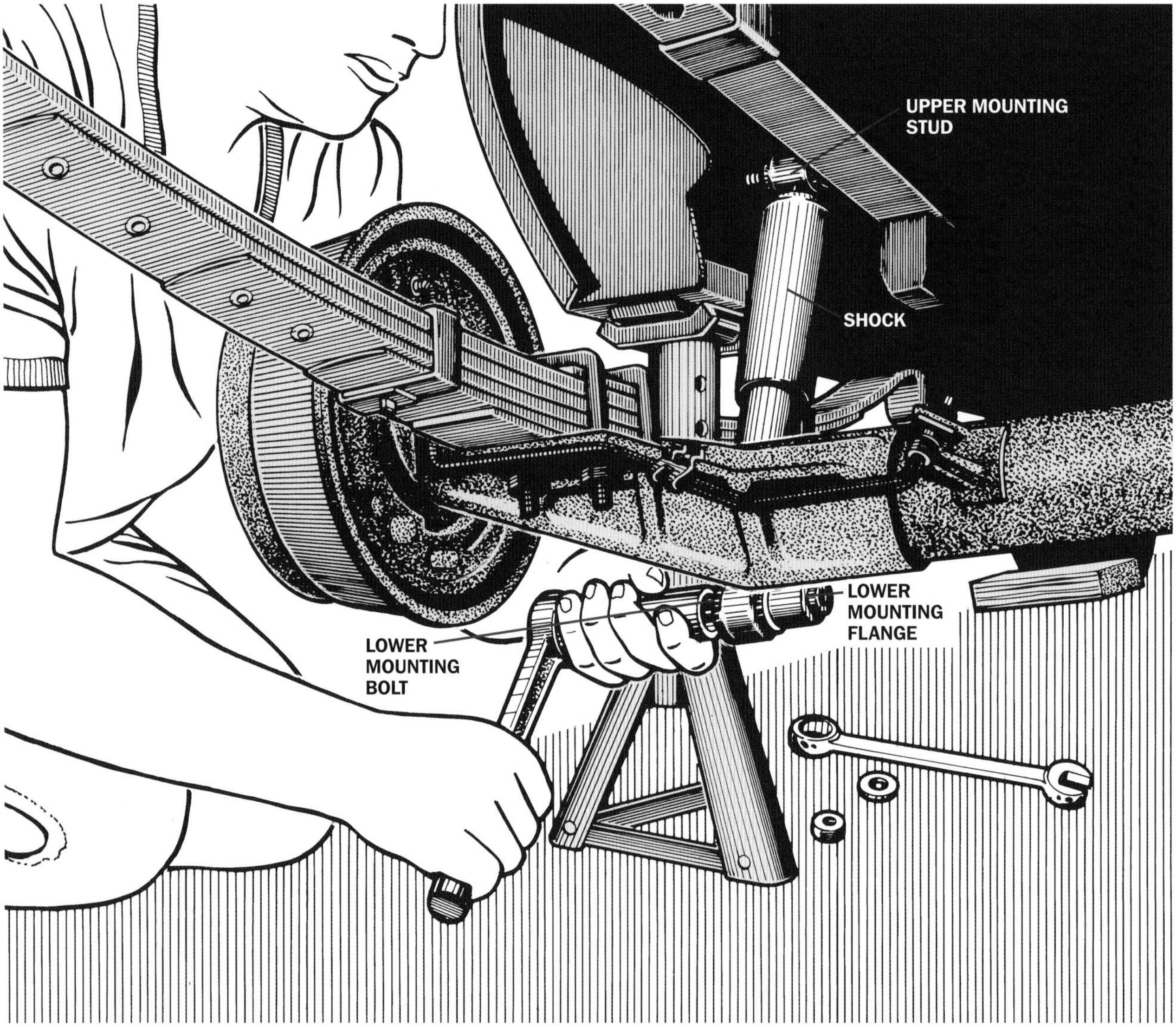

(Fig. 1) **Removing shocks is usually straightforward, but getting under the vehicle and applying sufficient torque to remove large-diameter rusted-on fasteners can be daunting.**

Your wife has started to sound like a detergent commercial, bragging about the spilled coffee stains she's gotten out of your shirts. The kids are making excuses about why they'd rather ride their bikes to the mall than get a lift in your car, and even the dog has started to get carsick. Wake up, Bunky, and realize that your vehicle's ride has gone, literally and figuratively, downhill. Hey, there are over 60,000 miles on the odometer, and the tires are starting to develop little concave "cups," sure signs it's time for new shocks.

Of course, you could get the jouncy ride of worn shocks at much lower mileage, perhaps because you drive briskly on bad roads and accelerate the wearing-out process. Or maybe the shock mountings have loosened. Occasionally, a shock produces a visible leak of fluid, but some hint of weep is normal, and most shocks we've seen that were well worn out, also looked bone dry.

That's right, we're talking about shock absorbers. The MacPherson strut is in wide use, but conventional shocks are on lots of cars, plus almost all those SUVs, pickups and at least the rear suspension of minivans. Isn't replacing them just like changing struts, just easier because you don't have to compress and remove the coil spring? No, although some things are similar (a strut is really a type of shock absorber), the mountings—and therefore the replacement procedure—are different.

Those Mountings

Both shock mountings on most late-model vehicles are in the underbody, so if you support the chassis on safety stands, you have access to the top and bottom. One problem is reaching them. Another is getting off the hardware (**Fig. 1**).

The first thing to do is see if the mountings are loose. If you can turn the mounting nut or bolt at the top or bottom without much effort, the mounting is loose. On some shocks there's a stud in a rubber bushing, and if it tears loose, you'll see and feel it turn as you try to tighten the nut. There's typically a hex on the stud, so you can hold the stud while you tighten the nut.

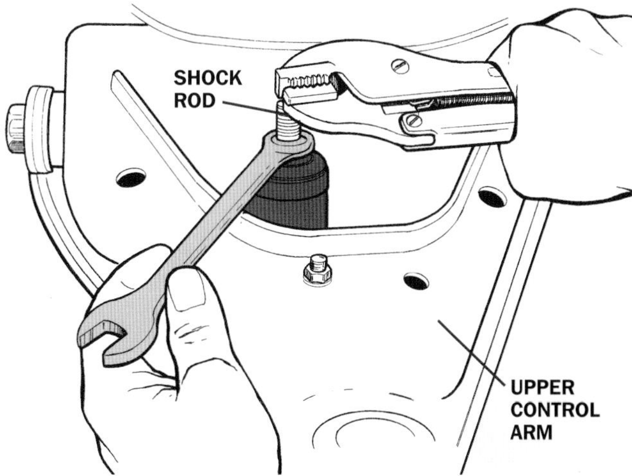

(Fig. 2) If the shock rod spins endlessly as you try to remove the upper mount, try Vise-Grips on the flatted end of the rod.

When a nut and bolt loosen, you may be able to just retighten. However, it will loosen again if you don't apply some thread-locking compound to the threads.

If the shock bushings' rubber is obviously cracked or badly distorted, you'll usually have to replace the shocks to get the new bushings. That's okay, because the shocks themselves don't figure to be in much better shape.

Replacement Shocks

The aftermarket manufacturers produce replacement shocks for just about everything, except some electronically controlled designs. Only a handful of electronic systems' shocks are not available from third parties, either because they're an oddball size or because the tie-in to the vehicle electronics would result in a ride/handling glitch if you installed nonelectronic replacements. It might be as little as a trouble code or warning light, but if there's major integration,

HOW IT WORKS

Shock Absorbers Don't Absorb Shocks

A shock absorber doesn't absorb shock (the spring does that, by flexing to absorb the energy of an impact). The shock absorber actually stops the vehicle from bouncing up and down on the flexing spring. It does this by transferring the spring-flexing energy to a piston in an oil-filled chamber, which dissipates it in the form of heat. Most shocks have twin-tube (chamber) arrangements, an inner chamber with the piston and a calibrated valve at the bottom, which has the entry passage to an outer chamber—the reservoir. When the piston comes down on compression, it forces fluid through the calibrated valve into the reservoir. When the piston moves up as the shock absorber extends, oil is drawn from the reservoir into the main chamber, and some also flows through orifices in the piston, as part of the ride control calibration. A charge of low-pressure gas in the reservoir reduces oil foaming, which would affect ride control. Many high-performance shocks, including some for heavy loads such as motorhomes, are of single-tube construction, with a high-pressure gas charge in the base. Fluid flow is between the areas below and above the piston, which has a sophisticated valve assembly. The higher pressure of the single-tube design is even more effective against fluid aeration, but at the expense of ride comfort. Strut replacement is sometimes a job for a pro with the right tools and coil spring compressors.

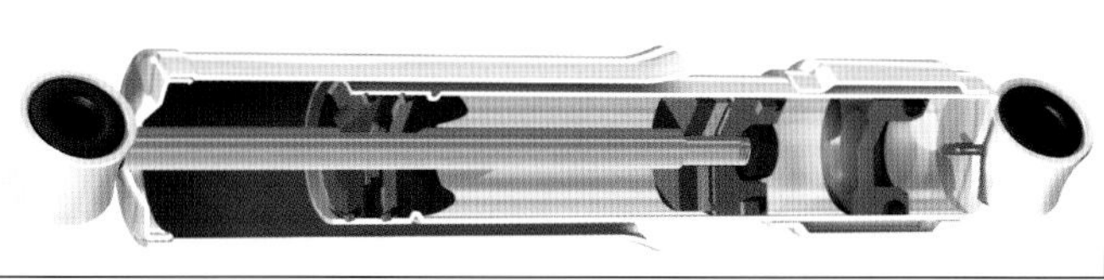

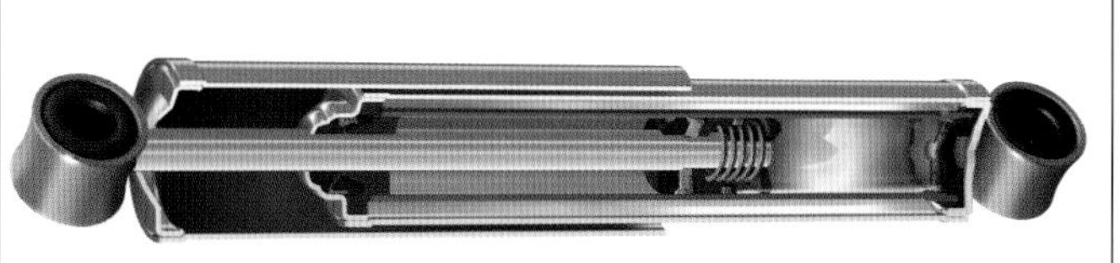

Single- and double-tube shocks are used on either the front or rear end of most vehicles. Struts are simply a shock that includes the spring perch and a bearing that replaces the upper ball joint.

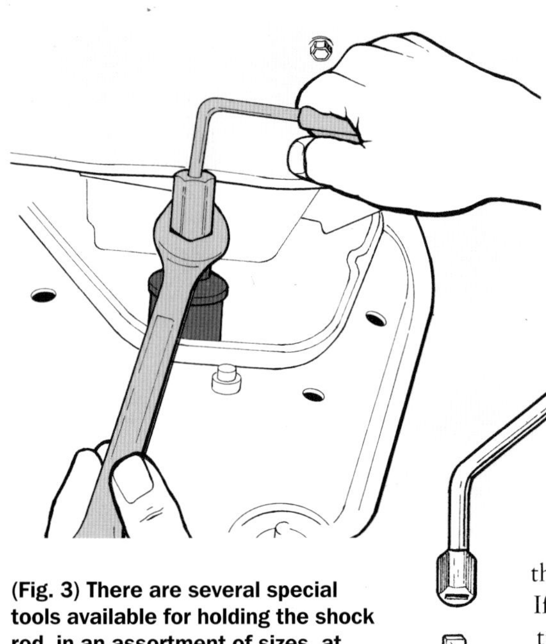

(Fig. 3) There are several special tools available for holding the shock rod, in an assortment of sizes, at auto parts stores. Use a box-end wrench to loosen the nut while you hold the rod stationary.

it could be more than that.

Just check the manufacturer's catalog, and if there are shock absorbers listed for your exact year, make and model, and the listing says it covers the electronic control system type, you're cool. You will be giving up the electronic control, but there isn't a system that's all that sophisticated on anything but a few premium cars, such as Cadillac, Mercedes, Corvette and some other high-end sports cars.

If the aftermarket catalog doesn't list a replacement, you're stuck with ordering replacement shocks from a dealer. On some Ford products there's an external motor drive, and you can unplug it from the old shock and install it on the new one.

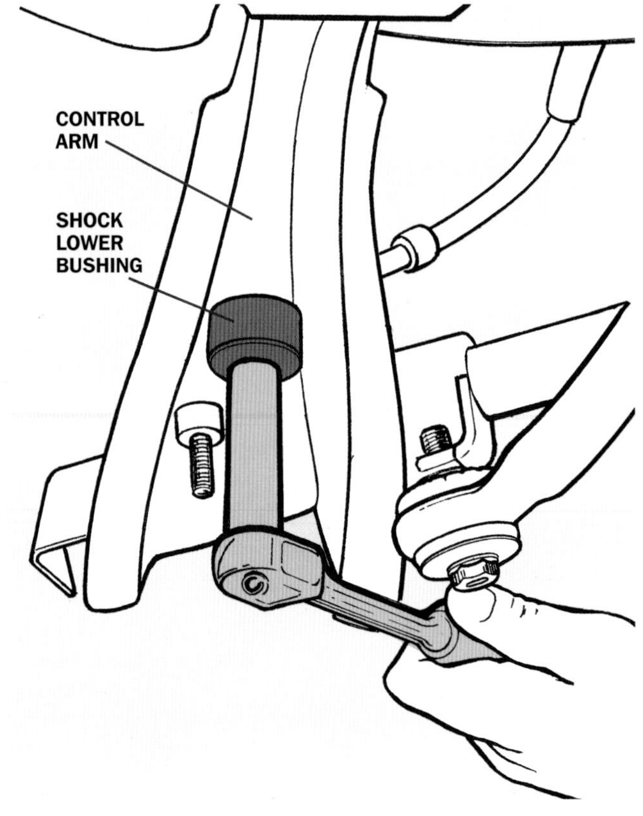

(Fig. 4) Generally, a socket will spin off the mounting hardware. New hardware is usually included with the shock.

In most other cases, you get a choice of shock absorber designs.

Getting the Shock Off

If there's an electrical connector, start by unplugging it. No electronics problem with installing conventional shocks? You could just cut the wiring, and tape securely. But if there's any chance you or a subsequent owner will want to re-establish the system, that won't work. If the connector is in the trunk, that's easy (just tape over it). But if it's underneath, find a safe location away from exhaust heat, pack it with pieces of plastic foam stuffed against the terminals, put it into a heavy plastic pouch, seal and hold it in place with a cable tie.

Loosening a rust-frozen nut and bolt is one of the major headaches in shock replacement. If a nut is exposed, you should be able to loosen it with a nut splitter, a clamp-like tool you often can rent from an auto parts store. No space for the splitter? Penetrating solvent, followed by heat from a torch, is another possibility. The most difficult is the type where the piston rod turns when you try to loosen the nut. One approach is to clamp locking pliers onto the "double-D" end of the piston rod, hold it from turning with the pliers and loosen the nut with a conventional wrench **(Fig. 2)**. Something better (particularly for recessed installations) is a special toolkit with a hollow hex that fits over the rod onto the nut, followed by a wrench (made to fit the double-D) that goes through the hollow hex onto the double-D end **(Fig. 3)**. Inexpensive kits, with three hollow hexes for most U.S. makes, or even some for specific models, are readily available in auto parts stores. It comes with three hollow hexes for most U.S. makes. There's also one specifically for some Ford products. If the shock piston end (or stud end) has a conventional hex, you can use an ordinary socket, of course **(Fig. 4)**.

Many shocks are mounted on studs, and we've even seen those where the shock upper mount has a retaining bracket held by an additional stud and bolt. It's not a major difficulty, just extra hardware to remove. When you get the nuts off a stud mounting, you still have to pry off the shock, working evenly at top and bottom so it doesn't cock.

If you're not sure of the condition of a bone-dry shock, just disconnect it from the bottom mount if possible (or remove it completely if it's on studs). Then slowly compress the shock (even low-pressure gas shocks will be easily

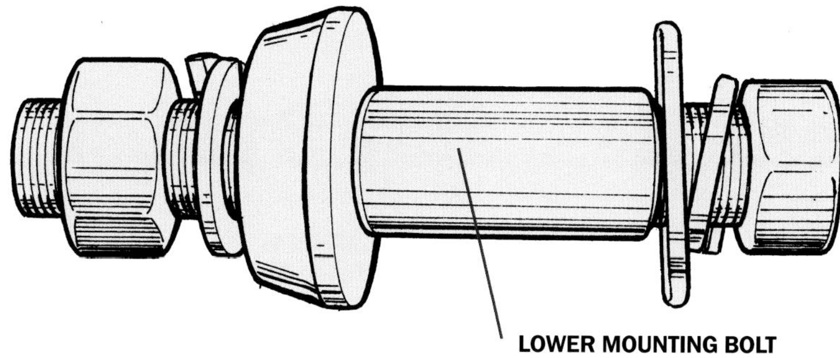

(Fig. 5) Lower mounting bolts are usually, but not always, included in the new shock's box.

compressed). If you feel any lost motion ("looseness" or unevenness), the shock is worn out.

Installing New Shocks

If you're on a budget and installing nongas shocks, it's a good idea to make sure they don't have air inside and bleed it out if they do. (Don't try this on old shocks. If they have air inside, it's from internal wear, and bleeding is not a cure.) With new nongas shocks, bleed by holding each shock upright (installed position): Extend it, and then turn it upside down and compress. Repeat the procedure a few times and the new shock should operate smoothly, with somewhat greater resistance on extension.

Using adjustable shocks? Some have soft, normal and firm positions, and although you can make adjustments after installation, start with soft or normal (firm is best for "ride restoration" after tens of thousands of miles of use).

The mounts for replacement shocks often are very different from those for the originals. That's okay, so long as you follow the instructions carefully. A common example is the aftermarket hardware for the "stud-in-bushing" design used on many General Motors cars. There's a specially shaped steel replacement stud assembly that goes into the lower mounting, and the bushing that's in the replacement shock just slides onto it (**Fig. 5**).

If the shock mounts on studs and the nut is tough to thread on, clean the threads with a wire brush and apply penetrating oil/solvent. If the nut almost spun off, apply a film of thread-locking compound to the stud. If you can tighten the shock hardware to specs without distorting the bushing, that's ideal. If the nut hits the end of the threads and the bushings are loose, you've got the wrong ones—or you're missing some hardware.

EASY

Maintaining Your Exhaust System

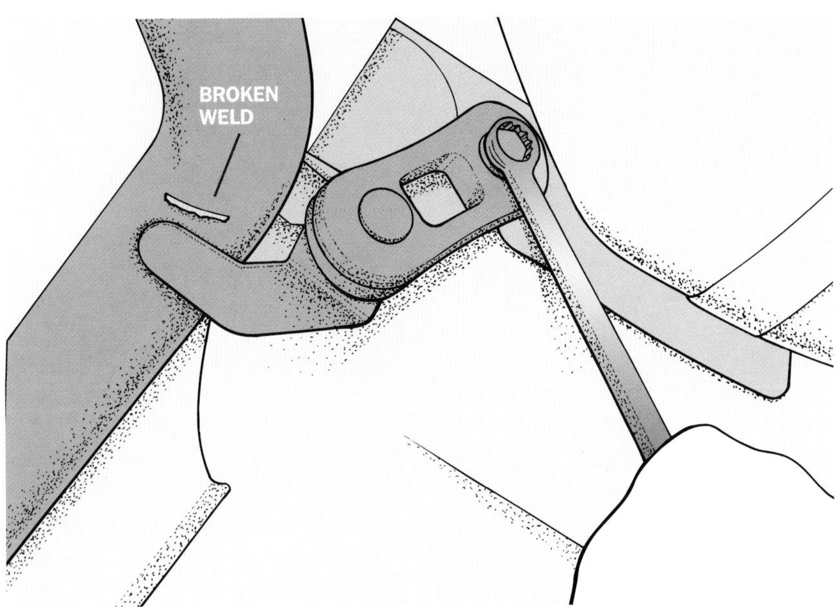

(Fig. 1) Tightening a loose clamp won't help if the bracket has broken loose at the weld line.

The sign says "DIP." And it's not advertising a samba school—there's a dip in the pavement large enough to lose a first-grader in. You touch the brakes lightly to keep from spilling your java as you traverse it. But there's a sudden graunching noise from under your car, followed by the scream as about a gallon of fast-food coffee flenses the skin from your thigh. You pull over to inspect your leg and the underside of your car, in that order. There are big, hot chunks of metal hanging loose under your chassis, and the exhaust system is nearly dragging.

Today's exhaust systems consist of a lot of expensive parts. There are one or more catalysts, an oxygen sensor, maybe even a 2-stage muffler. There's piping that's not only shaped to clear underbody lines, but also may be made of premium metals, in some cases dual-wall tubing. There are sheetmetal underbody heat shields to prevent the exhaust from igniting dry grass.

What's holding everything together? A few clamp joints and some welds. What's holding everything up? A few pieces of rubber with some brackets. What's keeping everything aligned? Those same few pieces of rubber and brackets. Failures are common and they range from cracked rubber to failed welds.

Before you suffer the same expensive fate we described earlier, take time to perform a regular underbody inspection—it's easy. To get started, jack up the car and support it on safety stands front and rear. Now you're ready for an in-depth look.

Hangers

If any hanger is broken, it has to be replaced, without delay—even if the exhaust system seems to be hanging level. One broken hanger means that when the system moves up and down as you drive, a whiplash effect goes through the clamped and welded joints. Eventually clamps loosen and welds crack.

Replacing a broken hanger used to be simple, because most companies used some type that bolted to the body and clamped to some part of the exhaust system. Today, the most popular design uses rods welded to the pipes and, often, to the vehicle underbody **(Fig. 1)**. These hangers also have a thick rubber section that resembles a flattened football or beach ball, with holes for a rod at each apex of the rubber. Welding positively locates all the parts, and although you may have to tug and pry, replacing the rubber piece when it becomes cracked is very straightforward.

You can install a brand-new pipe if the rod comes off the pipe, but if the pipe itself is good, that's an unnecessarily tough and expensive replacement. The alternative is to install a universal hanger, though this may require a bit of jury-rigging. First, remove the broken hanger. Then look for a nearby hole, perhaps even from the old hanger. Take a universal hanger that can twist and tilt and has an adjustable length setup, and attach it to the underbody with a bolt (and if it isn't threaded, also with a nut) through that hole. Next, make the connection around the pipe—a simple clamp and U-bolt usually works **(Fig. 2)**. Don't be surprised if a part of the welded-on bracket (from the broken hanger) has to be cut or ground off to provide space for the clamp that will attach to the universal hanger. You should try to make attachments very close to the locations of the original equipment setup. This will maintain system alignment and the balanced hang of the entire system.

If there is noise from exhaust system contact with the underbody or an underbody part, you should check for damage underneath. Exhaust system clearances are limited, and if you see the need to increase one, it may be possible to bend or shim an original-equipment hanger. If a rod-type hanger is welded in place, see if you can bend it with a piece of pipe over the rod's open end. If you need more than ¼ in. or so, look for an alternative. If the hanger is a bolt-on to the body, for example, you may be able to install washers as shims.

Some older imports have rubber hangers that resemble thick rubber bands. If the old band has broken off, you can get a replacement, but installing it is not a matter of simply stretching it over the retaining tabs. The band is so thick and stiff you probably will have to pry pretty hard to get it on.

Many exhaust systems have a bracket to provide firm support close to the transmission. If the bracket cracks—or if it was removed for service and never reinstalled—that can account for a lot of exhaust system flex and eventual cracking. If you can't get a replacement bracket, you may be able to get the old cracked one rewelded. But replacement is the best choice, and if the dealer doesn't have it, the wrecking yard may.

Shields

Exhaust system heat shields are prone to damage from driving on rough roads. To avoid the possibility of a grass fire, replace any that are missing or barely hanging on. If a shield is dented, unbolt it, and check the exhaust system for damage.

Exhaust Joints

If there has been a lot of exhaust system up-down travel because of a broken hanger, the clamps and joint may be damaged. If a welded joint is cracked at a muffler or resonator joint, you can replace the parts. Or to save money, cut away the piping and part of the neck joint, then install a short connector pipe and secure it with clamps.

If a clamped joint isn't cracked, but is leaking exhaust gas, remove the old clamp. If the pipe ends are badly distorted, you'll have to rent a pipe expander to reshape them. Otherwise, separate the pipes, sand them to remove any rust, then apply a coat of

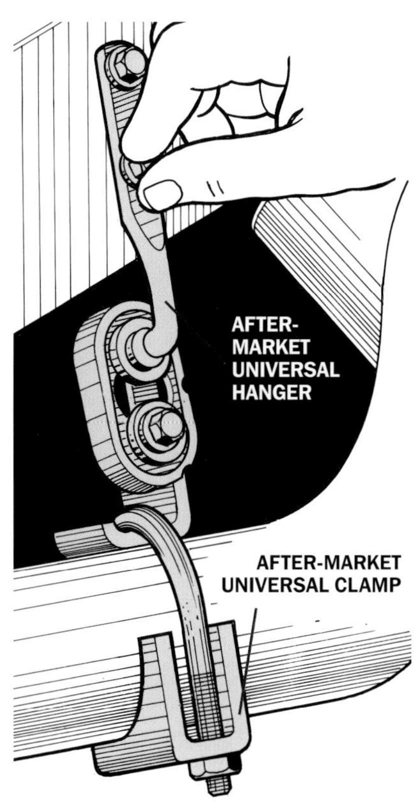

(Fig. 2) Sometimes a universal aftermarket clamp will fill the bill and let you reattach the OEM hanger.

HOW IT WORKS

Muffler

A muffler is a canister with internal tubular passages, shaped in part by baffles, designed to gradually reduce the pulsations of flowing exhaust gas. The slowdown creates back pressure in the exhaust system, all the way back to the engine itself. This slows down the exit of exhaust gas from the engine, reducing its performance. To get around this problem, many high-performance engines increase the exhaust flow with larger mufflers and accept some increase in exhaust system noise as a result. With careful design, however, including the use of silencing materials, the systems can be made to meet legal restrictions. Some back pressure is beneficial at low speed, because slowing down the flow pattern of intake and exhaust gases improves performance somewhat. Many engines have 2-stage mufflers with an internal spring-loaded valve. These mufflers maintain a specified amount of back pressure for good low-speed performance. But when the engine is at higher speed and there's more exhaust gas to flow through the muffler, back pressure builds up. Before it can become excessive, it pushes open the spring-loaded valve, and the gases take a far less restrictive flow through the muffler. This "second stage" permits the engine to develop considerably greater horsepower at higher rpm.

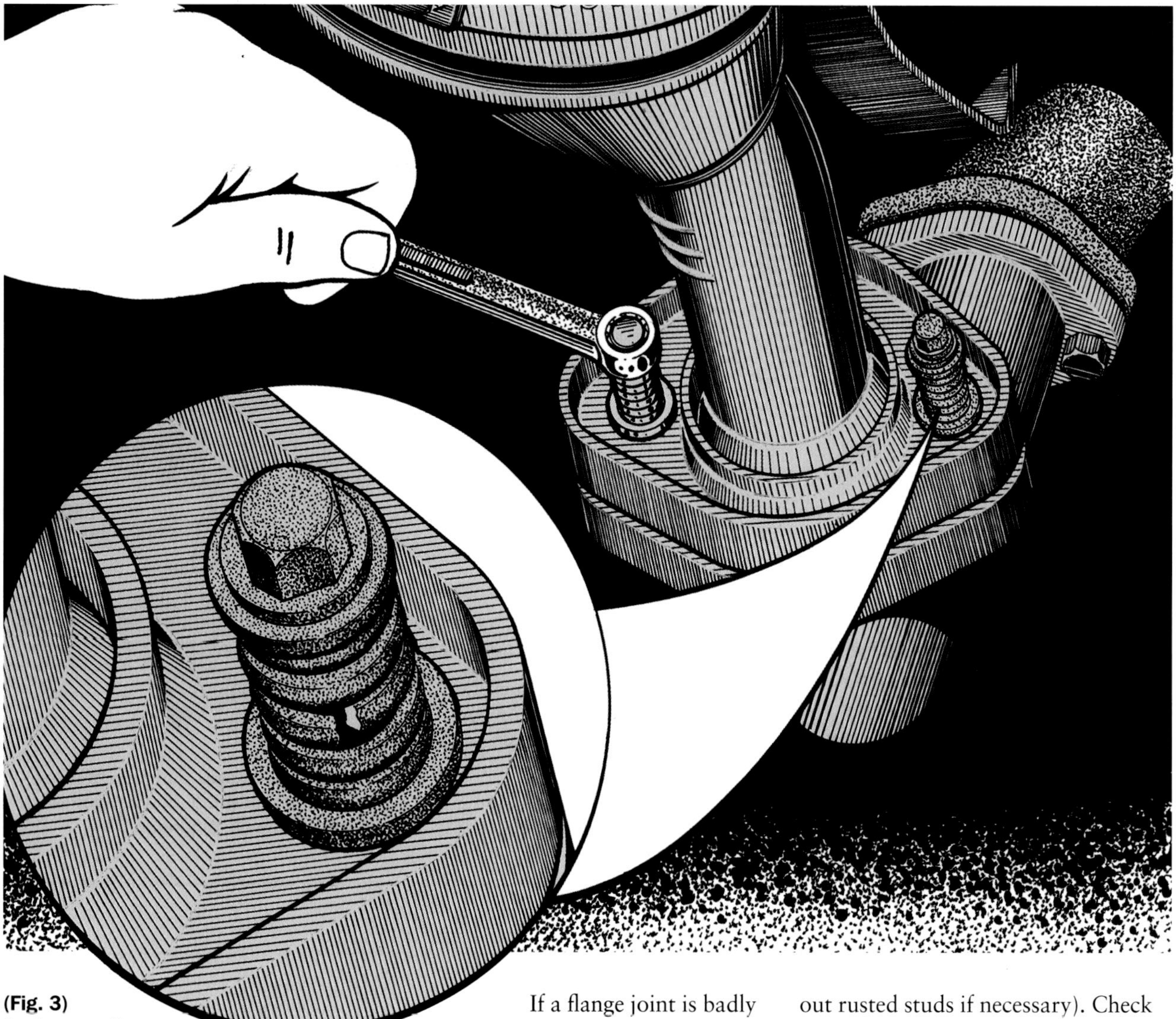

(Fig. 3) Springs on the bolts at the joint at the base of the headpipe allow the exhaust system to flex slightly as the engine moves on its mounts. Replace broken or sacked-out springs to prevent a leak.

exhaust pipe sealer. Reassemble and install a heavy-duty clamp, which can tolerate much more torque, to provide a leak-free joint.

Many systems have a flange joint at the exhaust manifold or at the manifold's Y-pipe. That joint is held together with spring-loaded bolts **(Fig. 3)**. The heat may weaken the springs, and the joint will loosen. Try simply tightening the bolts, but if the springs have cracked or are weak, replace the bolts. They're sold, with new springs, in auto parts stores.

If a flange joint is badly rusted, it's worth trying to free it up with penetrating solvent. Then, take it apart and see if it can be salvaged by sanding it clean, installing a new gasket with sealer and reassembling with new bolts and nuts (drill out rusted studs if necessary). Check at an auto parts store to see if a clamp-over repair fitting is available.

Damper Weights

Some exhaust systems have vibration dampers **(Fig. 4)**, which are weights that are attached to a pipe or are part of a flange connection. If a damper weight breaks off or is bent, the exhaust system will vibrate noticeably. This not only makes for an uncomfortable ride, but it can affect the life of welded and clamped joints.

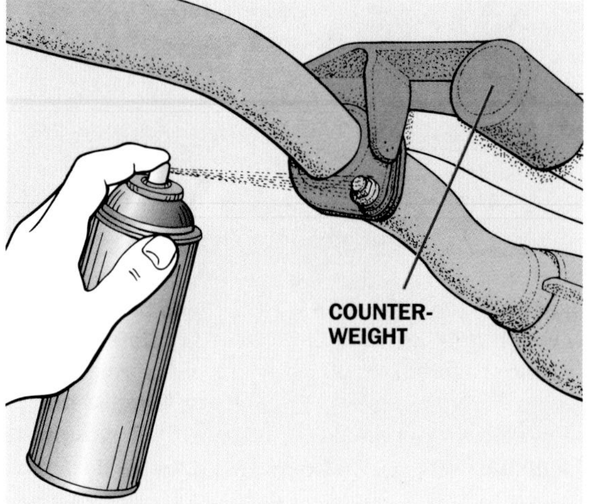

(Fig. 4) When using replacement parts, be sure to reinstall any original vibration-damping counterweights.

Replacing Your Belts

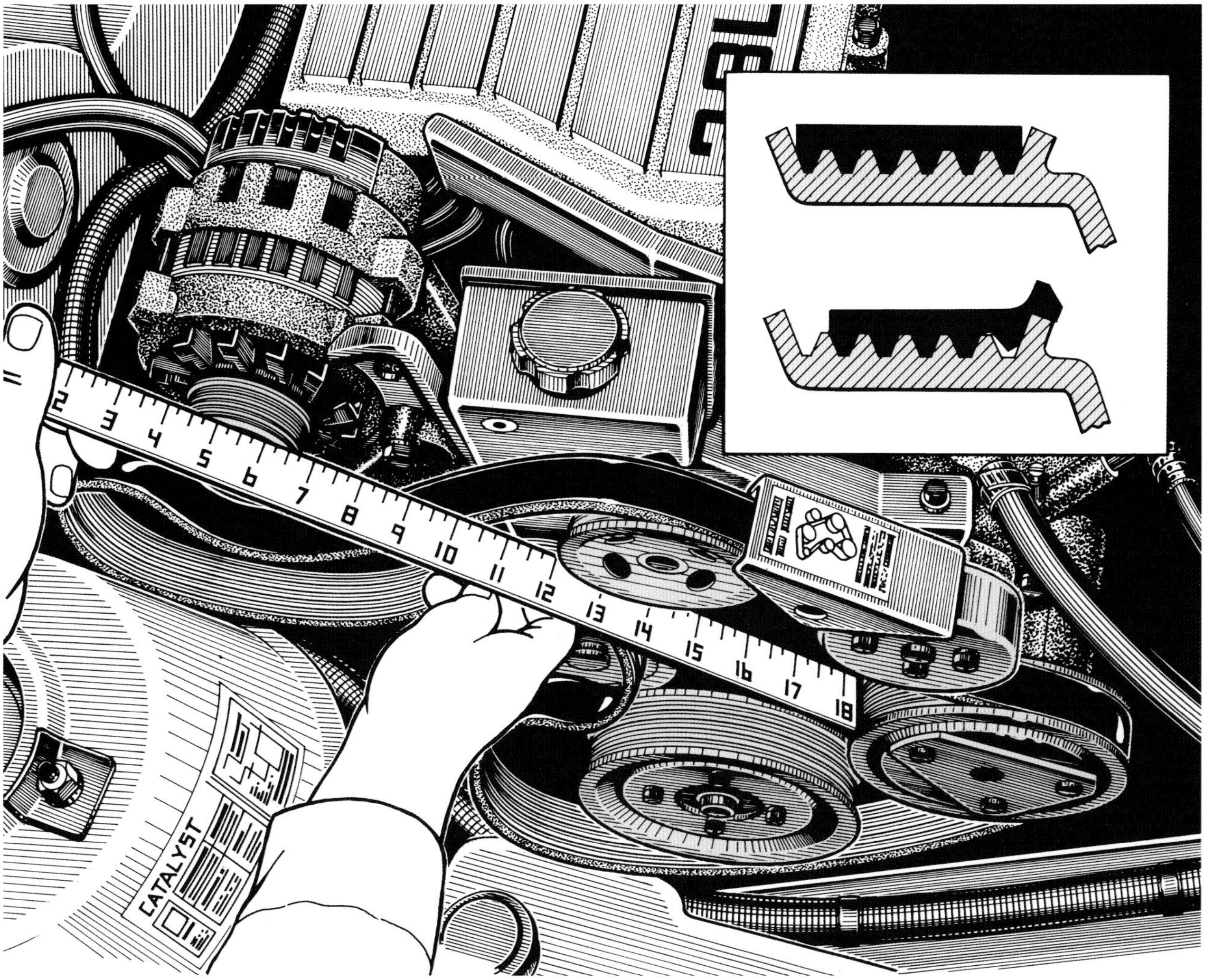

Not again! You crank the car through a turn and the steering suddenly gets almost rock hard. Both your heart and the steering wheel seem to stop. As you apply more muscle to the steering wheel, you hear sharp squealing from under the hood. On the dash, the alternator warning light shines brightly. As your vital signs normalize, you remember that you've had this happen before: The accessory drive belt for the power-steering pump either is slipping badly or has popped off.

Today's drive belts, particularly the ribbed belts, are supposed to last for years. You even know people who've never had to change them. Why do you have repeated belt problems?

The answer is that something's wrong with your belt's drive. Don't just put on a new belt, grumble and wait for the next belt failure. Find out why your car has an appetite for drive belts. Then make a more durable repair.

First, inspect all of the belts and each of the pulleys **(Fig. 1)**. Twist over each belt and check it thoroughly. On a simple V-belt, look at the sidewalls, and if they're glazed, that's a sign of slippage—typically caused by improper adjustment, but possibly a sign of a bad pulley, too.

(Fig. 1) A belt that's installed improperly, or one riding on improperly aligned pulleys, will not last long.

On a multiribbed belt look carefully for missing chunks of rubber. Specifically check for gaps at least a half-inch or longer on adjacent ribs.

If the belt hasn't lasted long, the reason will be found during inspection of the pulleys. There are lots of reasons why some cars eat belts.

Feel The Tension

Most cars and trucks use a single, serpentine belt (see "How it Works,"

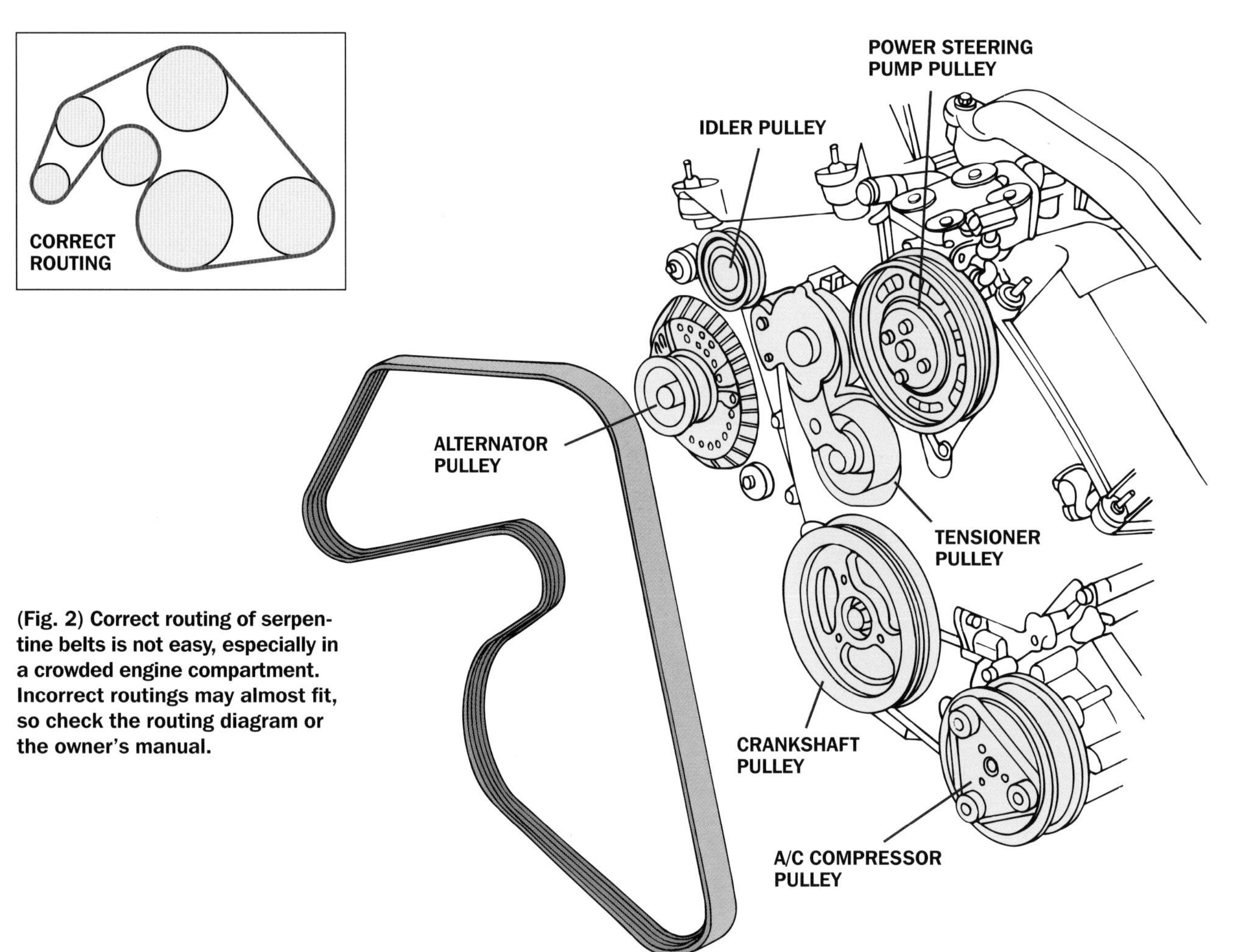

(Fig. 2) Correct routing of serpentine belts is not easy, especially in a crowded engine compartment. Incorrect routings may almost fit, so check the routing diagram or the owner's manual.

page 68) to drive a lot of accessories. These belts typically are tensioned by an idler pulley with an automatic tensioner. Just because there's an automatic tensioner doesn't mean it's working right. Any of the root causes discussed below can result in a belt getting chewed up fast, or popping off the pulleys.

There's a tension indicator on the idler and it should be reasonably close to midpoint. It should not be resting on the stop tab at the "loose" end. If it is at the stop—or very close—the belt has stretched and should be replaced before it pops off. You just put in a new belt, you say? Maybe you routed the belt incorrectly. Yes, it is possible to get the belt wrapped around all the pulleys in what seems to be the right way but have it wrong. Check the belt-routing diagram **(Fig. 2)**, which on many cars is on an underhood label.

Are you sure you have the right belt? Just because the tension indicator is in the right place doesn't mean you have the correct belt. It's hard to eyeball the difference between 7-rib and 8-rib belts, and if the pulleys have more or fewer grooves, the belt won't sit right. Even if the number of grooves matches, it's possible to install the belt too far inboard. While you're looking at the tensioner, also check for cracks in the housing which would allow it to flex enough for trouble.

Nothing obviously wrong yet? If the belt is still on the pulleys, run the engine and eyeball the accessory drive. If the tensioner is vibrating a lot but the pulleys are running smoothly, the damper bushing is bad and you'll have to install a new tensioner.

Put a wrench on the spring tensioner **(Fig. 3)**. Usually there's a square hole for a ratchet or breaker bar drive, and occasionally you can use one of those. If the tensioner on your transverse-engine car is buried so deep down between the pulleys and the suspension tower that you can barely see it, check out the assortment of special long, thin wrenches designed for those installations at your local auto parts store. The leading makers of these specialty tools will have theirs on display (Lisle Tools, K-D/Dannaher and Schley/SP). With the wrench on the tensioner, apply some light torque in the disconnect direction, and if the wrench moves very easily a short distance and then gets stiff, the tensioner housing spring either is out of position or broken. This condition often causes the tensioner and its idler pulley to vibrate.

Not today? Keep applying effort with the wrench, and you should feel uniform spring tension all the way to the belt-off position. If you feel binding or lost motion at any point, replace the tensioner. Never "let go" of a tensioner. Aside from the possible physical danger, the sudden release can cause internal parts of the tensioner to snap (including the spring). Release it very gradually. If you do need a new tensioner, don't think you have to get it from a dealer. Reputable aftermarket tensioners are available from automotive parts stores.

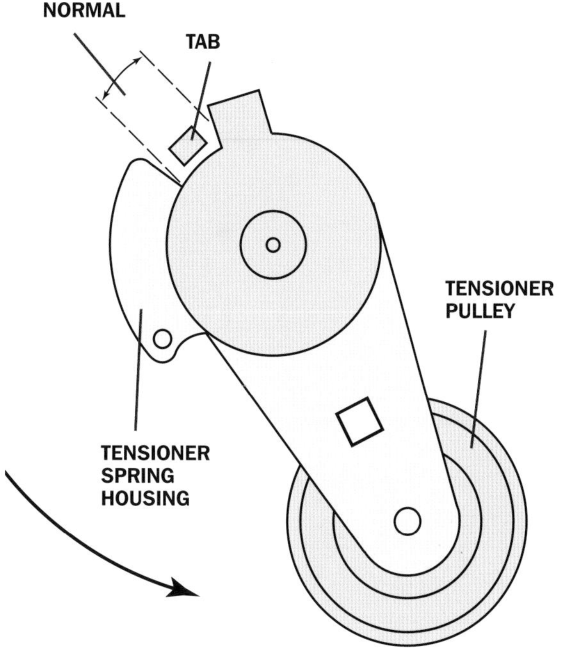

(Fig. 3) Most automatic tensioners provide a square hole for a ½-in. ratchet.

Playing With Pulleys

If there's wobble in the idler or any one of the other accessory pulleys, the pulley could be cracked or worn loose. Just one damaged pulley anywhere in the accessory drive also can affect the operating appearance of the tensioner. Replace the wobbling pulley—easier said than done on some accessories. Besides the problems of near-impossible access on a front-drive's engine, you may need to rent a special pulley-puller tool if you don't own one.

If the pulleys aren't wobbling but the belt isn't tracking well—seems to twist slightly or move in and out as it spins the accessories—there may be pulley misalignment. That is, one pulley is just too far forward or behind another. This happens on new cars when manufacturing tolerances are exceeded, but it doesn't just "develop" unless you did some front-of-engine work and failed to tighten all the accessory mountings carefully. It also could happen if an accessory recently was changed, and that accessory's pulley doesn't line up. (Did you just put in a new alternator? Power steering pump? Air-conditioning compressor? Water pump?)

If there's enough access room, lay a stiff mechanic's straightedge or a thin steel rod across the pulleys to help you decide if the pulley on that new accessory is misaligned. Unless you want to take back that accessory and check out another one, however, the only fix is to shim out the accessory with washers, which is a bit of cut-and-try.

Do some touchy-feely on the idler pulley. Try to turn it, and if it's seized, the tensioner has to go. If it turns, feel for roughness (which indicates a bad bearing) and if you come up with a dab of grease from the bearing area, that indicates a grease leak past a bad seal. Try to rock the pulley: In-and-out movement may be a sign of a loose bolt, but more likely a damaged pulley. If a pulley is steel and it's clearly rusted, that not only indicates the coating has worn off (normal, in time), but that it is damaging the underside of the belt and you have to replace it.

Pulley alignment okay and mountings are solid? No matter how badly they're buried, inspect all the pulleys. Look for chips and other physically damaged sections that also could come in contact with the belt. If any of the grooved pulleys are packed with road film, belt debris, etc., wire-brush them clean. If the smooth pulleys (idler and water pump) are obviously worn on the belt-tracking area, you'll have to install new ones or a new tensioner assembly.

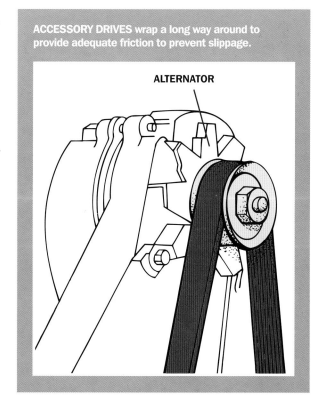

ACCESSORY DRIVES wrap a long way around to provide adequate friction to prevent slippage.

ALTERNATOR

Doing It By Hand

A lot of older engines—particularly on Japanese cars—still have simple V-belts. Many also have ribbed belts with manual adjusters. The typical adjuster is a jackscrew; just loosen the lock bolt and turn the jackscrew, counterclockwise to loosen the belt, clockwise to tighten.

Even if the pulley is for a simple V-belt, it can accumulate debris in the groove. So clean it out with a wire brush, just as you would a multi-groove. The days of getting an accurate sense of belt tension by pressing down on a belt with your thumb are long gone. It takes a tension gauge **(Fig. 4)**.

Although there are expensive professional gauges, we've found the Gate Krik-It gauges do a good job and fit into really tight places. Look for the longest belt span you can reach, preferably at least a foot. Just lay the Krik-It gauge at midspan, press down slowly on the center until you hear a cricketlike click, then stop pressing. The gauge bar rises as it encounters belt tension, and stops when you stop pressing. You can lift the gauge away and read the point of alignment of the edge of the bar with the linear dial on the gauge housing. Just turn down the jackscrew to get the specified tension, then tighten the lock bolt.

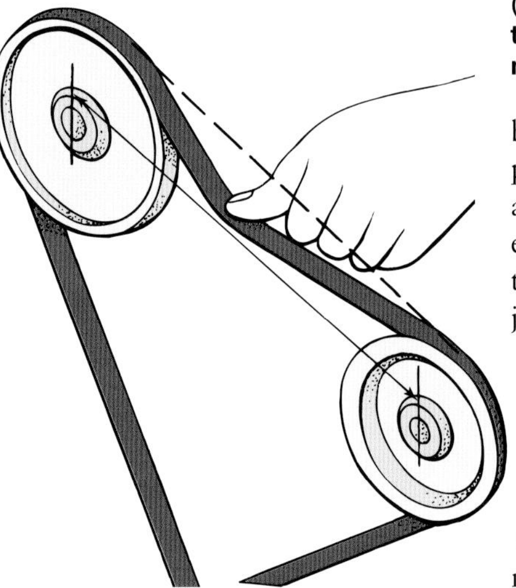

(Fig. 4) Don't check for correct tension with the time-honored one-thumb method. Use a gauge.

You're probably familiar with "belt dressing," an aerosol spray for belt squeal. Use it only to make a quick check of the belt as a source of noise. Repeated use ruins most belts.

HOW IT WORKS

Serpentine Belt

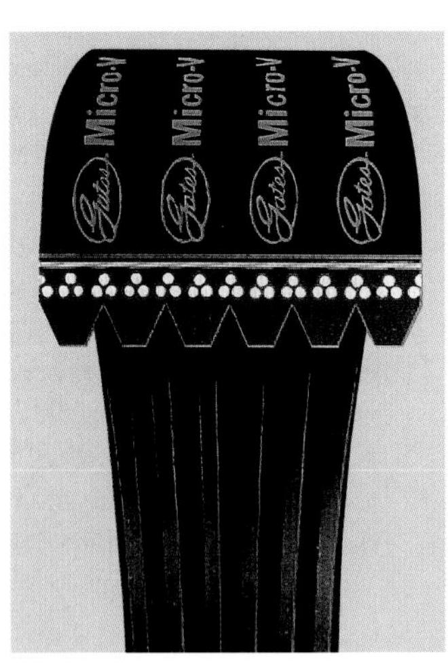

The serpentine belt is so named because its routing resembles the shape of a serpent. Carmakers developed the system so one belt would drive several, if not all, underhood accessories. A single belt, no matter how long, saves space under the hood since all the pulleys and accessories are on the same plane and there's no need to stack or stagger them. The ribbed side of the belt fits into grooved pulleys (each one a "mini" V), and the smooth back side of the belt often wraps around the water pump pulley and one or more idler pulleys. An idler is used to route the belt so there's plenty of "wrap" around each accessory pulley for good power transfer. To maintain adequate tension for good power transfer, and still eliminate the need for periodic adjustment, an automatic tensioner is usually used.

There's a nearly infinite variety of tensioner designs, but they all have a powerful coil spring inside. The poly-V belt design used on serpentine belts is capable of transmitting more power with less frictional loss than traditional V-belts. A properly installed and automatically tensioned serpentine belt system could remain troublefree for four to five years or 100,000 miles.

EASY

Replacing Hood and Hatch Struts

While topping off your transmission fluid one Saturday morning—hunched over the front of the engine, dog at your side—you feel the touch of cold steel on the back of your neck. You've received a weak "stab" from the car's hood latch. Time, weight and wear have conspired to force an unexpected surrender of the gas-charged hood support struts.

Unfortunately, gas struts do wear out—and sometimes at the most inopportune moments. Weak ones are more likely to fail in cold weather, when the gas pressure inside drops a little. Consequently, you'll find that these same weak struts work perfectly well on a hot summer day. But they should still be replaced for safety's sake. The good news is that one manufacturer recently introduced a temperature-compensating gas strut that should eliminate seasonal performance variations.

Sizing up the job

Large, modern auto parts stores often have parts catalogs dangling at the end of each aisle. So you may be able to look up strut applications on your own. If not, just go to the parts counter and ask for help. Be careful either way. Hood and hatch struts come in many different sizes and with several different mounting ends.

Some employ a ball-joint mount at each end. Others make do with any combination of the following at either end: a ball joint, a nonarticulating hard mount with an integral hinge or a flattened piston-rod end tab that mates with a stationary mounting peg. Some hood struts even

AFTER SECURELY PROPPING your hatch, examine the support struts' mounting ends to determine what socket or driver you'll need to begin removing the mounting hardware.

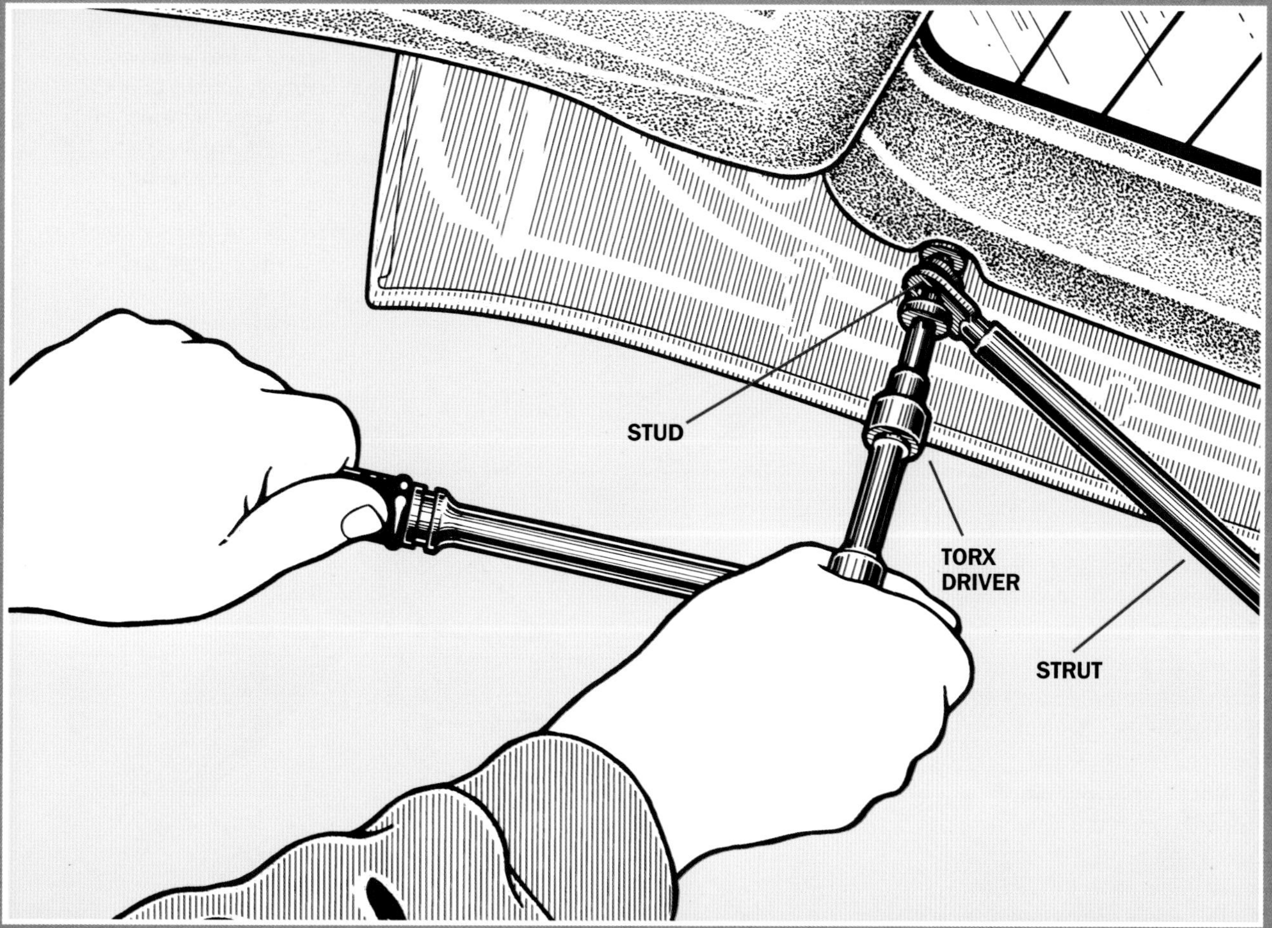

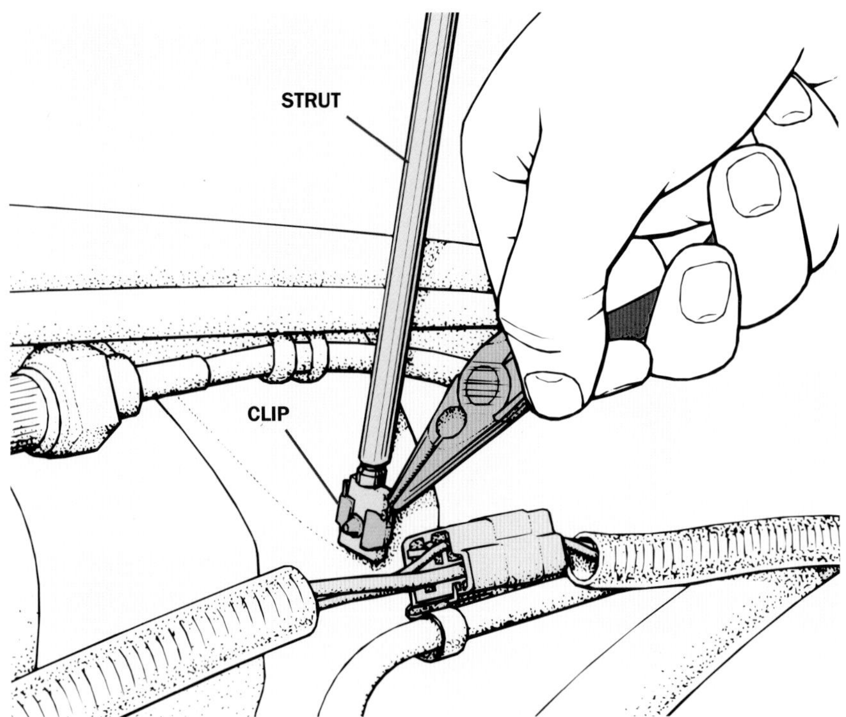

(Fig. 1) Slide the locking clip away from the mounting leg to allow strut removal. You might have to push or pull the clip to release it.

have two stages. On the Volvo 960, for example, unlocking a plastic clip on each strut allows the hood to continue opening past vertical for easier engine service.

Measure the full-open length of your existing struts before heading out to the parts store. Then, check the length of the new ones before going home. Or, take one of the old struts with you for comparison. It may save you a return trip. Be aware that some support struts for older cars may no longer be available in the traditional aftermarket. (The 1981 Datsun 310GX is one example.) If that's the case, you'll have to visit a dealer. Or maybe you'll get lucky and find the struts you need in the J.C. Whitney catalog.

With the correct unit(s) in hand, open the hood or hatch and prop it up with a stout piece of wood. On a 1-strut setup, the wood will be the only thing keeping the lid from meeting your head with a thud. On a 2-strut deal, the wood allows you to work on either side without worrying that the other strut is going to let go.

Doing the double-joint strut

With all the prep work done, replacing the old struts should take all of about 10 minutes. Those ball-joint ends are usually held together with some sort of clip: either a flat C-clip that mounts through the back of the socket and grabs the underside of the ball, or a wire C-clip that slides through the bottom of the socket and under the ball to prevent release.

Wedging a big screwdriver between the sheetmetal and the ball joint for leverage is not the best way to pop the strut. A little finesse, please. Use either needle-nose pliers or the smallest screwdriver you own to gently pull or pry clip away from the socket (**Fig. 1 & 2**). Then, simply pull the socket off the ball. Do the same thing at the other end. Save the clips if they're not broken. Sometimes an extra one comes in handy.

Be careful when working on hatch struts mounted near the rear-

(Fig. 2) This clip holds the socket onto the ball stud. Carefully remove the clip to release the sockets so you can pop off the struts.

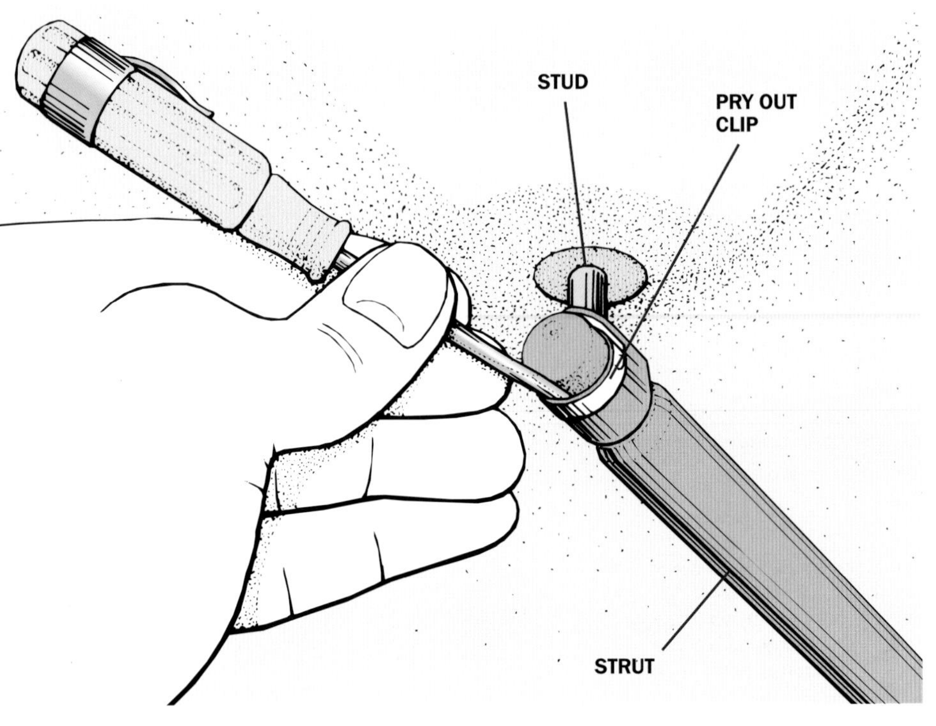

(Fig. 3) **Insert the new strut's integral ball stud into its mounting hole and fasten it with the nut.**

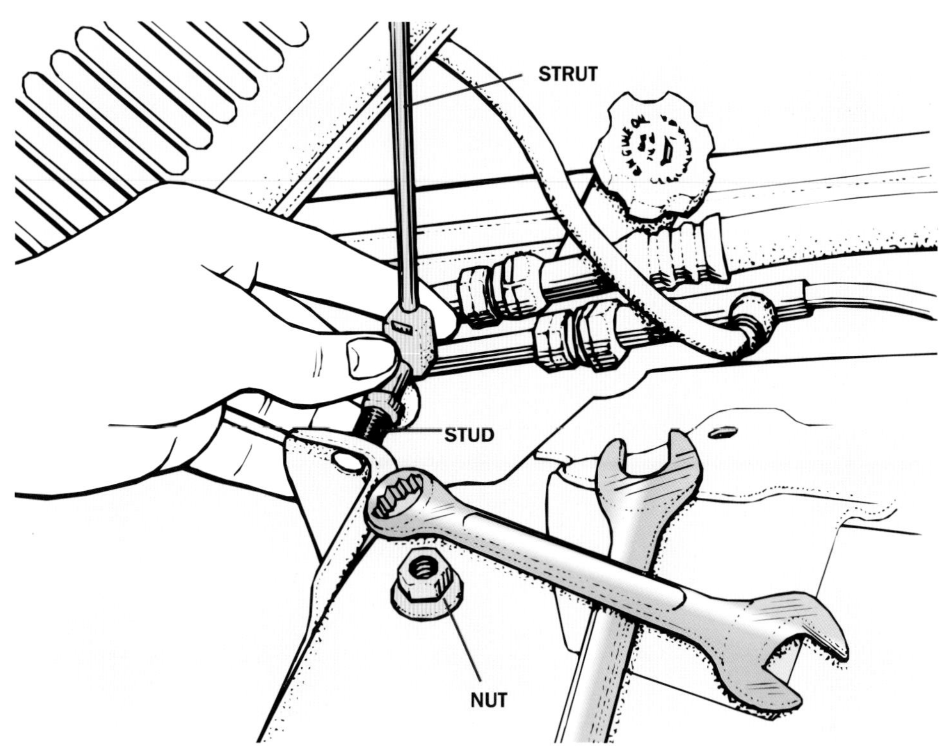

window defogger grid. If you slip with the screwdriver or pliers, you could ruin the defogger element.

Pop 'em in

To ease installation of the new unit, mount the clip(s) in a partially open position on the new socket, and put lube on the inside of the socket with a little silicone grease. Stick the socket over the ball, then snap the clip home. Repeat this for the other end (and the other side, if applicable) and you're done.

If you come across a ball joint that's not held together with a clip, see if the ball end of the joint is screwed into the sheetmetal (**Fig. 3**). If so, it's very likely that a hex is included for removing the old ball while it's still attached to the strut and screwing in the new strut's ball with an open-end wrench. Look at the new strut for guidance.

For the hard-mount type of strut end, just undo the bolt, screw or nut that holds the old strut in place, remove it and attach the new piece (**Fig. 4**). If you're dealing with a peg-style mount, you should find an E-clip of some sort or a cotter pin preventing the strut end from sliding off the peg.

E-clips generally need to be pulled or pushed in one direction or another in order to release them. Sometimes just a gentle nudge with the tip of a screwdriver is enough to pop them off. Otherwise, you may need to grab one of the clip's end tabs with needle-nose pliers and pull the clip out of position. Then, remove the old strut, mount the new one and slide the E-clip back home until you feel it click or can see that it is locked in.

Although the strut's piston rod has a hardened corrosionproof and weatherproof finish, you should still take care not to nick or scratch the polished surface. This would result in the marred metal ruining the strut's main seal. If the seal is damaged, the nitrogen gas would leak out and your brand-new strut would be trash.

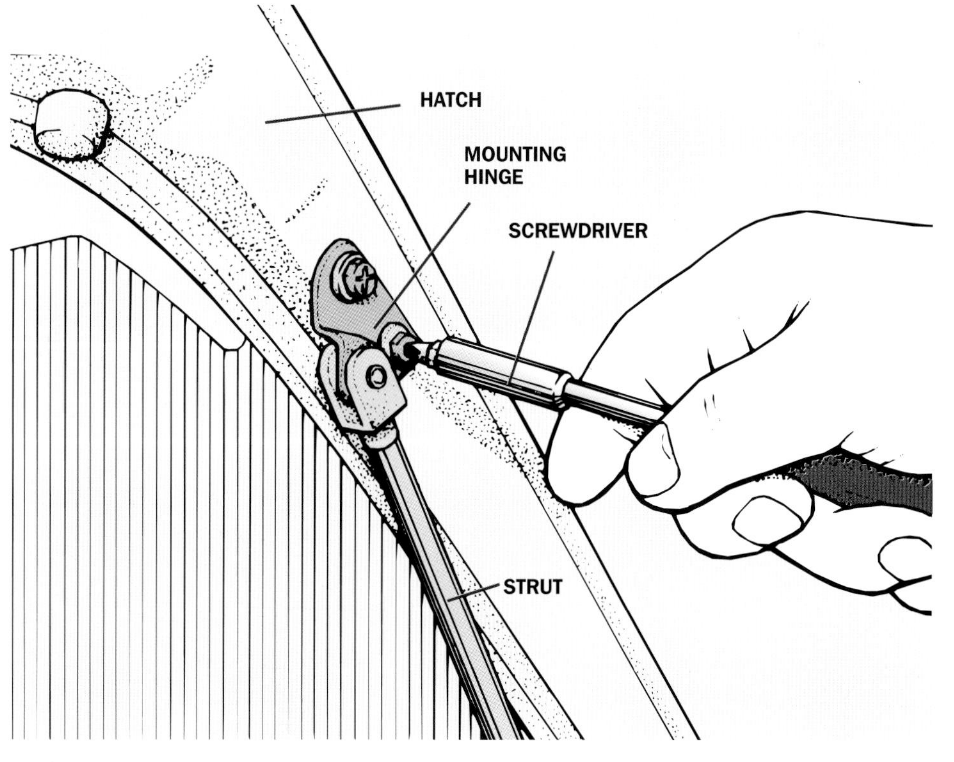

(Fig. 4) **Unscrew the hinge from its mounting point on either end to remove this type of strut. You may even be able to use a ratchet wrench and socket.**

Also, don't inadvertently mount the new unit piston-side up, especially if the old one was piston-side down. Most applications—those that contain some hydraulic oil as well as nitrogen gas—perform more smoothly if oriented with the rod end down. This allows the more effective oil compression damping to occur later in the strut's stroke for nifty end cushioning upon opening.

With the installation complete, pull out the wood prop and enjoy the convenience and safety of your hoods and hatches staying open on their own.

HOW IT WORKS

Support Struts

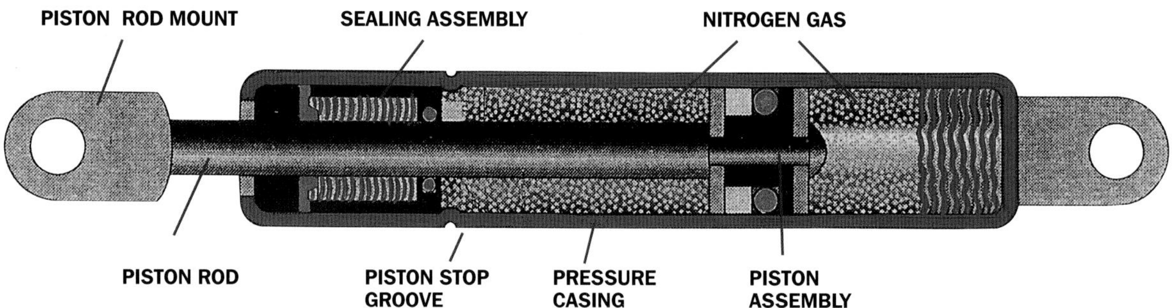

In the old days, your heavy metal hood and trunklid required beefy, space-robbing, spring-loaded hinges to stay open. Then the carmakers tried flimsy prop-rods for holding up the hood. But they invariably get in the way during service and tend to wear out and break at the pivot point on the radiator support.

So, as a result, gas-charged hood and hatch support struts, or gas springs, have steadily infiltrated the market. They're compact, light, durable and relatively inexpensive—key for auto manufacturing in the '90s.

One of the slickest applications around is on the Chrysler Cirrus/Dodge Stratus trunklid. No bulky suitcase-crushing hinges here, thanks to two stubby gas struts that open the lid past vertical to allow for easier trunk access.

How do they work? Like tiny shock absorbers really. But instead of being filled primarily with fluid for 2-way damping, they're charged with nitrogen gas for 1-way expansion. One end is fastened to the inner fender or cowl, the other to the hood or hatch. When you lift the lid a little bit, it extends the strut's piston rod enough for the gas to push on the piston and keep expanding the strut. The lid has nowhere to go but up.

On closing, you're actually pushing against the gas pressure to compress the strut back to its original size and position. A typical gas support strut is designed to last for at least 50,000 operations. They're maintenance-free throughout their life cycle but must be replaced when worn out.

Resetting Your Emissions Maintenance Reminder (EMR)

Your older minivan has been a trusted member of the family. It has helped you move your sister across town, kept your kid's Little League van pool rolling and faithfully transported the beloved dog to the vet. But it sure caused havoc last weekend. Leaving at 5 am with your buddies and a week's worth of fishing gear, it sputtered, spewed black smoke from the exhaust and wouldn't even idle. Walleye washout!

It's bad enough your fishing pals won't talk to you, but now the truck's got to go in for service. And the only way to get to work is by municipal bus because your wife needs the Bimmer to make all her sales calls. Peachy.

Your Dash Is Talking To You

Hold on. Have you been ignoring that warning light on the dash because your "car guy" brother-in-law said it's not important? Well, maybe it is. You see, that warning light, widely used on

(Fig. 1) Press button on EMR relay to reset reminder light for another 30,000 miles. This is an older Nissan engine.

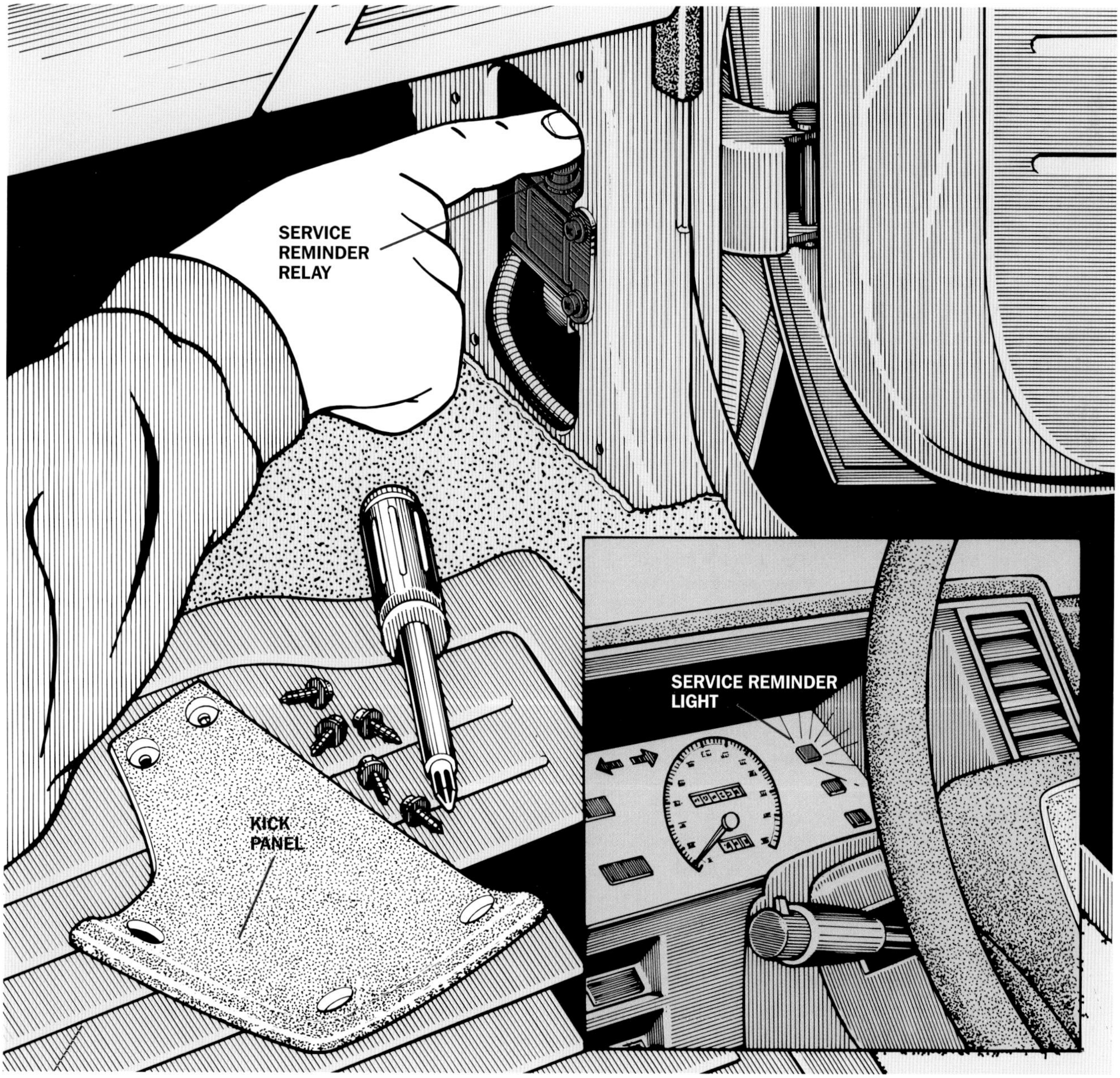

pre-OBDII vehicles (before 1996), is designed to come on at about 30,000-mile intervals, depending on the vehicle. (Check your owner's manual for the specifics.) It's called an emissions maintenance reminder, or EMR, and it definitely shouldn't be ignored.

When the EMR indicator glows, it doesn't necessarily mean trouble. But each time the light comes on, the emissions system should be checked. The idea is to work on the engine before the engine works you over. After giving your okay, the light has to be reset so the system starts counting down for the next EMR cycle.

There's a different reset procedure for just about every EMR system. Some indicators, such as those on most Chrysler light trucks since 1989, can be reset only by tapping a scan tool into the on-board computer controls. If you don't have a scanner, it's off to the repair shop or the dealer for assistance. Some setups are reset by replacing a module. After a certain number of miles, the module is simply left disconnected. There's no resetting provision at all on some vehicles. Just disconnect the plug or connector to shut off the light.

Still other EMR lights, such as the sensor warning on most Nissans **(Fig. 1)**, require nothing more than a screwdriver and about 5 minutes of your time to either push a button on a relay or pull apart a connector—that is, after you've given the emissions controls a once-over.

Only under the following three conditions should you consider resetting the EMR light without inspecting the emissions system: 1. You've had no driveability trouble and no CHECK ENGINE light, 2. You've noticed no appreciable change in fuel economy, and 3. Your vehicle always passes the state emissions test with flying colors.

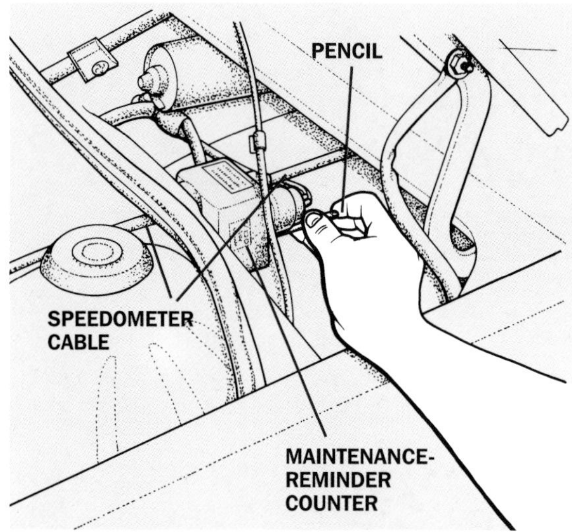

(Fig. 2) Stick a pen or pencil in the back of the mileage counter in the cowl tray on Audis and Volkswagens to reset EMR system.

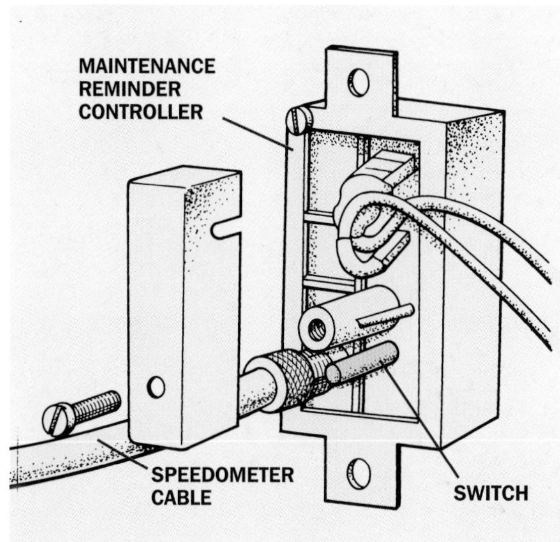

(Fig. 3) You'll find Volvo's mileage counter under dash. Press reset switch to turn off light.

Checking Emissions System

The key element in your emissions system is the oxygen sensor that's mounted in the exhaust manifold. It senses if the engine is running too rich or too lean. When the O_2 sensor gets lazy and stops reporting accurate information to the electronic engine controls, driveability trouble can begin—and fishing trips can be ruined. So check out the O_2 operation first.

Next on the list is the exhaust gas recirculation (EGR) valve, if your engine has one. Apply a vacuum to the valve's nipple and make sure the valve seat opens and closes smoothly. On late-model computer-controlled EGR systems, there may be no way to check the solenoid/valve mechanism without special tools. If you haven't heard any engine ping or knock lately, idle quality is okay, and if the CHECK ENGINE light hasn't come on, the EGR system is probably fine.

Other operations you can check include the smog pump (or pulse-air system) on engines that use them. Examine the pump belt for cracks, wear and proper tension. Follow the tubes from the pump to the diverter valve and down to the exhaust manifold and catalytic converter. Make sure the rubber hoses are intact and the metal pipes and check valves aren't rusted out. You might even be able to reach under the vehicle and rap the catalytic converter with a mallet or hammer. A rattling noise means the cat has broken down internally—and its better days are behind it.

If you can see the fuel-system charcoal-vapor canister (sometimes it's buried in a front fender), inspect the integrity of its rubber lines and fittings. And while you're at it, look at the air filter, air-box breather element and the engine's vacuum lines. Make sure the positive crankcase ventilation valve still rattles when you shake it. Check the spark plugs and wires and the distributor cap and rotor (if applicable) for wear. Ultimately, all powertrain components make up the emissions system, so check whatever you can get to.

Finding the Reset Location

Although it varies, reset-switch locations can generally be broken down into three areas: the speedometer cable/firewall area, the kick panel/under-dash area and the instrument panel area. The positions often

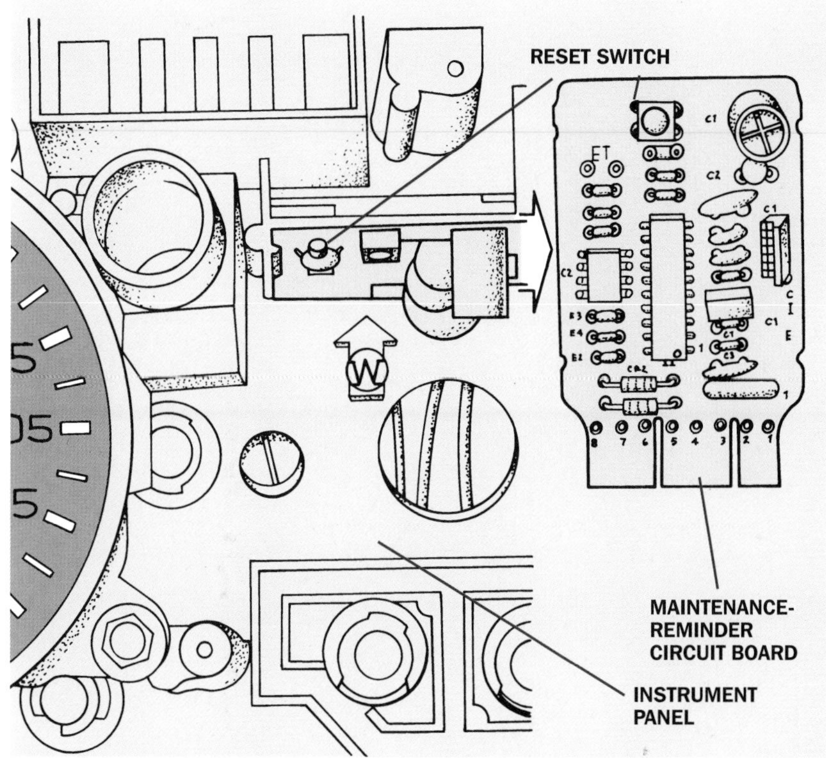

(Fig. 4) On Chrysler minivans, you must remove the fuel gauge or tachometer to get to the emissions-maintenance-reminder reset switch.

change from model year to model year across the same vehicle make, so always approach your search with an open mind. And check your owner's manual.

The speedo cable resets are usually the easiest because the cable sticks out like a sore thumb, and there's usually plenty of room to work. Vehicles in this category include many models from the early 1980s.

Audis and Volkswagens are a breeze. You'll find the mileage counter in the cowl tray at the base of the windshield (the speedo cable leads right to it). There's a hole on the back of the counter. Stick a pen or pencil in the hole and press in the reset button (**Fig. 2**). You'll feel the button lock in place. That's it. On Volvos, the mileage counter is also in line with the speedo cable. Once you've found the counter, press its reset button with your finger (**Fig. 3**).

Still others are done from the inside. Drop the lower steering-column cover. Feel for the sensor reset cable to the left of the speedo cluster. Yank on the cable until you see the flag reset itself on the left of the odometer.

Hunting for Switches

Vehicles that fall into the second category number too many to call out separately, but they all have some sort of EMR module, relay, connector or pair of connectors.

On some models, you'll find a cancellation switch on the right side of the fuse panel. Press the switch to the OFF position. Older Fords hide EMR modules behind the passenger kick panel on their trucks. Stick a small rod in the hole marked RESET. While holding the button down with the rod, turn the key to RUN and continue to depress the button for 5 seconds. On older Jaguars, the mileage counter is behind the trim in the trunk. Press the white button with the key on to reset the light.

Pulling the Instrument Panel

This third category can get complicated because you usually have to dismantle part of the dash to remove the instrument cluster or a gauge to get in behind the cluster, as on Chrysler's minivans (**Fig. 4**). According to a diagnostic hotline we are friendly with, these vans are the cause of the most EMR reset calls. The circuit-board-mounted switch is tricky to find if you don't know what to look for. It's mounted behind the fuel gauge on the standard cluster or behind the tachometer on the optional cluster. Sometimes you'll find a 9-volt battery in there, too. It must be replaced with an alkaline battery. Some Chrysler captive import light trucks have a reset switch on the back of the cluster near the speedo junction or on the lower righthand corner of the cluster, behind the face panel.

On early-model GM vehicles, pull the instrument cluster lens and use a small tool to push on the stem of the orange plastic flag that pops up near the odometer. An alignment mark should appear in the left center of the odometer window when the flag is properly reset. Late-model GMs use no specific EMR indicator. The CHECK ENGINE light illuminates if there's a problem.

Early-model non-turbo Audis have a cancel switch labeled oxs on the back of the instrument cluster that must be removed from the pod to gain access. Late-model turbos hide a mileage counter with a reset button under the rear seat. Some late-model BMWs use a resettable mileage counter. On 1989-93 Geo Trackers, locate the 3-wire cancellation switch in the main wiring harness behind the instrument cluster or in the steering-column lower-access panel.

You'll find the reset on the back of the speedo on Isuzu Troopers. Pull the tape from Hole B and swap the screw from Hole A to Hole B. Tape over Hole A. Mazda MPVs are similar. Swap the screw from Hole NO to Hole NC. Late-model Mercedes-Benz cars use no EMR indicator. However, 1980-85s, other than the 280, require bulb removal. On VW Rabbits and Pickups, remove the instrument panel cover trim plate to get to the mileage counter release arms at the top left of the speedo housing. Good luck!

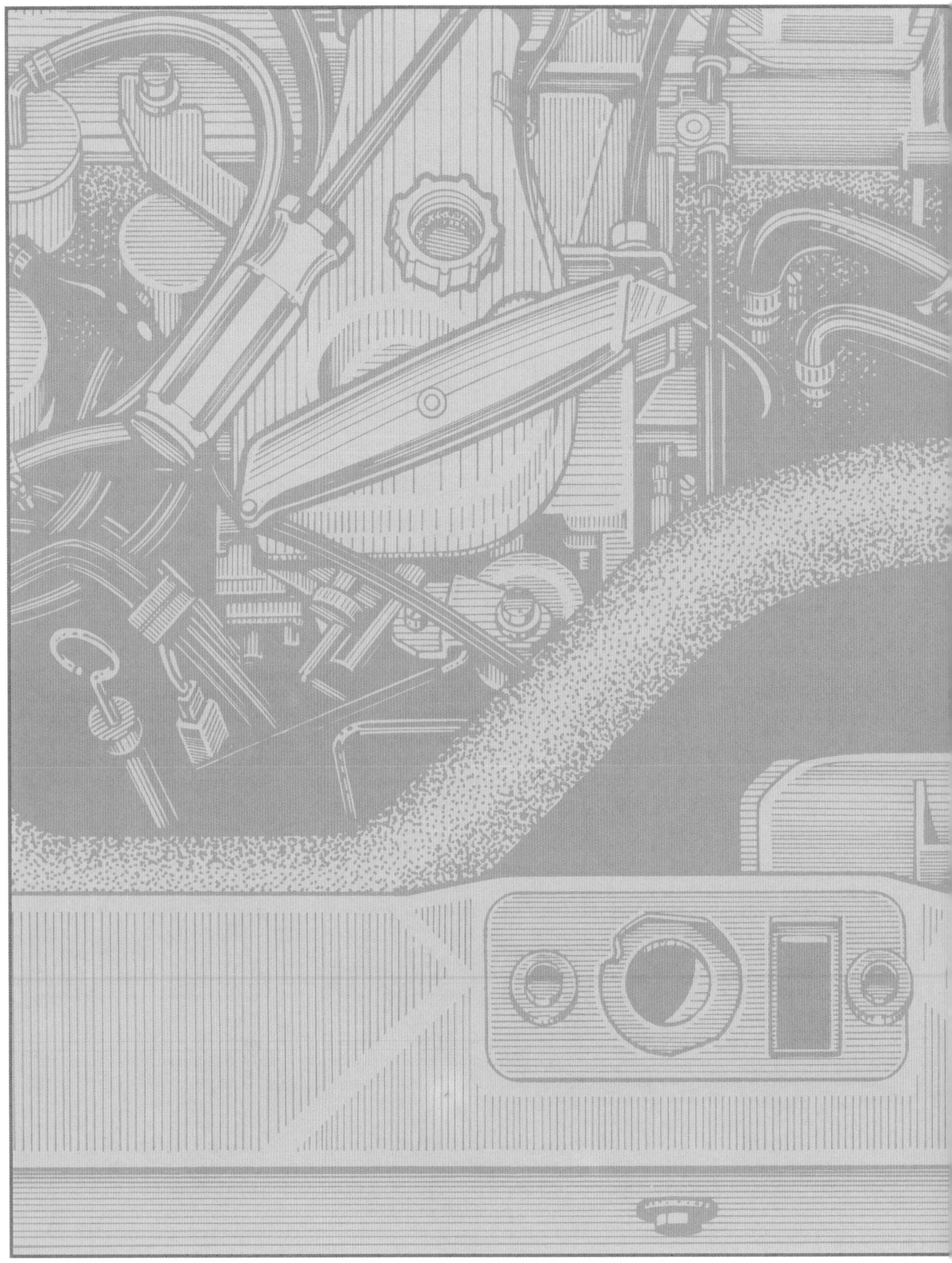

CHAPTER TWO

Engine

Today's Tuneup

RETAINING CLIP

NEW FILTER

OLD FILTER

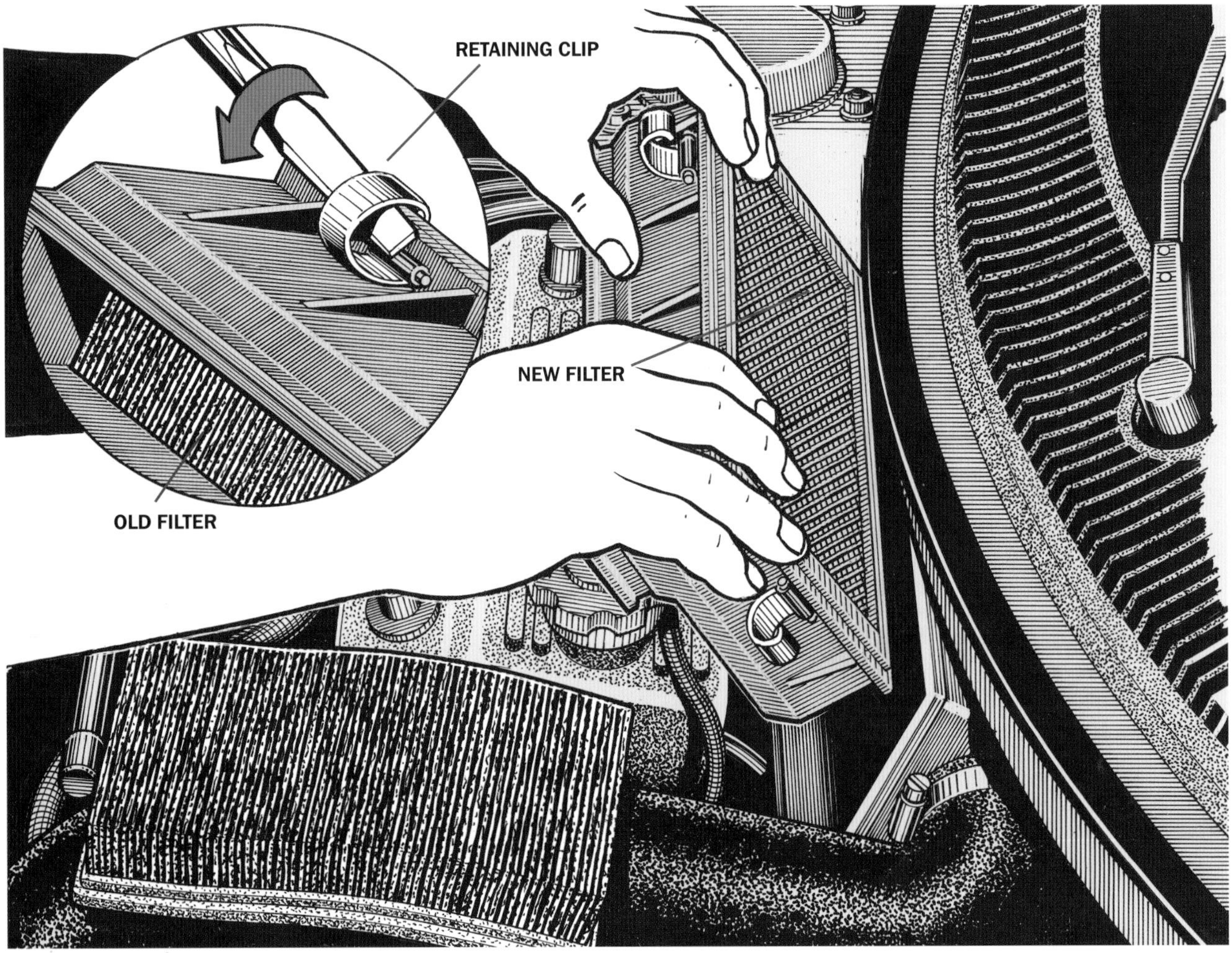

(Fig. 1) Replacing the air filter will require popping off a couple of clips. Slide the new filter into place, be sure it seals properly, and replace the cover.

There's the thruway exit, but you're stuck in the left lane. Hey—a break in the traffic. You flip up the turn signal, floor the gas pedal and try to edge into the right lane. Whoops! Your V8 is embarrassed by a 4-cylinder econobox with the same objective. It was behind you, but it apparently has better acceleration. You hit the brakes, crank the wheel to get back into the left lane, cruise to the next exit miles and miles ahead, and make the time-wasting U-turn. The Wife suggests a tuneup. But we don't tune up today's engines, right? They're computerized and there's nothing to adjust.

Wrong. It's true we stopped replacing ignition points over 20 years ago. If it's really a late-model vehicle, it may not even have a replaceable fuel filter under the hood. The battery is a fill-free design. And there's no ignition timing to adjust. However, while it has changed significantly—even in the last seven or eight years—the concept of a tuneup itself is anything but gone.

Emissions regulations may have tightened, but ambient air is still dirty. So the air filter still plugs up, and the engine gasps for breath until a clean new filter is installed (**Fig. 1**). Gasoline is unleaded, so spark plugs don't lead-foul anymore, and the new precious-metal designs last much longer. But they aren't guaranteed to last a lifetime, and engine performance often can improve when plugs are replaced well before the owner's manual dictates.

Underhood Checks

A good way to start today's tuneup is to look for trouble codes, using a scan tool. The only codes that turn on a Check Engine light are those that directly impact emissions, provided the computer can detect them, to keep people from getting nervous. Most codes show up only with a scan tool. On the other hand, "no code" driveability problems are also extremely common.

If you find a trouble code, you should trace the circuit to pinpoint the problem. Sure, it could be just a bad sensor, but it may be a bad wiring connection, chafed wire or damaged hose. You'll need the factory service information to be able to do this.

No trouble code? Inspect under the hood. Look for damaged vacuum hoses that should be replaced, loose connections at any of the sensors and solenoids, tears in the air cleaner ductwork, a disconnected duct or poor spark plug wiring connections.

Test the behavior of the engine controls and their sensors. There still are timing marks on many late models and if your vehicle is one of them, you can check basic timing (at idle) with a timing light. No marks? You still can check ignition timing on the scan tool by reading the ignition advance data item. Look for a steady increase in ignition timing as the throttle is gradually opened from idle to a midthrottle position.

Even if the timing is all right, check the throttle position sensor and intake airflow (mass airflow) sensor readings, which also should show gradual increases as the accelerator pedal is depressed. At the same time, tap on the mass airflow sensor with a screwdriver handle and if the engine hiccups or the scan tool reading spikes, the sensor is defective.

A coolant temperature sensor should show a continuous increase in the reading until the engine is fully warm (195°F to 230°F). A MAP (manifold absolute pressure) engine vacuum sensor should show changes when a pinched-closed hose supplying vacuum to it is released **(Fig. 2)**. The engine should read about 750 to 850 rpm at idle with the engine warmed, and increase gradually as the gas pedal is depressed.

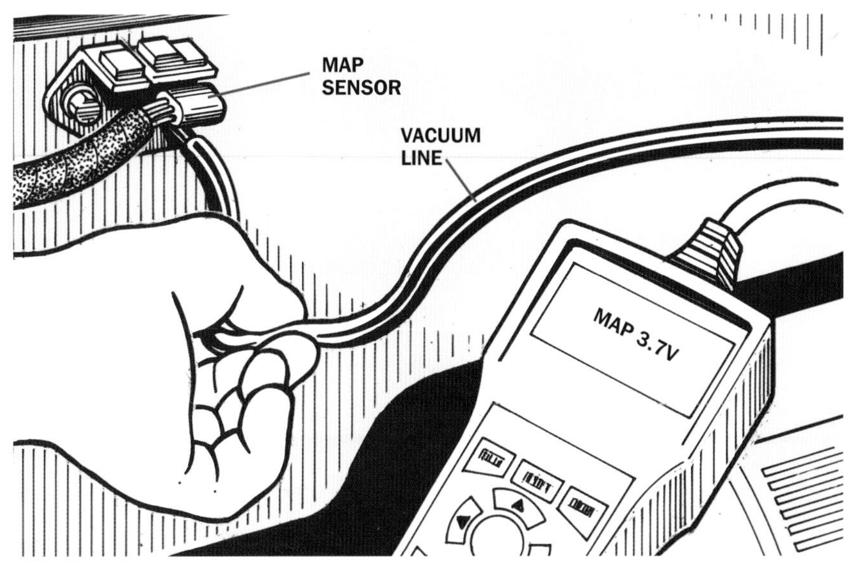

(Fig. 2) Check the MAP sensor with a scan tool by pinching its hose.

Still no reason for a driveability glitch? You need to access the powertrain computer. It may be located under the hood or under the dash. The most common under-dash location is behind the passenger-side kickpad. Remove the kickpad and, while a helper is slowly accelerating the engine, flex the computer wiring connectors and tap on the computer housing **(Fig. 3)**. If the engine hiccups, there's a bad connection or possibly cracked solder joints on the circuit board. You may need a replacement.

Replacing Spark Plugs

Time was, spark plugs were always visible, even if it took a struggle to reach them. Now they're often recessed into the head, and in many cases there are no plug wires. A mini ignition module, perhaps with the coil built into it (or into the plug boot), is used instead. You may have to remove a cover that holds the ignition modules and plug boots for access. Whatever the design, very carefully make any necessary electrical disconnection at the plug prior to plug removal. If there are plug wires, grasp and lift by the plug boots. Never pull on a plug wire or it may separate internally. Look inside the boot and if it appears soaked in oil or cracked by heat, replace it. If the ignition coil is built in, expect it to be pricey.

Inspect the plugs. If they all have a coating of black carbon, that indicates a rich fuel mixture and likely a bad oxygen sensor. A scan tool should be able to pinpoint a malfunctioning oxygen sensor even if it didn't log a trouble code. If there's just a single carbon-blackened plug, you probably have a leaking fuel injector.

When you're ready to install the new plug, apply a thin film of antiseize compound so the new plug doesn't heat-seal in place. Use a torque wrench to tighten the plug.

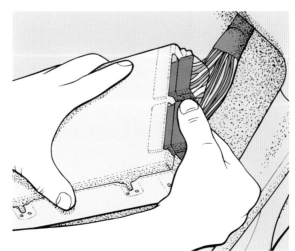

(Fig. 3) Wiggle the wiring connectors while the engine is running to check for misfires.

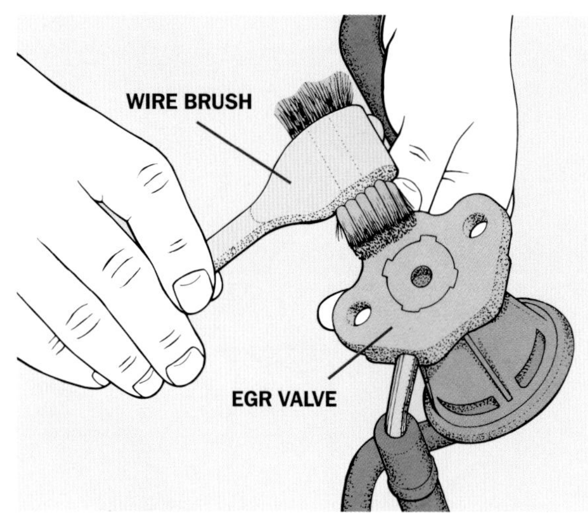

(Fig. 4.)You may not be able to clean the pintle on a recessed EGR valve like this one.

Exhaust Gas Recirculation

Exhaust gas recirculation (EGR) valves may stick open, fail to close completely or just not operate smoothly. If so, the engine will hesitate and may stall, fuel economy may drop, and emissions may be affected—even if you pass the state inspection test. The EGR valve meters some exhaust gas back into the cylinders to lower peak temperatures of the air-fuel charge during combustion. This not only reduces a key pollutant (oxides of nitrogen) but often improves fuel economy. The EGR valve, typically a diaphragm-actuated device with a pin-type valve, is pulled open by engine vacuum, but that vacuum must be precisely regulated. Too much vacuum results in too much exhaust gas flow, which can cause the engine to lose power, even stall.

Late models with OBD II computers have sophisticated strategies to detect severely malfunctioning EGR. However, this basic check will work on all vacuum-controlled EGR systems. Locate the EGR valve and if it has a vacuum hose connection, unplug it. Run the engine at idle, and connect a spare hose from a source of engine vacuum or use a manual vacuum pump and apply vacuum to the hose neck. The engine should slow significantly, probably even stall, if you apply full engine vacuum (17 to 21 in.).

If there's no significant change in engine idle—in fact, if the engine has been idling rough—the valve may be sticking open. Remove it and if you can see a heavy accumulation of deposits in the port, and if it's an exposed pin-type valve, clean it with a wire brush (**Fig. 4**). If the end of the pin is recessed in the port, it can't be cleaned. Replace it.

Battery Terminals

Clean the battery terminals, then reinstall and tighten. Today's batteries—top-post and side-terminal—are subject to continuous drain with the engine off, to keep alive the memories of many computers (from powertrain to car radio). Just a slight coat of corrosion—perhaps too subtle to be visible—can reduce battery charge. Disconnect the cable terminals. On a top-post battery, brush around the post and inside the cable terminal (**Fig. 5**). If the post or cable terminal is badly corroded, replace it with a premium terminal, the kind that often includes a cable section. Forget the cheap screw-together terminals—they'll become severely corroded and cause more problems than they solve. With a side-terminal battery, brush both contact faces even if they look clean. Make sure the bolt threads in without a feeling of looseness, and if there is any, don't try to muscle the bolt supertight with a wrench. You're more likely to make things worse.

Where To Get Service Information

Diagnosing failures that produce trouble codes, and finding out normal readings for engine sensors, is not subject to rule of thumb procedures. You need the latest factory diagnostic sequences and specifications. Vehicle makers have Web sites with this service information, and you'll be able to access the data for a day at a time. Many sites charge for this information—you can pay using a credit card. At present, General Motors information is available at www.acdelco.com (click on ACDelco TechConnect). Or you can get a low-cost subscription from www.alldata.com (a leading source for professionals, with information on all makes). In addition, AutoZone offers free scan tool connections and readouts at its stores.

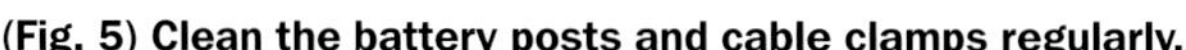

(Fig. 5) Clean the battery posts and cable clamps regularly.

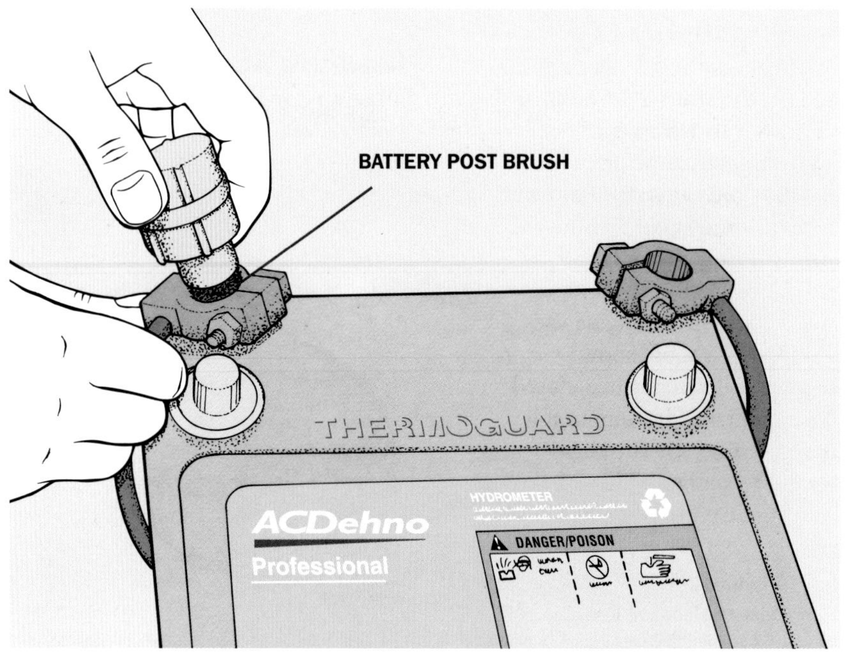

EASY

Smoothing Out a Lumpy Idle

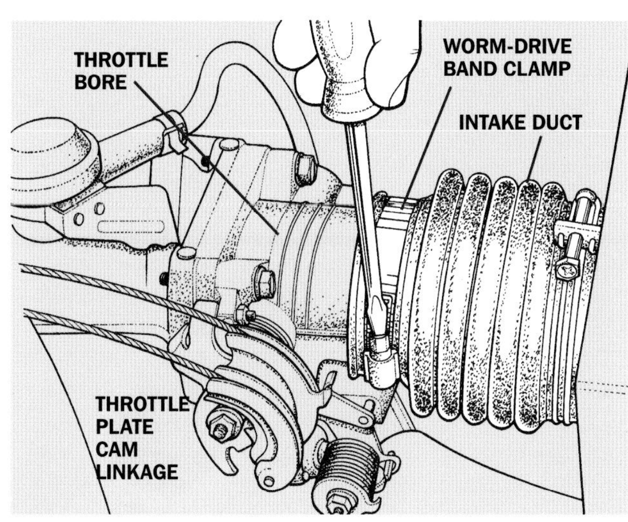

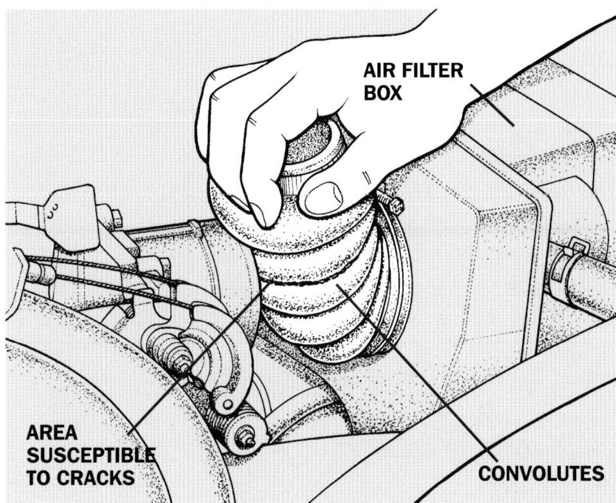

(Fig. 1, left) Make sure all the clamps sealing the intake duct are tight.
(Fig. 2, right) Pull back the intake duct to check for hidden cracks underneath.

Fearful pedestrians glare at you as they pass in front of your bumper at crosswalks. Out of embarrassment, you try to ignore them by glancing around nonchalantly, stroking your hair as you look in the rearview mirror or tuning the radio. Meanwhile, the size of your right thigh is growing to Dan Jansen proportions from the force being applied to the brake pedal. Your engine's idle speed is surging up and down, creating crescendos that would make Pavarotti proud: WAAAAaaaah, WAAAAaaaah, WAAAAaaaah! It's all you can do to keep your maniacal car from lurching forward into a lawsuit.

There are a number of generic steps you can take to see what's ailing your wheels. And if there ever was a time to step back and remember the basics, this is it.

Pop quiz: What is an internal-combustion engine?

It's basically little more than an air pump. The more air that gets in, the faster the engine runs. And airflow controls idle. By allowing a certain volume of air to bypass the closed throttle plate(s), idle rpm can be maintained at a healthy level. Even to accelerate, we don't "step on the gas," we "step on the air" by opening the throttle plate farther. Fuel is added a nanosecond later, in response to the greater intake airflow.

Check Your Intake Tract

If your engine uses a remotely mounted air filter in an air box, inspect everything from there back to the throttle plate(s). At the air box, check all hose connections and make sure the clamps are tight (**Fig. 1**). Replace the air filter if it's so dirty that light from a 100-watt bulb doesn't pass through the element. Make sure the new one seats properly in the air box and that the cover sits flush and clamps down evenly. Follow the intake tract toward the throttle plate, tightening all the clamps as you go. If there's an inline mass airflow meter in the tract, take extra care to examine its connections for leaks.

Big, convoluted rubber tubing-style intake tracts are susceptible to developing cracks between the convolutes on the underside of the tube. They're generally not visible unless you remove one end of the tube and bend it back to get a good look below (**Fig. 2**). If the engine controls measure airflow by means of a manifold absolute pressure (MAP) sensor, this type of leak shouldn't affect idle quality. But the hole still needs to be sealed, or else dirt and debris will find its way in. If the engine uses an airflow sensor, this type of leak tends to audibly reveal itself when the engine torques forward on its mounts and opens wide the convolute crack.

Then the engine gets an unmetered gulp of air and revs up on its own. The idle speed control may try to catch the speed burst by closing down the bypass channel. Then, when the engine returns to its normal position and the convolute crack closes, the idle speed is too low. In response, the idle controls may open up the channel again to raise the idle. This scenario can turn into a cycling condition that produces a lumpy, rolling idle.

If you don't mind getting your engine bay a little messy, another quick way to go about checking for intake tract and runner leaks is to simply spray carburetor cleaner around connections and the intake manifold while the engine is running (**Fig. 3**). If you get an rpm change when you spray, it means the vapors are getting in somehow. So you have to play spy to find the leak. Don't spray near the distributor—if you have one—because there's a chance the solvent will ignite and leave you minus your eyebrows and nose hair.

Keep Your Bore Clean

When you get to the last clamp at the throttle bore, unscrew it and remove the intake tract. Take a look inside the bore with a flashlight. If the muck is so thick that it's a wonder the throttle plate can move at all, you've found a major cause of your lumpy idle. In addition to the idle air-bypass channel, a small amount of air must be able to pass around the throttle plate itself. When blowby vapors from the PCV system (and EGR exhaust gases) sludge up the bore over time, the idle air-bypass function is seriously affected.

Steal an old toothbrush from your kids (so your wife doesn't blow a gasket) and pick up some noncaustic fuel-injection intake cleaner at an auto parts store. With the engine off, spray some cleaner in the bore and start scrubbing with the toothbrush. Pay particular attention to the circumferential area where the throttle plate sits when closed. Also clean both sides of the plate and its edges.

If the externally mounted idle air-bypass valve is easily removed and its channel easily accessed, try to get cleaner to pass through the channel into the bore. Be sure to clean the valve's pintle tip, too (**Fig. 4**). (Also see page 122.)

Wash Down the Residue

With the bore and channel clean, stick the intake tract back on and start the engine. If the engine doesn't use an airflow meter, you can pull the tract off with the engine running and spray some more cleaner in the bore to wash down the residue. Goose the throttle a couple of times. Then tighten the clamp and let the motor idle so that the engine-management system can relearn the parameters necessary for increased throttle plate air bypass.

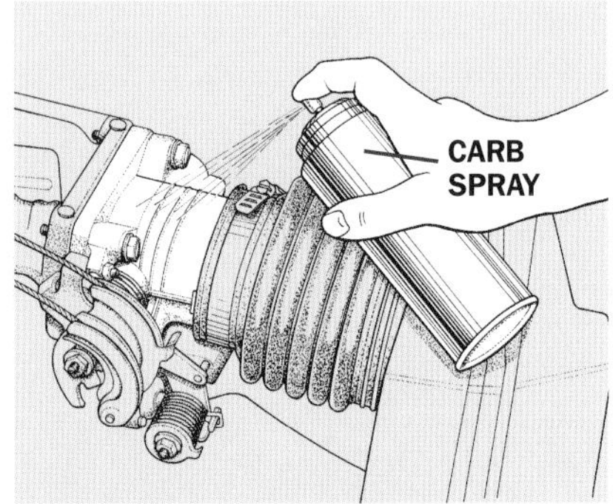

(Fig. 3) Spray carb cleaner around the throttle bore to find air leaks.

If your engine does use an airflow meter, it'll probably stall when you pull the intake tract off the bore. Get it started again and just pull the end of the rubber tract back a bit with one or two fingers to spray some more cleaner down in the bore. The engine will stumble for a second, but that's okay. Whatever you do, don't spray the cleaner into the tract before the airflow meter. You could damage the meter.

Single- and dual-point injection throttle bodies typically don't sludge up much because they're up top on

HOW IT WORKS

Engine Management

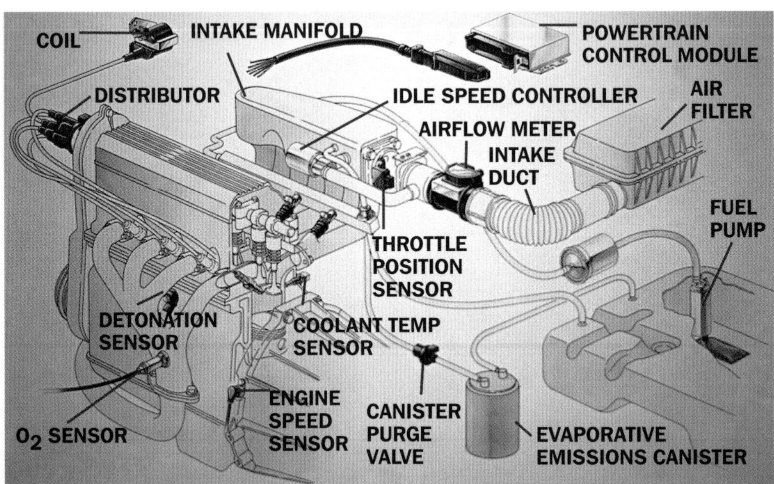

An automotive computerized engine-management system works like any computer as it controls idle speed. The central processing unit relies on various inputs to calculate necessary outputs. On modern motors, however, the inputs to the processor, or powertrain control module (PCM), are called sensors. The outputs are called actuators. And the PCM is programmed to control the actuators under any condition that the sensors deem necessary.

Key sensory inputs of most engine-management systems include engine speed, coolant temperature, crankshaft position, intake airflow, manifold vacuum, throttle position and exhaust oxygen content. Many systems go further, factoring in such inputs as camshaft position, barometric pressure, intake air temperature, detonation detection, EGR valve position, misfire detection, engine-oil temperature, power-steering pressure, air-conditioning pressures, gear-lever position, vehicle speed, automatic-transmission-fluid temperature, catalytic converter efficiency, system voltage and others.

Key actuators on many systems include the fuel injectors, idle speed control motor, EGR valve, evaporative canister purge, ignition coil timing and dwell (saturation time), torque converter clutch, smog pump diverter valve, cooling fan, alternator output and fuel pump.

the engine and PCV vapors flow in below them. However, if the plate(s) looks really dirty, it's okay to hit it with some cleaner. Just be careful not to drown the fuel injector sitting directly above the plate.

Assuming no one has ever played with the base idle settings (the screw may be sealed) and there's nothing wrong with the powertrain control module's programming (the malfunction indicator lamp has never illuminated), that covers the basic idle controls. Unless the manufacturer has issued a software update, today's engine-management systems are smart enough to take it from here and continue to provide a smooth, carefree idle until the next time that throttle bore has janitorial needs.

Loaded to the Hilt

When you consider the number of belt-driven accessories hanging off the typical engine today, in addition to all the mechanical and electrical loads, it's a wonder the pistons can continue pumping at all. That's why some vehicles today have 120-amp alternators and 140-amp fuses.

In rainy, cold weather at night, your alternator is working overtime to make enough amperage to power everything. Problem is, it's also trying to stop the engine from turning. Here's where your idle speed control really shines. As soon as alternator output drops to a certain level, the voltage regulator does its thing and the engine-management system sees the need for increased idle rpm to keep charging-system voltage between 13½ and 15 volts.

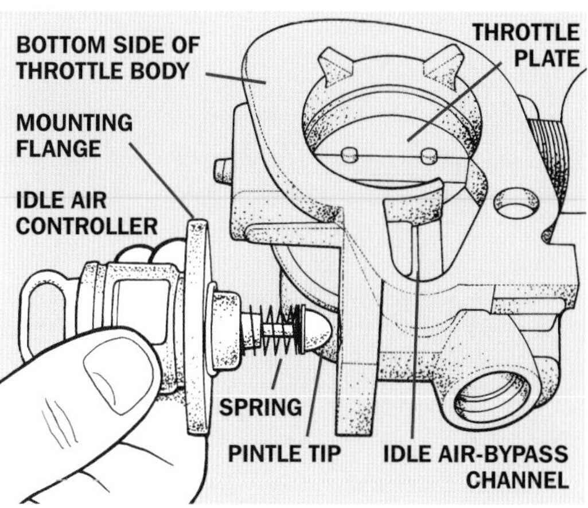

(Fig. 4) Pull the idle speed controller out of its bore to inspect the pintle tip, spring and air channel.

If a signal gets lost through a short or an open circuit or an intermittent connection, however, you're likely to get a lumpy or just plain low idle. Here's where you really need the specific service manual and wiring diagrams for the vehicle, because there are too many variations in form and function to discuss these systems in general terms. Some simple things you can do, however, include visually checking for corroded—and even burned—connections at the alternator and battery terminals. Eyeball the condition of all the fusible links around the battery, and check for fouled spark plugs (**Fig. 5**). Make sure the accessory belt(s) is tight and unfrayed.

Every time the a/c compressor kicks in at idle, engine speed would drop a couple hundred rpm were it not for the idle speed controls keeping things at an even keel. Here again, intermittent connections and a faulty pressure switch or two could cause the climate control to cycle in and out. A low or contaminated refrigerant charge might do the same thing.

Sometimes there's a pressure switch monitoring your power steering system, especially on 4-cylinder engines. During a tight parking-lot maneuver, when power-steering pressure skyrockets, the engine controls take the reins and bump open the idle speed control motor so your engine doesn't stall or bog down to the point of misfiring. A bad connection or leak at the switch would affect this system and possibly lead to a hunting idle. Periodic power-steering-system flushes go a long way toward preventing clogged switches and orifices.

An engine with high mileage that's tired and worn out may not pull a healthy vacuum of 18 to 20 in. Hg at idle (closed throttle plate) anymore. That means the MAP sensor will always read the engine as under load (low vacuum=high voltage) and—just doing its job—inform the powertrain computer to add more fuel. When the oxygen sensor picks up the rich mixture in the exhaust stream, it will call for a leaner mixture. Common strategy is to open the idle air-bypass valve to let some more air in. But an engine that's just on the borderline of wheezing may intermittently "loosen up," leading to a roller coaster idle. It may have trouble breathing when cold, but once warm—with expanded piston rings, gaskets and the like—show a perfectly healthy intake vacuum.

What it all boils down to is that there's a whole lot more than just a carburetor's throttle stop screw controlling your engine's idle speed these days. Simply understanding the system, however, is half the battle toward finding and fixing the offending troublemaker.

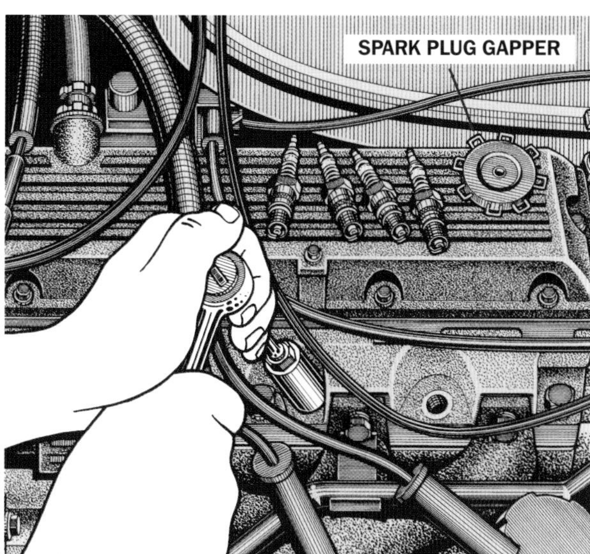

(Fig. 5) Fouled spark plugs can lead to misfiring at idle. They can be cleaned and regapped or simply replaced.

Replacing Your Water Pump

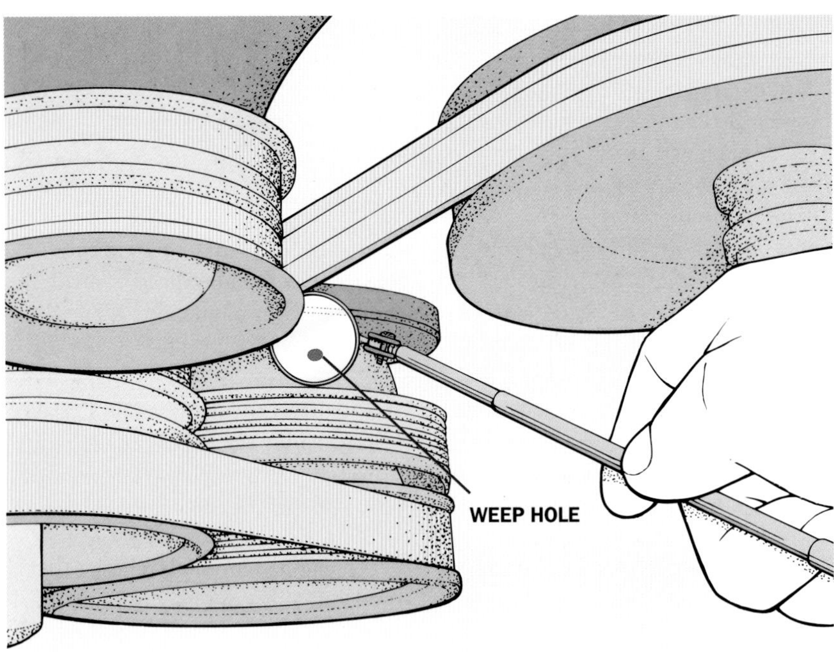

(Fig. 1) Wet liquid seeping from the weep hole signifies the end of the service life of the seals in your pump.

Bombing down the interstate, you glance at the odometer and realize you've just reached an automotive milestone: 100,000 miles with no major repairs. Time was a car that had passed its belly over that much real estate was considered pretty much used up, but yours still runs great and looks practically new. Amazing how technology has advanced.

Then you notice the temperature gauge. Holy smokes—pegged! You put it in neutral, coast off onto the shoulder and shut her down. There's that maple-syrup-spilled-on-the-radiator odor again—you've smelled it before, but filed it under "things to think about later." Sooner would've been better—now you're walking.

Seal Deal

The biggest change in water pump design occurred decades ago when the spring-loaded mechanical seal was adopted. However, its rubber parts may disintegrate if the engine overheats, and its polished sealing faces can wear and warp if the engine is run dry. Typically, pumps will start leaking catastrophically shortly after a boil-over.

This kind of failure can be worse than it sounds. Besides the vastly expensive internal engine damage that running without coolant may cause, a leaking seal can wash away the shaft bearing's lubricant, perhaps resulting in a seized shaft, and a flying fan or belt pulley can destroy the radiator or even dent the hood.

So, leakage is the No. 1 failure. Noise is second, and is always indicative of a terminal condition. While service literature on water pumps often will show a picture of a badly eroded impeller that contributes to overheating, technicians say that's not as common as it once was. Another possible problem with the same consequences is an impeller that's come loose from its shaft. Erosion of the inside surfaces of the pump chamber caused by cavitation (a weak cap or a chronically low level, perhaps?) can open up the working space and reduce flow, as can corrosion from weak antifreeze in the coolant mix.

Evidence Gathering

If you start to smell the distinctive odor of engine coolant, or you notice that the level in the overflow bottle is dropping rapidly, it's time for a careful exam. (If you're lucky, it may be just a leaky hose connection, but look the radiator over, too. If the smell is strong in the passenger compartment and the windshield tends to steam up, think about the heater core. In cases where none of the above is the culprit, better check out the water pump.)

First, use an inspection mirror and a good light to view the vent hole that's at the bottom of the pump casting's nose **(Fig. 1)**. Or, support the front of the car safely on jackstands and look up from underneath. All seals are supposed to weep slightly (a little coolant is needed to lube the faces), but drips mean you'd better go shopping for an estimate.

Next, grasp the fan or water pump pulley and see if it rocks from side to side. If there's anything but slight movement, the bearing is on its way out. Also, you can remove the belt and see how the bearing feels as you rotate the pump shaft **(Fig. 2)**. Roughness isn't acceptable.

A low-flow situation that results in hot running can be hard to diagnose. Drain the level down to the top of the radiator tubes, get the engine hot, and then shut it off for 10 minutes and let it heat soak to make sure the thermostat is wide open. Now, fire it up again and run it at 3000 rpm. On Japanese cars using the radiator fill neck on the top tank, look down into it with a flashlight and you should see strong circulation **(Fig. 3)**. Another possibility is to squeeze the upper hose to feel

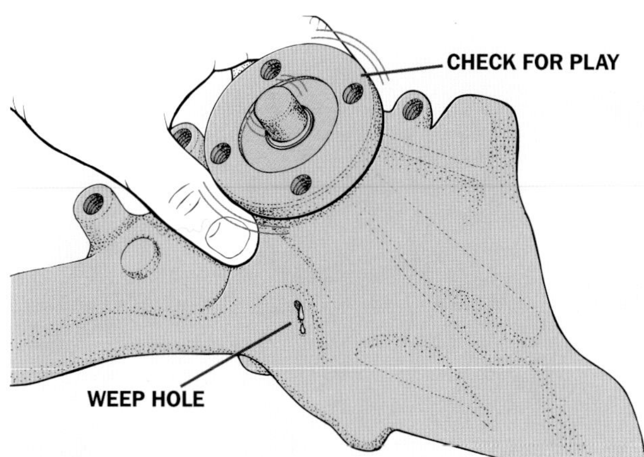

(Fig. 2) Almost any radial play in the water pump shaft is grounds for immediate pump replacement before something fails.

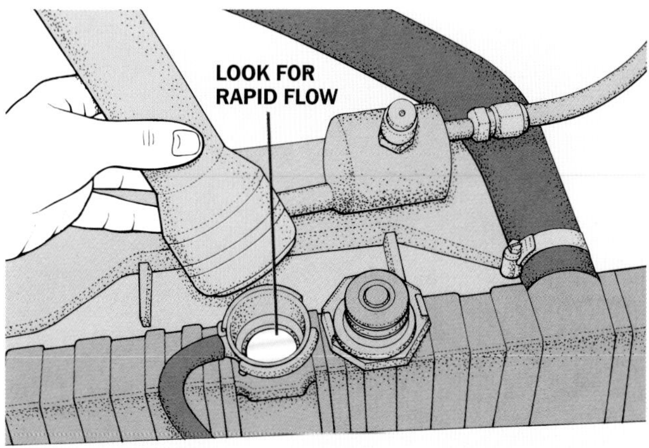

(Fig. 3) With the engine warm enough to open the thermostat, but not hot enough to pressurize the system, look for vigorous flow at 3000 rpm.

for flow, but that's pretty subjective. Unfortunately, there's no good way for the do-it-yourselfer to differentiate a weak pump from a clogged radiator.

Major Undertaking?

On some front-wheel drives the job is a horror story. Make sure you resist the temptation to get into this repair if you're not prepared to invest the time required. Find out the flat-rate hours by asking a local garage owner or dealer service manager. It's a job that could take several hours, depending on what you drive, particularly if the pump is recessed into the engine block.

The first steps in removing any water pump are to let the engine cool off completely, and then drain the cooling system by either opening the radiator petcock or disconnecting the bottom radiator hose and removing engine coolant drain plugs. Next, do whatever is necessary to remove the accessory drivebelts. If the car has a longitudinally mounted engine as found in every rwd and some front-

HOW IT WORKS

Water Pump Shaft Seals

Two perfectly flat rings, one stationary and the other rotating with the pump shaft, are pressed together by means of a coil spring. The rings may be made of carbon or may be ceramic, phenolic, porous bronze, cast iron, etc., in any combination. This allows only enough seepage to keep the elements lubricated. It has a weak link, however, in the form of its rubber parts—the bellows that seals the spring and the rubber seat cup between the rotating element and the shaft. If the engine is ever run dry, the temperature of the pump is apt to rise far beyond what the rubber can survive, and a leak occurs. Another possibility is warpage of the sealing elements, also from overheating.

There's conflicting evidence on whether silicates and phosphates from antifreeze, or other hard particles such as casting core sand, can actually damage the seal faces. Engineers have told us the running clearance is way too small to admit solids of any appreciable diameter.

Since cars are lasting longer than they used to, and since we've become such a litigious society, carmakers are working harder than ever to make water pumps last. After all, when a pump goes you've got to get out and walk, which exposes you to dangers that horrify auto company lawyers.

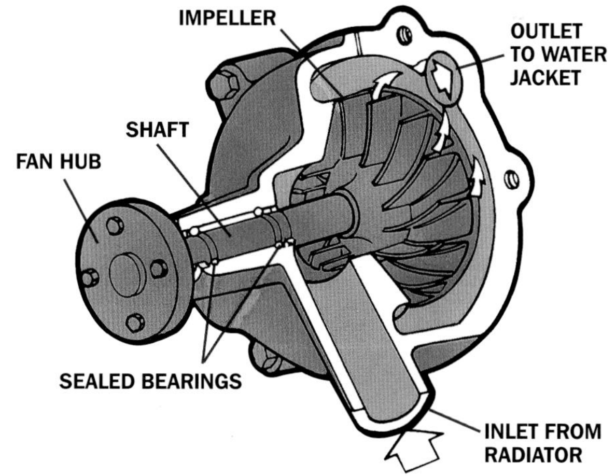

So, there has been a push for water pump seals that will rarely, if ever, fail. One design that looks promising is from Michael Ostrowski and John Crane International, the leading supplier of conventional water pump seals. Called the Advanced Metal Diaphragm seal, it uses a flexible stainless steel diaphragm that acts as both the spring and the bellows, and incorporates an improved method of mounting the seal faces.

(Fig. 4) **This is an easy one, because it's near the top. Your job would be a lot tougher if the pump were near the bottom.**

drivers, remove the air shrouds (in some cases, the radiator, too), and then the fan and its clutch, which bolt to the front of the water pump shaft.

Now you can start on the pump by disconnecting the hoses. Those for the heater will probably be stubborn, so you may need to split their ends with a utility knife (if they're long enough, you might be able to trim them off square and reuse them).

Extract the pump-to-engine bolts and keep them and any brackets they retain in strict order or you'll regret it at assembly. There may be hidden bolts, so take a look at a diagram.

The pump should come off with a good tug (**Fig. 4**). If not, make sure you didn't miss any bolts, and then tap on the inlet or outlet neck with a mallet or a block of wood and a hammer. Don't use a screwdriver to pry the seam open or you'll make a nick that the gasket may not seal.

Pumps seal against the engine or backing plate with a gasket, an O-ring or RTV silicone. Get the mating surface clean with a scraper.

If you must use silicone sealer, use one rated for automotive use. It should also be labeled low-volatility. Outgassing from the curing sealant can poison oxygen sensors—so leave the bathtub caulk with your plumbing tools.

We should mention a potential problem. Suppose you're installing a water pump on a car with a serpentine belt. Engines on many older models were equipped with a regular ribbed or V-belt, but the water pump for the old model may fit physically on the new one, if you change over the pulley. Can you guess the possible mistake? Think about direction: The serpentine belt might drive the impeller in the opposite direction from that of the V-belt, so you could end up installing a pump that runs backward, causing a seemingly incurable overheating situation. Make sure you get exactly the right part, and compare the impellers. Also, heed that routing diagram (**Fig. 5**).

(Fig. 5) **Vehicles with serpentine belts have a belt routing diagram under the hood somewhere. Read and obey.**

After everything is buttoned up, figure out how much coolant your system holds. This should be in your owner's manual, or in the shop manual. Using the appropriate manufacturer's coolant, add half that amount and then top off with water. This will give you a 50-50 mix. Be sure to follow the service procedure for bleeding the air bubbles out of the system.

Curing a Clicking Starter

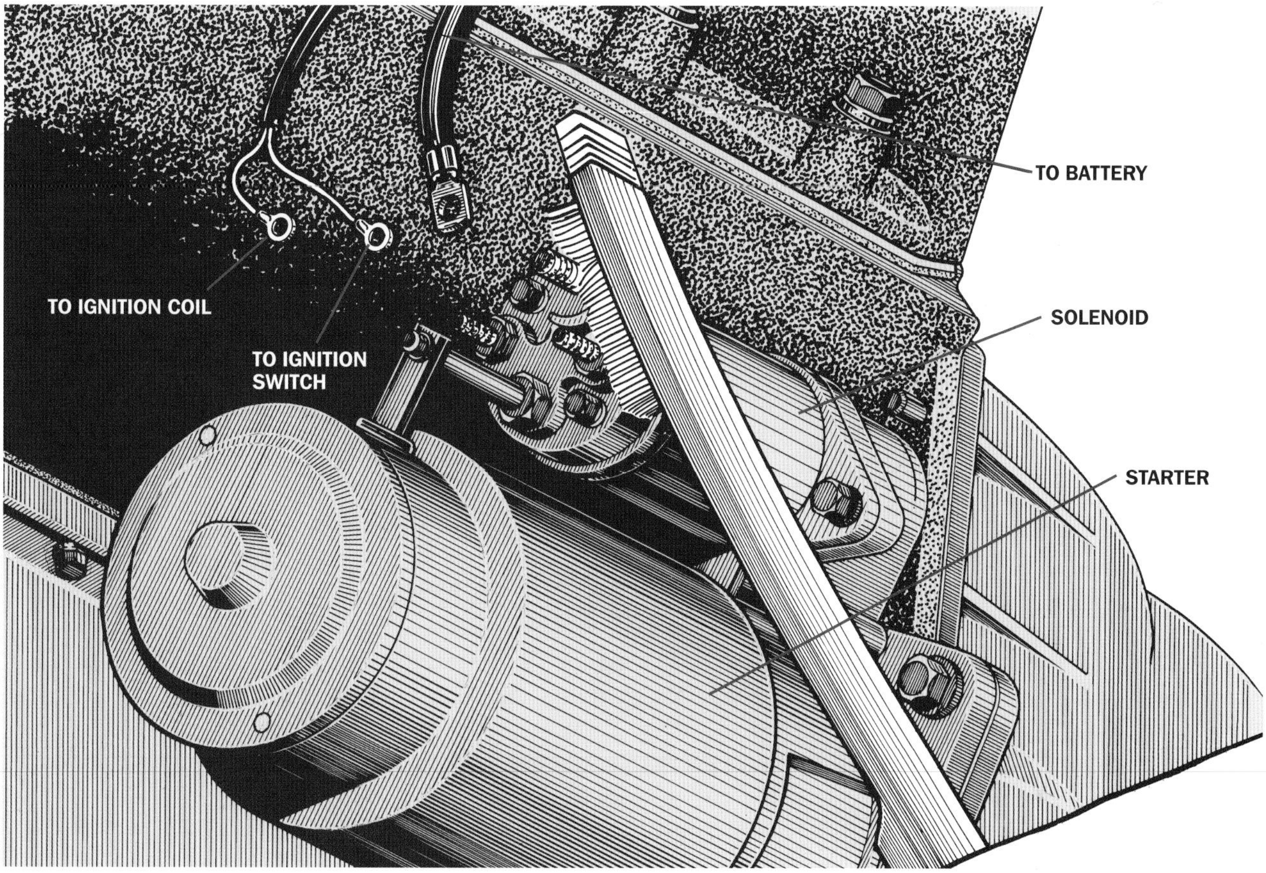

TO BATTERY
TO IGNITION COIL
SOLENOID
TO IGNITION SWITCH
STARTER

(Fig. 1) Loose or corroded starter cables can cause enough voltage drop to cause a clicking, intermittent connection. Clean with a wire brush and then rinse with warm water.

You twist the ignition key to start your engine, and instead of the syncopated whirling of a cranking starter and crankshaft, you hear a click or a series of chatterlike clicks. The engine that started every day for so long is not going to start today. Time to hitch a ride to work. If it's a weekend, you get the chance to find out why your vehicle has died and fix the problem before Monday morning.

That clicking noise is from either the starter solenoid or the relay. The solenoid is part of the starter. Typically it has a terminal for a thick power feed wire from the battery (**Fig. 1**), and a thinner terminal for the current supply wire to a switching mechanism in the solenoid. The relay is a remotely mounted switching device between starter and battery that controls either the thick power feed or the thinner electrical feed to the solenoid's switch terminal.

The first step (although at this point it doesn't tell you the root cause) is to find out where the click is coming from. If you have a helper turn the ignition key to start, you'll be able to trace the underhood click. If it comes from the starter, your problem is in the solenoid.

Ford and Chrysler products may have a relay in the circuit. If the solenoid isn't the source of the click, tracing the sound should take you to the relay on those models.

Even after you know what part is clicking, begin your real diagnosis at the battery. If the battery top has an "eye" indicator (actually a battery hydrometer that indicates the state of charge), recharge if the indicator is black. If it's green, it's got a normal charge. If it's yellow, get a new battery because the electrolyte is too low.

There's no indicator eye? Connect a voltmeter across the battery terminals (positive lead to positive terminal, negative lead to negative terminal). If the meter reads under 12.4 to 12.5 volts, it's borderline or undercharged (depending on the design of the battery). Recharge it for the day. Batteries do run down as a result of a temporary series of operating condi-

(Fig. 2) Check for voltage drop between battery post and starter terminal while a helper cranks the engine. Up to 0.50 volt is acceptable.

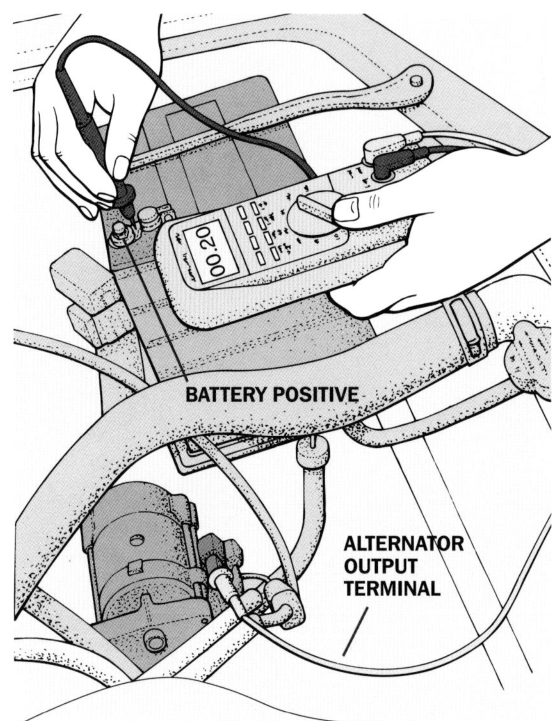

tions (lots of short trips, for example), but if the problem recurs, you'll have to check charging system output and the possibility of a short circuit.

If the reading is 12.7 to 12.9 volts, that's a good starting point. After a recharge, operate the headlamps for 15 seconds to remove what is called the "surface charge." The meter reading should not drop more than about 0.2 volt.

The reading is okay? Have a helper turn the ignition key to start, and in 15 seconds, read the meter. If it's below 9.5 volts, the battery may not be strong enough. Professionals have battery load testers to make sure. Your alternative: If the battery voltage was normal when you started, but is low during the attempt to crank, try a jumpstart. If the engine cranks normally with a boost, the battery probably is bad.

Corroded, Distorted Terminals

If the engine still won't crank, next inspect the cables and their connections at both ends. If you see corrosion or a possibly poor connection, make a voltage drop test **(Fig. 2)**. First, connect the voltmeter negative lead to the battery ground terminal and the positive lead to the engine block, close to the starter. With the key held in the start position, the voltmeter should read under 0.5 volt. If it's 0.5 volt or higher, the drop is excessive. In fact, if it's above 0.2 volt, that's really too high and could be a contributor to the problem if the battery is marginal. Perform the same check with the power feed side of the circuit (in this case, connect the voltmeter's positive lead to the battery, and the negative lead to the starter's battery cable terminal).

Get a high reading? Repeat the test, taking care to make contact at the battery post or side-terminal bolt, not the cable end. If the voltage drop now is within reason, the cable terminals are the problem. A simple cleaning may be all that's needed, but if a cable's

HOW IT WORKS

Starter Solenoids

A solenoid is an electromagnetic device that is capable of doing work, and in some starters, it does two jobs. 1) It moves a plunger that makes electrical contact between terminals for the battery and the starter motor, so the motor turns. If that's all it does, it's really just a switching device. 2) In some starters, the movement of the plunger also pushes a linkage that moves the starter's drive gear into mesh with the flywheel ring gear.

The solenoid has two wire coils. One is large, draws a lot of current and produces a strong magnetic field. That's enough to move the plunger. Once the plunger is in position (having completed the circuit and moved the starter drive), the large coil is disconnected and the circuit for a small coil is completed. The small coil draws a small amount of current and produces a weaker magnetic field—just enough to hold the coil in position. This saves battery energy for the big job of cranking the engine. If there isn't quite enough battery electrical pressure (voltage) to provide the current flow, however, the plunger won't lock into position so the small coil can take over. If this happens, all you hear is a solenoid click, and the plunger springs back. Some solenoids have an extra small-gauge terminal. This bypasses the ballast resistor, ensuring a hot spark while cranking.

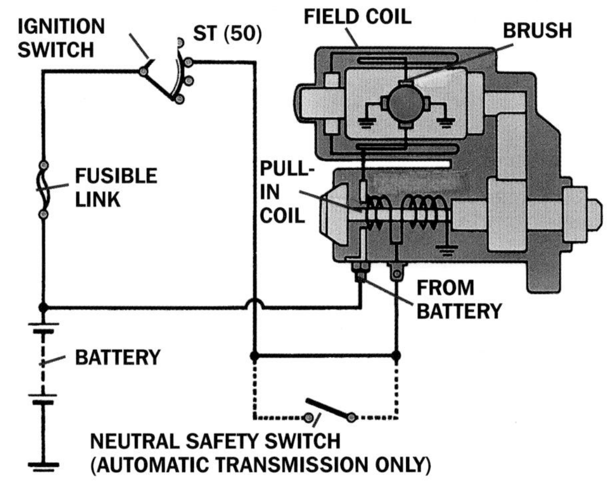

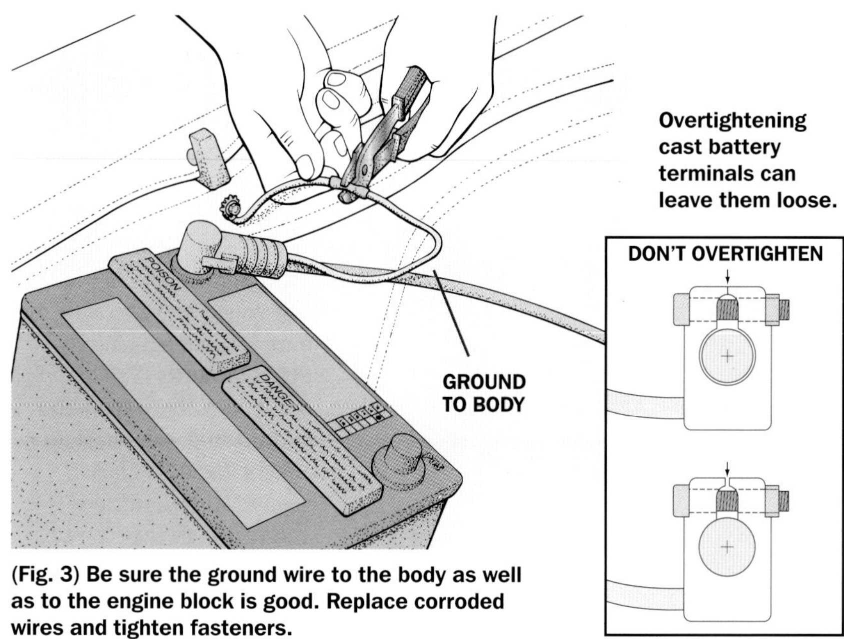

(Fig. 3) Be sure the ground wire to the body as well as to the engine block is good. Replace corroded wires and tighten fasteners.

post terminal is distorted, the jaws may be tight even though the inside surface is not making good contact.

If the cable end is distorted or corroded, replace it (**Fig. 3**). Get a quality cable end, which includes a section of cable with a protective sheath, not just a terminal. Cut the corroded cable back to where the copper wire is absolutely free of any corrosion. Install the new cable end and join it to the remaining cable (some repair cable sections have heat-shrink insulation, and others have screw retainers or crimp on).

No sign of corrosion on a ground cable? Remove the grounding bolt at the engine, clean the cable end and bolt, reinstall and tighten.

Checking the Starter Terminals

At the starter, inspect the terminals for both the battery (thicker wire) and solenoid switch for corrosion and physical damage. If the corrosion is minor, you may be able to remove the retaining nut and battery cable and wire-brush corrosion away. If the corrosion is so severe that cleaning it off leaves the threads damaged, install a repair stud, which cuts new threads onto the damaged studs (**Fig. 4**).

Now try to crank the engine. No improvement? With good connections at both ends (battery, ground and starter), try direct wiring with jumper cables, and if cranking still is weak, the starter apparently is bad.

Don't Have a Good Meter?

If you don't have an accurate voltmeter, you still can eyeball and make hands-on inspections for tightness of the cable connections at both ends. Clean and tighten the cables and see if the engine will crank.

Still no success? Disconnect both battery cables and make direct connections with booster cables, one from the battery's negative post to engine ground, one from the battery positive terminal to the starter solenoid terminal. Do a follow-up test with the booster to the starter battery terminal, plus a jumper to the solenoid terminal. These test procedures can be physically difficult to perform on many vehicles, particularly those with a side terminal battery, but they usually can be done. Just take the time to make good connections with the jumpers. If you can get the engine to crank this way, the problem obviously is in the cable connection.

If a Ford or Chrysler product's relay is the source of the click, it may not be operating properly. If running jumpers to the solenoid or starter (bypassing the relay) gets the engine to crank, test the relay.

On Ford products, connect a booster cable across the thick-wire terminals of the relay, and if the engine now cranks, replace the relay. On Chrysler vehicles, find the power feed (it's the wire terminal that turns on a grounded 12-volt test light). Connect a jumper wire from that terminal to the one for the power output wire (usually red) that goes to the starter solenoid. Needless to say, be sure the vehicle is out of gear and the wheels are blocked before making any attempt to turn the engine over.

On models with plug-in relays, you may have trouble finding the color codes, but the wiring diagram should indicate the power feed and output terminals and their numbers, which you'll find on the relay itself. Turn on the ignition. You now can use a grounded test light to find the power feed terminal, but you'll have to eyeball the relay's terminal numbers to figure out which is the output wire terminal (to the solenoid) in the underhood center itself. Connect a jumper from the power feed to the output, and if the engine cranks, replace the relay.

Make cleaning and tightening all the connections a spring and fall ritual and your engine will make reliable cranking a year-round habit.

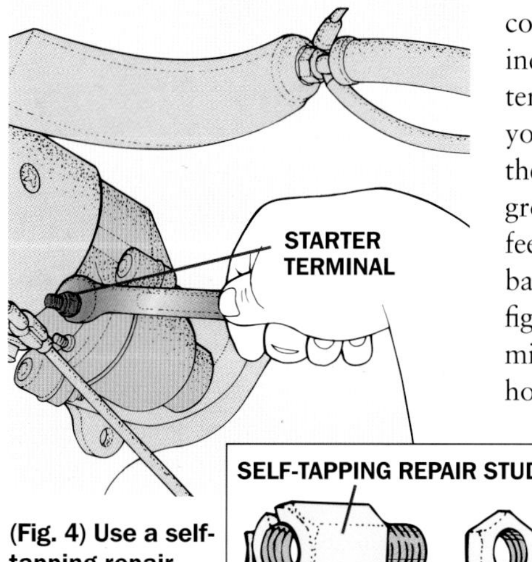

(Fig. 4) Use a self-tapping repair stud rather than replacing the whole starter if the terminal threads are damaged or stripped.

Repairing Cooling System Leaks

Okay, you replaced your lower radiator hose last week after it burst on the freeway, and the syrupy, turkish bath odor of boiling glycol coolant hitting a red-hot exhaust manifold is something you can live the rest of your life without ever smelling again. Lying face-up in a spreading pool of cooling coolant to change the hose is pretty low on the list, too. So it's a bad omen when that smell hits you at a tollbooth a week later—and a worse omen when you open the hood and realize the new hose is leaking from both ends. What gives?

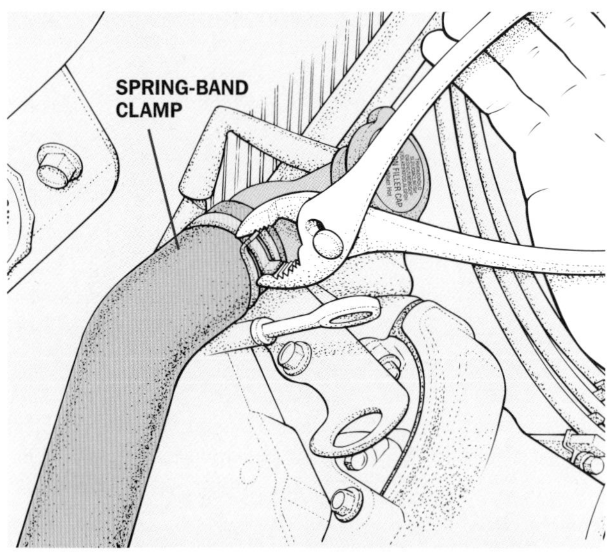

(Fig. 1) Spring-band clamps can usually be removed or replaced with pliers or locking pliers.

(Fig. 2) Shrink-fit hose clamps will continue to shrink as engine warms up, ensuring a tight seal.

Drip Patrol

There are about two dozen coolant hose connections underhood today, and it's a constant effort to find and fix the loose ones that leak coolant. Ingesting air is a routine issue. It used to be simple: Look for an antifreeze stain, then just tighten the hose clamp, right? Sorry, but that's not always true anymore.

First, the powertrain compartment is so tight that you can hardly spot a leak without a dedicated inspection. You're more likely to look closely at a hose connection when you have to disconnect a hose to reach something else. In either case, when you do look at the coolant hose connections under your hood, you may see very few of the type you loosen and tighten with a screwdriver.

Today's engines have complex coolant flow patterns and the compartments are so tight that the engineers have to use special hose designs to provide safe routing. Some of those hoses have plastic fittings, called quick-connects, to help an assembly line worker make errorfree connections.

Depending on the age of your car and whether or not clamps were replaced, you could have a variety of hose clamps. You can tighten some of these, but not all. (See page 121.) These are the ones you can tighten:

SCREW-TOWER—The screw is perpendicular to the band, and turning it down tightens the band. It's been around forever, it's cheap and it rust-freezes in place, so tightening an old one usually is impossible. To get it off, spray it generously with penetrating solvent, loosen the tower screw and slip in a slim screwdriver if necessary to pry it open. Or just cut it off.

DOUBLE-WIRE OR BAND WITH RETAINING SCREW AND NUT—A double-winding of wire or a band is held together by a tangential screw at one end that fits into a nut at the other. When it's overtightened, the wire type digs into the hose and may cut through.

WORM-DRIVE CLAMP—This has been the longtime favorite, and even was considered a premium design. Some worm-drives are, but most aren't. One reason it's popular is that it can be opened up and taken off without disconnecting the hose, although that feature has limited utility.

The quality worm-drives have such features as: rust-resistant plating; rolled up edges so the band doesn't dig into the hose if overtightened; offset teeth that keep the band from twisting when tightened; and even "teeth" that aren't cut through the band, so the hose rubber doesn't extrude into the slots.

CONSTANT-TENSION WORM-DRIVE—The

best ones (by Oetiker, a leading European maker with extensive U.S. marketing) have an internal band that glides through a slot inside the main band, bridging the joint of the worm-drive. Result: The clamp provides true 360° clamping. That clamp also has a coil spring to provide constant tension even if the hose underneath takes a compression set.

Spring-Band Clamp

Today most carmakers are using a clamp that you can't tighten, so it also never can be retightened. It's the spring-band (**Fig. 1**), an inexpensive form of constant-tension clamp. It may not be everywhere under the hood, but it usually is in a lot of places. Because it can't be pretightened to any spec, it's sized so even if the hose takes a set underneath, it maintains some tension, hopefully adequate to prevent a leak, but only if the hose neck is in perfect shape.

Shrink-Band Clamp

Would you like a low-cost non-adjustable clamp that not only maintains tension but seals well even if the hose neck is far from perfect? It's here, and it also can help with other problem clamping situations: the plastic shrink-band clamp.

You must buy a shrink band that's sized for your particular hose diameter. The band comes on a thick cardboard roll so it doesn't shrink in storage. Just crush the roll, remove the band, lube the hose neck with antifreeze, slip the band onto the hose and the hose onto the neck. Unlike a conventional clamp, the shrink band should be positioned so it extends onto a bead on a hose neck.

Apply heat with a hair dryer (**Fig. 2**) or heat gun (from within a couple of inches or so), and in a couple of minutes the band conforms completely to the neck and bead, increasing leak resistance. And the heat from the coolant will cause it to continue to shrink in service to compensate for any compression set in the hose.

How do you get it off? If you're replacing the hose, just cut it with a single-edge razor blade. If you're planning to reuse the hose, you have these choices: 1) Cut the band itself with a soldering iron, but be careful; 2) Force a feeler gauge between band and hose, and run the razor blade through the band just over the feeler; 3) If you plan to use these shrink bands everywhere on your cars, get a band-slitter, a tool that does basically the same thing but is easier to use.

Those Quick-Connects

In many cases, today's cars and trucks use quick-connects instead of clamps for many heater circuit hoses and also for some radiator hoses. The quick-connect is a fitting with an O-ring

---

HOW IT WORKS

How Coolant Hose Leaks Occur

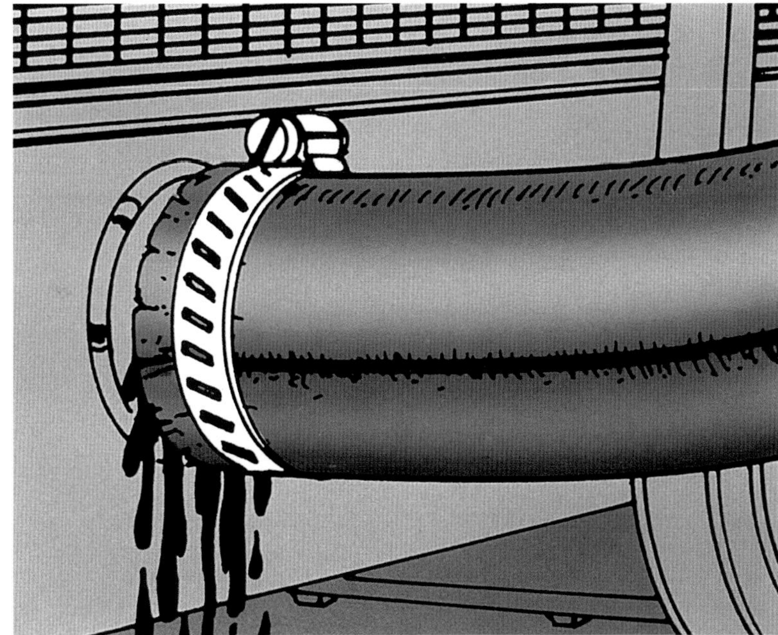

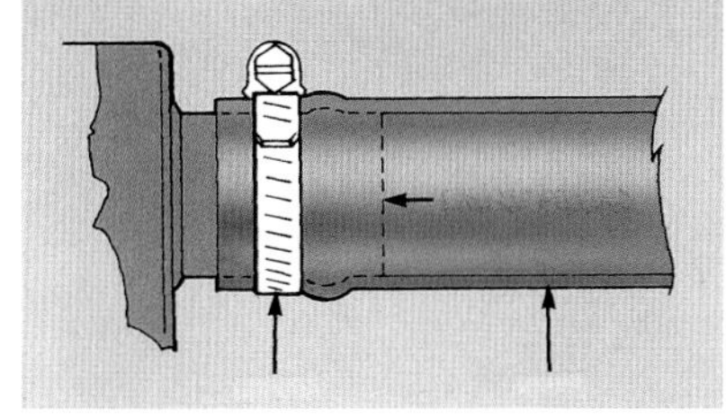

Why does a coolant hose connection leak after you've tightened a conventional clamp? After all, the clamp itself doesn't loosen. What happens is this: Both the hose neck and the hose expand when the coolant warms up. The clamp, however, is relatively unchanged, so it squeezes the rubber underneath even more, and this causes the rubber to become permanently compressed, which is called a set. When the engine cools, the neck contracts more than the hose. Many hose materials become virtually glued to the neck, so a seal is maintained. Others do not. In fact, silicone is almost immune to heat-sealing. That makes the silicone hose easy to replace, but it is the most prone to cold coolant leakage. Always install the clamp next to, but not overlapping, the raised bead on the fitting to keep from trapping a bubble of coolant in the void space inboard of the bead.

seal, and if it ever leaks, you have something else—one or two O-rings—to check and replace.

Every quick-connect comes off a bit differently, but it's usually obvious. On GM pickups you unthread a retainer, then turn a metal tab that provides a secondary hold and pull the hose. The hose end is a plastic fitting with O-ring seals. Just peel them off and install new ones. Clean out any debris from inside the female metal fitting on the engine.

So if the leak is from the quick-connect, get a replacement from the car dealer, then just pry open and remove the old quick-connect's permanent clamp and install the new quick-connect on the hose.

If you can't get a new quick-connect, you may be able to cut through a metal section in a long underbody coolant line, install a short hose section (secure it with some form of constant-tension clamps), and that should give you the extra hose length at the end that has the leaking quick-connect. Then you should be able to remove the quick-connect and make a hose-to-metal fitting clamp joint.

The Hoses

Many of today's hoses, particularly for the heater circuit, have crimped-on sections, and crimps are known to leak. A brand-new hose is a simple but expensive solution. An alternative is to grind or saw into the crimp, just enough to be able to break it apart.

Even without crimp sections, the coolant hoses themselves are anything but simple, flexible lines of rubber. On cars with pressurized coolant reservoirs (where the cap is on the reservoir, not the radiator or engine), the upper radiator hose typically has a tee fitting with a secondary hose to the reservoir (and the lower hose may have one to the heater circuit). So unless a repair tee is available, don't be surprised if the hose prices out at $100. Other hoses (also not cheap) are permanently crimped to metal lines, much like an air conditioning line or power steering hose. And even where there is a simple-looking hose, it may be a molded design, so that it fits into a very tight area (perhaps so it can connect to a metal line) without the possibility of kinking.

THEY MAKE SPECIAL PLIERS for wire-band constant-tension hose clamps, but ordinary pliers will usually get them free. It's a lot tougher in constricted areas, though.

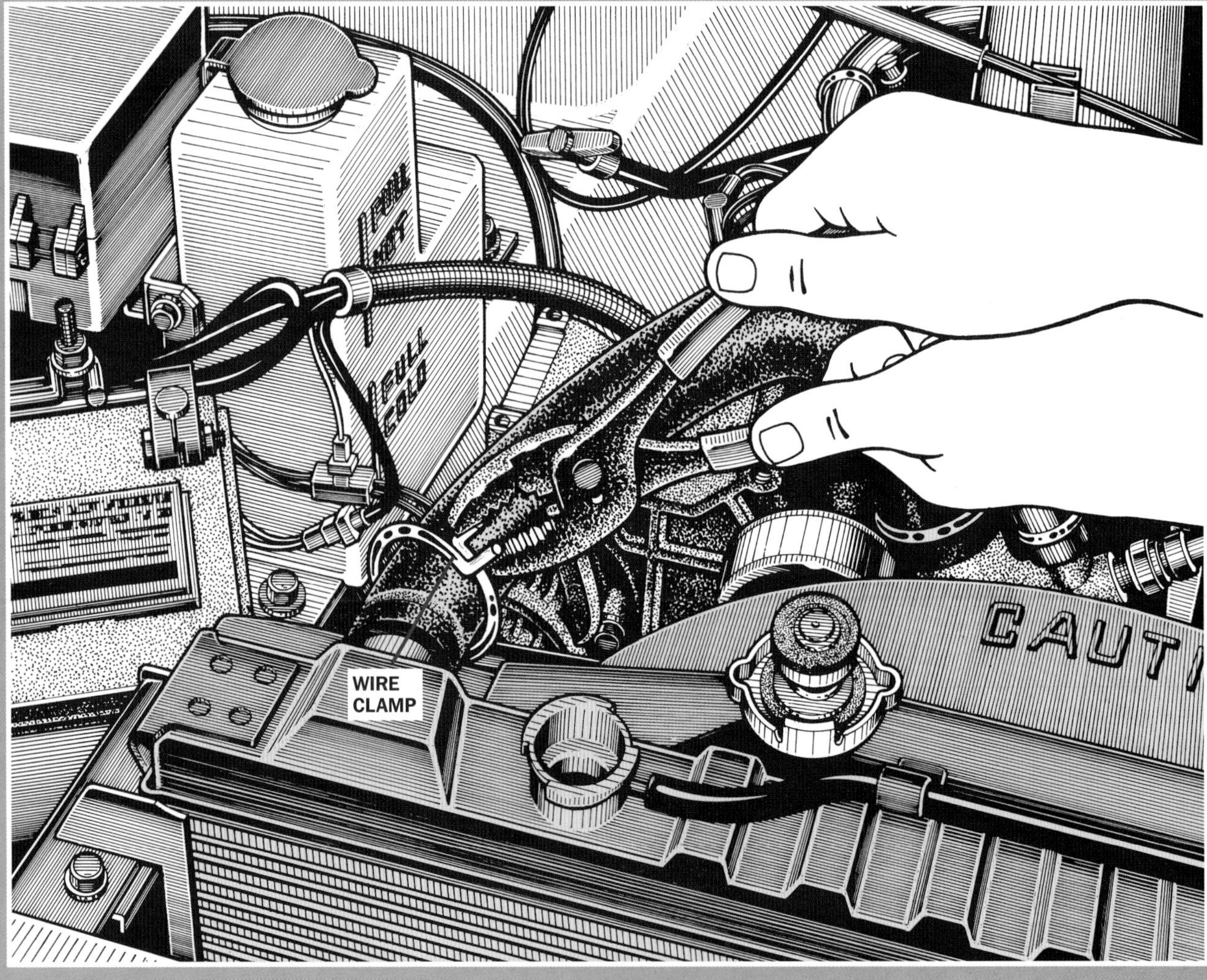

Curing Slow Cranking

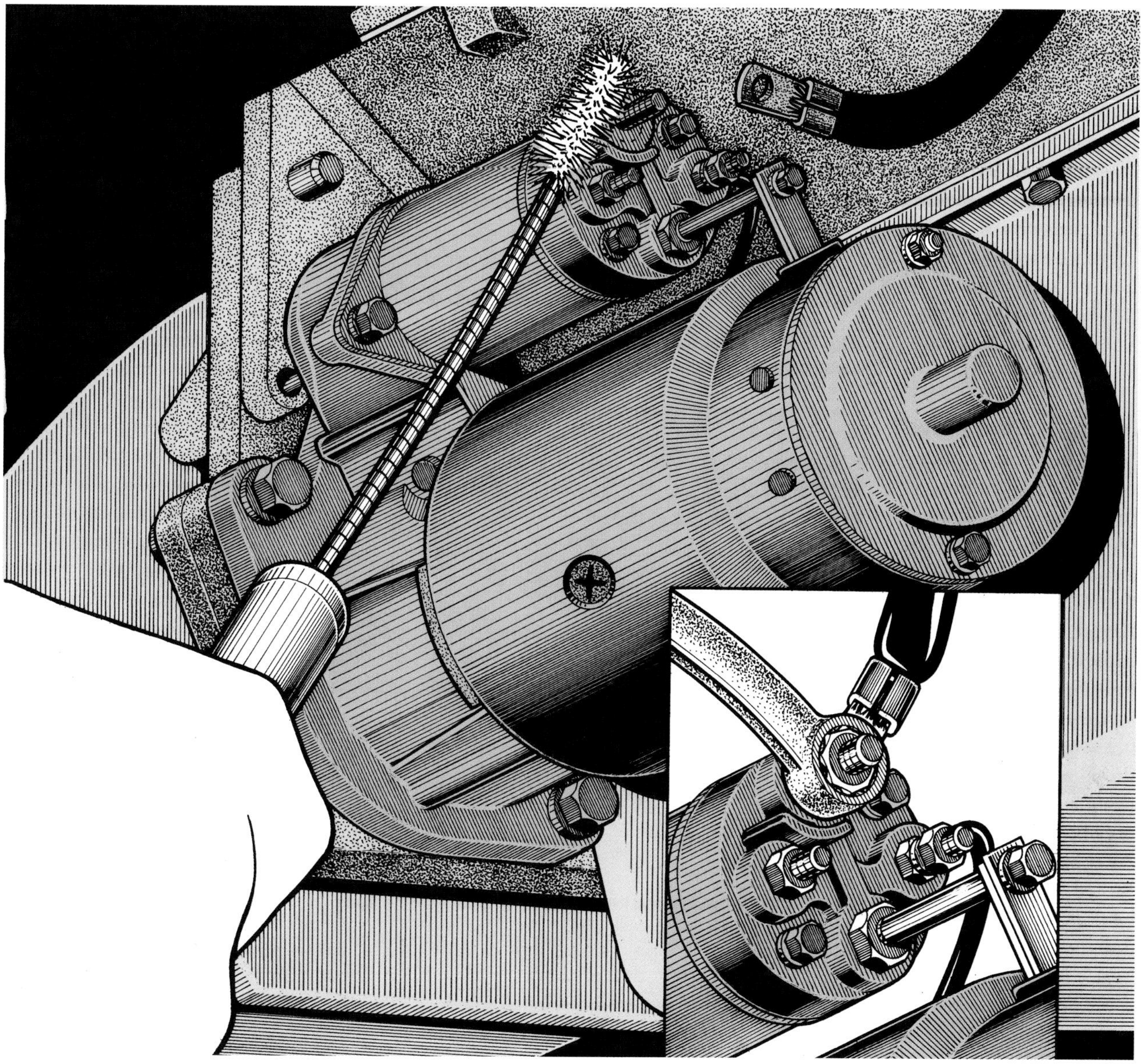

(Fig. 1) **Remove the wires from the starter motor or solenoid and clean off any corrosion with a wire brush and warm water. Rinse thoroughly and reassemble. Smear protective grease on the terminals to keep them clean.**

You've just treated your date and yourself to a postprandial double-caf no-fat cappuccino, and the caffeine courses through your veins like lava. You're pumped for a night of dancing as you head for the nightclub. The world seems to be in slow motion as the caffeine hits your brain—especially when you twist the key and your car engine grinds over very slowly, far too slowly for the engine to start.

The ugh-ugh-ugh of an engine that's cranking too slow to start is a sound that everyone can identify. And the immediate—if temporary—cure is to call for a battery boost. The long-term fix, however, requires careful examination to make a diagnosis.

Thinking Positively

If the battery positive-cable terminal on the starter is easily visible, begin by inspecting it for white/green corrosion and feeling the cable end for a loose connection. A wire-brushing to remove corrosion from the stud, nut and cable terminal, or just a tightening, may be the simple fix (**Fig. 1**). Perhaps the cable terminal has become loose because at some time it had been reinstalled on damaged starter-stud threads, or the nut had been cross-threaded when installed. Poor-quality rebuilts, used starters, goofs during cable or starter replacement are some of the usual suspects. In fact, these problems are so common that you can buy an inexpensive (less than $5) starter-terminal repair stud kit at auto parts stores. This cuts its own threads as it is threaded onto a stripped stud (example: Thexton Nos. 530 and 531). See page 89.

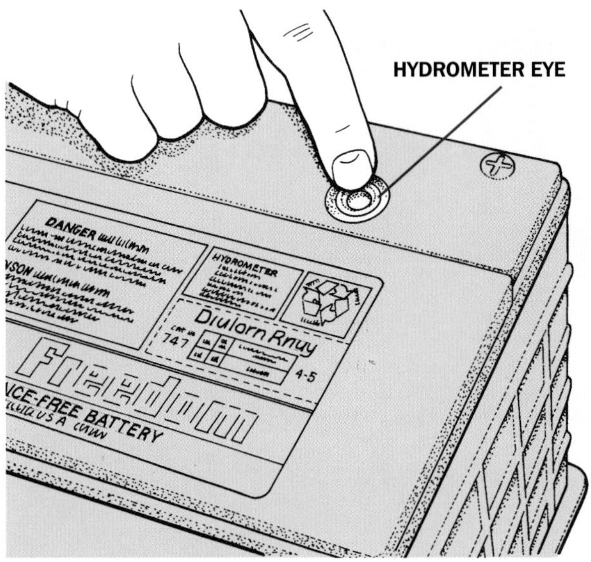

(Fig. 2) Check the battery's hydrometer eye for enough electrolyte or low charge.

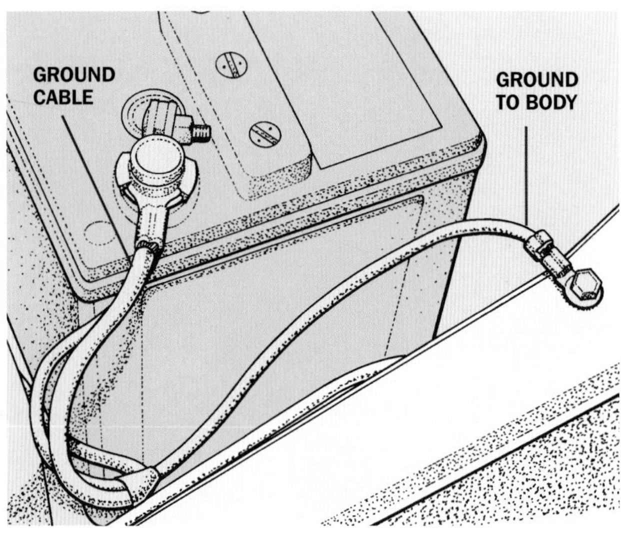

(Fig. 3) Check the ground connection to the vehicle's body for good contact.

Having a Heat Wave?

When the slow cranking occurs only on a hot restart in warm weather, you have to consider the possibility of high internal resistance in the starter, which is often caused by underhood heat. Some starters are factory-equipped with heat shields, particularly those in recreational vehicles, and the shield may have been bent or taken off and never reinstalled. Or it could just be that the starter wasn't designed to handle the heat well—a problem both with some original-equipment starters and with rebuilts that may fit physically but aren't designed to take the heat of a heavy-duty application.

If the engine starts easily after it cools off, the starter is one possibility. An easy check is to spray the starter with cold water if you get slow cranking during a hot restart. Now it cranks well? If there's no missing heat shield, check with a dealer to find out if a heavy-duty starter with better hot-starting ability is available.

If there's no sign of a problem at the starter, or if it's buried and you want to begin somewhere else, then move on to the battery. But we're not really giving the starter a passing grade just yet.

Batteries Not Included

Discard the old advice that says a small, cheap battery is adequate for a 4-cylinder, and only a big V8 needs a battery with a high energy rating. When you crank an engine, the electronics all wake up and the air starts flowing through the throttle body into the cylinders. It takes much higher cranking speeds to produce the necessary airflow through the complex flow paths to start today's Fours. And with the power demands of the electronics and the fuel system, a light-duty battery just can't hack it.

So if the old battery died and you installed the lowest-price replacement you could get, that could be the reason behind the slow cranking. In the days of carburetors, the battery-rating rule was one cold-cranking amp for each cubic inch of engine displacement. Well, we talk about liters for displacement today, but even if you look for 61 cold-cranking amps per liter, that's just not enough. There's hardly any late-model engine—or any engine—that will start reliably in all conditions with a battery rated at under 500 cold-cranking amps.

Also, you can't just look at the battery to determine its condition, even a battery with the circular window ("eye") in the top **(Fig. 2)**. That eye is over just one of the six cells. That cell might be okay—and you'll see a dark green, the indication of health—while there's weakness in another cell. Maybe you're ready to blame the battery because you can't see the "healthy" color. Try tapping on the eye before you start shopping for a new battery. The color may change.

The only reliable check is a load test, which requires a special tester. However, at least you can check the battery voltage with a meter connected across the battery terminals. But don't just look for something over 12 volts because it's a 12-volt system. If it's under 12.7 to 12.8 volts, the battery is undercharged, and at 12 volts it's 75% discharged. Yes, discharged.

If the battery is undercharged, you have to find out why. With the engine running at fast idle, you should check charging voltage across the battery terminals. If the voltage isn't well over 13, something's wrong. Unless there's a loose or glazed belt you can plainly see, inspect the battery-cable connections to make sure they're clean and tight. You can't see what the contact surfaces of side terminals look like without taking them apart. An almost-invisible coating of corrosion can constitute a charging barrier, so wire-brush them even if they appear good. Then, recheck the charging voltage.

If charging voltage still is low, inspect the other end of the ground (negative) cable. If the ground cable is a split design, the cable to the vehicle's body or chassis may be the easiest to see. But it has less to do with charging and starting, so more carefully check—and tighten if necessary—the cable to the engine, which may not be quite as accessible. Warning: Some cars have just a single ground cable from the battery to the body (**Fig. 3**). But don't stop there. Somewhere else on the car there will be a second strap, from the body to the engine or transmission (**Fig. 4**). It may even be buried underneath the car, so look around.

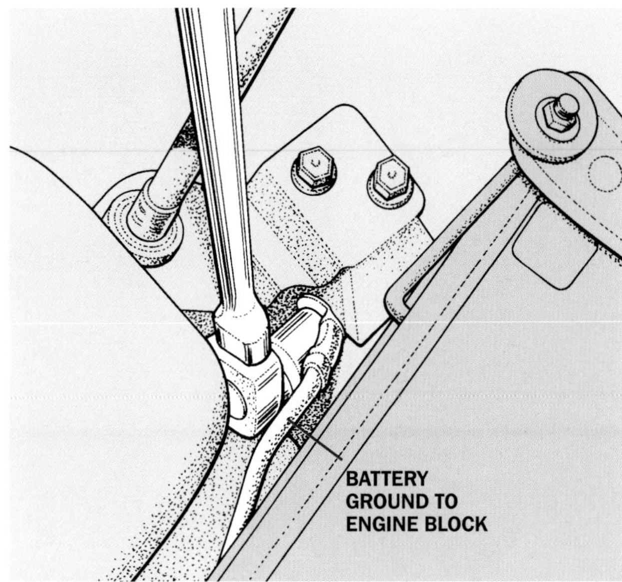

(Fig. 4) Check the ground connection to the vehicle's engine for contact as well.

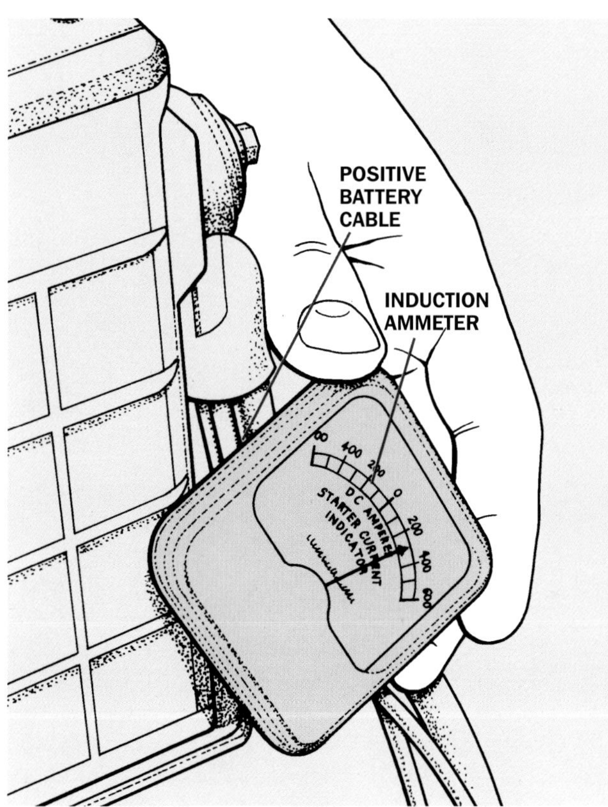

(Fig. 5) You can monitor the cranking current with an inexpensive induction ammeter.

With a fully charged battery, you're ready to find out if the starter circuit is pulling normal current. A low-cost induction ammeter (**Fig. 5**), which clips onto the battery cable, may not be a precision instrument, but it's close enough to pinpoint excessive current draw. Compare the reading with factory specs, if they exist. If they don't, here's a general guideline: Average starter draw is 150 to 200 amps, with 250 at the high end of normal.

Oil Is Thicker Than Water

When all the battery connections are good, there are two common causes of high draw: engine/transmission friction and a bad starter.

In cold weather, the friction may be caused by engine oil that's too thick. If you were using a few cans of oil-thickening additive during the summer to try to cure an oil-pressure problem, poor compression and so on, and haven't changed the oil since, you should do it before the cold weather hits.

If the vehicle has a manual transmission but can normally be cranked in Neutral without having the clutch pedal floored, a thick gear oil may be slowing down engine cranking. The thick gear oil may silence gear noise during warm weather, but by winter you may need something much lighter, both for easier starting and better shift quality. Some carmakers recommend automatic transmission fluid in a manual transmission oil for cold weather. Throw in the clutch pedal and if the engine now cranks normally, that's the tipoff. Check the owner's manual for acceptable lubes.

In hot weather, engine friction has the opposite cause: engine oil that's too thin. If you don't change the oil frequently enough, the additives in it will wear out and the oil won't provide the thin-film lubrication the cylinder walls need. Synthetic oils are better at maintaining their lubricity, but they're also slightly more expensive.

In addition, if your engine is running on the hot side—not overheating, just running a bit hotter than it should—that thins out the oil a bit more. The extra engine heat also may heat up the starter, which then will draw more current than normal. If the coolant temperature gauge is reading on the high side, get a precise reading, and if it's pushing 245°F or even 250°F, that's just too high.

When everything else seems all right, make the following checks:

- Is the ignition timing being upset by electromagnetic interference from the battery cables during engine cranking? This is most likely to happen if the battery or ignition wiring has been moved, even slightly, during service. Perhaps a cable wasn't reinserted in a clip or guide. A simple check is to disconnect the ignition primary wiring, such as from a distributor or distributorless ignition module (**Fig. 6**). If the engine now cranks faster, look for a mislocated cable. If the engine has a conventional distributor, also lift the cap to see if it's cracked or has carbon tracks between terminals. Either could disturb spark-plug firing enough to affect cranking.
- If the battery and ignition pass inspection, and the slow-cranking problem came on suddenly, check to see if the camshaft-timing belt jumped a tooth or two (**Fig. 7**). Unless they snap, timing chains are almost-forever items. However, a belt can jump a couple of teeth, and more than half of overhead-camshaft engines have belts, not chains. When a belt jumps time to advance valve timing, this can keep the engine from cranking and starting smoothly. If the cranking sounds unevenly slow and the engine seems to be trying to start but won't, valve timing definitely moves to the top of the list of possibilities.

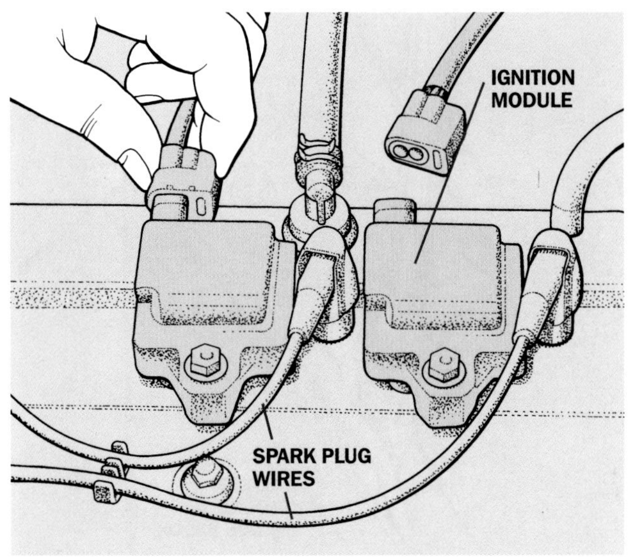

(Fig. 6) Pull the primary wiring to the ignition module or coil to check for misfires during engine cranking.

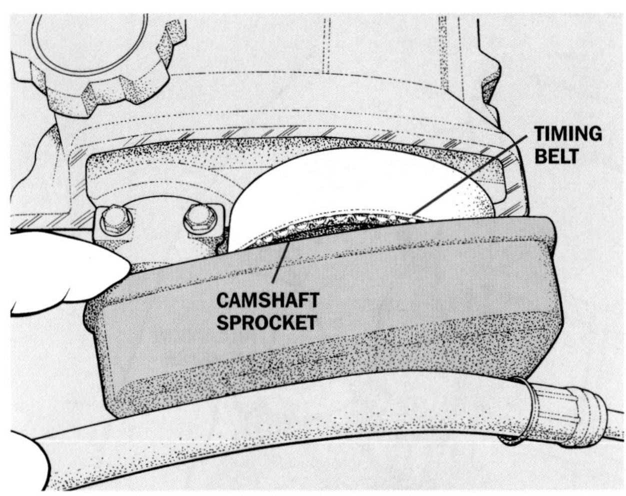

(Fig. 7) A camshaft drive belt can jump a tooth or two and affect cam timing and cause slow cranking.

Access to the belt on a transverse engine may not be easy, and checking the cam timing rarely is a 5-minute operation. Even the old Chrysler 2.2/2.5-liter 4-cylinder, which was one of the easiest to get to (thanks to an access window in the timing belt's upper cover), takes a bit longer than that.

On most cars, it is fairly easy to take off or at least substantially loosen the upper-half belt cover, gently flex it away and inspect the belt. If you see damaged belt teeth, that's a strong indication that belt timing may be off, and it's worth the extra effort of a timing check and a more careful belt inspection. Few late-model overhead-cam engines are "free-wheeling" (capable of tolerating a snapped belt without major engine damage). If you find the belt is near the end of its life and has jumped time, too, you not only could cure slow cranking, but save the engine or at least a cylinder head. And if the belt hasn't jumped but is well-worn, replacing it is great insurance, so you really haven't lost anything with the effort.

EASY

Finding Oil Leaks

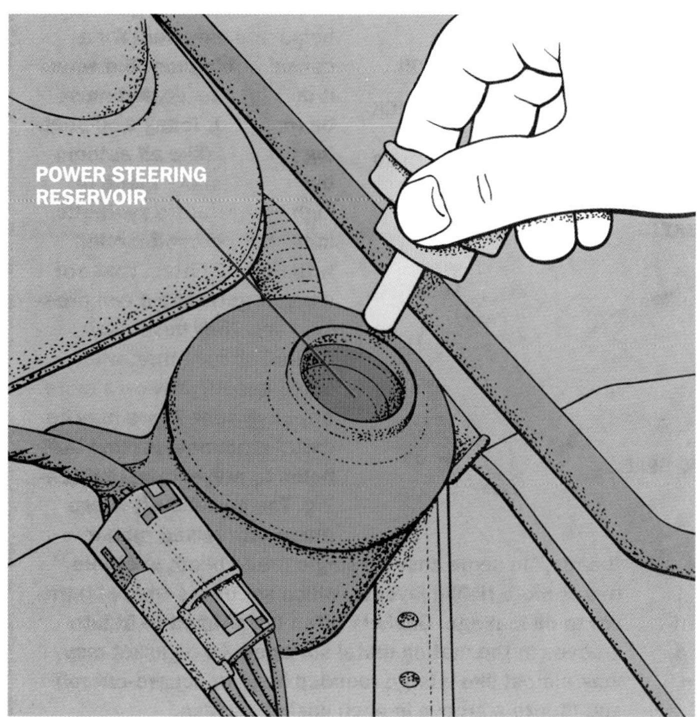

(Fig. 1) Check the dipsticks to see where your leak is starting.

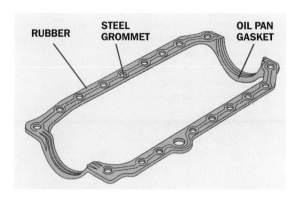

(Fig. 2) Oil pan gaskets may be a simple cork cutout or a pricey engineered rubber molding with metal inserts.

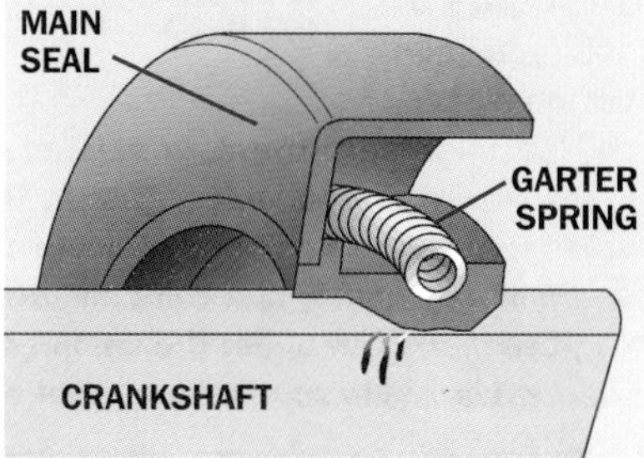

(Fig. 3) A leaky main seal will spray oil all over, and will need to be replaced.

Your tabby cat crawls into your lap, purring. Nice, but there's a huge patch of smelly, slimy, oily goo covering most of its back. Ick. Backtracking oily little catprints leads you into the garage, where a pool of oleaginous fluid has mysteriously stained the concrete floor. What is it and exactly what part of your car is oozing it? Time to put the cat down and get under the car. But there's leakage all over the engine compartment, and even a distinct pattern of windblown drops freckling the trunklid. Where's it coming from?

Begin by finding out what kind of oil is leaking. You can usually determine the color by putting a few drops on a sheet of white paper. Normally, engine oil turns black. Automatic transmission and power steering fluid is red but may discolor to brown or even be so dark that you can't tell it from engine oil. Washer fluid is blue and antifreeze is, well, it could be green, gold, orange, brown or blue, depending on the supplier. Feel the fluid. If it's very oily, it's lubricant. Antifreeze may have a light oiliness.

Your initial analysis points to oil, but you're not sure about the color or where it's coming from. Start pulling dipsticks. The power steering reservoir is a good place to start if the oil seems reddish (**Fig. 1**). If the reservoir is topped up, and the leak is at the front, check the automatic transmission cooler lines, particularly if they have sections of rubber hose with clamps.

If the oil is definitely black and the drops are directly under the engine, it's engine oil, which is the most common leak. But, once again, you're faced with that same question: Where is it coming from? A slow leak follows ribs on the engine block, is blown along the top of gasket joints, and oil gets everywhere. Put a lot of light in the engine compartment and take a look. You might get lucky and see the source. But unless you're sure, don't replace anything yet. A lot of gaskets are not only tough to replace, but they have sophisticated designs that are anything but cheap (**Fig. 2**). It would be a shame to waste a day replacing a costly gasket and still have the leak.

Oil also may be seeping past a worn crankshaft or camshaft seal (**Fig. 3**). The rubber lip that seals to the rotating shaft will eventually wear to the point at which the tension in the garter spring won't keep oil from leaking. This type of seal will only leak when the engine is running—and when it does oil will spray everywhere from the spinning shaft.

Because pinpointing an engine oil leak can be difficult, you should get all the help you can and, fortunately, a method preferred by the professionals is within easy reach: trace dyes

HOW IT WORKS

Gaskets

When you look at a pair of machined surfaces, or even today's well-finished engine surfaces, you may wonder why a gasket, an O-ring or other type of seal is needed to prevent an oil leak. Except for seals around rotating parts, wouldn't clamping the parts together tightly be enough to prevent oil leakage?

The answer: close, but no. Sorry, even mating joints bolted together look a lot more precise than they really are, and fluids can seep past them. It takes a flexible material in the joint to compensate for any unevenness and looseness to prevent, or at least minimize, leakage. That flexible material is a gasket. The design of a gasket itself is a complex art. Simple materials such as cork compress nicely and compensate for a fair amount of unevenness, but under the compression of a line of bolts, cork gaskets soon take a "heat set," also called a "compression set." Retightening gaskets helps and may work for a considerable time. But when it doesn't, the gasket must be replaced. Today's oil-sealing gaskets (like all automotive gaskets) are made of high-temperature synthetic materials, in combination with natural fibers, that are more resistant to a compression set. They have engineered shapes that, when compressed, provide a more effective seal. There may be metal grommets around bolt holes to prevent overtightening. The gaskets often are made with raised rubber "beads," in some cases a single broad bead, in others, two or more riblike layouts, which set up a series of barriers to oil leakage. Gaskets often are shaped to fit into grooves in the mating metal surfaces. Or a gasket may look almost like a large rounded band or square-cut rail and fit into a groove in each gasket surface.

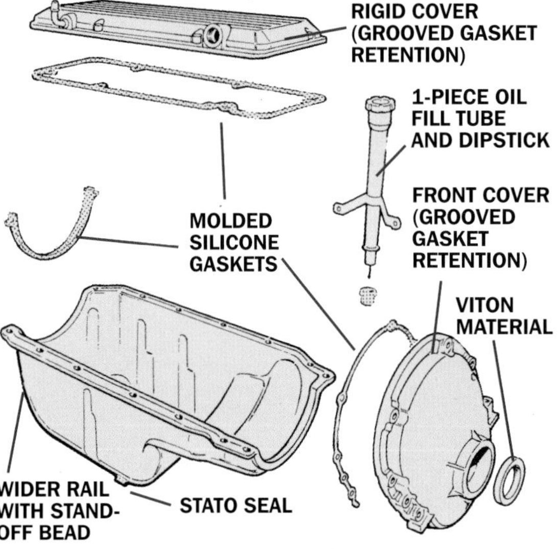

with ultraviolet (UV) light (**Fig. 4**). These can be used for all fluids—oils, fuel, coolant, even a/c refrigerants. The trace dye is fluorescent, so under UV light (so-called black light), it produces an unmistakable yellow/green glow. Aim the light, and a small dye stain may show you the source of the leak. The newest trace dyes were formulated in response to complaints from mechanics about low visibility of the dyes and the difficulty of positioning the large UV lamps. Now you can find kits with compact, flexible lamps, improved trace dyes and coated yellow glasses that enhance the appearance of the dye.

The kits typically include two bottles of dye, one for oils and another for antifreeze/coolant. The trace dyes for a/c refrigerants are very specific formulations, and they require special injectors. They are not part of the general purpose kits, but are sold in specific a/c kits.

We used the Tracer Products Leak-Finder Kit, a product that won a *Popular Mechanics* Editor's Choice Award at the 2000 Automotive Aftermarket Industry Week trade show. It's under $60 and includes a compact UV lamp with a flexible head, so it can be aimed into all sorts of underhood nooks and crannies. It also comes with a 10-ft. cord that has alligator clips to connect to the battery terminals, yellow glasses, and 1-ounce bottles of trace dyes for both oils and antifreeze/ coolant. You can buy individual bottles of any trace dye you use up.

Start by mixing a dose of oil-leak trace dye (½ ounce, which is half the amount in the see-through bottle) with as much engine oil as you have left in your top-up bottle, then pour that into the engine. You could just pour the 1⁄2-ounce dose into the engine, but if there's a leak you're probably down on oil anyway. If you just pour in the trace dye dose, it will coat the oil filler neck, and take a lot longer to be washed away by engine oil and mixed thoroughly into the oil supply. And it will take longer for the leak to show up.

(Fig. 4) Ultraviolet light will make trace dyes glow brightly.

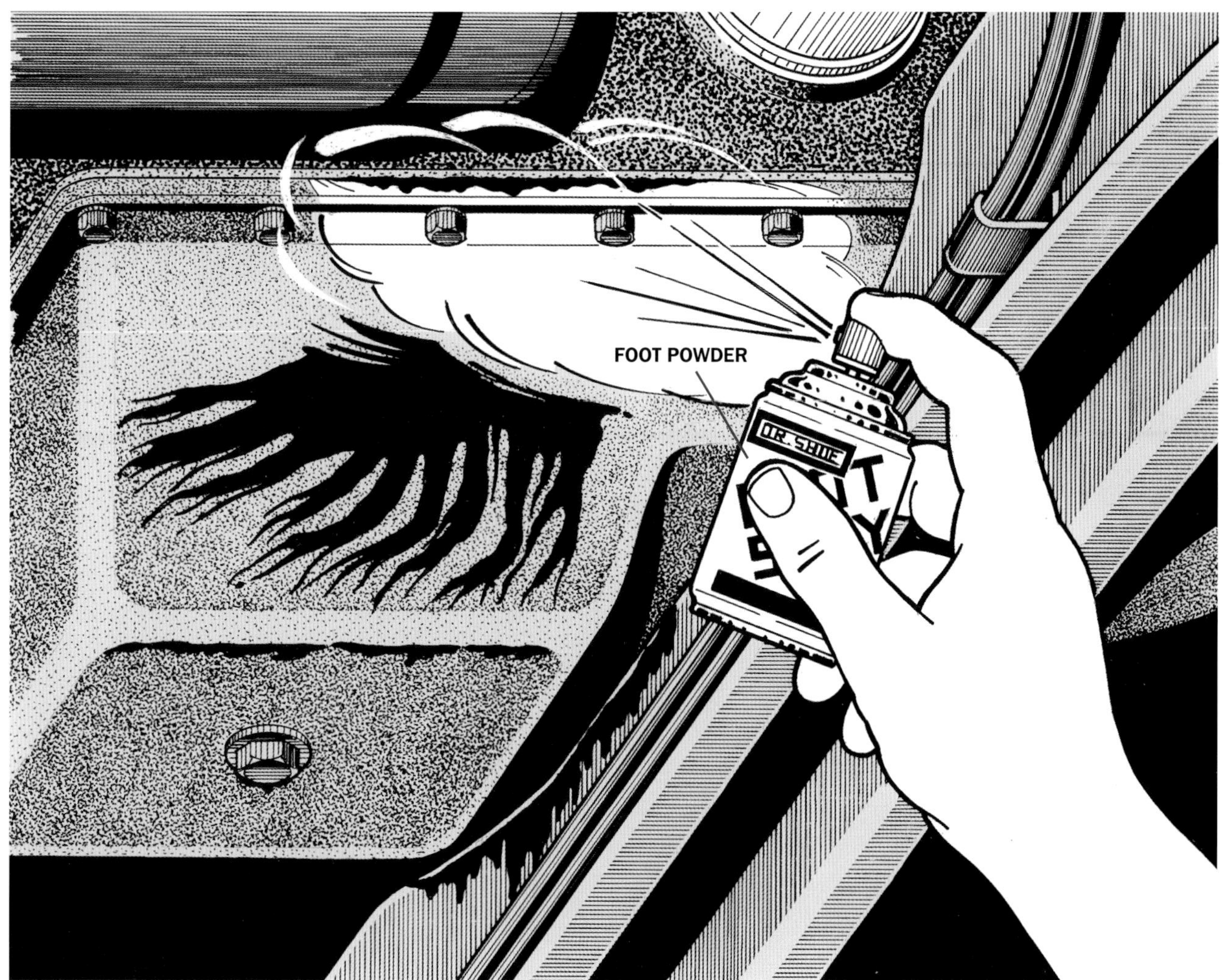

(Fig. 5) Clean the suspected area thoroughly and dry it. Coat liberally with powder to locate seepage.

After driving the car long enough to allow oil leakage, park the car over newspaper to catch the leaking oil. Check the drops on the paper with the UV lamp. If the drops glow, you're ready to look for the leak. Jack up the vehicle, support it on safety stands and connect the lamp clips to the battery. Then, put on the yellow glasses, aim the light up from underneath and press the switch.

Because leaking oil may follow a twisty path, look for the highest point of any oil trace, and that should lead you to the source. In our case, the path started at the oil dipstick tube, which had a leaking O-ring seal. In most cases, you'll find a loose gasket joint, which you may be able to tighten. However, in many cases, the gasket will have taken a severe "set" in the joint, and retightening won't stop the leak.

If you don't want to make the investment in a trace dye kit, there is an alternative method for finding a leak. You can use a couple of products you may already have at home—one in the garage, one in the medicine cabinet.

The garage item is aerosol engine degreaser/cleaner. Use the aerosol cleaner to loosen road film, then remove the film from the engine, transmission and adjacent underbody with a water hose. Drive the vehicle to dry it off—or when you jack it up and support it on safety stands, wipe the area clean and dry with a cloth. That's what you may have to do anyway to remove a lot of the road film. The objective is to clean the underbody well enough so road film and leaking black oil aren't confused.

From the medicine cabinet, get aerosol powder, such as that used to treat athlete's foot, and spray the underside of the general area of the leak, going as high up the block as possible (**Fig. 5**). The powder will adhere to and coat the metal, producing a white haze. Then, drive the vehicle until the oil leaks—be careful to avoid wet, muddy roads in the process. The hope here is that the leak will take a single large, reasonably direct downward path (even if there are some streaks from airflow). If it does, it will show up as a primary "stream" down the engine. You may have to perform a similar treatment closer to the top of the engine to really pinpoint some leaks, particularly those from intake manifold gaskets. However, if the oil stream is blown through a complex path along the engine before a drop hits the ground, using a trace dye and UV light is a surer way.

Flushing Your Cooling System

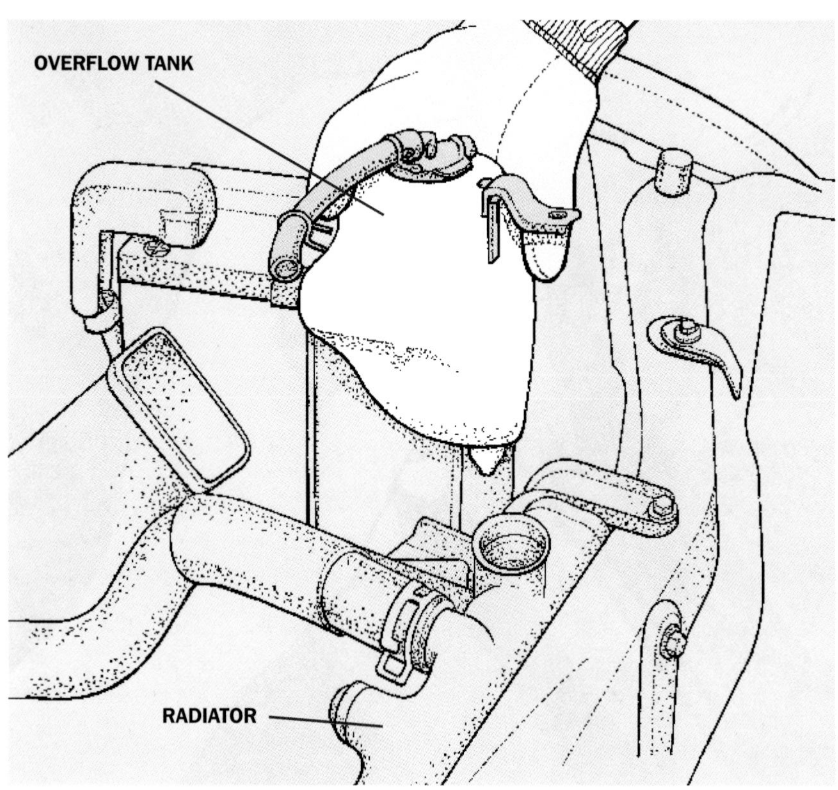

(Fig. 1) Remove the overflow tank, and carefully pour the coolant in it into your drain pan.

You take off the cap and look at the coolant. It's a nice shade of green, or maybe red, or maybe even orange. It looks good. Should you leave it in? Unless it's recommended by the vehicle or coolant maker for extended life, the answer is no, especially if it's been two years or more since the last time you drained it.

Today's engines are loaded with aluminum components: cylinder heads, water pumps, manifolds, even engine blocks. And the two primary heat exchangers—radiator and heater—are also aluminum. Aluminum needs great corrosion protection to survive, and the corrosion protection in conventional antifreeze is used up in about two years. If your car came with conventional, you can't switch to extended life without a fair amount of preparation. And if your car is much more than four years old, a switch is not likely to yield long-term coolant life—you'd still face the usual 2-year drain interval.

Glug, glug

First, let's do a proper job of draining the coolant. Start by checking the specs to see how much is in the system. This is important, because capacities vary all over the lot. Some Toyota Fours and V6s, for example, hold only about 5½ quarts. Other systems hold 14 to 18 quarts. This way, you'll know what percentage of the coolant drains out.

Start with a cool engine. If the pressure cap is on the engine or radiator, look at the overflow reservoir (**Fig. 1**), and if it's easy to disconnect and empty, go ahead. Then, remove the radiator cap and open the radiator drain cock. If the drain cock is in tight quarters, use a special socket available at most auto parts stores (**Fig. 2**). Let the coolant drain into a pan. Unless your town has a coolant collection setup, pour the old antifreeze into a household drain, clothes-

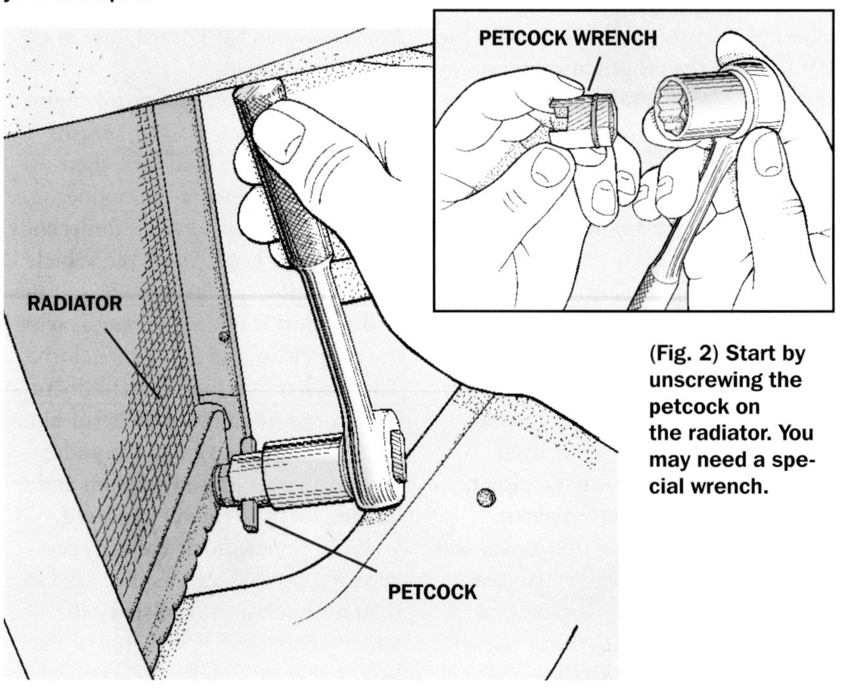

(Fig. 2) Start by unscrewing the petcock on the radiator. You may need a special wrench.

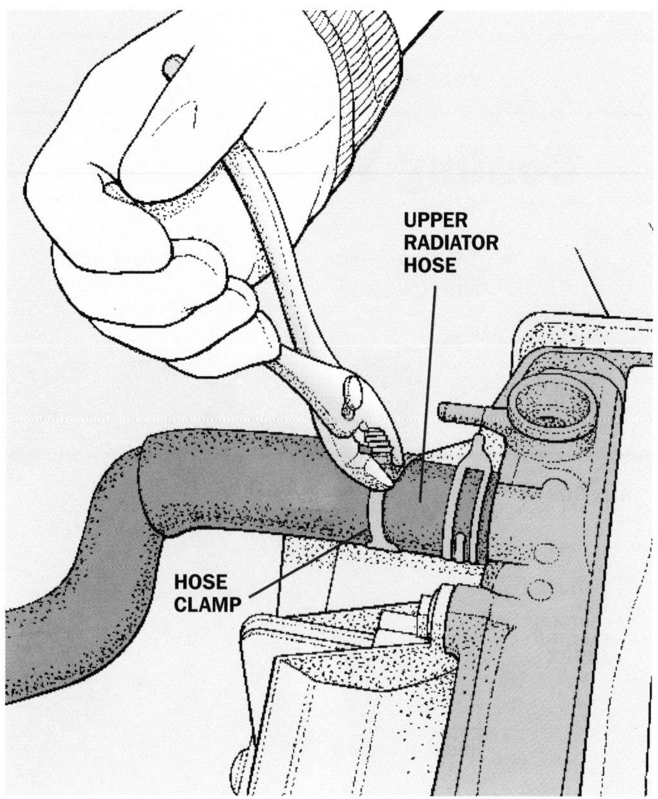

(Fig. 3) It may be necessary to remove the radiator hoses to completely drain the system. Remove the clamps and twist the hoses off.

washer pipe or a toilet. That's an environmentally safe approach. Don't pour it on the ground or into a storm sewer. If your car has a copper radiator or heater core, the coolant may be contaminated with lead solder. Many municipalities have hazardous-waste disposal facilities that will take it. Also, in most of the United States it's illegal for professional mechanics to dump used coolant, so you may be able to take it to a shop or the municipality for recycling.

Next, move the dashboard temperature lever to HOT, so if your car happens to have a heater coolant control valve, it will open. If the pressure cap is on the plastic reservoir, remove the cap, then open the drain cock. No radiator drain cock? Disconnect the lower radiator hose from the radiator (Fig. 3). Move the hose clamp back from the radiator neck, slip a thin screwdriver between the hose end and radiator neck to free up the hose, then twist slightly to disconnect the hose. Draining the radiator alone normally should remove 40 to 45% of the coolant. After the first drain, fill the system with water, then warm up the engine and let it cool. Drain the radiator again and fill it once more with water. Repeat. Or remove engine coolant drain plugs if they're not corroded in place.

Let it bleed

Now comes the hard part—filling the system. If the system holds 12 quarts, you want to install 6 quarts of undiluted antifreeze, or exactly half of the cooling system's capacity (Fig. 4).

The cooling system has lots of nooks and crannies that trap air, making it difficult to fill the system with coolant. The fill cap and neck are supposed to be at the high point of the system to help air bleed out, but often they aren't. And even if they are, you need all the natural help you can get. So jack up the front of the car, which gets the coolant fill neck as high as possible.

Check for air bleeds on the engine. Sometimes you'll see an obvious air bleed, such as a boltlike item threaded into a hose. If there's an air bleed, open it. If there are several, open them all. If you have access to factory or after-market service information for your car, check it for a coolant fill procedure.

Pour in the required amount of antifreeze slowly until you see coolant oozing out of the open air bleeds. Then close the bleeds and top off the system with the remaining antifreeze and then plain water.

(Fig. 4) Refill the system to half its capacity with coolant. Then add water to fill, achieving a 50 percent concentration of coolant. Check the concentration with a hydrometer.

HOW IT WORKS

Cooling Your Engine

A coolant pump, or water pump, circulates the antifreeze and water mixture between the engine and the radiator. After the coolant circulates through the engine, the pump pushes it out the upper radiator hose into the radiator, a heat exchanger made of metal tubes (aluminum on today's cars) to which fins are attached. The fins draw away heat and dissipate it to the air that is drawn through the radiator by fans and the forward motion of the car. The cooled coolant is drawn from the radiator through the lower radiator hose and back into the engine by the pump, and the cycle starts all over again.

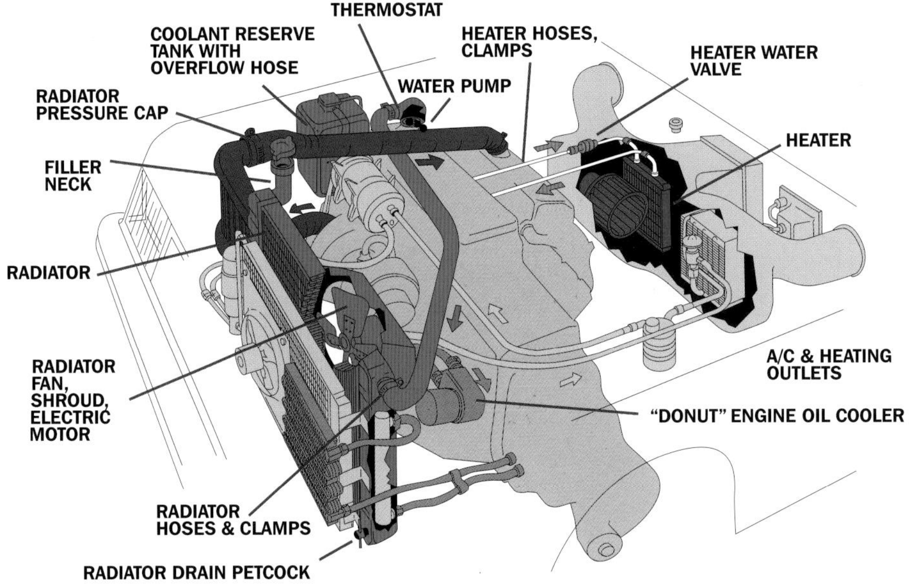

When the engine is cold, coolant circulates only within the engine, so engine heat warms it up faster. At about 195° F, the coolant heats a temperature-sensitive valve (the thermostat) that opens to allow the coolant to flow through the radiator. The thermostat may be located at the engine outlet, in line with the upper radiator hose, or at the inlet to the water pump (the preferred location on today's cars).

The coolant also flows through hoses into and out of the heater, which, like a miniature radiator, gives up its heat to the surrounding air. In this case, however, the heated air is blown into the passenger compartment.

Raising the cooling system's pressure also raises the coolant's boiling point, so the radiator cap (which also could be on the engine or on the separate reservoir) has a pressure valve to raise the pressure in the cooling system by about 15 psi. This increases the boiling point of the coolant by about 40° F. So, the boiling point of a 50/50 mix of antifreeze and water in a properly functioning system is about 265° F or higher.

If the system has a heater coolant valve, close it by moving the temperature control lever or knob to COLD. With the engine running at fast idle and warmed up, have a helper move the lever or knob to HOT while you listen at the coolant valve. If after the first rush of coolant you hear a continuous gurgling noise, there's still air in the coolant, and you should be prepared to watch the coolant level in the reservoir over the next few weeks.

Picking the right antifreeze

Most antifreeze is made with a base chemical called ethylene glycol. Green, yellow, red, orange, pink, and blue dye is used. The dye is not an indicator of the formula. Extended-life antifreezes, rated for four years/60,000 miles, were on the market until the mid-1990s. But the newest entries are superlong-life antifreezes with totally new rust/corrosion inhibitors, in some cases developed originally for diesels. The original, from Texaco (used as original equipment by GM), is called Dex-Cool. Other Dex-Cool antifreezes also are available from Prestone and Zerex, perhaps others. Dex-Cool is recomended for five years or 150,000 miles. Ford and Chrysler Group use a different antifreeze called a "hybrid," recommended for five years or 100,000 miles.

The rust/corrosion inhibitors vary, but if antifreeze is a major brand that is not extended life, but is in a car with a lot of aluminum components, change it in two years or 30,000 miles—whichever comes first. You can push that to a third year if the engine is all cast-iron. "Toyota Red" is a specific formula, but if you drain it, you can replace it with any name-brand American formula. Here again, the replacement interval is two years or 30,000 miles.

If you have at least 5000 miles on the antifreeze, the chemical bond with the aluminum components is "solid." So if you want to get extended life with a coolant installa-

THIS TIME-HONORED method of flushing your radiator is acceptable, but dispose of the used coolant into a sanitary sewer.

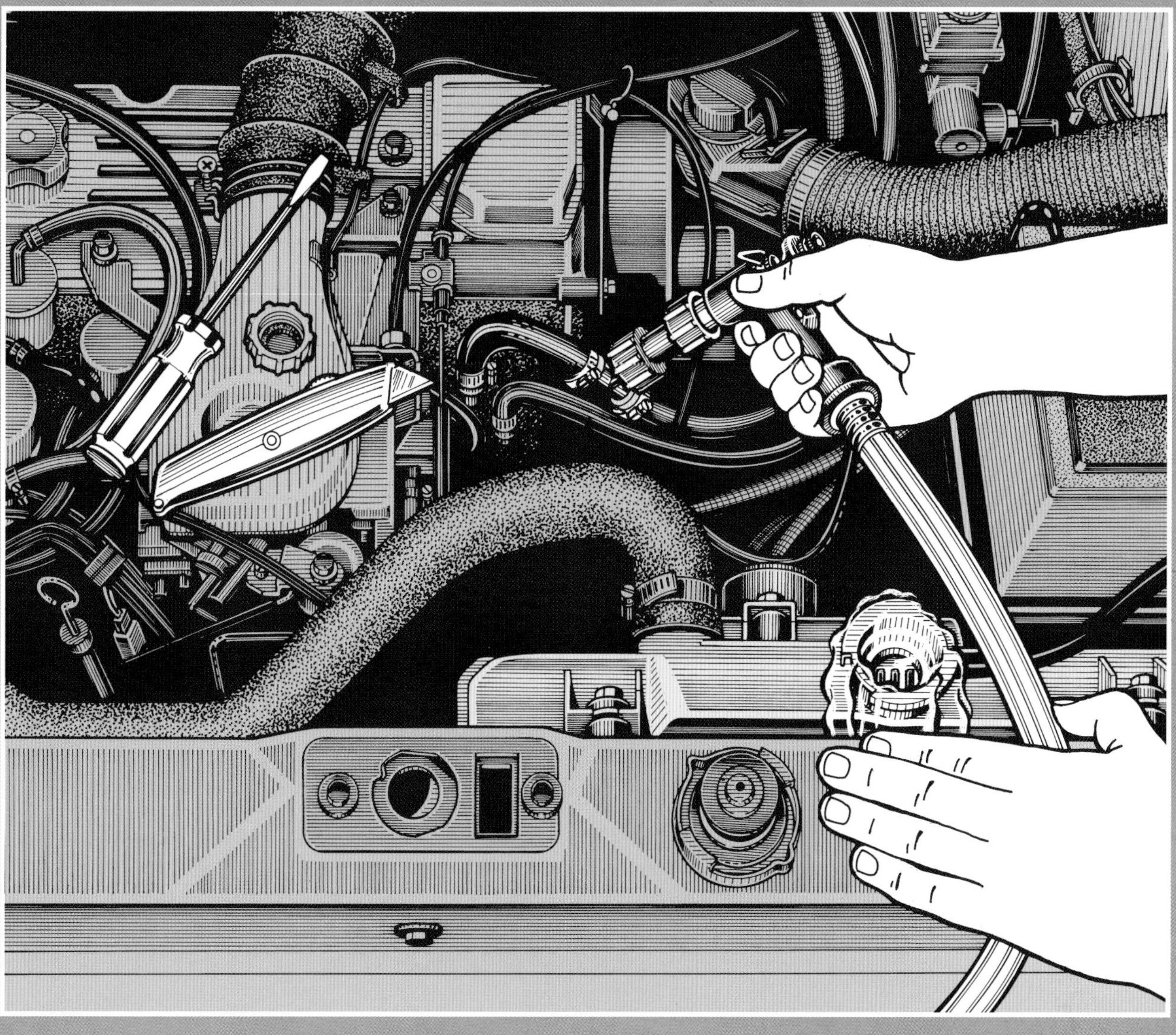

tion, just do a thorough drain-by-dilution, at least three times. The coolant you drain out should be virtually clear, like the color of water. If it's still colored, you have to repeat the process until it's all out.

With the radiator and reservoir drained, pour in the amount of antifreeze necessary—there should be plenty of room—and then top up with water. Follow the procedures we've discussed to ensure a full system.

Remember: You should do this only as a maintenance procedure, not as a final step when replacing a part, such as the water pump and radiator.

What about "pet-friendly" or "safer" antifreezes made with a base of propylene glycol? The name brands (Sierra and Prestone Lo-Tox) will do the same job as ethylene glycol. But they cost a little more and actually require a greater quantity to provide the same freeze protection, and in truth, they're only a bit less hazardous.

They aren't sweet, and consequently aren't as likely to be consumed by toddlers or pets. Don't rely on this, however. Store all unused coolant, low-tox or not, safely. Dispose of all drained coolant in a sanitary sewer or in accordance with local regulations.

EASY

Checking Your Ignition Timing

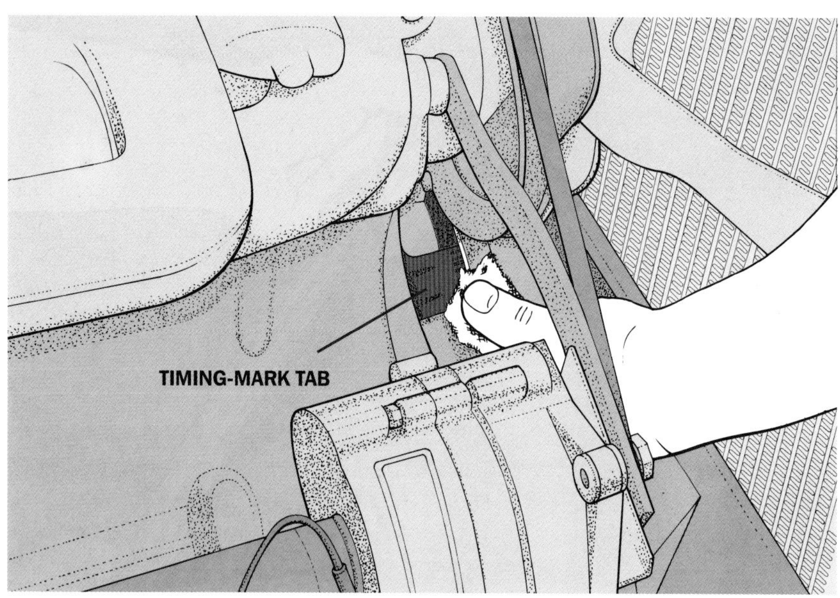

(Fig. 1) It's deep and dark in the engine compartment, and filthy to boot. On a cold engine, clean the timing tab and scale for better visibility.

You floor the accelerator to pull around a line of exit traffic, and you realize that your car is barely responding. A taxicab is camped half an inch from your rear bumper, and the cabby is alternating between using one of his fingers to semaphore his displeasure with your forward progress and leaning on the horn button. Your car's acceleration, nonetheless, remains a fraction of its former self. What could be wrong? The engine runs smoothly, but simply lacks power. There's no Check Engine light or trouble codes.

Pardon our asking, but when was the last time you checked the ignition timing? Ignition timing? Hey, you're driving a '97 model with a big, fast engine computer. All of those electronic gizmos handle that stuff, right?

Actually, you may need to dig out your old timing light and put it to use. Checking and, if necessary, adjusting ignition timing may have become lost skills, but a majority of cars and trucks on the road still have timing marks—and they weren't put there just for show.

If the sparks arrive at the plugs too early or too late, engine performance drops and the vehicle is likely to fail an emissions test. Sure, changes in ignition timing have been controlled by the engine computer on cars and light trucks for many years. However, the basic timing still has to be right.

There is a movement toward "coil on plug" ignition, eliminating spark plug wires (and the convenient attachment for the timing light) and the timing marks, too. If your engine has no marks, you'll have to check timing with a scan tester, which reads the sensor data processed by the computer. However, if there are marks, you can make the most meaningful check—the actual timing rather than a computer-processed signal.

If you have a car with a distributor, the timing probably is adjustable. It may have very little range for adjustment, but if you see any sign of a slot in the distributor's holes for the retaining bolts or nuts, timing can be reset.

Even if there is no distributor, there is a base timing specification, and if it's incorrect, the engine won't run right. The problem could be caused by a bad signal from a sensor or even by a bad computer, but unless you check the timing, you won't know.

Most pre-'96 models were equipped with an emissions diagnostic system called OBD (On-Board Diagnostics). A large number of these models, including two best-selling cars, Honda Accord and Toyota Camry, have adjustable ignition timing. In 1996, a far more sensitive, complex system called OBD II came into use. With either system, there's no guarantee that an ignition timing error will produce a Check Engine light or even a trouble code.

Checking ignition timing is a straightforward procedure—if you have a good timing light that's right for your car. The type you need depends on the type of timing marks on your engine. Get the timing spec from a shop manual or an after-market service information system.

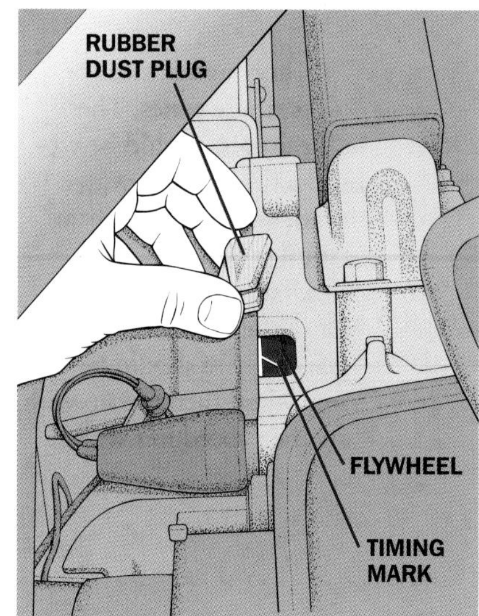

(Fig. 2) The timing mark on the flywheel may be under a dust cover or plug.

Finding Timing Marks

Locating the marks may not be easy if they're on the engine's front and are covered with dirt (**Fig. 1**). The marks may be found on an opening in the transmission bellhousing. (A rubber plug may be used to keep road film out of the bellhousing. Remove the plug for the timing check (**Fig. 2**).) Clean off the marks if necessary, and highlight the specified timing with a piece of chalk or white nail polish (**Fig.3**). Keep the highlight thin since a wide mark can span several degrees. You want the timing to be right on.

When a timing light is aimed at the timing marks with the engine running, a fixed mark should align with the illuminated mark on the spinning part, be it the crankshaft pulley or damper, or the flywheel. If the marks don't align, make the necessary adjustment of the distributor or go through a shop manual diagnostic procedure to find out if a sensor or the computer is bad.

If there's just a fixed point and a single line on the crankshaft damper or pulley, you probably can't check timing with a simple timing light. When those two marks are aligned, the timing is zero unless otherwise marked. Zero means the spark would arrive when the piston is at the very top of its stroke—"top dead center." The actual timing is typically some number of degrees before (or even after) top dead center. If there's no mark for that specification, all you'll see when the timing light flashes is that the two marks are some space apart. Is it the correct number of degrees? You need an adjustable timing light. With it, you can change the timing of the strobe light so that the light flashes earlier or later. You then read the dial or digital display to determine how many degrees you had to change the flashing of the timing light before the timing marks

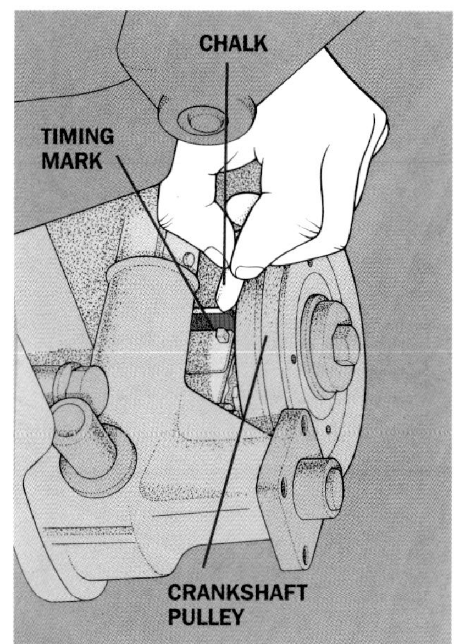

(Fig. 3) Chalk or light-colored touchup paint will make it easier to see the timing mark.

HOW IT WORKS

Distributorless Ignition

An electronic module with a double-ended ignition coil for each pair of companion cylinders is the most common type of distributorless ignition. The companions are cylinders with pistons that are in the same position in their respective cylinders at the same time—one on compression stroke ready for spark ignition, the other on exhaust. The coil module also contains electronic circuitry that communicates with the engine computer and executes its commands for ignition. There are three key inputs to the computer: the crankshaft and camshaft position sensors and a detonation (knock) sensor. The first two generally are electromagnetic devices that react to precisely located gaps in trigger wheels on the shafts. Changes in voltage caused by changes in electromagnetism provide signals from these sensors that tell the computer when each piston is rising on compression stroke. So, the computer can tell the coil module exactly when to discharge an ignition coil to provide a spark. The computer then can keep track of the sequence of cylinders for the electronic coil module to fire (so long as the engine is running). All the system continues to need are the crank sensor signals. If the weather, fuel quality or operating conditions produce engine knock, the detonation sensor sends a signal to the computer, which retards ignition timing. Each ignition coil discharges a spark from both ends, but only the one in the cylinder on compression has a fuel mixture to ignite. The other spark dissipates harmlessly in the exhaust gas of the companion cylinder. Ignition timing, along with fuel injection, is computer-adjusted primarily according to changes in throttle position, rpm, altitude and vehicle speed.

COMPUTER-CONTROLLED COIL IGNITION

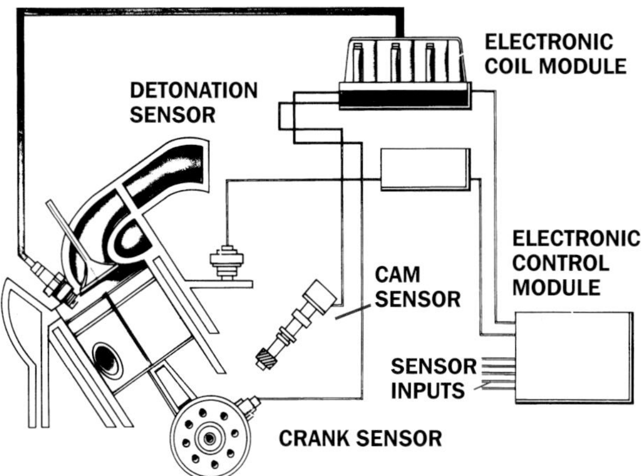

This ignition uses a separate coil for every pair of cylinders, usually in a pack of three or four coils mounted together.

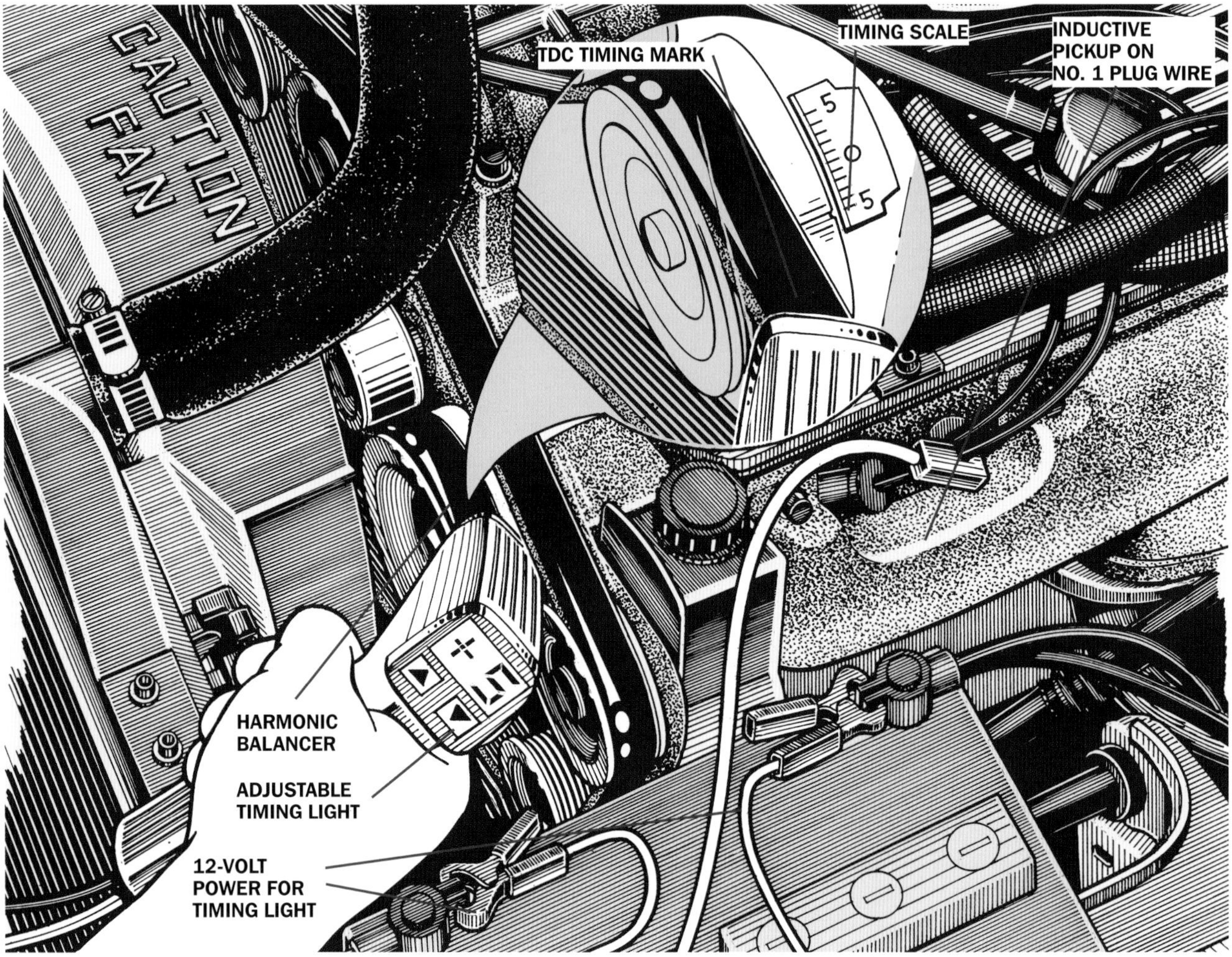

(Fig. 4) Modern timing lights often have an adjustable delay/advance function that allows you to set ignition timing at a value that's not printed on the timing tab.

appeared to align. If you changed it 16° in the retard direction, the timing really is advanced 16°. If the factory spec is 10° advance, the timing is too far ahead. If you changed it 6° but the timing specification is 10° advance, the timing is retarded. In either case, an adjustment is needed.

Okay, that's the way it should work. Let's go through a real timing check to demonstrate. First, the timing marks have to be clean and visible. Visibility often is tough, because of engine-compartment crowding. You may have to unbolt and hang a fluid reservoir out of the way to get a straight-on viewing angle. That's important, because if your viewing angle is bad, you get what's called "parallax error," and it can mislead you by several degrees.

Connect the timing light. The power and ground lead go to the battery, the lead with the plastic clip (called the pickup) goes to the No. 1 spark plug (**Fig. 4**). The pickup must be squarely positioned on the plug wire. On an inline four-cylinder or six-cylinder engine, the plug nearest the belt-and-pulleys end of the engine is virtually always No. 1. If you have a V-type engine, you'll have to check the manual, since No. 1 could be the first plug on either side.

After connecting the timing light, start the engine and warm it up, so it runs at idle speed. It's rare, but some manufacturers specify checking timing at a speed other than idle. If the timing isn't correct, you've got to find out why. The usual reasons are a defective crankshaft sensor (the part that reads crankshaft position for timing adjustment by the computer) or throttle-position sensor. There may or may not be a trouble code to guide you, but with an ignition-timing check, you've made a good start. Scan-tool and multimeter tests of the sensors can take you the rest of the way.

THIS FORD REQUIRES its connector to be disconnected before you check the base timing.

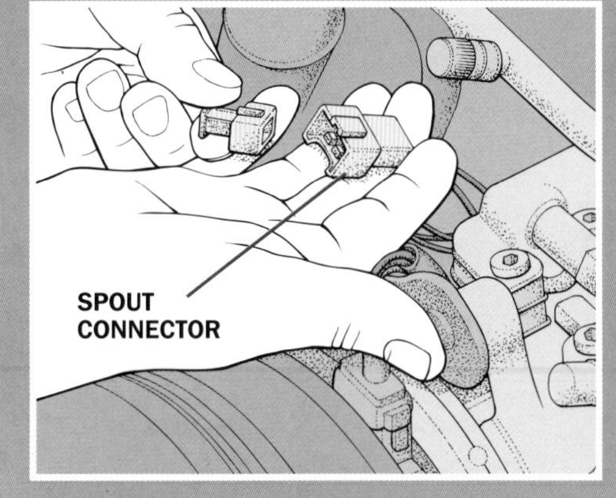

Replacing Engine Mounts

DOGBONE

RIGHT FRONT STRUT TOWER

STRUT

RUBBER BUSHING INSERT

NOTE DETERIO-RATED BUSHING

RIGHT SIDE MOTOR MOUNT

(Fig. 1) Check for deteriorated rubber bushings in the dogbone (shown) and other engine mounts that may permit the drivetrain to move too far and shake at idle. Replacement is usually straightforward.

You pull up to a traffic light and once you've stopped, you can feel the engine shaking. Okay, it's not so bad while you're stopped, but as you accelerate you can feel the engine clunk and shudder. Hey, you just did a tuneup last month, and you know it should last for a couple of years. You start to think, "I must have left a plug wire loose or something like that."

Lift the hood and check every wiring connection in sight, every air-duct clamp, every vacuum hose. Nothing looks out of place. But the engine is shaking. If you have a rear-wheel drive with an engine-driven fan, you may see the hint of a fan "scallop" on the rear of the radiator core, a clear-cut sign that the engine is tipping forward on acceleration. It's time to check the engine mounts and "dog bone" struts before there's a major failure and possible sticking of the gas pedal (**Fig. 1**).

Today's engine mounts are anything but simple two-piece metal brackets with slabs of rubber bonded between them. They have engineered shapes, specific durometer measurements (hardness) and often have strangely shaped cutout areas called "voids"—air gaps that tune the mounts' operation. In some cases they have hydraulic chambers that are filled with silicone fluid, and also in limited use are ones with electronic controls.

Okay, your car isn't brand-new and that's why the mounts are likely to be worn. The rubber may have been soaked with road film and oil (from a leaking valve-cover gasket). But it's more likely, particularly at 50,000 to 60,000 miles and up, that the mounts have cracks and distorted shape from the high temperatures common in today's engine compartments. If the weatherstripping along the cowl is missing, for example, that breaks the seal for the back of the powertrain compartment, allowing air to flow over the top instead of circulating through the compartment to cool the mounts (and other components).

The mount at the drivebelt (front) end of the engine has the biggest job in today's transverse-engined models. It reacts to both vertical and fore-aft shake, so check it with a pry bar (**Fig. 2**) and look at the rubber. If it cracks open at the internal edges of any voided area, or if it exhibits virtually no resistance, it is not providing much control.

Check fore-aft mounts, also by prying. In these cases, however, you'll probably have to force the bar against the metal edges of the mounts to be able to pry hard enough.

(Fig. 2) It might be necessary to use a pry bar to look for extra play in engine mounts.

What? Leaking Silicone?

Mounts with hydraulic chambers are circular and have a metal shell as part of their structure. It is possible for them to leak internally, but you're more likely to encounter an external leak. Surface cracks in the rubber generally are harmless, but run your fingers around them and if you pick up some thick, black goo that's not road film, it's the silicone oil leaking out. As with an all-rubber design, the only fix is replacement. You often can obtain aftermarket rubber/metal mounts to replace hydraulics at a significant savings. Are they likely to be as smooth? Probably not. Are they likely to satisfy you after experiencing the shake of a leaking hydraulic mount? Probably, particularly if the car is not destined for many, many years of additional use.

Replacing Engine Mounts

Although the powertrain end mounts on a transverse-engined car can be replaced individually if the one at the opposite end is good, it's better to replace both. When a fore or aft mount is bad on a transverse powertrain, always replace both. Ditto for the mounts on the driver and passenger sides of a north-south powertrain.

Support the engine with a hydraulic floor jack. If you have to place the jack on the oil pan, put a block of wood on the jack lifting pad to protect

HOW IT WORKS

Electronic-Hydraulic Engine Mounts

The Honda electronically controlled mount is typical of high-tech mounts used in a variety of cars to dampen the last little bit of shake produced by the powertrain. It's a hydraulic engine mount with two fluid chambers connected by a large orifice (kept closed by a rotary valve) and a small orifice (always open). The small orifice allows the mount to operate much like a simple, fairly stiff shock absorber. At idle, however, a vacuum diaphragm unit operates the rotary valve to open the large orifice, permitting more fluid flow between the chambers. It's like a shock that suddenly becomes softer, in this case absorbing the idle shake of the engine. The vacuum (from the engine) is fed through a solenoid valve that is controlled by the powertrain computer. This system operates when the engine is idling, perhaps triggered by turning on the a/c (which produces a load that affects engine idle). The computer opens the solenoid valve, and the engine vacuum flows to the vacuum diaphragm unit at the engine mount. When the solenoid valve closes above idle speed, the vacuum is vented and the engine mount goes back to single-orifice operation. If the vacuum reading fails to hold steady, there's a vacuum leak in the mount and it should be replaced. The next stage in electronic control of engine mounts already is in limited use (on some Lexus cars): A diaphragm pulsates in the hydraulic mount. The diaphragm creates a proportional counter-vibration to the frequency of the engine shake in the 600-to-900-rpm range, canceling the shake so the engine idles smoothly. If one of these mounts ceases to work, you may need to troubleshoot the wiring and check the mount itself.

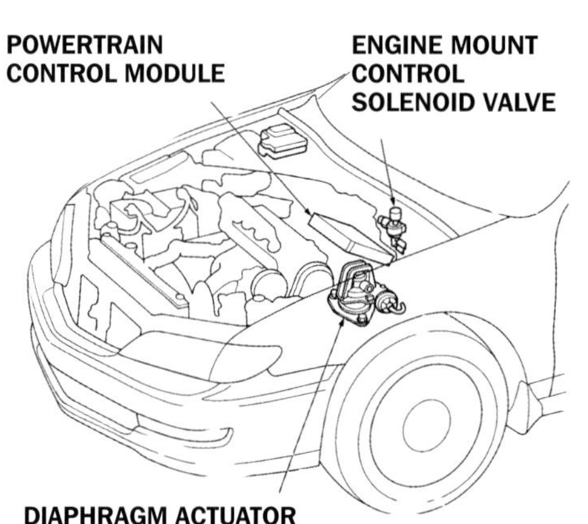

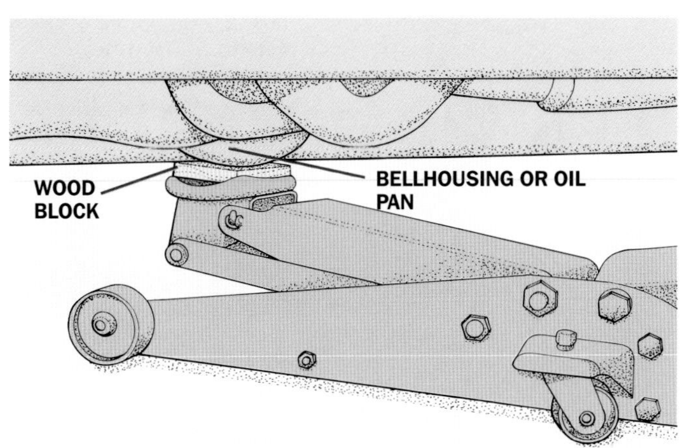

(Fig.4) Pad the nose of a floor jack with a block of wood to support the engine while you replace the mounts.

THIS MOUNT USES a soft rubber bushing. Install it with equal gaps on both sides of the bushing.

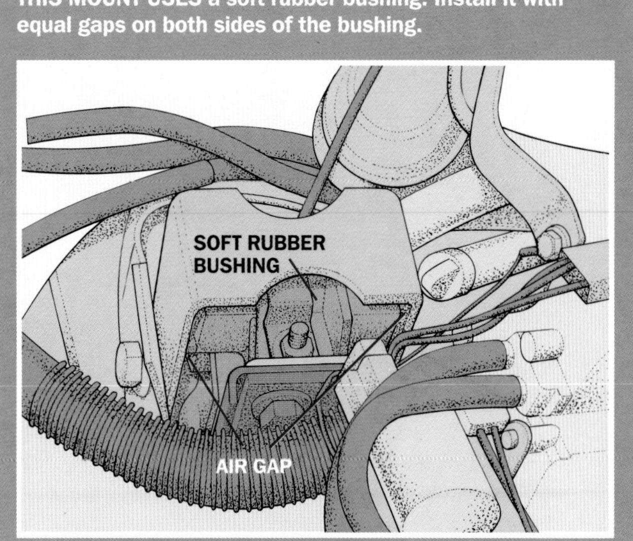

the pan (**Fig. 3**). If the mount's nuts or bolts are frozen, spray them with penetrating solvent so you can loosen them with a wrench and not have to resort to a chisel and hammer. In most cases, removing the fasteners and jacking the engine up slightly is all that's necessary to slide out a defective mount and insert the replacement. If you have to jack up a lot, there's a chance you could stress another mount unless you loosen it. Check before you pump the jack handle.

If there's a stud in the mount you're replacing, make sure you have it aligned precisely with its hole before you lower the engine. On many vehicles, you have to work both from underneath and above to insert and tighten nuts and bolts, and you occasionally will need a helper to pry on the engine while you get a bolt started through its mounting hole. If the mounting holes are slotted, run the engine and let it idle for a minute or two so the engine settles in the mount. Then tighten the nuts and bolts. Do the final tightening with a torque wrench.

Shock Absorber and "Dog Bone" Struts

Some engines have a shock absorber for vertical shake control. When used, it typically is bolted to the engine at the top end, and a chassis crossmember at the bottom. Disconnect the shock at either end and operate it by hand, just as you would to check a shock at a wheel. If you feel looseness or roughness with lost motion, that's a sure indicator of a worn-out shock.

Is there a dog bone strut or two? The dog bone usually is at the top of the engine compartment, at the fore side of a transverse powertrain. However, usually does not mean always. It may be installed at the top rear side (typically at the accessory-belt end, where it can directly assist the engine mount), or even at the bottom center on the aft side of a transverse engine. So if you don't see one at first glance, don't assume it isn't there.

(Fig. 5) This inexpensive vacuum pump will make it easier to diagnose bad actuators on some hydraulic motor mounts.

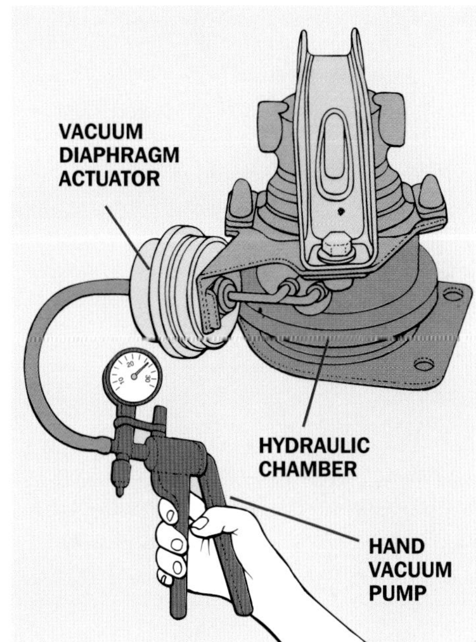

The ends of the dog bone have rubber sleeve bushings (**Fig. 4**), and if the rubber is cracked or distorted, replace the entire strut (the bushings are not replaceable). It's a straightforward job. Just unbolt it at each end, and install the new one. The engine will shift slightly when the old dog bone is removed, in which case you'll have to pry it forward into alignment with the bolt holes. You also may need a helper for this operation.

Some premium aftermarket dog bone struts include hydraulic chambers, much like a shock absorber—so the damping is done hydraulically instead of by squeezing rubber bushings. There's no noticeable difference in engine smoothness, but the hydraulic type reportedly has better long-term performance. The electronic-hydraulic engine mount (see page 108) may look complex, but it's easy even for a less experienced Saturday mechanic to check. Turn on the air conditioning with the engine idling, and then disconnect the wiring at the solenoid valve. If the engine shakes noticeably more, the system is working. If there's no difference, first disconnect the vacuum hose at the engine mount to check for vacuum flow through the solenoid valve. If there's vacuum flow, turn off the engine and apply vacuum to the diaphragm unit neck with a manual vacuum pump (**Fig. 4**).

Cleaning Throttle Bodies

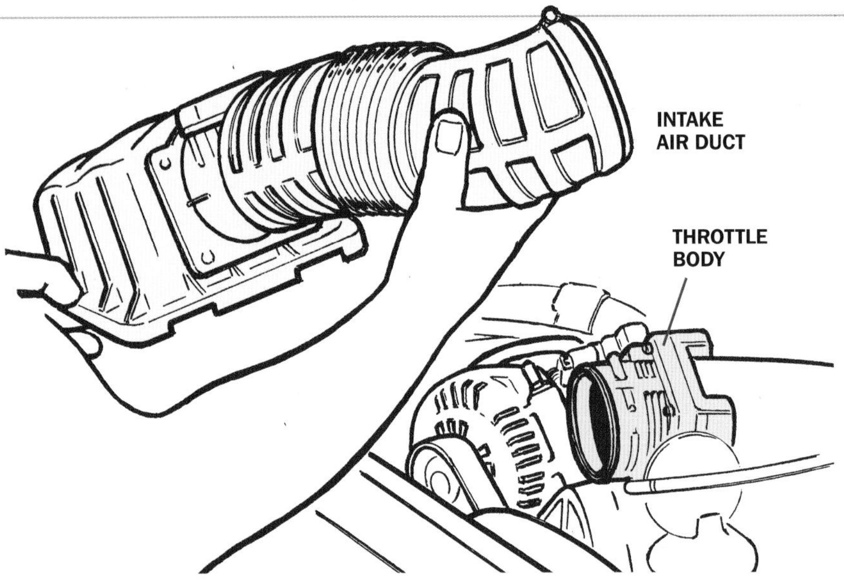

(Fig. 1) Remove the air duct and inspect it carefully for leaks or tears that might permit uncleaned air into the engine.

You slip behind the wheel for the morning commute. The engine starts easily, runs fine while fast-idling down the driveway and down the street for a few miles, but then stalls. You know instantly when the stall occurs because the air horn in the tractor-trailer rig immediately behind you curdles the fluid in your inner ear's semicircular canals when forward motion fails to proceed at an orderly pace. You restart, your car accelerates with a slight stumble, and when you coast to a stop at a traffic light, it stalls again. The stumble and possible stall problem doesn't go away when the engine is warm, so the common cold-engine poor-running possibilities are scratched from your priority checklist. This is more than annoying and as soon as the weekend arrives, the hood goes up.

Diagnosis: Deposits

All sensor wires are connected. There's no Check Engine light and there are no trouble codes. What do you look for now? A disconnected or damaged vacuum hose? Sure, that's a good bet, because many vacuum hoses can be pinched and damaged where it's really difficult to see. But take the time to check them all, making sure they're not only on tight, but not cracked or burned through due to contact with an exhaust pipe or exhaust gas recirculation tube. Don't be surprised if the last hose you check is the one that's damaged. If all the hoses are intact and on tight, there's another possibility that's just as likely: dirt and gum accumulation in the throttle body.

Get Dirty

To check for this, you've got to remove the intake air duct between the air cleaner housing and the throttle body (**Fig. 1**). First, disconnect all hoses and unplug any sensor wiring connectors (**Fig. 2**). If there's a chance you could confuse a hose connection or wiring connector, put a piece of masking tape on the hose or connector, another on the hose neck or sensor, and mark each with the same letter.

Next, loosen any clamps, work the duct off the throttle body and set it aside. With the wiring and hoses disconnected, you should not run the engine. Even if it starts and runs, it will log trouble codes, possibly triggering the Check Engine light. Then you'll have to go through a code-clearing procedure—extra work you don't want. Moreover, the computer may have to relearn some driveability trim settings, which may leave you with a marginally running engine for a while.

On some vehicles, it's possible to leave hoses and sensors connected and still move the intake air duct safely out of the way. In that case, it would be possible to spray a solvent into the throttle body opening with the engine running. However, there's no great advantage to this and, as you'll see, there are reasons why it's not such a great idea.

Take a good look inside the throttle body using a flashlight. Operate the throttle linkage to open the throttle plate so you can see past the outside surface of the throttle body. If you see a coating of dirt and oily film on the inside wall of the throttle body or the edge of the throttle plate, you've likely found the problem. The coating both upsets and restricts the airflow when the throttle is closed or slightly open.

Where do these deposits come from? Some are in airborne dirt that gets through the air filter or past a crack in the intake air duct. So be sure to check the intake air duct for cracks, particularly in the "accordion" area where they're not as obvious. Most deposits, however, are from oil gases transferred from the positive crankcase ventilation system and pushed forward by normal engine pulsation as the intake valves close and open, and from exhaust gases that seep in.

Some throttle body bores have a coating to reduce the buildup, but, in time, bores with protective coats can be affected. There are several ways to

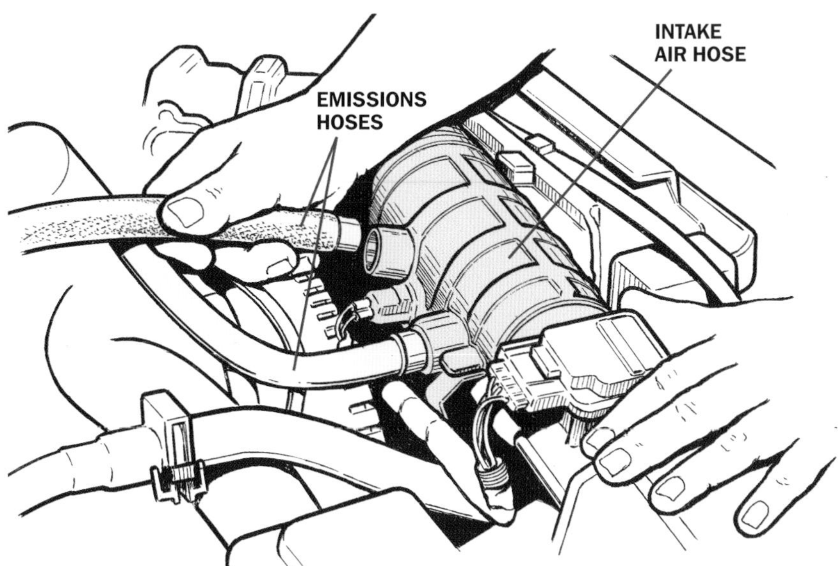

(Fig. 2) Remove any hoses or wires on the air duct connecting the throttle body to the air cleaner housing. Mark which hose or wire goes where to avoid confusion later.

clean out the area. The best is with a professional tool called the Intake Snake, which comes with an effective yet safe solvent, and the simplest is with an old worn-out toothbrush with soft bristles and a mild solvent.

There are three reasons why you have to be careful, both in choice of solvent and in application:

First, if the throttle body has a protective coating (as on many Ford products) to reduce the buildup, a strong solvent and hard brushing will remove it, so you'd have to do the job more often. If you see a warning label on a Ford product, that's why.

Second, there may be a sensor tip projecting into a small opening in the area of the throttle plate, and a strong solvent or hard brushing might damage it. In addition, a sensor O-ring seal may be damaged by a strong solvent.

Third, the throttle plate shaft is sealed at the mounting holes in the throttle body to prevent entry of unmeasured air (which would upset the fuel mixture). A strong solvent (and hard brushing) could damage the seals.

Stronger Than Dirt

Most aerosol carburetor and choke cleaners are pretty strong. Ditto for those aerosol cleaners that can be sprayed into the air intake with the throttle open for combustion-chamber cleaning. These aerosols have to be very strong to clean surfaces without the mechanical advantage

HOW IT WORKS

How A Throttle Body Works

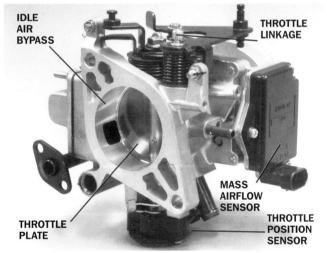

An engine runs primarily on air (about 15 parts by weight, to one of fuel), and the throttle body in a modern fuel-injected engine is the device that controls the airflow through its round opening. When the intake valve for a particular cylinder is open, the air flows through the throttle body, which is mounted on the intake manifold. The airflow continues into the intake manifold, through a chamber, and then through the open intake valve into the cylinder. At the same time the fuel injector sprays in fuel, the inrushing air and fuel mix, the intake valve closes and a spark from the plug ignites the mixture. The intake airflow control is provided by the throttle plate, a pivoting plate on a spring-loaded shaft that goes through the center of the throttle body's round opening. The throttle plate is a type of air valve, often called a "butterfly." When your foot is off the gas pedal, the throttle plate springs closed, and only a minimum amount of air, enough for engine idle, goes through a bypass around the throttle plate. One end of the throttle plate shaft also holds the movable contact arm of the throttle position sensor, a variable resistor-type sensor that tells the engine computer whether the vehicle is idling, accelerating or holding a throttle position. On many new engines, the gas pedal is just a variable resistor, sending a signal to the engine computer. The computer controls the throttle plate to produce the desired opening. This is called "drive by wire."

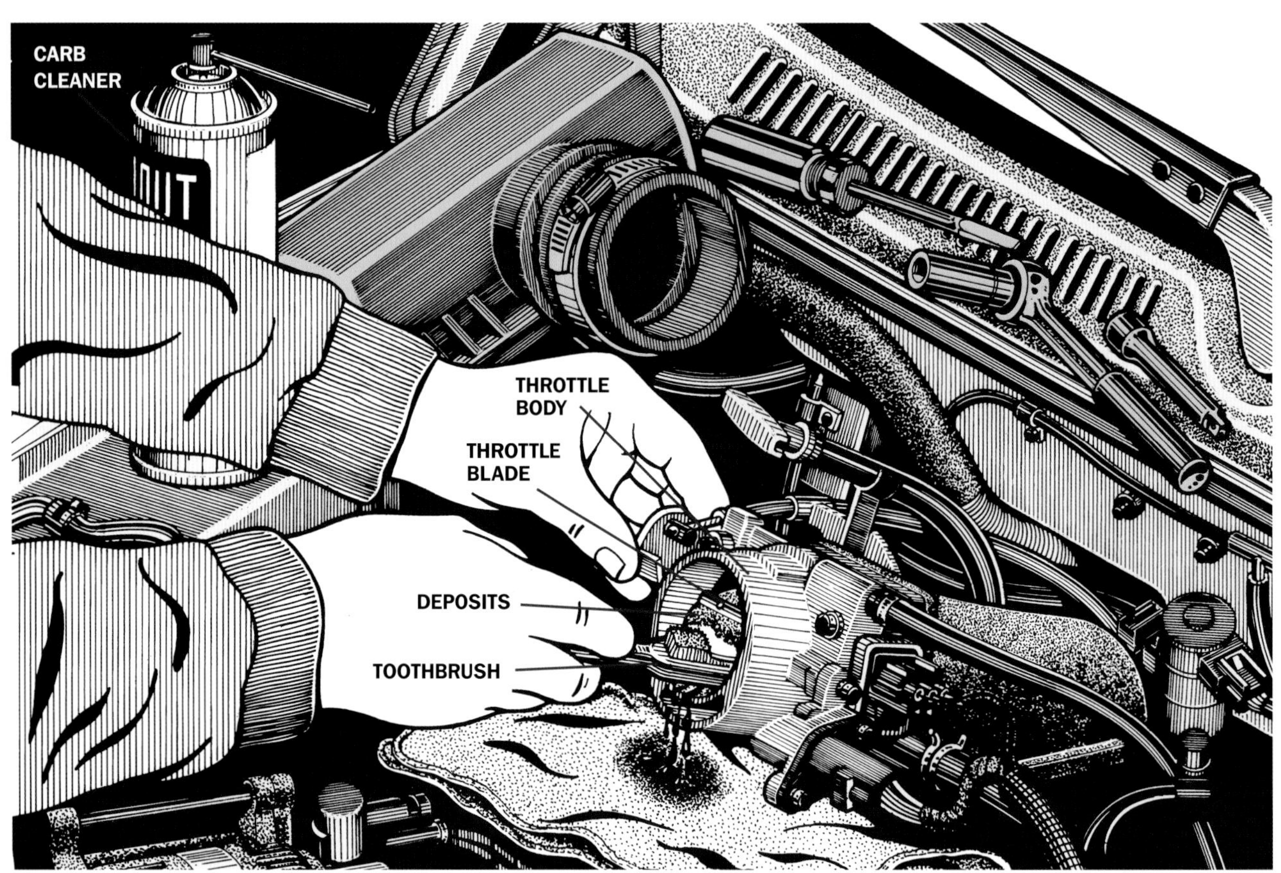

(Fig. 3) Spray-can carb cleaner may be a little too aggressive for safety—dilute it with gasoline to prevent damage to seals and sensors. Always remove the negative connection from a battery first and reconnect it last to prevent shorting the wrench out on nearby metal objects.

of a rubbing brush. A strong solvent can cause deterioration of not only sensor seals, but also throttle shaft seals. Further, you can't see which deposits have been removed and which have not. The aerosol spray will not clean all areas, particularly the back side of the throttle plate.

A tuneup/injector cleaner mixed with gasoline (1:4 or 1:5 ratio) should be safe (**Fig. 3**). You won't be using much, and you can pour the rest into the gas tank after you're done.

Start by cleaning the exterior of the throttle plate, and then hold it open using a wire tied to the throttle linkage so you can clean the inside perimeter of the plate. All you're trying to do with brushing is to loosen all the deposits.

Next, clean the throttle body wall, being careful to work around any electronic sensors, and around the throttle plate shaft holes. When you're done, remove the deposits with solvent and a clean rag.

Because this service is something your vehicle may need every few years, the professional kit (www.intakesnake.com) is a worthwhile investment at under $60. It includes a container of two cleaning tips (containers of two tips are available separately for under $15). The "snake" is made of a smooth plastic and won't scratch anything. It's 14 in. long and moderately flexible, so you can reach deep into the throttle body and follow any contours (**Fig. 4**). The tool holds the spongelike work tips that are coated with a hypoallergenic solvent that's also safe for sensors and throttle plate seals. Because the dirty film is held by the work tip, there's little or no wiping needed when you're done. Press a release tab and the dirty tip falls off the tool (into a garbage can).

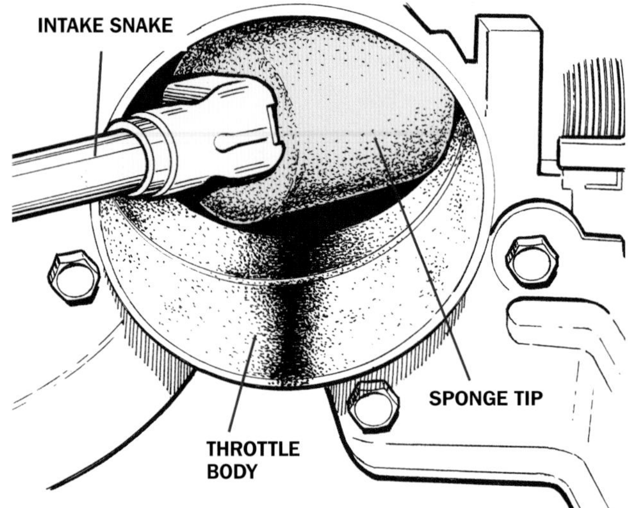

(Fig. 4) The Intake Snake is one way to safely clean throttle blades and throttle body castings of deposits.

EASY

Electric Cooling Fan Problems

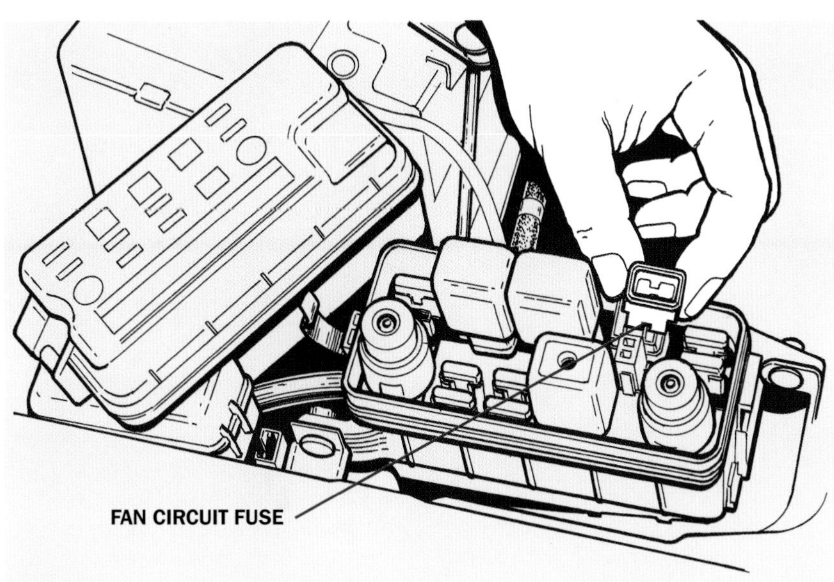

(Fig. 1) Check the high-amperage fan fuse in the underhood electrical box.

It's a really, really warm day, but the temperature gauge reads normal and the a/c is blowing out a lot of cold air, so who cares? Then the traffic suddenly slows to a crawl and doesn't get any better. Gradually the temperature gauge needle creeps toward the Hot end of the dial, and the air blowing out of the a/c registers is anything but cold. In fact, to forestall overheating, you shut it off. Even worse, you soon have to turn on the heat to try to prevent a boil-over, and open the windows to try to get a breeze.

If you're lucky, the traffic tie-up breaks, and you're cruising again. The gauge needle starts dropping, and you turn off the heater. Still sweaty, you turn on the a/c again, and even if the air isn't frigid, it's cold enough to make you feel better.

Later, you lift the hood with the engine running near an overheat and the a/c on—the radiator electric fans aren't running. But why? The fan may be under the complex control of a powertrain computer, but the basic circuit is pretty straightforward.

On almost all cars the fans should go on if the a/c is turned on, triggered by the powertrain computer or by an a/c pressure switch. The fans may not go on instantly, but certainly within a couple of minutes. If they don't, proceed to a circuit diagnosis.

The simplest first circuit check you can make is the current feed, starting at the fuse, which on late models is in an underhood fuse box (**Fig. 1**). Just pull it out and look. Replace it if it's blown. On older models it's often a fusible link—a short section of wire typically four gauge numbers higher than the wire of which it's part. You may see it's singed. Even if it isn't, pull on the ends of the wrap, and if it stretches, the wire underneath is broken.

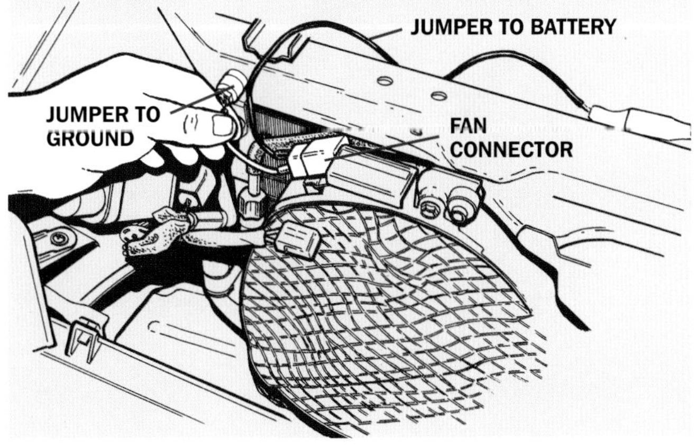

(Fig. 2) Try jumping the battery direct to the fan to see if it spins.

Checking The Fan Motors

Fuse okay? The most practical approach is to go next to the end of the circuit: the fans themselves. Most cars have two fans. Unplug one fan's wiring connector and (referring to the wiring diagram color codes) hot-wire the fan motor's half of the connector. Run one jumper wire from the current feed terminal of the connector half to the battery's positive terminal. Attach a second jumper wire to the other terminal of the connector and run it to an electrical ground (**Fig. 2**). The fan should run. If it doesn't, the fan motor apparently is defective.

Some cars have a single fan that runs at two speeds. In these cases, the connector may have:

- Two terminals (one from a dual power feed—through a dropping resistor for low speed and a resistor-bypass circuit for high speed—plus the second one for the ground). There's a splice or connector for the dual power feed earlier in the circuit. If you check by hot-wiring at the fan motor itself, it will run at high speed.
- Three terminals (one for low-speed feed, one for high-speed and a common ground). Check each power feed terminal separately, using the common ground in each case.
- Four terminals (high, low and two grounds).

THERE MAY BE SEVERAL temperature sensors and switches on the engine. Find the correct one and check it with a test light or an ohmmeter.

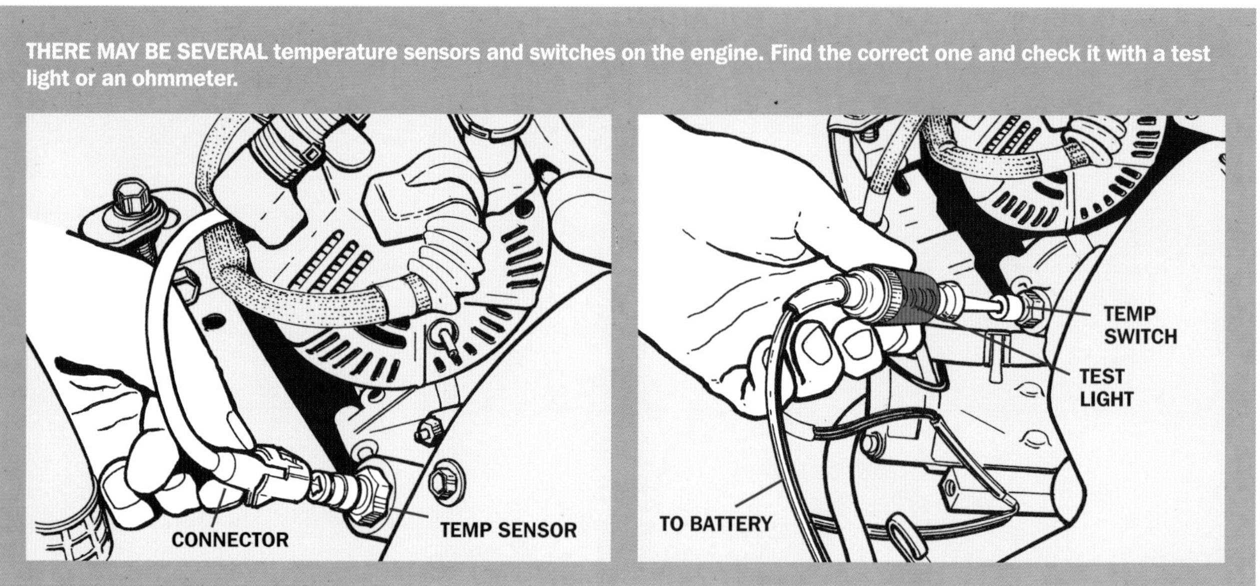

Hot-wire each pair separately with your jumper wires.

Testing Coolant Switch Or Sensor

If both fans run when they're hot-wired, the problem is somewhere between the current feed at the fuse and the fan motors. On older systems where the trigger for the fans is a coolant temperature switch, unplug the switch connector. Be sure you have the right one, as some vehicles have as many as three: one for a dashboard warning light, one for an overhead console and one for the powertrain computer.

With the engine running and with the coolant switch unplugged, the fan should come on because the powertrain computer logs a trouble code for a failed switch and turns on the fans in most systems. If it doesn't, and the switch is a typical domestic design, it has a normally open type that stays open until coolant temperatures are high, when it closes to turn on the fan. To double-check, just ground the unplugged connector's single wire terminal, using a jumper wire. The fan should spin. Many older Japanese cars have circuits with normally closed switches. They open with high coolant temperatures to turn on the fan, so a simple unplugging (with the ignition on) always should get the fans to operate with this setup.

Most late models have a coolant temperature sensor. It isn't a switch, but a temperature-sensitive resistor (thermistor) that sends a signal to the powertrain computer. The computer, which also has some control over a/c operation, then decides when the fans should operate and at what speed. You may not be able to get a response by simply unplugging the sensor connector or even by grounding it. Instead, check its calibration by connecting an ohmmeter (**Fig. 3**). The thermistor develops lower resistance as the temperature goes up, higher resistance as it

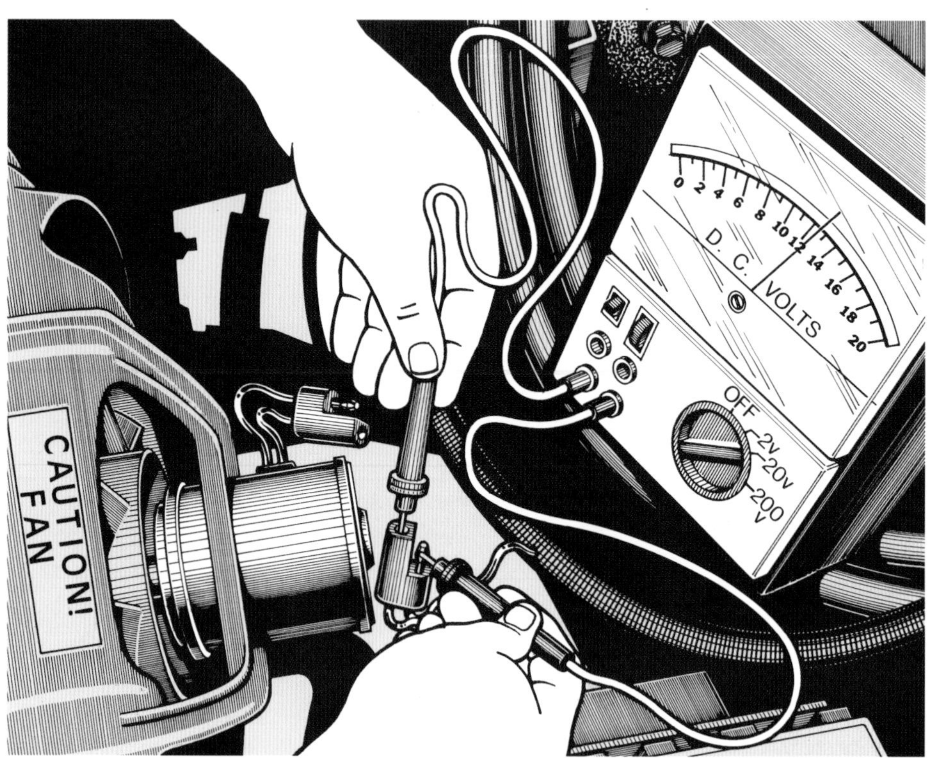

(Fig. 3) Connecting an ohmmeter is one reliable way to check the thermistor.

drops. If the sensor reads a thousand ohms or more (which signals low temperature) when the engine coolant is warmed up, it's out of calibration. Replace it. Even easier is to use a scan tool which will give you a reading in degrees (C. or F.).

Relay Diagnosis

Head for the fan relay (or relays—some systems have low- and high-speed fan relays) **(Fig. 4)**. Turn on the ignition, and locate the relay terminal for the wire from the switch. When you ground its terminal with a jumper wire, the relay should click and the fan should run. If it does, the relay and its circuit to the fans are good. Any problem is in the wiring between the coolant temperature switch and the relay.

If the fan still won't spin, continue at the relay, which has two current feeds, one to the electromagnetic coil, one to the electrical contacts. Probe the two current feed terminals of its wiring connector with a grounded test light. With the ignition on, it should go on in both cases. No light in one? There's a break in the wiring from the fuse to that relay terminal.

On systems with computer control via a sensor signal, make a similar test of the relay current feed terminals with a grounded (computer-safe) test light and the ignition on.

If the current feeds are good, ground the relay's switch terminal (the one with the wire that goes to the coolant switch). If there's a sensor and the switch terminal wire goes to the powertrain computer, unplug the wire before grounding the terminal. The relay should click and operate the fans. If it doesn't, replace the relay.

You may have trouble doing this with relays that plug into an underhood relay "center." Unplug the relay, turn on the ignition and with your test light probe the two current feed terminals in the relay center. If they pass (turning on the test light), make up short jumper wires to connect to the unplugged relay and one long jumper (that you run to an electrical ground) for the switch terminal. If the relay still doesn't work (ignition on), replace the relay. If the relay does click, probe the output terminal to the fan motor with a grounded test light. Light goes on? The problem is in the wiring from relay to fan motor.

HOW IT WORKS

The Electric Fan

The fan is powered by an electric motor, which is wired to a relay. The relay is a magnetically controlled switch. It typically has four terminals, two of which are current feeds from a fused source of 12-volt electricity. At the relay, there is one current feed into an electromagnetic coil, and one feed into a set of contacts for the switch, which is open. The other terminal for that open switch is connected to the electric motor for the fan. The fourth terminal, also for the coil, is wired to the powertrain computer, which may look at various signals to determine whether or not to provide an electrical ground for that coil. If, as in this circuit example, it gets a high-temperature signal from the coolant temperature sensor, also wired to it, the powertrain computer can choose to ground the coil terminal. This energizes the coil, creating a magnetic field that pulls the arm on the power feed contact, so that it touches the terminal for the wire to the electric motor. That closes the switch of the relay. Current flows through the closed contacts of this switch to the electric motor, which spins to operate the fan.

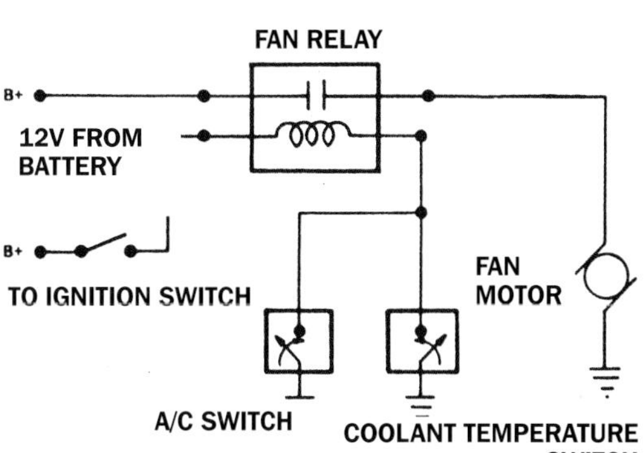

Your diagnosis may point to the powertrain computer. It's rare, but a computer failure can be responsible—without a Check Engine light or trouble code. Perhaps just a single driver has blown, so the computer itself seems to be performing normally. In addition, in a number of cars, particularly some GM models, the powertrain computer turns off the fans if the vehicle is cruising 40 to 45 mph or higher. This strategy relies on the vehicle speed sensor, which may be misbehaving. If your speedometer is way off, or not working at all, it's something to consider if the relay works when grounded. Want to work through one of these problems? Open your factory service manual, plug in a Saturday Mechanic-level scan tool and go through the trouble-tree diagnostics to find the answer.

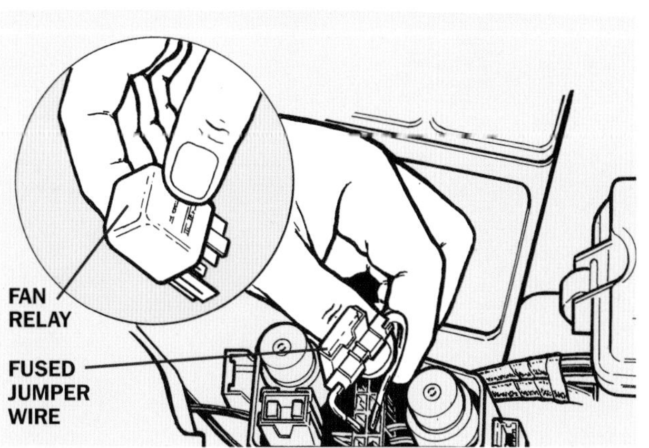

(Fig. 4) You can jump across the fan relay to confirm the relay's failure.

Finding Engine Knock

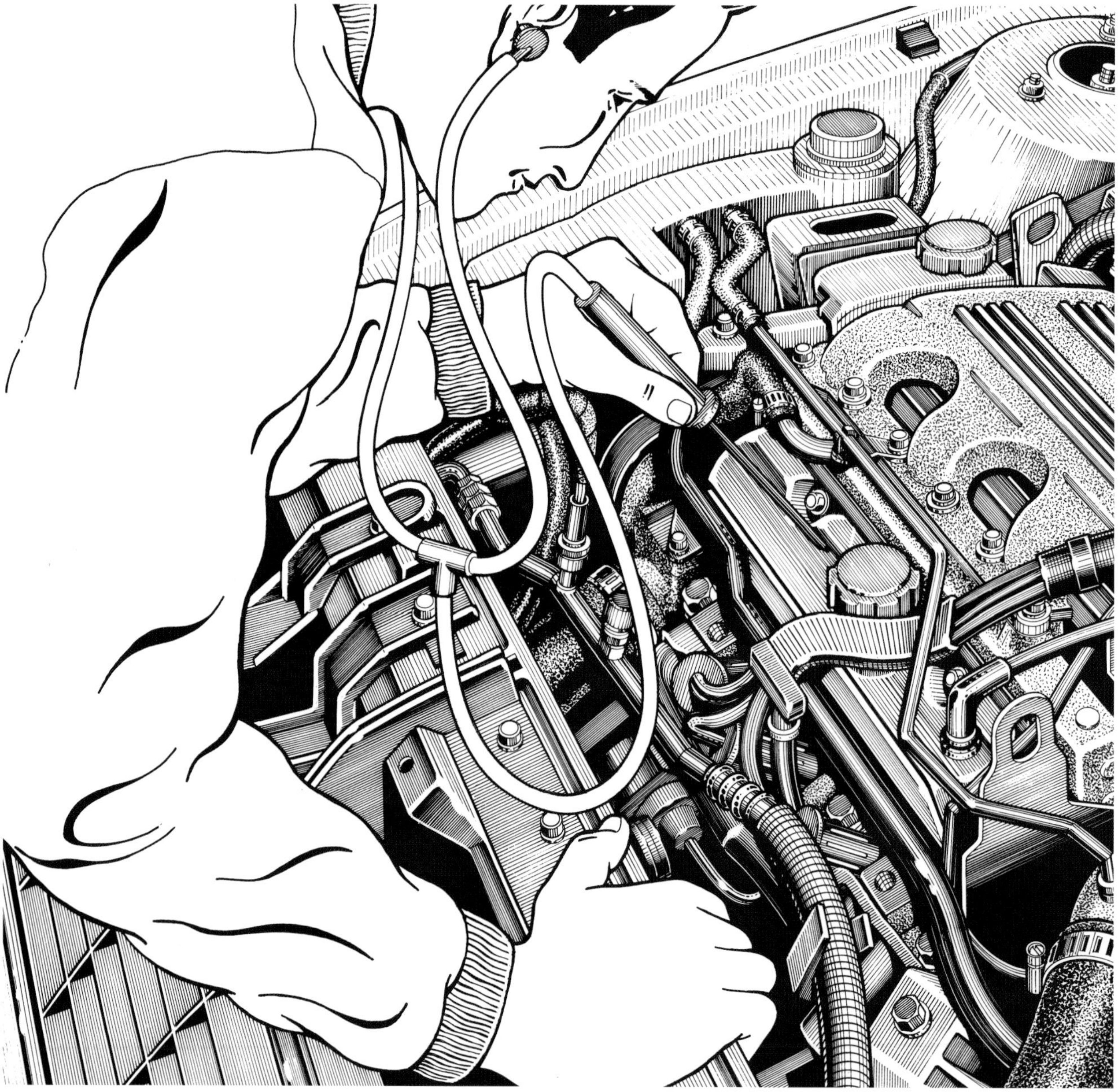

Fig. 1. Try to isolate engine noises with a mechanic's stethoscope. You can usually determine which cylinder is at fault. Try pulling one plug wire or injector harness at a time to see if the noise changes.

You're waiting in the drive-up line at the bank, all the better to redeem some of your hard-earned cash from the vault. But as you inch your way to the teller window, your engine misses so badly that it either stalls or has to be held at high idle with your right foot. The teller sends you a note through the pneumatic tube, "Sir, you forgot to endorse this check, and please get your car fixed—I can't hear a thing." It's off to the garage instead of the beach.

Days later, you're at the end of your rope. Above idle, the engine purrs like a kitten. But below 2000 rpm, there's a steady miss in the No. 4 cylinder. You've checked everything you can think of. Spark, compression and the fuel injector to that cylinder are working just fine. Yet the miss remains.

Complete Engine Testing

Many people—even mechanics—think that the beginning and end of internal engine diagnosis lie in using a compression tester. But the truth is that many internal engine problems (such as a weak valve spring, for instance) are not revealed by compression testing alone.

"A weak valve spring is easy to spot, if you use a vacuum gauge," said Dave Hakim, an engine and fuel system specialist with Federal Mogul Corp. "Connecting the gauge to the intake vacuum would reveal normal vacuum at idle. But when a valve spring is bad, the vacuum needle would fluctuate rapidly between 12 and 24 in. when you raise the rpm."

You can diagnose most internal engine problems using a vacuum gauge, a compression gauge and a leakage tester. And you can usually get to the root of mysterious internal engine noises by being a good listener.

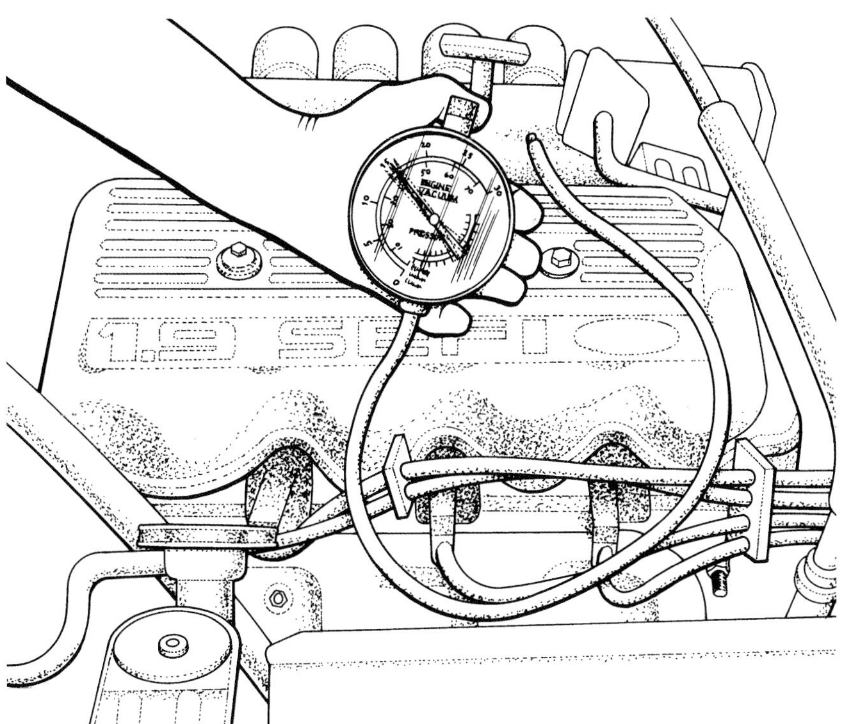

Fig. 2. With low, rapidly pulsating vacuum, this engine probably has valve guides that are worn out.

Engine Noises

The most common source of engine noise comes from the valvetrain. The noise—usually a clicking or tapping at half the engine's rotating speed—is caused by excessive clearance between components or a bad hydraulic lifter. On camshaft-in-block engines, you can isolate valvetrain noises by briefly running the engine with the valve cover off and pressing on each valve rocker with the end of a hammer handle. When the pressure from the handle removes the clearance, the noise disappears and you've found the problem.

Diagnosing valvetrain noises is more difficult on overhead-cam engines because you can't run them with the valve cover off.

Running the probe of a mechanic's stethoscope along the length of the valve cover with the engine running should allow you to isolate the noisy valvetrain component (**Fig. 1**). If you don't have a stethoscope, use a long screwdriver as a probe and listen by placing your ear against the handle.

Other internal noises include main- and rod-bearing knocks, wrist-pin noise and piston slap. A main-bearing knock has a deep metallic sound and is usually loudest when the engine is under load. If the knock is because of a failed bearing, low oil pressure may accompany the sound. Connecting-rod noises have a lighter rapping sound under light engine load. Disconnecting the spark plug to the offending cylinder usually results in a marked decrease in the noise. Piston slap, caused by excessive piston-to-cylinder wall clearance, causes a dull rattle. Disconnecting the spark plug makes it go away. Wrist-pin noise usually gets louder when the spark plug is disconnected.

Keep in mind that there are many external engine noises that can mimic internal noises, such as a loose flywheel or broken flexplate. Drivebelt pulleys can also cause noise, which can be isolated by running the engine briefly with the drivebelts removed.

Vacuum Testing

A good manifold vacuum gauge costs only about $35, yet it can quickly tell you a lot about what is going on in an engine. A vacuum gauge can reveal how well the valves are working, whether the piston rings are sealing adequately or whether camshaft timing is retarded.

To perform a manifold vacuum test, begin by connecting the vacuum gauge to an adequate source of intake-manifold vacuum.

On most engines it's easiest to tee the gauge hose into a vacuum hose such as the hose that runs from the intake manifold to the vacuum brake booster. With the gauge connected, start the engine and let it warm up to operating temperature. On most properly running engines, the gauge will hold steady between 15 and 20 in. If the needle fluctuates at idle, it indicates that one or more valves are leaking. Doing a compression test or an engine leak-down test will reveal the leaking valve or valves.

A slightly low vacuum-gauge reading, along with a slight flutter of the gauge, may indicate that the valve guides are worn (**Fig. 2**). On engines without overhead camshafts, you can verify guide and seal conditions by removing the valve cover(s) and squirting engine oil on the tops of the valve guides while the engine is running. If the vacuum-gauge reading increases and blue smoke starts to appear from the tailpipe, it's a good indication that the valve guides are worn.

If the vacuum reading fluctuates between 5 and 7 in., it indicates that valve timing is excessively late. A skipped tooth or excessively worn timing chain or belt are all likely causes.

To check for weak or broken valve springs, increase engine speed to 2000 rpm. If the gauge needle fluctuates between 12 and 24 in. and the fluctuations increase as engine speed increases, the valve springs are weak. If the fluctuation is irregular, it's likely that one valve spring is weak or broken.

If intake vacuum appears normal in the above tests and the engine oil is in good condition, you can do a quick test to determine piston-ring sealing. To do this, bring the engine speed up to 2000 rpm, then let the throttle snap closed. If the vacuum reading jumps 5 in. or more over the normal reading, it indicates that the piston rings are in good condition.

Compression Testing

A compression test can reveal a lot about an engine's internal condition, but only if it's performed properly. Many people mistakenly do compression tests with old diluted oil, the engine cold or with the throttle closed.

Begin by warming the engine to normal operating temperature. Then, use compressed air to blow all the spark plug wells clean before removing the spark plugs.

Disable the ignition, then connect the compression gauge to the No. 1 cylinder, according to the instructions supplied with the gauge. Have an assistant hold the throttle wide open while cranking the engine over until five complete compression strokes have been completed (as indicated by pulses on the gauge). Record the compression readings on the first and fifth strokes. Repeat the process for each cylinder.

A cylinder has good compression if it achieves two-thirds of its total compression on the first stroke and reaches the minimum factory compression specification by the fifth stroke. If the compression reading is low on the first stroke and builds with following strokes but doesn't reach minimum compression, the piston rings are probably not sealing well. If the gauge reading remains low on all five strokes, it usually indicates a leaking valve. Low compression in two adjacent cylinders indicates a blown head gasket.

Fig. 3. A leakage tester can pinpoint which cylinder is bad and where the leakage is.

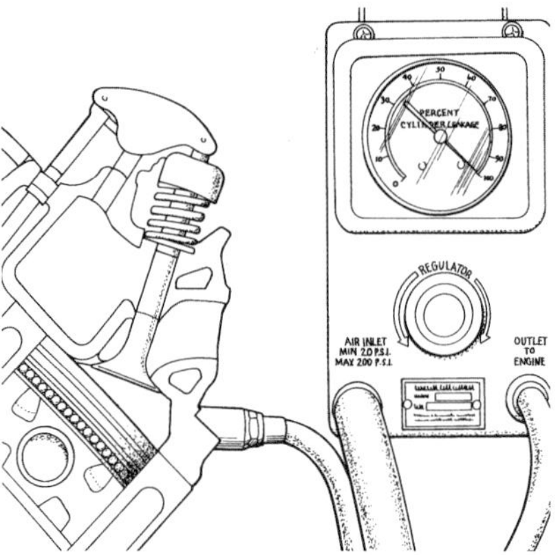

Fig. 4. To look for combustion leakage into the cooling system, hold a bag over the radiator filler. The emissions probe should show no CO_2 when the engine is running.

If all engine cylinders achieve proper compression, then you're done. If any of the cylinders had low compression, however, you'll have to confirm the cause by doing a "wet compression test." Squirting oil into combustion chambers with low readings temporarily improves sealing of the piston rings. If compression goes up 10% or more when you repeat the compression test, then the rings are bad. If compression stays the same, then the compression leakage is most likely from the valves.

Keep in mind that a wet test won't work on horizontally opposed Volkswagen, Porsche and Subaru engines.

Leakage Testing

Long favored by professional racing mechanics as the most accurate method for testing an engine's combustion-chamber sealing, a cylinder leakage tester works by pressurizing the combustion chamber with compressed air and then measuring total leakage as a percentage.

A leakage tester, which costs about $75, will not only tell you the condition of the rings and valves, it can tell you if the leak is coming from an intake or exhaust valve (**Fig. 3**).

To do a leakage test, warm the

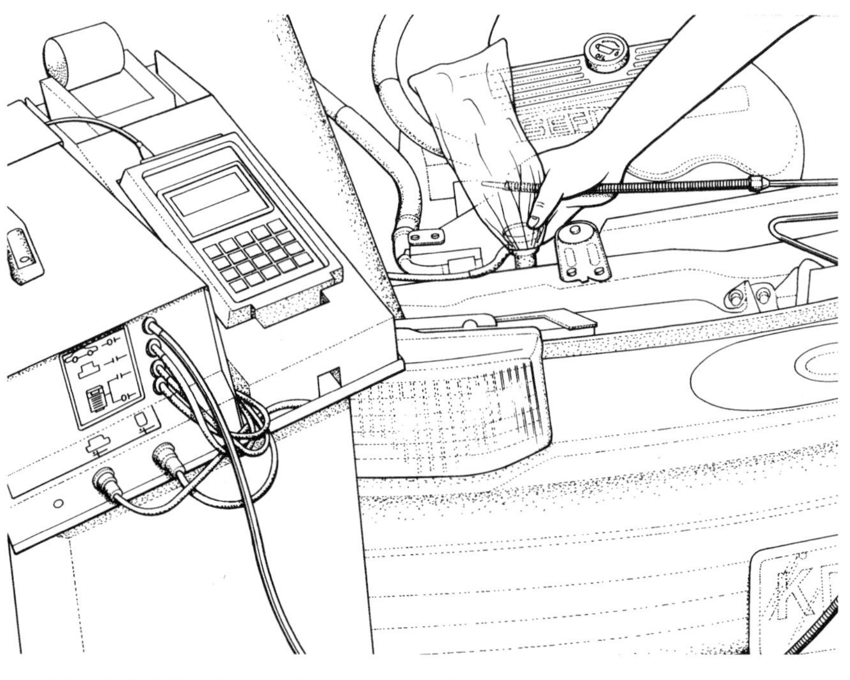

engine and remove the spark plugs. Remove the air cleaner and block the throttle wide open. Rotate the engine so the No. 1 cylinder is at the exact top dead center (TDC) on the compression stroke. Install the fitting from the leakage tester in the No. 1 spark plug hole, then connect an air-compressor line to the tester. Pressurize the cylinder and note the percentage of leakage on the gauge.

AN ENGINE WITH GOOD compression will show readings on the gauge within a 20-pound spread or less.

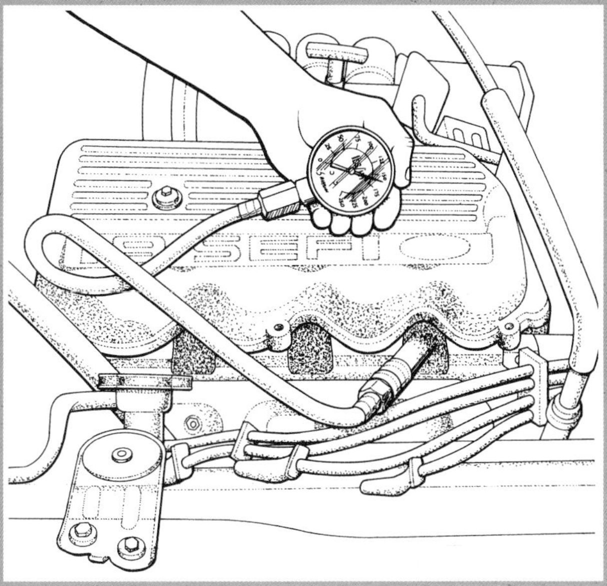

An engine in great shape will have cylinders with 5% to 10% leakage. An engine with 20% leakage is still in pretty good condition. If the engine has a cylinder with more than 30% leakage, however, you should isolate the cause.

You can do that by listening for escaping air while the combustion chamber is pressurized. If the sound comes from the intake manifold, the problem is a leaking intake valve. From the exhaust manifold, it's a leaking exhaust valve. If you hear air escaping from the oil/-filler cap opening, the problem is with piston sealing. You can even look for bubbles in the engine coolant at the radiator cap to check for a blown head gasket. And, like the compression test, high leakage readings between cylinders equals a head gasket leak.

It's also possible to find head gasket leaks at the local emissions inspection station. Warm the engine and ask the mechanic to place the emission tester's exhaust probe in a plastic bag. By placing the plastic bag over the radiator opening while the engine is running, the probe will be able to pick up any exhaust gases that are leaking from the combustion chamber into the cooling system (**Fig. 4**).

Plugging Leaks

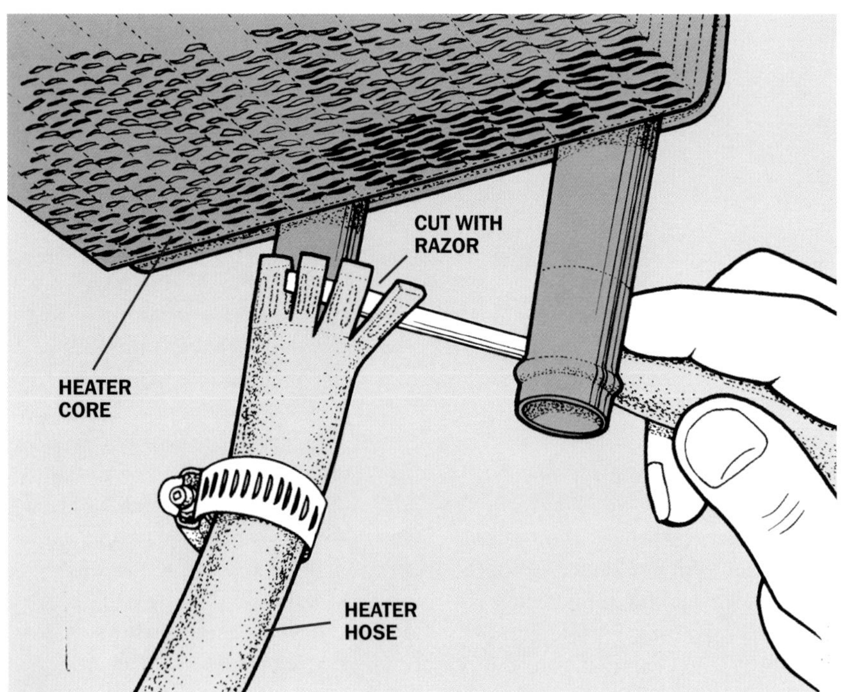

Fig. 1. Remove a stubborn hose by carefully slicing it. Don't nick the neck it fits over.

The sweat pours down your brow as you lift the hood while gasoline gurgles into your tank in the self-serve lane. Through the shimmer of heat that escapes from underhood you lean over to check the level of bright green coolant in the translucent overflow tank. Empty, again.

You've topped it up a few times—but the last few tankfuls it's been dry inside. In fact, coolant seems to be disappearing at an accelerating rate. The weather is getting hotter, and you're about to take a vacation. It's time for some action.

It should be easy to prevent most major coolant leaks since they usually occur when a hose fails. And you should be able to spot the bad hose before it bursts by those telltale signs of heat cracking and other deterioration, right? Wrong. While coolant hoses near the end of their useful lives used to show the classic warning signs, they no longer necessarily do. Today's hoses are so much better you can't tell only by looking.

You should also be able to easily spot a coolant leak, even a small one. After all, the antifreeze contains a green dye that leaves a stain. Well, the truth of the situation is that your current model engine may have more than a dozen hose connections—and other joints sealed by gaskets and O-rings—and many of them are buried. To top off the problem, there are ways that coolant can escape from the system without leaving so much as a trace.

Even when you find the leak, it may take some special steps to fix it. Result: Finding, fixing and preventing future coolant leaks involves a lot more than it used to. But if you take the time to do the job right, you'll be able to avoid the repeated need to top up the system, and the disaster that would occur if you forget.

Fixing Obvious Leaks

If a leak is obvious, such as a leaking radiator, cracked hose or badly leaking joint, that's great—a solid starting point. If it's an O-ring type at a coolant pipe, clean the groove if necessary with ultrafine sandpaper or steel wool. Wipe clean, and then replace the O-ring, lubricating it with antifreeze. Leaky radiator? Check with a radiator shop, and you may get away with an inexpensive repair.

It might be possible to resolder a split seam or a leaking joint at the neck/tank junction on an old copper-brass radiator without even removing the radiator from the car. Even leaky plastic-tank radiators can sometimes be repaired by replacing the O-ring between the end tank and the aluminum core. This is definitely a task to leave to a professional, however. It's a hose? If the clamp is not tight, and the leak is from the hose end, perhaps the hose has taken a compression set under the clamp. Try a simple retightening—but don't overdo it, or you'll distort the hose and neck, and just end up with a worse leak than you had.

Tightening the clamp doesn't help? Replace the hose. Uh-oh, it's stuck. Grab it with pliers and twist? Not unless you want to crush the hose neck and make it impossible to seal properly. Better to cut it off instead.

With a razor blade, slit the leaking end of the hose at several points around the circumference, gently pry up each slice, then peel the rest of the hose end. Don't nick the neck on the radiator or engine, or it'll never seal again. Clean the neck—on the radiator, engine, heater core, connector pipe—with a wire brush and wipe clean. Then install the replacement hose, using fresh antifreeze as a hose lubricant.

Radiator necks are generally pretty sturdy, but heater-hose pipes are usually very fragile. Twisting and prying

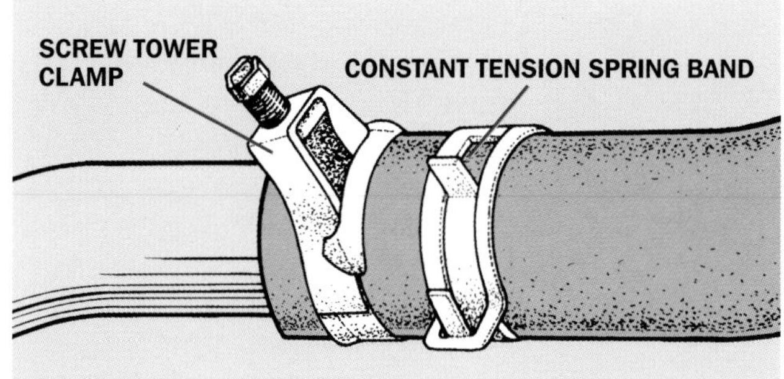

Fig. 2. OEM screw-tower clamps don't seal nearly as well as spring clamps. A regular worm-drive clamp provides a tight seal, too.

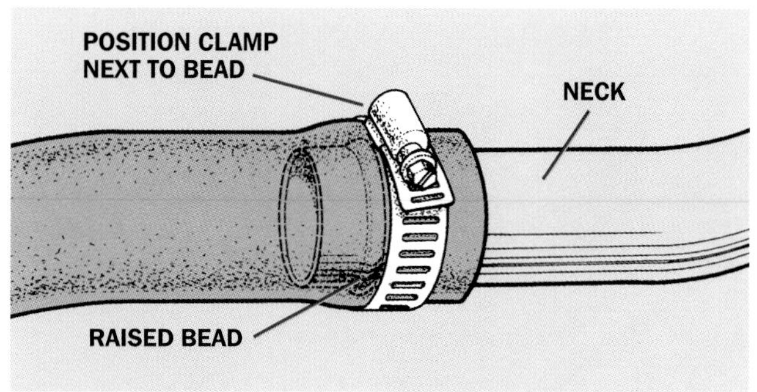

Fig. 3. Don't give coolant a place to collect between the clamp and the sealing bead, or you'll give corrosion a place to start on copper-brass radiators.

to remove a hose—or replace it later—can easily break the seal between the pipe and the heater core's tank. And removing a heater core to repair or replace it can involve removing half of the underside of the dashboard—an operation that can consume a dozen hours or more. Use caution.

Unless there's lots of slack in the hose, don't try to trim the cut end and reuse it. What's left probably will kink and ultimately restrict coolant flow.

Use a new clamp and position it correctly for a leak-free connection, being extra careful if there is any damage or distotion to the hose neck. The two best types of clamps are the constant-tension spring band and the 360° adjustable double-band. A decent-quality, worm-drive tangential-force clamp, with a slotted band that won't dig deep into the hose rubber or cut it when you tighten, also does a good job. The screw-tower clamp, widely used as original equipment, is tolerable for a brand-new system, but is about the least effective for resealing.

Install the hose as far as possible on the neck, and if there's a stop, right up to it. Position the clamp carefully so that it's about midway between the end of the hose and the end of the neck, typically about one-half inch or more from the end of the hose. If there's a raised sealing bead on the neck, position the clamp flush against the back side of it. If it's any distance away, it won't seal as well and it will force a crevice between the hose and neck. Coolant will collect and stagnate in the crevice, accelerating corrosion (and erosion) of the neck on copper-brass radiators, eventually resulting in a significant leak. If a hose neck is badly distorted or eroded, get it reshaped or repaired by a radiator shop if you expect it to seal.

Finding Hidden Leaks

Sure, you have to look hard to inspect all the hose connections, O-rings and gasket joints, but you can get some help if you first pressurize the system with a cooling-system pressure tester. Pump up the system to its rated pressure plus a couple of psi. If the gauge reading holds for 2 minutes or so, the cooling system isn't leaking—at the moment. However, you may still be losing coolant.

Does the gauge's reading start dropping almost immediately? That tells you the system isn't holding pressure, and if you start looking you should see leakage from the offending joint or possibly the water pump's weep hole. All water pumps seep a minor amount of coolant (there's no such thing as a perfect seal), but if you see steady dripping or more, the pump seal is bad. Replace the pump.

Okay, the pressure gauge reading hardly budged, and you're still losing coolant. Now the diagnosis gets a bit tougher, because there are these possibilities

- Although cold engine leaks are more common, it's also possible the leakage only occurs with a hot system. Run the engine to warm up the system and retest.
- There is minor seepage from many joints and it all adds up. If your engine's cooling system has a lot of connections, inspect them all for even the slightest trace of coolant staining. Simple retightening of all the hose clamps may do the job.
- The leakage is from the

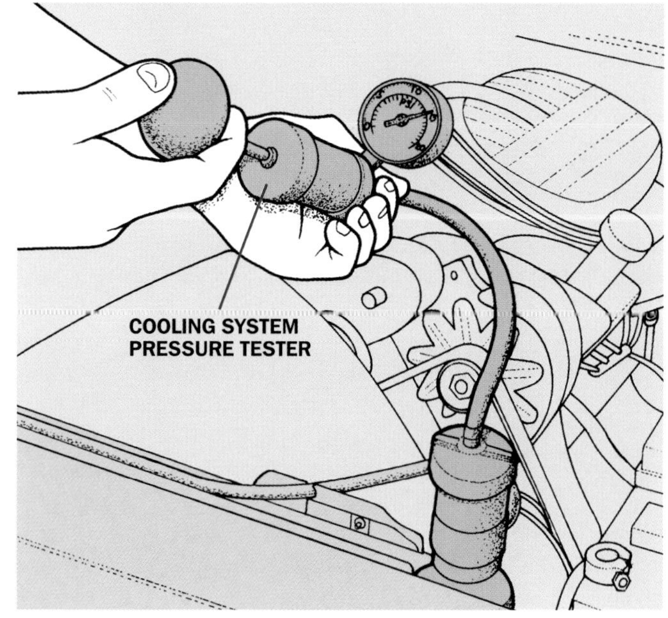

Fig. 4. Pump your system up to a couple of pounds higher than the rating on the radiator cap to check for leaks. You can rent the tool for an afternoon.

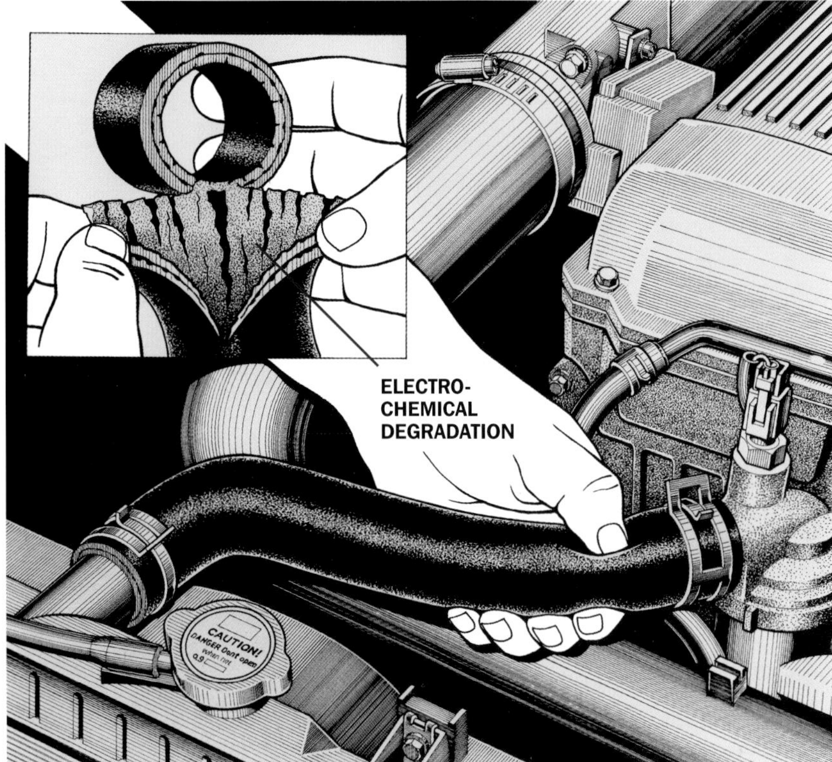

Fig. 5. Check your hoses for electrochemical degradation by pinching and rolling the hose between your fingers and thumb. Feel for cracks in the inner liner.

overflow reservoir, which on many cars is at atmospheric pressure and isolated from the pressurized part of the cooling system. Hairline cracks in reservoirs often result in leaks that travel along body seams and are detectable only if you are really looking for them.

•The engine periodically runs so hot that coolant fills the atmospheric overflow reservoir and overflows it. Or the pressure cap valve is weak, so that coolant flows from the system into the reservoir even under normal operating temperatures. Check the coolant level in the reservoir immediately after getting stuck in heavy traffic. If coolant is ready to pour out of the reservoir vent, pressure-test the cap to see if it's holding the specified pressure.

On systems where the reservoir is pressurized, inspect the radiator-cap valve seal for deterioration. A bad seal can allow coolant to be lost by evaporation.

If the cap is good, next check the antifreeze concentration with a hydrometer. If the percentage of antifreeze is low (below 50%), the coolant will boil at a lower-than-normal temperature and contribute to the problem. If the problem is the coolant running too hot, a poor cooling system condition may be responsible. This would include low coolant level, an electric fan coming on too late (or a mechanical clutch fan slipping), a defective water pump, a plugged radiator or even something as simple as a bug-and-road film coating on the front of the condenser or radiator. Such a coating blocks the cooling airflow.

Preventing Future Leaks

Today's hoses fail more often from the inside, because of a problem called electrochemical degradation, the catchy ECD for short. The metals of the cooling system and the hose material, combined with the coolant, form an electrical cell that produces a low DC voltage, particularly at high coolant temperatures. Over a period of time, the electrical flow is enough to cause fine cracks to develop inside the hose, starting at both hose ends and working along the length of the hose. Eventually, the hose develops a pinhole leak or may even burst.

You can't see this damage, but you can feel it. Wrap your thumb and two or three fingers (not your whole hand) around the hose at the end and feel with your fingertips for soft "channels." Run your fingers around the hose to develop a mental picture of what the inside circumference of the hose must look like. Work your way from each hose end toward the center of the hose, and if the hose feels more solid as you approach the center, it's probably suffering from ECD. According to studies by Gates Rubber Co., most upper radiator hoses, for example, are ready to leak (if they haven't already) after about four years of service.

So if any of your cooling system hoses fails this fingertips test, drain the system, cut the hose and peel it off. And install new premium hoses designed to resist ECD. You can get silicone hoses, but newer designs of another synthetic, EPDM, are less prone to tearing and are designed to resist ECD. Secure them with good-quality clamps and your engine should keep its cool.

If you're topping up your system after a leak, all you really need to do is add a 50/50 mixture of coolant and water to the radiator. But if you've been topping up with water, you have no real idea of the relative concentration of the two fluids. Perhaps you've been using water from some roadside ditch or rain puddle—a better proposition than walking or melting an engine for sure, but one that requires you to drain the cooling system completely and flush it.

If you've flushed the system for whatever reason, don't just start pouring 50/50 coolant into the radiator. There still will be a lot of water in the system that won't drain from the radiator (see page 101) and they'll leave you with a low concentration of glycol. Instead, look up the capacity of your cooling system in the owner's manual or the shop manual. Add half that amount of undiluted coolant, and top it all off with pure water.

You did collect the drained coolant for proper recycling or disposal, didn't you?

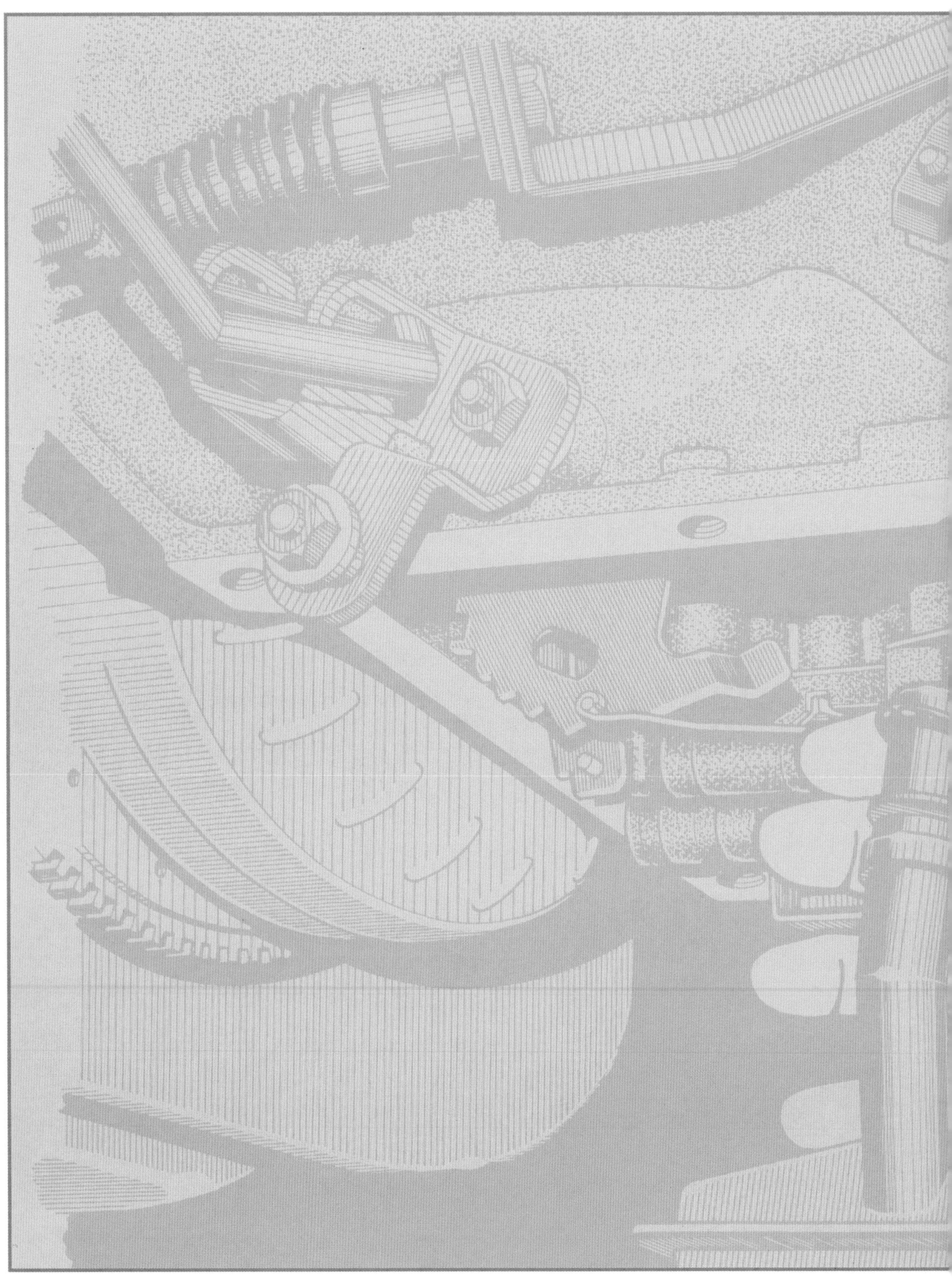

CHAPTER THREE

Drivetrain

Curing a Harsh-Shifting Automatic

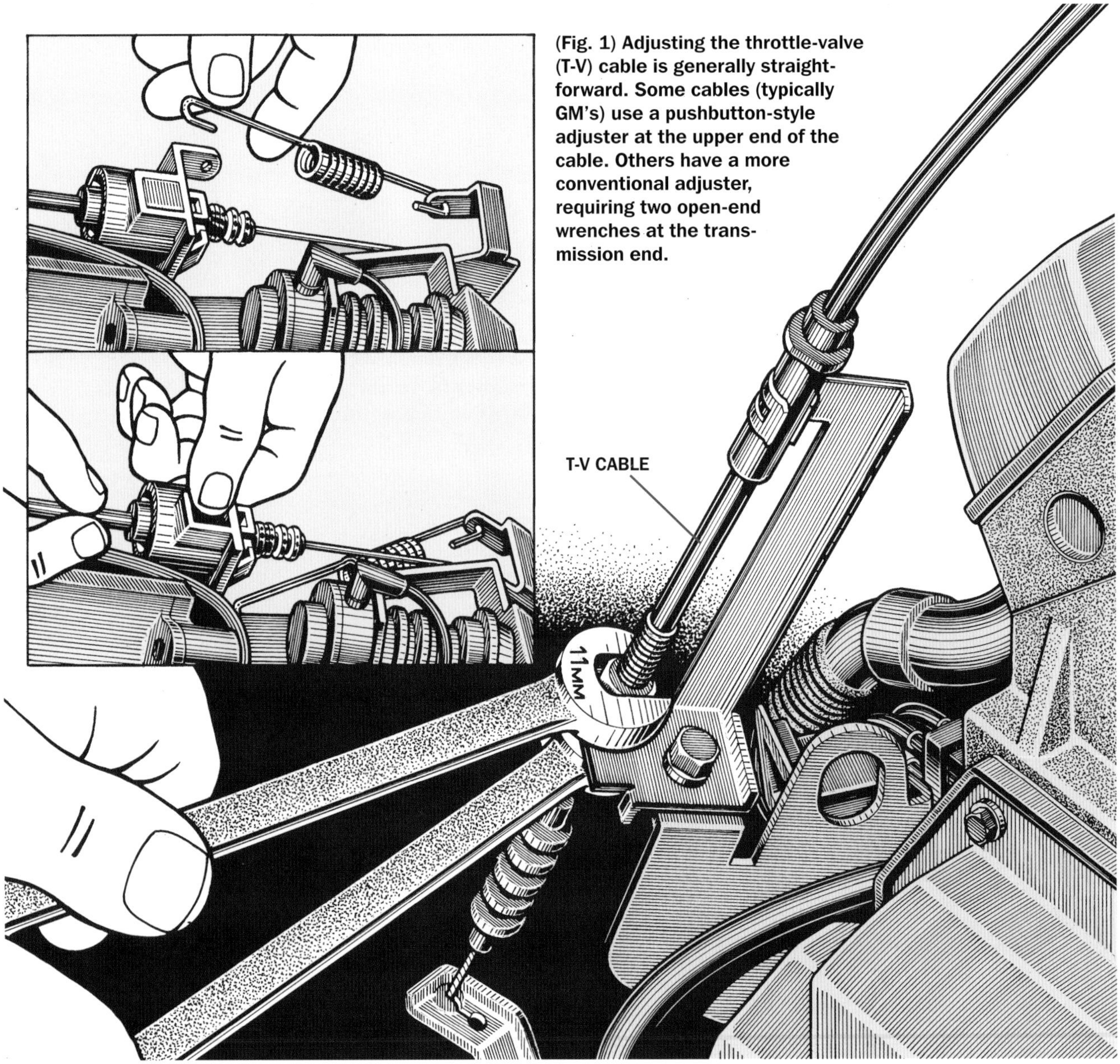

(Fig. 1) Adjusting the throttle-valve (T-V) cable is generally straightforward. Some cables (typically GM's) use a pushbutton-style adjuster at the upper end of the cable. Others have a more conventional adjuster, requiring two open-end wrenches at the transmission end.

T-V CABLE

11MM

There's coffee all over your shirt, the dog refuses to ride in the car and your teenagers have threatened you with a class-action whiplash lawsuit. The fact is, when you were a teenager, you would have paid plenty for a car that got rubber in Second—but when it happens leaving every traffic light, it stops being cool.

An automatic that clunks into gear and suffers from irritating vibrations in the process is not something you have to live with. Nor is it a problem you have to drop a few weeks' pay to correct. Most of the causes are things you can fix or prevent, and although you'll need a good service manual for adjustment procedures, specs and parts locations, you won't need a collection of special tools or instruments.

There are two basic types of automatics: the fully hydraulic and electronic hydraulic. In a fully hydraulic automatic, found primarily on older vehicles, all the shifting is controlled by piston-type valves that slide in a valve body and direct the pressurized fluid to the appropriate bands and clutches. The road-speed signal comes from a centrifugal hydraulic device called a governor and the engine load (acceleration) signal comes from a cable or linkage between the trans-

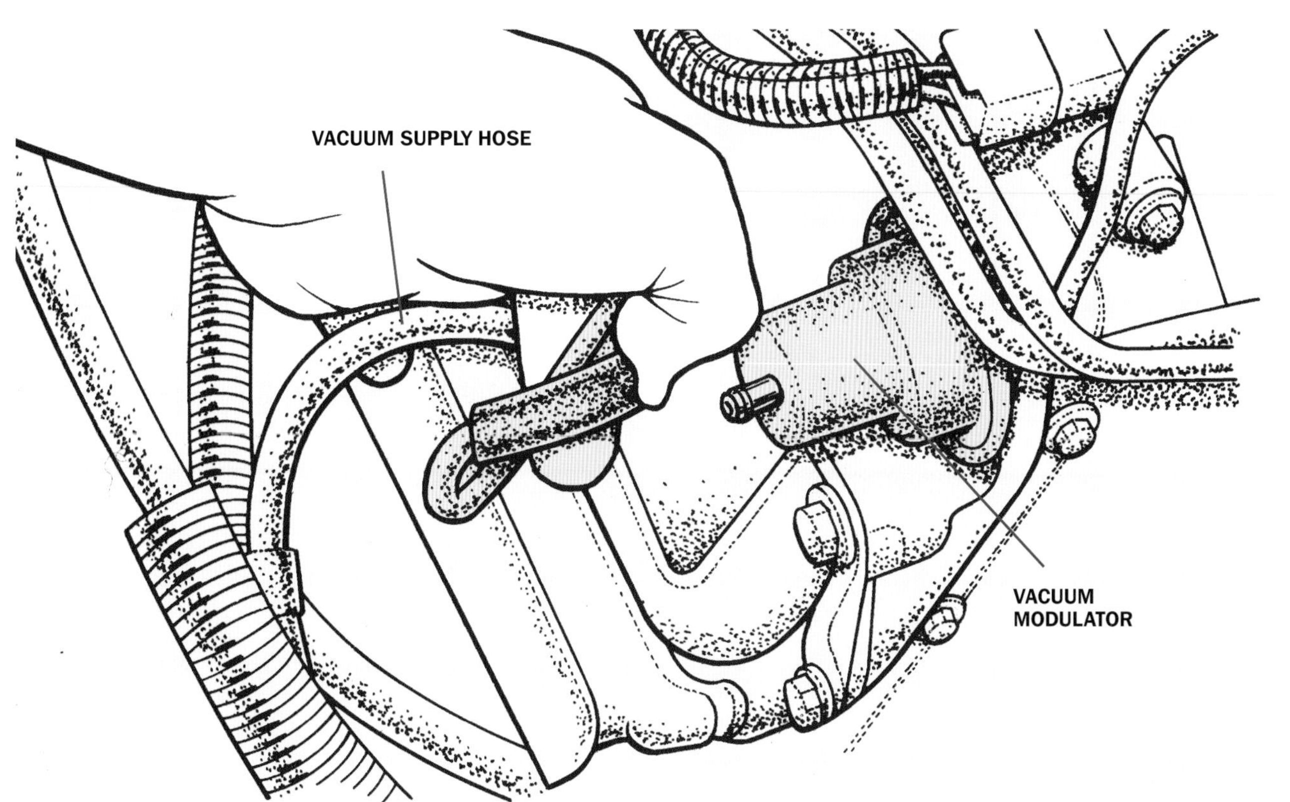

(Fig. 2) The vacuum line at the modulator should exhibit healthy suction when disconnected and the engine is at idle. Look for ATF inside the modulator.

mission and the throttle body. Shift quality and engine load also may be signaled by a vacuum modulator, a diaphragm unit connected by a hose to engine vacuum, and by a link to a piston-type valve in the valve body.

The electronic hydraulic may have a hydraulic valve body with electronically controlled solenoids that provide signals for directing fluid flow. Or it may have a set of solenoids that directly control fluid flow. The road-speed signal comes from a vehicle-speed sensor and the load signal from the throttle body's throttle-position sensor.

Garage Shifts

If the Park or Neutral to Drive shift—called the "garage shift"—is rough, but other shifts are normal and the idle speed is high, then high idle is very likely to be the reason. There are many possible causes of high idle speed on cars with computer-controlled idle, including vacuum leaks, a maladjusted throttle-position sensor and leaking O-rings around fuel injectors.

Idle speed normal? If you'd been pulling a trailer, particularly in hot weather, the automatic transmission fluid may be oxidized. This is a common cause of harsh shifts, particularly with the garage shift. You won't always get a bad smell from oxidized fluid, but if you've done the kind of high-load operation that could overheat it, a fluid and filter change might help.

All Shifts

If all the shifts are harsh, the mileage is high, the fluid has never been changed and the service has been severe (such as hot-weather trailer towing), it's possible that all the control hydraulics are sludged or sticky.

You could drop the oil pan for an inspection and if that's what you find, a straightforward fix is to bolt in a replacement valve body. That's still just a moderate investment. However, before you go this far, check out all the other possibilities that can be easily fixed.

For example, when the harsh shifting is in every gear, the hydraulic-pressure feed, or line pressure, is likely to be too high. Also, on some transmissions the design is such that harshness could result from pressure that is too low, so don't forget a fluid-level check with the dipstick.

Note: Some late model automatics may suffer poor shift quality if they were drained and filled with other than a specified fluid. A fluid designed for Ford Type F applications will cause problems in a Ford transmission for which Type H is specified, for example (see page 132).

Before you go further on a car or truck with an electronically controlled automatic, watch the speedometer. If the readings bounce around a lot, perhaps from zero to 2 or 3 mph when the car is stopped and idling, the vehicle-speed sensor apparently is misbehaving and a bad road-speed signal may be what's upsetting the shift quality. Note: The sensor could be misbehaving without the speedometer effect. The best check is with a scan tool.

On vehicles with fully hydraulic transmissions, the hydraulic governors that supply the road-speed signal may cause late or mushy shifts, but are not likely to cause harshness.

Road Load Signals

The transmission's hydraulic pressure is modulated by a throttle valve,

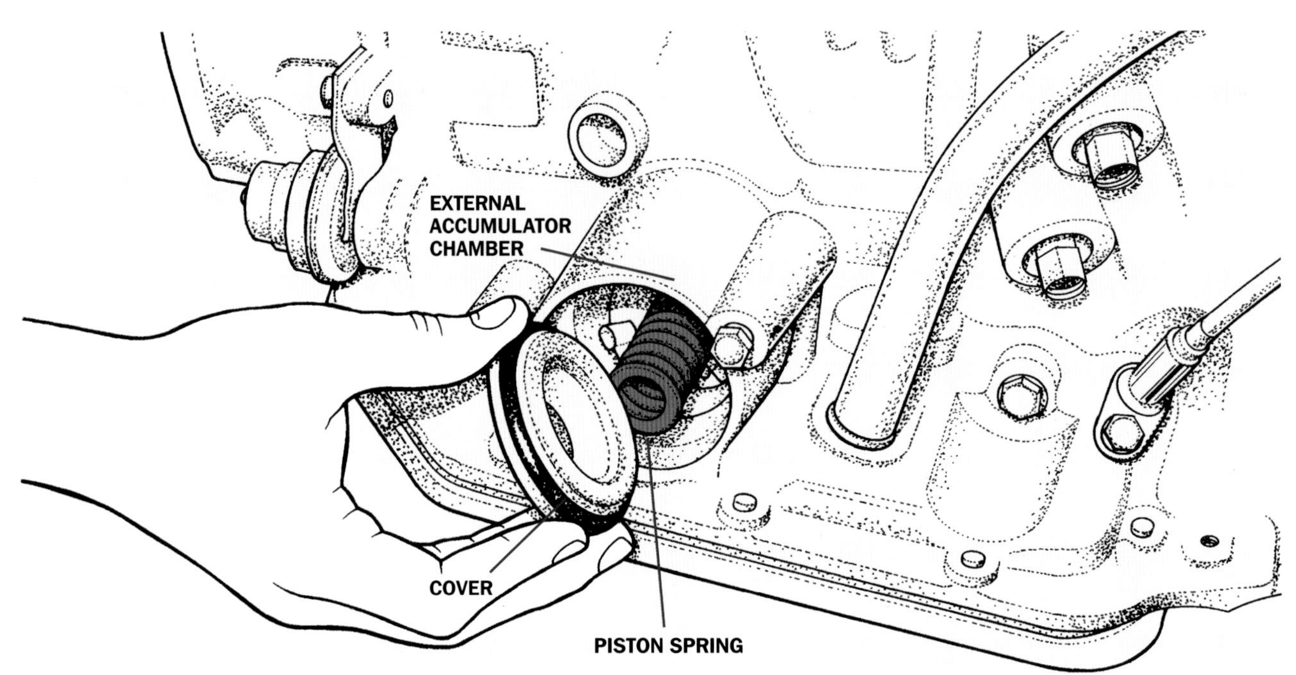

(Fig. 3) Check for sludge or heavy varnish inside the accumulator, which could also indicate sludge in the valve body. Check the spring as well.

which responds to how hard you're accelerating. The valve is in the transmission's valve body, the assembly of hydraulic valves that routes the pressurized oil to make the shifts in most transmissions. And with an automatic transmission that is controlled hydraulically instead of electronically, the valve is connected to external linkage and a cable that goes to the engine's throttle body to provide that throttle-position signal.

However, almost all 1980s and up to mid-1990s cars and trucks use a cable from the transmission to the throttle-body linkage, and that cable has an adjuster at one end. On most General Motors and Ford products, it's at or close to the throttle body. On late-model Chrysler products with the 3-speed (basically hydraulic) transaxle and many imports, including Honda and Toyota, the adjuster is at the transmission end **(Fig. 1)**.

The adjuster has some provision for varying the length of the cable assembly, and it has a spring that takes up backlash. The details of adjustment vary (which is why you need a service manual), but the principle—including inspection—is similar among most makes.

Inspect the spring to see if it's broken or weak (so it doesn't compensate for free play in the cable). Replace a bad spring. Check the cable-retaining brackets to ensure they're not loose or bent, and that they hold the cable housing properly. Look for a bent link at either end of the cable. Next, operate the throttle linkage and watch the cable, which should function smoothly and progressively at both ends. If it doesn't, make the adjustment.

On General Motors vehicles, a typical procedure would be to press the release button on the adjuster and pull the cable slider through the adjuster with the throttle linkage held closed, leaving just a hair of free play so there's no binding.

On a Honda Accord, the usual method begins with running the engine at idle, pulling on the cable housing toward the throttle body to remove all play and checking for some free play between the bracket and the locknut on the throttle-body side (about .040 in., which you can measure with a feeler gauge) **(Fig. 2)**. If there's not enough or too much free play, hold the locknut on the transmission side (the lower locknut) and turn the locknut on the throttle-body side (the upper one).

Things vary somewhat for electronically controlled transmissions. Because the throttle-position sensor provides the upshift/downshift signals, it's the primary item to check. If the throttle-position signal to that throttle-valve assembly is wrong, the shift quality goes down. To see if the sensor is operating within factory specs, perform a scan tool test. Or probe the signal terminal of the sensor with a high-impedance (minimum 10 megohms) digital voltmeter, following the service manual procedure.

Both fully hydraulic and electronically controlled transmissions may use a vacuum modulator. And the modulator is a major factor in shift quality in either case. The modulator takes the engine vacuum signal and uses it to control the shift characteristics, so if vacuum is low (because the engine is out of tune or because there's a vacuum leak), the transmission will behave as if the car is being accelerated and "stiffens" the shifts. With the engine idling, disconnect the vacuum hose and feel the hose end for a strong vacuum (at least 13 in. if you want to check with a gauge). Also test for a leaking diaphragm by inserting a cotton swab into the neck. If there is any transmission oil on the swab, the diaphragm is leaking. Replace the diaphragm unit.

High altitude and low vacuum can affect shift quality, so if you've moved up to the mountains, ask the local

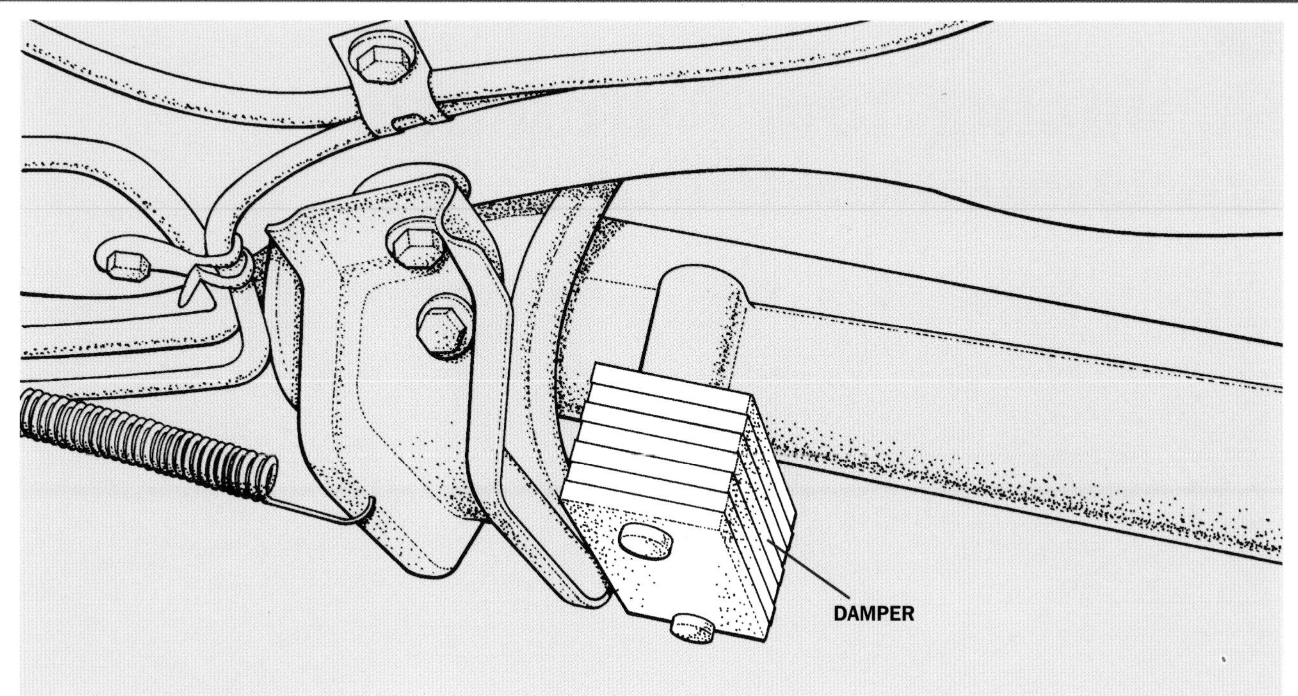

(Fig. 4) Some transmissions use an external damper bobweight at the end of the tailcone to control vibration. If it's missing or loose, you could have poor shift quality.

dealer if there's a special modulator with an altitude compensator.

Only One Shift

Does the harsh shifting occur only in one gear change, such as First to Second or Third to Fourth, for example? The accumulator is something to suspect on fully hydraulic and partly electronic automatics. Most hydraulic clutch/band circuits have an accumulator, which is a spring-loaded piston assembly in a chamber, to prevent shift shock. If the chamber is filled with sludge or the piston spring is broken, it could be responsible (**Fig. 3**). If the accumulator is external, you can remove the cover and look inside.

Of course, a sludge-filled or varnished accumulator chamber could indicate a varnished valve body under the oil pan. So one harsh shift now could become all harsh shifts soon. However, just cleaning out the one external-access accumulator now could be smooth-shift news for a long time.

If the accumulators are on the valve body, the job is more difficult because you'll have to remove the oil pan. But at least you get a look at the valve body too. Refer to a service manual to see what's involved in an inspection.

Shudder and/or Vibration

The automatic transmission lockup clutch, used on every modern automatic to help the carmakers meet fuel-economy standards, is responsible for all sorts of shudders, particularly if it engages at the wrong time. A simple way to determine if it's the reason for poor shift quality is to unplug the wiring connector on the transmission. Do this only for a brief test, as many transmissions will overheat fluid if they don't get clutch engagement. And be sure to unplug the right connector, as many automatics have more than one, particularly if they have electronic controls.

If the transmission becomes silky smooth with the clutch circuit disabled, check with the dealer to find out if there's a factory fix. On newer cars there may be a reprogrammed computer or a new computer module to raise the shift speed. Or there may be a recalibrated pressure switch (to accomplish the same thing) in a hydraulic passage for the transmission-speed governor.

Another cause of shudder or a vibration is a loose, broken or missing vibration damper that may be attached to your transmission (**Fig. 4**). Not a lot of cars have a damper, and the damper alone doesn't directly affect shift quality. But if it's not intact and tightly mounted, the overall response of the transmission is affected, and that may worsen the feel of the shifts.

Whatever you do, don't try to cure shift problems by pouring some additive, particularly a limited-slip differential oil, into the transmission. Limited-slip oil contains a large dose of special friction modifiers that cures harsh shifts and shudder. But it also causes so much slippage that the clutches and bands will burn out fast.

What about harsh downshifts on acceleration? Well, the typical downshift, made at full throttle or close to it, generally is harsh. If it's the only harsh shift and it suddenly becomes much harsher, check the fluid level. If the fluid level is normal, and you have a fully hydraulic automatic, open the manual and look for a downshift cable adjustment. It often is similar to the throttle-valve cable adjustment, but made at wide-open throttle. Check the manual.

The odds are very good that you'll find the reason for your car's harsh shifts somewhere among the basic items we've covered here. Then, you can send those nasty little shifts back to charm school.

EASY

Replacing Your Automatic Transmission Filter

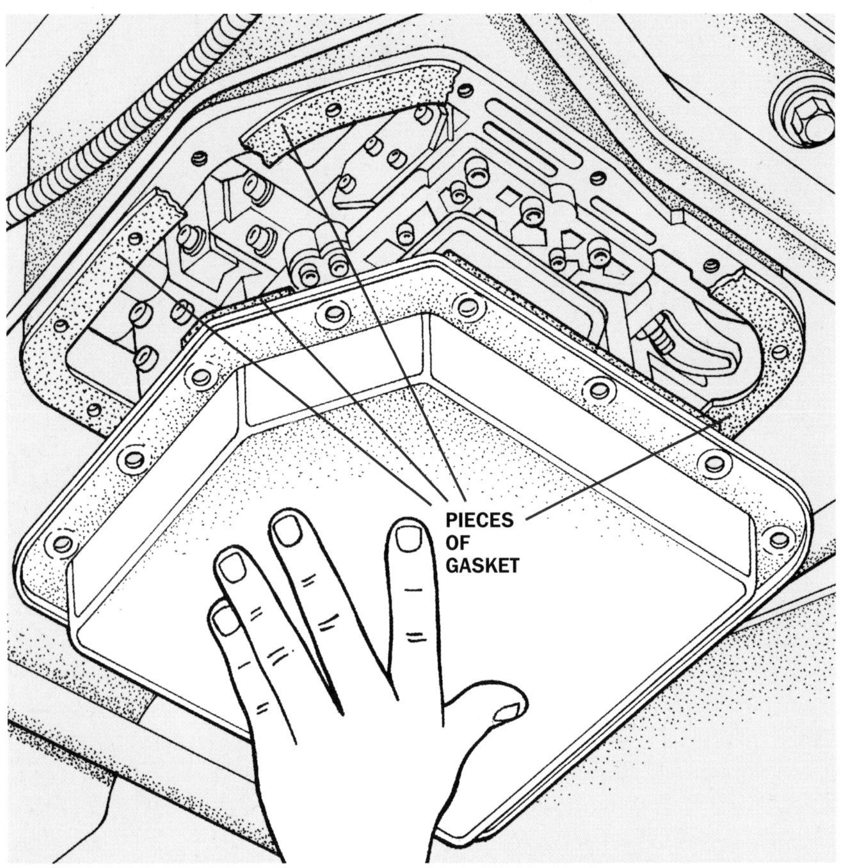

(Fig. 1) **Jack up the car and get a good-size drain pan. Loosen and remove the bolts on the transmission pan from rear to front, then drain the oil.**

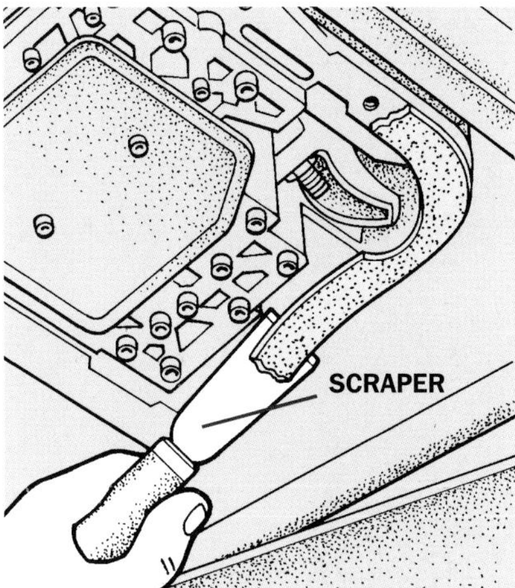

(Fig. 2) **Use a scraper to remove the remains of the old gasket, being careful not to scratch the aluminum transmission casting.**

You've just spent the hottest 4 hours of your life creeping through a colossal traffic jam. You pull into the driveway and collapse into your favorite comfy chair in your air-conditioned den. Later, in the cool of the evening—before you begin packing the family car for a get-away—you check the car's vital fluids. The oil and coolant are okay, but the automatic transmission dipstick is still too hot to touch—the fluid on it is as black as squid ink and smells like the bottom of a barbecue grill after a picnic. Time to change the transmission oil and filter.

The oil in your automatic transmission can get very hot—often approaching 300°F—when you're pulling a heavy load or moving slowly in hot weather. But it also can get every bit as torrid when the wheels are spinning and slipping on icy roads in winter, so this is a year-round issue. And the oil becomes contaminated with particles that have worn off the transmission's clutches and bands, even metal shavings from the pump and other moving parts.

Don't wait until the oil sample on the automatic transmission dipstick has a burned odor to change both the oil and the filter. Unlike engine oil, the automatic transmission oil not only has to lubricate, it also has to provide hydraulic pressure to operate the clutches and bands that produce the gear-ratio changes.

Factory recommendations for transmission oil and filter changes range widely. GM, for example, says 100,000 miles, but that's under ideal conditions. And the recommendation comes down to as low as every 15,000 miles given one or more of the following: you drive in a lot of traffic and high temperatures, periodically pull a trailer or other heavy load, let the car sit idling for long periods or subject it to other operation similar to taxi, police or delivery services. Mom's taxi service surely falls in the latter category, so a transmission oil and filter change every two years or every 30,000 miles is good practice.

Getting Greasy

Jack up the front of the car, support it on safety stands, put a large catch pan underneath the transmission and loosen the transmission-pan bolts (**Fig. 1**). Remove the bolts at the rear, then loosen the others, so the oil drains out one side into your catch pan. On the typical car, several quarts will come out, which is less than half of the oil inside—and there's no practical way to get out any more oil. Consider that

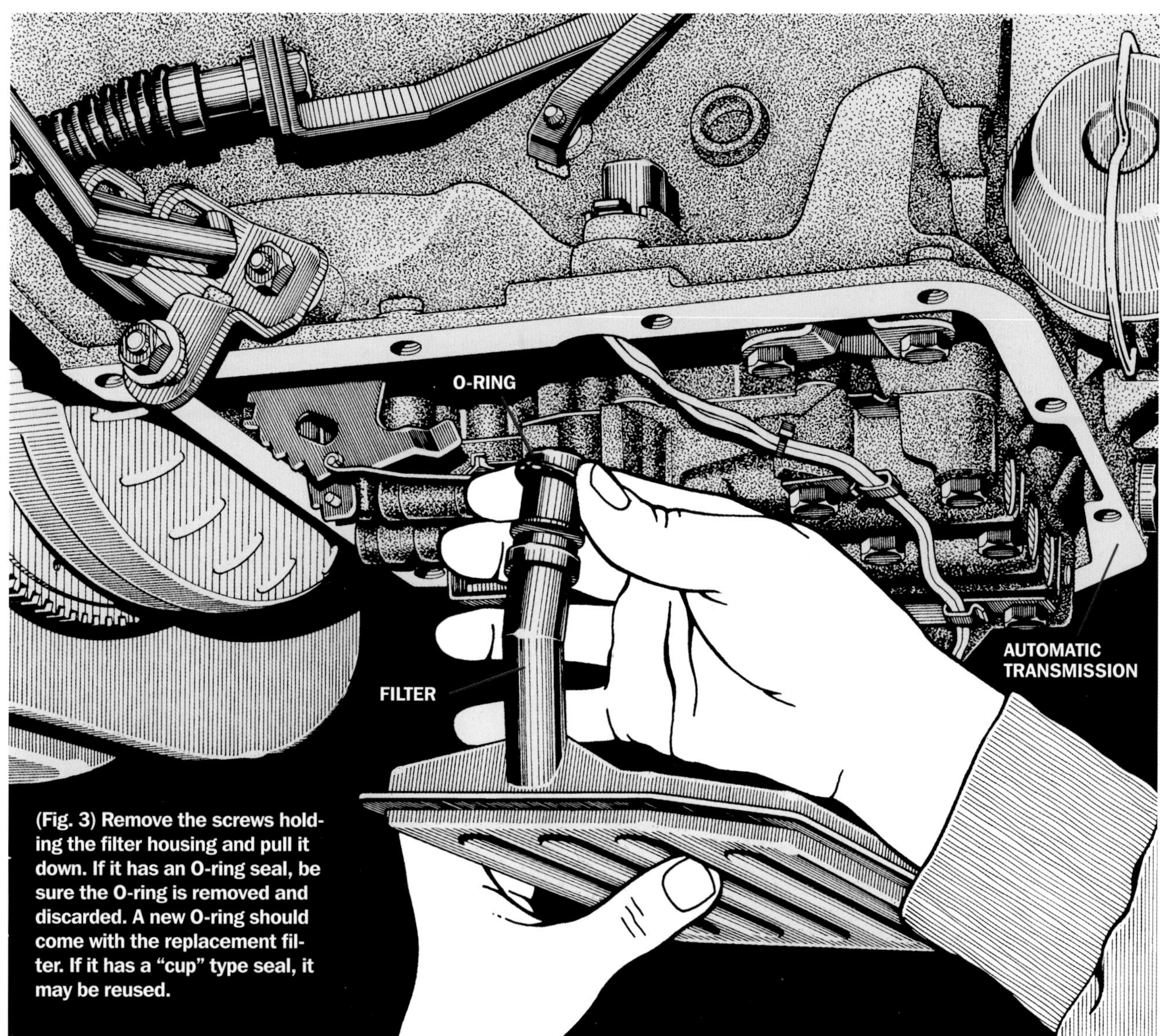

(Fig. 3) Remove the screws holding the filter housing and pull it down. If it has an O-ring seal, be sure the O-ring is removed and discarded. A new O-ring should come with the replacement filter. If it has a "cup" type seal, it may be reused.

the next time you want to postpone a transmission service. Finally, remove all the bolts and lower the pan. (And no, most transmissions don't have a drain plug.)

Scrape the gasket from the pan, taking care not to gouge the flange surface (**Fig. 2**). Wire-brush any gasket residue from the pan. If any piece of gasket sticks to the underside of the transmission, gently remove it with a scraper—not a screwdriver, as the surface normally is soft aluminum and prone to being gouged. A gouged surface may not seal, even with a new gasket. If the gasket is rubber with a raised center section, it's reusable if it is still in perfect condition. Just clean and dry the gasket surfaces on the pan and transmission. If it's damaged, replace it with one of the same type.

Clean the pan thoroughly, as there will probably be a fair amount of silt in the corners, from sludge, worn friction-clutch material and tiny bits of metal. Big flakes of metal might indicate a problem, but expect a certain amount of shiny stuff.

If the oil-pan bolt holes are distorted by previous overtightening, place the edge of the pan on a heavy metal surface (your workbench, for example) and with a ball-peen hammer, tap them down flat to ensure a good seal.

This Is a filter?

It probably looks more like a fine-mesh window screen, but this is what passes for a filter. It's adequate to screen out chunks, but very small abrasive particles pass right through, another compelling reason to service the tranny regularly.

Remove the old filter, which typically is held by screws. Pull it down slowly, as it may have a neck with an O-ring, and you should remember where that ring is (**Fig. 3**). Some O-rings sit on the neck, but are prone to sticking inside the case when you remove the filter. If you don't remove the old O-ring and add a new one with the new filter, it won't seat properly. Most General Motors cars have an O-ring, but there's a cup seal that goes in the case on some models since 1994. The filter neck is inserted into it, and there's no O-ring at all. Consider retrofitting this new filter

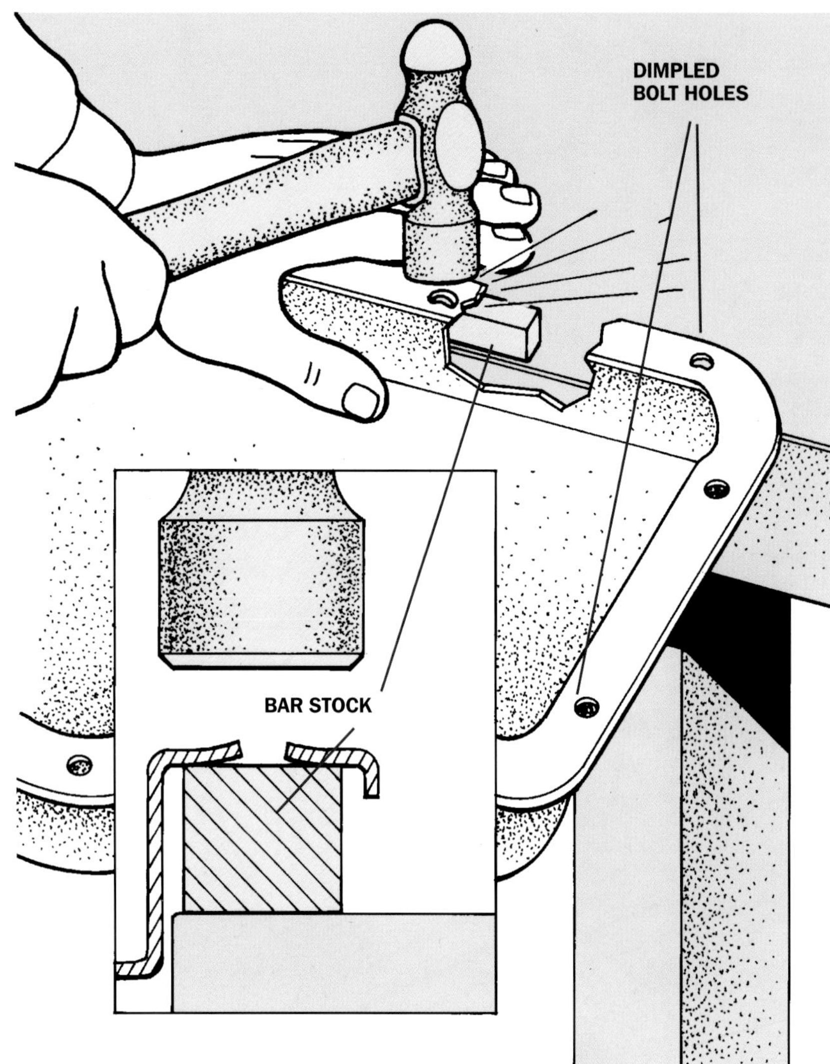

(Fig. 4) Overtightened bolts can distort the pan's sealing surface. Flatten the dimples with a hammer against a hard surface.

and cup seal to the earlier-type tranny.

Apply a thin film of nonhardening gasket sealer to the oil pan, lay the new gasket on it and install a bolt through each corner to hold the gasket in place.

Hand-start each bolt. Don't tighten any bolts more than two or three threads until they're all in place (**Fig. 4**). Then run them down with a ratchet until the gasket is in contact all the way around. Tighten the bolts to factory specifications with a torque wrench, using a spiral pattern starting from the center of the pan and working alternately to the ends. Go in steps, a few foot-pounds at a time, up to the torque spec.

Glug, Glug

Finally, add fresh oil. Not all cars use the same type. Most late models take Dexron IIE or Dexron III, although Ford recommends an oil that meets its Mercon standard (including some older cars for which a "Type H" fluid was prescribed). Check your owner's manual. Major brands of oil are formulated to meet all these carmaker requirements, and you should use one of them. A few European cars and older Fords (some through 1981) may require a Type F fluid, which is nothing like the Dexron and Mercon formulas. If Type F (or the virtually identical Euro-spec Type G) is listed in the owner's manual, that's what you should pour in. New Nissan products may call for Type J or Type K fluid, which is not a Dextron type.

Oil is generally added to the trans through the dipstick tube and you'll need a long skinny funnel or a funnel and a hose to get it in. Some GM automatics have no dipstick and removal of a fill plug is necessary.

Whatever type of oil you need, follow the carmaker's precise recommendations for checking fluid level. Typically, you have to cycle the shift lever from P to L and back a few times and add the oil with the engine running. Do it slowly, recheck repeatedly, as less than a pint can be the difference. Overfilling causes as many performance problems as a low fluid level, so if there's any transmission oil left in the quart bottle, don't pour it in. Put the cap back on and save it. If someday down the road you find the dipstick reads low, what's left in the bottle should be just the right amount to top it off.

DIFFICULT

Replacing Your Front-drive Car's Clutch

The problem was almost imperceptible at first: Going up a slight hill at highway speeds, you noticed that the engine was revving higher even though your car wasn't going any faster. Backing off the gas or dropping into a lower gear made the problem go away each time.

But that was a month ago. Now you spend your days looking for routes that have no hills, because even a slight incline causes the engine to rev wildly while the car slows down. There's also the smell of burnt buttered popcorn in the air as you downshift in a feeble attempt (the semi driver on your bumper is blasting his air horn) to reduce the engine load and get the car going again. Your biggest fear is that you'll end up backing down the hill. The problem isn't in the engine or transaxle. All that slipping is caused by a worn-out or misadjusted clutch.

Compared to other automotive devices, the clutch (**Fig. 1**) is decidedly low-tech (see How It Works, following page). And while replacing and adjusting the clutch doesn't require exceptional skill or high-tech equipment, there are some things you should look out for.

Please Release Me

It couldn't be simpler: Push the clutch pedal in and the clutch should disengage. However, if the clutch doesn't fully disengage, you'll hear a lot of grinding during shifts or when you try to put the car in gear. "A lot of people immediately think there's a problem with the clutch disc or pressure plate when the clutch doesn't disengage," says Gabe Vajda, a technician with LuK, a maker of clutch parts.

"Any play in the clutch-pedal parts soaks up travel, so the clutch won't fully release," Vajda cautions. He says that before you remove the transaxle

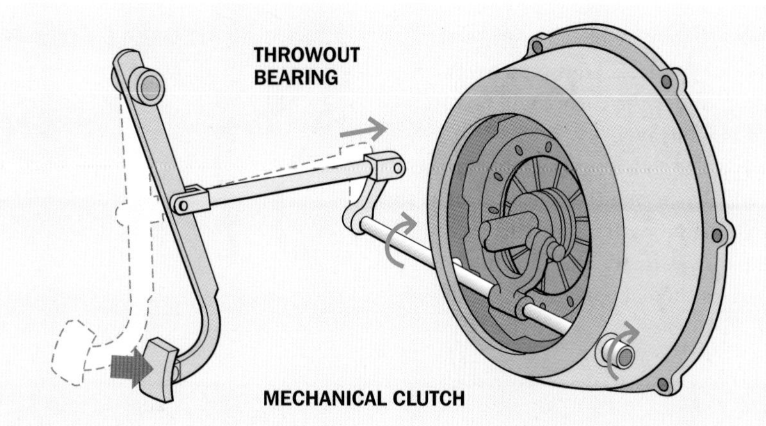

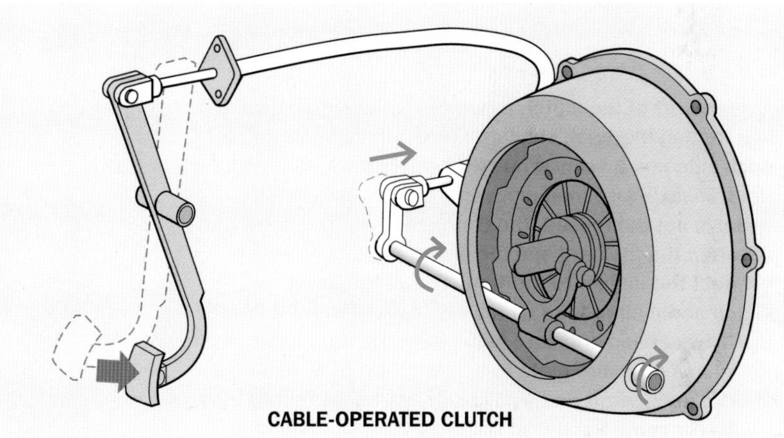

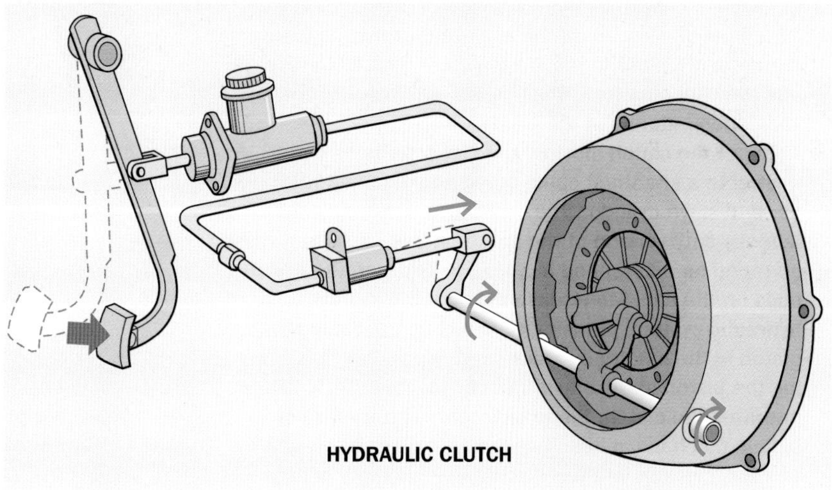

(Fig. 1) Regardless of method, depressing the clutch pedal will push the throwout bearing against the pressure plate. There should be some adjustment mechanism as well.

and clutch, it's wise to check the pedal-arm bushings and the actuating cable, or, on cars with hydraulic systems, the slave and master cylinders. Also, a nonreleasing clutch could even be caused by something as simple as carpeting under the pedal that's too thick, which has been the case with some 1988-90 Chevy Beretta and Corsica models. Trimming away insulation under the carpet will restore full pedal travel.

If a clutch isn't releasing, start by manually prying the release arm at the bellhousing with a screwdriver. If the arm moves freely and the clutch releases there, chances are good that the problem lies outside the bell-

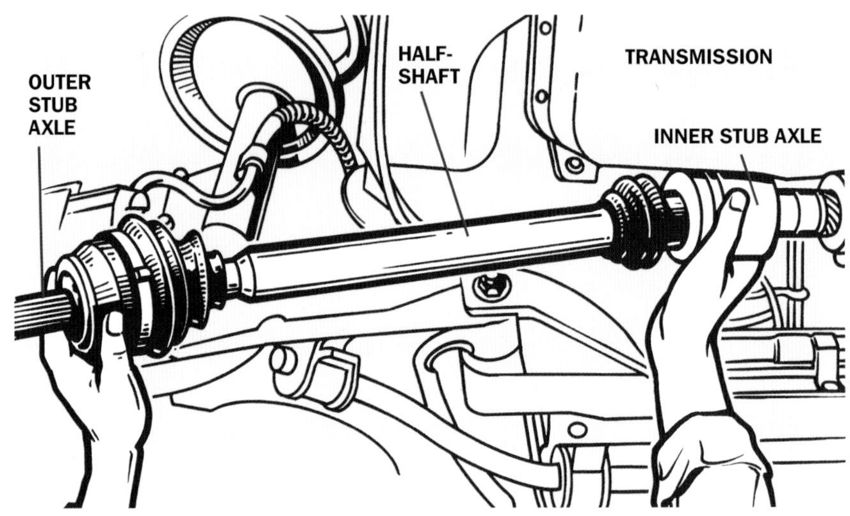

(Fig.2) Remove the outer stub axle from the hub, and then pull the entire axle free of the transaxle. You may need to plug the inner socket.

HOW IT WORKS

Clutch Play

At the heart of the clutch assembly is the clutch disc. It has friction material, similar to brake-lining material, on each side and a splined hub that slides back and forth on the transaxle's splined input shaft. When the clutch pedal is not depressed, the clutch disc is tightly clamped between the flywheel and the pressure plate to firmly connect the engine to the transaxle. Depressing the clutch pedal allows the clutch disc to spin freely between the flywheel and pressure plate, allowing the engine, flywheel and pressure plate to spin on their own, while the splined input shaft and transaxle freewheel with the disc.

The clamping force that engages the clutch comes from a large spring, or series of springs, located inside the pressure plate called a diaphragm. Depressing the clutch pedal presses on the diaphragm spring, causing the pressure plate to move away from the clutch disc, and the clamping force diminishes until the engine can spin independently of the transaxle.

To get the clutch moving, the clutch pedal is connected to a sheathed cable or a hydraulic master cylinder and slave cylinder. The cable system works much like a heavy-duty version of the brake-caliper cable that can be found on a 10-speed bicycle—depressing the pedal pulls on the cable to release the clutch. With the hydraulic system, pressing on the clutch pedal moves a piston in the master cylinder, which displaces fluid, causing the piston in the slave cylinder to move. This, in turn, operates the clutch. Some older cars and trucks use a simple mechanical bellcrank linkage instead of a cable or slave cylinder, but the mechanical principle is the same: Depress the clutch pedal and the clutch is released. How?

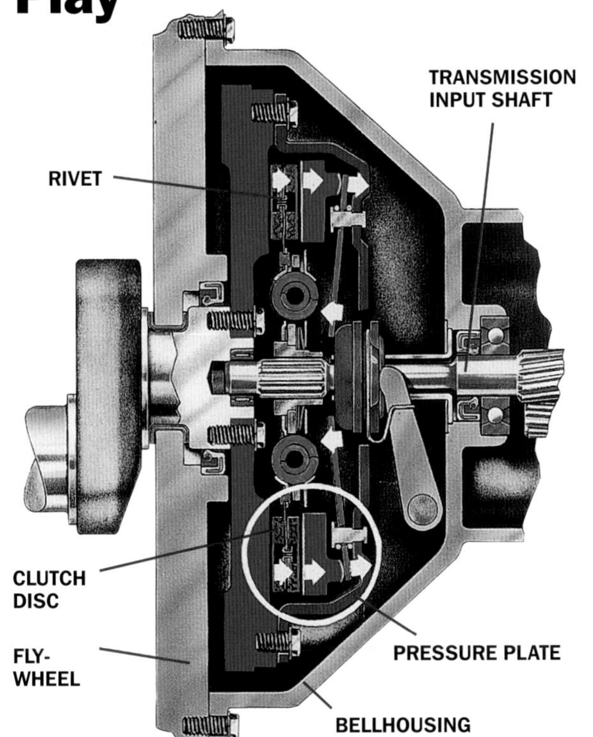

Whether the clutch-pedal system is operated hydraulically or by cable, it moves a release fork that pivots on the bellhousing. The pivoting action moves the end of the fork toward the pressure plate. A throwout bearing (also called a clutch-release bearing) at the end of the release fork applies even pressure to the diaphragm spring and the pressure plate moves back, releasing the clutch disc. Let the clutch out, and the pressure on the spring releases and the clamping force on the disc returns.

housing. On cable-operated clutches, there could be too much play in the cable, which can reduce travel. To reduce cable play, find the adjusting nut at the top or bottom of the cable and adjust the cable to the proper specifications. On hydraulically operated clutches, air in the lines, or a worn master or slave cylinder, can result in reduced travel. To bleed the air, top off the master cylinder reservoir with brake fluid. Place a piece of hose on the slave cylinder's hydraulic vent, then place the other end of the hose into a partially filled glass bottle. Open the vent, then have an assistant repeatedly depress the clutch pedal slowly until any bubbles coming from the end of the vent line disappear. After tightening the vent, clutch travel should return to normal. If it doesn't, then the slave and master cylinders should be replaced.

Removal and Inspection

Barring adjustment, the only way to fix a slipping clutch is to replace it. Installing a new clutch is very straightforward. But you have to make sure the work is done right, since fixing any mistakes usually means removing the transaxle—something you don't want to do more than once. It's best to consult a service manual for instructions specific to your vehicle. The following is a general procedure for replacing a clutch.

Start by disconnecting the battery positive cable. Then, while working under the hood, prepare the transaxle for removal by disconnecting the clutch cable or hydraulic slave cylinder. Also, remove or disconnect items that prevent the transaxle from being removed, such as backup-light wires, air-cleaner ducting, exhaust pipes, the starter motor, speedometer cable and other items. If you are in doubt as to exactly what needs to be removed, consult a manual.

Next, chock the rear wheels and jack up the front end of the car and support it with stands. Working from under the car, remove any additional parts that you couldn't reach from under the hood, including the bolts that hold the axle shafts to the transaxle on most vehicles (Fig. 2).

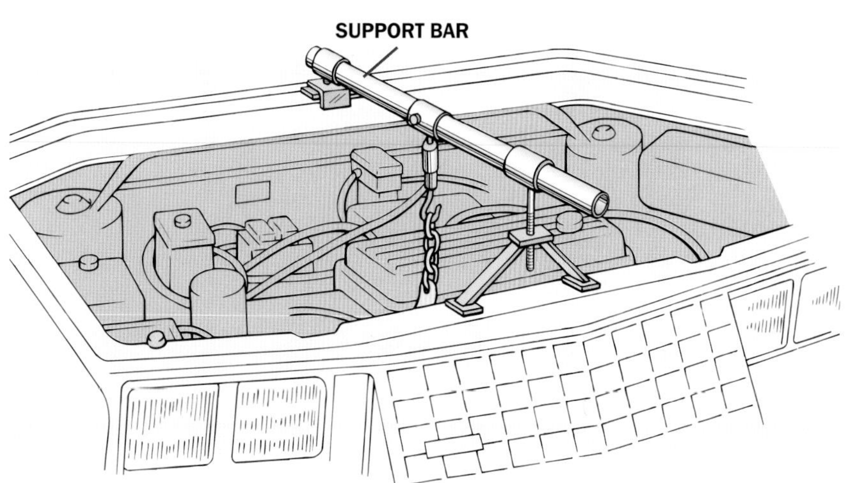

(Fig.3) A support bar or a stout piece of timber will be necessary to support the engine while the tranny is out.

To remove the transaxle, you normally have to remove one or more engine mounts. But before you can start removing them, you'll have to support the engine. With many cars, it's possible to support the engine from underneath by placing a jack under the oil pan (with a third piece of wood on the lift pad to prevent damage to the pan). But on other cars, a special engine-support rod that allows the engine to hang while the transaxle is out must be installed under the hood. (Fig. 3) Again, consult a manual for the proper method.

To disconnect the transaxle from the engine, support the transaxle with a jack and remove the bolts from around the flywheel bellhousing. Next, slide the transaxle away from the engine until the transaxle input shaft clears the pressure plate, then lower the transaxle to the ground and roll it from under the car and out of the way.

Once you have removed the trans-

(Fig.4) The clutch is readily accessible—but only after removing the transaxle from the engine. You'll need to remove or unhook the axles as well.

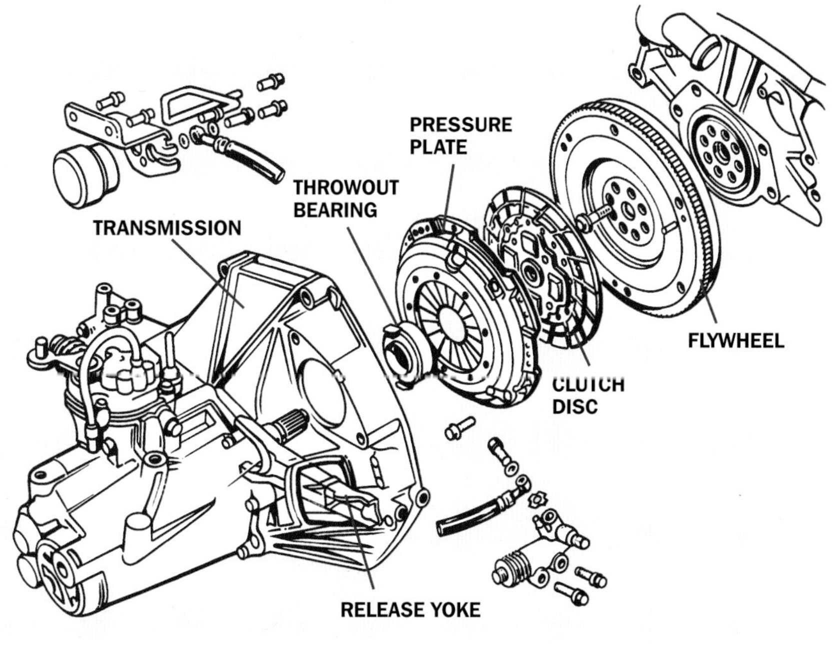

(Fig.5) You'll need an old tranny input shaft, this special arbor, or a wooden dowel to center clutch disc on flywheel as the pressure plate is installed and torqued down.

axle, you will then be able to access the pressure plate and clutch disc **(Fig. 4)**. Remove the bolts from around the pressure plate, then remove the plate and clutch disc. Inspect the friction surface of the flywheel. If it is scored, checked or shows signs of hot spots, it must be removed, machined at a machine shop and then reinstalled. Keep in mind that it's good practice to have the flywheel machined so the clutch disc has a proper surface to break in on. If you don't have the flywheel machined, sand it lightly with medium-grit sandpaper wrapped around a small block of wood, then wipe clean with a damp cloth.

When inspecting the flywheel, also inspect the pilot bearing or bushing at the center of the flywheel. The needle bearings (if applicable) should be lubricated and show no signs of galling. If there's any doubt about the quality of the bearing, remove it with the appropriate tool and install a new one. You should also inspect the back side of the flywheel for signs of oil leakage at the engine's rear main seal. If oil reaches the surface of the clutch, chattering and grabbing will result. Some cars have "stepped" flywheels, which is when the clutch disc rides on one surface and the pressure plate bolts to a surface that's stepped above the clutch surface. It's important that both surfaces be machined the same amount, or slipping or failure to release could result.

If the flywheel is machined too much, it moves the clutch and pressure plate away from the release bearing. This can keep the clutch from fully releasing. You might be tempted to use shims between the crankshaft and flywheel to move the clutch assembly toward the release bearing. However, it's possible for a thin flywheel to burst at high rpm. The only safe alternative is to replace the worn flywheel with a new one.

Inspect the transaxle's input shaft

seal to be sure it isn't leaking. (There's no need to inspect the clutch disc, pressure plate or release bearing, since you'll be replacing those.) If the seal is leaking, replace it. Next, look for leakage at the engine's rear main seal. If there's more than a hint of seepage there, this may well be the reason for the early demise of the clutch disc. Mark the flywheel so you can reinstall it back on the crankshaft in the correct index. Remove the flywheel and remove the old seal. Carefully install the new seal without gasket sealer by tapping it in with a seal installation tool, or at least a large socket or a piece of wood. Check the crankshaft's sealing surface for a depression where the seal has eroded the metal (this is particularly common in dusty areas). There may be a repair sleeve available for your engine, so check with your machine shop if you think you have a problem.

Installation

Before you install a new or freshly machined flywheel, make sure the crankshaft flange is clean. After placing the flywheel on the flange, tighten the bolts in a star pattern to the proper torque specification. There are two tricks to installing the clutch disc and pressure plate. First, the disc is designed to go on in one direction. If you look at the center hub, you'll notice a series of damper springs. On one side of the clutch, this damper hub sticks out from the friction surface. That side always goes toward the transaxle. Put it in the other way, and you'll soon be taking the transaxle out to do it all over again. Second, you'll need a "clutch pilot tool" to install the clutch disc so it aligns with the pilot bushing in the crankshaft (**Fig. 5**). To install the disc, slide it onto the pilot tool, then securely stick the center of the tool into the pilot bearing. Install the pressure plate over the clutch disc, torque all bolts to specifications using a star pattern, then remove the pilot tool.

Before installing the transaxle, install the new release bearing onto the release fork, then make sure that the fork operates freely. Jack the transaxle into position and slide it forward so that the input shaft slides into the splined hole in the clutch disc. You may have to turn either the input shaft or the engine's crankshaft (and the flywheel and clutch along with it) to get the splines to align. Don't force the input shaft into its splined hole. When everything's properly aligned, the shaft will slide right in. If it doesn't slide right in, don't force it. Back it out and try again.

Never let the transaxle hang unsupported from the engine, since this can lead to damage to the pilot bearing, input shaft and front input shaft bearing.

After installing and torquing all the bellhousing bolts to spec, you can reinstall any motor mounts that you had removed, the drive axles, as well as any other components under the car. Once the underside work is done, remove the jack holding the transaxle and lower the car to the ground. Reinstall any underhood components.

You don't really have to replace the clutch cable at this time, but because it costs less than $75, replacing it is good insurance against trouble later on. In any case, adjust the cable to the proper amount of free-play.

Most hydraulic clutch actuators are self-adjusting and, therefore, have no free-play. Still, you'll want to make sure the self-adjusting action is working properly. To do that, simply push the slave cylinder piston back into its bore. If it moves, the system is working properly. If it doesn't move, it means the slave cylinder's pressure-relief orifice is clogged and the slave cylinder should be replaced.

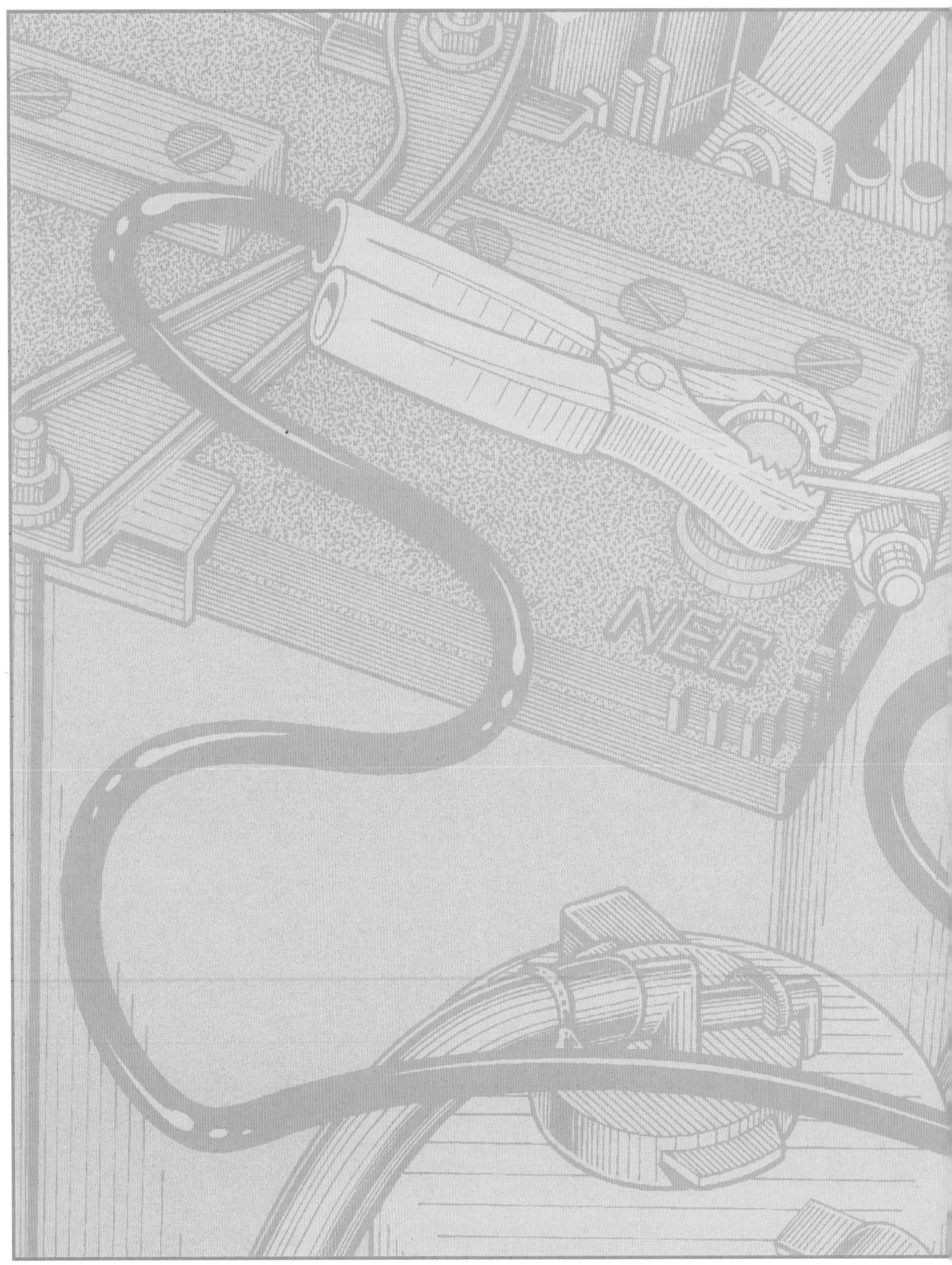
NEG

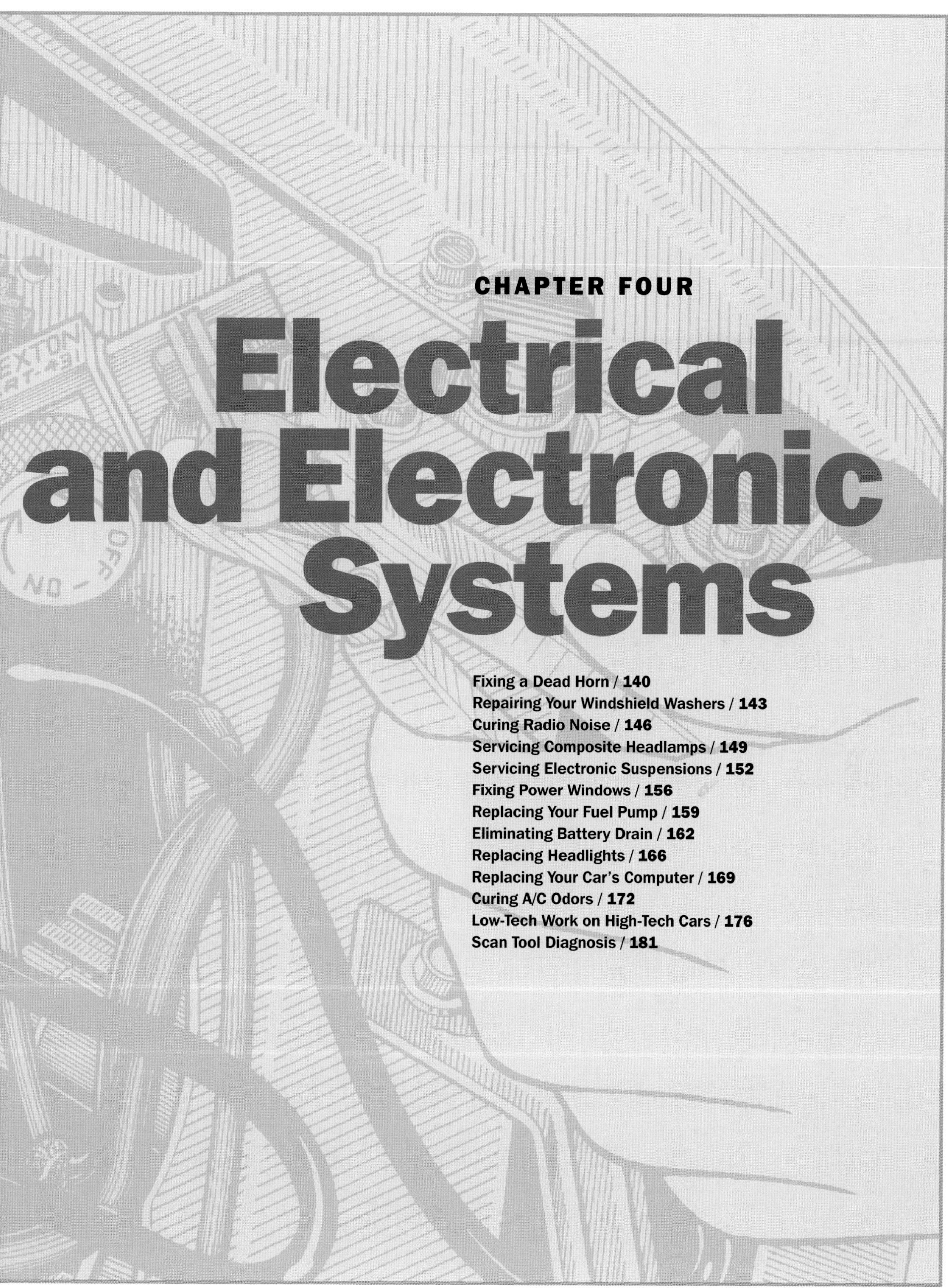

CHAPTER FOUR

Electrical and Electronic Systems

Fixing a Dead Horn

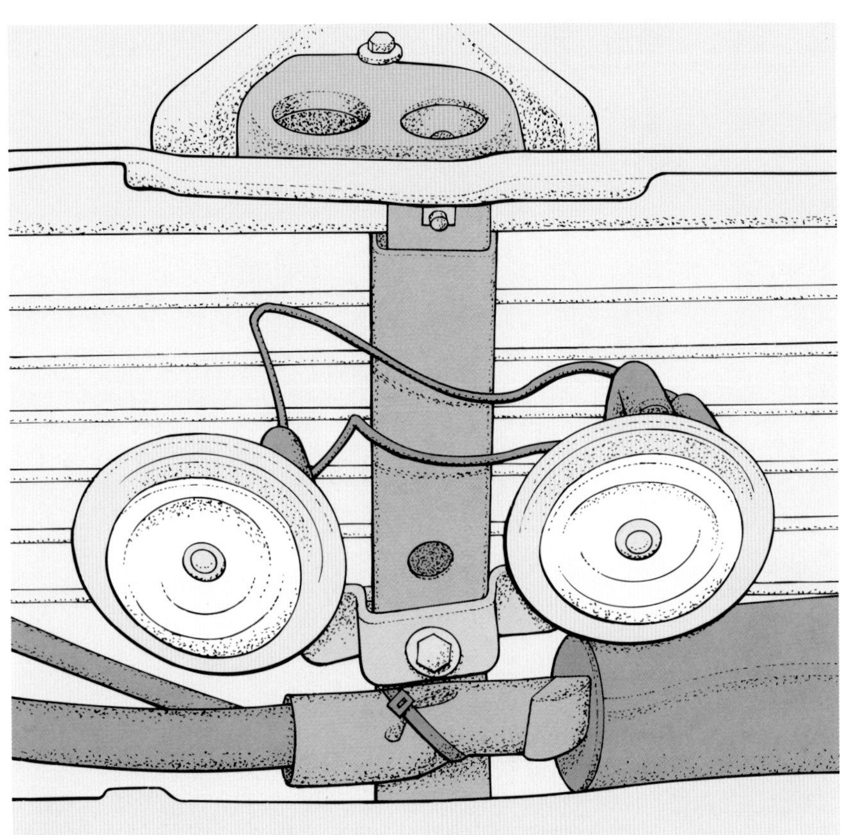

(Fig. 1) The horns are usually mounted behind the grille and in front of the radiator, although they may be to one side, higher or lower.

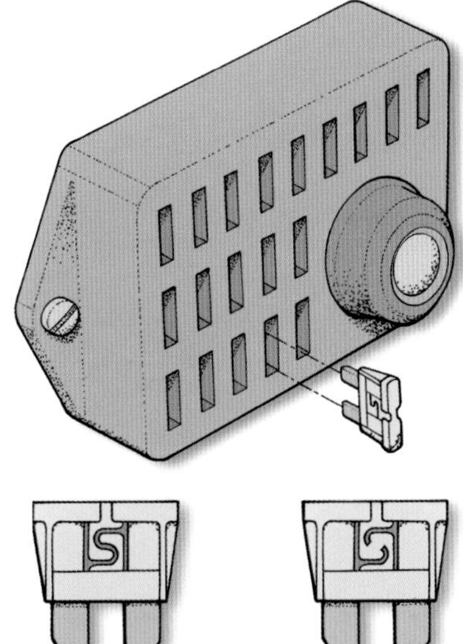

(Fig. 2) See the panel cover or manual to know which fuse protects the horn's circuits. If the S-strip is broken (fuse at right), replace the fuse.

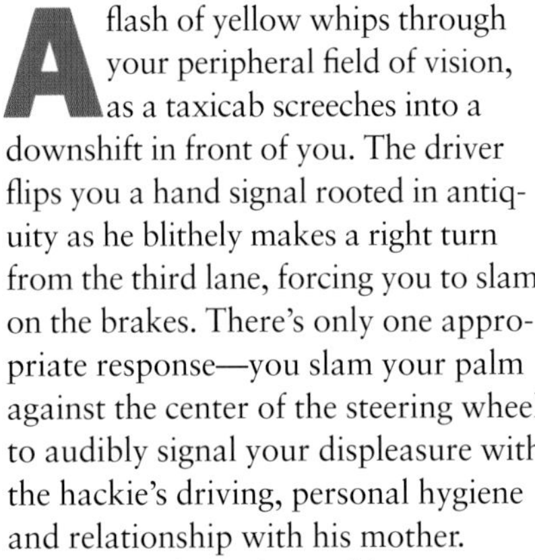

A flash of yellow whips through your peripheral field of vision, as a taxicab screeches into a downshift in front of you. The driver flips you a hand signal rooted in antiquity as he blithely makes a right turn from the third lane, forcing you to slam on the brakes. There's only one appropriate response—you slam your palm against the center of the steering wheel to audibly signal your displeasure with the hackie's driving, personal hygiene and relationship with his mother.

But your horn doesn't blow. A sound more akin to the utterings of a dyspeptic goat emanates from your grille for a few seconds—then silence. Your horn is broken. The moment is gone. And your mood sours even further.

This Has Got to Stop

Actually, blowing your horn as a sign of sheer displeasure is totally inappropriate. The cab driver will undoubtedly continue to drive dangerously despite any message you might have delivered. Some municipalities prohibit blowing a horn within the city limits unless there's a traffic situation that genuinely requires it—if not, you may get a ticket. But horns do have more purpose than letting your teenage son signal to his date that he's waiting in the driveway. A brief tootle can gain the attention of a pedestrian about to step off a curb without looking, and may be the best way to get the attention of that soccer mom driving a 7000-pound SUV while talking on her cellphone and looking in the rearview mirror at her whining kids.

The horn is required equipment by law—you'll need to get it fixed or you may not be able to pass inspection. A zealous police officer may even find it appropriate to write you a citation if your horn isn't functioning properly.

Less-Than-Adequate Honking

In our scenario, the horn blew for a few seconds at reduced volume. This means that the circuitry that feeds the horn with 12 volts is alive and well. Most vehicles actually have two horns, wired to sound at the same time. They usually will be of a different pitch, sounding a chord instead of a single note. Some luxury cars use three horns for a more complex, melodious sound. The horns generally are mounted to the radiator core support or somewhere behind the vehicle's grille **(Fig. 1)**. A cursory rooting around in the engine compartment should find them.

If one or more horns are inoperative, the sound will be slightly reduced and less pleasant. If you sus-

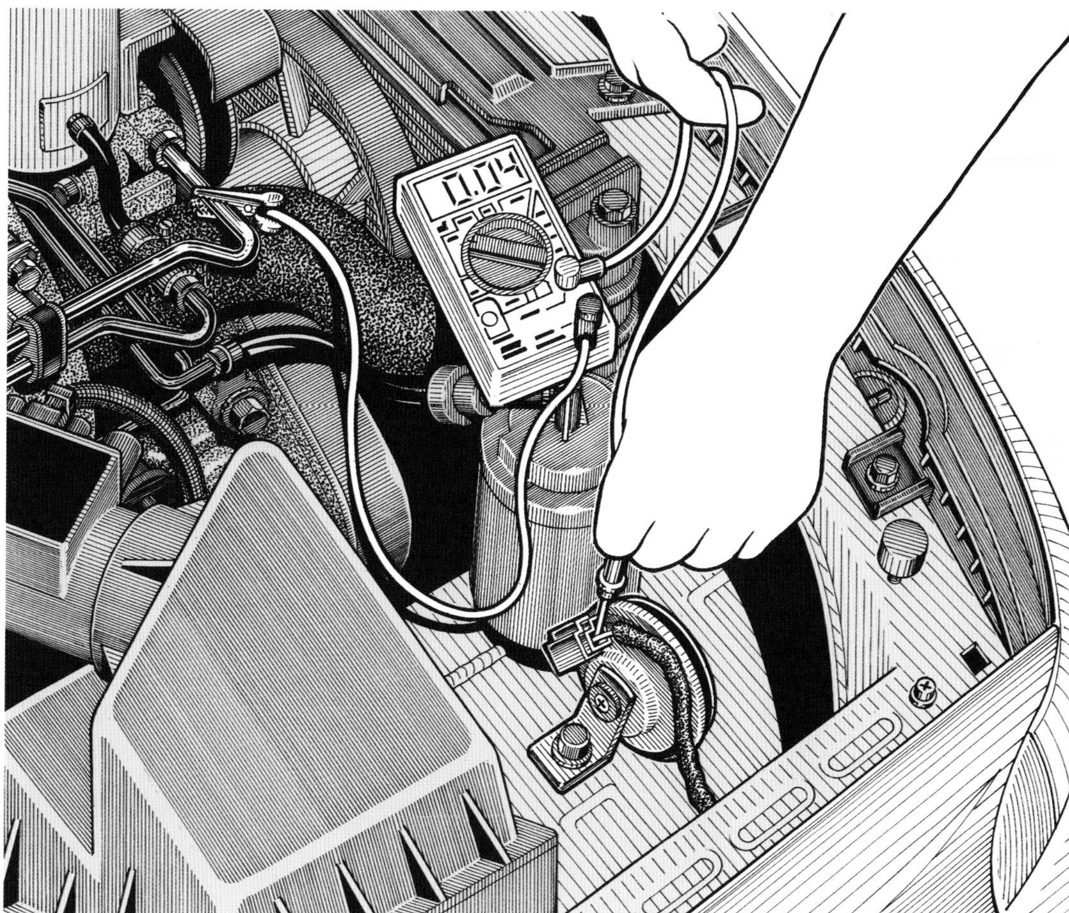

(Fig. 3) Using a simple voltmeter, backprobe the horn's connector to see if 12 volts is present when the horn button is depressed and the key is on.

pect one of your horns isn't sounding, have a helper depress the horn button briefly (key on) while you touch the suspected horn with your fingers. (We recommend earplugs, for obvious reasons.) Sound vibrations? Remove the wiring connector, clean up the spade lugs and then reinstall the connector. Still nothing? If the horn has only one wire running to it, it relies on its mounting bolt to complete the circuit to ground. Unbolt the horn, clean up any corrosion and reinstall it.

If there's still no sound, make sure that a bad horn is indeed the problem by running a jumper wire directly to the battery terminals. If one horn is defunct, replace it. Generally, the horn will have an imprint or a sticker identifying it as a High or Low tone. To preserve the OEM horn character, you'll need an exact replacement. This will ensure that the horn's frequency (pitch) will be the same. If you're not fussy, any universal replacement will work, although the mounting may not be the same and you'll have to adapt it.

Sound Off

Not so much as a squeak from either or any of the horns? Then the problem lies elsewhere in the wiring. Now's the time to check the fuse, which probably is buried in the bottom of the dashboard, the driver's kick panel or under the hood—or

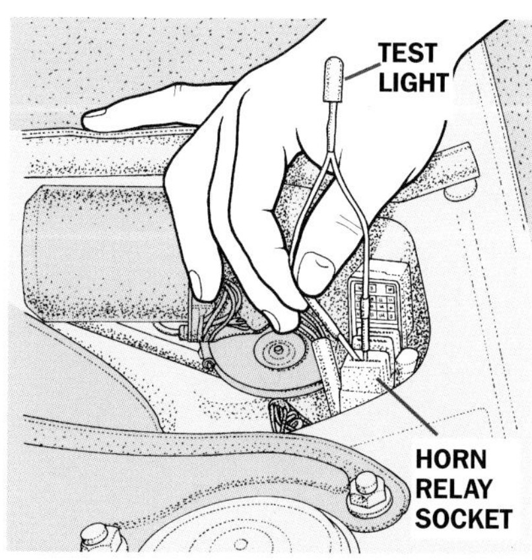

(Fig. 4) Check at the horn relay for 12 volts when the key is turned on.

almost anywhere on the front half of the vehicle if it's not in one of those obvious places. Check the owner's manual for the location of the fuse box and of the specific fuse (Fig. 2). If it looks like the metal strip inside the fuse has failed, replace it with one of the same amperage rating. Once in a blue moon, fuses will seem to fail for no apparent reason. If the fuse is bad, odds are you've got a problem that will make it blow again, sooner or later.

The Fuse Passed Inspection

Now you'll need a 12-volt test light or a voltmeter. You also should find a shop manual or, at the very least, a schematic diagram of the horn circuit.

Start by testing for 12 volts at the connector to the horn (Fig. 3). One side of the circuit is carried by the car's metal frame, so you'll need to check between a good ground point and the wiring connector for the horn. If there's no voltage at the connector, try checking the horn relay (Fig. 4).

The horn relay switches a large current to the horns at a signal from the low-current horn button in the steering wheel (**Fig. 5**). It's a simple, inexpensive single-pole single-throw (SPST) relay, packaged in a small metal or plastic box with five spade-lug connectors. If you're unlucky, your vehicle uses a relay that's integrated into a larger box of sparks that also controls several other functions on your car, such as the headlights or the turn signals. This part is considerably more expensive. Sorry. Consult the shop manual for the location of the relay, as it, like the fuse box, may be hidden almost anywhere underhood or under the dash—and not necessarily near the fuse box. A simple SPST relay will have a constant supply of 12 volts to it, a lead that runs through the harness to the horn, another lead that runs to the horn switch in the wheel, and a ground. Check that voltage is coming into the relay at two terminals and leaving it at two other terminals when the switch is pushed. If it's not, try grounding the lead that goes to the horn button to make the relay pull in. If the horn sounds, the relay is good but the horn button or its wiring is bad. You may be able to simply replace the relay if it's the problem. Otherwise, you'll need to do some serious detective work to chase down the open circuit.

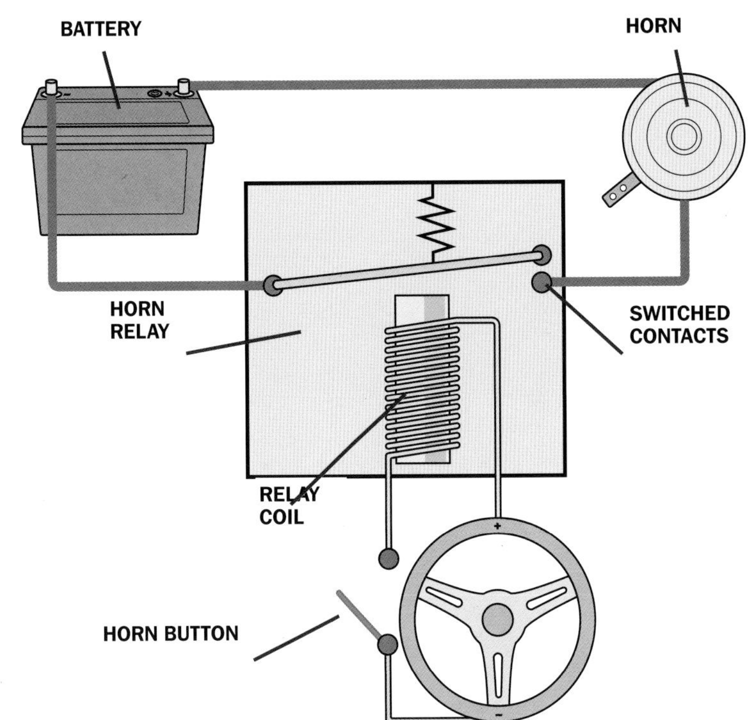

(Fig. 5) The horn relay steps up the low current from the horn button to the higher current needed by the horns.

Button, Button, Who's Got The Button?

If you have a "panic" button on your keyfob/remote, you can check to determine if the horn circuit works. If it sounds the horn, but the horn doesn't work when you press the button, the problem is in the horn button or its wiring to the relay. Every late-model car has an airbag camped in the middle of the steering wheel. This airbag, if improperly handled, can expand with lethal force. Even the static from dragging your clothing across the seat can set it off. And the horn button (or buttons) is generally attached to the top of the airbag shroud. That means you should get a trained technician to remove the airbag for you and then reinstall it after your horn has been fixed. He can test the airbag system to be sure it will go off when it's supposed to and not go off when it's not. The airbag must be removed to access the slip rings or clock spring that carries voltage up the rotating steering column from the relay to the horn button (**Fig. 6**). If you need to access this, we recommend you leave the job to a service technician who has training and service manuals detailing the correct procedures. Incidentally, a horn that intermittently blows on its own generally is caused by a bad clock spring that shorts out to ground randomly. Older car "budget" alternative: Clip the horn button wire near the relay, splice an auxiliary wire to it (and wrap the splice with electrical tape). Run the auxiliary wire to an aftermarket universal horn button you can mount on the dash or console. It's not eye-appealing and you do have to "learn" the location, but it costs just a few dollars.

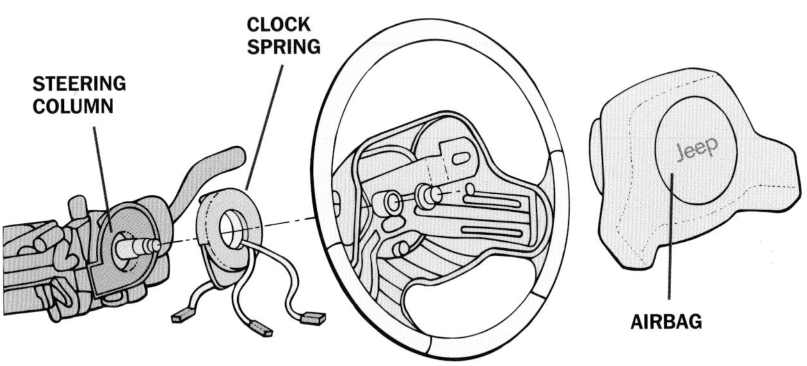

(Fig. 6) The clock spring allows the wheel to turn in circles while still making an electrical connection to the car's wiring system.

EASY

Repairing Your Windshield Washers

(Fig. 1) Replacing a nonworking pump is simple once the reservoir is empty.

It's a light drizzle—barely enough to wet the windshield. So you press the washer button and turn on the wipers. There's nothing—or maybe just a weak squirt—out of the washer nozzles, and the wipers quickly slow down and just streak the windshield to cover up whatever clear areas there had been. Traffic becomes a blur, and you're forced to slow down, pick your way through a slalom of cars and trucks to a side street, and just shake for a few moments until you have the presence of mind to get out and clean the window by hand.

Where's the Liquid?

You just filled the reservoir last week and haven't used the washers since. So the reservoir should have plenty of fluid, right? It was a washer anti-freeze solution? Okay, is the reservoir still full? It's empty? There must be a leak. Even if that solution contains a dye, you still are likely to have a tough time finding a cracked seam in the reservoir, particularly if the reservoir is under the battery or in a fender well, the late-model location of choice for space-deprived power-train compartment engineers.

Fill the reservoir and run your fingers along any seam, and also around the pump seal, which may be a simple rubber grommet. If you're losing fluid at a noticeable rate, you should be able to find a wet spot pretty fast. If it's a seam, empty the reservoir, dry the exterior and apply a bead of windshield sealer or epoxy. If it's the pump grommet, pull the pump out (just work it side-to-side or up-and-down with an outward tugging motion). Replacement grommets are not necessarily easy to buy, so if you can't get one, it's worth trying to apply beads of RTV silicone sealer around the pump opening in the reservoir and around the barbs of the pump. Allow adequate time for the RTV silicone to "skin" (partly cure) so it doesn't extrude out of position when you reinstall the grommet and pump.

The reservoir is full? Next question: Is the pump working? Have a helper press the washer button while you listen at the pump. If you hear it working, disconnect a hose that runs from the pump, aim it into a container and repeat the test. If there's a solid stream, repeat the test at the hose connection to a spray nozzle. If a car has two nozzles, it's unlikely that both nozzles would plug up simultaneously, but it is possible that the hose from the reservoir is kinked, that a check valve (installed in some lines) has closed up or an inline filter is plugged. So if you get a solid stream from the pump, but nothing at a hose connection, work your way back to the pump. If all you can find is a check valve or an inline filter, remove it and make a temporary splice with a plastic hose connector. You may find the washer system operates well enough to make that your permanent repair.

If the pump isn't working, either it has failed or there's a break in the circuit leading to it. Unplug the wiring connector and again have your helper press the washer button while you probe the terminals with a grounded 12-volt test light. It should go on with the probe in one of the two terminals, and when you identify that one (the current feed), try to jump across the two terminals with the test light. Again it should go on. If you can't get the light to go on in the first test, there's a break in the current-feed side of the circuit from the washer button, and you'll have to trace it from there. If you can't get the test light to go on when you jump across the two terminals of the connector, there's a bad ground.

The connector passes both tests? The pump is the problem. On most late models, you can just pull it out (the rubber grommet may come out with it).

On many older cars, where little more than the end of the pump sticks out, look for a serrated retainer you can pry out with a thin-blade screwdriver. Then pull the pump itself with slip-joint pliers on an edge of the electrical terminal **(Fig. 1)**.

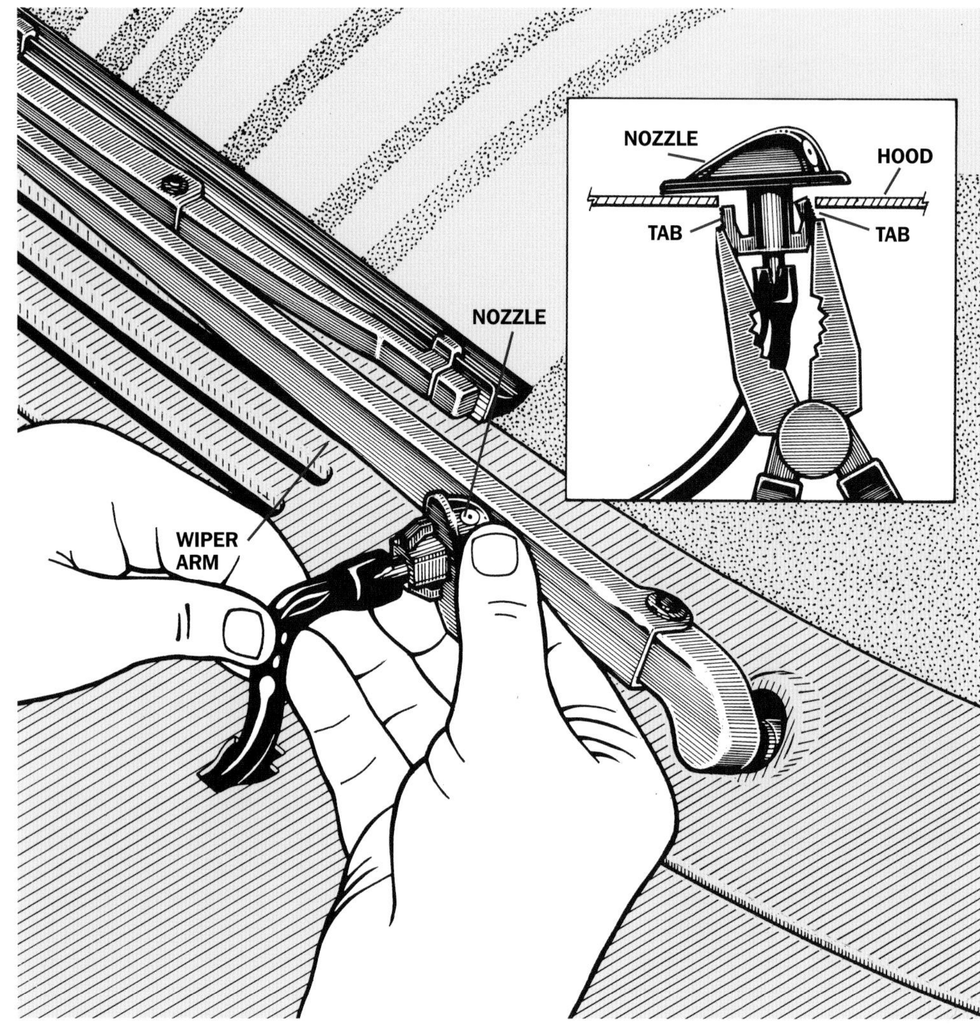

(Fig. 2) Replacing a damaged hose or nozzle is simple: Squeeze the plastic tabs together with pliers and the nozzle should pop out of the hood.

Just a weak squirt from the nozzles? If there's a solid stream from the hose connections, the nozzles apparently are plugged. The easiest approach is to just replace them, if you can get new ones. Most nozzles are held by retaining screws or built-in squeeze clips. Some nozzles have just a single-side clip (press toward the nozzle and push the nozzle out). Others have clips on both sides of the nozzle (squeeze together and push out the nozzle). If the opening is large enough, you may reach in with fingers to squeeze the clip(s). Otherwise, use needle-nose pliers **(Fig. 2)**.

Can't get new nozzles? On some old cars you could work in a needle to clear out the passage, but today, few nozzles have passages straight enough to do that. And if the car has a single, centrally located nozzle, it's probably a "fluidic nozzle." It seems to apply a super-wide-angle spray to the windshield, but actually it produces an oscillating stream that is so fast it deceives your eye **(Fig. 3)**. There are no moving parts within the fluidic nozzle, but it does contain a complex set of passages that produces the oscillation that swings the spray from one side to the other.

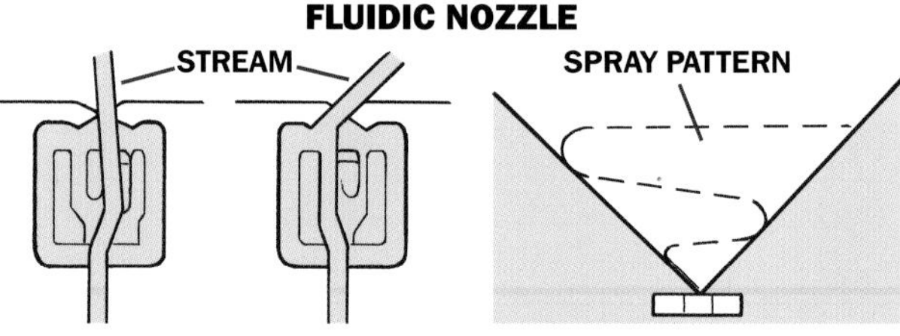

(Fig. 3) Fluidic nozzles cover a large area from a single point.

Soak the clogged nozzles in vinegar, at least overnight, to dissolve deposits, then blow compressed air through the nozzles, and that should restore the spray pattern.

Nozzle Aim

If the spray doesn't go where you want it to, it may be possible to make an adjustment. Typically, if the mounting pad is round, and the nozzle head has two or three spray holes, it can be adjusted side-to-side, up-or-down or both, by inserting a thin probe tool into a spray hole **(Fig. 4)**. Some nozzles have a rectangular hole between two spray holes, meant specifically to accommodate a probe for adjustment **(Fig. 5)**.

On older cars, the nozzle may be a simple piece of metal tubing (with a calibrated orifice inside), held by a retaining screw. With a pair of needle-nose pliers, make a very tiny bend, at a joint if there is one, near the base if there isn't.

You can't reshape plastic, and most nozzles are rectangular and fit into a position that defies change. If it's held by a screw, you may be able to slip a thin piece of plastic or aluminum under the fore or aft end of the nozzle to lower or raise the spray tip, so the spray hits the windshield higher or lower. However, if it's retained by plastic clips, you can't do this, or the clips won't seat. If a nozzle starts to spray off the usual pattern, that's usually the result of front-end bodywork that included hood adjustment, and it may take some readjustment to correct.

Nozzles in Wiper Blades

When the washer nozzles are in the wiper blades, a damaged hose can allow leakage that weakens the spray. Or the hose may have become kinked from careless cleaning of the windshield. The nozzles are never adjustable, so if you can't clean them, you'll have to pop in replacements.

Rear Systems

Some vehicles, particularly wagons, minivans and sport utilities, are equipped with rear washers, which often means a second pump and dual-chamber reservoir, plus a long hose to the rear to check out. If there are dual sections, most are designed so the rear drains into the front when the front is nearly empty. So the fact that you haven't used the rear, and it now doesn't work, could mean a problem with the front system, particularly a leak from the front chamber or a front circuit hose.

There's also a second washer pump, so be sure to check the right one. Washer system service isn't complex, but it may require working in tight, dark quarters. So use a bright droplight and spend the extra minutes to do it right.

HOW IT WORKS

A Washer System

When you operate the washer button, you complete a circuit to the system's electric pump, typically mounted in the bottom of the reservoir.

The pump draws fluid from the reservoir and pushes it through a hose to one or two nozzles in front of the windshield, typically in the hood or the cowl area just to the rear of the hood. On vehicles with a rear window washer, there's a second pump with its own hose, and generally a single nozzle at the rear. Some rear washers have their own reservoirs as well.

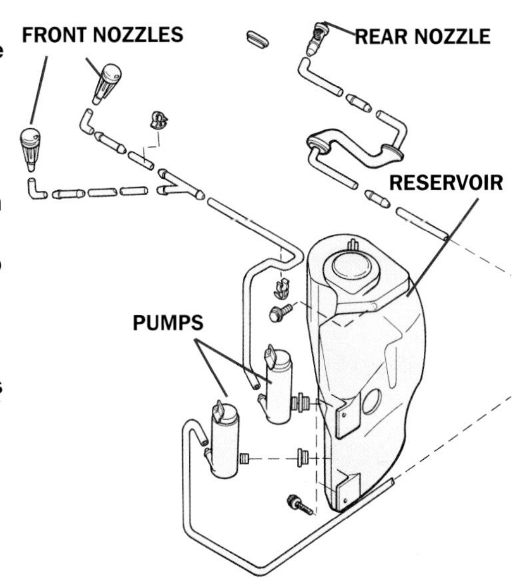

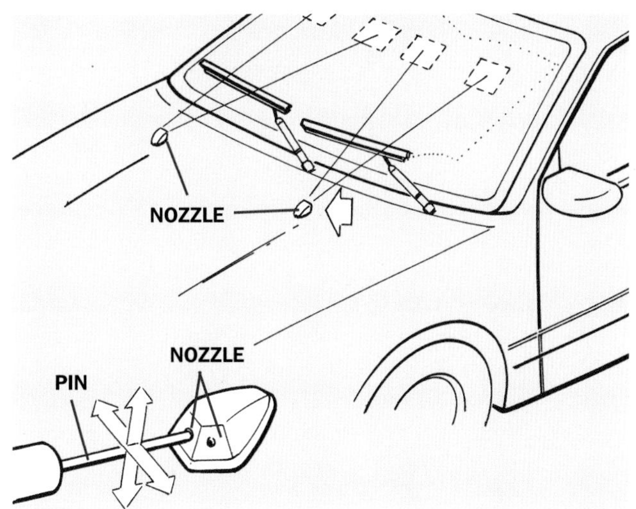

(Fig. 4) Some nozzles can be aimed with a straight pin inserted in the hole.

Inside a Fluidic Nozzle

The single fluidic nozzle seems to apply a wide-angle fan spray across the windshield, but actually it's an oscillating stream. Fluidics is the name of the operating principle. The internal passages of the nozzle are shaped so the incoming fluid goes through a main passage, sort of "leaning" against one wall (a deflector in the main passage "biases" the nozzle to start the flow to one side). As it flows, some of the fluid is diverted through an opening on that wall into a feedback passage that produces a second fluid flow against the incoming flow at its entry point. The pressure of the second flow deflects the incoming flow to the opposite side wall of the main passage. There's also a feedback passage on this side, and again the second fluid flow deflects the main flow back to the opposite wall. This goes on so fast that it appears to be a spray. But because it's an oscillating stream, the flow from one centrally located nozzle covers the entire windshield.

Fluidics works on airflows as well, and the same principle was used in the defroster nozzles of the 1990-96 General Motors minivans, where two standard-size defroster nozzles with normal airflow could cover the large windshield.

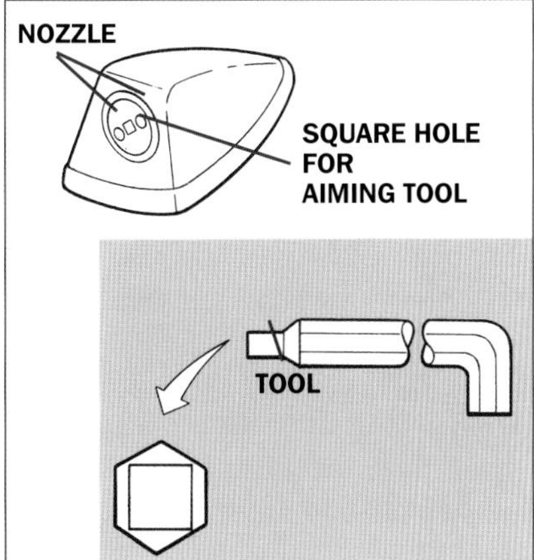

(Fig. 5) Other styles of nozzles provide a receptacle for a special aiming tool.

EASY

Curing Radio Noise

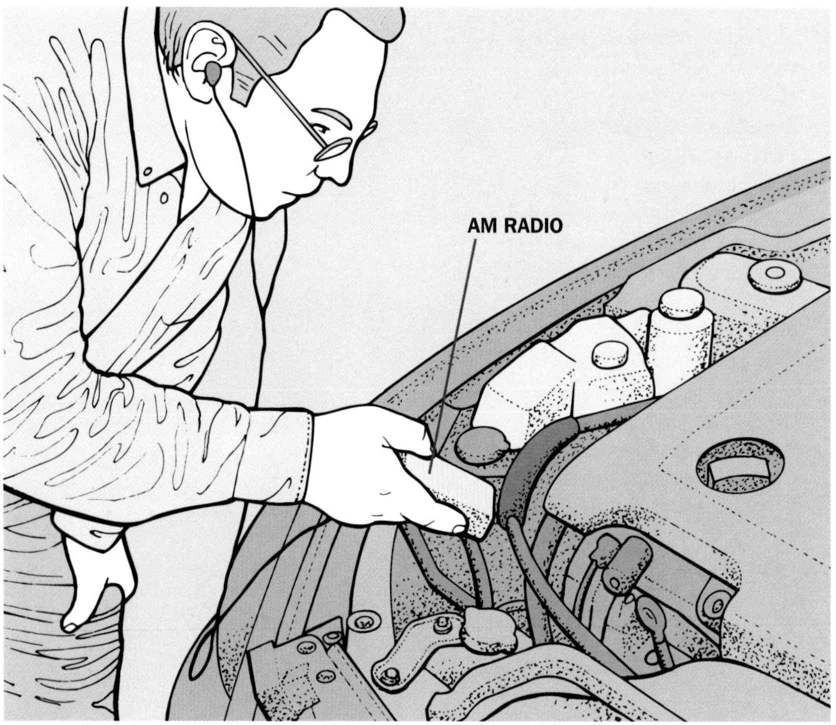

(Fig. 1) A cheap AM radio makes a good Geiger counter-style device for hunting down RFI. Here, we're looking for an alternator with a bad diode. Mind your fingers.

You're looking forward to the chance to listen to the ballgame, having just dropped your purple-haired teenage daughter off at her first semester at college. A lot of ballgames, actually, now that you don't have to listen to her headbanger music, with its shrieking vocals and droning guitars. But instead of the first inning, you hear what sounds like some awful guitar note—and it changes pitch as you speed up and slow down, turning to a maniacal rhythmic clicking as you wait for a traffic light to change. There's no tape in the player. What you have here is radio frequency interference (RFI).

Finding the Source

There are three classes of RF noise—constant, intermittent and engine-speed following. Our hapless father's problem was in the last category—his noise varied up and down in pitch and volume as his engine sped up and slowed down. This type of noise is caused by something that varies its speed with the engine. Likely culprits include the ignition, the alternator or even a fuel injector. Constant-speed noises are usually caused by an electric motor—most likely the electric fuel pump found in the tank of most modern vehicles which runs at a constant speed anytime the engine is running. An electric fan motor will also run at a constant speed—until you change the fan setting or turn it off. Intermittent noises are easier to associate with a source, such as an electric seat adjuster or a power-window motor. In other words, even though the noise comes from a radio speaker, it may be caused by any manner of device anywhere on your vehicle.

Constants

The one motor that's guaranteed to be on whenever the car is running is the fuel pump's, and unfortunately it's usually buried inside the fuel tank. Here's one sure way to tell. Turn the key to the Run position without starting the car. The pump should run for 2 or 3 seconds. Then, when the computer senses that the engine isn't running, it will shut off the pump to prevent spilling fuel and draining the battery. Other almost-constants are heater fans, wipers and electric radiator-cooling fans.

Engine-Speed Noises

Candidates here include the alternator/voltage regulator, a faulty fuel injector and the ignition system.

Geiger-Counter Test

Here's our favorite low-tech tool for hunting down and killing wild noises—a cheap AM radio (**Fig. 1**). Tune it to an empty channel around 1400 kHz, crank up the volume in your headset, and use the radio to sniff out the noise. These cheapo radios use a ferrite-bar antenna that has good reception along its side, but poor reception along its length. Once

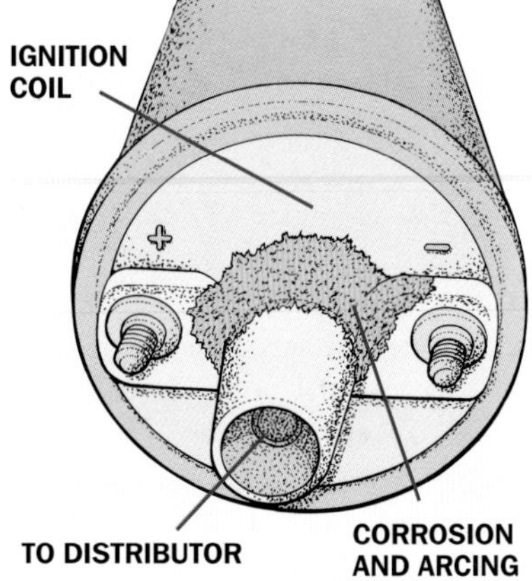

(Fig. 2) Carbon tracking in the ignition system is a noise source.

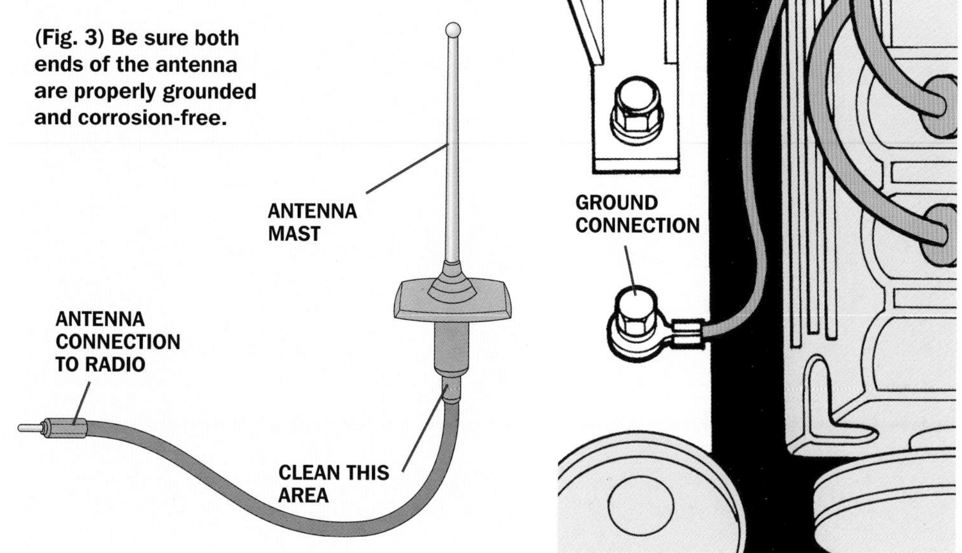

(Fig. 3) Be sure both ends of the antenna are properly grounded and corrosion-free.

(Fig. 4) Check grounding points by loosening, cleaning and tightening.

you find the noise within a few feet, turn the radio 90° to minimize the noise. The top of the radio will point at the source like a gunsight.

Making Sure

Find some way of disconnecting the source of the RFI and check to see if the noise ceases. This will be difficult in the case of the fuel pump or ignition, but you can pull the belt off the alternator. (Don't disconnect the alternator electrically—the back EMF [voltage] may smoke the diodes.) If you think it's a fuel injector, try disconnecting it from the harness.

Plugged Up

Virtually all cars today use resistor-type plug cables if they use spark plug wires at all. If your vehicle is more than a few years old, degraded cables may be the source of the problem. Remove and replace the cables one at a time, clean them of grease and dirt with mild detergent, and check the connections to the ends. Now get out your ohmmeter and measure the cables' resistance along their length—they should measure approximately 10,000 ohms per foot. Resistance in the megohms or single digits may well be the source of not only your RFI, but a nagging misfire. Replace any suspect wires with factory or high-quality aftermarket wires. Check the plugs, coil and any distributor for evidence of carbon tracking or arcing as well (**Fig. 2**).

Intermittents

These noises are easy to associate with the source. Any RFI that sounds only when one window is going up or down will be easy to blame on the window motor.

Which Way Home?

Now that you've pinpointed the noise, what can be done about it? It depends on whether your RFI source is broadcasting or cabling the noise to your radio. This matters because the cure is different. Try pulling your radio's antenna lead out. If the noise goes away or is substantially quieter, it's coming in through the antenna. If the noise stays the same or gets louder, it's coming in along the 12-volt power cables.

Try removing the antenna from the fender and cleaning the fender sheetmetal and the antenna mount. Clean down to the shiny metal, using sandpaper to remove any corrosion (**Fig. 3**). Smear the area lightly with Vaseline and reattach. This will provide a proper ground at the antenna. Be sure the radio chassis is properly grounded to the car body (**Fig. 4**). Aftermarket installations are more likely to have a radio that's grounded only by the shield in the antenna co-ax. A simple wire added between the component's metal case and the car's sheetmetal will often eliminate any RFI.

There are two ways to reduce noise: by using an inductance in a power cable to keep the high-frequency noise from traveling, or by using a capacitor to shunt it off to ground harmlessly. Sometimes both ploys are necessary. In fact, most of the electrical motors in your vehicle use some sort of capacitor for noise suppression. Any good car stereo shop or Radio Shack will have the parts you need. The noise filter we show below is one example (**Fig. 5**). It has a large inductance in series with the 12-volt power cable to a buzzing aftermarket stereo, as well as a couple of small capacitors in parallel. The inductance prevents noise from entering the amplifier through the power leads, and the capacitors bypass any leftover noise.

Electric motors, as we mentioned, often have a capacitor in parallel with the armature for the purpose of reducing RFI. If the motor's brushes are worn and sparking, the noise may overpower the capacitor's filtering. Most automotive electric motors are not serviceable, and they'll have to be

(Fig. 5) This RFI filter goes in line with both power and ground connections.

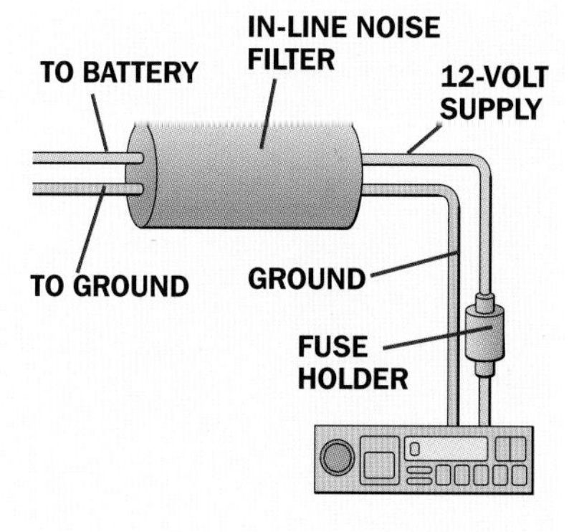

replaced if a simple filter doesn't quiet them.

As we said earlier, fuel pumps are difficult to get to—in most modern cars they are mounted inside the fuel tank. To access the pump, or even the wiring that connects to the pump, it's necessary to drop the tank out from under the car, which is a lengthy, messy and potentially dangerous job. Be careful if you attempt to add a filter to the external tank wiring, as the filter itself is large and bulky. You'll need to securely mount it to the top of the tank to keep it from breaking loose over potholes and bumps.

Soldering

One of the most common sources of RFI is poor connections. If you find a poor, corroded connection or a loose electrical joint, don't just crimp the connector tighter onto the wire. Remove the connector and clean the wire. It may be necessary to trim the wire back a few inches to get past any corrosion inside the insulation. There's only one acceptable technique for splicing wires if you're having RFI issues—and the common automotive-style crimp connector isn't it. You'll need a good, clean, high-wattage soldering pencil or gun, rosin-core 60-40 solder and PVC shrink tube.

Start by using proper, stranded automotive-grade wire. Unstranded household wire will fracture and eventually break. Start with wire of at least the same diameter as the wire you're adding to. If you're adding a power cable, a ground connection or a filter, use 12-ga. wire for ultralow resistance. Strip and pre-tin both wires to allow you to twist them together for a sound mechanical connection. Slip a length of PVC shrink tube over one wire, twist together, and solder. Use enough heat and a sparing amount of solder to make a shiny, wet-looking solder joint. Allow the joint to cool without disturbing it. This will prevent the liquid solder from crystallizing as it cools.

Cover the joint with the PVC tubing and shrink the tubing with a heat gun, or carefully with your lighter if you must. If the solder joint you're making will be exposed to the elements, use shrink tube that has waterproofing adhesive inside it to keep corrosion from creeping into your fresh joint. Silicone seal or liquid electrical tape is a good alternative.

Dress any new wires carefully to prevent chafing on corners. Support any components you've added. Remember that even a foot or two of heavy-gauge wire can flex itself to the breaking point if it's unsupported.

THIS STEREO POWER amp is getting an in-line noise filter added to its power lead. Solder and PVC shrink tube make for a noise-free, high-current splice.

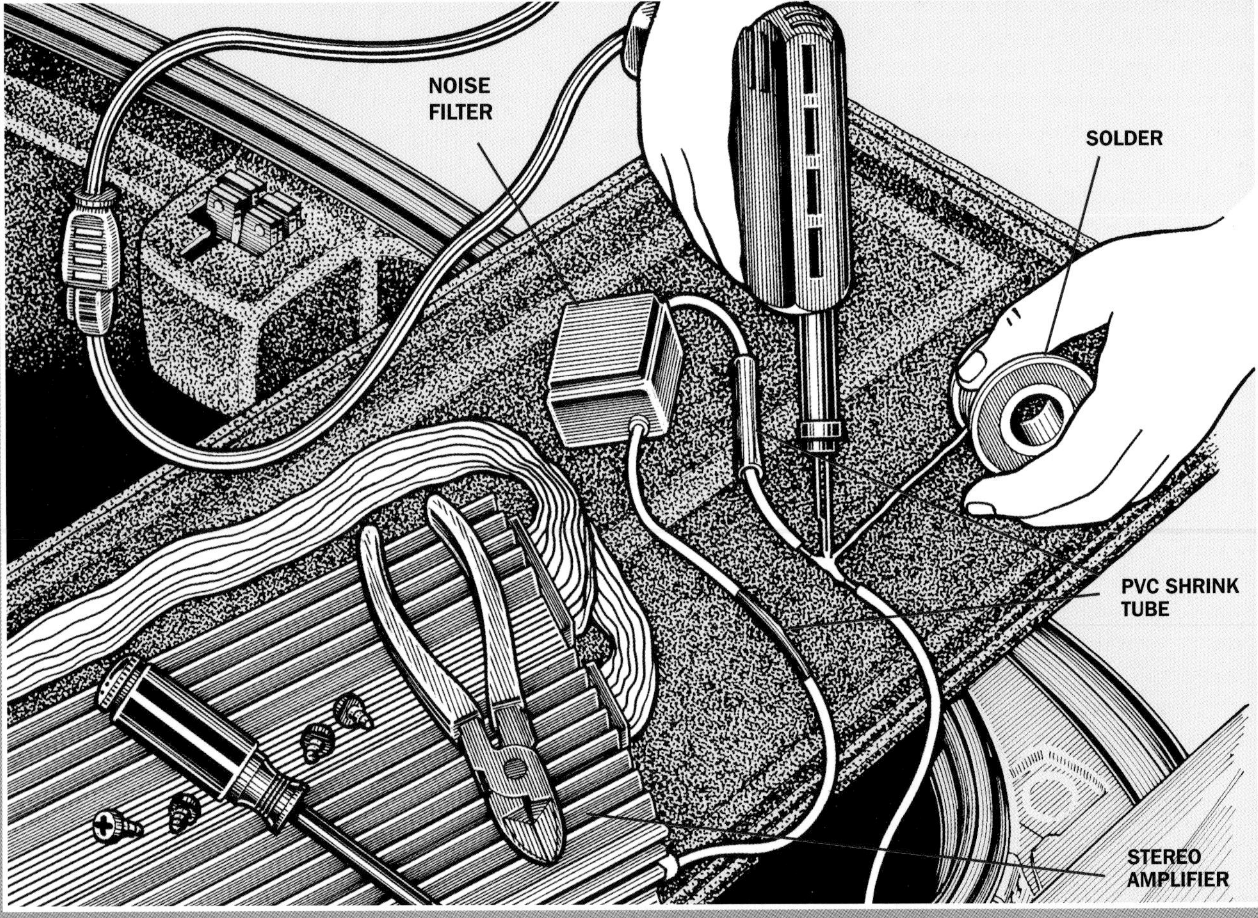

EASY

Servicing Composite Headlamps

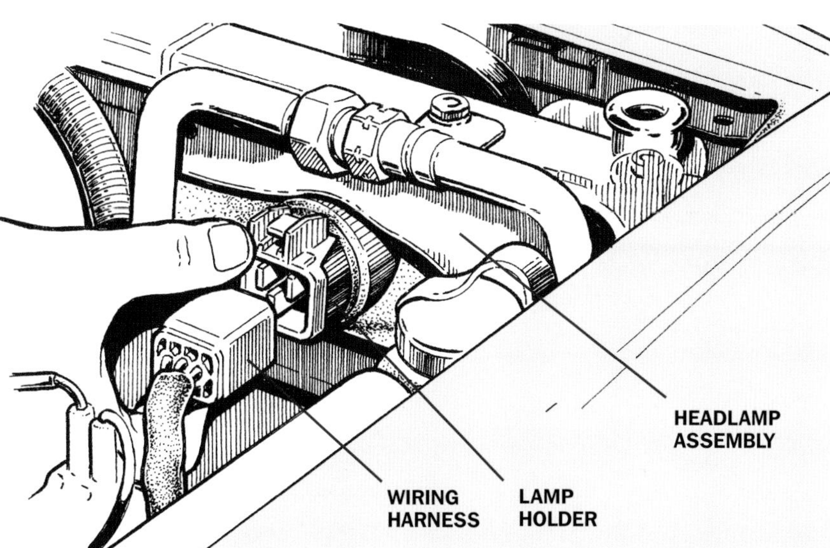

(Fig. 1) The first step to replacing a lamp is to disconnect the wiring harness from the lamp holder. Never touch the glass on the replacement bulb with your fingers.

It's your first chance in months to get out of Dodge. It'll be great to pack up some cold ones, a couple of fishing rods and some old clothes and escape to the country for a day or two. But as you leave the mercury-vapor-illuminated metroplex, you realize what you forgot—carrots, lots and lots of carrots, because you can barely see the road in front of you in the starlight of the countryside. Relax, it's not your failing eyesight. It's a burned-out headlamp.

Older Ways

For generations, American cars, and any car sold in the United States, had the same kind of headlight—a sealed-beam, either in a single or a quad arrangement. This fragile blown-glass envelope was filled with an inert gas and worked pretty well until it burned out. It had only modest performance, but the Department of Transportation mandated its use.

Most modern cars use what's called a composite headlamp—a plastic reflector bonded to a plastic or glass lens and fitted with a bulb. The bulb is of a quartz-halogen design. The "glass" bulb is actually made of silica quartz, which is highly resistant to heat. The filament is engineered to run at a much higher temperature, producing more light and heat. The silica envelope is filled with a mixture of halogen gases (iodine or bromine) to scavenge evaporated tungsten filament from the inside of the quartz, keeping each bulb's brightness constant until it fails.

Simply replacing a bulb is easy. A socket holds the bulb in place at the back of the reflector assembly. Unscrew it and pluck the bulb out. New quartz bulbs are always packaged in a bag or sleeve. This is to prevent the oils on your fingers from contacting the quartz. Temperatures at the surface of the bulb are high enough—several hundred degrees—that the oils will carbonize onto the surface, creating a localized hot spot. This hot spot will overstress the silica, resulting in a crack that lets air into the bulb, blowing the filament out within minutes. Never allow your fingers, or anything that isn't squeaky clean and dry, to touch the bulb (**Fig. 1**). If you do, clean the bulb with alcohol and a clean cloth. The easiest way to avoid problems is to leave the protective sleeve on until the bulb is in the socket and ready to reinstall. When reinstalling the lamp holder, a small smear of silicone grease over the O-rings will help it slide back in and keep moisture away. For more detail on this work, read "Replacing Headlights" on page 166.

Foggy, Foggy Nights

Both of your headlights are lighting up but you still can't see? Are the sur-

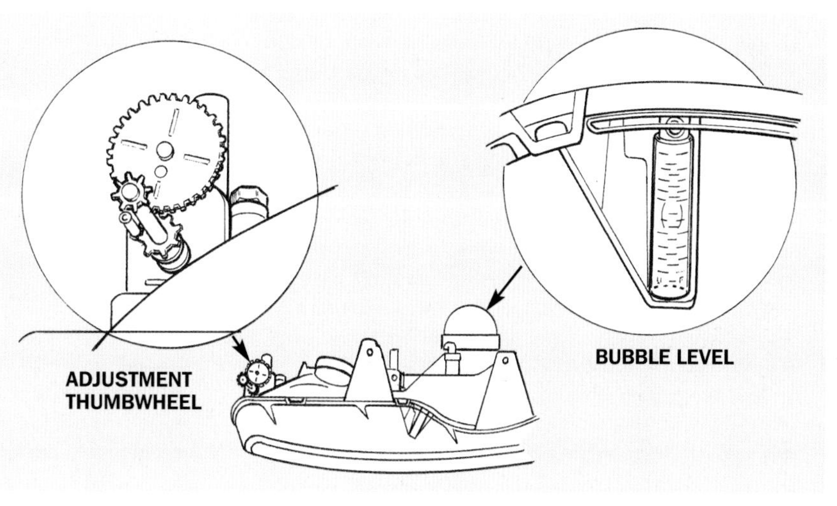

(Fig. 2) Many modern headlamp assemblies have a bubble level to assist in aiming the light beam. You'll still need a marked wall to see the beam pattern.

faces of your headlamps fogged? Plastic lenses are covered with a special UV-resistant coating. After years of exposure to pollution and UV-containing sunlight, it can fog. Using rubbing compound to remove the haze is a short-term solution. With the coating polished off, the lens will yellow and haze. Your only solution is to replace the entire assembly.

If moisture has crept into the assembly and fogged the interior, you may have a problem with the housing's vent system. Look for collapsed vent hoses, or hoses plugged with mud, insects or rustproofing.

If the vehicle has been immersed in muddy water, you'll need to remove the entire housing and flush it out. Dry thoroughly inside and out before reassembly. Corroded plating on the inside of the reflector is grounds for replacement.

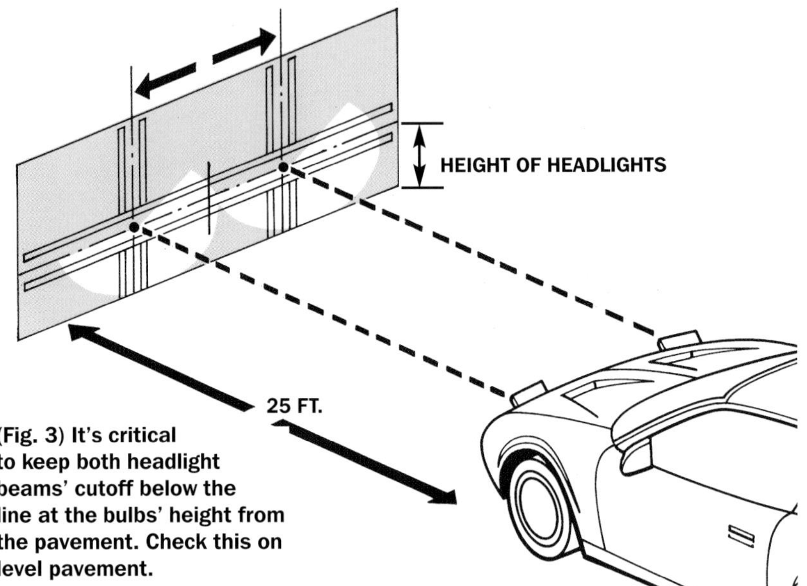

(Fig. 3) It's critical to keep both headlight beams' cutoff below the line at the bulbs' height from the pavement. Check this on level pavement.

Aim High

Be sure to set the aim correctly. Old-style sealed-beams were not fussy about aiming, but the modern quartz lamp in composite headlamps has a very sharp horizontal cutoff to keep light out of the face of oncoming traffic. Consequently, the aiming of the beams is critical.

Sealed-beam lamps used a relatively crude aiming mechanism that required a Phillips-head screwdriver to turn adjusting screws, which invariably got more difficult to turn as the socket aged and corroded. Sooner or later, the heads of the screws stripped, and you aimed your headlights poorly or not at all.

Some headlamp assemblies are adjustable by means of a large Phillips-head screw accessible from the front of the vehicle through holes

HOW IT WORKS

High Intensity Discharge Lighting

Some high-end vehicles are available with an extremely bright, tightly focused type of lighting known as High Intensity Discharge (HID). Unlike conventional lighting, there is no filament to burn out, as the light is generated by incandescent gases in a quartz tube. How hot is it? Hot enough to create a plasma of the molecules by stripping the electrons away from their nuclei. This requires, at least initially, nearly 20,000 volts to discharge across electrodes in the bulb. The plasma envelope's shape is easier to focus than a springy tungsten wire, so less stray light goes into oncoming traffic's windshields and more, far more, goes onto the verge of the roadway. There's nothing to burn out, so the lamp should outlast the vehicle. Aftermarket retrofit kits are available to upgrade your vehicle. We've installed a Xenarc low-beam kit from Sylvania on one of our vehicles, and it has given us a new appreciation for the number of deer browsing near the side of the road at night.

Just remember that correctly aiming these types of lights is far more critical than conventional lamps, because their intense light can potentially blind oncoming traffic if they're aimed too high. Warning: Before you replace a bulb with this system, be sure the switch is off, battery is disconnected, and ballast connectors are unplugged. High voltage is hazardous.

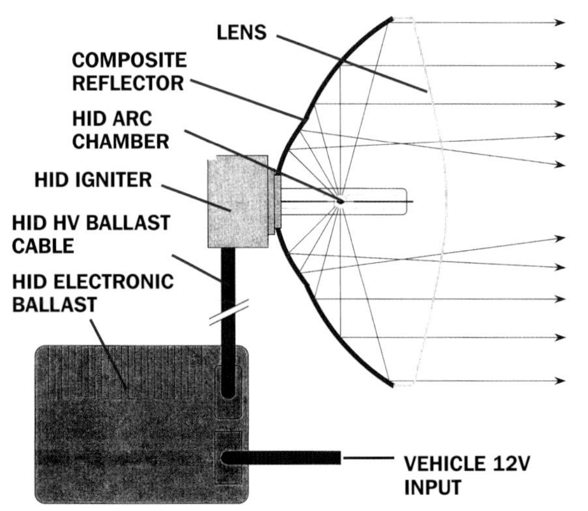

in the grille. Others may have thumbwheels that you simply crank up and down and left and right without any tools (**Fig. 2**). Vehicles vary, so you'll need to check your owner's manual or the shop manual for specifics—but here are the generic instructions.

Park your car in front of a light-colored wall in a dark spot indoors, or outdoors at night. Position the car so that the headlights are 25 ft. from the wall, and be sure the car is parked at right angles to the wall. Measure the height of the center of the headlights from the ground. Make a line on the wall with a marker or masking tape at this same height (**Fig. 3**). Now mark a pair of vertical lines directly in front of each headlight. With the adjustment thumbwheel, you can now slue the beam up or down and left or right. If you have trouble visualizing one beam because the other obscures its light, try pulling that lamp's connector, or just covering it with your jacket.

The specific numbers vary with each vehicle manufacturer, but at the very least, the left and right beams should be the same with respect to their individual centerlines. The cutoff line should be just below the line at the headlamps' center. The kickup to the right of the beam should start just to the right of the centerline. Do all the adjusting with a trunkful of luggage, a tankful of gas and a warm body in the driver's seat.

Many late-model cars incorporate a small bubble level directly into the headlamp housing (**Fig. 2**). Observing the level will help you to make adjustments when you are aiming the light beam. Remember that this is only an initial adjustment. You'll still need to visualize the beam on a wall to trim out the correct alignment. This is because manufacturing tolerances don't always place the filament in the lamp in exactly the same position relative to the lamp's metal base—which can make the beam's alignment quite different when the lamp is replaced. The level will let you make headlamp adjustments when you have to drive a heavily loaded vehicle. Check the settings on the bubble levels, load up the trunk, reset the bubble levels and go. Don't forget to raise the beam after you unload.

REPLACING A BROKEN HEADLAMP assembly is straightforward. Most of the fasteners and mounting hardware will have to be transferred to the new housing.

EASY

Servicing Electronic Suspensions

You and your Corvette have been terrorizing the same back road on the way home for months. A warning lamp that says SERVICE RIDE CONTROL winks at you from the dash. No problem, you say—I'll take it to the dealer for service next week.

That sensuous, sweeping switchback turn is disappearing—rapidly, very rapidly—under your front tires. You've been through this turn a hundred times before, but this time something is different. A small pothole suddenly makes your outside front tire start to skitter across the asphalt as you mow down a solid hundred feet of weeds between the verge and the ditch before regaining control.

Suddenly the need to see the dealer has become much more urgent. Then the dealer says it may cost as much as (gulp!) two grand to fix. Time for the Saturday mechanic to get busy.

Finding the Problem

Consider the fact that the warning light mysteriously came on after the car was jostled around on some broken pavement. That means there's a good chance you're dealing with just a bad electrical connection. Or maybe one of the Bilstein shock absorbers was severely worn and just needed that last pounding to jam the adjustment mechanism. In retrospect, the right front corner has felt a bit mushy lately, hasn't it? Luckily the Selective Ride Control (SRC) system in the Corvette is one of the simplest setups, if not *the* simplest, of its kind. OE replacement parts aren't cheap (the shocks cost about $300 apiece), but at least you don't have to pay labor when doing the job yourself.

Pity the guy who has problems with an air-strut setup, such as those found in Lexus LS 400s, some Mitsubishis and the Lincoln Continental **(Fig. 1)**. Except for the Infiniti's Q45 active suspension, these are the most complicated systems on the road. The Lexuses and Mitsus adjust damping rate, ride height and spring rate automatically through a computer. The Continental changes just damping and ride height. Unlike the Corvette and some other ride-control systems, the Continental's air struts can't be converted to a conventional suspension. Tough luck.

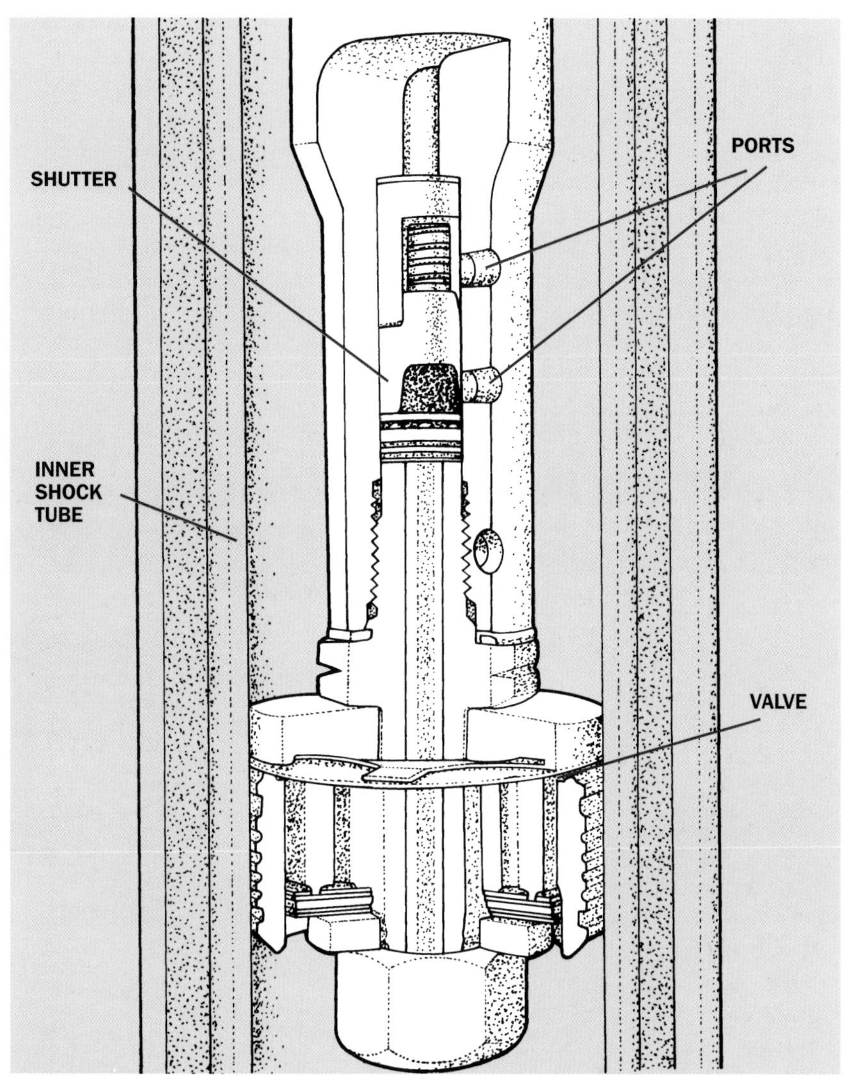

Fig. 1. Lincoln Continental's air-strut damper shutter varies oil flow through ports. Other systems are similar.

Check the Basics First

Roughly half of all the mainstream carmakers offer some type of electronic suspension system on some models. In general, they all make computer-controlled adjustments on response to one or more of the following inputs: road conditions, vehicle speed and weight/load, brake

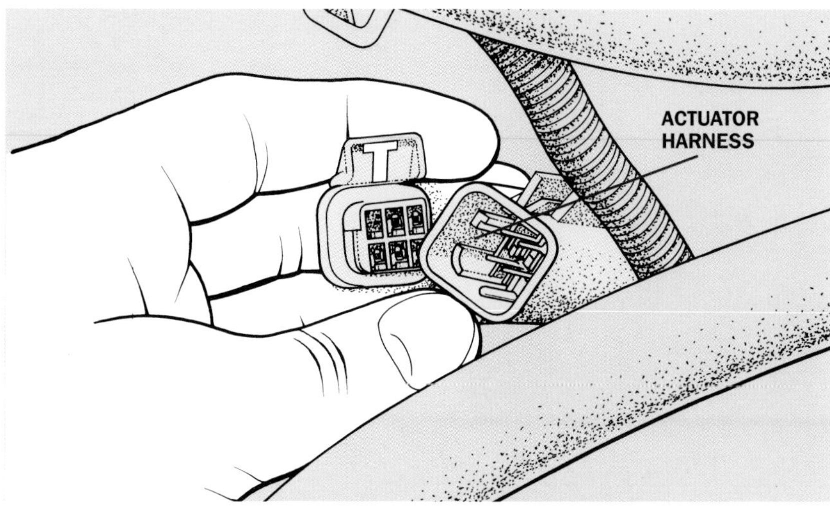

Fig. 2. With no trouble codes stored in a ride-control system's computer, begin the diagnosis by visual inspection of the parts and wiring.

application, steering-wheel angle, power-steering pressure, throttle position, lateral/longitudinal acceleration and the position of a dash- or console-mounted driver-selectable switch.

But don't let this list overwhelm you. The key to any modern automotive system is to keep it simple and check the basics first, then move on. One prerequisite for working on almost any modern car is adequate documentation. Beg, borrow or steal the manual for your car, which may involve ordering it from the dealer. Without some sort of manual, you'll be guessing, and probably not only won't be able to make the repair but you might inadvertently damage some pretty expensive parts.

In the case of your Corvette, there should be at least one trouble code stored in the computer. So you would jump right to "Corvette diagnostics" on the page 155, because it would probably lead you to the problem a lot faster.

If the computer hadn't turned on the warning message but you felt something wrong with the suspension (or you don't have the self-diagnostic information for the system you're dealing with), you would start by taking a close look at the adjustable shocks for some signs of oil leakage as if dealing with plain ol' shocks. If you see any stains or drips, the first piece of business is to replace the bad unit and hope the system is

Fig. 3. Air suspension must be off before jacking up Lincoln Town Cars or Mark VII/VIIIs.

fixed. The same logic applies to all electronic suspensions, be they air, hydraulic or both. No matter how complex the system is, the damping portion of the shock/strut is still filled with hydraulic oil and needs to be sealed.

Next, do a visual inspection for any air/fluid lines that have burst and for damaged or misadjusted height sensors on those setups that use them. Look around for any obvious harness connector trouble and check the shock/strut actuators and their connectors (**Fig. 2**). If you hear the air compressor running constantly, it usually means a height sensor is out of whack, there's a small air leak or a relay is stuck in the ON position. If the compressor never turns on, you can suspect a bum height sensor, a stuck-open relay, a clogged air bleed-off valve, a blown fuse or even the compressor itself.

Ford issued a technical service bulletin on this exact subject back in the mid-90s. It seems that on 1990-93 Crown Victoria/Grand Marquis and Town Car models, the rear air suspension may not pump up when loaded because the air-supply line at the Y connector near the No. 4 crossmember tends to rub on the underside of the car body. The constant rubbing eventually wears through the line and creates a leak. An improved air line with a protective shield was issued to remedy the problem. The OE part numbers are F2AZ-5A897-B (Crown Vic/Grand Marquis) and F2VY-5A897-A (Town Car).

Corvette Nitty-Gritty

Understanding how the SRC system works will help to diagnose and fix it and will make other setups easier to comprehend. SRC consists of four adjustable gas-charged shocks, an actuator motor on top of each shock and a computer to drive the actuators. SRC can adjust the damping rate only—the ride height never changes. Inputs to the computer include a 3-position driver-selectable switch, the vehicle speed sensor and signals from each actuator's Hall-effect position sensor. Based on the car's speed and where the driver has the switch, the computer powers the actuator motors so that they rotate a certain number of degrees. Every time the key is turned on, the computer rotates the actuators back to the 0° stop.

Inside the conventional-looking shock shaft is a thin rod, called the damping rod. It extends from the top of the shaft down to the piston. On top of the damping rod is a gear. When the actuator is mounted, its gear fits over the gear on the rod, which enables the actuator to rotate the rod up to 160° inside the larger shaft. Because the bottom of the rod is beveled, as it turns clockwise it gradually closes off the bypass orifice machined in the side of the larger shaft. The smaller the orifice

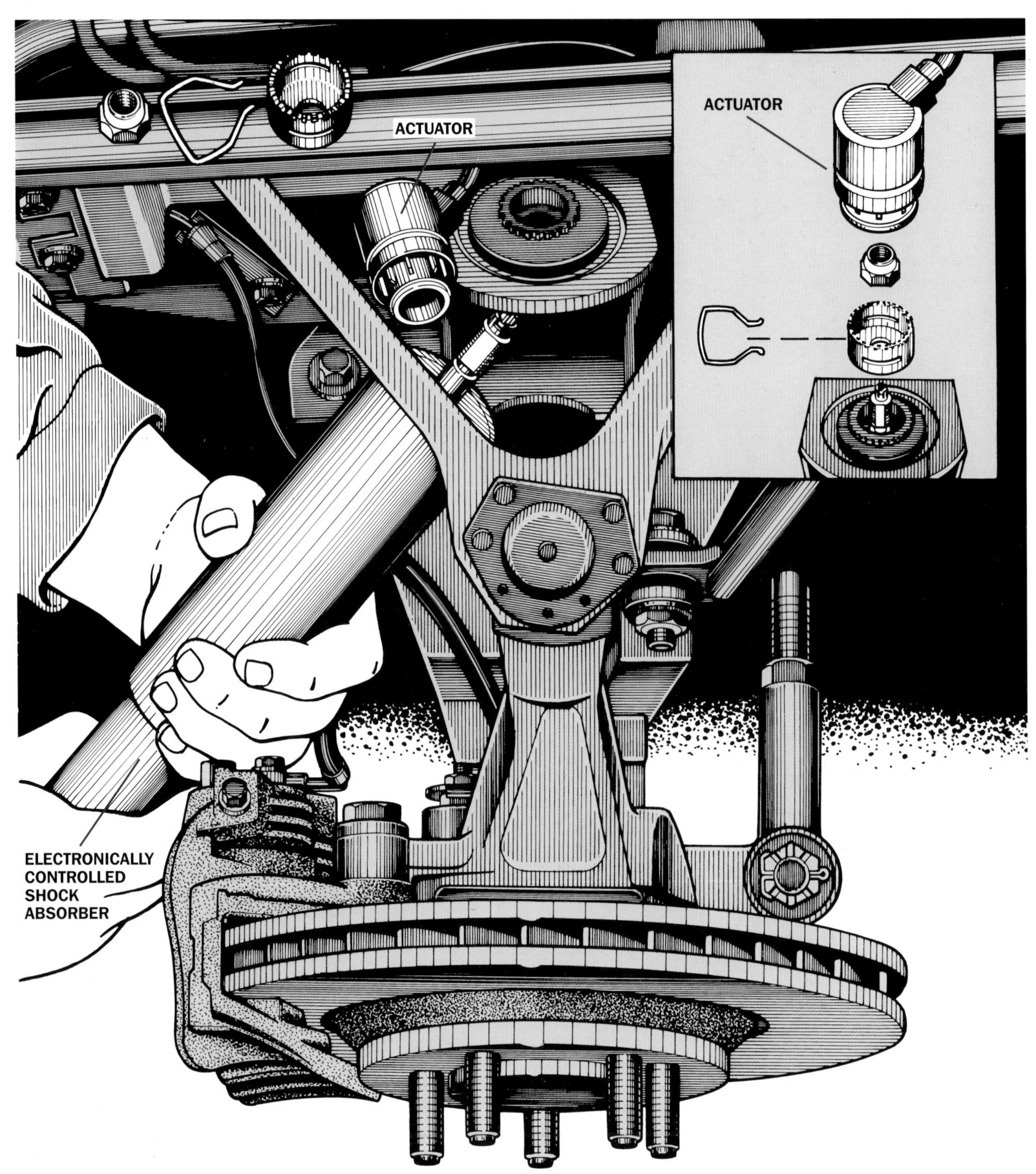

gets, the stiffer the shock gets. Mechanically it's simple. As long as the electronics don't screw up, only normal wear should affect the system.

Other electronic dampers work in basically the same way but they vary in design. For instance, the Continental's air struts use a shutter-type mechanism with different size orifices to vary the oil flow.

Replacing the Shocks

If you find a leaker or one shock that's clearly worn out, replacing it is about as straightforward as any conventional shock. Start by loosening the lug nuts of the wheel that has to come off and jack up the appropriate end. Remove the wheel. (On some air systems, such as the Lincoln Town Car and Mark series cars, you must flip

Fig. 4. The Corvette SRC actuator must mesh cleanly with its shock's damping rod gear or the computer will set a trouble code. The locking clip should slide easilty into place.

off the air suspension switch in the trunk before jacking up the vehicle—don't say we didn't warn you (**Fig. 3**). Next, pull the actuator's locking clip and pull the actuator straight up off the shock to expose the damping rod's little gear. Lay the actuator gently on a frame rail if possible. Don't let it hang on the harness. If there's no place to set the actuator down, either tie it out of the way or pull its connector from the main wiring harness and remove the actuator and its harness completely.

Now, you just need to remove the upper and lower mounting bolts and pull the shock. You may need to pump up like Arnold Schwarzenegger for a few seconds to compress the stiff gas shock enough to slip it out between the control arms. The same goes for slipping the new unit through the arms into place. Be careful not to damage the new damping rod gear. The actuator must remesh smoothly with the new gear. Anything that prevents the actuator from doing its job will set a trouble code in the computer **(Fig. 4)**.

Actuator Precautions

Don't hit the Corvette's actuator with anything during installation—press it on gently by hand. Never whale on the upper retaining nut with an impact gun or you'll jam the damping rod. The nut must be torqued to 33 ft.-lb. Hold things steady with a wrench on the flats of the retainer insulator while tightening the nut. Make sure there's a good mesh between the damping rod gear and the actuator gear, and a good fit for the locking clip **(Fig. 5)**.

Once mounted, make sure the actuator harness pigtail points directly rearward for a front shock and directly forward for a rear shock. This prevents the harnesses from rubbing against the fender splash shields and frame rails.

The actuators on other electronic shocks/struts are usually held in place by two screws, so they can be installed in only one position. This means the computer doesn't need to take a zero reading with each key cycle.

There's no way to install an SRC shock backward because the actuator position sensor keeps tabs on the damping rod angle. However, this doesn't necessarily apply to all electronic suspensions. Be sure to check the manual for the latest information.

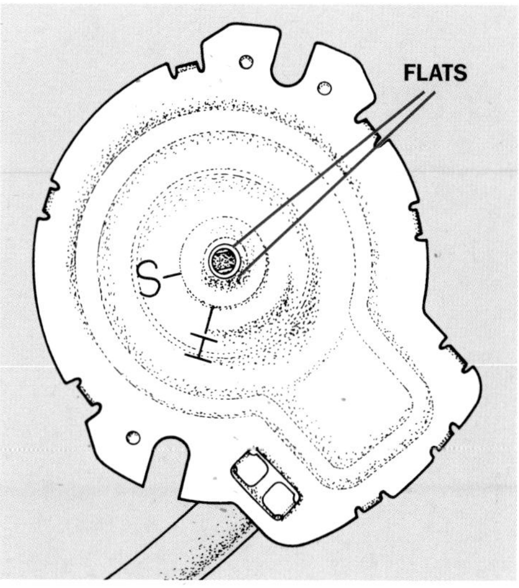

Fig. 5. Actuator must align with top of damping rod to maintain proper soft/hard positions.

Corvette Diagnostics

Remember that SERVICE RIDE CONTROL warning? When it's on, it means the system is in a fail-safe mode and the computer has locked all the actuators in the 60° position until the problem is fixed. With the car stopped and the ignition on, jump terminals A and B (1989 only) or A and C (later models) of the ALDL (assembly line diagnostic link) located under the knee bolster with a paper clip or a piece of jumper wire to make the SERVICE RIDE CONTROL warning message flash out 2-digit codes. There are 13 possible codes that can be spit out, but you'll need a service manual to decipher them and to do the proper tests.

Four things can prevent the warning light from flashing codes or from coming on with the key for a bulb check: a burned-out bulb, a blown fuse, a bad harness connection at the computer or a bad computer. The electronic brain for this system is found in the bin behind the driver's seat in the Corvette. In other cars, it's usually mounted behind the rear seat in the trunk area. Only two problems won't set codes in the SRC system: a leaking or worn shock and system voltage out of the 10- to 16-volt range. To clear codes after the repair has been completed, jump ALDL terminals A and B (1989) or A and C (later models) three times 2 seconds each.

The Real Time Damping system on late-model Corvettes (mid-late 1990s) also permits on-board trouble code diagnostics without a scan tool, through the Central Control Module. Codes are displayed on the Driver Information Center. Refer to the factory service manual (or the service information website—www.acdelco.com).

Fixing Power Windows

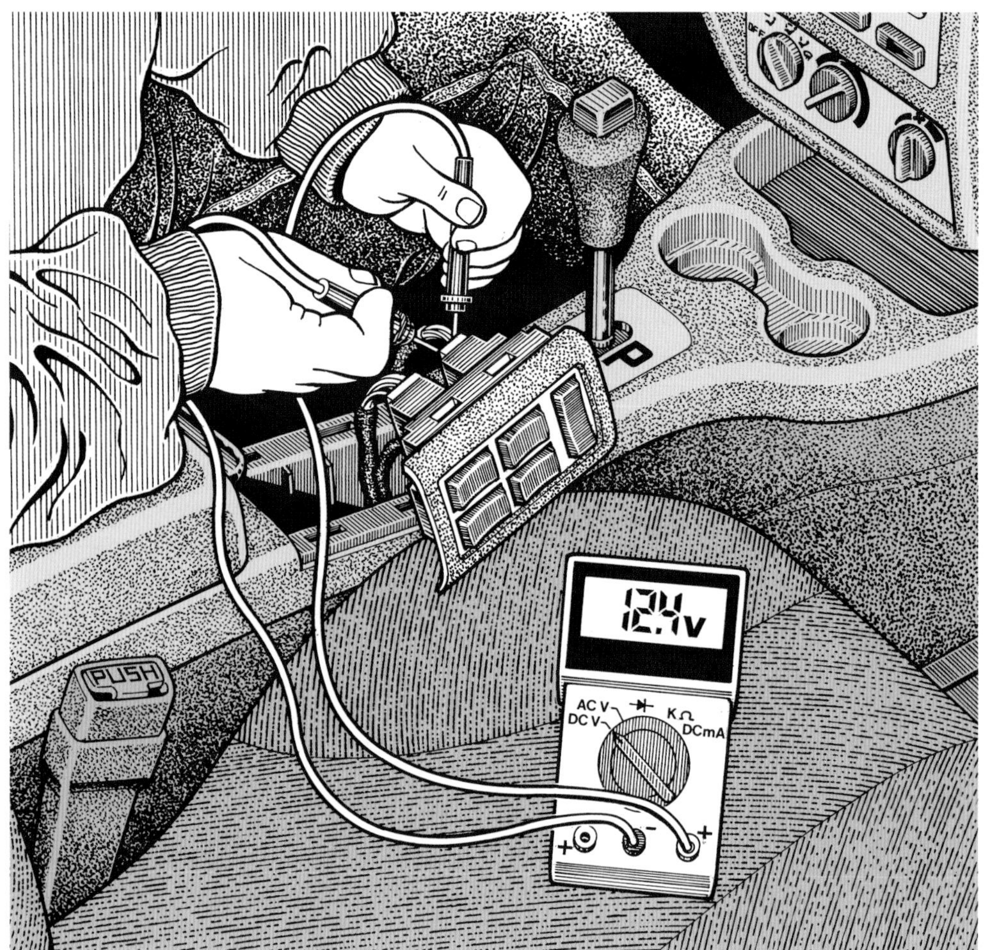

(Fig. 1) Carefully backprobe the window switches to isolate any electrical faults in the switches, connectors or wiring.

Another toll-booth, another mile—or at least it seems as if the tollbooths come every mile on this road, with a half mile of traffic idling its leisurely way up to the token monster. Within an arm's length of the bin, you toggle the power window switch with one hand while the other hand fingers a token, preparing to whip it into the basket just as you floor the throttle. All goes as planned—except the window doesn't move, the token bounces back into your face, and you have to jam on the brakes, crack the door and pitch a second token backhanded to keep from getting a ticket as a toll evader, all to the tune of horns blaring from the cars behind you.

Fortunately, power windows are usually one of the more reliable systems on a late-model car. And diagnosis and repair are usually pretty straightforward.

What's Up?

The most common power window mechanism is pretty basic. There's a simple regulator mechanism, usually similar to the mechanism used on garden-variety hand-cranked windows. It comes in several varieties—rack, sector and cable drive. Troubleshooting is pretty straightforward, once you get the door panels off—but your problem may be terribly simple and may not require removing any trim at all.

First: Are all of the windows on the fritz? Or just one? If you can't move any of the windows, the first place to look is at the fuse. Window regulators are high-current devices, and the fuse is sized to just barely be able to open all four windows together. Age and a few sticky window channels can pop a fuse.

Turn the key to the Run position, but don't start the car. If the fuse is blown, pushing a window button will do nothing at all: The motor won't groan and the glass won't quiver. If the fuse is good and you can hear the motor, or the glass acts like it wants to move, then you've got some sort of mechanical problem. If not, check the fuse. If the fuse box isn't labeled, check the owner's manual to see which fuse is the culprit. Don't go yanking fuses willy-nilly looking for a bad one—you might interrupt the power to the engine management computer, causing poor driveability for 30 minutes or so—or you might reset all the buttons on your car radio to that undersea-alien rock-gospel station.

Fuse okay, but the window still won't budge? Again, are all the windows dormant? Or just one? If it's just one, you still may get an opportunity to go spelunking inside the door. If it's all four, maybe it's something simpler you can troubleshoot under the dash.

At this point, if you've narrowed the fault down to some electrical problem that's not as simple as a blown fuse you need to round up a schematic of your car's electrical system and a voltmeter or 12v test light. All that's necessary now is to start at the fuse panel and follow the wiring to the switch, and from there move on to the motor, testing along the way for 12 volts. Somewhere, you'll find a loose or corroded connector interrupting the voltage to the motor. Or, the switch itself might be bad. If the driver's door switch won't open the right rear door, but the switch in the door will, look for either a bad switch in the driver's door or a fault in the intervening wiring.

Open Sesame

At this point, you probably need to be able to access the inside of the switch panel. On some vehicles, like the one in our lead illustration, you can simply pry the panel up with your fingers and backprobe the connectors (**Fig. 1**). Other vehicles may require that you remove the panel.

Door panels are held on with a bewildering variety of fasteners. Start by pulling off all of the door pulls and handles. The perimeter of the panel is customarily held on fragile plastic studs intended for one-time use. Pry them up carefully, and you should be able to reuse them.

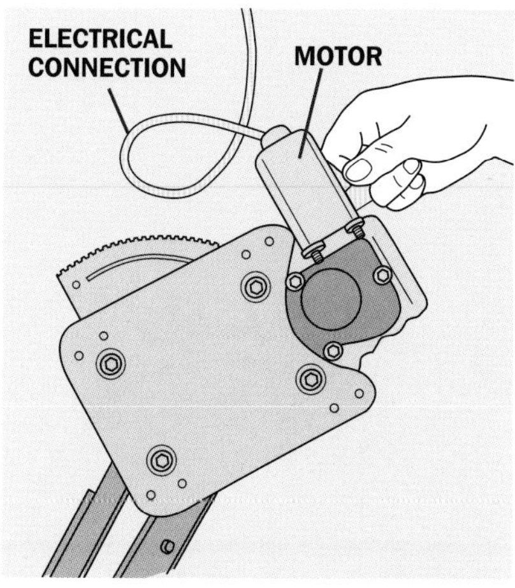

(Fig. 2) It may be possible to replace a bad motor, or you may need the entire mechanism.

Once you've got the door panel off, carefully remove the weather sheeting. You'll need to replace this later, and you may need fresh contact cement to do so.

Warning: You now have the ability to put your fingers into places where fingers normally don't go. As our mechanic pal Lefty points out, "A power window motor has enough torque to put a serious hurtin' on ya if it's actuated while errant digits are in the gears."

Proof Positive

As an absolute proof that the problem is electrical, try running a jumper wire direct from the battery positive terminal to the positive side of the motor to see if it comes alive.

Be aware that a few window regulator systems supply 12v constantly, and switch the ground side of the circuit. Check the schematic. Also, most vehicles have the ability to lock—and deactivate—the rear windows. Check this switch if only the rears are balky. Occasionally, the true problem is a bad motor (**Fig. 2**). You'll have to replace it. Otherwise, you can simply trace the wires until you find the problem.

Sticky

All windows have gaskets and seals to keep wind noise and rain out. If the window has a slow spot or won't open or close properly, check the gaskets. A gasket that's misplaced or torn can prevent proper operation. If the gasket is loose, or even torn, you may be able to repair it. If the gasket is simply loose, get some 3M Super Weatherstrip Adhesive at the auto parts store. Clean off the old adhesive with lacquer thinner and reglue the gasket into place. Allow this to dry overnight with the window closed, and be certain you're not gluing the window to the gasket.

If the gasket is torn, you might be able to use a super glue to simply repair the tear. You may be able to judiciously trim a loose corner of gasket away with a single-edge razor blade. Be particularly careful about doing this on the part of the gasket that sits outside of the glass, because it may admit rain and salt spray to the inside of the door in quantities too large for the door's internal drainage system to cope with.

HOW IT WORKS

Automatic Windows

Some late-model high-end cars have frameless windows that automatically crank themselves open a quarter-inch or so as the doors are opened. It happens so fast that you may not notice it. The window opens rapidly, clearing the seal before the door latch clears. It then closes automatically about a second after the door latch latches. There are two advantages to this. First, the slightly open window vents interior air, which can actually make doors on tightly sealed cars hard to open by springing the door back open against air pressure. It also lets the manufacturer use a vastly different style of seal on the top of the window. The seal can more closely resemble a sedan door seal, with a small lip protruding over the top of the glass. This type of seal won't work on frameless windows because the glass has to clear the seal as it opens and closes. This type of seal allows less water and noise intrusion. A similar automatic system is used on those high-end convertibles with fully automatic tops, to provide clearance for the moving parts of the top. The downside with any automatic window system is with the logic control module needed to achieve this. Repairs will probably need a factory shop manual and, potentially, some expensive parts.

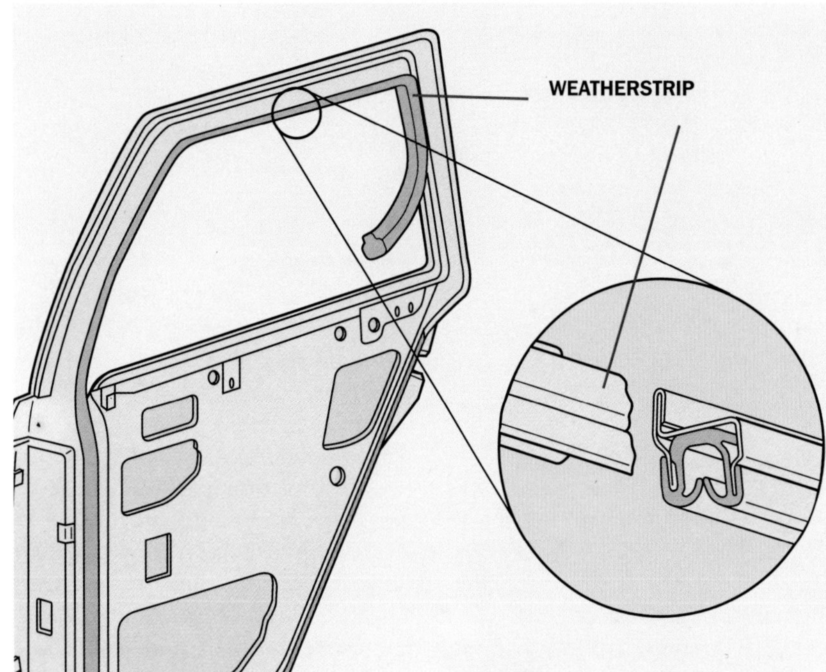

(Fig. 3) Check the weatherstripping and window channel for torn, loose or folded rubber parts, or foreign objects in the way.

Replacing a gasket or seal with a new part is generally straightforward. If it's not obvious that the gasket is astray, inspect the entire gasket and channel carefully. Look for damage, but also look for such things as pine sap, fossilized Froot Loops or other foreign objects that might make the window stick or bind. Clean the surface of the gasket and window with lacquer thinner to remove oxidized rubber and scum (**Fig. 3**).

There's a fair amount of friction between the gasket and the window glass. Almost any misalignment can dramatically increase the friction to the point where the motor no longer has enough torque to move the glass properly.

Lubricate the entire channel with silicone spray or protectant, because the reduced friction just might get your window working again.

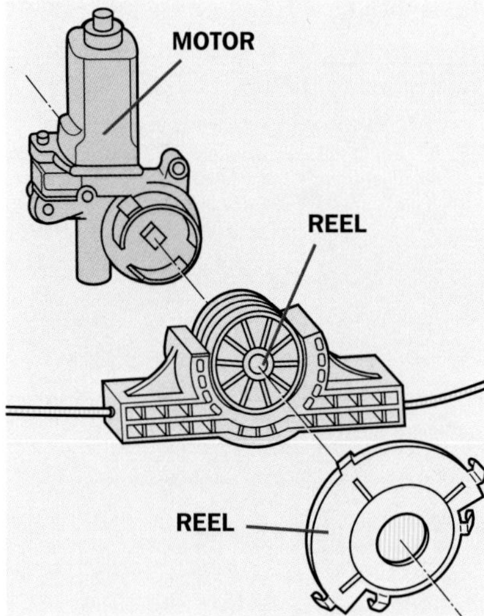

(Fig. 4) Reel and cable window regulators are simple mechanisms, but can be fussy about cable routing and may snag if jammed.

It's also possible that the problem is deeper inside the door. If so, you'll need to pull the door panel and go poking around. Remember to pull the fuse to prevent amputating your fingers. You can use either a rubber wedge doorstop or a couple of feet of duct tape to anchor the glass up while you work.

Sometimes the problem is nothing more than a loose bolt allowing the door's inner structure to move around, misaligning the window track. Many doors have slotted holes for the attachment points for internal parts, so careful consideration of the misalignment will sometimes let you simply slide one adjustment a quarter-inch or so and straighten it all out. All bets are off if the door has been damaged in a crash. It may take a long time to get everything working right.

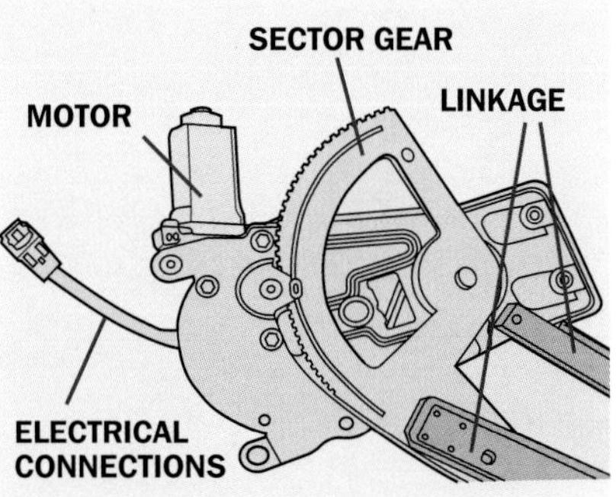

(Fig. 5) Severe misalignment caused by loose fasteners can jam gear-type regulators.

Lastly, the mechanism that runs the window up and down may be faulty. Whether it's a gear-and-sector, scissors lift or cable-operated mechanism (**Fig. 4**), you'll need to watch it moving up and down a few times. Again, keep your fingers out of the works. Sometimes the problem will be a loose fastener or rivet, sometimes a broken or missing bushing (**Fig. 5**). Cables can bind on the drum or become sticky. Lube all the friction points with white grease. Don't forget there are gaskets in the window track down below the top of the door, and you may need to reglue, repair or lubricate them.

Replacing Your Fuel Pump

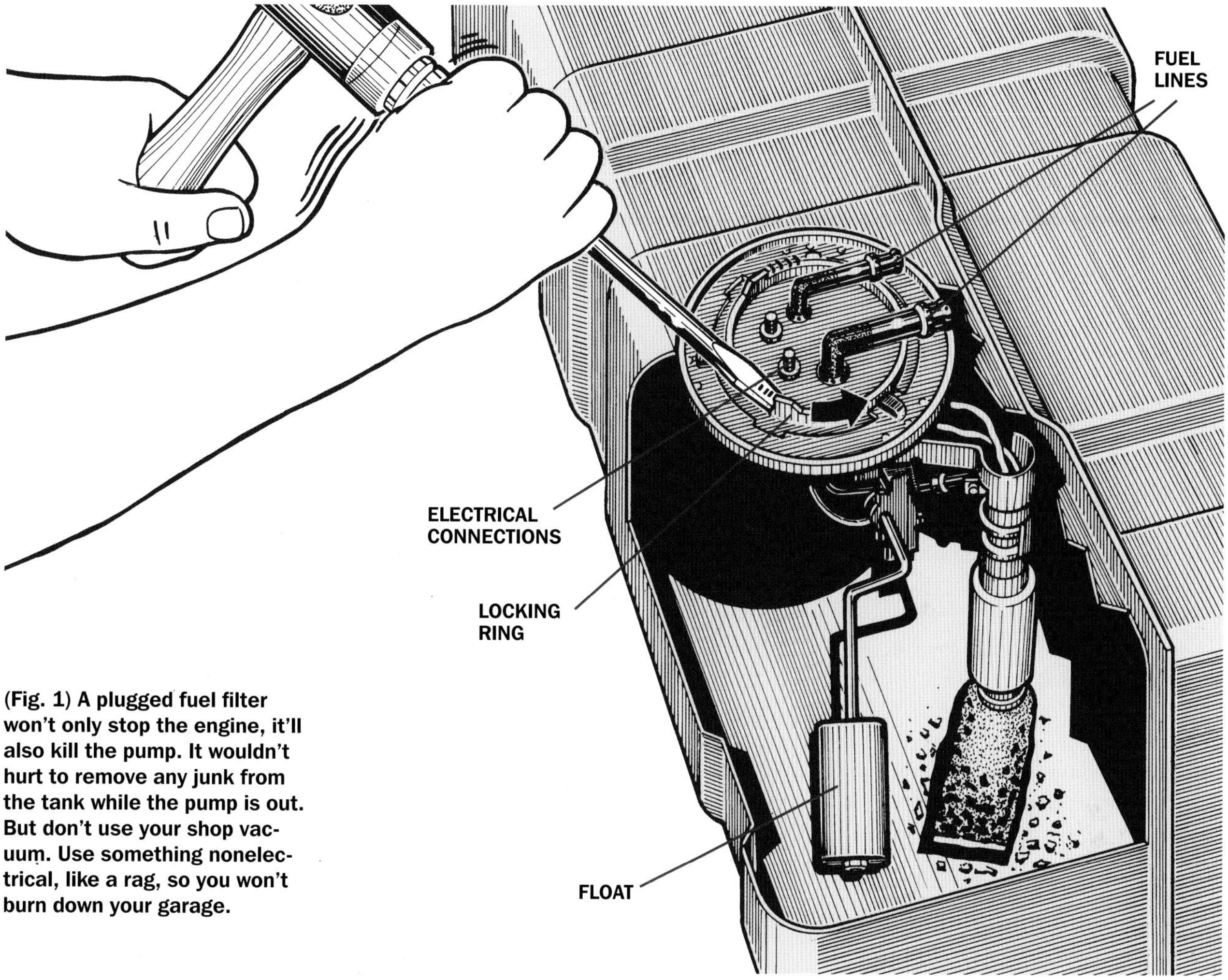

(Fig. 1) A plugged fuel filter won't only stop the engine, it'll also kill the pump. It wouldn't hurt to remove any junk from the tank while the pump is out. But don't use your shop vacuum. Use something nonelectrical, like a rag, so you won't burn down your garage.

Ten minutes late. Gulp half your coffee, sprint out to the car. Twist the key and she cranks. And cranks. And cranks. No fire, and your ulcer potential increases along with your blood pressure. It always seems to happen when you're behind schedule, as if the gods of internal combustion are eternally against you. You should've paid attention to that occasional bucking on the highway.

If there's anything over 60,000 miles on the odometer, but more commonly 100,000 plus, there's a good chance that the cause of this distressing no-start condition is an electric fuel pump that's no longer capable of forcing fuel forward with sufficient pressure. Even if the condition hasn't reached the point of grounding you, pump inadequacies can cause numerous driveability problems, such as momentary cutting out, hesitation, low power and stalling at inopportune moments (typically, it'll start again after it's cooled off).

For years, the car companies have been looking for a pump life of 10,000 hours (say, 400K miles) as a bogey. Now, they're asking their O.E. suppliers for "life-of-car" (that many miles isn't a car's life span anymore?). To reach this goal, pump makers have lowered amperage draw and balanced armatures more precisely. That's all very admirable, but ask any service technician and he'll tell you that they simply don't last anywhere near that long in most cases. What's happening?

In a word, crud. Many (most?) of the fuel filters replaced are so jammed up you can't blow through them (**Fig. 1**). If you had checked the pump's amperage draw before removing the old filter, you might have seen up to twice the expected number—perhaps eight to 10 instead of four to six. It shouldn't take much of an intellectual leap to realize that a plugged fuel filter at the outlet site will make a pump work harder, and all that extra current will wipe out the brushes and groove the commutator, killing the pump prematurely. Also, the pump's already digested whatever's causing the restriction.

While on the subject of pump fatalities, another reason pumps burn out is because immersion in gasoline is necessary for cooling, yet people run around on "E." So, try to keep your tank at least half full.

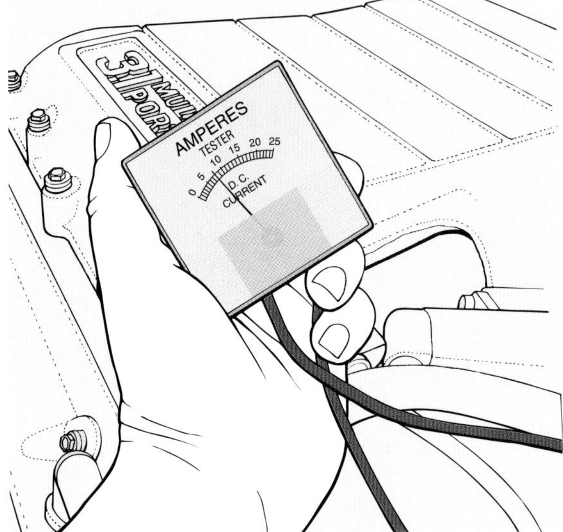

(Fig. 2) Find out how many amps the pump is drawing with a current draw test. Just bypass the wiring and run jumpers from the battery.

Two-Legged Tripod?

For a century, mechanics have been taught that spark, compression and fuel are the legs of the tripod that support an engine's ability to run, and that's still true. So, before you jump to any unfortunate conclusions about your fuel pump, do a spark check (a story for another day) and make sure the camshaft is still connected to the crankshaft (remove the oil filler cap and watch the cam or rockers while you have a helper crank the engine). If these two essentials are okay, you can start thinking gasoline.

Turn the key on and listen carefully. In most cars, you'll hear the pump run for a few seconds. No? Then check the fuse. If it's blown, and the car starts after you replace it, you should still find out how many amps it's being forced to carry. If pump electrical draw is too high, a fix now will head off a future breakdown.

You'll need either a low-reading analog ammeter (**Fig. 2**) or a DMM (Digital Multi-Meter) with sufficient current-carrying capacity. Amperage testing is done either by hooking up the meter in series with the load, or with an inductive pickup that you clamp around the wire. The latter works best with big current flow, such as you'd find in the starter circuit, so we prefer the former for diagnosing fuel pumps.

That means you've got to break into the circuit. Connect one of the ammeter's leads to the positive battery post and the other to the pump's hot wire. Look this up in a service manual. Ditto for the specs, but we will say that if you see anything over 5 amps with a low- to mid-pressure system (13 to 45 psi), or 7 amps with a high-pressure version (60 psi) you've got a problem.

Will on-board diagnostics help you here? Not very often, although a problem in the pump relay circuit will set trouble code No. 42 on a typical Chrysler product, or code No. 87 on a garden-variety Ford.

Excluder and PSI

Have you replaced the fuel filter at the recommended intervals? How about ever? If you've been lax in this regard, it's certainly one of the first things to check. Even if it's not the reason the engine won't fire up, it's critical maintenance that you should be doing anyway, so you're not wasting your time.

Important: Filter removal will be a lot less dangerous and messy if you relieve system pressure first. Wrap a rag around the Schrader-type valve on the fuel rail and press down on the valve's pin (**Fig. 3**). Or, remove the fuel pump fuse, and crank for 20 seconds.

Checking fuel pressure is one of the basics of troubleshooting, and reasonably priced gauges are available. Most screw onto the Schrader-type valve, but with some imports you'll need a special banjo connector or a special fitting.

Turn the ignition on and read the gauge. No or low pressure may mean the pump's electrical circuit is faulty. This could be because of a defective control relay, but check for bad connections before you think about a new relay. Examine all the connectors for evidence of corrosion or looseness. Test for the presence of battery voltage at the pump's positive terminal or wire, and check for a bad ground as well.

By the way, an inertia-type safety switch in the pump's circuit, as found on many Fords, can be tripped by a minor impact, such as bumping into a snowbank.

Voltage-drop testing is the best way to locate high resistance. With the circuit powered up, use an accurate voltmeter to see if you get a reading across connections and lengths of wire. Anything more than about 0.2 volt is too much.

Other possible causes of too few psi to start the car are the already-mentioned clogged filter, a pick-up sock in the tank that's blocked, a crimped line or, of course, a weak pump.

If key-on/engine-off pressure was within specs, use a test light at the

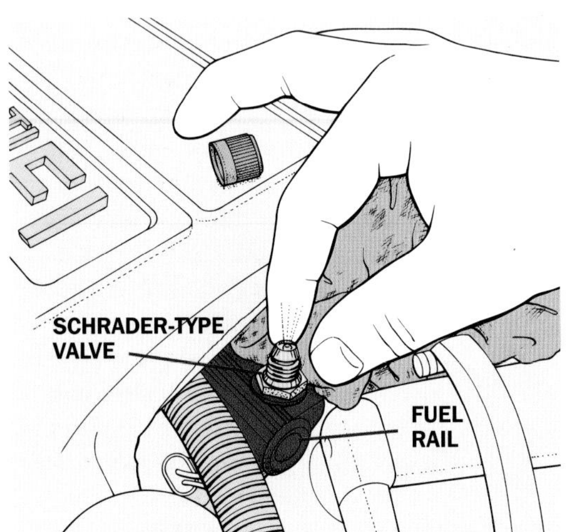

(Fig. 3) Before you open any connections, relieve system pressure.

HOW IT WORKS

Fuel Pumps

Unlike mechanical fuel pumps, which are necessarily attached to the engine, the electric variety is mounted back in or by the tank. There are three types: turbine, gerotor and roller cell. The first uses rollers in a notched rotor to catch gasoline and force it into a small-volume area of the housing. It has lots of moving parts and can be noisy. Gerotors are similar to some oil pumps—they squeeze liquid by means of the eccentric action between a star-shaped rotor and a matching element that surrounds it. Today, however, the O.E. trend is toward the turbine type.

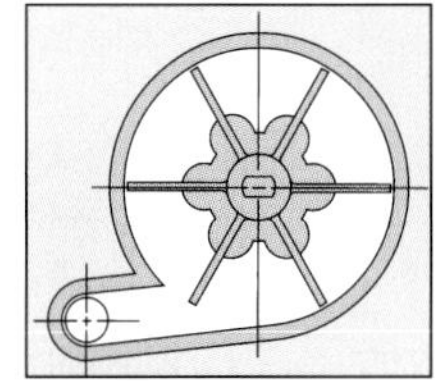

TURBINE

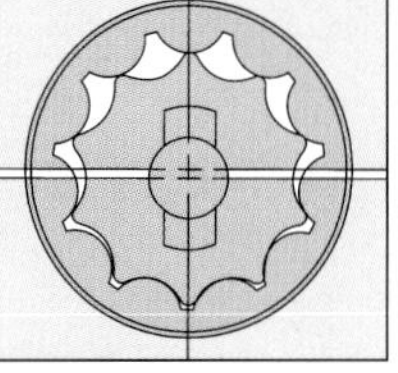

GEROTOR

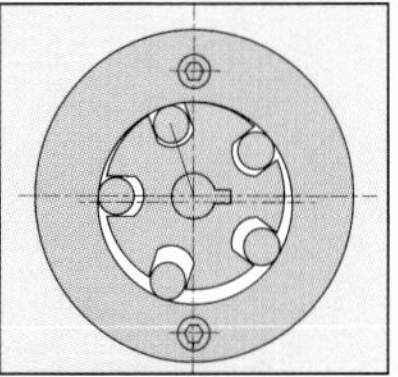

ROLLER CELL

With throttle-body fuel injection (also called "wet throttle plate"), electric pumps typically put out 15 to 20 psi, whereas port injection requires 45 to 60 psi.

If you're still wondering why mechanical pumps aren't used with fuel-injected engines, think pressure and volume. The former has to be higher than the 3 to 5 psi a typical mechanical unit supplies. Otherwise, you won't get that nicely vaporized plume that burns so well. Plenty of fuel has to be flowing all the time, too. Only a small percentage of what's available is actually used even at full throttle. The rest serves to keep those injectors and rails cool as it recirculates to the tank. That, plus the location of the pump way back in or by the tank, pretty much eliminates vapor lock problems.

appropriate injector wire (or, pull an injector connector and plug one of those inexpensive "noid" lights into the harness). No flashing? Then the injectors aren't firing, which means troubleshooting will have to graduate to a whole other level of complexity as you look into the electronic engine management and EFI systems.

It Starts, But ...

In cases where the engine runs, but has a driveability problem, concentrate on your gauge readings. You should see violent needle swings between dead-head and running pressures (**Fig. 4**). A slow rise means trouble. Pull the pressure regulator's vacuum hose and you should see an increase. Too many psi may be due to a defective regulator or a restricted return line.

Just because you've got specified pressure doesn't mean there's sufficient flow. Total system volume at the Schrader-type valve of 1 pint in 20 seconds will run any car. (While a typical pump may flow 30 gal. per hour, less than a tenth of that is needed to run the engine. The rest is returned to the tank, which helps keep everything cool.)

Kaput

Pump replacement may be easy or difficult, depending on the design. On vehicles with in-tank pumps, access is sometimes just a matter of removing a seat, or folding back the trunk mat and removing a panel. Others require that you drop the tank, which can be quite a ponderous undertaking, especially if you've just filled up (gasoline weighs 6 pounds per gallon). We use the term "drop" in a mechanic's sense here—we don't really mean to drop it. You can siphon it down—dump what you get into your other car, or give it to a neighbor. If you have a good floor jack, put a big square of plywood between it and the tank. Remember that there's still a certain amount of fuel in the tank after you've drained it. No smoking, and dry up any spilled fuel right away. It'd be a really good idea to work outdoors, too. Remember that gasoline vapor is heavier than air, and will spill down the basement stairs until it finds the pilot light for the water heater. *Poof!*

Speaking of flammable, don't even think about working on an electric fuel pump until you've disconnected the negative battery cable. On some cars, the tank is above a rear-suspension subframe, so access requires unbolting it.

Once you've got access, the actual removal and installation is pretty straightforward. Special spanners are often recommended for unscrewing the pump assembly locking ring, but we'll bet you'll figure something out. Just make sure you get that sock or strainer on there right.

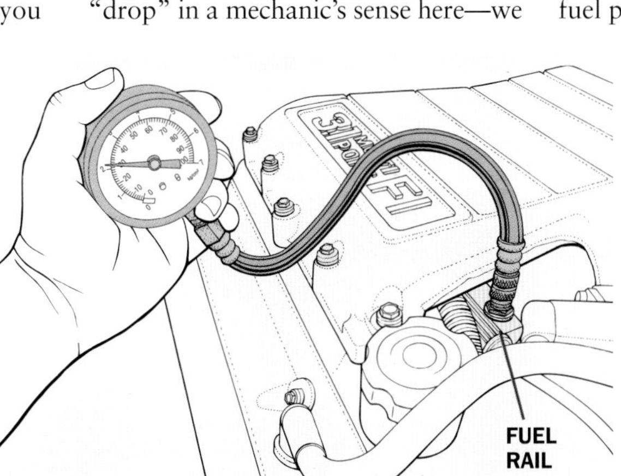

(Fig. 4) A fuel pressure gauge can tell you plenty. Take readings dead-head (key on, engine off) and running.

EASY

Eliminating Battery Drain

It's a familiar feeling, twisting the key and being rewarded with little more than a groan from the starter. Your mechanic diagnoses it as nothing more than a tired battery, and a simple transplant cures the problem. It's *déjà-vu,* as you've heard the same thing every winter—your car's battery needs replacement on an annual basis. It's time to get to the bottom of the problem.

Given normal circumstances and use, a car battery should last four to five years or more. Sure, there's a warranty, but it's typically pro rata, which means that unless the battery dies an almost instant death, all you will get is a partial credit toward the price of a new one.

There are a lot of reasons why a car eats batteries. If you've had hard luck with the ones you've been buying, the problem almost surely is not the fault of the battery manufacturers. Oh, there's an occasional dud, but most of the time the reason is in the car itself. Deep-discharging a few times will damage a battery, and so will constant over- or undercharging.

All Charged Up

First, make sure the battery really is damaged before you spring for a new one. The simplest test is to fully charge it and see if it takes that charge. If it takes a charge, it's still good—but if it doesn't, it must be bad.

Here's where we get to the procedure that convinces many Saturday mechanics that they need a new battery. They connect a trickle charger overnight, and then conclude the next day that the battery can't take the charge. But there's a flaw in this approach: If a modern low-maintenance battery goes stone dead for some reason, it may need a real jolt to accept a charge. The discharged battery's internal resistance is very high, and many smaller chargers won't supply enough voltage to get over the hump **(Fig. 1)**. There are professional chargers that start out with well over 12 volts (typically 18 to 24 volts) to break through, and your trickle charger (or even a reasonably decent homeowner-model charger) just won't kick out that much. You'll have to take the battery to a service station that has a premium charger. If you insist on trying to use your own small charger, it may take several days. Remember that the dashboard gauge really doesn't tell you much. Check the voltage across the battery terminals when you're done (charger off and headlights on for 15 seconds to remove a "surface charge"). It should be at least 12.7 volts, preferably about 12.8 volts.

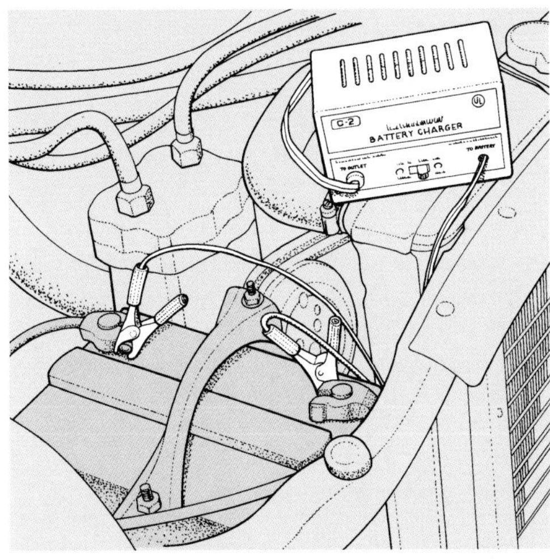

(Fig. 1) Inexpensive low-current trickle chargers may not revive a completely discharged battery.

Even if your battery isn't so run-down that it needs breakthrough voltage to start taking a charge, it does need good connections from the charger. Unfortunately, the side-terminal battery has a small contact area for the cable's alligator clip. Unless you have a specially shaped clip, you really need a charging adapter, made of copper, that clamps all the way around the side-terminal contact area **(Fig. 2)**.

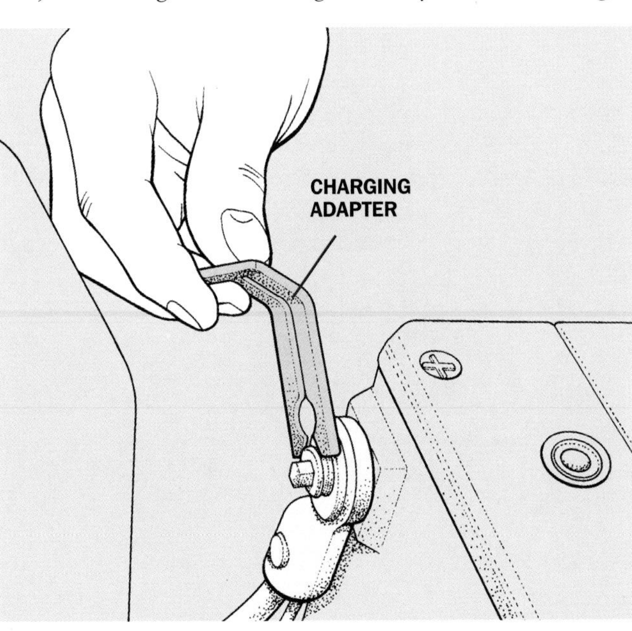

(Fig. 2) It may be necessary to use a battery-charging adapter to let the jumper cables get a good bite on side-terminal batteries.

If the battery takes a charge but runs down in use, there's a problem that has to be traced. Otherwise, the car will seem to eat the next battery, too, even if it's a higher-capacity model.

Now that the battery is charged, you can check the charging voltage. With

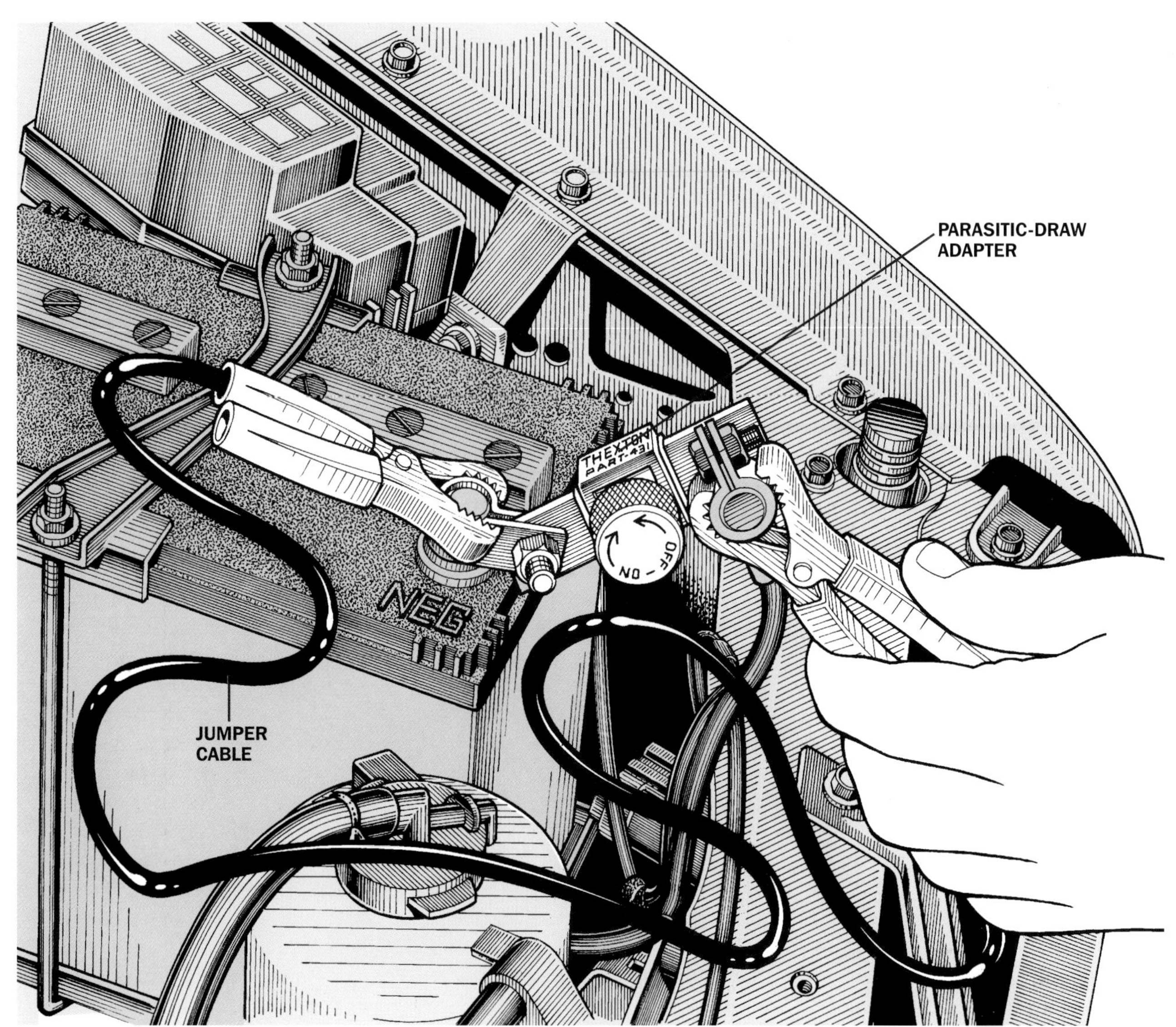

(Fig. 3) An inexpensive parasitic-draw adapter can simplify the diagnosis of key-off current-drain problems. Connect it in series with the battery's ground lead.

the engine running and warm and all the power-consuming accessories switched off, the voltage across the battery should read at least 13.8 volts. Next, turn on the headlights and rear-window defroster, and set the heater/air-conditioning fan on high. The voltage should still be above 13.5 volts. Anything less means you may have a malfunctioning alternator.

When demand exceeds supply

Let's see if you're pulling more juice than the charging system can replace during your normal driving cycle. If you have a high-performance sound system and a cellular phone, and run other accessories, this kind of usage really sucks amps. But you still should be okay—if you drive the car far enough. A half-mile in the morning with the a/c on and a half-mile back home at night with the a/c and lights on, perhaps with your favorite CD blasting through the speakers, is a great recipe for battery rundown. Drive your car long enough to pay back the battery for what you've borrowed, plus interest, at least once a week.

In addition, today's cars pull a fair amount of current even when everything seems to be off, just to keep alive the memories for all the electronics: the engine computer, keyless-entry receiver, the radio presets and the alarm system, to name the most common.

To keep the draw from depleting the battery, the electronics are supposed to go into a deep sleep, during which they require only a few milliamps. If they don't take this snooze, they can add to the current loss. To check, disconnect the battery ground cable. Install a parasitic draw adapter (Fig. 3) in series with the battery and cable terminals, then connect an ammeter to the terminals. Open the adapter to see if the draw is less than 50 milliamps. Normally, you have to wait until the electronics go into snooze mode, which can take 60 to 70 minutes on some cars. Until then, the current draw may be sev-

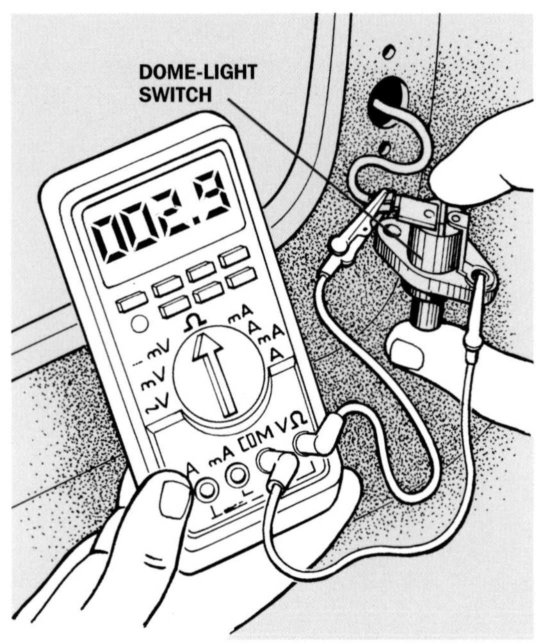

(Fig. 4) Check the dome-light switch for intermittent or abnormal resistance with an ohmmeter.

eral hundred milliamps, or even as much as several amps.

However, even if the draw is near 50 milliamps or so when you actually take your reading, it might be far too high before the snooze, or perhaps the electronics are awake for far too long. So, next, wake up the electronics and see what the readings are.

To do that, disconnect the ammeter from the parasitic-draw adapter. Connect a battery booster cable from the battery terminal to the cable terminal, bypassing the adapter. Turn the ignition key to the run (not to start) position. Wait a few seconds, then turn the key back to lock and take it out. Reconnect the ammeter, disconnect the booster cable and take the current-draw reading, which should be the awake number.

If the awake number is acceptable, make sure the electronics go to sleep within a reasonable amount of time. If the electronics still are awake and pulling hundreds of milliamps—or even an amp or more—hours later, something is very wrong. You can isolate a high current draw to a specific circuit by pulling one fuse at a time and rechecking. Just make sure the ignition is off.

A high-current-drawing short will cause a battery to go dead in hours. More likely, there's a small-to-medium draw that's bleeding the system, or a charging system that's not performing up to speed. Sometimes, you can spot the problem if you look hard. Many cars have interior lighting delays, but occasionally a key part of the delay system doesn't shut down. It might not be the in-plain-view dome light, but perhaps the dashboard lights or some floor lighting. If they're still on 15 minutes after the dome light is off, you've found a circuit glitch. For instance, 1990 to '91 Chevy Luminas had a problem caused by an electrical feedback from the radio. Even though the electronic timer said "Lights out!" and other bulbs were extinguished, the instruments continued to glow.

The lights for the glovebox, luggage compartment and hood are out of sight unless those areas are open, in which case the lights are supposed to be on. Peek inside as you just lift the cover, decklid or hood slightly to see if the light already is on or just coming on. If it's constantly on, then you've found your culprit.

A bad doorjamb switch can cause a lot of problems. If it's making intermittent contact, it's repeatedly waking up the electronics and turning on the interior lights.

The simplest overall check is to remove the fuse or fuses for the courtesy lamps to see if the battery stops running down. If that seems to be a possible cure, check out each doorjamb switch. Disconnect the battery ground strap, then remove the switch from the door opening and connect an ohmmeter (**Fig. 4**) from the switch terminal to its metal bracket, which provides the ground. The ohmmeter should read close to zero (a couple of ohms is okay). Repeatedly press the switch plunger part of the way and see if the ohmmeter reading goes to infinity (fully off position). If it takes a lot of plunger travel, or if the plunger response is inconsistent, the switch is probably bad.

Also check for a sticky radiator/condenser fan relay that keeps the fan going with the ignition off for a longer period of time than any computer strategy dictates, until it finally pops open. In fact, the relay could keep the fan on until the battery is dead. Look and listen for this one.

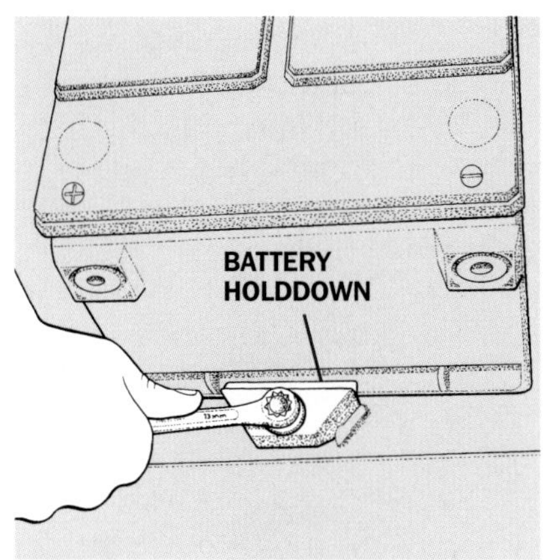

(Fig. 5) Check and tighten the holddown to keep the battery from vibrating.

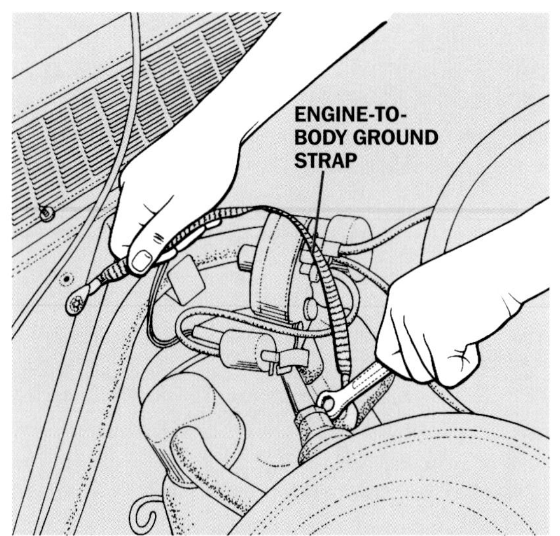

(Fig. 6) Make sure the ground strap is connected and in good shape. It's often hidden and neglected.

Rocking the Boat

If the current draw is acceptable and the issue seems to be that the battery just suffered from short life, make sure that the battery case is in good condition and the battery holddown is tight (**Fig. 5**). Even a slightly loose battery can vibrate enough to suffer a short life. Just because a top holddown looks tight doesn't mean the battery actually is secure. See if it rocks, even a little. Many holddowns arc against a bottom lip on the battery, almost out of sight, so if the battery mounting isn't rock solid, check a down-low holddown.

Are the cables in good shape and securely tightened? The alternator may be pumping, but if the cable connections are bad, the juice won't actually get to the battery. The battery ground usually is the big offender.

In some cases, there's a split ground cable, and you can see one of the cable ends, in plain view and clearly tight. But the other part of the cable (usually the one to the engine) is buried deep, and what's out of sight shouldn't be out of mind. Find it, and put a wrench on it to see if it's snug (**Fig. 6**).

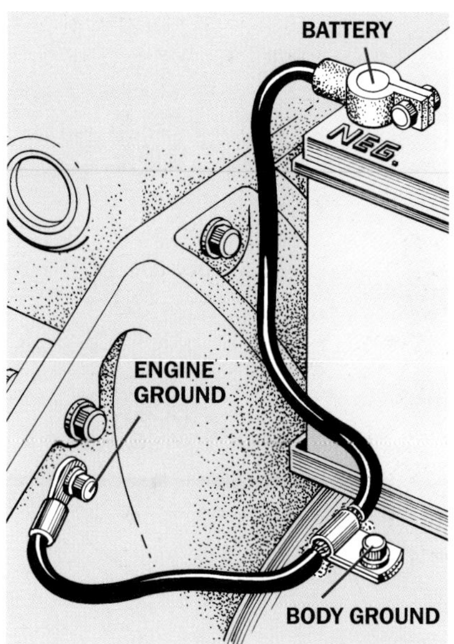

(Fig. 7) Check all three ground points on this type of ground strap for corrosion or looseness.

Many cars have a separate ground strap between body and engine, and it's usually nowhere near the battery (**Fig. 7**). In fact, if it's underhood, it's often disconnected for service and never reconnected. So the car's electrical system "forces" the juice through less efficient routes, and the battery is one of those that suffers. We've even seen engine-to-body ground straps that actually ran from the transmission to some part of the underbody. These ground straps fray, come apart and are far from any place you normally would look.

So if you don't see a clear-cut route from the battery negative (ground) terminal to both the engine and the body, look again—everywhere. Some older Ford products have a single ground cable to the engine, but with the insulation stripped at midpoint, and the body ground made by a clip from the stripped section to the fender-well sheetmetal.

Okay, the battery takes a charge and the cable connections are good. Well, perhaps the accessories you use are simply pulling more juice than the car can provide in your short-trip operation. A regular diet of trickle charging every night should provide the vitamins your battery needs for a normal life span.

EASY

Replacing Headlights

You're cruising down a 2-lane road late at night. Oncoming cars flash their lights and toot their horns at you. Or they come straight at you and suddenly veer away. No, they're not partied out. Unless you're blinding them with your high beams, one of your headlamps probably is out.

Replacing burned-out headlamps is a straightforward procedure, if the problem is just the headlamp. Although most are about $15, some headlamps are special numbers, available only from a dealer and can cost up to $45 apiece, even for an econobox. And there are even higher-tech (and higher-priced) systems, such as High Intensity Discharge (HID) headlamps, in some luxury models. They may look like ordinary headlamps—just as halogen sealed beams resemble the conventional sealed beams used years ago—but the manufacturing processes, the coatings, the materials and the gases used inside the bulbs are totally different and produce totally different lighting.

Don't leave in a headlamp with a cracked lens just because the light hasn't gone out. Even if only a small part of the lens is missing, dirt gets in and coats the bulb inside, which reduces light output. And if there's a chunk missing from the lens, the light beam isn't diffused as it should be and can blind oncoming drivers. With normal vehicle vibration, the lamp also may not hold its aim and you won't get the best view of the road. Also read "Servicing Composite Headlamps on page 149.

Circuit Check

If it seems that a headlamp is burned out, make a simple circuit check. With just one of two or four on the blink, the odds are that the sealed beam is the problem. It's unlikely that two headlamps will go out simultaneously.

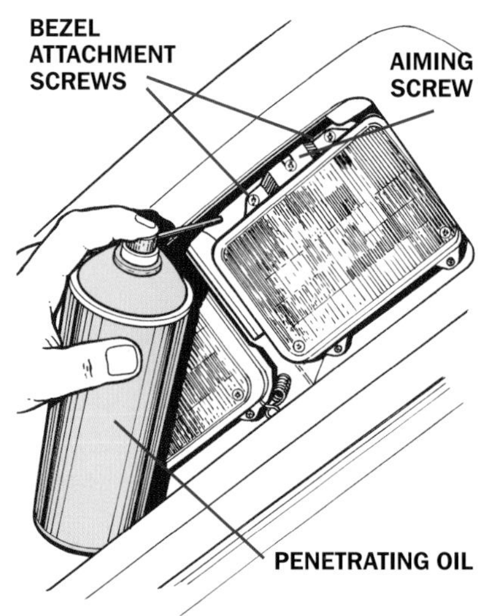

(Fig. 1) If the trim bezel screws are hard to turn, use penetrant to loosen the threads.

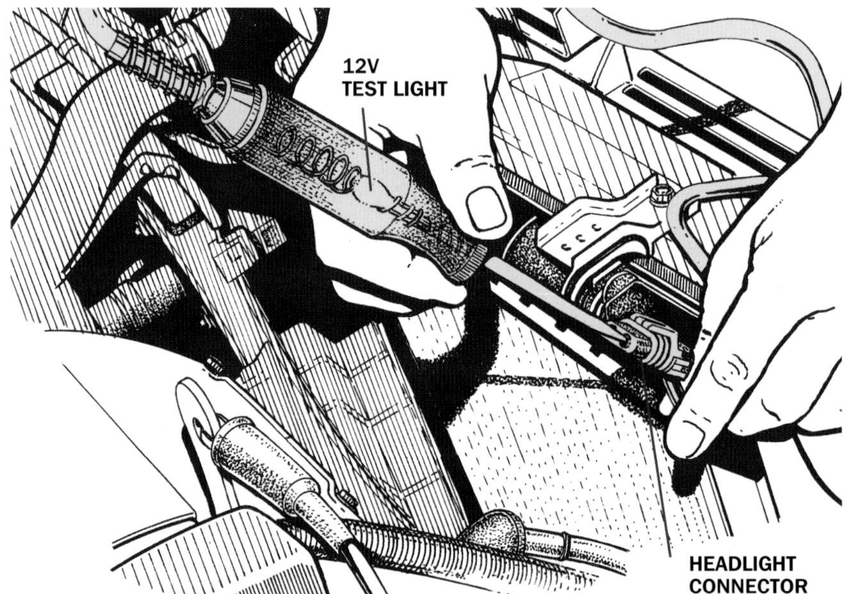

(Fig. 2) Use a simple 12v test light to confirm operating power and ground circuits before replacing an expensive bulb or sealed beam.

Of course, if the low and the high beams are in a single bulb, it is possible, but it's much less likely when they're separate lights.

Checking or changing a burned-out headlamp begins with gaining access. If it's a sealed beam, there's probably a trim plate in front, which comes off first. Most trim plates are held by either Phillips or Torx external screws. A few may be on studs that project through to the back of the lamp assembly—these are accessible from under the hood.

Next, look for and remove the four screws holding the headlamp rim or bezel. Be careful not to confuse them with the screws that control headlamp aim—the ones with coil springs under the screwheads. Are the screws rust-frozen in place? Don't try too hard to turn them, or you may strip out the screwheads. Spray them with penetrating solvent and allow it to soak in (**Fig. 1**). The attachment screws usually have a Phillips head, but—like the trim screws—they may be Torx.

Once the rim is out, pull the sealed beam forward and unplug the wiring connector from the back. You'll see two or three terminals on the lamp and connector. A 2-headlamp system always has three terminals. A 4-eye lamp may have two or three, depending on how the entire circuit is wired.

A simple check of the circuit is to see if there's power at the connector and a complete electrical ground. Take an ordinary 12v test light (**Fig. 2**), connect the alligator clip end to a ground and check each connector terminal with the probe. The headlamps should be turned on. The test light should go on in at least one terminal. If the sealed beam is a 2-eye with three terminals, flick on the high-beam switch and the test light should go on with the probe in a second one of the three terminals.

Next, unground the test light and gently press the alligator clip end (with a nail inserted, if necessary) to make contact with the other (ground wire) terminal—ground is usually a black wire. The test light should go on again.

If the test light goes on during these two checks, install the new sealed beam. If it doesn't, forget the installation until the circuit problem is repaired. If the test light went on when the alligator clip was connected to ground, but not when you probed the other connector terminal for a complete ground, the problem is a defective ground connection—a common problem.

Check a factory manual or after-market information system, such as www.alldata.com, for the location of your car's ground. If the connection is corroded, wire-brush it clean. If it's loose, retighten it.

No power to the headlamp connector? That can be more difficult to trace, and you'll need a wiring diagram and parts locator again.

A new circuit complication is on the scene: daytime running lights, or DRLs. These may be the low-beam or high-beam headlamps, or other external lights such as turn signals.

Headlamps are wired in what is called a parallel circuit—each lamp receives full battery voltage. However, if your car is a newer-than-'96 model

HOW IT WORKS

Quartz-Halogen Sealed Beam

The conventional sealed beam of years ago had a tungsten filament inside a lens assembly with a reflector. Today's quartz-halogen beam is a separate bulb inside that lens assembly. It produces a brighter, whiter light—at least 25% more down-the-road visibility, with less power draw.

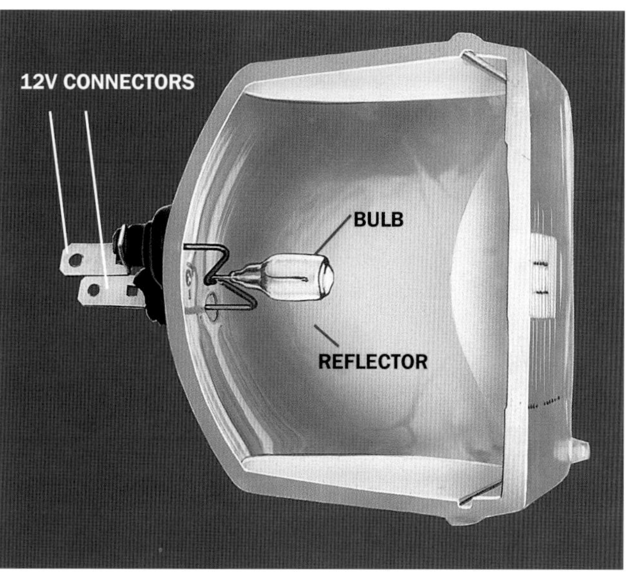

The bulb envelope is a high-temperature glass—the "quartz." The filament material is the familiar tungsten, but the bulb is filled with a special gas from a "family" called halogens, such as iodine or bromine gas (that family also includes a/c refrigerants, by the way). In a conventional sealed beam, the high temperature of the tungsten filament causes particles of the metal to vaporize from it. The particles deposit on the wall of the conventional sealed beam (darkening it), and eventually the filament burns out.

The quartz lens allows the bulb to operate at a much higher temperature to help produce that brighter, whiter light. The halogen gas inside the quartz envelope causes the "evaporating" tungsten particles to continuously redeposit on the filament, so it enjoys long life and consistent brightness virtually until it fails.

Headlamp technology is fast-moving. The High Intensity Discharge lamp (see page 150) is just one of the new approaches, but it's already installed as a low beam in some BMWs and Mercedes-Benzes and the Lincoln Mark VIII. This type has no filament, but instead it has two electrodes in an "atmosphere" of xenon gas. The current jumps the gap between the electrodes, producing a comparatively brighter light. You may have already seen these lights coming at you out on the highway. They're so white that they appear a little blue. But because there's no filament to burn out, the hour life of the xenon bulb is expected to go into six figures.

There are several other new headlamp designs on the market, including one on the '97 Lexus ES 300 that uses multiple reflectors. All the new lamps—including the high-performance halogens—are capable of producing a lot of brightness with reasonable power consumption. And introduced in some 2003 models are "smart" headlight systems that use signals from sensors to pivot the headlamps side to side for the road conditions and the way you're driving the car. These combination bright/smart lights are in part a technological fix for the declining night vision of a graying population.

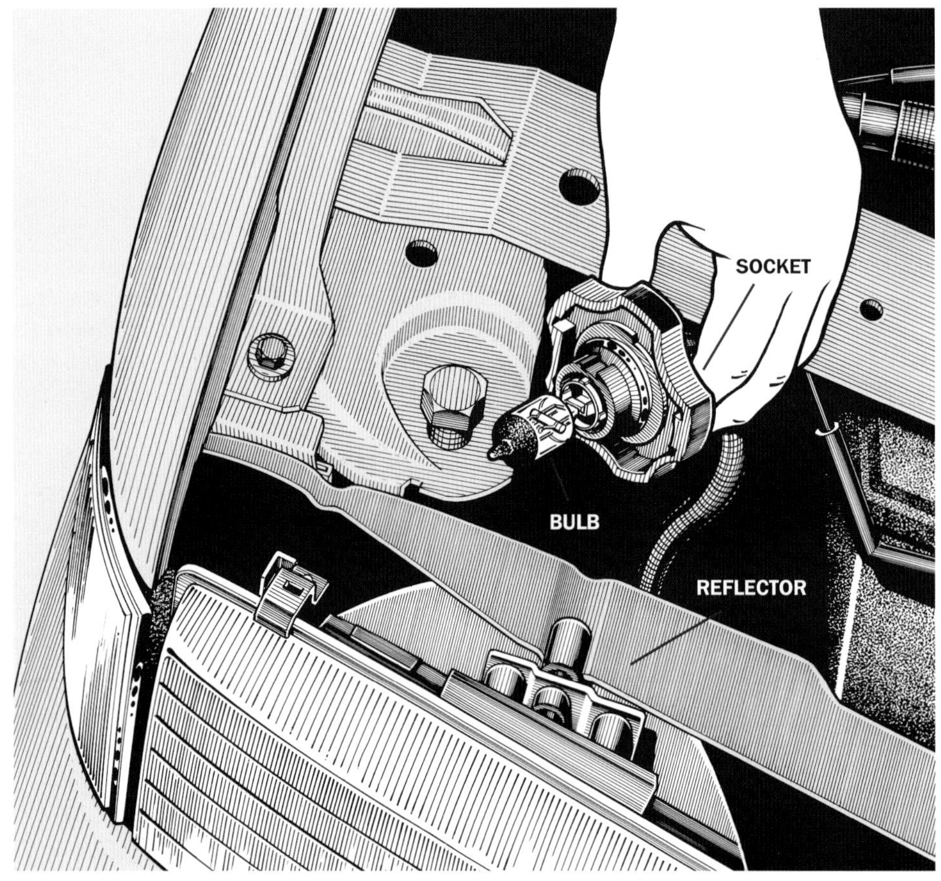

(Fig. 3) Newer cars use bulbs that can be replaced without using tools. Unscrew the socket from the reflector and change the bad bulb, then replace the socket.

with daytime running lights and the headlamp high beams are used, there's a second circuit controlling them through an electronic module. The high beams could be wired to the module so that they can be fed current for DRLs in a series circuit—the current flows through both, so that one acts as a resistor for the other. The result is less brightness, but also less current flow for reduced power consumption. If you have a problem with the high beams, a defective DRL module is one of the new possibilities of which you should be aware, both for sealed beams and replaceable bulb designs. Some cars have DRLs that are also designed to shut off when the parking brake is applied. Read those circuit descriptions carefully!

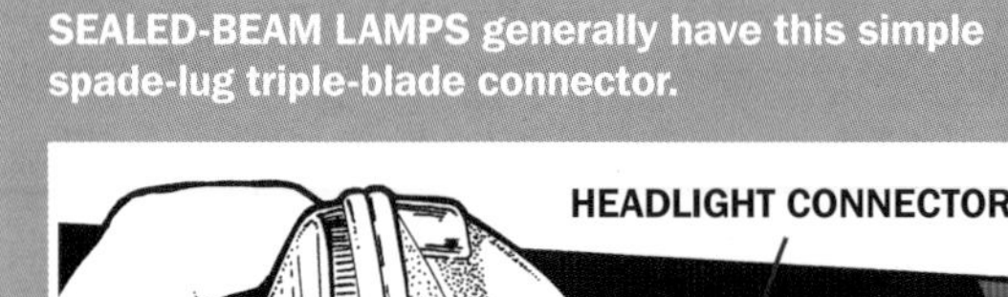

SEALED-BEAM LAMPS generally have this simple spade-lug triple-blade connector.

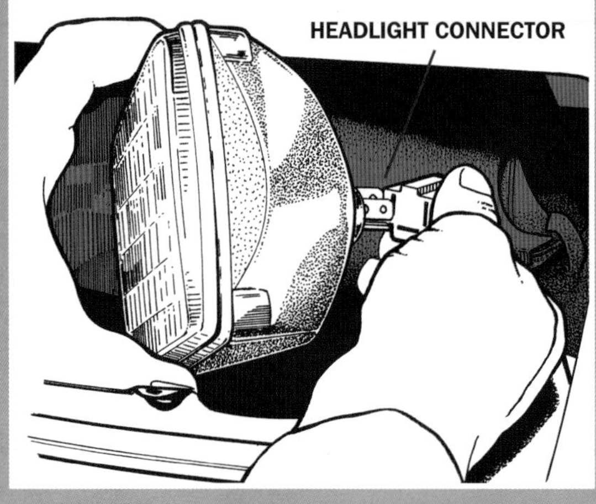

Replaceable Bulbs

Many late-model cars have a replaceable bulb plugged into the back of the lens assembly (**Fig. 3**) instead of the sealed beam. (European cars have always used this type.) Typically, the bulb has a wiring connector held by a plastic locktab, and a plastic lockring to hold the bulb.

Pry up the tab (with a thin screwdriver, if necessary) and hold it up as you pull the harness connector off the terminals on the bulb. You can probe the harness connector the same way as on the sealed-beam design to make sure the bulb is at fault. An alternative: If the bulb is easy to remove, take it out for inspection. Turn the plastic lockring, which may come out or stay loosely in place. Then grasp the bulb by its connector and gently rock it out (it seals with an O-ring to keep out dirt and moisture). If the bulb filament is burned out, that tells you it's most likely the problem. Warning: Replaceable bulbs are usually quartz-halogen—and touching the bulb with your fingers will leave fingerprints that will crack the quartz glass within a few hours. The new bulb will be wrapped in cardboard or foam, so don't remove the wrapping until last and avoid touching the bulb. Too late? Clean the bulb with alcohol and a clean cloth.

When you install the new bulb, work it in very carefully, then push smoothly to seat it in the lens housing. This ensures that the O-ring seals properly instead of being twisted or dislodged.

A bulb or sealed-beam harness connector may have a ribbed-rubber moisture seal if the location poses a problem with road splash. When you see this setup, make sure it enters the bulb connector uniformly and seats evenly.

Replace it with the same type of bulb or sealed beam as the one that came out. You may see high-performance versions of the type you removed on the auto parts store shelf. If you want to install one of these instead, replace the one on the other side too, for even lighting.

EASY

Replacing Your Car's Computer

Experiencing bad engine performance? Your vehicle may need brain surgery, and believe it or not, it's something an experienced Saturday mechanic can do. Yes, we're talking about the powertrain computer—the "brain" behind the operation of your engine, transmission, even the air conditioning.

Today, you can order a computer from your neighborhood parts store, which can choose one from a long list of reliable aftermarket suppliers. The computers are reconditioned, and in many cases you change over a program module, which holds the specific calibration instructions for the powertrain, such as ignition timing. If you're careful, you can do the job. In fact, in many cases you'll find you don't have to replace the computer, but can perform a lower-cost or even a no-cost "minor operation."

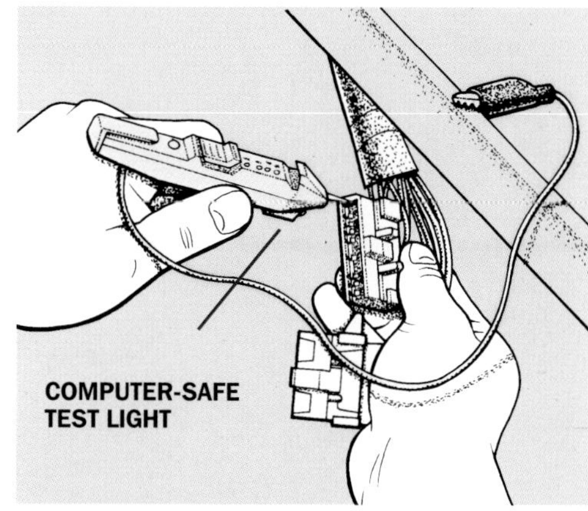

(Fig. 1) Check the feed with a high-impedance voltmeter or a computer-safe test light.

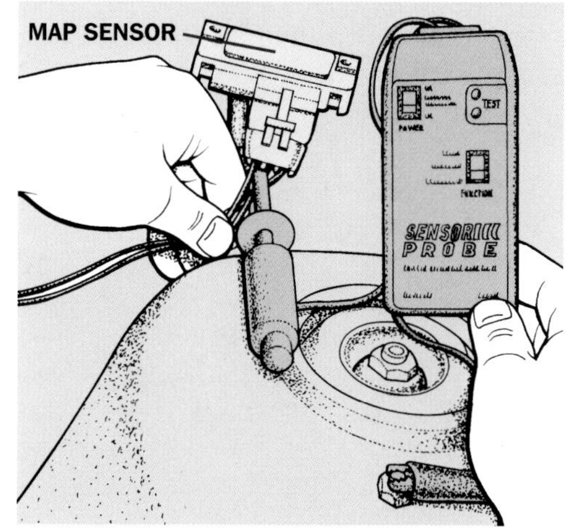

(Fig. 2) Check sensors with tester or voltmeter to rule out noncomputer problems.

Diagnosis

Before you do actual brain surgery on your car, you have to find out if the engine is performing poorly because the brain is bad or if it's just responding to a "bad case of nerves" (bad signals from electronic sensors).

It could simply be a blown engine-computer circuit fuse, but if not, it's time for diagnosis. For this, refer to your vehicle's service manual—either a factory manual or an aftermarket manual with a complete engine-computer diagnostic section.

Check for diagnostic trouble codes. Although the procedure varies from car to car, on most pre-1996 vehicles there's a way that doesn't involve special equipment. Typically, you make a simple jumper-wire connection at the computer's diagnostic plug, which is under the dash or under the hood. Check your service manual. On later models meeting OBD II onboard diagnostic II regulations, you need a scan tool. More on OBD II later in this section.

Just a single code? Check that particular item, whether it's a sensor, switch, motor or solenoid. The manual will give you a "diagnostic tree," a series of steps to follow, typically using a jumper wire and a computer-safe (high-impedance) multimeter to isolate the problem **(Fig. 1)**, which could be in the part itself or somewhere in its wiring circuit. Or you can use a sensor tester **(Fig. 2)**, which comes with adapters and/or special tips so you can probe wiring connectors. Correcting a problem in any circuit tied to the computer is an essential first step in every case, as it can be responsible for a computer failure.

In many instances, the diagnostic tree will conclude with REPLACE COMPUTER. You also could be led to the computer if there's a flickering CHECK ENGINE light, or no light at all (but the bulb is good).

Still another possibility: a laundry list of trouble codes. In many cases, the problem is in what's called a driver, a type of electronic switching device that is in the computer box. However, it isn't replaceable, so if it's bad, the only cure is a new computer.

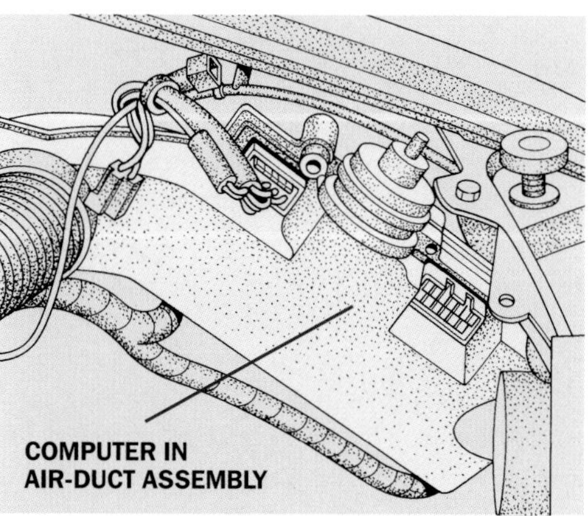

(Fig. 3) Some early Chrysler computers were housed in an air duct under the hood for cooling.

Minor Surgery

Computers typically have been located under the dashboard, accessible after removing a trim pad or the glovebox on the passenger's

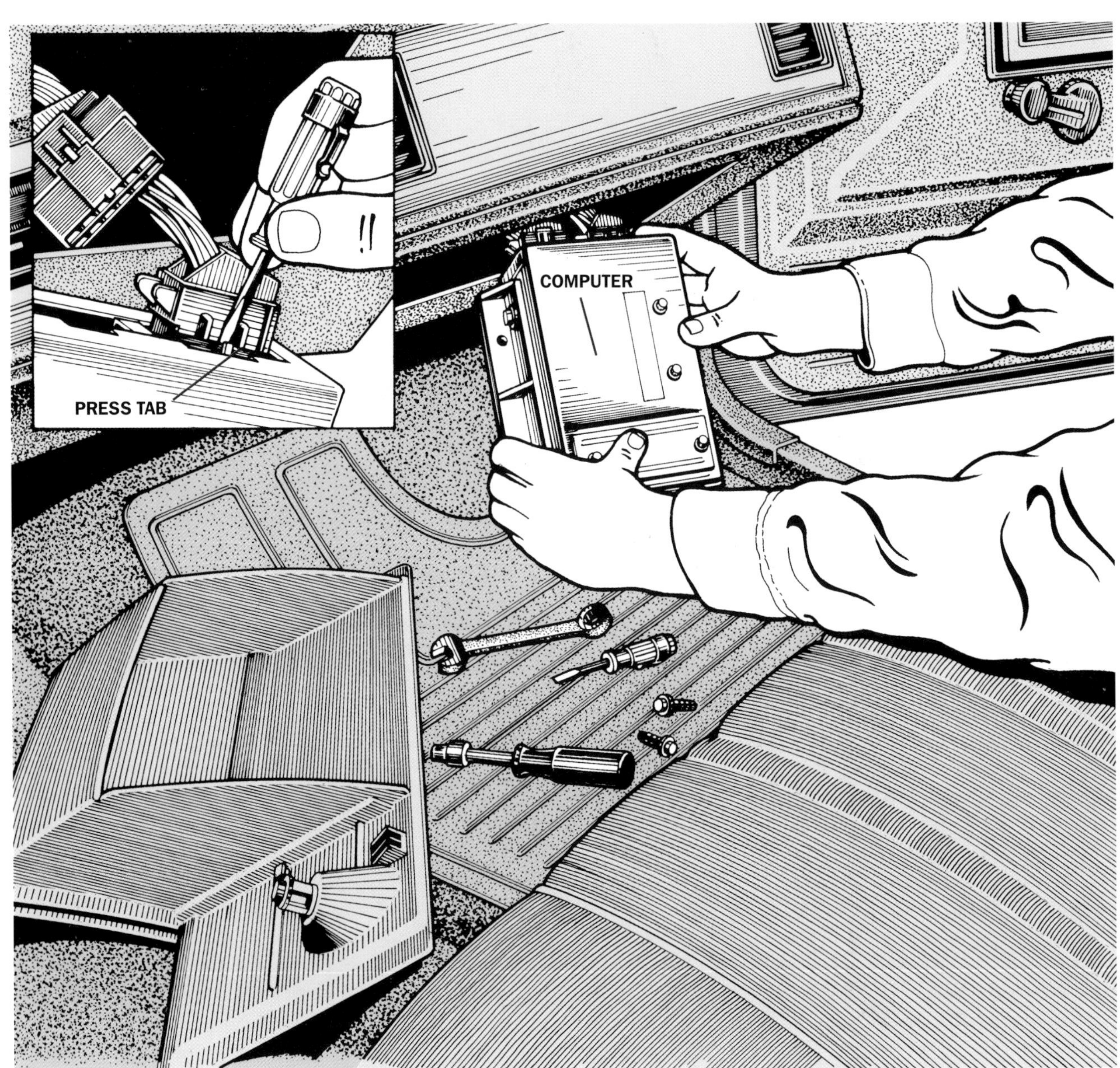

side. Older Chrysler computers usually are under the hood, integrated into an engine air-intake duct, but they were an exception for the 1980s (**Fig. 3**). Today, and as the electronics have become more heat-resistant, many computers are located under the hood.

Wherever the computer is located, the first steps are to turn off the ignition and disconnect the battery ground cable.

Next, unplug the computer's wiring connector. It often has plastic latches or locking tabs, so you should look carefully before you try to pry anything off and press tabs or latches wherever necessary (**Fig. 4**).

Eyeball the terminals in the computer and the wiring connector, looking for both corrosion and signs of bending. You can try to straighten a bent pin—but no rough stuff. And don't try to sand or scrape off corrosion, or you'll ruin the terminal. Brace the terminal with your fingers and clean it with a pink pencil eraser.

If everything looks good, start putting the connector back on by working it back and forth a few times, then pushing it all the way home. This may clean off a small amount of virtually invisible corrosion (enough to create havoc with electronics and produce multiple trouble codes) and get the computer system working again. If the problem comes back, well, at least you tried.

(Fig. 4) Once you've determined that the computer is really fried, replacing it is simple. It's often situated under the dash or behind the passenger's-side kick panel. There may be a locking tab holding the computer's umbilical connector in place.

Back to disconnecting the computer. With the wiring connector off the computer, probe the connector's terminal for the ground wire with a computer-safe test light or multimeter (set to volts), connected to a 12-volt source (either at the battery or at the fuse box). The test light should go on to full brightness, or the meter should read battery voltage. Also check the 12-volt power feed (or feeds) in the connector with a grounded test light or voltmeter. The results should be the same. If you get a low-voltage reading or a weak light, there's a bad connection. Whatever the result, always double-check all electronic grounds.

Brain Transplant

Is it a clear-cut case of a bad computer? Order the replacement and make the module changeover, if necessary (**Fig. 5**). General Motors vehicles and most European cars have computers with a plug-in program module, which doesn't come with the replacement computers. In fact, some have two modules, and you have to change over both.

Remove the module cover, then take out the module. Some of them are held by retainers—push them back and simultaneously lift the module straight up and out. With most others, you have to pry it out, and the safest way is with thumb and forefinger at the ends, applying an ever-so-slight rocking upward motion. The typical module is in a plastic carrier (don't try to separate the pieces). If space is too tight for your fingers, use two small screwdrivers—one at each end—to rock the module assembly up as evenly as possible. Do not pry one side up or you may bend the terminals.

Note the way the module comes out, as it has to go into the new computer the same way. It's possible to install it backward on some cars, which could destroy the new computer. Position the module on the mounting area of the replacement computer, push slowly (so you know that the terminals are lined up for engagement), applying pressure only

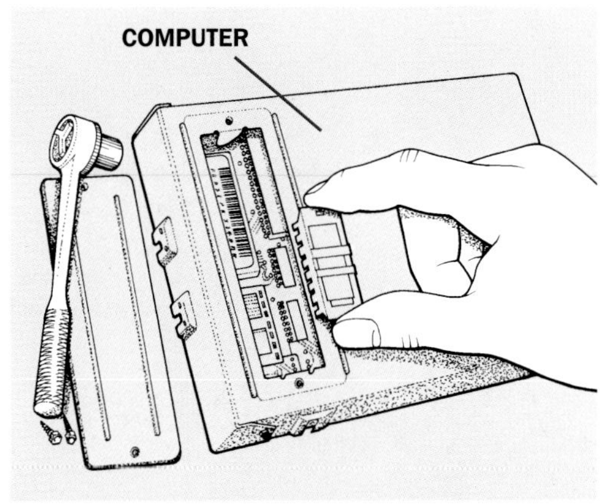

(Fig. 5) You may need to remove your old calibration module and install it in the new computer.

on the ends of the module, until it seats. Lock the tabs.

Reconnect the wiring harness to the computer. If you're working under the dash, you may build up a lot of static electricity while sliding into working position. As you make the harness connection, you could zap the computer with enough voltage from the static electricity to fry it. Simply ground part of your body to an underdash ground, such as by keeping a bare elbow against a metal brace.

Make sure you not only seat the wiring connector, but that you close any latches that hold it in position. Reinstall the computer, engaging all clips and tightening all bolts, screws and nuts so the computer is held securely in position.

Reconnect the car battery. The installation instructions with the replacement computer will provide a basic test of the system (similar to checking for trouble codes), and once that's done, you should be ready to drive. But all modern engine computers must go through a period of "learning" how you drive and making compensating adjustments (primarily to fuel-system calibrations). So be prepared for perhaps 100 miles or 4 to 5 hours of so-so performance as the new computer (even with an old program module) learns how to do its job.

This is something to keep in mind if you are doing a test run to see if one of the minor operations (cleaning corrosion, tightening a ground and so on) fixed a problem. Disconnecting the battery cable erases the trouble codes. However, if the faults remain, most trouble codes show up again within a half-hour of vehicle operation, even though it takes much longer for overall engine performance to return to normal after a successful fix.

All models since '96 have computers that conform to On-Board Diagnostics II (OBD II), an enhanced computer system with some standardization of trouble codes and diagnostic routines. One scan tester (computer-system data analyzer) will fit the underdash diagnostic plug on all OBD II cars, and there are models for Saturday mechanics for under $200 (see page 181).

The OBD II computers on many vehicles are reprogrammable through the diagnostic plug. With previous systems, carmakers offered factory fixes by having the dealer replace the computer or the program module. With the specific OBD II system, they now have the dealer simply reprogram the computer. A few cars have had reprogrammable computers in past (pre-OBD II) years, but with OBD II, it's basically across the board on U.S. nameplates and most imports.

Curing A/C Odors

(Fig 1) The simplest cure for odor is to run the air conditioning in fresh-air mode to lower humidity in the evaporator plenum.

It's a sweltering day. You get behind the wheel, start the engine and hit the max a/c button. But instead of refreshingly cool air hitting you, there's a blast that smells like a basketball team's locker room after a hard game. Your car's air conditioning is suffering from what could be called "jock socks odor." And you're not alone—it's one of the most common complaints that *Popular Mechanics* receives from readers.

If you take the car in to a dealer, he'll tell you it's a fungus growth in the under-dash a/c case that holds the evaporator. That's the heat exchanger that pulls the BTUs out of the passenger compartment. His solution is an expensive cleanout of the a/c with disinfectant. And after you've spent a lot of money, the smell is gone—for a while. It may be back before the air conditioning season is over.

Is there a less costly and more durable way to fix it yourself? Can you prevent the problem from occurring in the first place? The answer to both questions is yes.

The price of prevention is free, and the most important step doesn't even require a tool. Just don't use max a/c. If you have a car with an air-recirculation switch or lever, just move it to the outside-air position (**Fig. 1**). The evaporator case is a humid environment because it's where the air is dehumidified (as well as cooled), and when you shut off the engine, heat builds up inside the evaporator housing. A hot, humid environment with stagnant air is the perfect setting for fungus growth.

The recirculation switch closes off outside air, and causes the a/c to merely recirculate the air in the passenger compartment. With little or no entry of hot outside air, the interior gets cooler faster and remains much colder. It's okay to use recirculation to help with the initial cool-down on a sweltering day, but after a few minutes, you should shift out of recirculation to bring in fresh air.

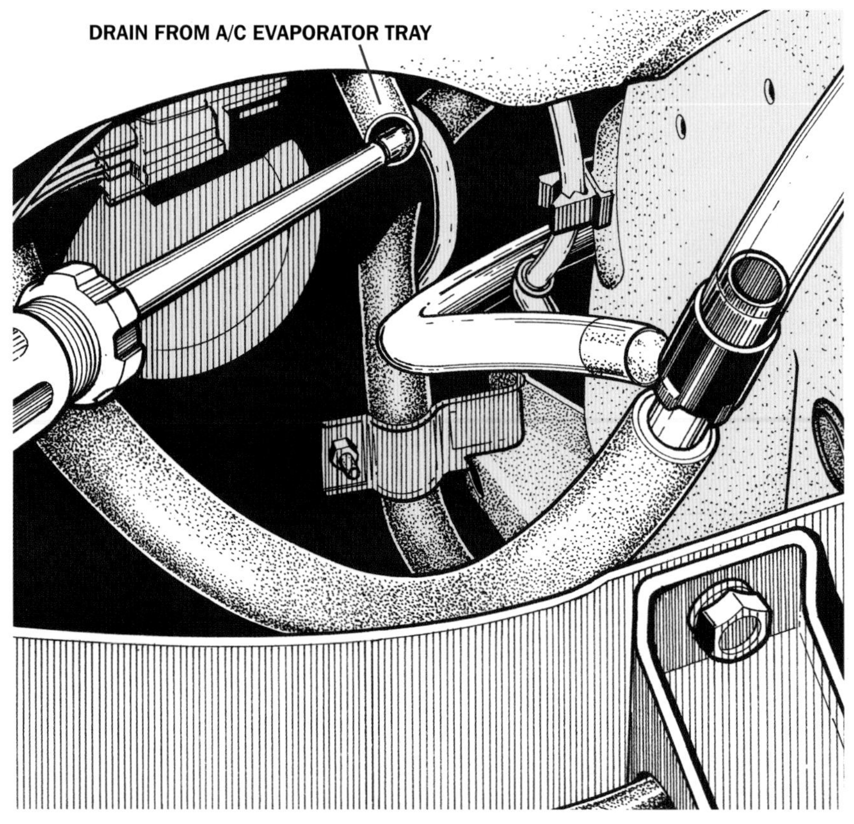

(Fig 2) An evaporator-tray drain that's plugged with dirt and debris might keep moisture from draining onto the ground.

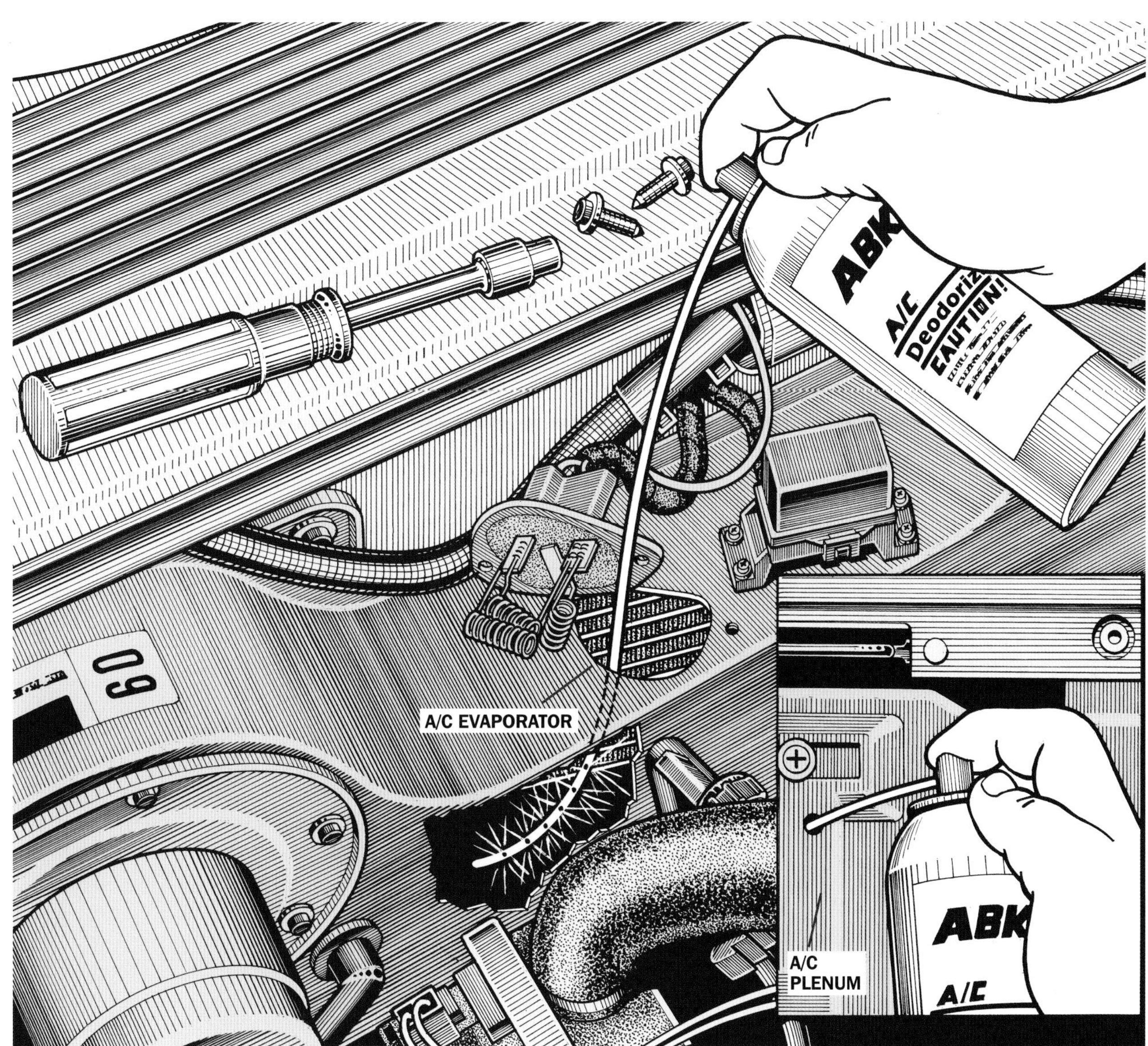

(Fig. 3) There are effective and ineffective cures for a/c odor. This aftermarket disinfectant works when sprayed directly onto the evaporator core. Before spraying, tape over the blower resistor opening (illustrated), making a small opening for the straw.

Many manual and automatic temperature-control systems are in recirculation when in max a/c or at the lowest temperature on the automatic system's dial. In this instance, you should also shift to a slightly warmer setting.

Garbage Collection

The next step is to lift the hood and inspect the air intake at the cowl. If it's packed with leaves and other debris, you may have a miniature compost pile forming. The odors from it are drawn into the passenger compartment by the blower fan. These odors are equally unpleasant, and you will need to dig out the debris or clean it up with a shop vacuum and wash out the area to get rid of them.

After you've cleaned it, remove the air intake grille, insert a fine window-screen mesh underneath, seal the perimeter with plumber's putty, then refit the screen. Periodically check the screened area and remove debris to ensure a fresh air supply. Most late-models have an intake air filter that removes smoke and pollen from the outside air. These filters also keep out debris and may have a replacement interval of typically one year or 15,000-20,000 miles.

When you're doing an oil change or other regular maintenance under the hood, inspect the evaporator-tray drains **(Fig. 2)**, which are one or two hoses on most vehicles. If the hose ends are plugged or badly damaged, the moisture that the evaporator wrings from the interior air will not drain properly, leaving a stagnant pool for fungi. Dig out any road film with a thin screwdriver. Many hose ends have built-in check valves, which should be carefully inspected for damage. The ends are specially shaped, so don't trim them flat with a razor blade. Open the check valves gently, and if the ends are not damaged or plugged, leave them alone. If the ends are damaged, however, the best route is to replace the hose.

The next step is at the evaporator case. But before you do any work, check with the car dealer to determine if there's a specific factory solution that goes beyond disinfecting and other steps we'll be covering. For example, many 1985-94 Cadillacs have evaporators with such tight spacing between the fins that the evaporator holds too much moisture, increasing fungi growth. General Motors has replacement evaporators that may decrease cooling a few degrees, but drain moisture more readily.

Late-model Chrysler products since 1992, particularly minivans, have been known to suffer from air-conditioning odor. It doesn't smell like dirty socks, but it is offensive, and the cause is an overly thick coating of a corrosion treatment. Here again, the only fix is a new evaporator. See your car dealer.

For the overwhelming majority of cars, the treatment is to disinfect the evaporator case. Some shops use expensive professional equipment that takes several hours to use correctly. It's the best treatment, but it's fairly costly. You can save some money and get very good results with a quality handheld disinfectant spray if you work carefully (**Fig. 3**). A household disinfectant such as Lysol can be used, but it isn't made for this problem, and any results will be too short-lived to justify the effort. Listerine won't work either, despite the fact that it's often recommended by people who don't know any better.

There are several products you'll find in auto accessory stores, and

A FEW SIMPLE SPLICES are all that's necessary to graft the afterblow electronics into your car's harness. Newer kits come with twist-lock connectors.

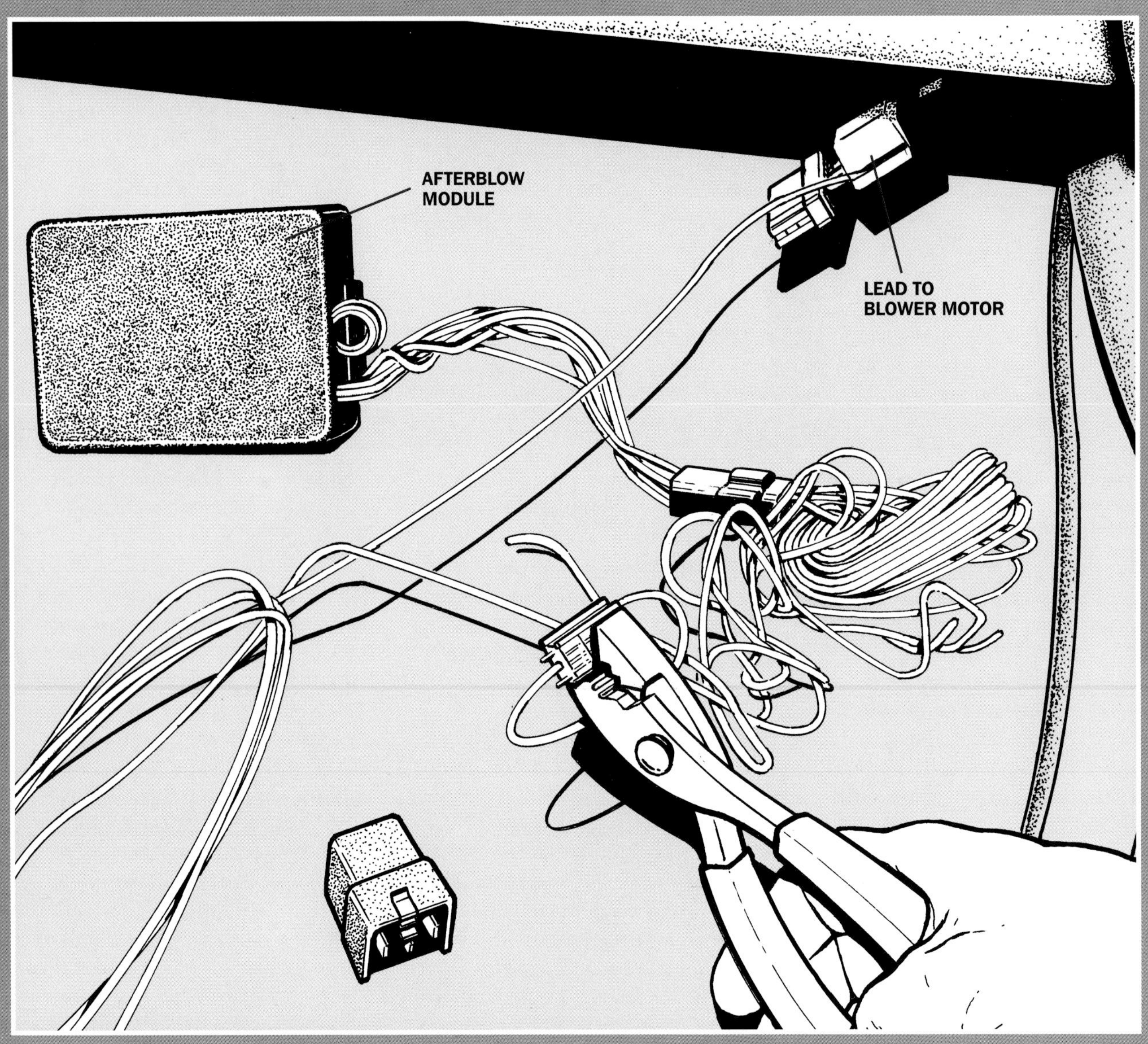

those with which we're familiar seem to work to some degree. The only one we know that has a successful track record is an expensive aerosol (about $25-$35) called ATP Clean 'N Coat. This is sold under other labels, and nationwide by GM as AC-Delco air-conditioning deodorizer (Part No. 15-102). The aerosol includes a special straw with strategically placed pinholes that produce a fogging spray, which thoroughly saturates the evaporator housing and all of the fins.

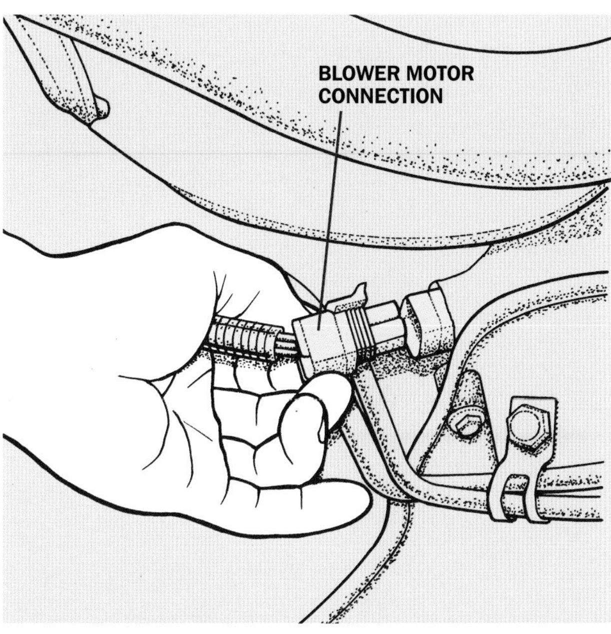

(Fig. 4) Start installation of the afterblow module by finding the power connector for the air conditioner's blower motor.

The basic approach to using the disinfectant begins by disconnecting the air-conditioner compressor. Just remove the wiring connector (typically two wires) between the clutch and the compressor body.

Next, run the system on high blower speed, in maximum heat and in recirculation (outside air shut off). If you have an automatic temperature-control system that seems to refuse to do this, override the automatic functions and pick a manual mode. Let the blower run on high speed for at least 20 minutes. This should dry out the evaporator case.

Find a spot to insert the disinfectant spray can's straw between the blower fan and the evaporator. Don't try to spray into the cowl air intake and rely on the blower to blow the disinfectant to the evaporator. If you do, virtually all the disinfectant will stick to the blower wheel.

On most cars, you can remove the blower resistor. If you look inside, you should see the evaporator, which vaguely resembles a radiator. Tape over the resistor opening and make a small hole for the straw. If you can't get to the blower resistor, find a suitable location between the blower motor and the evaporator (you may have to check a service manual to see the layout of the HVAC case). Drill a 1⁄8-in. hole in a safe place between them. Be careful not to drill in the wrong place or too deep, or you risk the danger of drilling into the evaporator or even the heater core.

Attach the straw to the can, insert the straw and hold the can relatively upright. Restart the engine, switching the a/c to outside-air mode, maximum heat and the highest blower speed. Spray in one direction, then the other. Just keep turning the nozzle and straw back and forth, spraying in each direction until the can is empty. Then stop the engine, let the disinfectant soak in for 30 minutes, then restart and run the blower for another 20 minutes, fan on high, temperature on maximum heat, system in recirculation. Finish up by shutting off the engine and reconnecting the wiring to the compressor clutch, then reinstalling the blower resistor or sealing the 1⁄8-in. hole with plumber's putty. This disinfectant is toxic, so don't leave the cat, the kids or delicate houseplants in the car while you're doing this. Opening the garage door or working outdoors is a good idea, too.

The Afterblower Solution

Now let's talk about a long-term fix: the afterblow electronic module. Its strategy is to run the blower at high speed for about 5 minutes an hour after the ignition is turned off—if the a/c has been on for at least 4 minutes. General Motors developed it as a factory solution for Cadillac and found that it worked so well at drying out the evaporator case that the electronic feature was incorporated into the a/c computer software on some Cadillacs in 1994. The kit was redesigned and released for other GM models. If you find a GM kit for your GM car or truck, it comes with connectors and a wiring schematic customized for your specific model vehicle.

Then, someone got the bright idea to use the module in a generic kit for any make. So Air Sept, AC Delco and others are selling it with an all-makes approach to the wiring and a batch of screw-lock connectors. You can install it in almost any post-1997 car.

Wiring

Just locate the blower motor's wiring connector (**Fig. 4**) and, with a grounded test light, isolate the current-feed terminal if there are two wires. The module's wiring is very straightforward, and when it's installed, the module turns on the blower at the appropriate time in high ambient temperatures when a/c operation normally would occur. It really is easier than it sounds. The most difficult part will probably be finding a good place to sinstall the module, which is held by a Velcro strip.

And when you're done, you'll not only enjoy cool fresh air, but the sweet smell of success, too.

Low-Tech Work on High-Tech Cars

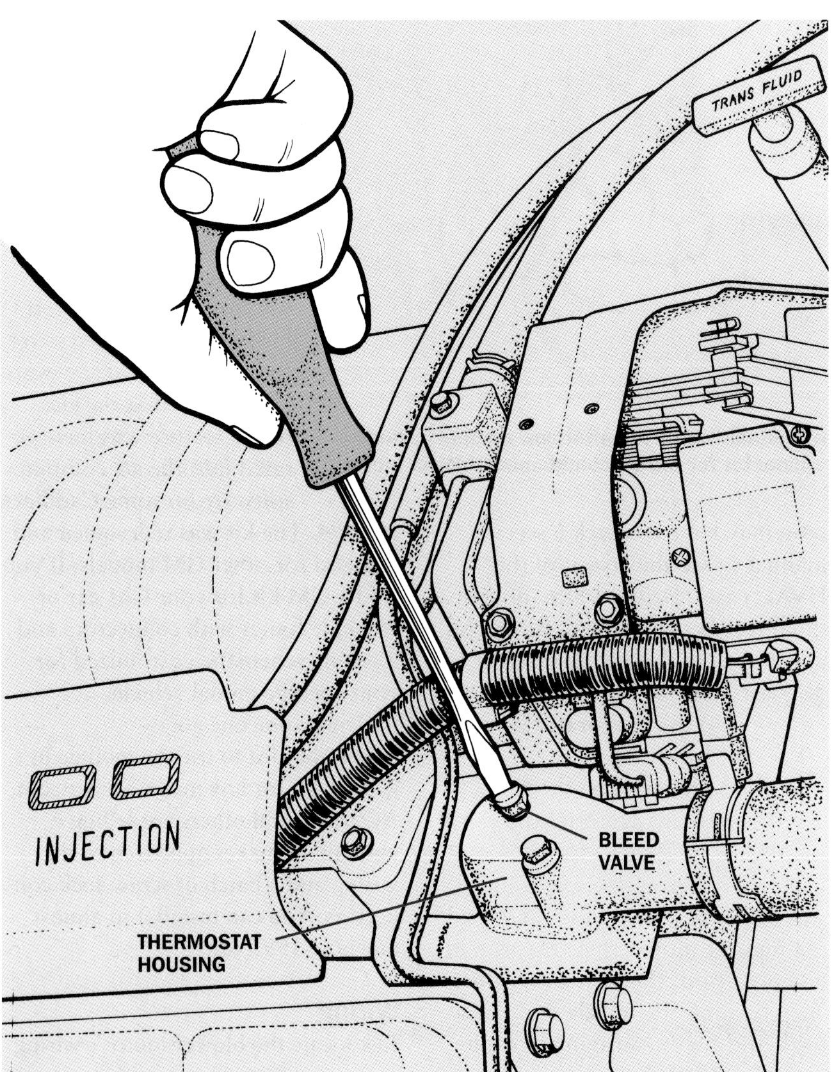

(Fig. 1) Many late-model cars with low hoodlines require bleeding the cooling system, not simple topping up.

You've finally gotten the new car through the warranty period, and the dealer's ministrations aren't necessary—or affordable—any longer. Time to start performing some of that maintenance yourself, a daunting proposition on most computer-controlled technorides. Without returning to college for degrees in engineering and computer science, how's a Saturday mechanic supposed to stay ahead of the maintenance curve? Not to mention having to buy a shop full of tools and test equipment.

Fortunately, most of the work necessary on your car is "low tech." It's routine maintenance such as replacement of lubricants and parts, basic electrical diagnosis, brakes, shocks and struts, spark plugs, cooling systems and belts, and gaskets. It's all the kind of work you can do without a major investment in equipment and shop manual "book learning." However, there's so much in today's cars that you can't avoid it, even if you stick to the basics.

Gaining respect for the sensitive items and learning how to avoid mistakes that produce problems is a learning experience (although less involved than the high-tech work itself). Here are the important beginning steps.

Strapping In

Draining the cooling system and refilling it with a fresh mixture of antifreeze and water is the No. 1 do-it-yourself job, and it's worth doing right. That means opening the engine block drain (if there is one) as well as the one on the radiator and getting out all the old coolant. You then face the problem of completely filling the cooling system. Because the radiator or surge tank neck on many cars isn't the high point of the system, air is trapped elsewhere. Even if it is the high point, there are nooks and crannies in modern systems, many of which were developed with sophisticated computer programs for an efficient flow pattern.

Start by jacking up the front of the car, to help expel air. Then fill the system as well as you can and start the engine. You have to either crack open the little bleed valves **(Fig. 1)**—and some systems have several—or you may have to remove a plug. Even with these precautions, you should check the coolant level repeatedly over the next few weeks and keep topping up as necessary. If you don't, the engine will feel the difference in summer and you'll feel it in winter, when the heater output is low. If there's a really big bubble trapped in the system, the engine could overheat. Check your service manual for specific bleeding instructions for your car.

Need to replace a drive belt? The new multi-V ribbed type is almost universal. If you get the right belt (not just one that's close), follow the

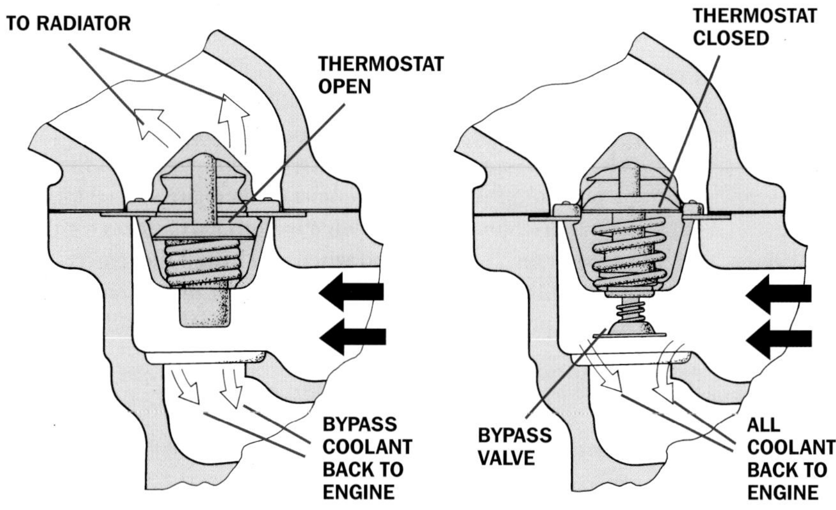

(Fig. 2) Bypass-style thermostats force all the cold water back into the block during warmup and all of the hot water into the radiator at running temperatures. If you use one that doesn't have the needed bypass valve (as at left), coolant flow will not go to the radiator for proper cooling.

underhood decal's routing diagram and make sure the belt is properly aligned in all of its grooves, and it will transfer power smoothly.

If you have to change a thermostat, don't just get one that fits. Many late models have a stat with a bypass valve, intended to make *all* the hot water—not just most of it—flow through the radiator (**Fig. 2**). If you replace the thermostat with one that doesn't have a bypass valve, the engine will warm up slowly, and it may run hotter in summer and heat poorly in winter. A thermostat also may have a jiggle valve, a pinlike device that balances pressures in the system and helps bleed air.

Even if you get the right thermostat, you have to install it correctly so it operates normally. On many Japanese cars with thermostat jiggle valves, for example, there's a specified position for the valve, such as being aligned with a tab at 12 o'clock.

The gaskets that seal the thermostat housing and water pump also are very different from the fiber/paper type you may be familiar with on older engines. In fact, new gasket designs are all over the powertrain.

Gaskets

The simple precut gasket is still around, and it may even be a good choice on older cars for replacing formed-in-place silicone, which can smear during installation and therefore seal poorly.

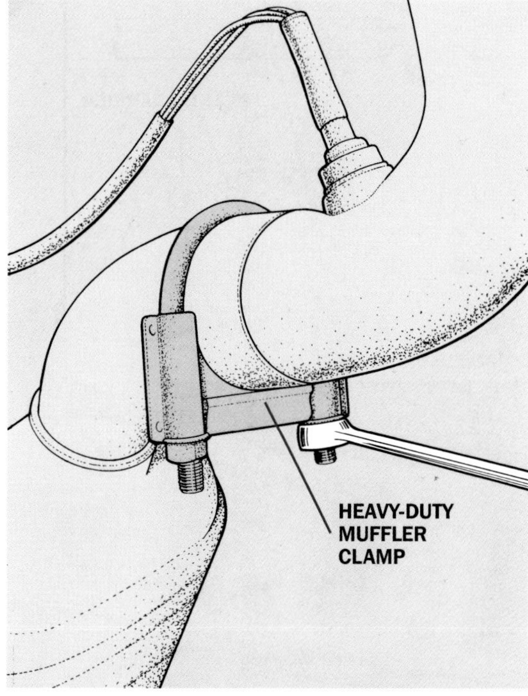

(Fig. 3) Stainless-steel exhaust systems necessitate heavy-duty clamps to properly seal pipes.

However, more of the gaskets used today are high-tech designs that resemble giant O-rings. Some of them have a round cross section, others are oval or even an indescribable engineered shape that is designed to seal when clamped down a precise amount. Still others, which resemble conventional gaskets, have torque-limit buttons, which are metal or hard plastic rings for the bolt holes, to resist over-tightening. Others use a hard-plastic carrier to carry an engineered-shape rubber sealing ring, as shown in the illustration on the following page. Intake manifold gaskets are traditionally difficult to seal on V-shaped engines, especially when there's a combination of aluminum cylinder heads and a cast-iron block.

You could use a conventional gasket in place of these high-tech wonders, and it will cost less—but it had better be made by a reputable gasket company specifically listed for your car's exact year and application.

Usually the torque required to seal a gasket properly is a lot less than you would think feels right, and if you over-tighten, you distort the O-ring and it will leak. You have to use a torque wrench to be sure.

Exhaust System

Today's high-temperature stainless-steel exhaust systems are anything but cheap, and they're either welded together or held by super-duty clamps (**Fig. 3**). If you have to cut a weld to replace a pipe or muffler, get a high-quality clamp to ensure it holds the joint on today's heavier pipes. You may have to shop around, or even place a special order, because many parts stores stock only the inexpensive clamps with bent metal saddles. The premium clamps have welded or double-crimped saddles and are probably two or three times the price of the more common variety, but they are the only kind that can take the 60 ft.-lb, or more of torque needed to clamp the thicker pipes.

Brakes

If your car has antilock brakes, be careful not to damage the wheel sensor when you pull a caliper for brake lining work. In fact, it's a good time to inspect the sensor connector for physical damage and the trigger wheel for badly chipped teeth. You may find a reason for misbehavior of your high-tech brake system that's repairable with some pretty common do-it-yourself parts replacements.

Bleeding brakes at the wheels after you replace a caliper should not be a problem with antilock brakes—just stuff a tapered plastic plug into the brake hose end when you disconnect the caliper, to help keep out air.

However, replacing the master cylinder might be a special problem. If it's physically separate from the antilock hydraulic components, you can bleed a master cylinder very well on the bench (or in some cases on the car, just before you reconnect the brake lines)—there are special kits available in auto parts stores for this. And when you install the master cylinder on the car or reconnect the brake lines, the pedal should be firm.

THE HIGH-TECH ENGINEERED SHAPE of this intake-manifold seal does the sealing, while the plastic carrier plate holds the seal in place and ensures that it's properly crushed. The complex shape of the end seal is the result of similar high-tech engineering.

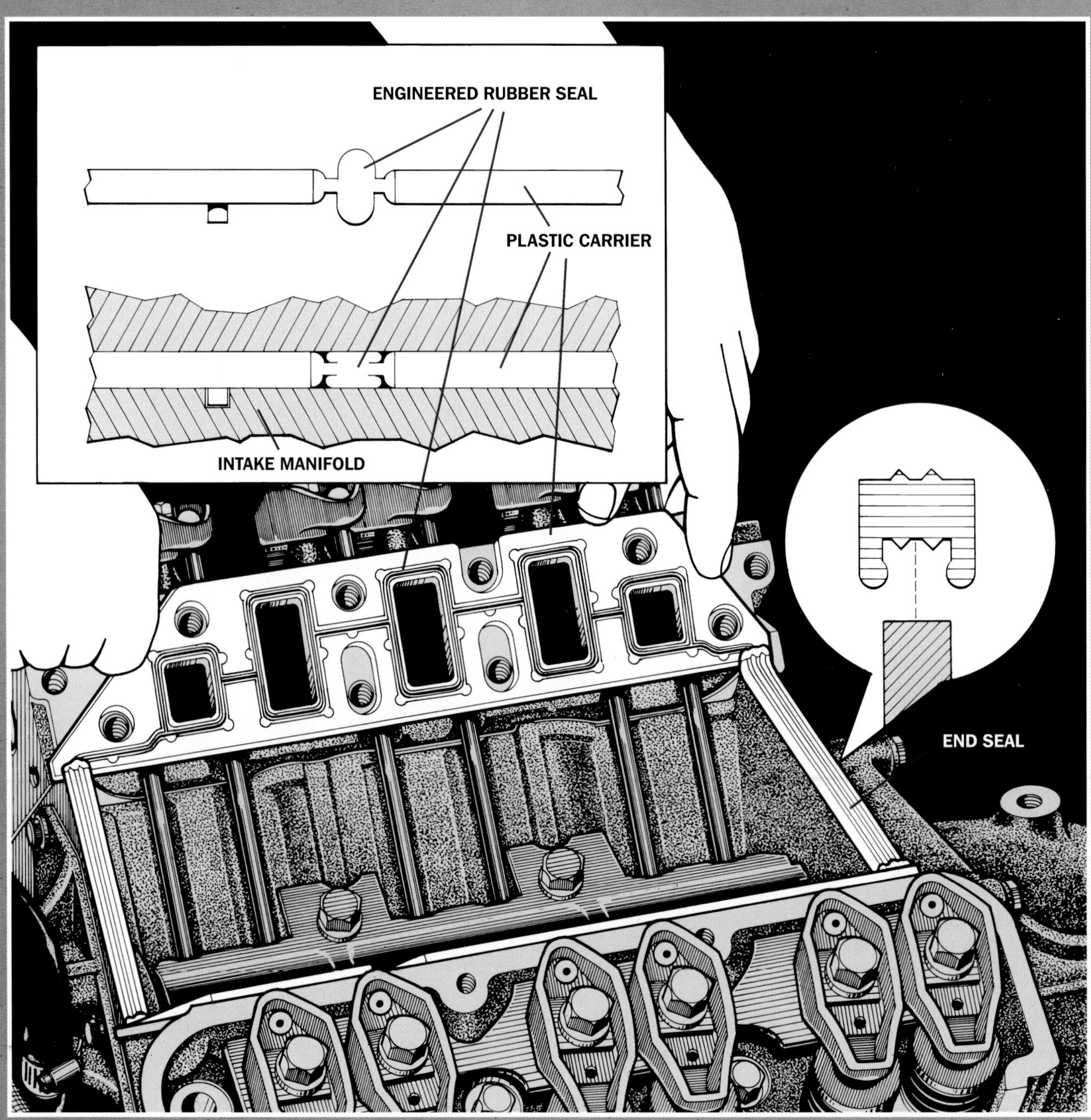

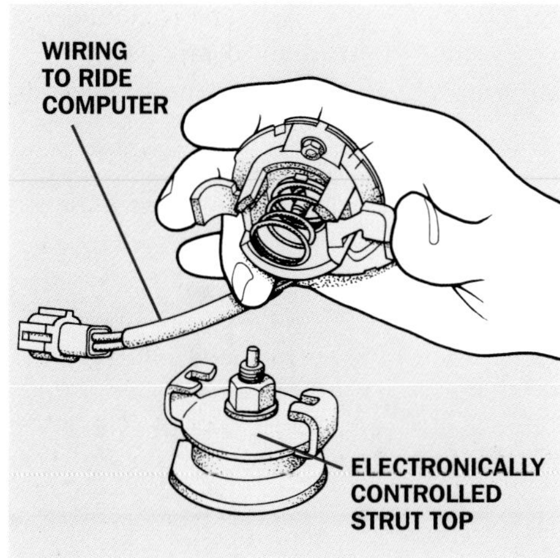

(Fig. 4) Replacing ride-control shocks doesn't necessarily mean replacing the actuator.

Just plug any hydraulic lines you disconnect to keep out as much air as possible when you start the job.

If the master cylinder and antilock system are a single assembly, you may have to follow a specific shop manual procedure to bleed it. Sometimes this is d-i-y doable, and sometimes it isn't. For example: The master cylinder/antilock assembly on many Fords requires a special procedure. But, the late-model Taurus/Sable also calls for a special electronic switching device and a breakout box (a special adapter for testing circuits) to bleed the single assembly which (for now) makes it a job for a dealer.

Shocks and Struts

Those computer-controlled shocks may have seemed like a neat feature when the car was new, but they may cost hundreds of dollars a pair at replacement time. If you want to maintain the electronic control, on many cars you can transfer the electric motors that operate the originals to a pair of new shocks and save some money (**Fig. 4**). Even with switching over the motors, you can be in for major expense with electronically controlled shocks, and it may not seem worth it on an older car.

Fortunately, on most cars you can unplug the computer at a connector in the trunk and then install conventional shocks. There are some cases where doing this confuses the car's electronics. This problem afflicts late-model Thunderbirds and Cougars with Programmed Ride Control, early Mazda 626s with Auto Adjust Suspension (but not the later models), Nissan 300ZX Turbos and more exceptions to come. We suspect, however, that there will be computer bypass kits available eventually.

Tuneup and General Electrical

Tuneup and general electrical are areas where you have to be careful, but if you are, you should not let fear of smoking some expensive component keep you from doing work. Here are a few guidelines to follow:

- When you have to disconnect a fuel line on most Ford and Chrysler products, you'll generally find it doesn't have a threaded fitting, but a quick-connect type. It takes a special but inexpensive tool, available from auto parts stores (**Fig. 5**). Don't try to pry the fuel fitting apart, or you'll damage it. These fittings often have O-ring seals, which should be replaced. Be sure to get these in a packet for the exact application. Ford, for example, uses spring-lock couplings on both fuel and a/c lines. The O-rings are not only a slightly different size, but a totally different rubber. Fuel-line O-rings won't live in a/c and vice versa.
- If you have to disconnect a wiring terminal from a plastic connector, such as for an electrical test, you can't just shove in a small screwdriver blade to disengage it, or you could damage the terminal and create a problem where none existed. Virtually all late-model cars have special terminals and plastic connectors for positive retention, and these usually require special tools. The pick-type tools for General Motors and many Ford cars are available from auto parts stores, but you could have difficulty with other makes. In '93, Chrysler switched to a new line of connectors that require a half-dozen special tools that we still haven't seen in auto parts stores.
- If you have to disconnect a battery cable, consider the use of a computer memory saver. It not only will keep the time on the electric clock and hold the preset radio stations, it will maintain the long-term calibrations of the powertrain computer. If you lose these, the car's driveability may be poor until the computer "relearns," which could take 100 or more miles of driving.

There are two basic types of memory savers. The 9-volt battery with one type is okay, but just a small voltage drop could kill the memory. So you must keep all electrical accessories and lights off (that means door domelight switches, too, so either keep the doors closed or install hold-closed clips on the switches). An alternative is a saver that hooks up to a 12-volt battery. If your battery is okay, just carefully make the connections as you dis-

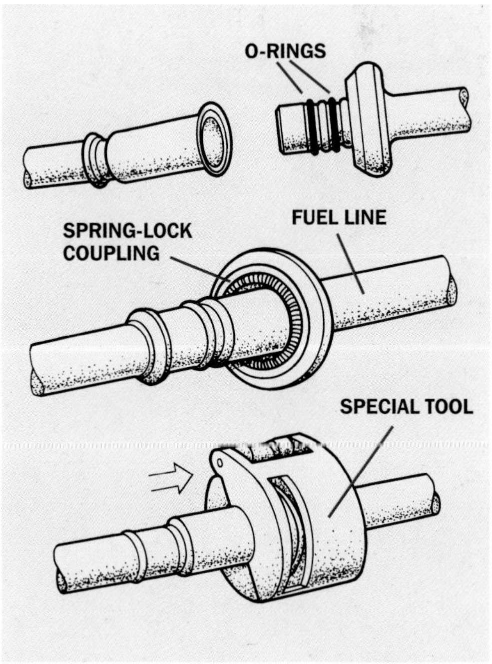

(Fig. 5) Spring-lock fuel and a/c connectors need a special inexpensive tool to open them.

connect the cable. Or use the battery from another car or a lantern battery.

• Use a computer-safe test light. A standard 12-volt light may allow enough current draw through a circuit with electronics to measurably shorten the life (or even fry) some solid-state components. Computer-safe test lights start at under $15, and even the best—which plug into a cigarette lighter socket and identify both power feed and ground—are under $60, including one that has a built-in flashlight (for probing under the dash) and a buzzer if you're probing a power feed in a blind spot.

• The test meter should be a "high-impedance" type (10 megohms or greater), for the same aspects of safety for electronic circuits as the test light. Name-brand multimeters may go over $500, but there are suitable volt-ohmmeters that start at under $50.

If you have to probe a circuit and want to do it safely, one way is to buy a "bed of nails" test lead that makes mini holes in a wire, and when you disconnect the lead, they self-heal. You can pierce the insulation with a dressmaker's hemming pin, but it may not make good enough contact with the copper wiring inside.

• Don't reposition wires underhood. This applies not only to spark-plug wires, but to any harness, including a battery cable (particularly if you get a replacement that's a different length from the original, or is outside a harness and is not easy to route the same way). The reason is the high-voltage electricity from spark-plug wires may produce electrical interference in adjacent low-voltage circuits, particularly if they contain electronic components. Because many electronic components operate on 5-8 volts, even the sudden flow of 12-volt high-amperage electricity through a battery cable during cranking can cause big trouble.

• Never disconnect or connect a circuit, or an electronic module, with the ignition key in the ON position. In fact, to avoid static electricity damage, unplug an electronic module with one hand held to a body ground. Static electricity that discharges from your hand may not totally trash an electronic module, but it can shorten its life from years down to weeks or even days. Professionals who face this problem all the time may wear a grounding strap on one of their wrists.

As you get familiar with your car and read the manuals, you will be able to move into higher-technology service. You'll discover that it takes careful attention to the diagnostic procedures in the manuals, but it isn't rocket science, and it doesn't take a degree in computer science, either. The high tech you've already learned in doing the low-tech service will get you started.

Scan Tool Diagnosis

DIAGNOSTIC CONNECTOR

SCAN TOOL

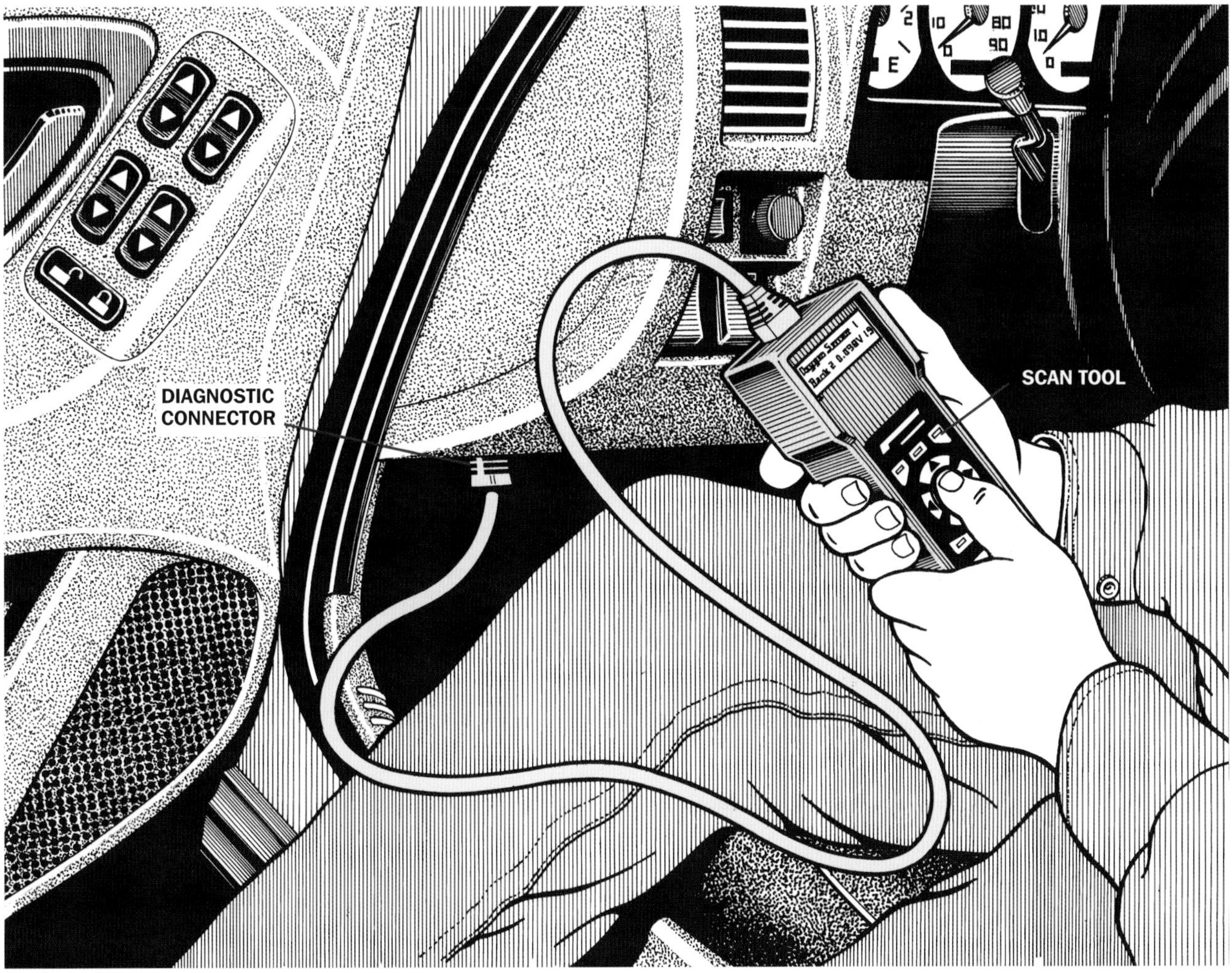

(Fig. 1) OBD II scan tools hook to the car's engine-management computer via a connector under the steering wheel.

It's state inspection time and you're ready to leave bright and early for the inspection station with the family's '98 minivan. You're starting the day in a less than jovial mood because your daughter said "the light came on" last night on the way home. She said she threw a few dollars of gas into the tank to make it home. Turns out your annoyance is misplaced. Sure enough, the light's on all right, but it's not the fuel warning, it's the CHECK ENGINE warning. You stop for gas anyway, and then you pull into the inspection lane.

Well, full tank or not, the minivan does not pass muster.

Failure Is Not an Option

This is a late-model vehicle with what's known as OBD II, the second-generation on-board diagnostic system that replaced OBD I starting in 1994. It's industry-wide and federally mandated. One of the problems with OBD II for the do-it-yourselfer is that you can't get trouble codes by counting the blinks on the CHECK ENGINE light like you can on earlier computer-controlled vehicles. You could take your minivan into a high-tech shop, where the minimum charge for diagnosis and inspection could run you somewhere into three figures. Or you can learn about OBD II yourself, but you will need a piece of diagnostic equipment that you probably don't have—an OBD II scan tool (**Fig. 1**).

If the Check Engine light came on, it should be no surprise that the vehicle failed an emissions test. With OBD II, that light comes on only if there's a failure that significantly affects emissions. That makes the scan tool even more important since it will reveal a lot of the problems that do not cause the warning light to come on.

With many problems, the light

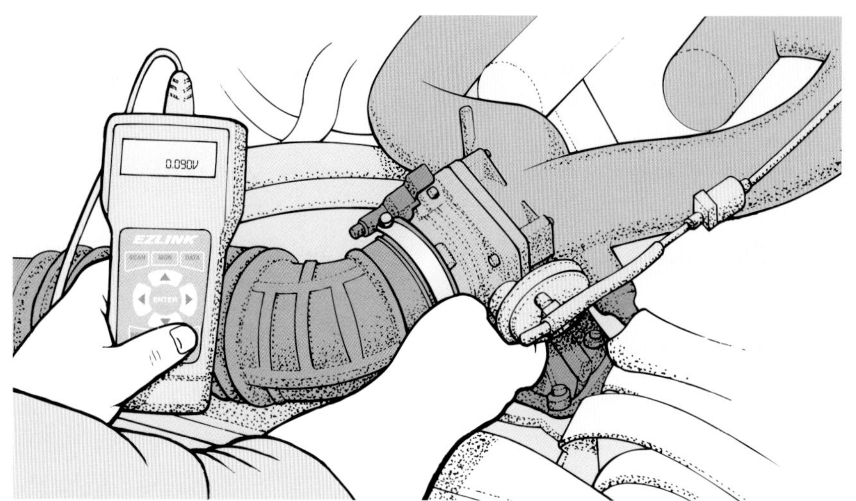

(Fig. 2) Datastream scan tools will let you investigate the functioning of most sensors, like the throttle position sensor being checked here.

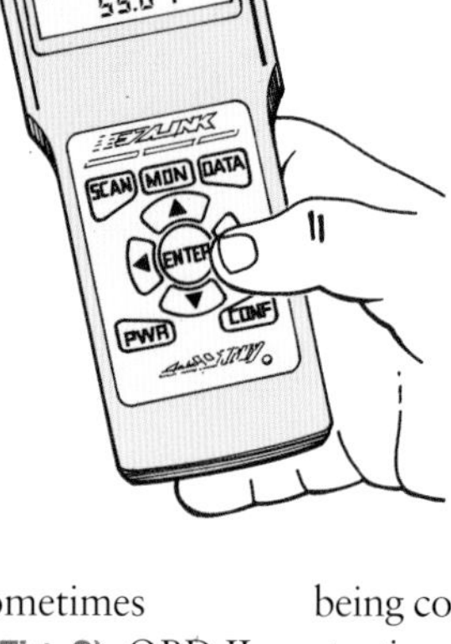

(Fig. 3) Units with more features will let you snapshot and store data while the car is being driven.

stays on after the repair is made and the code remains in the computer memory for a certain number of ignition on/off cycles. Your daughter didn't tighten the gas cap correctly, causing a code for the evaporative emissions system to set. Eventually the light will go out and the code will self-erase, perhaps after the next time you start and stop the car. You also can use the scan tool to erase it immediately.

With many other problems, however, the only way to turn off the light and erase the code is with the scan tool. Just a warning: If you erase trouble codes with a scan tool or disconnect the battery for any reason, you also erase the computer's continuous monitoring system. So if you take your car in for a state inspection before enough normal driving, the computer might not have completed all its tests, and your car will fail inspection for that reason.

The OBD II scan tester not only will enable you to find answers to the simpler problems, but will tell you into what areas the seemingly more complicated ones fall. Then you will have a better understanding of what the technician is (or should be) looking for.

Cracking the Code

With an OBD II scan tool you also can read a certain amount of engine operating data: typically rpm, ignition timing, fuel-injection calibrations, readings from a variety of sensors (such as the oxygen, throttle position, barometric and mass airflow sensors), a "calculated load" value and sometimes switch position signals **(Fig. 2)**. OBD II also includes a "capture" mode, in which you can use the scan tool to take a "snapshot" of what the sensors were reading at the exact instant a driveability hiccup occurred **(Fig. 3)**.

Sensor Scan

With enhanced scan tool capability, you can discover problems that do not trigger the engine-warning light. For example, we recently turned up a generic PO713 code on a late-model car. This is listed in the shop manual as "transmission fluid temperature sensor circuit—high input." If the transmission fluid is running very hot, the transmission could completely fail, and quickly.

A scan tool could save a lot of worry and effort if it has enhanced diagnostics. You can do much of the troubleshooting from the driver's seat the way we did. First we cleared the code with a simple push of a button on the tester. Then we rechecked: The code came back quickly. We cleared it again and looked at the reading that was coming from the transmission temperature sensor to the powertrain computer. It was 131° F, nothing abnormal.

The problem apparently was in the sensor or the circuit, possibly a bad connection. The wiring was good and when we started poking around, we found physical damage that clearly indicated the problem was a defective sensor.

So Many Choices

If you have a late-model vehicle, you have OBD II. However, just because it's generic, and the wiring connector from any OBD II scan tool will plug into your vehicle, doesn't mean any OBD II scan tool will work on your car. The Europeans are the problem, as the ones after 1998 require a software upgrade. Korean cars are also problematic, and how well they work with any given scan tool needs to be investigated on a case-by-case basis.

Further, new cars are being converted (on a phase-in basis starting with Saturn and Saab in 2003) to "CAN" (Controller Area Network). This is a new diagnostic "protocol" and most scan tools will need an adapter module, or complete replacement.

The OTC Mind Reader for OBD I can be upgraded with an additional chip to read generic OBD II in domestic, Japanese and earlier European models (but not the later Europeans).

The Actron ScanTool for OBD I can be updated to the same level of OBD II as the OTC Mind Reader with a plug-in cartridge (or you can buy an OBD II-only model).

AutoXray produces a programmable scan tool. Although it doesn't have the OBD I Chrysler command tests of the Mind Reader, it is the one home mechanic's scan tool we've tested to date that covers all generic OBD II models (including the Europeans) with more on the way and covers the new CAN diagnostic with just a software

THIS TESTER WILL let you check sensor outputs directly without using the vehicle's on-board computer.

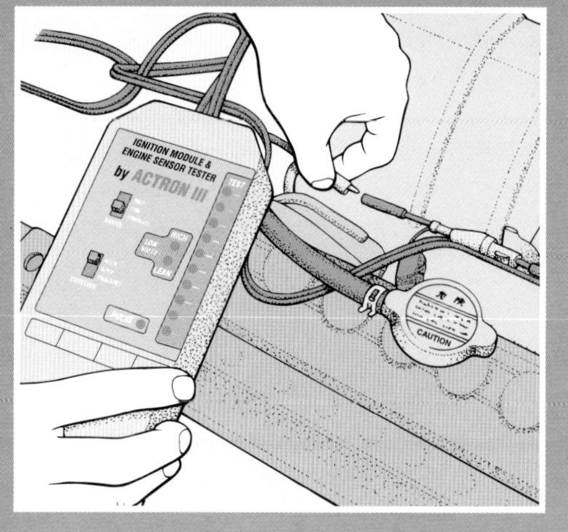

(Fig. 4) Simple code readers/ resetters like this one do not give you sensor data.

update. The software is sold over the Internet. You'll be able to store it on your personal computer and then download it to your scan tool via a cable available from the manufacturer.

Any AutoXray scan tool is designed to be upgraded electronically, from one-make OBD I coverage through the latest models. Although the professionals have had this software (and a lot more) in their scan tools, you have to wait for it in the consumer market. Other scan tools may be upgraded to enhanced status and beyond with new cartridges, CD-ROMs or via the Internet. Ask about upgrades before you buy.

Although Actron has a line of OBD II scan tools, its top tester for car owners is the Actron CP9087, a simple code reader with read-codes and code-erase buttons. You get no sensor readings or other data items (**Fig. 4**). It's a low-cost device (under $200) that comes with a good assortment of wire leads for making test connections—including a back-probe adapter that has a thin, curved metal terminal. This terminal lets the probe slip through a water-sealed connector to reach a wiring terminal for a test connection.

OBD II has been in use on all vehicles since 1998, so the earliest vehicles that have this system are well off warranty. OBD II is complex and we've given you just a basic introduction. The OBD II powertrain computer is getting a lot better at finding problems and logging codes. But, the computer won't tell you a thing unless you hook up a scan tool.

HOW IT WORKS

How OBD II Transmits Data

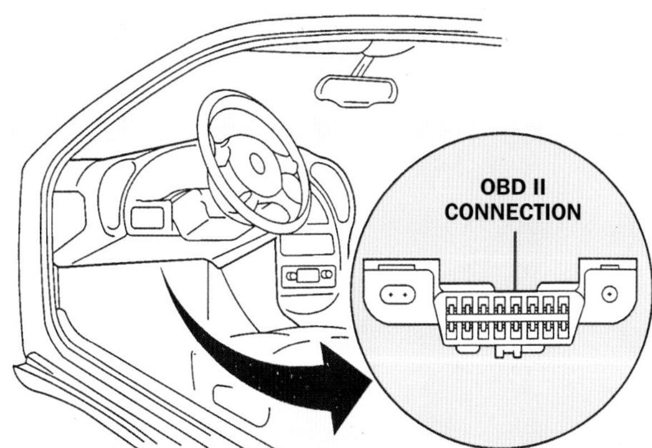

Today's powertrain computers are at the heart of a vehicle's communications network, circulating information from switches and sensors to the other computers that control antilock brakes, air conditioning, transmission, suspension and safety systems. The powertrain computer is also in charge of systems that affect engine emissions, so the information it processes has to be available for evaluation by a technician. That information travels along a wire to a standard 16-terminal diagnostic connector (although, generally, fewer than a half-dozen terminals are live in any given vehicle). Because manufacturers do not all use the same data transmission protocols, the scan tool must be programmed to recognize which one is being used. Fortunately, there has been some standardization, but we're not down to one transmission protocol for all, hence the problem with late-model European cars (including the Cadillac Catera). There are four different so-called standard data pins in the standard connector, and at least four different types of data transmissions that could be used, plus enhanced versions of the standard stuff (other pins are available for additional manufacturer-specific data, such as vehicle diagnostic systems for a/c and ABS).

As anyone with a household PC knows, "plug and play" doesn't always work, and OBD II scan tools can encounter compatibility problems. Some European and Korean cars don't always work when they're suppossed to. How can you tell? Checking a scan tool manufacturer's Web site for updates is the way to keep your tool current.

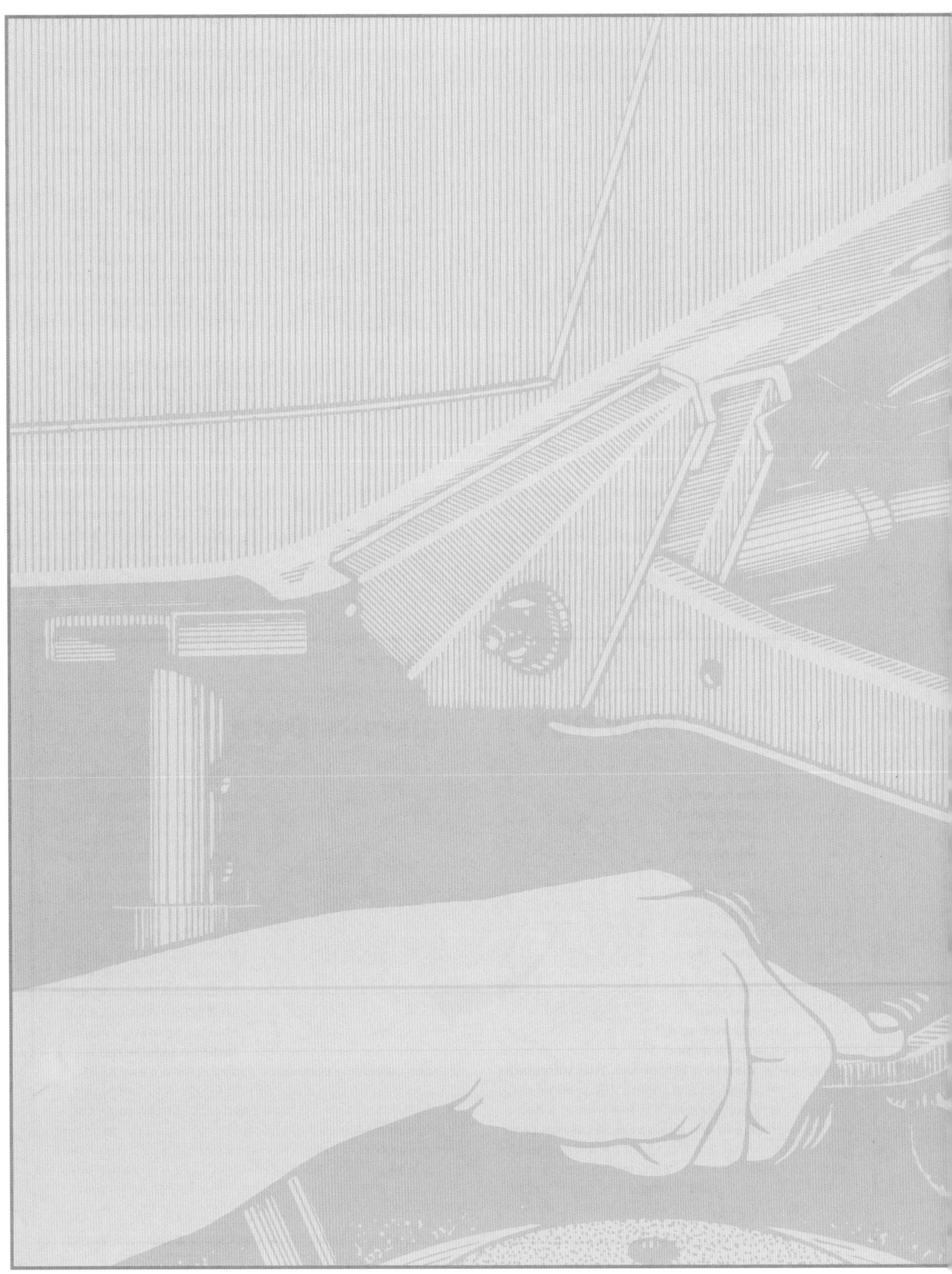

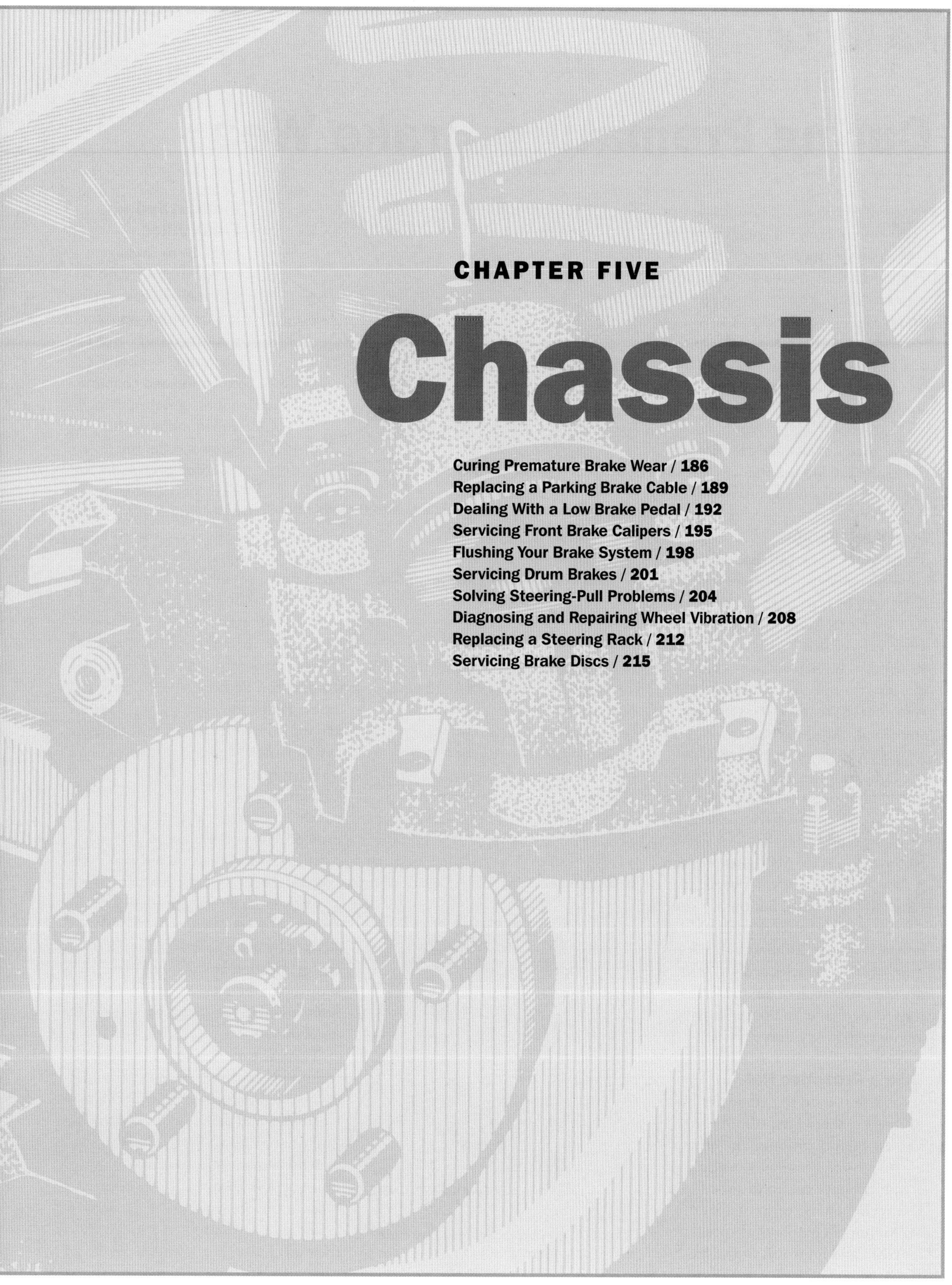

CHAPTER FIVE

Chassis

DIFFICULT

Curing Premature Brake Wear

You're taking a pleasant ride in the country, enjoying your car's performance. A stop sign. You step unhurriedly on the brake pedal—what the heck? You let off and try again. There's no mistake. You hear a high-pitched squeal that you recognize as a pad wear indicator sounding off. Those front linings are going, going, gone.

That wouldn't be so troubling except that you distinctly remember doing a brake job less than a year ago. Hey, what's going on?

Low-Life Linings

Thirty years ago when disc brakes were becoming common, we were impressed by how long linings lasted. Not anymore. Many late model cars and trucks eat their pads quickly. The tendency is to blame new friction material formulas for accelerated pad wear, but the real reason is usually something else altogether.

Now, you've got overdrive, a low-friction V6 and an aerodynamic design that not only lets the car coast farther, but also cuts airflow to the brakes.

Another factor in the short-lived pad scenario is the SUV phenomenon. A typical Blazer or Explorer might weigh 4800 pounds, but the brakes are not enough better than those designed for the 3000-pound pickups most of these vehicles evolved from. It doesn't take much of an intellectual leap to see that even normal driving amounts to heavy-duty service.

Take a Proactive Role

What can you do to extend the life of those brakes? First off, buy the highest-quality brand-name linings you can find. These may be "full-ceramic," have ceramics added to the semimetallic mix, or have a sacrificial titanium coating that speeds break-in and improves initial feel.

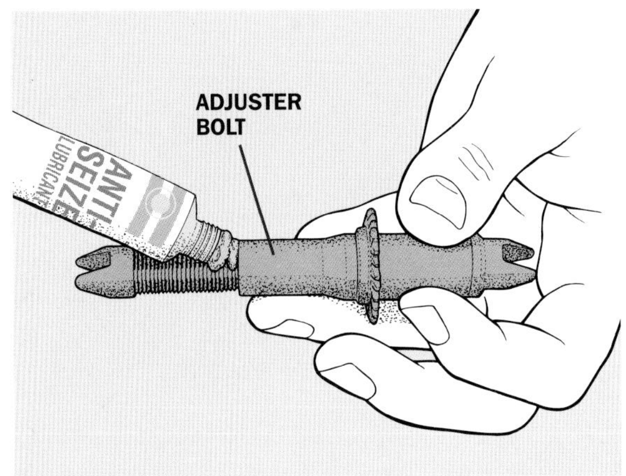

(Fig. 1) Coat those star-wheel adjuster threads with grease or antiseize compound.

That's not, however, all there is to the job by a long shot. You've got to look at the brake system as a whole.

Many motorists just don't use the parking brake. Some may think it's an emergency stopping system only. But with many common rear-disc designs and some rear drums, lining-to-rotor/drum adjustment simply doesn't occur unless the parking brake is applied (a symptom is a low pedal). So, adopt the sensible habit of engaging this device every time you park instead of just depending on Park to keep the car from rolling away.

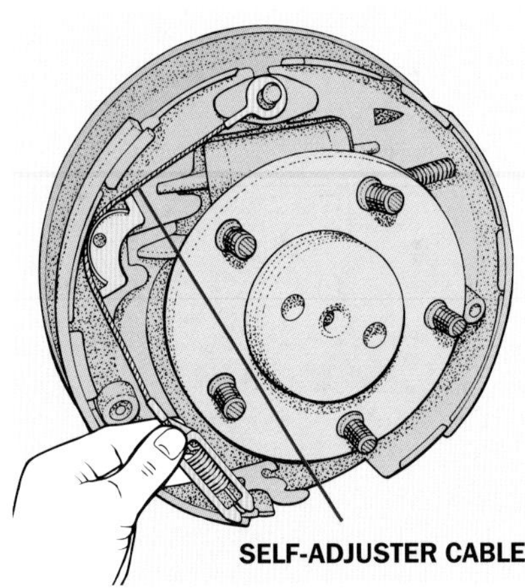

(Fig. 2) Drum brake self-adjuster hardware is frequently faulty.

Innards and Fresh Juice

Even the most diligent person in this regard is still going to have problems if the self adjusters of the rear discs aren't operating. Typically, corrosion and contamination jam the piston and immobilize the screw mechanism.

Some professionals have switched from overhauling rear calipers to installing quality remanufactured units, saying that it wasn't worth the labor and headache to pull them apart and put in a kit—it's hard to get the adjusting mechanism to work properly. Great, except calipers can be expensive in some cases. That's the price you pay for driving a modern car and neglecting maintenance.

What maintenance is that? Brake fluid changes, of course. With that parking brake/self-adjustment mechanism present and immersed, internal corrosion is to be strenuously avoided. Ergo, periodic fluid changes are even more important than with disc/drum systems. This has been advised by many import manufacturers for decades, and is now starting to show up in the service recommendations found in the owner's manuals of domestics.

This car-care item can save you serious money in the long run. Besides disc brake internals, consider ABS. Corrosion and debris in the control unit can result in a disastrously expensive repair—$1500 isn't unusual! Use a turkey baster to get most of the old stuff out of the master cylinder reservoir, refill it with fresh, then use a clear bottle and hose setup

(Fig. 3) A partially clogged brake line can let pressure build up in the caliper.

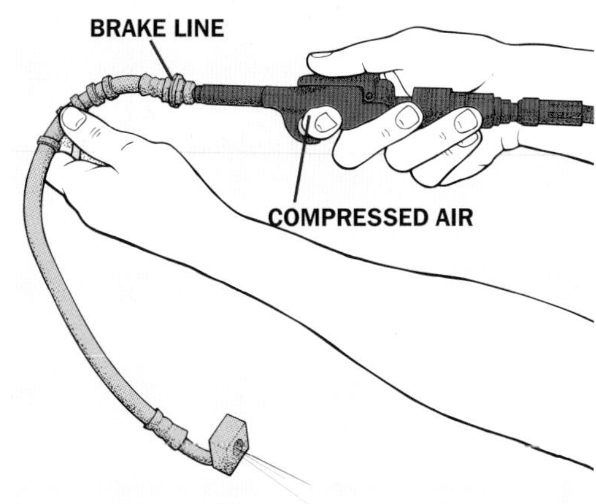

at each of the bleeders and pump until you see a nice, clean liquid appear. Do this every other year.

Beaten Drums

Rear drum brakes often shirk their duty, too, resulting in burned-up front pads. Seized star-wheel screws **(Fig. 1)** and otherwise inoperative self adjusters **(Fig. 2)** are practically an epidemic, so you're asking for accelerated front lining wear if you don't inspect and lubricate the hardware involved, and replace any items you're dubious about (frayed or fatigued cables, for instance).

We fixed a car recently that had fried pads and a badly grooved rotor on one side. It turns out the hose was plugged—it allowed pressure to gradually build up in the caliper, and then the piston couldn't retract **(Fig. 3)**. Another possible cause of drag is overfilling the master reservoir, which can apply the brakes as the fluid expands.

Broken In or Just Broken?

We know people who still believe that the right way to seat new linings is to really stand on the brakes a few times. That's an anachronistic idea left over from the days when linings were supplied "green." Panic stops would indeed get that friction material hot enough to cure it. But you don't get uncooked pads and shoes from manufacturers anymore, so this whole idea belongs to a bygone era, a time of ignition points and bias ply tires.

There's no way to overemphasize the importance of proper lining break-in (some authorities say overlooking this procedure is the No. 1 cause of noise and hard pedal complaints). The ideal way to start new linings off is to make 30 slow stops (spaced 2 minutes apart) from about 30 mph using light to moderate pressure. You may not be willing to take that much time, but you'd be foolish not to make at least 10 moderate stops at 30-second intervals (you

HOW IT WORKS

Pad Wear Indicators

Mechanical pad wear indicators, which have been around since the early '70s, are so simple and can head off so much damage that it's surprising they didn't show up even before then. All that's required to warn the driver that he's almost down to the rivets is the addition of a light steel tab that contacts the rotor when the linings are getting too thin for comfort. This produces a high-pitched squeal that appears suddenly and is unmistakable. The tab is too flimsy to cause any damage to the disc, unlike the rivets, which will grind away at that nice stopping surface, leaving wide, deep grooves. With bonded linings, the steel pad plates will do the same, and have been called "full-mets" by brake guys with a twisted sense of humor. By the time you hear and feel either, considerable rotor damage has already begun.

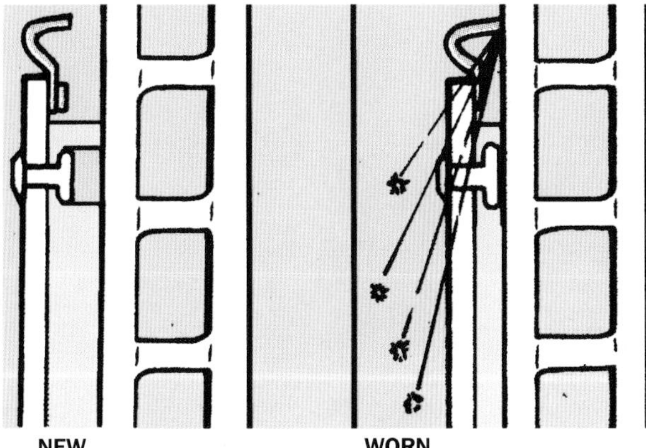

Unfortunately, many of the cars out there still aren't so equipped, and often replacement pads for cars that had wear indicators as O.E. don't include this helpful device.

A slightly higher-tech variation on this theme is the electrical pad wear warning system, which first appeared a couple of decades ago on such cars as Toyotas and Mercedes. Here, the pad is drilled for an electrical contact that stands slightly proud of the lining rivets. When wear reaches the point that this touches the rotor, the ground circuit to a Brakes warning light on the dash is completed, and the lamp winks on. Again, unfortunately, some companies that manufacture replacements for these applications don't bother to include the contact, with the result being that the wire ends up tied off in the suspension somewhere.

should be able to feel the action smooth out), then avoid heavy braking for the first 200 miles.

What if one pad is worn-out, but the other still has lots of friction material left? Think about the way a single-piston caliper operates. The piston pushes one side directly against the disc, and this action pulls the other side into contact. If anything interferes with the sliding or floating movement that transfers and divides the force, only the pad that the piston actually bears on will wear. So, every time you put in a new lining, clean and lubricate the machined grooves of sliding calipers, using special brake grease (**Fig. 4**). Ditto for the bushings and pins or bolts of the floating variety, and make sure any rubber parts are in good shape.

Voice of Experience

When lubrication is called for on an internal mechanism, use silicone grease. Anything else will attack the rubber parts.

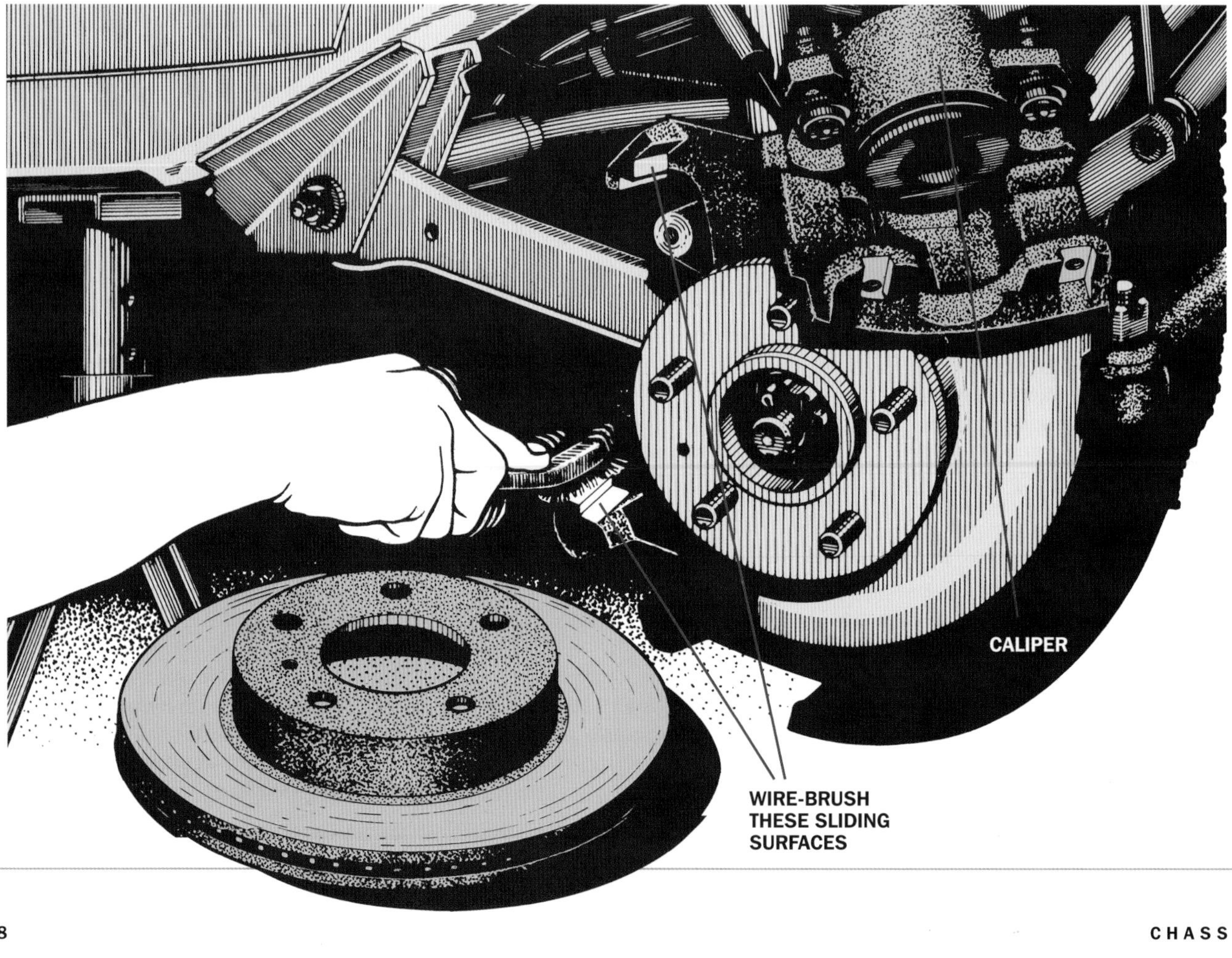

(Fig. 4) If the caliper won't slide on its grooves or pins, brakes will wear fast. Clean, and then lube sparingly.

CALIPER

WIRE-BRUSH THESE SLIDING SURFACES

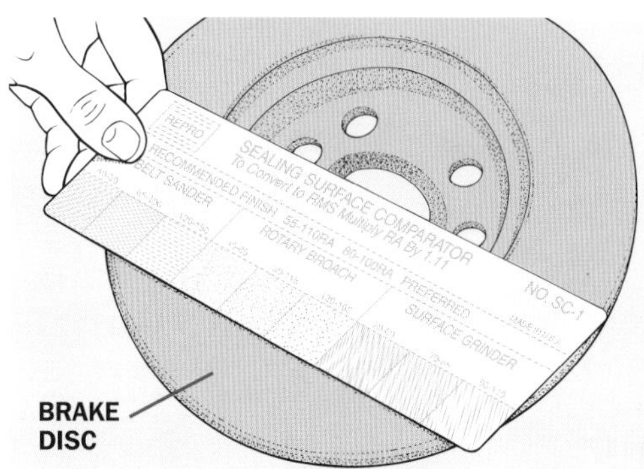

Don't force caliper pistons back for pad replacement without opening the bleeder. The line comes in near the bottom of the cylinder where the sediment is, and this forces debris up into the ABS unit—often resulting in a glowing antilock warning light. In fact, many brake experts say just opening the bleeder isn't good enough. They want you to clamp that hose (use a special tool or pad the jaws of locking pliers with heater hose).

Don't believe you can get away with the rough directional disc finish that worked fine with asbestos. Smoothness is the rule today. If you're familiar with roughness scales, where 80-100 RMS or 73-91 RA was once considered correct, now 40-60 RMS or 36-55 RA is recommended (you can check this with a surface comparitor gauge). In other words, finish that rotor up with 120- to 150-grit paper instead of the traditional 80-grit (**Fig. 5**).

(Fig. 5) Discs need to be refinished to a finer finish for today's pad material.

Regardless of whether the rotors have been refinished, you absolutely must take the time to clean them. Otherwise, hard particles will become embedded in the new linings and you'll get noise and scoring. But brake cleaner isn't the answer because it won't float those iron filings away. Use detergent and water, and then dry with a paper towel.

Replacing a Parking Brake Cable

You've just parallel-parked your manual-transmission car on a steep side street, carefully setting the parking brake by pulling it up farther than you've ever pulled before. So far that it actually pops a little as it edges up that last click. Exiting the vehicle, you turn to lock the door—just as your car slides forward 3 ft. and nudges the luxury car in front of you in the bumper. Setting off the alarm. Hurriedly, you restart your car and back up to your original position, determined to pull the brake up far enough to anchor the *Titanic* this time. Unfortunately, this time the handbrake offers no resistance whatsoever until the mechanism tops out—and you have no parking brake at all, forcing you to find a flat parking space three streets away and walk through the rain to your job interview.

Not to mention having to replace the parted handbrake cable.

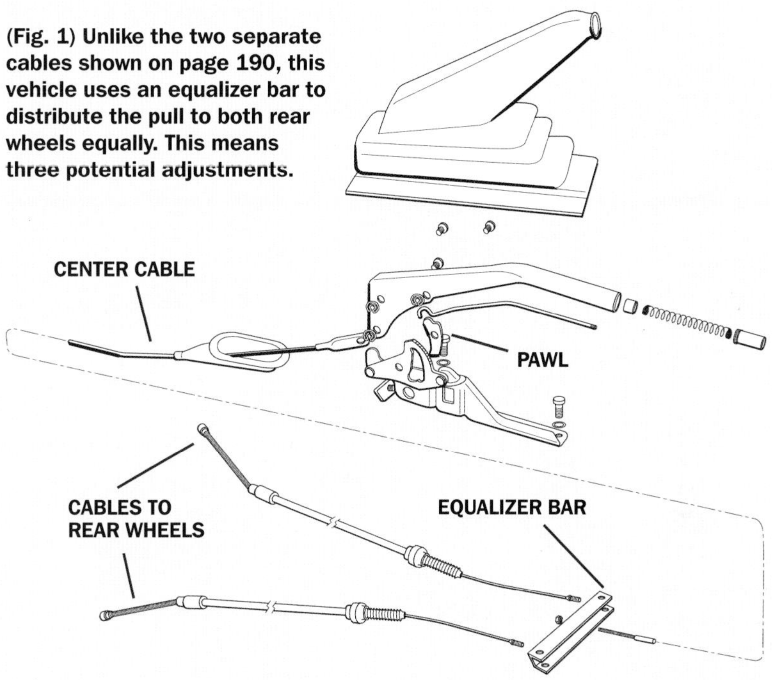

(Fig. 1) Unlike the two separate cables shown on page 190, this vehicle uses an equalizer bar to distribute the pull to both rear wheels equally. This means three potential adjustments.

Why It Failed

Parking brakes are operated by a long, steel cable that runs between the handle in the cockpit and the rear wheels. It has crimped-on ends that can potentially slip off (unusual but not unknown). More commonly, the rubber-covered outer cable that runs between the car and the rear brakes tears or splits, allowing moisture and road salt to corrode through the inner steel cable. Sooner or later, the corroded cable fails under tension.

Live in the desert where it's flat, and never use your parking brake? Or maybe you have an automatic transmission and just put your car in Park. Then you face another issue—the cable needs to be exercised regularly or it will seize up. So you should use the parking brake regularly. Ever have trouble getting your transmission out of Park when parking on a grade because the parking pawl in the tranny is jammed against its gear? Setting the parking brake before putting the trans in Park and letting the car roll forward will prevent this.

Getting Dirty

First, you need to determine which cable has parted. Remove the boot over the mechanism between the seats and see which cable is slack. If there's only a single cable to the handle, you'll often need to pull up the rear seat and look for the equalizer bar (**Fig. 1**). One cable to the bar will be easy to pull straight out. Warning! Parking brake cables are generally lubricated with thick black grease that will get everywhere, and generally destroy your car interior and your clothes. Be ready with rags to contain the mess.

Now, you need to check the outer cable that leads to the rear wheel. If it's damaged, you'll need to replace that as well. You may have no option if the inner and outer cable are sold as an assembly, which they often are. To actually look at the outer cable, you'll need to get under the car. This means either backing onto ramps or jacking up the car and resting it on jackstands. If you're using jackstands, loosen the lug nuts first. (Never get under a car that's lifted on a jack, even a floor jack.) Be sure to block the wheels.

Check the outer cable, which leads from the backing plate of the brakes over to the car body. Don't confuse it with the brake hydraulic line, which is a steel tube connected to the body at some point with a short rubber hose. The brake cable will be much thicker and rubber-covered along its whole length. Look for cracks, abrasions and deteriorated rubber, and don't forget both sides—if the other side is damaged you may as well replace both cables now.

Inside the Brake Drum

Once you've determined which cable(s) to replace, get the car up in

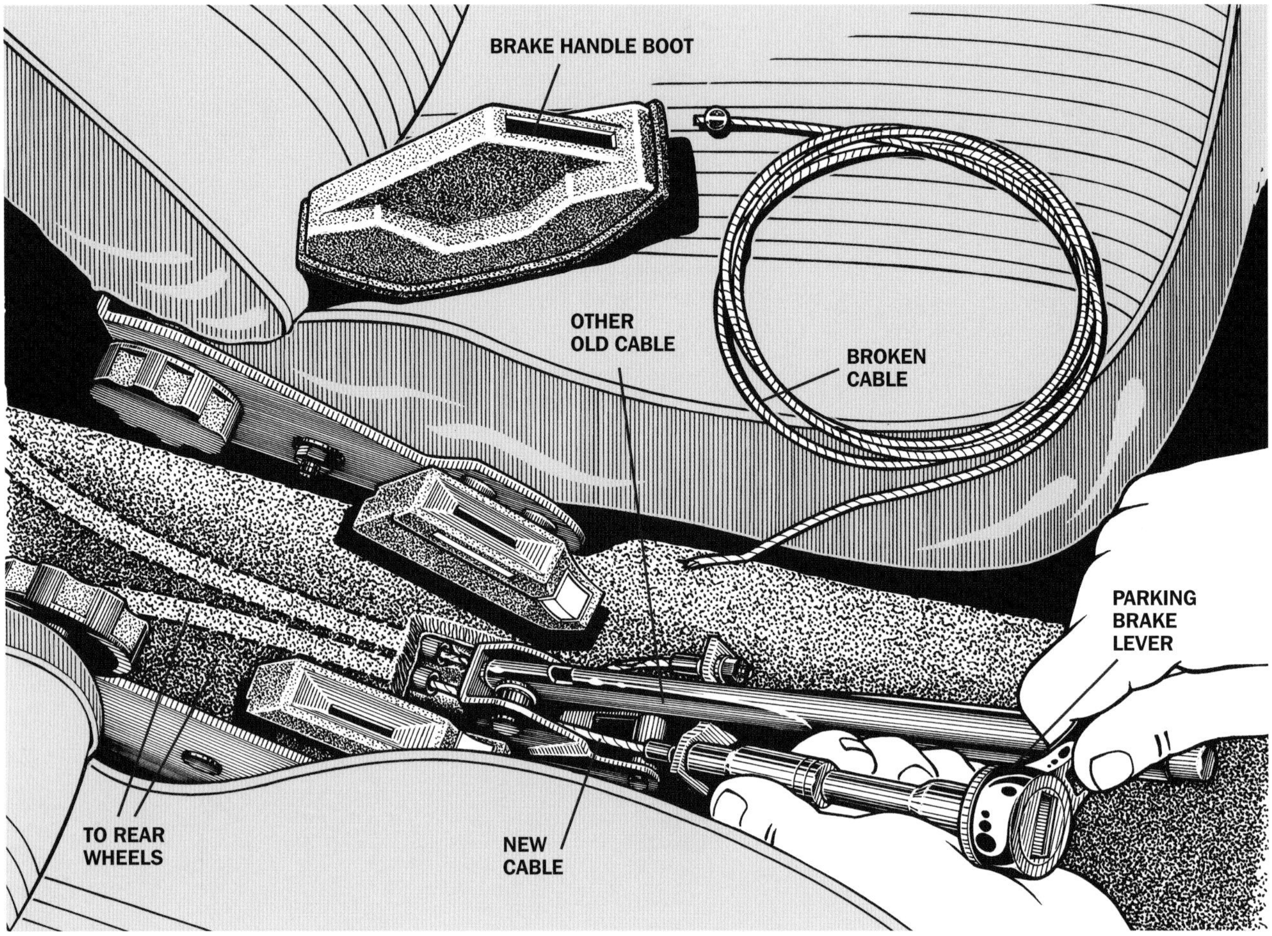

(Fig. 2) The final adjustment of the new cable is usually done at the handle inside the car. You may need to hold the new cable with locking pliers to keep it from turning as you use a socket on the adjuster nut.

the air and the wheel or wheels off. Now you need to remove the brake drum. Generally, the drum is simply sandwiched between the axle flange and the wheel, retained by a small sheetmetal clip or Phillips setscrew to keep it from landing on your foot when you remove the wheel. Occasionally, they will become intimately attached to the hub and need persuading. Judicious application of penetrating oil, light hammer taps near the hub, profanity and moderate heat will see them loosen. You may need to back off the adjuster mechanism to get the shoes out of the way if the drum has developed a wear ridge on the inner lip.

Now you can see the brake shoes and mechanism. (This might be a good time to replace the shoes if they're worn down to anywhere near the rivets). If you're replacing only the inner cable, simply disassemble the mechanism far enough to pull out the old cable and thread the new one into place. If you need to replace the outer cable as well, it's probably pretty well rusted onto the backing plate. Spray it with penetrating oil, and twist with pliers until it lets loose. Some cables are retained by snap rings or a small collet-style clip—check the new cable for its attachment style.

Clean It Up

Now's your chance to wire brush rust and dirt from all the hardware and mating surfaces on the brake mechanism, and sparingly lubricate all the moving parts with antiseize compound or high-temp grease. Replace any suspicious hardware like springs and clips. Be sure to clean the mating surface of the axle flange and brake drum, to prevent foreign matter from keeping the drum from seating properly on the flange. Lightly lube the mating surfaces with antiseize so you won't have to cuss the next time you need to take it apart. Reinstall the brakes and drum, hooking up the new cable to the actuating arm. Adjust the brake shoes properly if you needed to back off the adjuster.

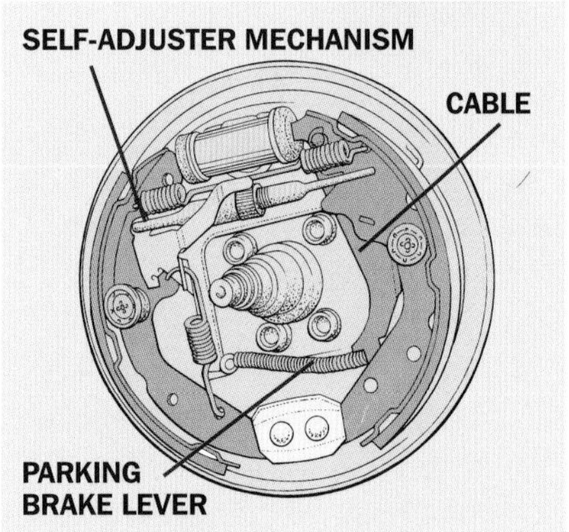

(Fig. 3) Be sure the rear brakes are properly adjusted before trying to set the parking brake adjustment.

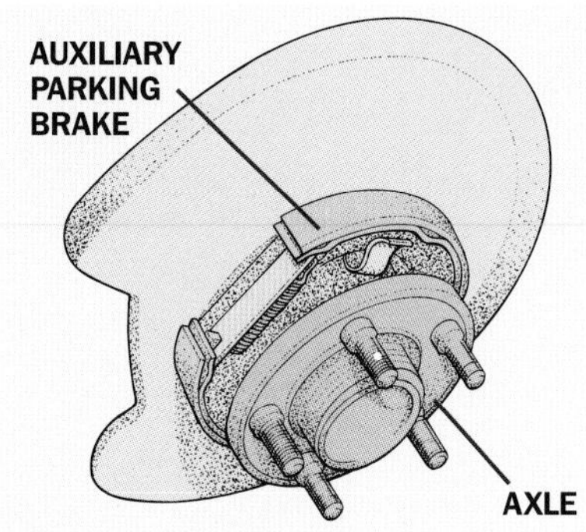

(Fig. 4) Some cars with rear discs use a small set of brake shoes dedicated to the parking brake.

Back Inside

Now it's time to hook up the inner cable's forward end (Fig. 2). If it didn't come with a new nut, you'll have to rescue the old one. It may be a locknut, or there may simply be two nuts jammed together. Thread the threaded end of the cable into the equalizer bar or the handle, and lightly run the nut down. Pull the handle up (or depress the pedal) three clicks, and then tighten the adjusting nut until the wheel lightly scrapes as you rotate it. This assumes you had the brake shoes adjusted correctly and they don't scrape with the handle down.

If you don't have the brake shoes correctly adjusted, and then you adjust the handbrake, bad things can happen. As the brake shoes' automatic adjuster mechanism (Fig. 3) kicks in over the next few days, the slack in the handbrake cable will gradually disappear, and your brakes will start to drag. Be careful for the first few days that the handbrake retains two or three clicks of free play.

Is the equalizer bar straight? Not cocked over at some wacky angle, but reasonably close to perpendicular to the cables? If not, adjust the nuts appropriately. If your brakes use two separate cables with no equalizer bar, adjust the individual cables so both rear wheels have equal tension when the brakes are actuated.

Four-wheel Discs

If your car has four-wheel disc brakes, your job is simpler, because the attachment of the handbrake cable to the caliper is generally much simpler to get

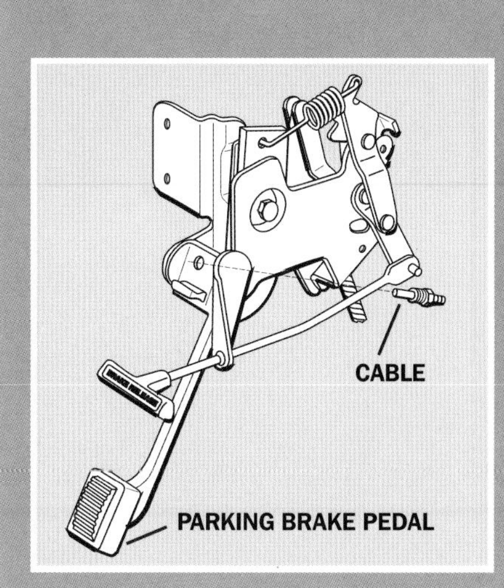

at than with drum brakes, requiring less disassembly and readjustment. Some rear disc brakes actually have a small drum brake system just for the parking brakes (Fig. 4), but the cable arrangements are pretty easy to deal with. You generally can replace the cable without removing the disc or caliper.

One last word of advice: Regardless of the state of health of your brakes, always turn your front wheels into the curb when parking on a hill.

HOW IT WORKS

Self-adjusting Brakes

Self-adjusting brakes are universal now, except for some elderly Volkswagens still on the road. The service brakes are actuated by a hydraulic cylinder that forces the two shoes apart, jamming them into the inner diameter of the brake drum. But as the lining material wears, a mechanical escapement mechanism is necessary to keep the shoes close to the drum. Otherwise, the pedal would gradually get closer and closer to the floorboards as the friction material wore down. This self-adjust mechanism is actuated by the slight vertical movement of the trailing brake shoe that occurs whenever the brakes are applied in reverse. Normal driving will keep the clearances appropriate. If you have a circular driveway, never back out of parking spots or generally back up like Granny, the mechanism may not be doing its job. Try a few smart applications of the brakes while backing up (needless to say, this needs to happen where you won't hit anything). You don't need to go fast—just walking speed. Hit the brake pedal good enough to stop rapidly, but not fast enough to chirp the tires. You may be surprised—your wimpy handbrake may regain some authority, and your braking may improve. Repeat as necessary. If you've been rocking about with the manual adjuster, you may need to do this a number of times. You'll need to do it if you've disassembled the rear brakes as well.

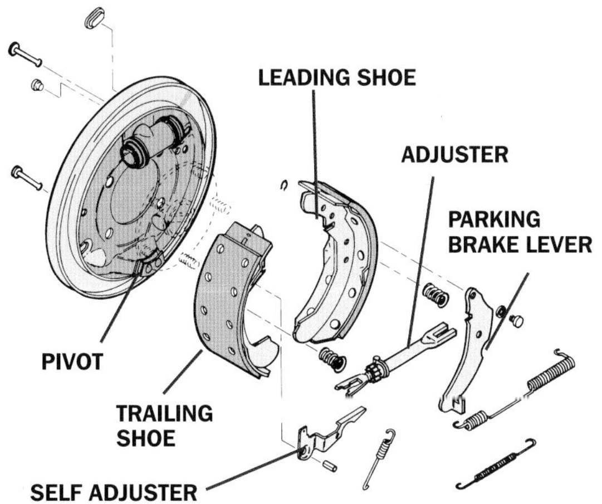

DIFFICULT

Dealing With a Low Brake Pedal

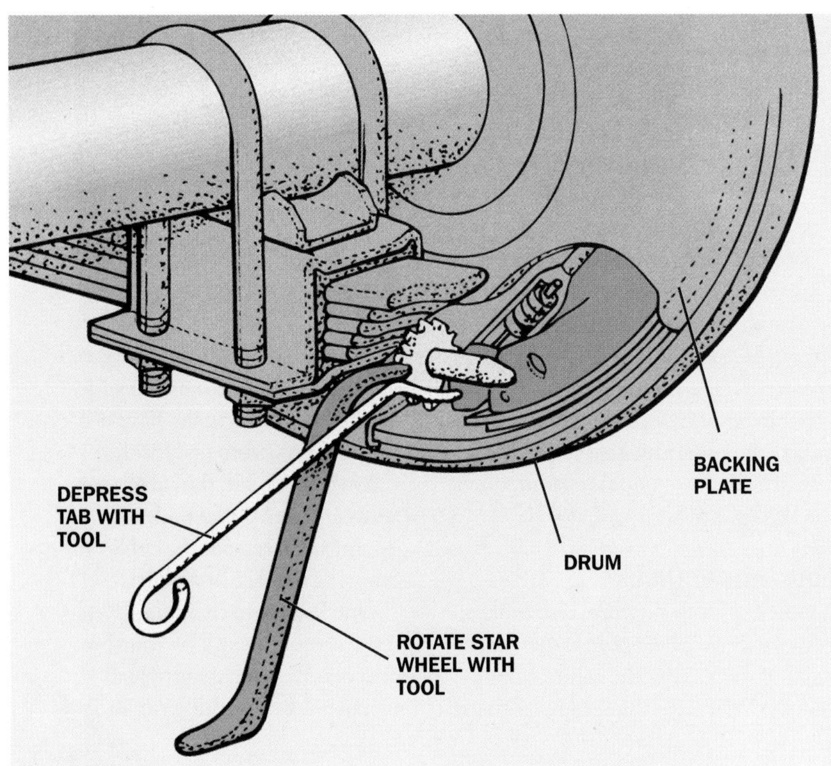

(Fig. 1) Depress the tab while you rotate the star wheel to close up the clearance. When the wheel scrapes lightly, go back one click.

(Fig. 2) Brake drums will be marked clearly as to how far they can be machined safely to remove out of round.

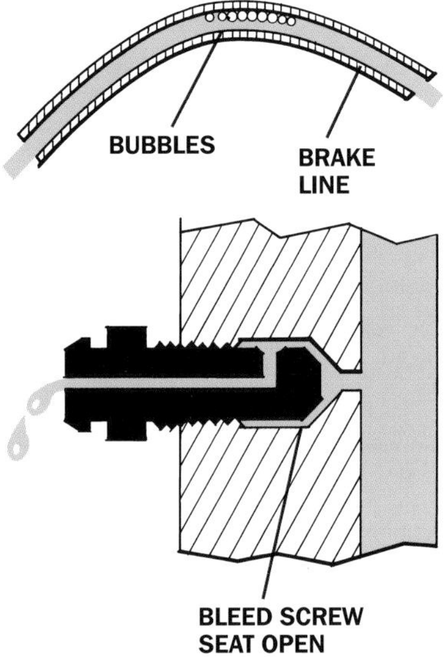

(Fig. 3) Bubbles collecting in high spots in the brake system need to be removed by opening the bleeder valves to flush them out.

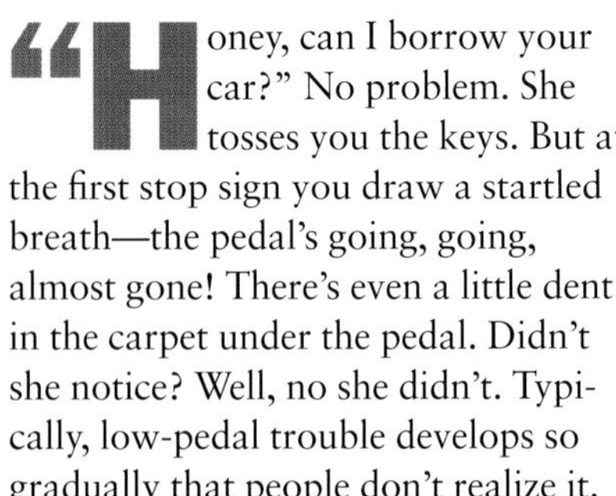

"Honey, can I borrow your car?" No problem. She tosses you the keys. But at the first stop sign you draw a startled breath—the pedal's going, going, almost gone! There's even a little dent in the carpet under the pedal. Didn't she notice? Well, no she didn't. Typically, low-pedal trouble develops so gradually that people don't realize it.

Hydraulic brakes have been around since Duesenberg introduced them in 1921, but apparently a long history is no defense against troubles. And professionals and do-it-yourselfers alike are often guilty of misdiagnosis—they blame the master cylinder, though it is seldom the culprit.

There are only two plausible reasons for a low pedal: air in the system; and excessive movement between linings and rotors or drums (due to lack of adjustment, an out-of-round drum, or a wobbly disc that's knocking the pistons back so that there's extra space to take up before braking action begins).

Isolation

You can find out all you need to know about the master cylinder by removing the lines, screwing brass or plastic plugs into the outlets, and then applying the brakes. If the pedal's high and hard now, the master has been properly bled and its seals are okay. The pedal would sink gradually if it were bypassing—that is, if fluid were finding its way around the sliding seals. You've also confirmed that the booster is okay. Reattach the lines.

Continue the process of elimination by clamping hoses to isolate each wheel. Use a suitable rounded-jaw tool, either the locking-pliers type or one of those inexpensive J-hooks with a knurled screw. Releasing one at a time should locate the problem.

Use That Parking Brake

If you never engage the parking brake, self-adjustment of the pads and rotor simply won't occur, and that means a low pedal. Another impediment to adjustment is corrosion and contamination of the piston, cylinder and self-adjustment hardware. So, change your habits and start using the parking brake every time you leave the car, and replace those calipers if they're not just right. If the parking brake isn't used regularly, one of these days a parking lot attendant will apply it and your car will be immobilized until those corroded cables and other seized parts are replaced.

Beat the Drums

Rear drum brakes can cause a low pedal, too. Seized star-wheel screws and otherwise inoperative self-adjusters are all too common, and you're risking trouble if you don't replace the hardware when replacing shoes (**Fig. 1**). At the very least, clean the star-wheel threads and treat them to a coating of antiseize compound.

There's another factor that's usually not recognized: drivers who never stop aggressively enough in Reverse to ratchet the self-adjusters. It's a good idea to stomp on the brake pedal every week or so while backing up—preferably in a deserted lot or other safe place.

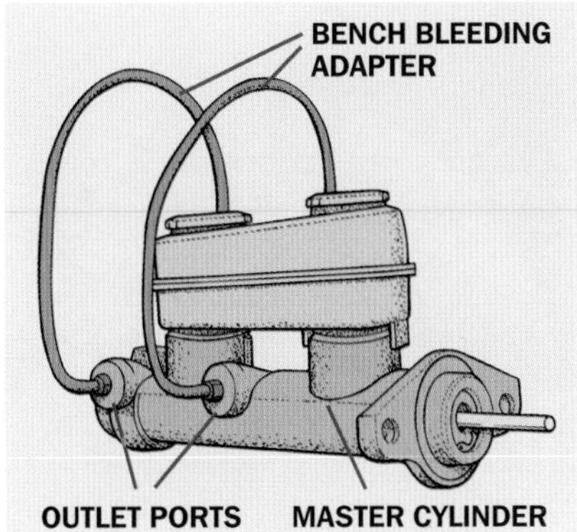

(Fig. 4) Bench bleed a master cylinder to get air out before installing it into the vehicle.

What about the drums themselves? They're frequently out of round (**Fig. 2**), leaving excess shoe-to-drum clearance and, of course, causing pulsation.

Bubble Trouble

For all practical purposes, brake fluid is incompressible. Air, on the other hand, can be squeezed down into a smaller-than-natural volume, and its presence will disrupt the operation of any hydraulic system. It promotes internal corrosion, too. Ergo, it must be expelled (**Fig. 3**).

One possible cause of pedal problems is failure to bench bleed a new master cylinder (**Fig. 4**). Screw the supplied fittings into the outlets and place the tips of the tubes in the fluid in the reservoir. Clamp one of the master's mounting ears in a vise—don't grip around the cylinder—so the unit is as level as possible. Use a rod or drift to stroke the piston slowly. Wait at least 15 seconds

HOW IT WORKS

The Dual Master Cylinder

Whether you call it the dual, split or tandem master cylinder, it has been used on every car sold in this country since 1967, although Cadillac had it in '62. Even so, most people don't understand its construction and operation. A typical modern specimen is of the composite variety—aluminum with a plastic reservoir—but iron 1-piece units are still around on older vehicles. Two pistons ride in the bore, and here's where we encounter some potentially confusing terminology. The rear piston is the primary, the one in the front is the secondary. This apparent misnaming resulted because the rear piston is the first to receive the signal from the brake pedal, so it does make a certain amount of sense. Kind of. Each piston has a primary cup seal at its front and a secondary at its rear. In normal braking, the pushrod from the booster forces the primary piston forward. No pressure is created until the primary seal covers the compensating or vent port from the reservoir, but once it does fluid is trapped in the chamber between the pistons and it becomes a solid column. Pressure is routed from this chamber to two wheels. A combination of the trapped fluid and the primary piston coil spring bears on the secondary piston, to which the line to the other two wheels is attached. The replenishing ports allow fluid to move freely between the chambers behind both pistons' primary cups and the reservoir, determined by demand and expansion and contraction from temperature changes. If a hose lets go or a saboteur has sawed through one of the brake lines, the other half will still provide a means of decelerating the vehicle, albeit with a lower pedal and reduced stopping power. This protective function is, of course, the dual master's reason for being.

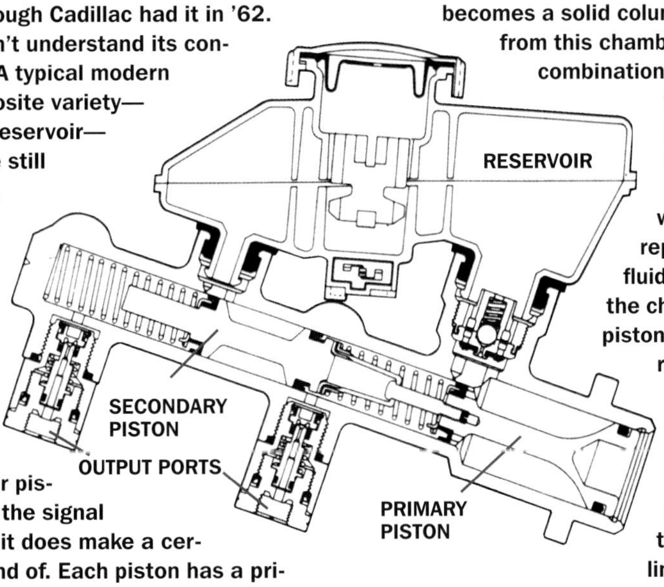

between strokes to allow the low-pressure chamber to release all its bubbles and fill completely. Keep stroking until there's no more evidence of air at the ports and tube tips.

If the car has a replacement cylinder that somebody didn't bench bleed, you might be able to do it with the master in place, provided you can jack the rear of the vehicle high enough to get the cylinder to be level. Again, pump slowly and allow time between strokes.

An important precaution to observe during any bleeding procedure that involves pumping the pedal is to limit pedal travel. You don't want the delicate lips of the master cylinder's piston seals to ride so deep in the bore that they encounter rough corrosion or deposits, which can scratch them. Just throw a chunk of 2 x 4 on the floor under the pedal.

When it comes to the bleeders at the wheels, most people just open them and let the fluid squirt. Not only will this result in slippery puddles on the floor, the fluid can shoot farther than you might expect—think about the 2500-plus psi of line pressure on some ABS-equipped cars. Brake fluid is a pretty effective paint remover, and it really burns when you get it in your eye. Wear eye protection.

One convenient setup is a tube and transparent bottle kept half full of fresh fluid (**Fig. 5**). There are also inexpensive 1-man bleeder hoses that contain a 1-way valve to eliminate the possibility of air being drawn back in when you release the pedal.

The bleeder cups and hoses that are often included in manual vacuum pump kits, such as those from Mighty Vac, work well. Once again, you can see what you're getting, and you don't have to keep climbing into the seat to pump the pedal.

(Fig. 5) The old-fashioned, low-tech way to bleed brakes is to use a jelly jar half full of brake fluid, a short piece of hose, and a patient helper to depress the brake pedal.

You should also be aware of special procedures. For example, on Teves Mark II ABS systems, you can't get fluid to the rear brakes unless you turn the key on and then apply the pedal slightly. Be sure to check the shop manual if your vehicle has an antilock braking system.

Finally, there's the bleeding sequence. Since you're supposed to do the longest line in the circuit first, the traditional order is right rear, left rear, right front and left front. But with the diagonally split systems you'll find mostly on fwd cars, the order is right rear, left front, left rear then right front. ABS-equipped cars may have special procedures to follow.

Servicing Front Brake Calipers

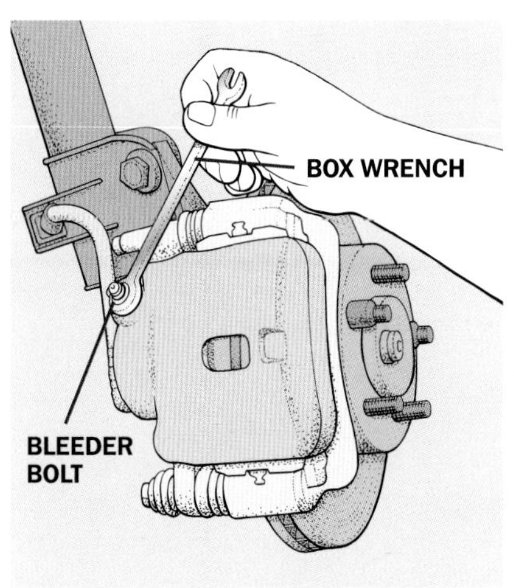

(Fig. 1) Before you go too far, be sure the bleeder isn't frozen. It may need to be retapped.

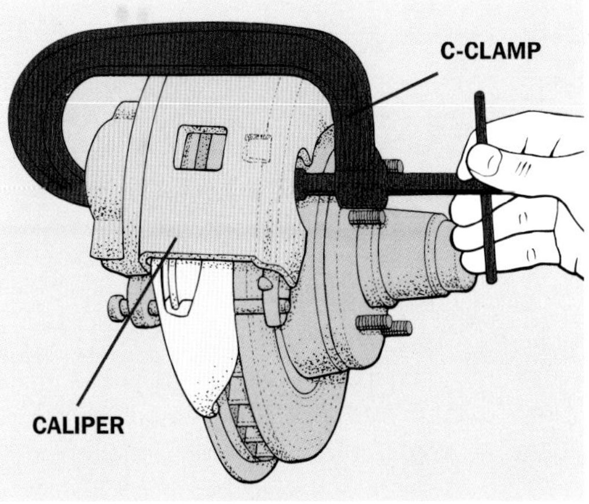

(Fig. 2) Some types of sliding calipers can be pushed back without removing them from the caliper mounts. Be sure it's not seized sliding surfaces that are binding, though.

Brake lights in front of you flash suddenly, and for no discernible reason. You mash the brake pedal to avoid rear-ending a driver who must have suddenly remembered leaving the stove on. Your car stops, but you've swerved well into the adjacent lane, where, fortunately, an alert driver slowed and pulled over to give you some clearance. Too close. Your panic braking attempt should have had two different results: Your car should have slowed more rapidly, and should have tracked in a straight line as it slowed. There's obviously something wrong.

Check It Out

Your car pulled to the left, but the problem is more likely to be at the right front wheel. It didn't brake as well as the left, so the car pulled in the opposite direction.

Remove the wheel and take a look. Don't be surprised if you see that both shoes have a reasonable amount of brake lining left. The problem is more likely to be a bad caliper, that big hydraulic clamp that forces the brake shoes against the disc-brake rotor.

Most cars have sliding calipers with a single hydraulic piston. When you step on the brake pedal and that piston is pushed out, it forces the inner brake shoe against the inner side of the rotor. The caliper simultaneously slides inward, pulling the brake shoe in the outer side of the caliper against the outer surface of the rotor. Some cars have fixed calipers with one or two pistons in each side of the caliper (two or four pistons total). When you step on the pedal, all of the pistons force the brake shoes against the rotor.

Check the brake fluid level in the reservoir and if it's been topped up to maximum level, siphon out a small amount (otherwise it may overflow during the test). Set up the clamp so the top edge of the C is against the midpoint of the inboard side of the caliper (behind the piston) with the tip of the forcing screw directly opposite. Depending on the shape of the caliper, the forcing screw could also bear against the back side of the outboard brake shoe or even against the rotor surface. If the vehicle has antilock brakes, loosen the brake bleeder screw (see page 188).

Turn the forcing screw and the caliper should move smoothly as the piston is pushed back.

If the caliper passes this test, make one more (if you haven't already): Check the bleeder valve to be sure it loosens (**Fig. 1**). If it doesn't, you can drill it out and install a replacement. But this can be a difficult operation, and installing a remanufactured caliper is a safer bet. If the caliper binds or moves only with unusual effort, there are two possibilities: The caliper piston is frozen in place (the most common), or the caliper is not able to slide because of corroded bolts (along which most calipers slide), cocked or damaged bushings through which the bolts go, or rusted sliding "ways" (guides) in the anchor that holds the caliper. You'll have to remove the caliper to see.

Sliding Caliper

Taking off a sliding caliper is a straightforward operation (**Fig. 2**). Usually there are two bolts that hold it to its anchor frame. Or, there's a single bolt at the bottom and a locating stud at the top, a design called a flip up. Clamp off the brake hose close to the caliper with a C-clamp or padded locking pliers to minimize loss of brake fluid and to reduce the necessity of after-the-job bleeding. Next, loosen the bolt that holds the hose to the caliper. Remove the bolt or bolts holding the caliper.

If the caliper is the type that is held in machined guides, there are two common setups. There is a lower guide that can be unbolted and driven off the anchor. Do this, and then lift the caliper up from the bottom of the anchor and off the upper guide. Or, there are bolt-on retainers at the top and bottom to hold the caliper against the guides. Remove both, then pull the caliper away from the anchor.

Replacement

With the caliper off the bracket, unthread the brake-hose banjo bolt and catch any drops of fluid with a rag. Install a replacement caliper, using new sealing washers for the brake hose (**Fig. 3**). Many caliper bolts are not recommended for reuse, so if the vehicle manufacturer says this is the case, get new ones (**Fig. 4**).

Making It Slide

If the caliper piston returns smoothly, you'll likely find that the caliper isn't sliding properly because the movement of the caliper bolts is hindered by corrosion or sticking in the caliper ear bushings. Or, the machined guides are rusted. You can use a wire brush to remove rust from the guides (and the caliper edges), then lubricate both with suitable water-repellent grease. Heavy rust may require a light touchup with a file. However, if the bolts are sticking in the bushings, replace them, and lubricate with the same type of grease.

If the O-rings are deteriorated, replace them, or they could allow the bushings to cock. In any case, clean the caliper ears, then relubricate the O-rings.

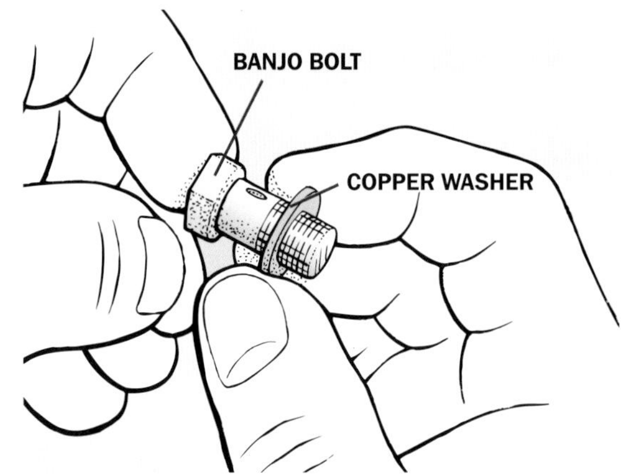

(Fig. 3) Always replace any copper sealing washers on brake line connections with new ones.

The Details

Don't leave out any dust or moisture boots from the caliper ears. And if the old ones are deteriorated, replace them (they could be the cause for corrosion seizure of the sliding caliper bolts in the bushings). If a sliding rear caliper is reusable and it incorporates the parking brake mechanism behind the piston, be sure to thread back the piston (turn back the internal screw mechanism).

Fixed Caliper

With a fixed caliper, you won't know if the pistons are sticking until you take it off. So don't loosen the brake hose (although you should determine if the bleeder valve is frozen). Remove the mounting bolts—usually just two but possibly four. Hang the caliper with wire to relieve any tension on the

HOW IT WORKS

Rear Disc Caliper with Parking Brake

If the parking brake uses the rear disc-brake shoes instead of a separate set of drum-brake shoes, there is a mechanism in the caliper piston cylinder to push the piston and apply the rear brakes when the driver operates the linkage. That mechanism, which is connected to the parking brake linkage, has a screw setup to compensate for the fact that in normal foot-brake operation, the piston automatically moves out to adjust for brake-shoe lining wear. The type shown here is a common design. There is a cone behind the piston and it moves with the piston when the foot brake is applied. When the parking brake is operated, the brake lever turns the screw on which it is mounted (it also is an adjusting screw threaded through an adjusting nut).

Rear calipers with parking brakes require special techniques to retract the pistons at pad replacement time.

The nut can't turn because it's splined into the cone. With the inboard brake shoe in place, the piston (and shoe) can't turn either. So the lever operation causes the piston to be pushed out to apply the disc-brake shoes. When the lining wears, some clearance develops between the piston/cone and the nut. When the foot brake is released, hydraulic pressure in the caliper cylinder also is released. The adjusting spring then causes the nut to thread out on the adjusting screw to take up the clearance.

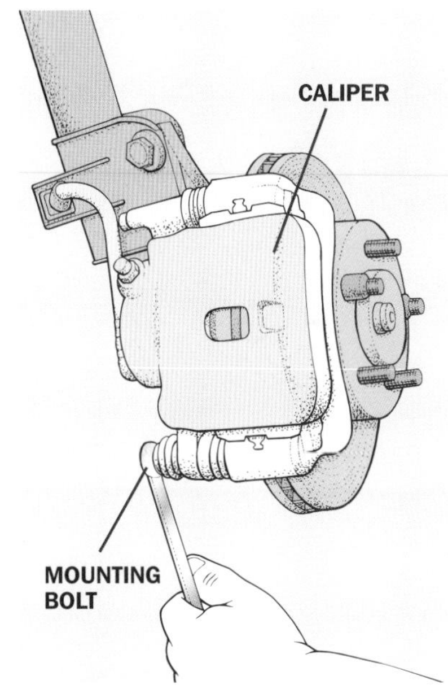

(Fig. 4) Some makers say that the mounting bolts cannot be reused. Check before removing.

brake hose (**Fig. 5**). Now use the C-clamp to check the pistons. Place a brake shoe against a piston (or pair of pistons) to distribute the force evenly, and put the C-clamp forcing screw against the shoe. Then, turn the forcing screw to determine if the piston moves smoothly. If it's sticking, replace the caliper.

A fixed caliper will be more expensive than a slider, and you may be tempted to salvage one by drilling out a frozen bleeder. Don't take the risk. Let a machine shop do it for you. Also note if the fixed caliper bolts are reusable.

Restricted Brake Hose

It's rare, but you may find that there's no leak and the problem isn't at the caliper. It's possible that the brake isn't applying normally because there's inadequate hydraulic pressure to the caliper, the result of a restricted hose. Have a helper apply the brake and see if you can turn the wheel with a wrench on a lug nut—make a real effort and use a wrench with a long shank. If the wheel can be turned at all, no matter how much effort you're applying, the caliper isn't getting full hydraulic pressure. To check, open the bleeder valve fully (with a hose over it and the other end in a glass jar) and have a helper apply the brakes. Look to see if there's a solid column of fluid coming out of the hose. There isn't? Either a brake line is kinked or the hose is defective.

(Fig. 5) Check for a frozen caliper by attempting to push the piston back. Don't hang the caliper by the hose—use a piece of wire.

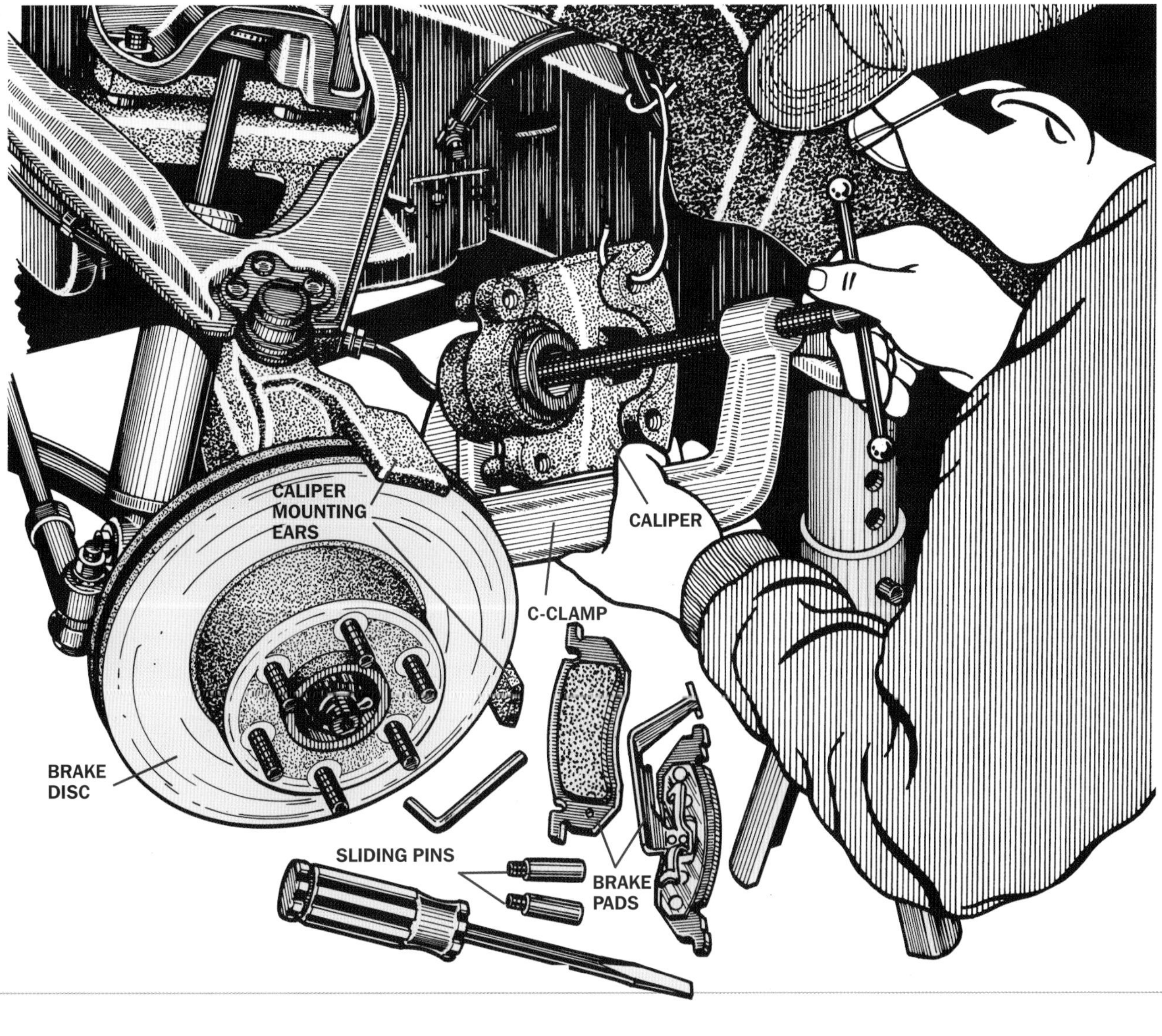

MODERATE

Flushing Your Brake System

It's a dark and stormy night, with steady rain and scattered lightning. But traffic moves along smartly—until it doesn't. You wind up hammering the brake pedal to keep from eating the license plate in front of you. Naturally, you expect—you count on—the antilock braking on your new car to ensure a safe, controllable, steady stop. Instead, the car begins to fishtail and it takes a monumental struggle to keep the car in a single lane as it comes to a stop. The extra distance you had from the car in front of you saves a collision, but you know something is wrong with the antilock braking system, a.k.a. ABS.

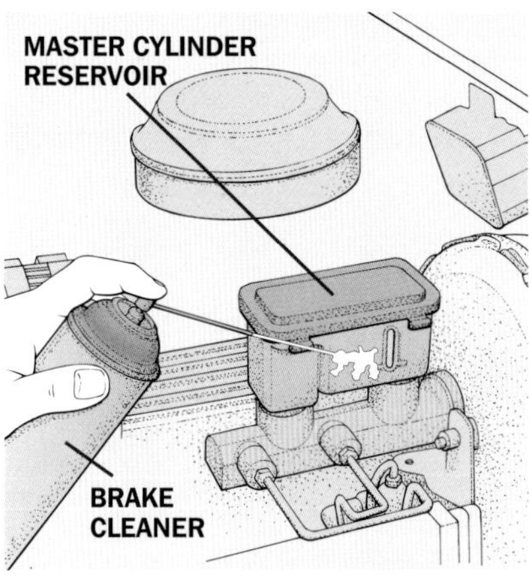

(Fig. 1) Clean the master cylinder reservoir to prevent dirt from falling in.

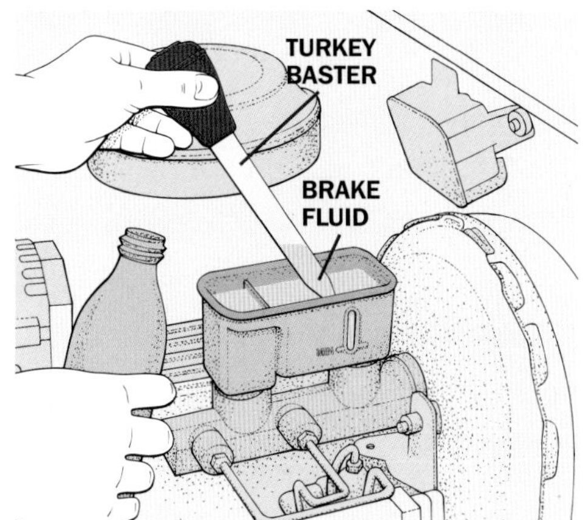

(Fig. 2) Remove almost all of the old brake fluid with a turkey baster before adding fresh fluid.

The shop gives you the bad news: The actuator is defective, and you can figure on $1400 for a replacement (or even worse, it's part of an integrated unit with the brake master cylinder and the price is even higher). No, it didn't log an ABS trouble code, but that doesn't mean anything. It's not a bad connection and it's not a factory defect. What caused it? Maybe even the technician will shrug his shoulders, but there's a good chance it's contaminated brake fluid.

The brake fluid reservoir is vented, so that's an entry point for dirt and moisture. And the rubber brake hoses are permeable—they allow even more moisture to get into the fluid. Dirt and moisture move through the lines. Most goes to the calipers and wheel cylinders, and some may get to the ABS actuator, where it can cause the delicate solenoids or motors inside to behave erratically.

And if you or the shop does a disc caliper brake job, and someone pushes back the caliper pistons, the possibilities are ominous. A lot of the dirty, moisture-laden fluid in the calipers is pushed back, where some of it gets into the ABS actuator. The prospects for an ABS failure go up, up, up.

Even if you don't have ABS, contaminated brake fluid can affect caliper and wheel cylinder bores. The older systems with the reservoir built into the master cylinder are even more prone to contamination, because the reservoir cover gasket may have taken a set and be leaking. Or a lot of dirt may have gotten into the system when the cover was removed as part of a brake job. Even simple moisture in the fluid is a real problem, because the heat of braking will cause it to boil, causing brake fade.

Flushing the system is not a difficult job. There is equipment for a one-man bleeding job, but the good stuff is expensive and we have reservations about trying to use the low-cost alternatives (hose with a one-way valve, and manual vacuum pump are examples). A simpler, effective approach is to have a helper step on the brake pedal. If you can line up someone, the only equipment you need is:

- Ramps or jack and stands to raise the vehicle a few inches in front and back, so you have access to the bleeder valves. However, it's possible to reach them on some vehicles with the wheels on the ground.
- Piece of clear hose to fit on the bleeder valve.
- Tight-fitting wrench for the bleeder (like a tubing wrench). Don't use an ordinary open-end wrench.
- Spray can of automotive cleaning solvent and a spray can of penetrating oil.
- Turkey baster to draw fluid out of the reservoir. A baster costs under $1, so don't try to clean and reuse one from the kitchen.
- A pint container of brake fluid for an econobox, a quart for a larger car. The brake fluid may be labeled DOT 3 (minimum boiling point of 400°F), DOT 4 (minimum boil of 450°) or even DOT 5.0 or 5.1 (500°F). Your system contains DOT 3 or DOT 4. These two are fully compatible, so you can mix them without worry, and one of these is what you should use.

Brake fluid is hygroscopic, which means it's like a sponge. But it's supposed to be, so if any moisture can get in, the fluid embraces it. However, moisture causes the normal boiling point of the fluid to drop. Just 2% moisture in a fluid is considered excessive. There are moisture testers, but we don't know a repair shop that has one. And there's no guarantee that the moisture level in the reservoir is the same as at the caliper—it may be higher at the caliper.

Warning: There are silicone brake fluids (labeled DOT 5) that are immune to moisture (5.1 is nonsilicone, but DOT 3 and 4 are what you should use). Don't even think about using DOT 5 silicone fluid in an automotive braking system, because it may cause faster wear of the seals, and if enough water gets into a system it could cause loss of pedal. DOT 5 and 5.1 have application in some racing vehicles.

Flush Twice

Now for the flushing job itself: Raise the vehicle a few inches on ramps or with a jack and stands.

Begin by cleaning the master cylinder's brake fluid reservoir (or top and sides of the master cylinder with the integral reservoir), using aerosol cleaning solvent and paper towels or a clean rag (**Fig. 1**). Don't remove the reservoir cover until the area is squeaky clean.

If it's an older style—the master cylinder with the integral reservoir—you'll find a rubber gasket. Inspect the perimeter for deterioration and replace the gasket if necessary. Otherwise, just clean it with some fresh brake fluid. Siphon most of the fluid out of the reservoir (**Fig. 2**), then add fresh fluid up to the level mark.

On front-drive vehicles, where the hydraulic system is split left front/right rear and right front/left rear, start at the left rear wheel. Next, go to the right front, then right rear and last, the left front wheel. On rear-drives with a diagonal split, do the same. If the rear-drive split is front/rear, however, start at the right rear, then left rear, right front and left front. The object is to begin at the wheel brake farthest away from the master cylinder and gradually work toward the closest.

If the bleeder valve can be loosened with the wrench, you're golden. If not, spray it first with penetrating oil (**Fig. 3**), let that work in, and try again with the wrench. Won't loosen? Clean the penetrating oil and heat the bleeder with a propane torch. Try again. If your wrench handle isn't that long, or if the fit isn't very tight, you

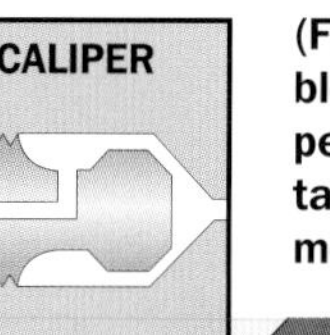

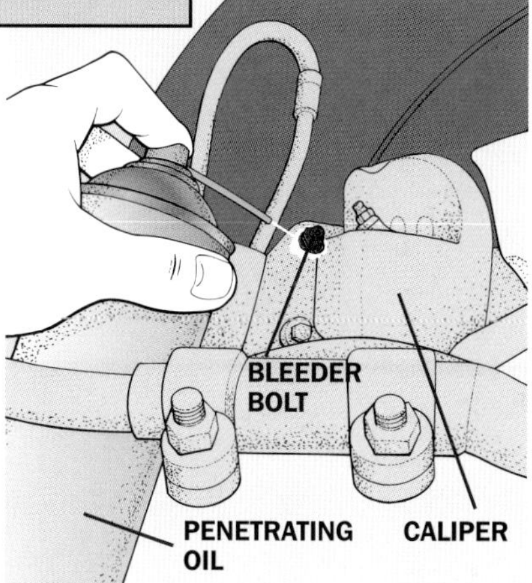

(Fig. 3) Spray the bleeder bolt with penetrating oil and tap lightly with a hammer to loosen it.

HOW IT WORKS

Testing Brake Fluid with Dip Strips

If the brake fluid in the reservoir is obviously dirty, flush the system. If it isn't, flush if it contains excess moisture, which you now can determine with "reagent dip strips." Reagents are substances used in a chemical reaction to detect other substances, and Wet Check strips for brake fluid now are marketed by Wagner Brake. Insert the strip into the fluid, remove it in a second, wait 30 seconds and compare the change in color of the two pads with a chart.

One pad merely identifies the type of fluid—DOT 3 or DOT 4. They're compatible, so this is not critical (and a 50/50 mixture of the two merely produced an ID color close to that of DOT 4, in our tests). The pad closest to the end, however, turns tan if moisture content is excessive.

We tested the strips in separate containers of DOT 3 and DOT 4, with different percentages of water. With pure brake fluid, the color was in the definitely okay range: dark green. At 1.64% water content, there was a very slight indication (some lightening of the green) that the fluids were less than pure.

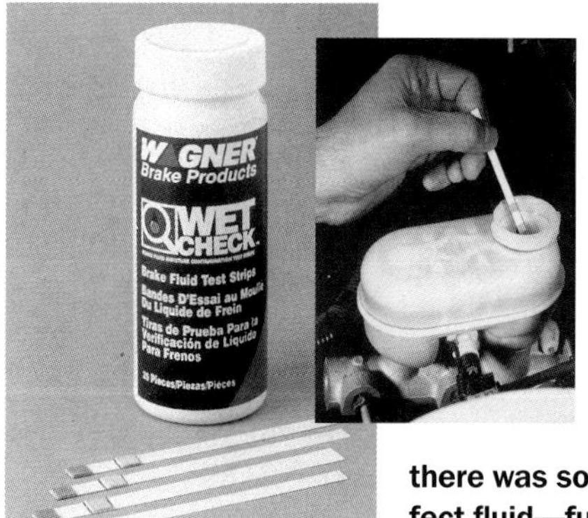

At 3.25% water, there would be at least a 25% drop in brake fluid boiling point with DOT 3. It could be as much as 50% with DOT 4. The color change to tan was unquestionable in three of four tests. In the fourth, there was some indication of less-than-perfect fluid—fuzziness in the light green—but not tan.

At 5% water the pad turned tan as soon as it was taken out of the fluid—we didn't even have to wait the 30 seconds. Read the strip almost exactly 30 seconds after removal from the fluid. If you read it too early, you might get an okay indication with 3% water. If you put the strip down for a few minutes, it can absorb enough moisture from a humid room to indicate contaminated fluid when none is actually present.

can try locking pliers (**Fig. 4**). Some tapping on the wrench or pliers end with a hammer may help.

When the bleeder just breaks loose, stop and push the end of the clear hose onto the bleeder nipple. Aim the other end of the hose into a clear glass or bottle (**Fig. 5**).

Put a block of wood under the pedal to prevent the piston from bottoming out in the master cylinder. Then tell your helper to step on the pedal and press down gently but firmly. Open the bleeder valve and watch the fluid as it flows through the clear hose into the clear glass or bottle (**Fig. 6**). If you don't get any fluid movement at the rear brakes on a car with ABS, close the bleeder valve. Have your helper turn on the ignition and apply the brakes once, then turn off the ignition and just lightly rest his/her foot on the pedal. Open the bleed valve slowly. If a stream of fluid flows from the valve, allow it to come for about 10 seconds, then close the valve and add fluid to the master cylinder. Depending on the system, the pressurized reservoir may push out enough fluid. Or the flow may continue only if the helper presses down on the pedal. On most cars, the flow will start and continue without the preliminaries—only the helper's foot pressing on the pedal.

When the pedal hits the wood block, tell your helper to hold it there. If you had a lot of trouble loosening the bleeder, remove it completely. Apply a thin film of anti-seize compound to the threads of the bleeder valve, then reinstall and close the valve. Add fresh fluid to the master cylinder reservoir again and repeat the procedure. When the fluid color changes from grungy black to something closer to what the new fluid looks like, you can stop. Close the bleeder valve and go to the next wheel brake. Be very sure to add fresh brake fluid up to the level in the reservoir every single time.

Before you do the final top-off, however, have your helper apply the brakes over and over, to exhaust the high-pressure reservoir of the ABS. This will cause the level in the master cylinder reservoir to rise slightly. It may take 25 to 35 pedal applications to do this, but when the level stops rising after a couple of dozen, that should be it. If you don't do this, the reservoir might overflow under some conditions.

When you're done, a hard brake application should extinguish the brake warning light.

And remember when you next do a disc brake job, don't just push back the piston with a C-clamp. First, clamp the brake hose with locking pliers, wrapping the hose with a protective sheath of thick rubber, perhaps from an old radiator hose. Open the bleeder (and with antiseize on the threads, it should cooperate quite nicely actually), attach a hose to the nipple, then push the piston back, collect the fluid in a container and discard.

This job is about more than saving money on an ABS actuator. No matter how new or old your car, it's about saving your skin.

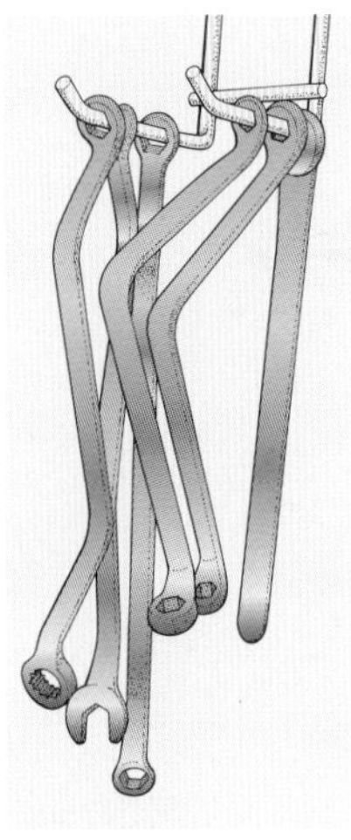

(Fig. 4) You may need to use a special wrench.

(Fig. 5) A hose over the bleeder bolt will keep fluid off of your arm and out of your eyes.

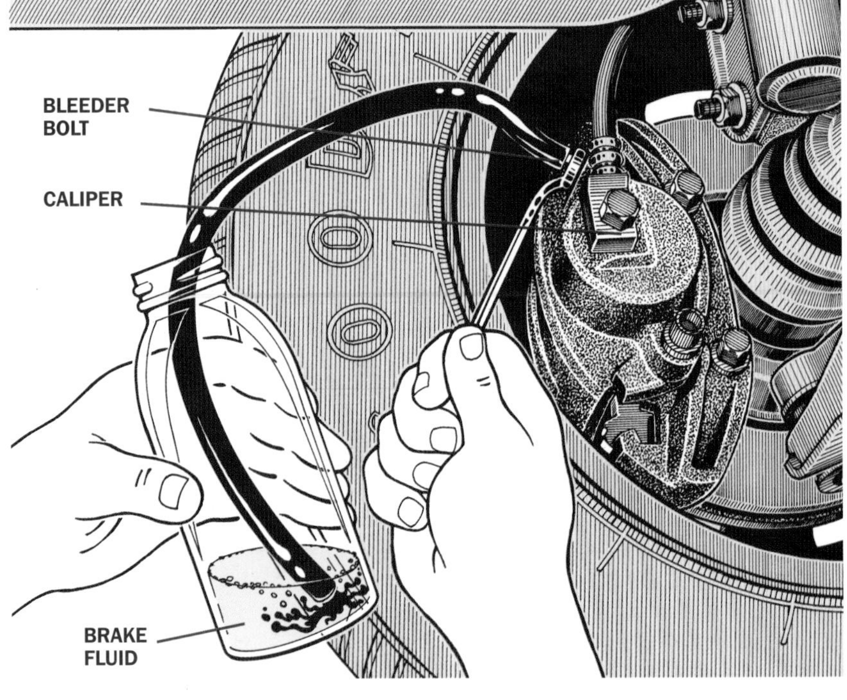

(Fig. 6) Use a box wrench or tubing wrench to loosen the bleeder bolt while a helper depresses the brake pedal. Tighten the bolt after brake fluid stops flowing, but before your helper releases. Repeat until clear fluid comes out.

Servicing Drum Brakes

You're halfway down the hill when you realize how much speed you've picked up. So you hit the brakes. Hard. Too hard, apparently, because the front tires repeatedly lock and aren't able to kill off much velocity. At the first turnoff, you check your front brakes—hot as a cup of McDonald's coffee. But your rear brakes are cool. Obviously, the front disc-brake job you had done over the weekend wasn't enough. It's time to look at those rear drum brakes.

Diagnosis

Block the front wheels. With the vehicle's rear off the ground and on safety stands—and with the parking brake off—turn each wheel. If you hear a uniform light scraping noise, that's okay. Otherwise:

- If the wheel is binding all the way around the rotation, the brakes aren't releasing properly. If that's the case, remove the drum and check for either one of two possibilities: 1. The brake shoes are not retracting fully because the return springs are weak, perhaps combined with the shoes hanging up on the backing plate; or 2. The automatic adjuster for the shoes is overdoing it.
- If you get an intermittent scraping or binding, maybe the drums are out-of-round, the shoes aren't retracting properly, a backing plate is warped or an axle problem exists.
- If there's no hint of a scrape—despite the fact that your rear brakes have been noisy or haven't been contributing to the car's braking—they may need to be adjusted. If there's an access opening in the backing plate or drum, turn the adjuster until the shoes make light contact with the drum. Then rotate the wheel to see if the lining drag is relatively even all around.

(Fig. 1) The surface of the brake drum should be totally free of any grooves, cracks and shiny spots.

If you can't turn the adjuster, take off the drum to free it.

Look As You listen

To gain a better look at the brake drum, remove the tires and wheels. Now, as you turn the brake drum, eyeball its relationship to the backing plate at various points. If the drum seems to move in and out or rock up and down—even slightly—the wheel bearing is bad, or the wheel spindle or axle shaft is bent. If the drum appears to turn evenly but its relationship with the backing plate is uneven, perhaps the plate is bent—also not an unusual problem. (If you're not sure, compare one rear drum brake with the other to see if the appearance is different while turning it.) Either way, you'll have to pull the drums to confirm the cause.

Inspect the drum where the wheel mounts against it. If a wheel is deformed, the drum may be deformed as well. Also, compare the tire sizes side to side and front to rear. Odd-size tires can trigger a vehicle's antilock brakes at the wrong time, affecting the rear-braking performance and, in some systems, setting off an ABS trouble code.

Drums Off

Pulling off stuck brake drums may require a penetrating solvent. You might even have to apply—gently—heat from a propane torch to the stud holes and the drum/hub joint. If a drum is still stuck, you may need to use a screw-type drum puller.

Once the drum is off, check its shoe-contact surface for any grooves in which you can catch a fingernail (**Fig. 1**). Discs work well enough with deep scores (although they may get noisy), but drums don't. And even if a drum is super-smooth, get it measured at a machine shop to see if it's out-of-round, worn past specs or misshapen in some way. Normally (but not always), a faulty drum will create an uneven lining wear pattern or cause short lining life.

Find a drum that needs cutting? Take both drums to the machine shop, and have an equal amount removed from each. There may not be enough metal remaining, which means new drums. After a drum is machined, clean it out with a detergent and water solution, then wipe it with a lintfree rag and a brake solvent. Wipe until the rag comes clean, and let the drum dry.

Next, inspect the linings. Even if they're thick enough to be left in (1/8 in. or more), they may have a glazed surface and need replacing. Don't try to sand off the glaze. The linings have undergone a chemical change from overheating, possibly combined with the effects of aging as well as climate.

The linings may also be glazed because the brake shoes were dragging. Perhaps the automatic adjust-

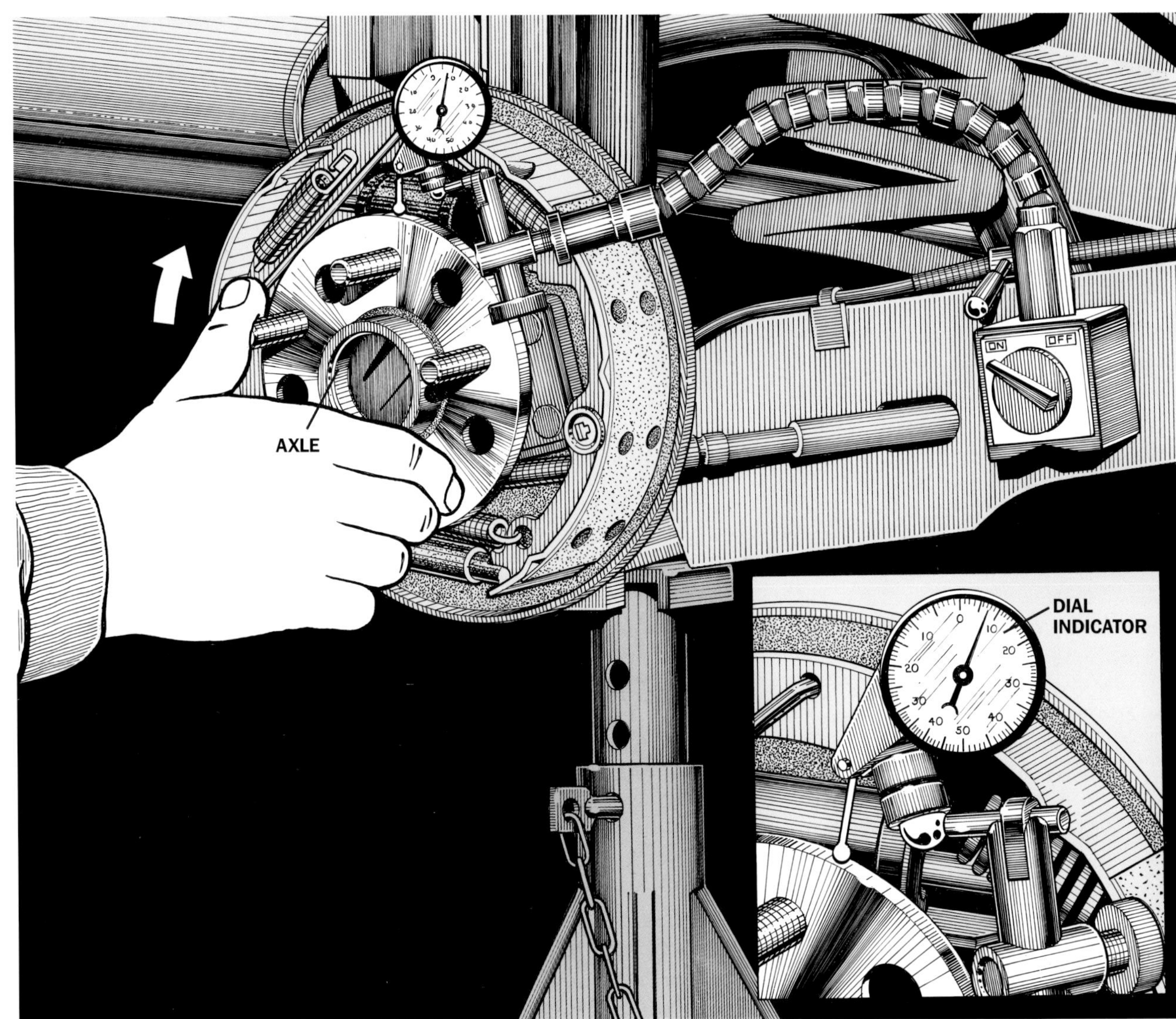

(Fig. 2) After you've removed the brake drum, use a dial indicator to check for both axial play and radial runout of the rear-axle hub. For good braking performance, total runout should be only a few thousandths of an inch. Excess runout probably indicates a bent spindle.

ment mechanism is bad—or someone keeps forgetting to release the parking brake before starting to drive.

Running Out—Literally

Did you encounter that intermittent scrape when you turned the drum in a pre-disassembly check? But despite the noise, did the drum and shoe hardware seem to be good? This is the time to check for a bent spindle or axle shaft, and/or a bad bearing. Use a dial indicator (**Fig. 2**). (If you don't own an indicator, you can rent one from an auto parts store or rental center.)

To check the radial runout, mount the dial indicator on the suspension, body or chassis so that the plunger is against the edge of the spindle or shaft hub. Then turn the axle shaft or spindle. Caution: Turn the axle slowly, so you won't be fooled by a burr or nick on the hub—particularly one on the edge—as you're checking radial runout. To get an accurate reading, you may need to clean up some corrosion on the hub with sandpaper or a wire brush.

To check for lateral runout on axle shafts with a hub, relocate the dial indicator so the plunger is touching the outer face of a hub. Then turn the shaft again.

Runout, in any case, should be within manufacturer's specs—typically just a few thousandths of an inch. If your brakes have objectionable shudder, you'll probably find that the runout is .010 in. or greater.

Putting It All Together

Ready to install new shoes, springs and other hardware that come in the typical drum-brake repair kit? Don't use a screwdriver or your neighbor's 15-year-old set of brake-spring pliers—a spring could fly off and smack you right in the mouth. Instead, get a pair of spring pliers (**Fig. 3**) designed for late-model cars—it has jaws that engage the spring hooks and the shape to actually expand the spring enough to remove it. Ditto for late-model brake holddowns, which come in more than one size and call for a

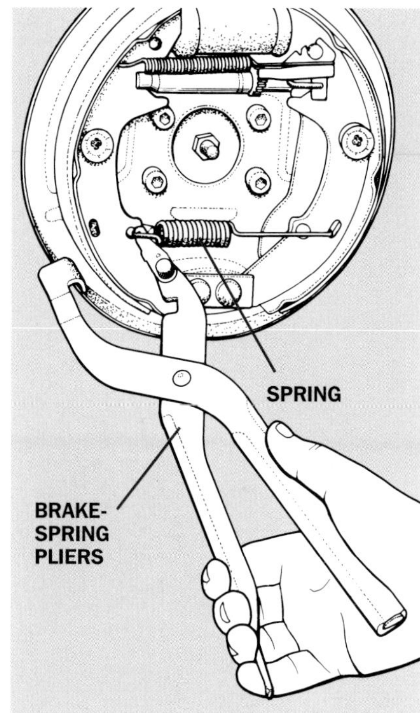

(Fig. 3) Brake-spring pliers make the process of reinstalling springs both safe and easy.

new tool with the two popular-size tips. Clean off the shoe side of the backing plate and make sure that the wheel cylinder isn't leaking.

How should you install semimetallic shoes if you live in an area with cold, wet winters? If they freeze to the drums after an overnight cold snap, the first brake application may be uneven. Chamfer the ends of the shoes (up to the first rivets) and they'll break loose more easily and retract

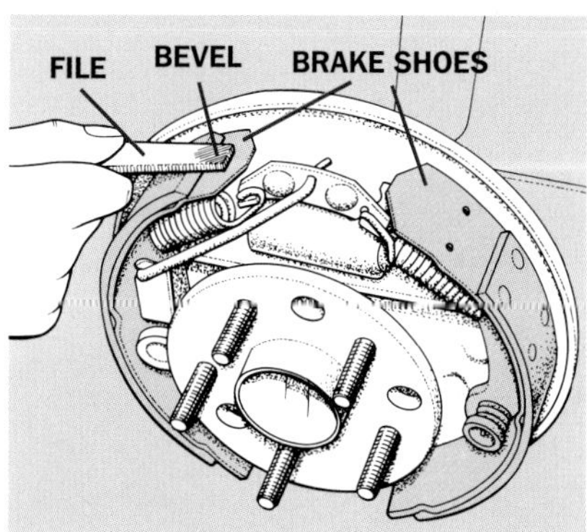

(Fig. 4) Chamfering the leading edges of the lining material can improve your car's braking performance in certain weather conditions.

when you take off (**Fig. 4**). If the problem occurs even at temperatures just above freezing, you might want to check with the car dealer—he may have a substitute lining (with a lower metal content) that's less affected by the cold weather.

If pre-disassembly checks indicate a warped backing plate, don't try to bend it back into position—install a new one. On many rear-drive General Motors cars built from the late 1970s through the early 1990s, there may be another problem: wear in the cutout for the clip-held wheel cylinder. The result is a loose cylinder. If you can force it to rotate even slightly—say, by moderate prying on each end of the cylinder with a large screwdriver—that's reason enough to install a new backing plate.

The "by-the-book" method of replacing a brake backing plate on a rear-drive car is to remove the axle shaft. This is a tough job, so if you need a new plate, it's a lot easier to install an aftermarket 2-piece plate (available for many GM cars) (**Fig. 5**). Just loosen and cut the old one with a hacksaw and you can bolt on the new one without breaking a sweat.

If the platforms on which the shoes slide are burred or rusty, they're probably a contributor (along with weak springs) to the shoes failing to retract quickly—not to mention overheating or premature wear. Smooth off the platforms using fine sandpaper, wipe clean and apply a coat of silicone dielectric grease. Also, you should sand smooth the edges of the new brake shoes where they ride on the platforms.

If you saw a lot of road film on the inside of the backing plate, or evidence of water/snow entry in winter, seal up the back of the plate. If any inspection/adjustment covers are missing, buy and install replacements. And if you can see any light coming through the wheel cylinder cutout in the backing plate, seal it.

Finally, bolt on the wheels and tighten them to specification with a torque wrench, using a crisscross pattern. This is not only important for

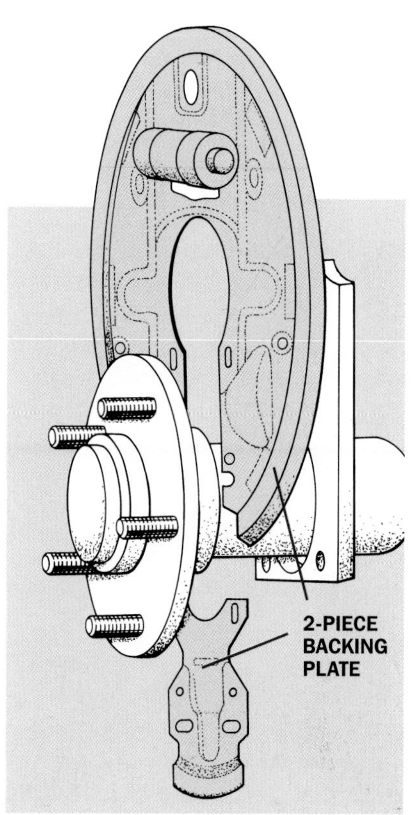

(Fig. 5) Aftermarket 2-piece backing plates can help you avoid the very difficult job of removing the axle.

front-disc rotors, but it will also keep rear drums from warping.

The bottom line? If you touch all the bases this time around, you'll get 100% braking action the next time you hit that pedal.

ADJUSTERS NEED TO BE free-moving. Check this while lifting the adjuster arm with a screwdriver.

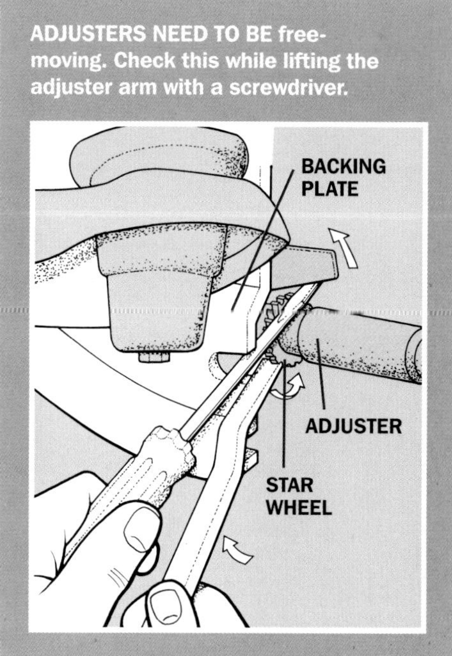

EASY

Solving Steering-Pull Problems

Your personal trainer mentions that the diameter of your left forearm is twice that of your right, unusual for a righthanded individual. Popeye would be proud. And your spouse nags you constantly to keep to the right lane of the freeway, because you're always brushing the edge of the shoulder in the fast lane at 5 under. Guess it's time to find out why your car pulls so hard to the left.

The tire pressures are correct. You haven't bounced the front end into a concrete embankment or over a rocky road lately, so there's probably nothing bent in the suspension/steering underbody. Is it just something you'll have to live with? Probably not. The sources of most pulls are pretty easy to pinpoint if you define the basic problem and systematically check the possible causes.

First question: What kind of pull is it? That calls for a road test, made under precise conditions: correct tire pressures when the tires are cold, no wind and a smooth, level road (no crown). Drive at a steady speed (somewhere between 30 and 45 mph), then shift into Neutral. Next, when there's no traffic around, remove your hands from the steering wheel. Note whether the pull occurs in gear and also in Neutral, and if your hands on the steering wheel make any difference.

If the pull is most noticeable under acceleration and goes away when you shift into Neutral, it's called torque steer. And, yes, torque steer also can occur at steady speeds. If it occurs with the transmission in Neutral, it's a typical pull. Still no pull or torque steer? Make a turn and allow the car to return to facing straight ahead. Then, repeat the test to see if the car pulls in the same direction as the turn that was made. This is called memory

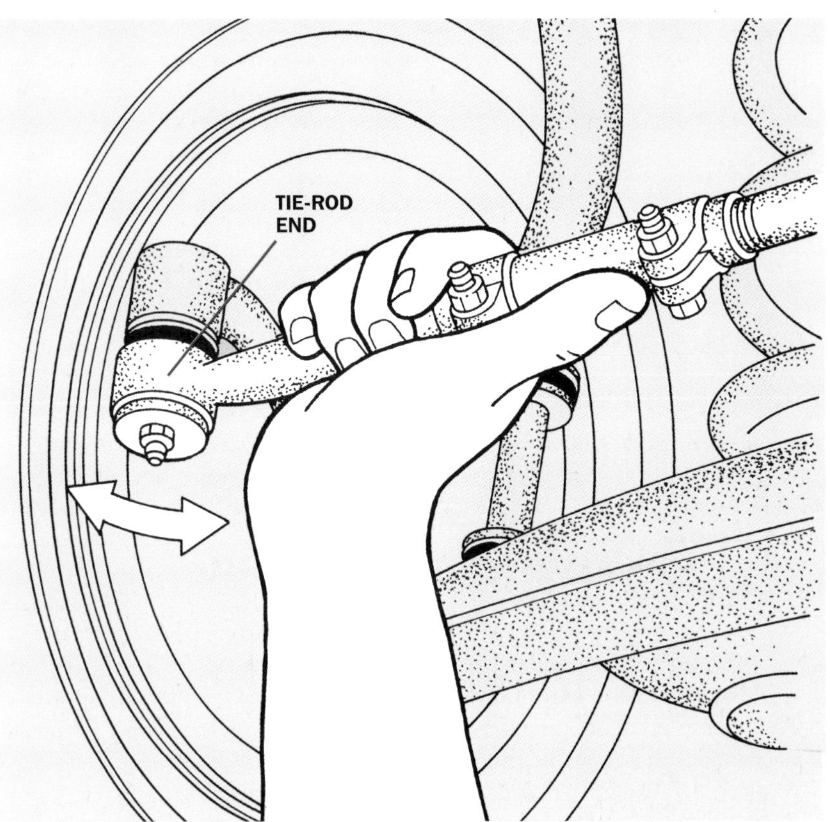

(Fig. 1) Rock the tie-rod ends to check for binding or wear. Some light resistance is fine, but there should be no slop.

steer, and you'll see that it's most obvious when you take your hands off the steering wheel.

Torque Steer

Torque steer results from more possible causes than any other source of pull, so it's tougher to isolate. If you have a powerful engine and you mash the throttle, some torque steer—particularly on acceleration—is normal.

Transverse-engine front-drive cars with high-performance engines are particularly prone to torque steer, although proper suspension design helps minimize it. When significant torque steer is evident, something is wrong and you should be able to trace it.

Checking for brake drag is a good first step. Even slight differences in

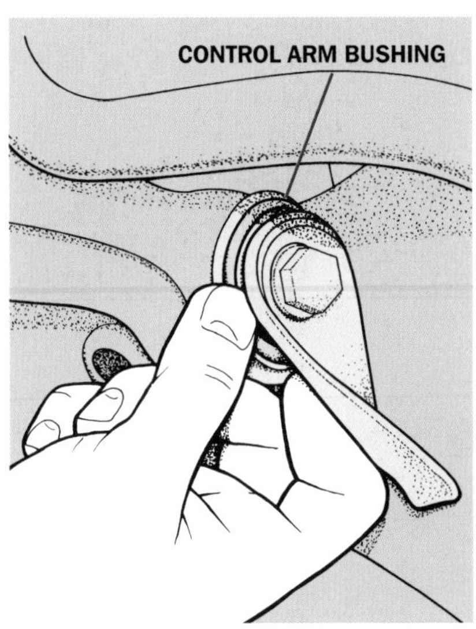

(Fig. 2) Worn bushings can often be detected visually—look for shiny metal where the bushing has been moving.

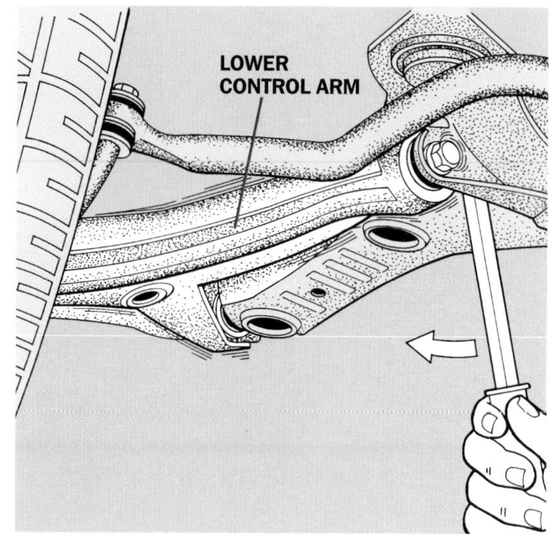

(Fig. 3) Pry the control arm lightly to find worn bushings. The arm should return to its original position when you release the pry bar.

drag or between the front tires can compound any tendency toward torque steer. A second check should be for a difference in looseness of the front suspension or tie-rod ends from one side to the other. You can feel major looseness by grasping and pulling/pushing on the tie rods **(Fig. 1)**. Or you can have a helper hold the steering wheel steady while you rock the road wheel side to side and up and down to look for play in the tie-rod ends.

In addition, eyeball any rubber bushings, particularly at the control arms **(Fig. 2)**. When these bushings are bad, they look it—cracked, distorted. Also, pry the control arms to feel for any looseness **(Fig. 3)**.

Next, measure the front suspension ride height **(Fig. 4)**. Factory service manuals detail the many possible measurement points, but the object is to compare readings between a pair of fixed points—one on the suspension and the other on the chassis. You'll need an absolutely dead-flat piece of pavement for this, and bounce the car up and down on the suspension a couple of times after you park.

One way to check for symmetry—or the lack thereof—in the suspension is to tie a string between the bottoms of the lower control arms (such as from the ball-joint grease fittings). The string should be very tight (and "straight as a string"). Measure from

(Fig. 4) With the car on a dead-level surface, check for correct symmetry in the suspension ride height. Stretch a string between a pair of convenient points on the shocks or ball joints, and measure to the frame rails. It should be level to within less than a half-inch.

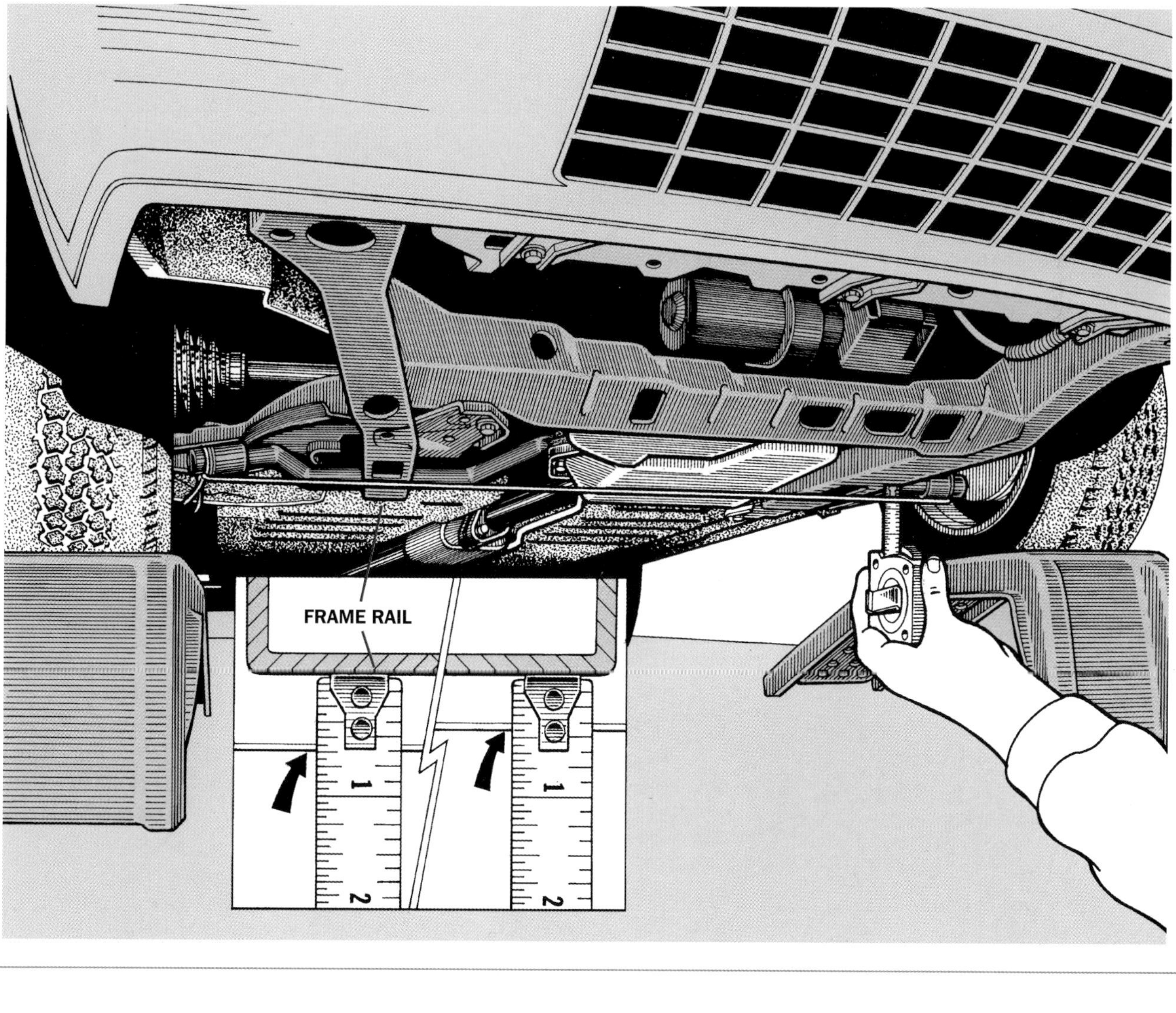

(Fig. 5) You may need to pull the strut apart to properly check the strut bearing for binding.

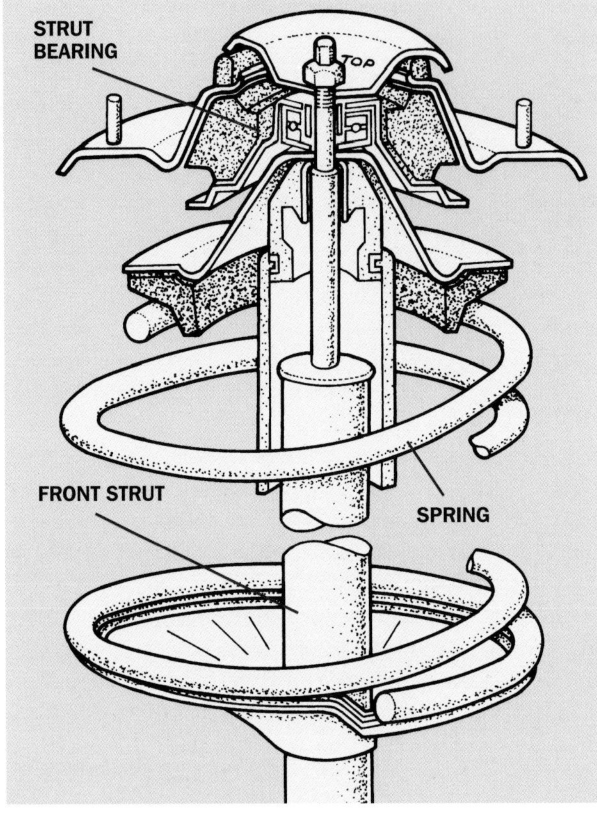

the string to the underside of the frame rail to which the control arm mounts, and the distance should be the same from side to side, within less than a half-inch. If it's greater, there's front spring sag, a common major contributor to torque steer. Replace the springs to fix this problem.

Badly sagged rear springs can cause a vehicle to pull as well, but you'll be able to see the height difference visually before the pull gets bad enough to notice while driving. Just look carefully at your car or truck from the rear when it's parked on that level patch of pavement.

Good springs? Check the engine mounts for deterioration, as weak mounts allow the powertrain to shift unevenly on acceleration, and that can move the car in one direction or the other. If the rear (transaxle) mount is an air-gap type and it's bad, the engine will rock backward, mashing the metal of the mount against the rubber center section. To check for this, have a helper hit the gas pedal while in Neutral.

Also check to see if the transaxle is level, which you can do with a carpenter's level. It doesn't have to be absolutely, perfectly level, but within a quarter-inch or so.

If it's not, try loosening the transaxle mount, running the engine at idle (have the parking and service brakes applied, once more) and, if you have an automatic transmission, shifting the transmission back and forth between Reverse and Drive several times. With a manual box, you can try prying the powertrain fore and aft a few times. This should resettle the powertrain.

Retighten the bolts and recheck the level. If it's still on a tilt, you can try shimming up the low end of the powertrain, using suspension shims.

STRUT BEARINGS CAN bind up and cause the steering to stiffen and pull to one side.

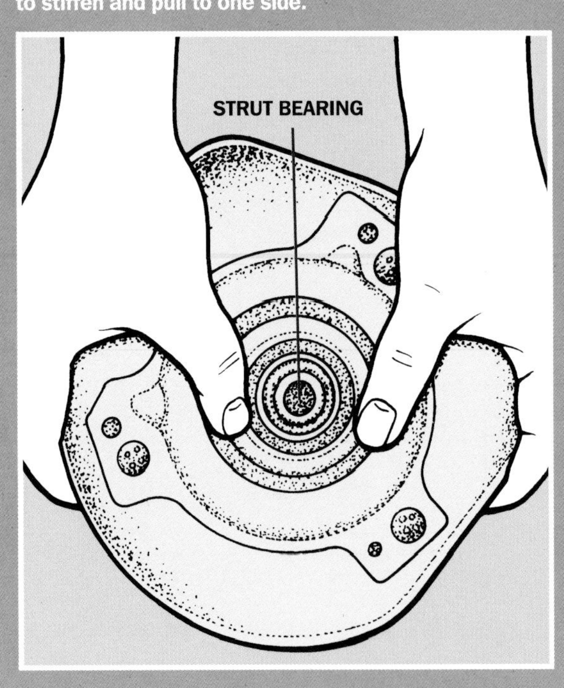

Still looking for answers? It's certainly possible that problems with the front tires, such as misaligned belts—under the tread and out of sight—are a factor. Normally, tire problems are going to cause pull even when you're not accelerating, but it is possible that you are more sensitive to it only during acceleration.

So let's look at the tires, and talk about a straightforward pull.

Tire-Related Pull

Hopefully, you had your alignment checked at a shop that uses first-rate electronic equipment, one that even checks caster and camber on "net-build' (nonadjustable) front suspensions. A good alignment shop knows what is acceptable as a suspension ages and springs sag slightly. And it can slant the camber readings ever so slightly to minimize pull in one direction.

Tires are the first do-it-yourself items to check, even if the pressures are the same and right at specifications. Are they exactly the same size and type, and worn about the same? If not, they're probably at least contributors to any pull. Even if they look exactly the same, the tread belts of one or more may have been damaged.

Get the front end of the car up in the air on proper jackstands for the remainder of these tests. Put the stands under the frame, not the suspension members.

Rotate each front wheel and feel for more than light drag. If you get much more drag at one front wheel than the other, you have a brake-system problem—either a bad caliper or something wrong with the hydraulic system, such as a crimped tube or even a bad master cylinder.

Equal or no drag on both front tires? Switch them left to right. If the pull is in the opposite direction, get new tires. Even if the pull changes somewhat, but not necessarily all the way in the opposite direction, the tires still are the most probable cause of the pull, and a new pair might be worth a try if nothing else pans out. If you're lucky, however, the pull will go away and you can pat yourself on the back for a cheap fix. Stop here if you're checking for a cause of torque steer. Let's try one more thing for a tire-related pull.

If there's no change after the front-tire swap, next switch the wheel on the driver's-side front with the one on the driver's-side rear. If that makes a significant change, get a replacement for the tire now at the driver's-side rear (the one originally at the passenger's-side front). If the tread pattern or amount of wear is significantly different between new tires and the rest that you have, you may have to simply replace all four tires.

Memory Steer

When toe is correct, and the car pulls in the same direction as the last turn, you're dealing with memory steer—almost always caused by binding in the suspension on that side of the car.

On a MacPherson-strut suspension, it's a good bet that the binding is in the upper strut mount bearing. Sometimes, you can feel roughness in the mount by reaching up from underneath and resting your fingers on it, while a helper cranks the wheel back and forth (front end up on safety stands).

More often, you'll have to pull the strut for a better test of the bearing. Check for binding in the bearing after you've pulled the strut **(Fig. 5)**.

No luck? It might be a binding tie-rod end, but that's not likely—they generally get sloppy rather than bind up. Give the tie rods a shake and a twist to check. Also unlikely but possible is a binding ball joint. You may need to disconnect it to confirm this.

It's possible that the binding is in the steering gear. As a final test, you can disconnect the tie rods. With them connected and then disconnected, you should be able to feel the difference by turning the steering wheel in each direction with the engine off.

Unfortunately, not all alignment shops are as methodical as they could be. And some shops will tell you that "all front-wheel-drive cars do that." But unless the pulling problem has been there since the day you received the vehicle, it isn't generic and you should conduct a careful road test and underbody inspection.

MODERATE

Diagnosing and Repairing Wheel Vibration

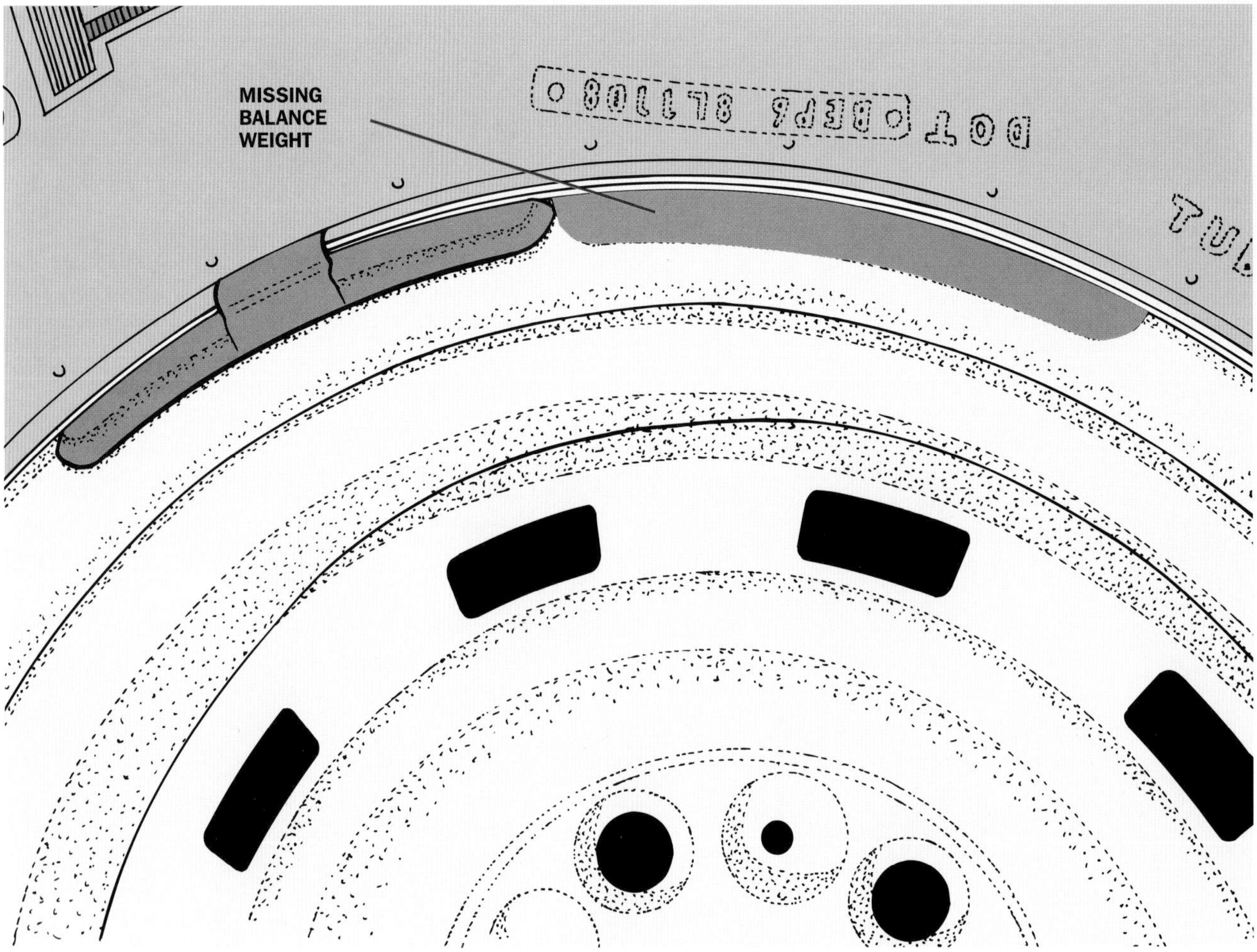

(Fig. 1) Missing wheel weights will leave marks on the rim. Check the inside of the rim, too.

At long last it's the weekend and you're headed for the mountains ... or the desert ... or the shore. Anywhere out of town. And for the first time in weeks you can point your hood ornament at the horizon instead of the license plate in front of you and actually achieve the speed limit on the interstate. Your hands shake with glee.

Actually, that's not glee, or even healthy anticipation. Nor is it some unspeakable neurological syndrome. It's a vibration that isn't even perceptible at lower speeds.

Maintain Your Balance

A simple wheel balance will cure most vibrations. But if that doesn't cure the problem—or if it cropped up suddenly within a reasonable time after a wheel balance—your problems may go deeper.

Begin by cranking the wheels over to the steering stop and looking at the inside of the rim. It's customary to split the amount of the balance weights between the inside and outside of the rim. If a weight (even an old one) has come off, that could be the problem. The weight should leave a clear outline, so you'll know exactly how much is missing **(Fig. 1)**. If the balance weight was added recently, you can take it back to the shop for a replacement.

Also inspect the rim—inside and outside—for any damage. Look for packed mud on the inside of the wheel. Also look at the tires—if you see any bulges or uneven wear of the tires, consider them in the "probable cause" category.

Nothing obvious? Take the car for a test drive. When the vibration occurs, is it while you're accelerating through a bend? That means it's both torque and speed sensitive. When you pull back to your garage, inspect the axle shafts, looking for damage

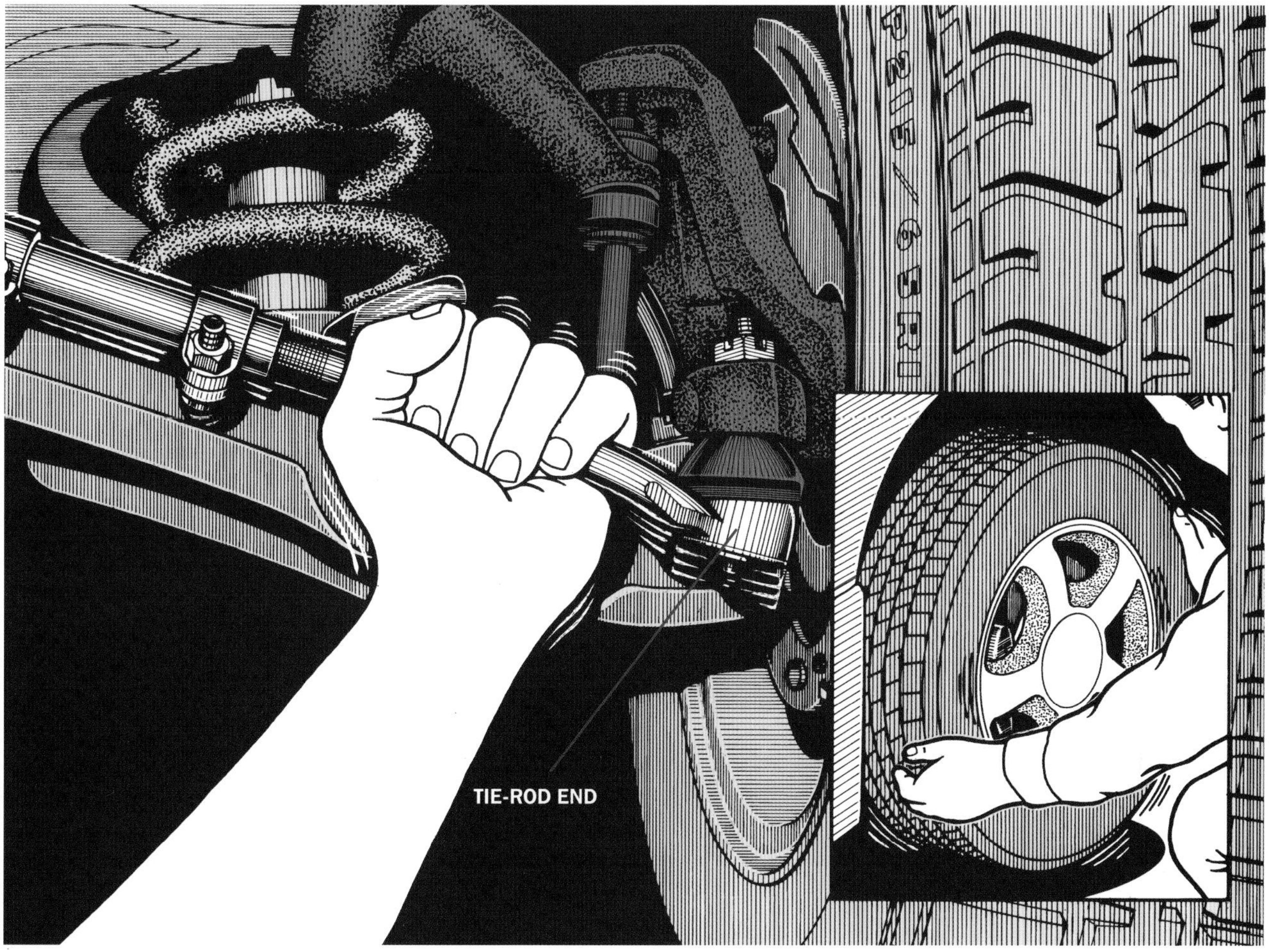

(Fig. 2) With the wheel off the ground, shake it in and out to check for a loose wheel bearing. Then check for loose tie-rod ends.

to the boots. Constant velocity joints can wear out. But if the boots are intact, the clamps are holding them at each end, and there's been no loss of lubricant and no intrusion of road film, then they're probably in good condition.

If the vibration is not related to torque, shift into Neutral and let the vehicle coast at the problem speed. Still have the vibration? It's speed sensitive pure and simple. This could be the source of your troubles, even if the wheels are balanced and the tires are good. It's not a powertrain or driveline issue.

Keeping Your Bearings

Jack up the front wheels by the control arms, so they're off the ground, and support them with safety stands. Grasp each wheel, holding it first at the sides, then at the top and bottom. See if you can rock the wheel in and out and if you can feel any looseness, which indicates a loose wheel or worn wheel hub bearings (**Fig. 2**). To replace wheel bearings on front-drive cars, you've got to remove the wheel hub. This job requires a slide-hammer puller, a tool typically available from the rental Peg-Board of many auto parts stores, and a torque wrench capable of the high torque usually required for the retaining nut (often well over 200 ft.-lb.). Front-drive wheel bearings (and the front bearings on many rear-drive cars) are well-sealed and often are life-of-the-car without lubrication. However, if you've been on a lot of secondary roads, or glanced off a curb hard enough to bend a rim, they could be worn or damaged.

If you have an older rear-drive car it probably has adjustable front wheel bearings, and finding a lot of

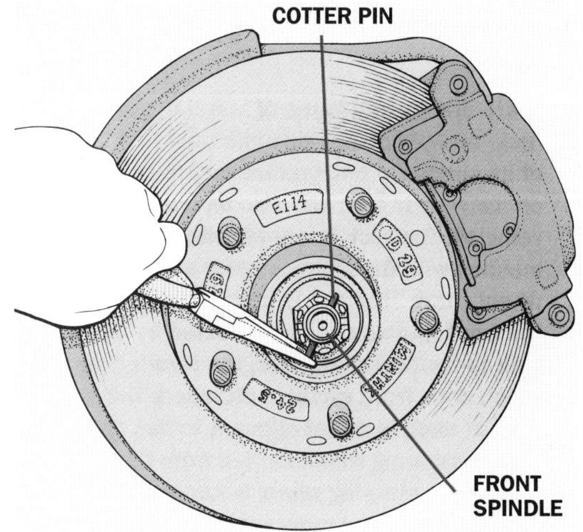

(Fig. 3) Remove the cotter pin to retorque a loose front wheel bearing on a rear-drive car.

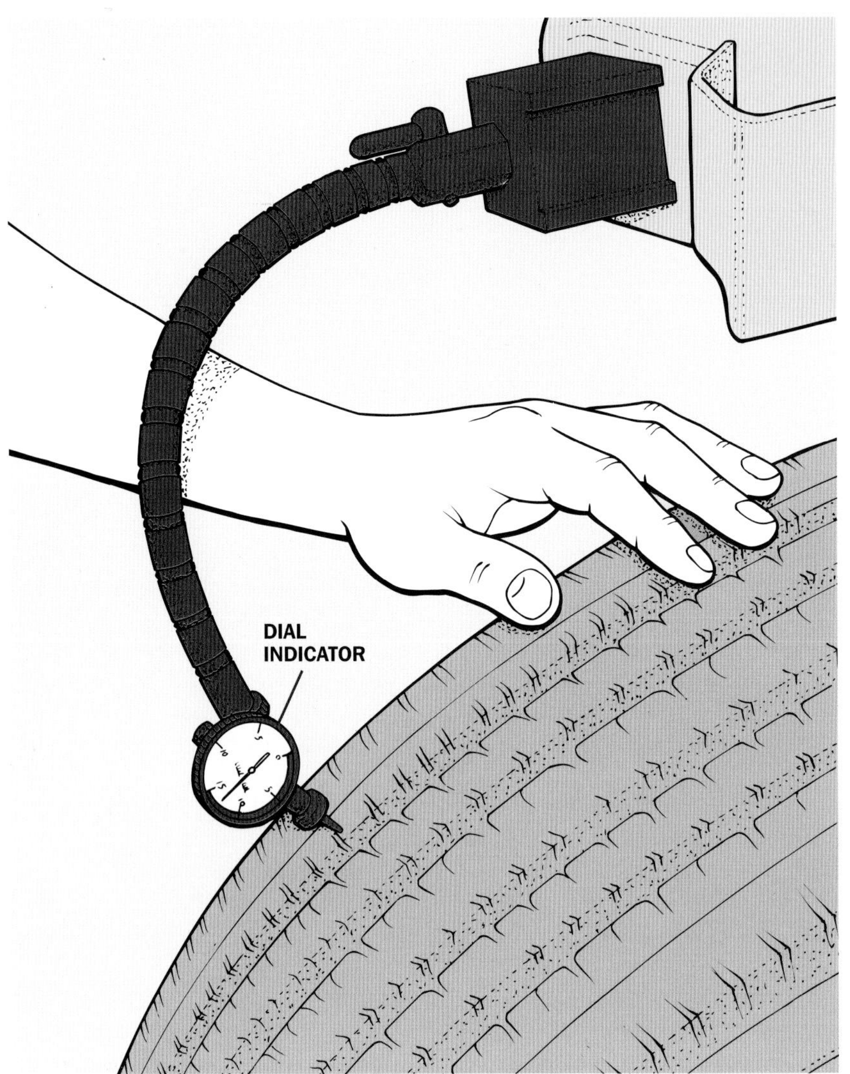

(Fig. 4) Total radial runout at the tire tread should be no more than .050 to .060 in.

free play in these is not surprising. To adjust, remove the cotter pin, tighten the wheel bearing nut to about 20 ft.-lb. to seat the bearings, and back off so they're just free but have so little play that you really can't feel it **(Fig. 3)**. Then line up the slot in the spindle with the nut and insert a new cotter pin.

Steering Your Way

You may not feel free play in a front wheel (front- or rear-drive), but try rocking it in and out with a bit more effort, but not enough to move the steering linkage. That could demonstrate free play from wear in the tie-rod ends or ball joints. If you're not sure where the free play is, pry up on the bottom of the tire and watch the ball joint to see if it has free play—¼ in. is a lot. To check a tie-rod end joint for looseness, try to flex it by hand. A good tie-rod end should feel snug, but not immobile or stiff.

On rack-and-pinion steering, it's a good idea to check the tie rods' inner sockets. They're covered by the steering rack boots, but you can squeeze the boots to hold the inner joint. Jack

HOW IT WORKS

Rack-and-Pinion Steering

There are several types of steering systems, but the rack- and-pinion has become the most popular because of its simplicity and precise response. It's used primarily on passenger cars and also on late-model sport utility vehicles. The rack is a shaft with gear teeth, and it meshes with the pinion, a gear at the end of the steering wheel shaft. The rack is horizontally installed between the front wheels and is connected by a tie rod at each side to a steering knuckle, the pivoting structure to which each front wheel is attached. The tie rod has a flex joint at each end that allows it to flex and pivot in transferring steering wheel motion from the rack to the knuckles. As the steering wheel is turned to either side, the pinion rotates and moves the rack to that side, pivoting the front wheels in the same direction.

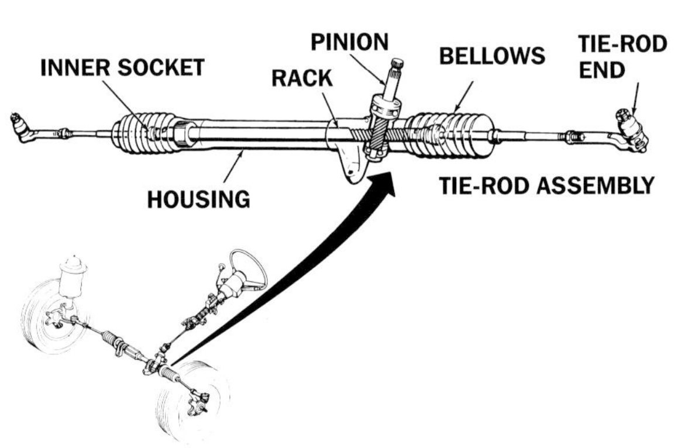

up the front end to take the weight off the front wheels. Have a friend slowly turn the steering wheel a partial turn to each side, while you feel for looseness.

Look Out for Runout

Just because you can't feel a lot of free play or "wobble" in a wheel doesn't mean there isn't enough to cause vibration. It doesn't take a lot to be responsible for objectionable vibration at speeds of 60 to 70 mph and above—any deviation from a truly circular spin is called runout. It can be vertical (up-down) or horizontal (in-out).

The only practical way to check for runout—front or rear—is with a dial indicator, another tool you can rent at many parts stores. There are several different checks to make to pinpoint the source of the runout.

Mount the indicator on something heavy that won't move, such as an anchor plate or wheel hub/knuckle. Position the plunger for the specific runout check. Example: For a radial runout test, rest it against a good tire tread groove. Slowly turn the tire and measure the amount of runout, ignoring jumps in the plunger that result from the shape of the tread or minor imperfections in it. If there are factory specifications for runout, use those.

If you don't have specs, see if the runout is about .050 to .060 in.—this measurement is considered rule of thumb (**Fig. 4**). The tire almost surely isn't the issue, although there is precision equipment that can check a tire for heavy spots. We know—you don't have it and can't rent it. Most professionals don't have it either, which tells you how common it is.

To isolate the source of the runout, check it at the wheel with the plunger on an underside horizontal surface. Ignore minor imperfections in the wheel finish (paint, weld, tiny dings) that cause the plunger to jump instantaneously. If the runout is over .045 in., the wheel should be replaced.

If radial runout isn't bad, check lateral runout with the plunger against the sidewall, even if the in-out rocking didn't show anything. Obviously, ignore any plunger movement from raised lettering, etc. If the runout is over .045 in., it's too much. Here again, isolate the runout by checking at the wheel with the plunger against a vertical surface. The rule-of-thumb specs are the same as for radial runout.

When the runout at the wheel is excessive, a new wheel normally is the answer, but not always. Remove the wheel and check runout on the wheel hub (**Fig. 5**). Making a lateral runout check is an obvious procedure because there's a hub face against which you can rest the plunger. For a radial check, it may be more difficult if the top surface of the hub isn't reasonably smooth because you have to use the threaded edges of the studs, and, typically, there are only four or five of those studs. So it does take some careful measuring to see if there's a significant amount. You have to look for the peak reading at each stud to be sure you're measuring at the outermost point. Unless almost all the radial runout is in the bolt circle, and that amount is at least .030 in., go for a new wheel. Replacing the hub and bearing on a front-drive is not a quick and easy job.

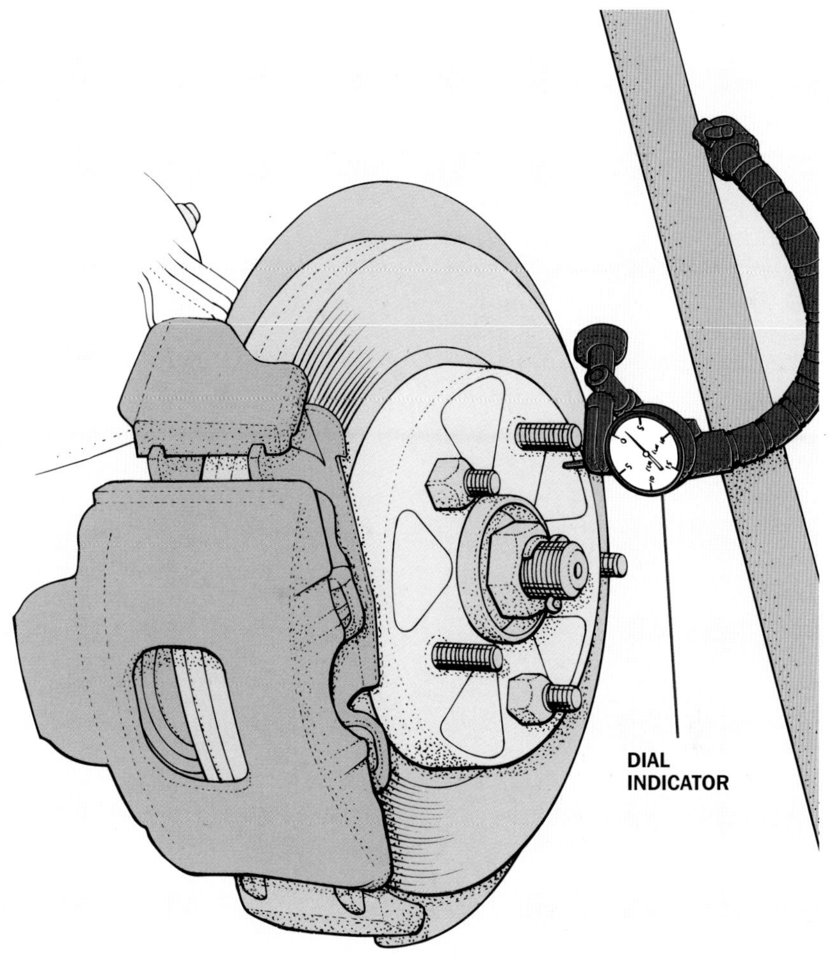

(Fig. 5) If radial or lateral runout is high, check both runouts at the hub to rule out a bent rim.

It can take a couple of hours to check out the possible causes of high-speed vibration, and you may be tempted to take the car in for wheel alignment to see if that helps before you spend time on all these other things. Sorry. Unless there's some evidence of wheel misalignment (such as irregular tire wear), a wheel alignment is not going to help at all. In fact, until you first isolate and correct the cause of the vibration, alignment would be a waste of time and money.

DIFFICULT

Replacing A Steering Rack

It's a crisp morning as you carefully back your car down the driveway. A quick turn of the wheel as the front tire clears the curb will swing your car up the street. But the steering wheel is strangely stiff. Instead of swinging the car's nose around, you run straight back, knocking over a trash can across the street. Fortunately, the damage is small: a crunched $14.95 rubbish barrel and a slimy mess to pick up in your second-best suit.

"What happened?" you wonder as you pop the hood. "The belt's still there and the fluid's up—although it does look black. Maybe the belt just slips until it warms up." After tidying up across the street and tidying up yourself, you try backing out again—with both hands on the wheel. The steering feels fine now—no groans and plenty of power steering boost.

If the belt is 4 years old or more, go ahead and change it because it's due anyway. But don't be shocked if the problem returns the next chilly morning. Power steering that awakens slowly on cool days has so-called "morning sickness." It won't go away.

It's caused by wear inside the steering assembly (a.k.a. the "rack"). The fluid's black, metallic look is a result of metal worn from the inside of the housing. The fluid is abrasive, and the wear will worsen with time. The rack is shot—replace it and use the opportunity to flush the junk from the pump and lines.

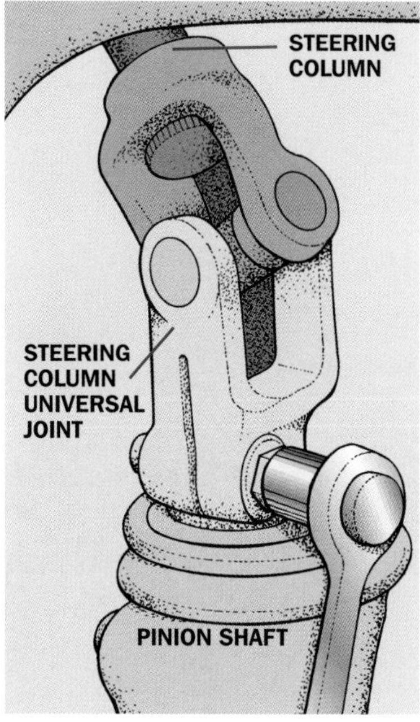

(Fig. 1) Disconnect the rack's pinion shaft from the steering column.

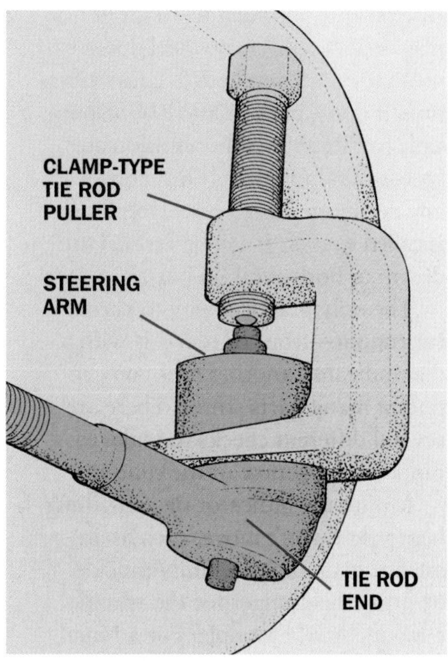

(Fig. 2) Use a special puller to remove the tie rod end from the steering upright.

Can I Do It?

Swapping a rack is simple in some cars, nasty in others. For example, a rear-drive car's rack, if bolted in front of the front crossmember, is usually easy to change. But it's more challenging in a front-driver with the rack bolted to the subframe behind the powertrain or against the firewall.

Should you do it yourself? A shop manual may tell you how tough the job will be, but not always. One General Motors manual says you have to lower the front subframe 3 in. to get enough clearance to slip out the rack. Maybe, maybe not. Legions of technicians just twist and wiggle it through the existing space with no problem.

But you should still check the service manual. For one thing, it'll let you know if there are nuts and bolts that must be replaced with new ones, for safety's sake, when changing the rack. You will also want to know the torque values for all fasteners. Are there any O-rings involved? They'll need replacing. The manual will tell you.

Before chickening out, look at a replacement rack. You'll see the location of bolt holes and the fluid pressure and return line ports—the only fluid lines you'll need to disconnect and reattach at the rack. Safely support the car and check clearances. If you find you can't grasp everything you need to work on from under the car or by reaching around the engine, you may opt to send the job out. Lastly, before deciding, talk with people who know the job, such as the front-end pro who'll align the car after you've swapped the rack, or a dismantler at a local salvage yard. They may know legitimate shortcuts.

Doing It

Ready to go? It will help if you remove the front wheels for better access to the wheel wells. Break all the lug nuts free before using the jack. Lift the car and support it safely on stands. Then, unbolt the clamp that connects the steering column to the pinion shaft **(Fig. 1)**.

Detach the outer tie rod ends. You may need to use a special tie rod end puller to get the tapered bolt to relinquish its grip on the steering upright **(Fig. 2)**. If you're reusing the old outer tie rod ends, don't take them off the knuckles with a fork-type remover—it could damage the grease seals. Use a puller-type remover. Better yet, you probably can leave them in the uprights. Just loosen the jam nuts and turn the tie rods with a pipe wrench. The rods will unscrew from the ends—clockwise on one side, counterclockwise on the other. Unbolt the rack from the chassis. Now you can disconnect the fluid lines and capture the power steering hydraulic fluid as it drains.

Flushing

In spite of having digested considerable amounts of crud, many power steering pumps survive morning sickness intact. Still, you'll need to remove contamination to preserve the new rack. Here's how to flush most of the junk out of the pump and lines.

Disconnect the return line to the fluid tank and let it drain into a small container through the return hose. This is the low-pressure side, usually secured with a hose clamp. Then block the hole. Vinyl vacuum caps work well.

Next, disconnect the pressure line from the rack and aim it into a bucket. Refill with fresh fluid and tap the starter—it may require pumping a quart or more to clean the line. Cap or plug any loose ends.

Now it's time to twist, wiggle and snake the old rack out of the vehicle (**Fig. 3**). Expel any minors from the garage, as they may find the language necessary to persuade the rack clear of the vehicle unacceptable. You may need to unbolt and slightly move some other components to get the rack out of its tunnel. Lift, twist and wiggle in the new rack and reconnect the fluid lines. It may be easier to get a wrench to swing on a fluid line attachment once you've unbolted the rack and moved it a bit. Also, reattaching the lines may be easier before the new rack is bolted in place.

Use a tape measure to check the overall length of the rack and tie rod assembly. Set the overall length of the new assembly to this same dimension by twisting the tie rod ends on their threads. Keep the rack centered and

(Fig. 3) Snake the old rack out of its mounting tunnel after disconnecting the steering shaft, the tie rod ends and the fluid hoses.

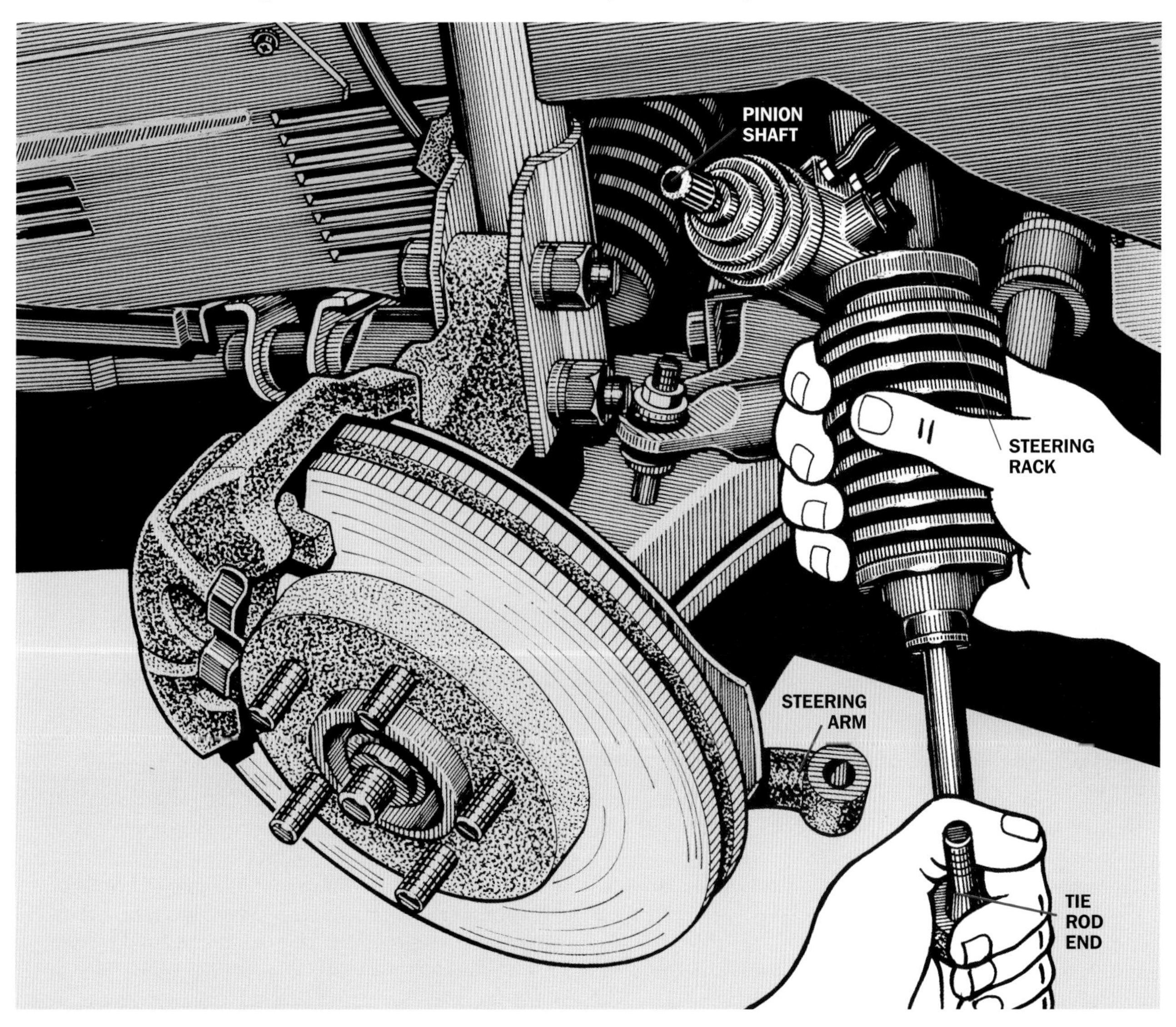

SEALING RINGS can wear grooves into the rack's housing, bypassing hydraulic fluid.

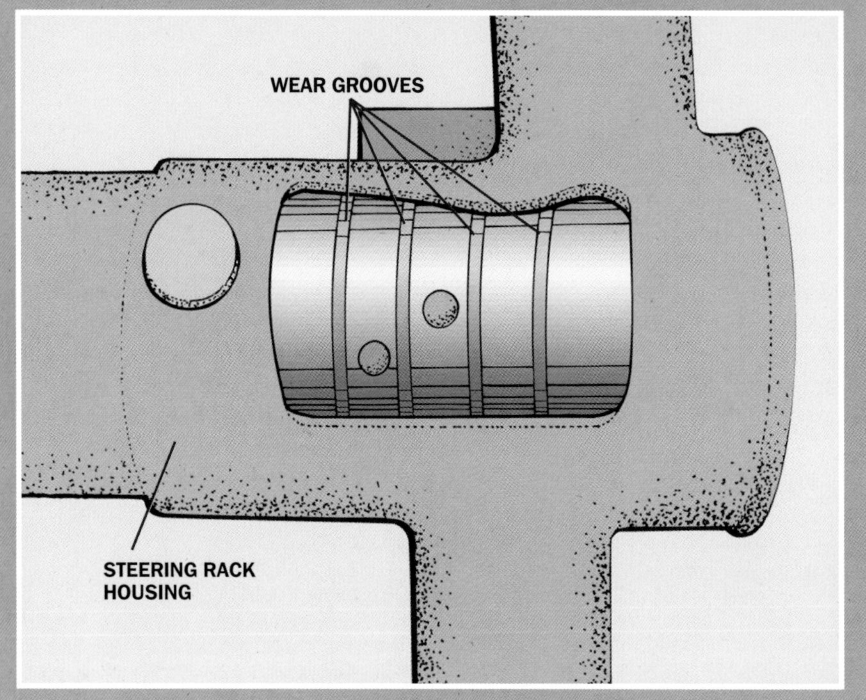

split the overlap difference between the left and right rod ends as you do this, or the steering wheel will be off-center when you're done. Connect all the lines, the steering shaft and the rack-attachment hardware. Use fresh cotter pins in the tie rod ends' castellated nuts. Reattach the front wheels.

Once the new rack's in, reconnect all hoses except the reservoir return line. Point it into a bucket, then refill. Start the car, and run fluid through until it looks clean. Reattach the pressure line. Note: You may be able to install an aftermarket inline filter so any crud you miss won't harm the new rack.

Have an alignment shop reset the toe-in adjustment or the car may handle strangely and wear out its tires rapidly.

The Fluid Situation

The last step is bleeding out all of the trapped air. While the car's still elevated on stands, fill the reservoir, idle the engine and steer side to side, from lock to lock, 10 to 12 times. Be careful to avoid banging into the stops. Tan or foamy fluid contains air. Shut down, let it sit 15 minutes, then top off and start again. Repeat until the fluid looks normal.

Don't forget to properly torque the lug nuts on the front wheels after you've taken the vehicle off the jackstands. And it wouldn't be a bad idea to change the power steering fluid in a few hundred miles to get out any crud you've missed.

HOW IT WORKS

Power Rack-and-Pinion Steering

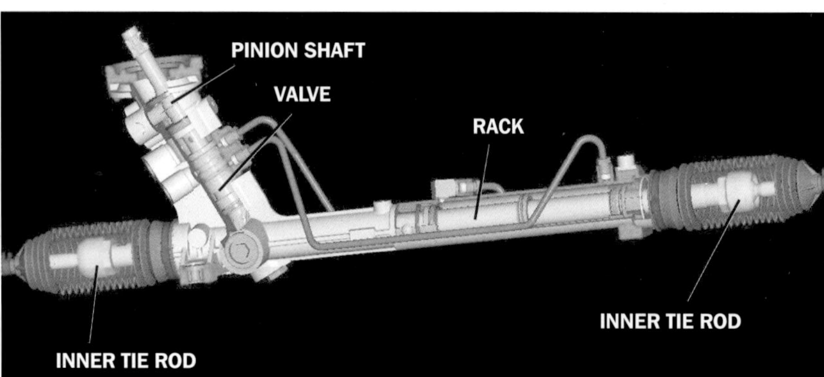

As you turn the steering wheel, a spool valve on the pinion shaft moves relative to ports in the housing. The ports connect to chambers on either side of a piston on the rack shaft. Steer left and the port connected to the chamber on the right side of the piston opens while the other port closes. This lets fluid pressurize the right side of the piston, helping push the rack shaft to the left and pointing the wheels in that direction. (This description assumes the rack assembly is ahead of the axle. If it were behind it, moving the shaft right would point the wheels left.)

Wear allows fluid to bypass the piston, wasting steering assist. "Morning sickness" results from light wear that closes up as heat expands the parts. As wear worsens, expansion will no longer take up the slack.

Intense competition has driven remanufactured rack prices down. A "reman" unit may be your best bet, since many originals wore out because their shafts bore directly on the inside of their aluminum housings. In remanufacturing, the housings are bored, then hardened-steel inserts are installed in areas subject to wear. You may be able to get a recently installed new or reman rack at a salvage yard.

EASY

Servicing Brake Discs

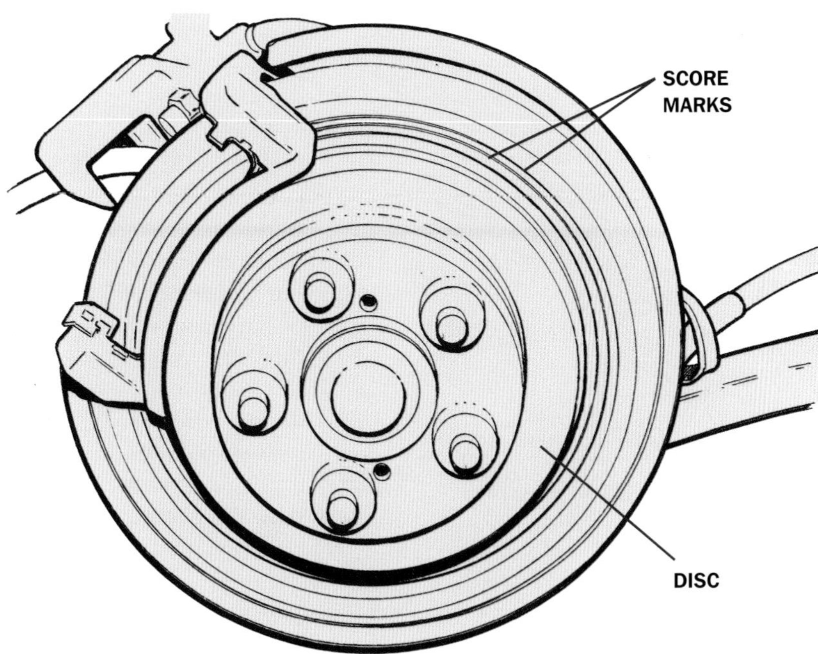

(Fig. 1) Surface grooves deep enough to catch your fingernail will need to be removed by machining the brake on a lathe.

You're up to highway speed and suddenly a car cuts across your lane to make an exit. You manage to slow enough to avoid a nasty accident, but the brakes definitely don't feel right. The brake pedal has had this kind of vibration for a couple of weeks, but only at low speeds. Now it feels like you're stepping on a running chain saw, and the front wheels don't want to go where you want them to.

Forget The Guesswork

Pull the wheels for a closeup look. With the wheels off, you can inspect the rotor-lining contact surfaces. First look for a crack that goes all the way through a vented rotor—or at least through one of its two surfaces. A cracked rotor causes severe pulsation, and the only cure is replacement.

Rust at the rotor edges is meaningless, as are moderate scores in the disc's surface, or a few off-color spots on the shiny areas swept by the pads. Be sure to check both sides of the rotor, however. When you pull the wheels, there should be an accessible area on the back side (even if there's a dust shield) where you can inspect the surface. Severe rusting of the lining contact surfaces is a problem. So are thick, deep scores, uneven thickness and lateral runout (warping).

If the rotors have never been resurfaced, it is theoretically possible to have them machined to remove significant rust and deep scores (about .060 in. deep). However, many late-model rotors are not very thick to start with, and can't take more than a .030-in. resurfacing. Unless the rotor is at least .060 in. thicker than the minimum thickness stamped somewhere on the rotor, forget trying to save it. Buy new rotors. How can you test the depth of a score? If it's thick enough, insert the head of a dime into it. If the dime goes in beyond the top of the president's head, the score is too deep. If a score is too thin for the dime to slip in, it's harmless. Another test is to run your fingernail across the surface radially. If your nail catches, the rotor needs to be resurfaced **(Fig. 1)**. If not, you're probably okay, provided there's enough thickness left on a true-running rotor.

Uniform thickness is critical. Measure each rotor with an outside micrometer at a number of evenly spaced points around the lining contact surface. A variation of .005 in. or more is enough to cause the pulsation you feel.

Lateral runout is caused by a rotor that's uniform in thickness, but is wavy. Uneven thickness and excessive runout often go together. That is, the runout causes the uneven wear on the rotor. So if you catch it early, the rotor may pass a thickness check, but it still could have excessive lateral runout. The high heat (then rapid cooling) from hard braking is a primary cause of runout, but close behind is uneven tightening of wheel lug nuts. Dirt or rust buildup between the rotor and hub also can produce runout **(Fig. 2)**.

To check for excessive runout/warping, you need a dial indicator, which you can rent from many auto parts stores. When you pull the wheels, the rotors might be loose on the studs, so refit the lug nuts and tighten them securely. Install the dial indicator, and mount it on the suspension. Then, aim the indicator plunger at the middle of the lining contact surface, at as close to a 90° angle as possible. Set the plunger so it presses lightly against the rotor-lining contact surface, then zero out the dial. Slowly rotate the rotor and watch the dial. If it exceeds .005 in., the rotor is not running true **(Fig. 3)**.

(Fig. 2) Whenever assembling brakes, remove any dirt or rust that might get between the brake and the hub to reduce lateral runout.

You may not have to replace or resurface the rotor. With the rotor off, you can look for and remove dirt or rust buildup. If that's not the problem, you can try re-indexing the rotor. That is, just remove it, rotate it one or two stud holes, install and tighten the lug nuts and recheck. Although the typical rotor just slides off the studs with the wheel removed (some advance spraying with penetrating solvent may be necessary), the caliper has to come off first.

First, remove the bolts that hold the caliper itself to its anchor frame or to the suspension. Then pry the caliper up, lift it off the frame and wire it to the suspension. This will relieve any strain on the brake hose. Many vehicles have "flip up" calipers. Remove one lower retaining bolt, flip up the caliper and slide it off a stud. If the brake shoes stay in the anchor frame, perhaps held by a retaining clip, remove those next.

Finally, unbolt the anchor frame, lift it out and the rotor should slide off. But first, if the rotor is not necessarily being replaced, make alignment marks on the hub section and the stud, so you can reinstall it in the same location. If it binds on the hub, that's normal rust buildup. Just spray the studs and holes and hub/rotor joints with penetrating solvent, rock the rotor with a pulling motion and it should walk off. Clean

HOW IT WORKS

Brake Rotor

The brake rotor, the disc in disc brakes, mounts on the hub with the wheel, and both rotor and hub are held by the same studs and lug nuts. When you apply the brakes, the hydraulic device called the caliper clamps the brake shoes (also called pads) against the rotor, and the friction material on the shoes stops the spinning of the rotor (and therefore the wheel). The friction material on the shoes causes the energy of wheel and rotor motion to be converted to heat, and the rotor temperature can soar to over 1000°F in a hard stop. That heat has to be dissipated very quickly so that the rotor can cool down for the next stop. Because front brakes do about 75 percent of the work in a front-drive car (over 50 percent in a rear-drive), the front rotors have to be able to dissipate a lot more heat than the rear brakes, drum or disc. As a result, the front rotors on virtually all cars today have two contact layers separated by a vent area, which resembles a paddle fan, to scoop up air. This design not only gives each brake shoe a separate disc, but the airflow through the center provides greater cooling. Some high-performance cars also have vented rear discs.

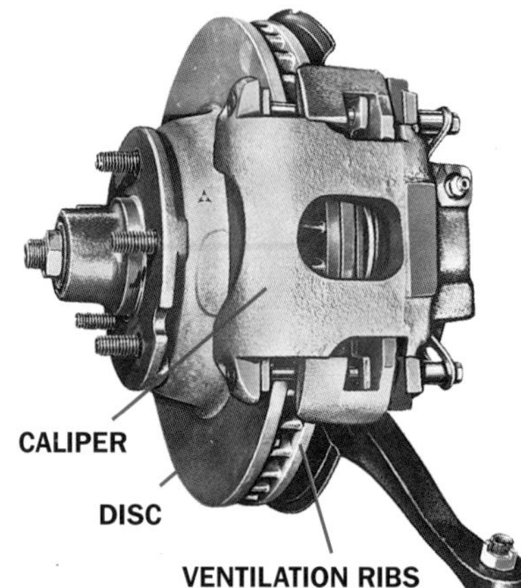

A typical vented disc brake assembly. The hole in the caliper is for inspecting pads.

(Fig. 3) A dial indicator will show you the total lateral runout—.005 in. is too much.

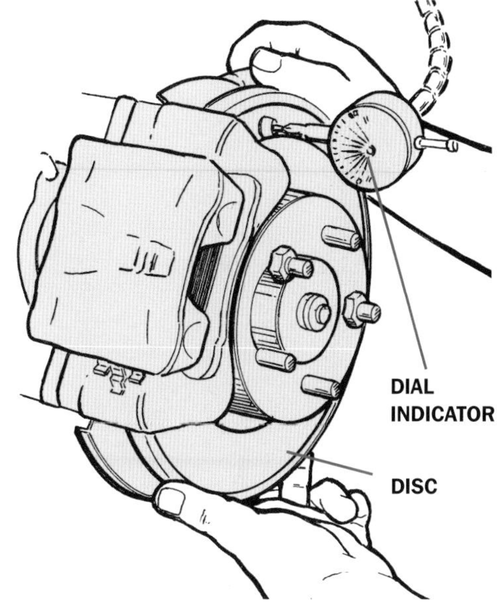

rust off the hub with ultrafine sandpaper or a wire brush. Clean the mating face of the rotor as well.

If you're working on rear discs, they're likely to have a mechanical actuator for a parking-brake function or a drum-type parking brake built into the hub. With the drum type, the rotor itself will have a deep "hat" section to fit the hub, and the inside of that hat is the drum for the parking brake. Normally, with the parking brake off, the rotor just slides off, but if the parking brake has a self-adjusting linkage, it's possible that it's overadjusted and the drum shoe linings are locked against the inside of the hat. In that case, you can reach in from the back through an access hole (in the hub and also possibly through a dust shield), and back off the adjuster (**Fig. 4**). With the type that uses an actuator on the disc brake lining pads, you may be able to just lift the caliper off. At worst, you'll first have to disconnect the brake cable from the actuator on the caliper.

Installation

If you need a new rotor, install it straight out of the box. Some of the lightweight rotors, made of a stamped steel hub with a cast-iron braking surface, could test as warped unless you check them with all lug nuts installed and tightened.

Note: There are some rotors that are a real bear to remove, so if the vehicle manufacturer indicates special tools or if a press is necessary, a rotor can be machined on the vehicle. You're best off leaving this to a properly equipped pro.

Both Sides, Please

Normally, what happens to one wheel happens to the other. If one rotor is gone and the other is marginal for machining, replace both. However, if one is particularly bad, perhaps the vehicle has been pulling, leaving the other side pristine. There may be uneven brake application, perhaps from a hydraulic or mechanical problem at the wheel. Trace the cause in addition to correcting the rotor problem.

Clean lug nuts and stud threads with a mild solvent and wipe dry. Don't lubricate them if the torque specifications are based on clean, dry threads. But a thin film of anti-seize compound normally is beneficial. One of the most important tools you can use is a torque wrench. When you're re-indexing a rotor, be sure to reinstall the lug nuts and torque them to specifications in at least three stages. Use a crisscross pattern for each stage until all are tight.

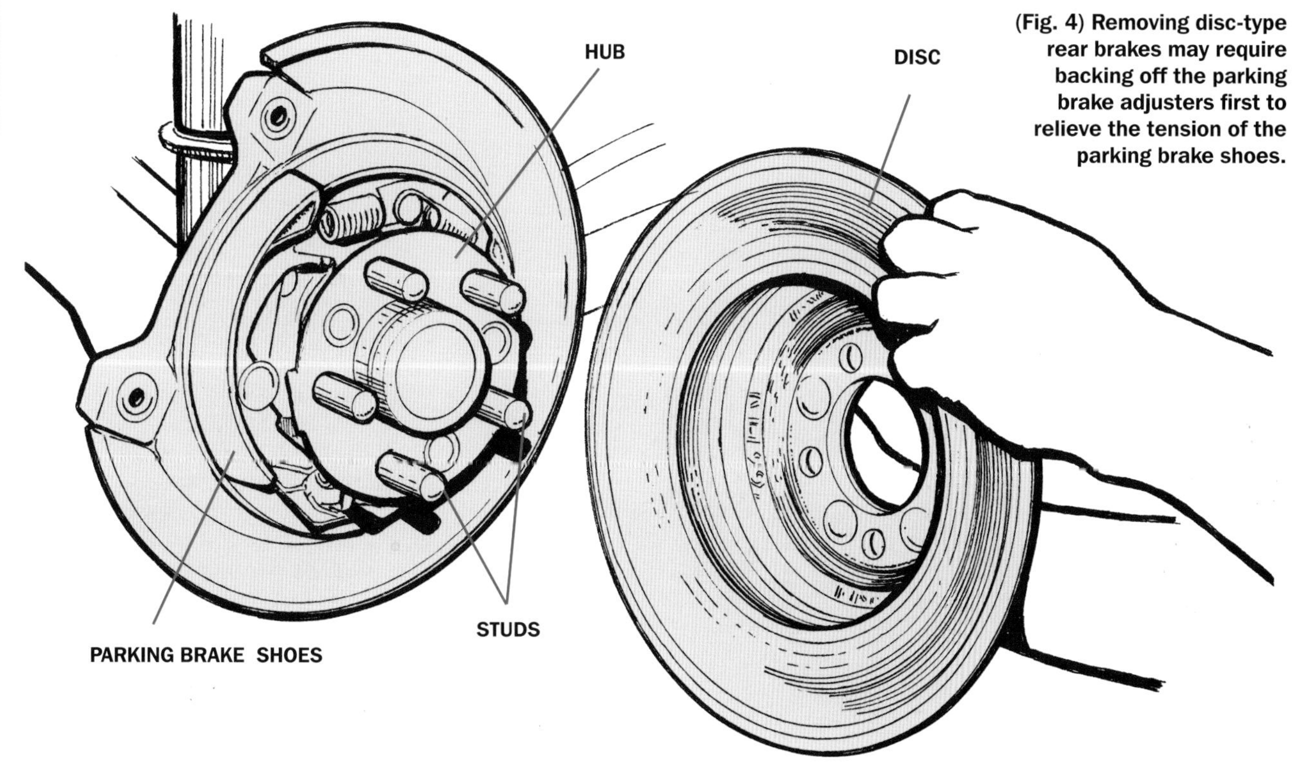

(Fig. 4) Removing disc-type rear brakes may require backing off the parking brake adjusters first to relieve the tension of the parking brake shoes.

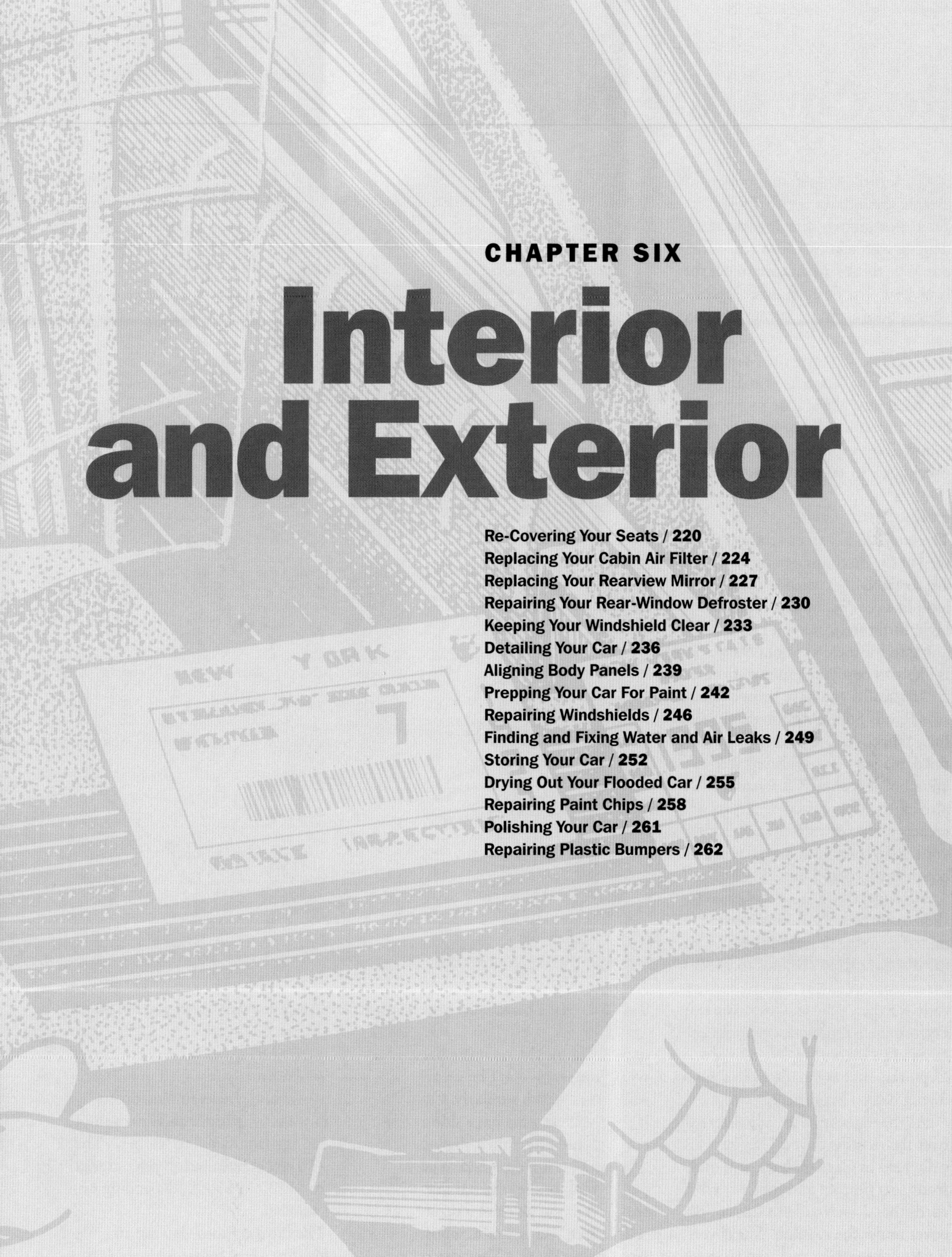

CHAPTER SIX

Interior and Exterior

Re-Covering Your Seats

It's Saturday night, and you're taking the in-laws out to dinner. Unfortunately, the dog has been digging—unbeknownst to you—for bones he thinks are hidden under the back seat. The ensuing divot leaves your spouse's mother sitting at a considerable angle all the way to Denny's.

Morning finds you duct-taping large and small chunks of foam rubber back into place. Late morning finds you calling upholstery shops, followed by a quick balancing of the checkbook to see if you can afford it.

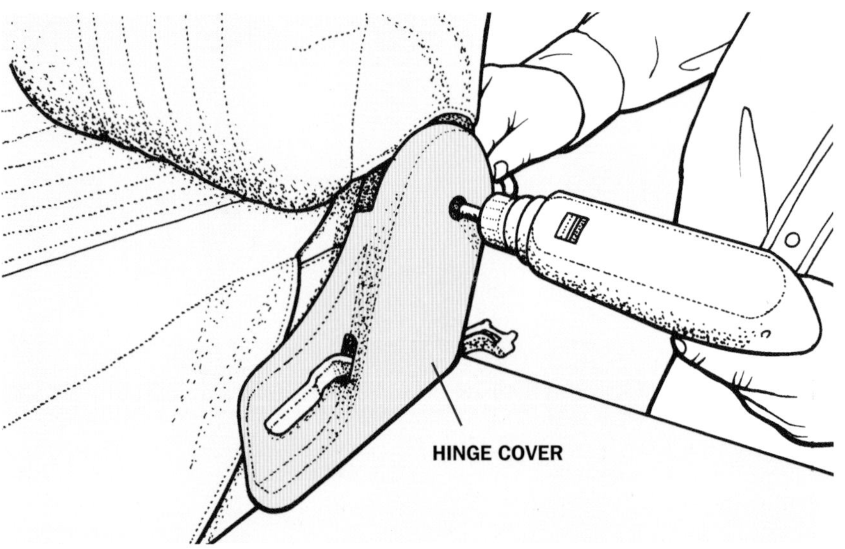

(Fig. 1) Start removing the front-seat top by removing the cover over the hinge.

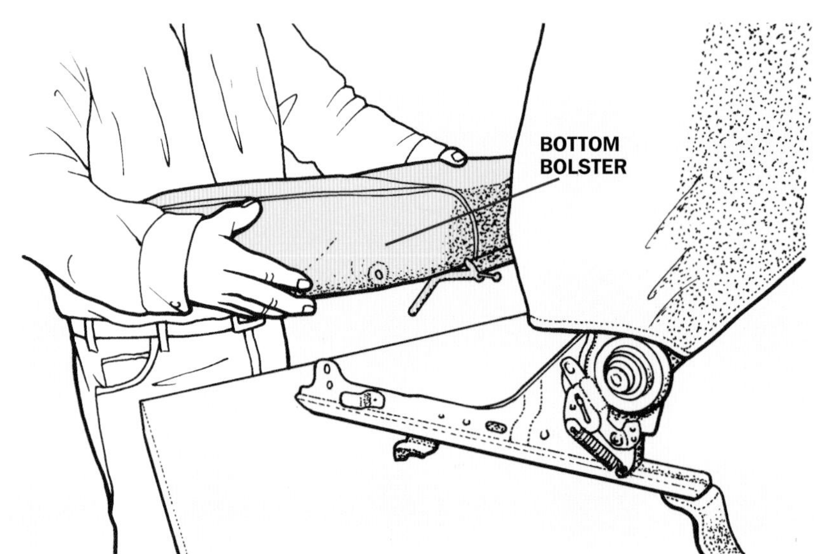

(Fig. 2) Once it's completely disconnected, pull the bottom bolster free of the frame.

Rolling Your Own

The one-size-fits-all covers you've seen at the discount department stores are certainly inexpensive, but they look like covers more suitable for lawn furniture. And you know that going to the local car upholstery shop is likely to cost you a minor fortune.

"Basically, you have three choices," says Randy Smith of Brougham Seats Inc., "slipcovers, re-covers or getting the damaged seat panels replaced at an upholstery shop." A fourth choice also exists: Get replacement seats of an acceptable cover from a wrecking yard. If all seats have been damaged, consider this possibility.

Slipcovers, which are designed to slide over the car's original seating material, range in price from $25 for the discount store cheapos to $400 for custom-fit covers designed specifically for each vehicle. One company, Performance Products, even sells slipcovers for Toyota trucks and Ford Explorers that are made from scuba-diving wet-suit neoprene.

As the name implies, slipcovers slip over the existing cover. They're typically held in place on back-seat and front-seat bottom cushions with flex cords that attach to both sides of the cover under the cushion. The covers for front-seat back cushions snap on or are held by Velcro at the bottom where the seams can't be seen. Headrest covers attach similarly. Caution: If your vehicle seats have side airbags, covers could affect their deployment.

Re-covers are designed to completely replace the original factory seat coverings. "It's not a do-it-yourself project," says Smith, whose company makes them. "They can only be purchased by upholstery shops, and they're normally installed in fairly new cars and trucks for customers who want to upgrade their car's interior, say from vinyl to leather." The cost? Typical installation prices range from $1500 to $3000, depending on the vehicle.

The third option—having an upholstery shop repair a vinyl, cloth

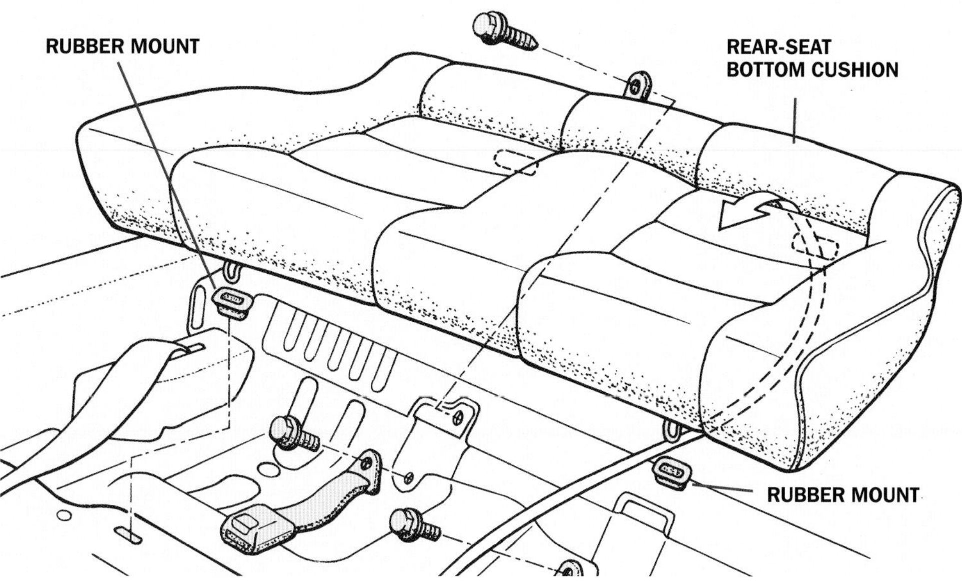

(Fig. 3) Rear-seat bottom cushions usually just clip in at the front.

or leather panel on a seat—might actually yield the most attractive result and may even be the least expensive option, if the damage or tearing is limited to a single panel on a bottom seat cushion or seatback. You can save additional money by taking the seat out yourself, removing the hard-plastic skirts, splitting the back from the bottom cushion and delivering the damaged cushions to the shop for repair.

Of course, the drawback is that your car will be out of commission for a while if the work needs to be done to the driver's seat.

If you're planning to go this route, check with the upholstery shop first so it can order matching material ahead of time, then make an appointment to have the work done to reduce your vehicle's downtime.

Seat Removal and Disassembly

Repairing an upholstery panel is not easily tackled at home, but you can remove and disassemble the seats.

And while you don't necessarily have to remove the front seats to install the slipcovers, the finished job will look better and smoother if you take them out and then separate the cushions before putting on the covers.

If you're doing all the seats, remove the front seats first so you'll have room to maneuver the rear-seat cushions from the car. Doing it this way is especially critical on 2-door vehicles.

Most front seats are bolted to the floor pan at all four corners. Begin by removing any plastic covers **(Fig. 1)** and then remove the bolts (**Fig. 2**). On power seats, disconnect the wires to the seat motor before lifting out the seats. Caution: If your vehicle has side airbags in the seats, refer to a factory service manual for instructions on how to disable them safely, as well as how to reconnect the system.

Typically, rear-seat bottom cushions must be removed before the back cushion can be removed.

Most bottom cushions are "hooked" to the floor pan in front (**Fig. 3**). Firmly pushing the seat cushion rearward and then lifting upward disengages the cushion from the hooks so the cushion can be lifted out.

The back cushion is usually bolted to the rear bulkhead near the bottom of the cushion, while the top of the back hooks to the top of the bulkhead. Remove the bolts and lift upward to remove the rear cushion.

With the seats missing, you'll want to pick up loose change, petrified food and other materials. Now is also a good time to give the carpet a thorough vacuuming and even a shampooing if it's gotten really disgusting.

To disassemble the front seat, remove the headrest by sliding it from the seatback. You'll probably unbolt the seat top at the hinge pin. First, remove any hard-plastic skirting. If the seat has a reclining lever near the bottom cushion, you'll also have to disconnect the reclining mechanism from the seatback (**Fig. 4**). After that, unbolt and separate the two cushions.

Installing Slipcovers

If the foam cushions are damaged, this is the time to patch or replace them. If there are chunks missing, you can simply carve matching pieces

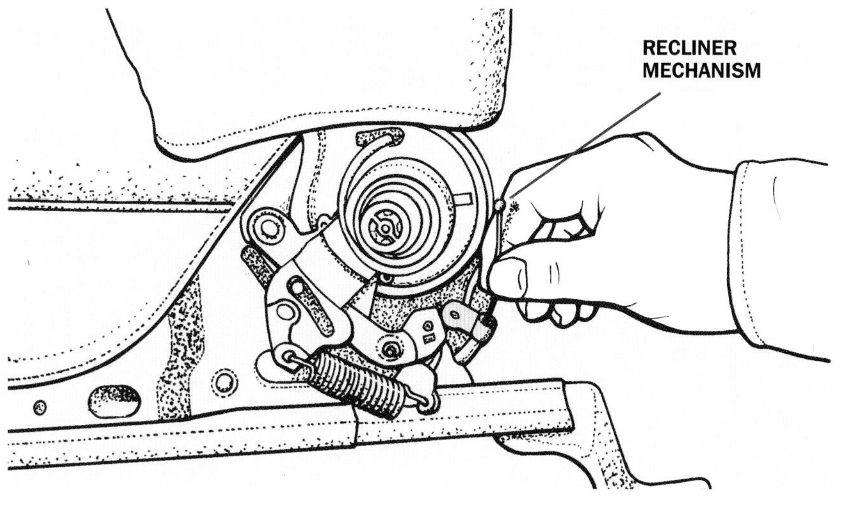

(Fig. 4) Disconnect the seatback recliner mechanism from the seat carefully.

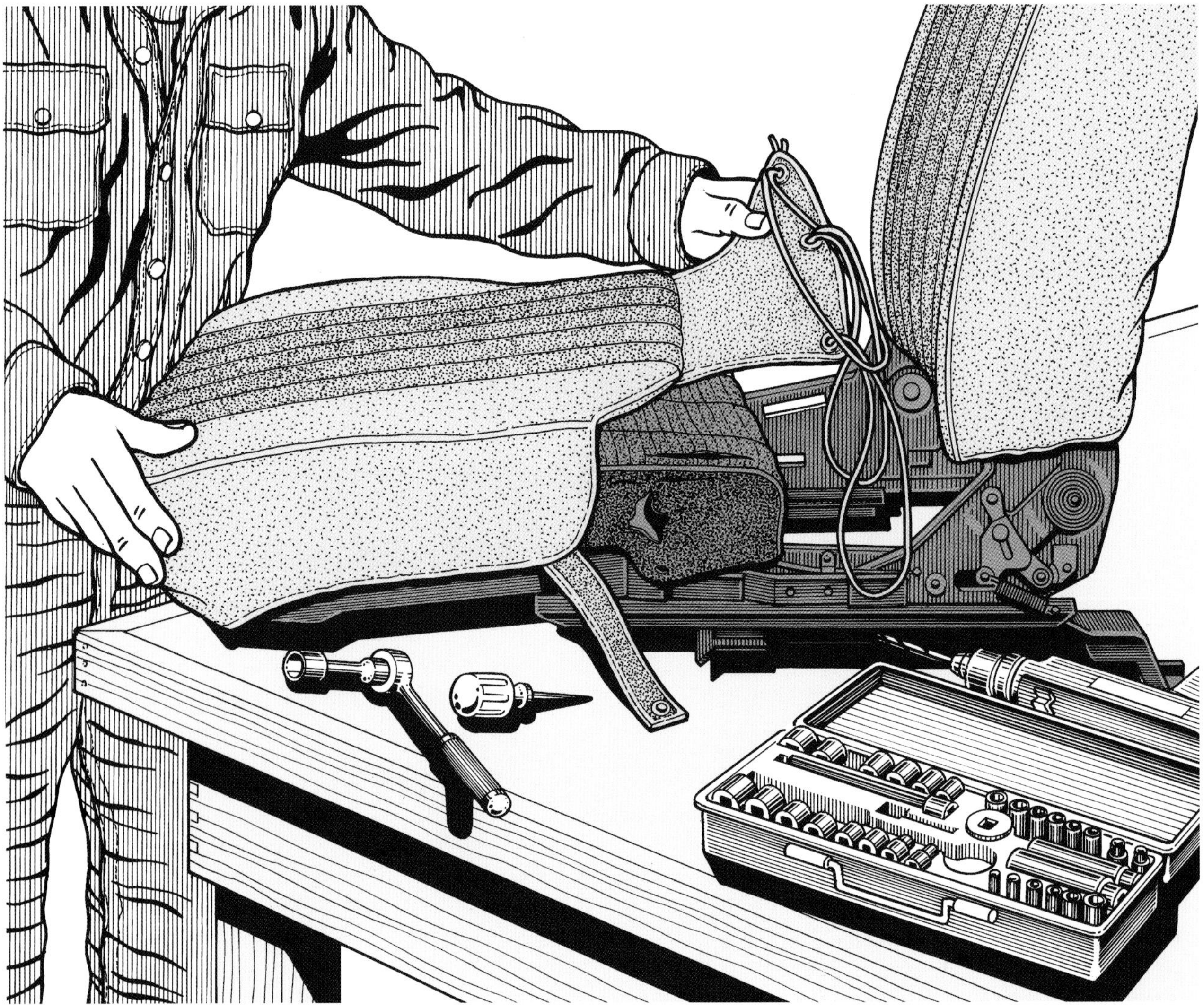

(Fig. 5) After you've removed the front seats from the vehicle, the new seat covers can be tugged over the seat bottoms.

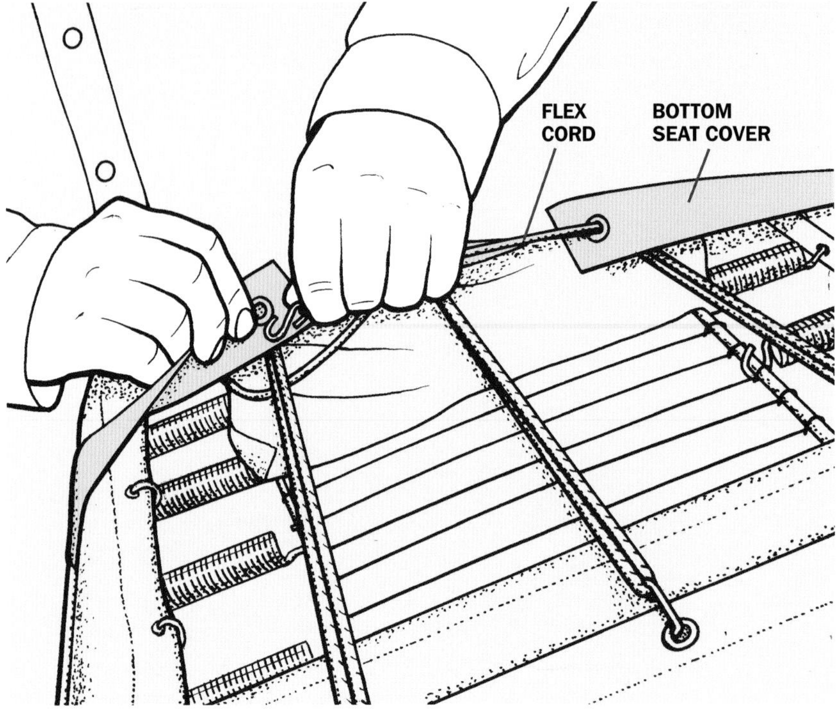

from upholstery foam to fit, gluing them to the existing foam in the cushion with contact cement.

Because durable materials are thicker and a tight fit makes for a better look, the more expensive the slipcovers, the harder they are to install.

Begin by sliding the cover onto the bottom cushion first (**Fig. 5**). You may need an assistant with strong fingers to help you pull on the cover and get it aligned on the seat. Once the cover is in place, move to the underside of the cushion where you can draw the flex cords to the other side. Attach

(Fig. 6) After the cover is on, add the elastic cords and connect the S-hooks.

them to the eyelets in the cover with the S-hooks that are provided with the cover (**Fig. 6**). To ensure that the flex cords stay in place, crimp the S-hooks closed with pliers (**Fig. 7**).

Next, slide the slipcover for the back cushion into place and snap or Velcro the bottom.

Install the headrest covers and any fold-down armrest covers. Before reassembling the seat's back and bottom cushions, make sure the slipcovers are properly fitted with no gaps or loose corners. If there are any, readjust the covers on the cushions until the gaps disappear.

After the seat cushions are reassembled, reattach the recliner mechanism and reinstall the plastic skirt.

The rear-seat slipcovers for both the bottom and back cushions install with flex cords in a manner similar to the front-seat bottom cushion. After the cords are in place, crimp the S-hooks with pliers and reinstall the cushions in the car.

Another suggestion is to take this opportunity to Scotchgard the new fabric while the seats are still out. This water- and dirt-proofing treatment is available at your local discount store in the automotive department, or at the auto parts store. It's a simple aerosol can, and you can avoid cleaning up overspray if you use it outside the car.

SUPPLIERS

- The Driver's Seat, 1400 Glades Road, Boca Raton, FL 33431; (561) 368-7966.
- JC Whitney, 1 JC Whitney Way, LaSalle, IL 61301; (800) 469-3894.
- Performance Products (Ford Explorer, Toyota 4x4s, Porsche), 8000 Haskell Ave., Van Nuys, CA 91406; (800) 553-2840.

Reinstalling Seats

When reinstalling the rear seats, make sure the lap and shoulder belts are properly routed through their seat openings. Also, make sure any hooks and fasteners are firmly engaged (**Fig. 8**).

When reinstalling the front seat, be sure to torque the mounting bolts to the proper specifications. Properly route the seatbelts and then make sure that both the sliding track and reclining mechanisms work properly.

On electric seats, reconnect the motor wires and then run the seat through its full range of adjustments to ensure the connections are correct.

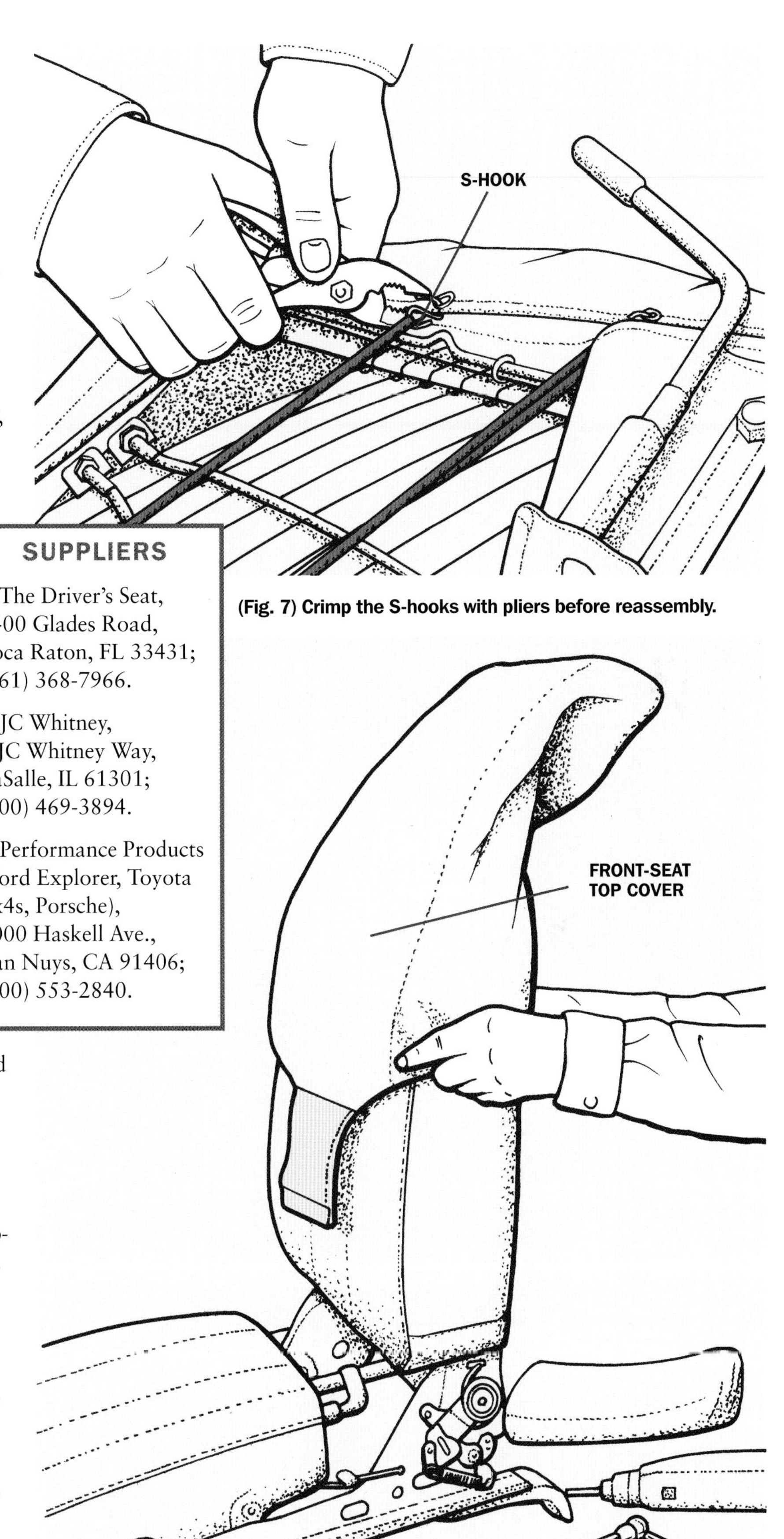

(Fig. 7) Crimp the S-hooks with pliers before reassembly.

(Fig. 8) Install the front-seat top cover in the same way you would pull on a big, heavy sock.

EASY

Replacing Your Cabin Air Filter

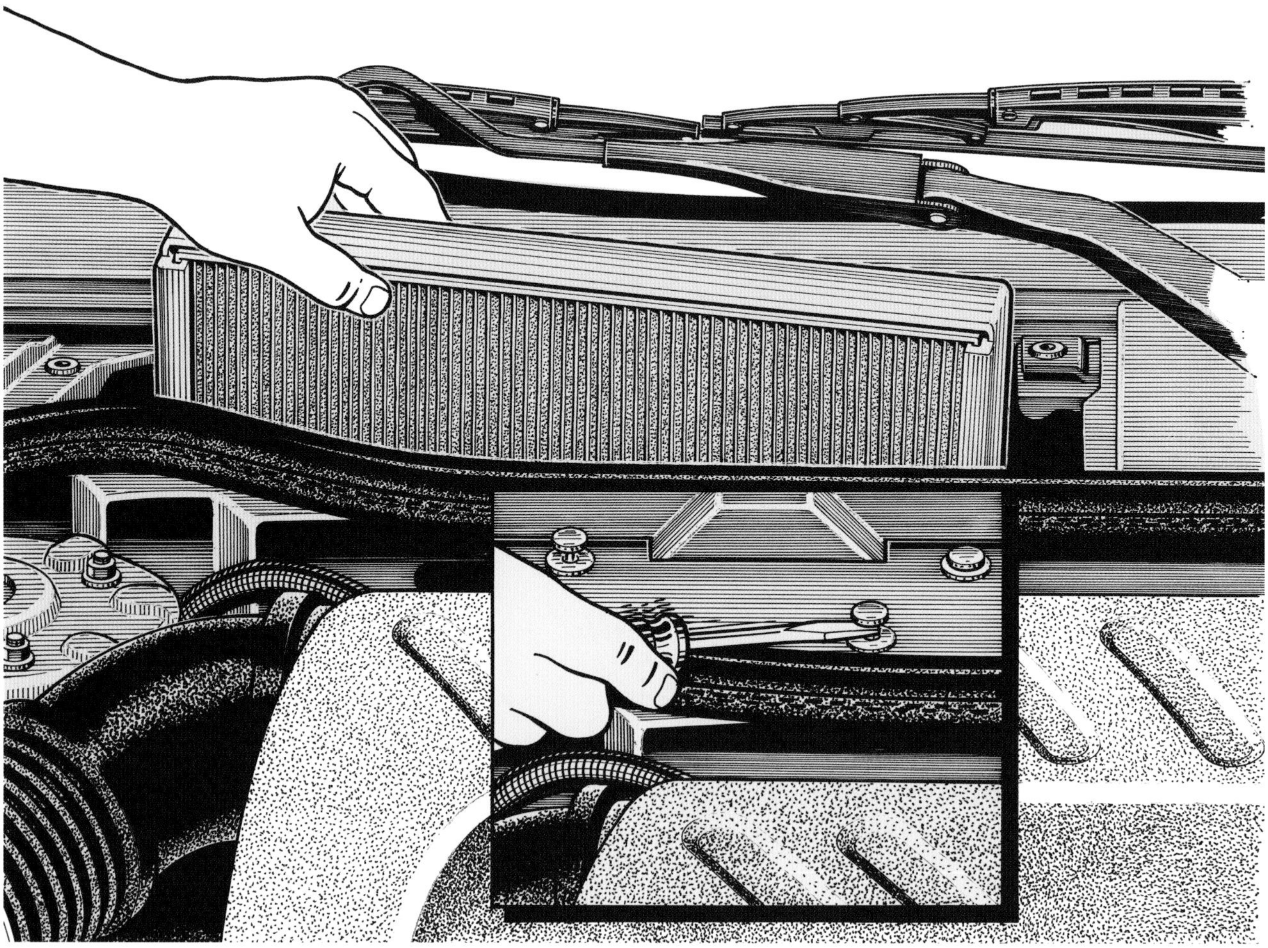

(Fig. 1) Underhood filter covers are often held in place with plastic button fasteners, which need to be pried up carefully.

It's Sunday and the big basketball game is this afternoon, but you can forget about getting tickets. So it's time to gather the crowd and drive to the sports bar. Minutes into the ride, the windshield is so foggy, you've got to hit the Defrost button. But why? The panel is set to outside air for heater operation, and there are no smokers in the car. You put your hand over the defroster outlets and there's hardly any airflow. When you turn the blower switch to high, the noise level goes up but the airflow is still weak.

Maybe you need to change the cabin air filter. If it's plugged, the passenger compartment might as well be a sealed cabin—and with a carload of friends the glass will fog in minutes. Filter life depends on the air quality in your area, but a year, or 12,000 to 15,000 miles, typically is the recommended replacement interval.

Cabin air filter? In the late 1980s and early 1990s, only some European luxury cars had them. It's more common on newer cars. In many premium cars, there may be two filters, even three. Sometimes they're parallel (side by side), sometimes they're in series (one after the other, with some space in between). Sometimes they're nowhere near each other.

Locating the Filters

A cabin air filter may be in the outside air intake, visible with the hood up and perhaps a cover lifted. Or it will be under the dash in one or both of two general locations:

- Above the blower in the back section of the outside air intake, a location well protected from moisture.
- Between the blower and the rest of the HVAC case.

If the owner's manual doesn't tell you the location, and you can't see it with the hood open, check behind the glovebox—perhaps you'll see an obviously removable (with a spring-tab or similar retainer) rectangular plastic cover. Next, look under the dash (on

(Fig. 2) If any debris has contaminated the filter plenum, vacuum it out and then wipe with a damp rag.

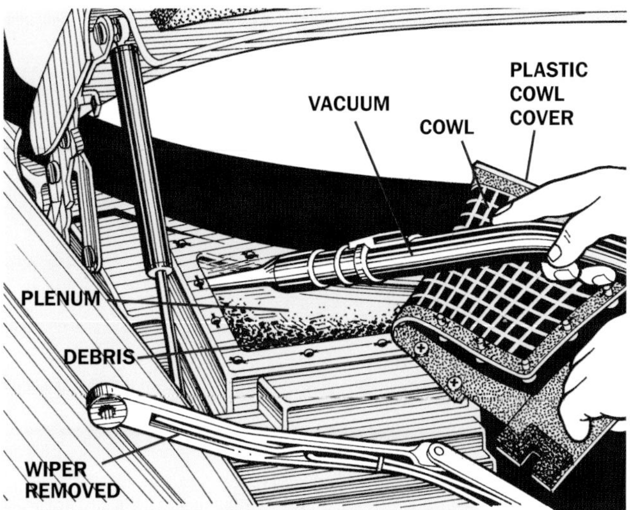

both the driver's and passenger's sides) for a removable plastic cover in the HVAC case. If you can remove its cover, look inside the HVAC case.

Still no answer? Buy the filters, something you have to do anyway. You've got two choices:

- Buy the factory filters at the dealership at full price. This way, you'll know for sure what they look like and get some idea about how they have to be installed. You'll also find out how many your vehicle has. The parts department should have a diagram to show you where the filters are located in the car.
- Buy aftermarket filters that come with step-by-step instructions from an auto parts store. The odds of the original equipment parts coming with instructions are extremely slim. Do all aftermarket filters have them? No, but if you're shopping at a parts store, you should be able to check in the boxes on the shelves. Also, these parts probably will cost less.

Replacing the Filters in the Air Intake

The filter in the outside air intake (even if there are other filters) takes care of most of the dust and pollen, so it's likely to plug first.

The typical procedure begins with removing the air intake screen, which is held by "Christmas tree" plastic fasteners. If the "tree" has a center pin, pry it up with a thin-blade screwdriver and then wiggle the tree out of the hole (**Fig. 1**). If the tree is a single-piece design, you'll have to pry it out. Most of the time, it will break and you'll have to replace it (blister packs of replacements are sold in most auto parts stores).

If there's a rain/snow deflector over the filter, remove it, then extract the element. The filter element may be held by a plastic tab, or it may slip into a retainer housing that you will reuse with the new element. Some dust may have gotten around or through the filter. Use a vacuum cleaner to clean the outside air intake duct (**Fig. 2**). Be careful when you reinstall the air intake screen, as well as any cover over the filter element. If the gasket surface around the screen does not seal, or if the cover (actually a shield, in most cases) is not reinstalled, rainwater can flow into the filter, saturating it.

In the Case, above the Blower

If the filter is in the case above the blower, most likely it is behind the glovebox. Removing the glovebox may be easy, but you may not have to remove it at all.

Many filters (such as on most Hondas and Toyotas) are just above the blower behind the glovebox, and you'll have to drop it for access. In the best of cases, you can flex the sides of the box so the pins clear the dash, then pivot the box down for clearance. In others, the entire glovebox assembly has to come out, which means removing a number of retaining screws, not all of which are visible.

Replacing Midcase Filters

The midcase filters may not always be easy, but remember, the setup was designed to allow filter replacement, so don't assume the worst.

There are pull tabs taped in place in GM sedans that have two or three filters in the same HVAC case located

SOME UNDER-DASH FILTERS can be replaced without any tools by simply opening a small access door.

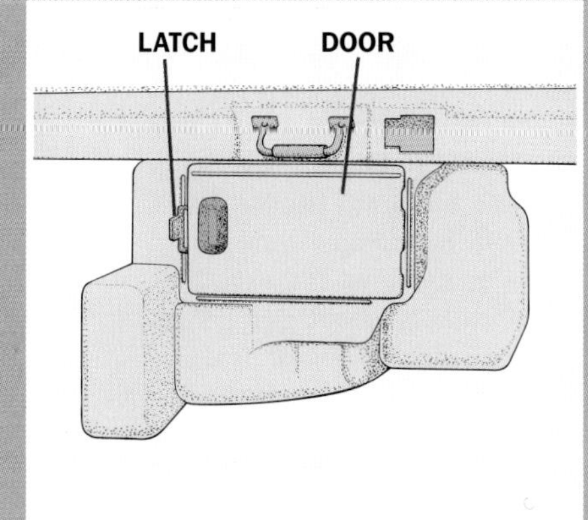

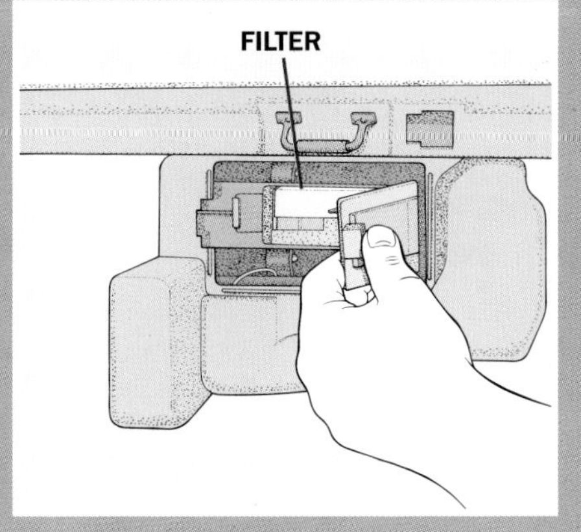

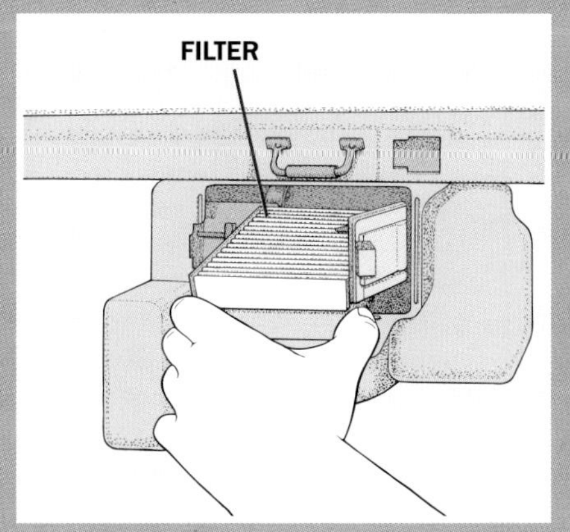

above the gas pedal. Pull a tape to release the tab, then pull the tab to withdraw the filter. Ditto for the others.

All filters need perimeter sealing, so air flows only through the filter element. With side-by-side filters, the sealing may be a simple foam rubber strip. Or there may be interlocking guides. On many cars the filter will come straight down and hit the floor without clearing the HVAC case. Nothing's wrong. Most of these filters are flexible, and you have to bend them to get them out and the new ones in.

INTERIOR-MOUNTED FILTERS may be stacked inside the plenum and housed in a plastic tray.

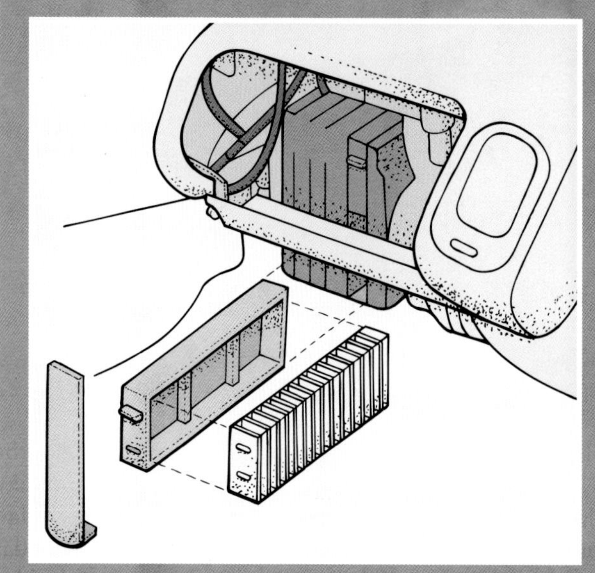

How to Buy

Even if the filter location is accessible, the toughest job may be getting the right replacement filter. One of the most common complaints among professionals is that the aftermarket catalogs haven't kept up with the year-to-year changes, particularly with filters that fit under the dash where the space provided may have changed.

If a vehicle has more than one filter, you may not find both in the same box, especially if they are in different locations. And they may have totally different part numbers. This is particularly true if one filter is in the air intake and others are in the HVAC case. The one in the air intake is more likely to be a simple particulate filter, one that just traps small particles. The one under the dash is more likely to have a charcoal layer for odor control.

No matter what the original equipment element is, the aftermarket one is more likely to be a particulate filter, rather than the more sophisticated type with a charcoal layer. Should you get the charcoal filter, which may cost a lot more? If you're in a densely populated area with slow-moving traffic, or your carpool partner fancies Mexican food, the extra cost is worth it.

If you're not facing an odor problem, you may save money with a low-cost particulate-only replacement for an original-equipment filter with a charcoal layer. An aftermarket particulate element does filter finely enough to remove pollen as well as dust particles, so if pollen and dust are your major concerns, save your money.

HOW IT WORKS

Cabin Filter

The cabin filter is a type of air filter that in some respects—such as pleating to provide a lot of surface area in a small package—may resemble an engine air filter. However, it usually is made of different materials, the main one being a charcoal layer in many elements. Like some engine air filters, the dust and pollen filtering element is electrostatically charged, which means it's made with fiber particles that have been given either a positive or negative static electrical charge. Airborne particles are negatively or positively charged, so they are attracted to the opposite-charge fibers.

In addition, the filter performs "mechanical filtration." This means that fiber material with pores of a specific size will trap particles larger than the size of the pores. The charcoal filtration layer removes odors.

The charcoal is "activated," which means it is treated with chemicals and heat to give it specific odor-control properties. Each manufacturer has its own recipe, based on tests with individuals who have "sensitive noses," including people who work as perfume testers. Charcoal traps odor-causing gases by adsorption (not absorption), holding them on the surface of the material. Because charcoal is porous, each pore is an exposed surface, so the filter has a very high capacity for trapping noxious gases.

Replacing Your Rearview Mirror

The traffic seems unusually light this morning. In fact, you haven't seen another car to the rear for 10 miles. Time to make a little time.

But then there's a strange noise following you. Sounds like a siren. Hmmm. No lights behind you, so where is that sound coming from?

It's coming from the police car that's riding your tail. You didn't see it because your glued-on rearview mirror isn't on the windshield. It's lying on the floor under the seat where your 4-year-old has hidden it after discovering he couldn't do chin-ups on it. Tell that one to the judge.

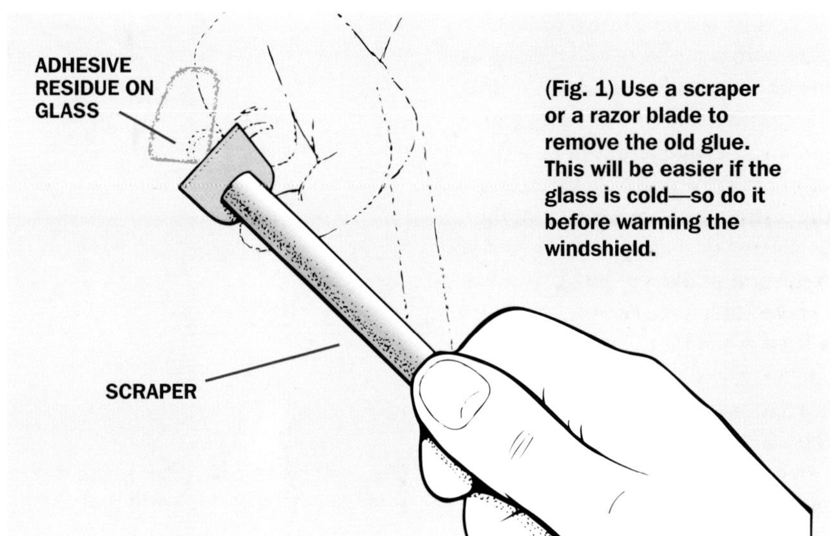

(Fig. 1) Use a scraper or a razor blade to remove the old glue. This will be easier if the glass is cold—so do it before warming the windshield.

HOW IT WORKS

The Antiglare Mirror

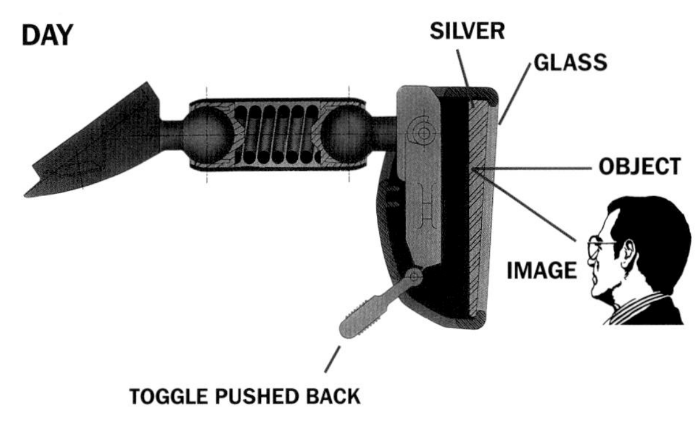

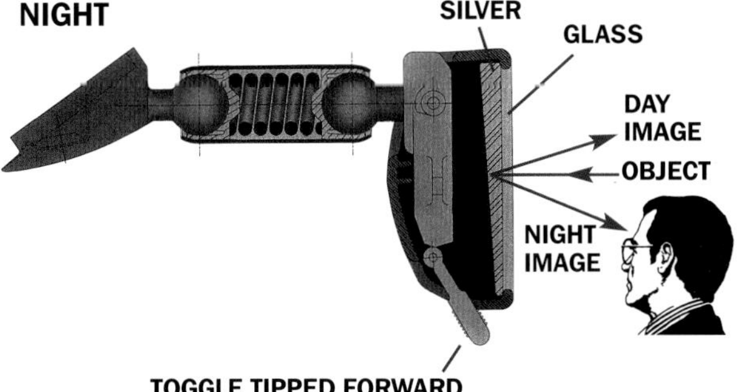

Most cars and trucks come with a manually dimmable day/night prismatic rearview mirror. You toggle a little lever from the day position to the night position. And the mirror glass is not flat, but rather beveled. The top edge is thicker than the bottom edge. Here's how the day/night function works.

In the day position, the image you see is reflected off the silvered surface on the back face of the mirror glass. The image is crisp and bright, because the silver provides an almost total reflection (80%) of the object.

In the night position, the toggle mechanism tilts the mirror glass upward slightly. Now, the bright day image is deflected off the silvered surface and up into the vehicle's headliner. And the front (plain glass) surface of the mirror takes over, providing a 5% reflective image. Everything appears very dark, but you can still monitor traffic behind you.

Many carmakers offer an automatically dimming electrochromic rearview mirror that provides an infinite number of brightness levels. These darken automatically according to ambient light conditions and the amount of headlight glare. Sensors feed input to electronics that determine how much voltage to apply to a special gel sandwiched between thin layers of reflective glass in the rear and clear glass up front. The more glare present, the more voltage is applied, and the darker the gel becomes.

Reattachment

Luckily, gluing your rearview mirror back on is one of the easiest jobs for a Saturday mechanic. What you need most is patience and a clean working environment. Warm weather helps, too, but it isn't mandatory.

Start by running down to your local auto parts store and picking up a rearview-mirror adhesive kit. It'll come with a vial of superstrong glue and a vial of accelerant to help the glue cure very quickly. There are usually instructions on the back of the cardboard packaging, too, should you need some guidance. You'll also need a razor-blade-type scraper, a small Allen wrench that fits the lockscrew on your mirror's baseplate, a grease pencil or some masking tape and, depending on your particular circumstances, a tape measure and a heat gun or hair dryer.

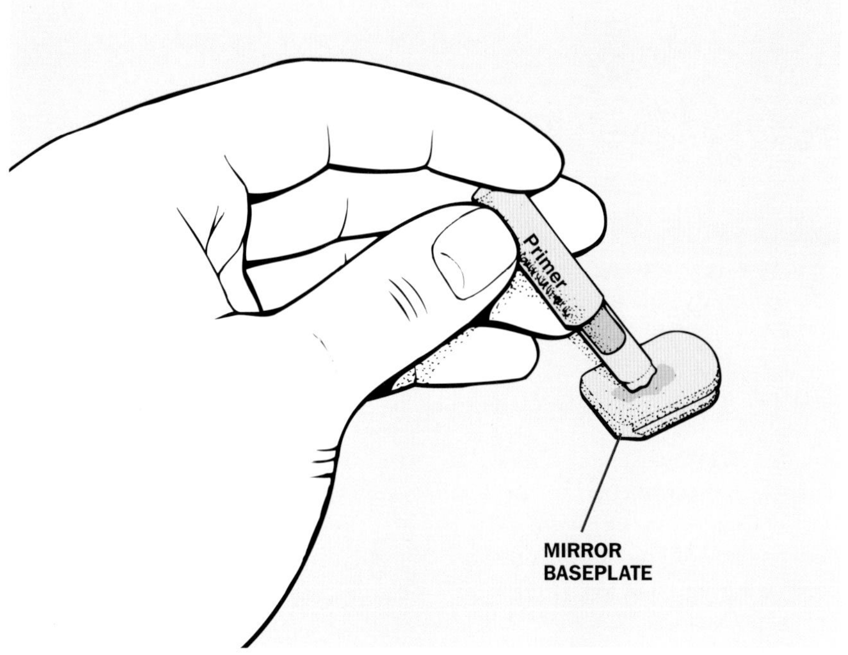

(Fig. 2) Applying accelerant to the mounting surface speeds the adhesive curing. Don't touch the surface with your fingers.

Ready?

Prepare to work outside with the windows open, as the adhesive kit will probably contain acrylic acid, methacrylic ester and trichloroethylene, which you don't want to breathe in large quantities.

Because the adhesive cures faster in warm ambient temperatures, plan on using the heat gun or hair dryer to warm the glass if you're forced to do this job on a cold day. But use common sense. Ice-cold glass will not appreciate being blasted by intense heat. You'll almost definitely crack the windshield this way. To avoid this, hold the heat gun or hair dryer about 12 to 18 in. away from the glass and waft the warm air back and forth to gradually increase the glass temperature. And make sure to scrape off the old glue before warming the glass or you'll create a gooey mess **(Fig. 1)**. An alternative is to park the car facing the sun for a few hours before beginning the job.

If the old mirror left behind an obvious amount of residue on the inside of the glass, you won't need the tape measure to locate the midpoint of the windshield. But if you, say, forgot to mark the spot before you cleaned the glass completely, simply measure halfway across the top of the window and about 3 to 4 in. down from the headliner, and that will be your new mounting point.

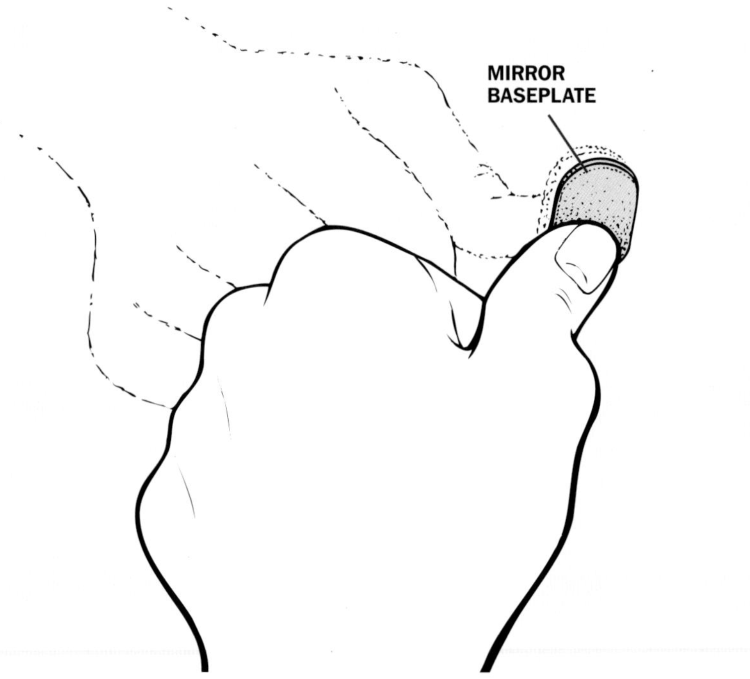

(Fig. 3) Press on the baseplate firmly for at least 2 minutes to allow the fresh adhesive to start to set up on the glass.

You can begin the remounting process by marking the outside of the window with a grease pencil over the area where the old glue is. Or you can cordon off the area on the inside with masking tape. (Some sort of mark is useful should you get interrupted after removing the old glue.) The latter is the neater way to work, but leave adequate room around the work area for scraping and cleaning. Now, go at the old glue with your scraper.

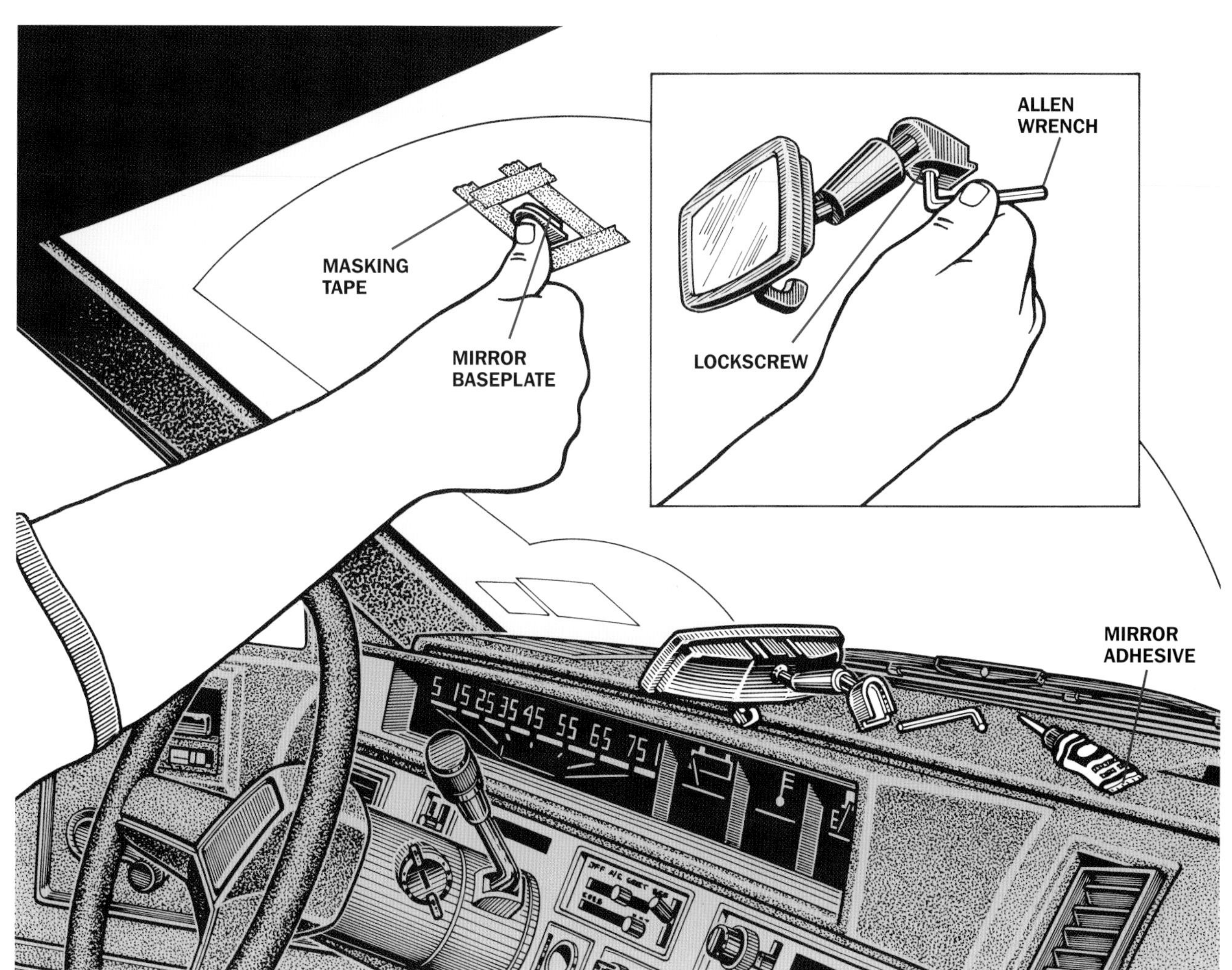

(Fig. 4) After gluing the baseplate onto the glass, mount the mirror and tighten its lockscrew with an Allen wrench.

Once you're down to smooth glass again, wipe the spot down with isopropyl alcohol to get it squeaky clean. Do the same thing on the back of the mirror baseplate so that you have clean metal to work with. Don't touch either surface once it's cleaned or the oil that comes off your fingers will contaminate it.

The Acceleration Phase

The accelerant (primer) vial will have a double wall of plastic. The inside wall is designed to crack open when you bend the tube. The outside wall simply flexes. This allows the accelerant to drench the felt tip of the vial without leaking out all over your hands. Apply the accelerant liberally to the mounting point on the glass. It needs 5 minutes to dry.

In the meantime, use your Allen wrench to undo the lockscrew and release the mirror from its baseplate. It's much easier to glue the baseplate onto the windshield first and install the mirror later. Working with the whole assembly is too awkward.

Once the baseplate is free, goop up its flat mounting surface with the accelerant and let it dry, as well (Fig. 2). Don't touch either of the treated areas as they're now ready to accept the adhesive, which will cure faster because of the accelerant.

Adhesive Time

Now you're ready to apply the adhesive. Neatly goop up the back of the baseplate and carefully press it onto the glass. Squoosh it around just a little bit to get good adhesion—and keep applying pressure. Don't let go for at least 2 minutes while the adhesive begins to set up (Fig. 3). Then let it dry for at least another 15 minutes. If it's really cold out, a little warm air from the heat gun or hair dryer should speed up the curing process. Remember, 15 minutes is a minimum. It's best to let the adhesive cure as long as it is convenient—even overnight—before reattaching the mirror to the baseplate and tightening the lockscrew (Fig. 4).

If you're a neatnick, trim the excess glue around the baseplate with a knife or one of the corners of your scraper blade. Then reattach the mirror and readjust it for a safe rearward view.

Oh. And don't pull on the mirror to see how tightly it's mounted. With Murphy's Law always in effect, you just might rip it off the window again. Just leave the mirror be—and keep your kid out of the front seat. The mirror will probably stay up there for the life of the car.

EASY

Repairing Your Rear-Window Defroster

It was a dark and stormy night. Snow has covered the entire car to a depth of several inches. It takes a few minutes to clear the snow, and by then the engine has warmed up enough to melt the frost clinging to the inside of the windshield, and has actually made inroads to the frost on the side windows. But the rear-window defroster clears only a narrow strip near the top and bottom of the window, leaving a wide strip of glass as translucent as a barrister's door, and absolutely no visibility to the rear.

A worse scenario: The rear-window defroster grid has packed it in completely, requiring you to either drive blind (bad idea), or resort to scraping the rear window clear with your trusty plastic scraper.

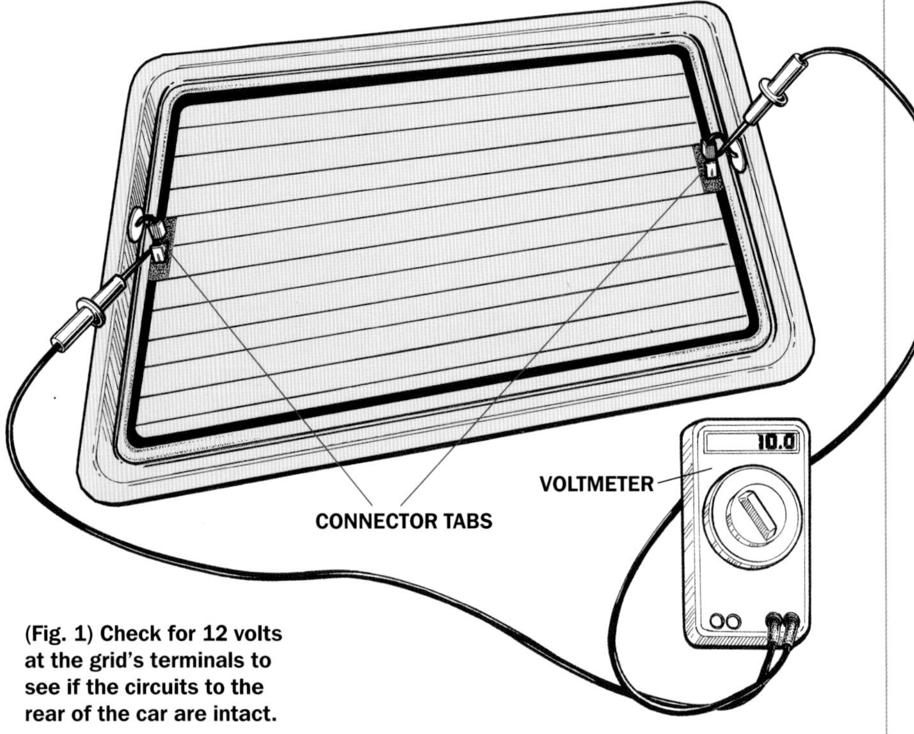

(Fig. 1) Check for 12 volts at the grid's terminals to see if the circuits to the rear of the car are intact.

Danger!

Let us make this perfectly clear: The resistance wires are silk-screened, essentially painted, onto the glass. They are very easy to scratch, and will not work properly if the scratch breaks the continuity along the wire. This means that it's possible for boxes, furniture or any other hard object one might place in a car to scratch the wire. Even a credit card can damage it. Don't cram stuff into the back, and don't let the load shift backward in your minivan so that it touches the glass. If your window has a defroster grid, the only thing that should ever touch the glass is a soft cloth dampened with window cleaner. If you must clean the rear glass, scrub gently, and in the direction of the grid, not across it.

You don't want to have to replace the glass to effect this repair. The compound-curve style of rear window is several hundred dollars, and a large hatchback's backlite on, say, a Camaro, can easily top a grand or more. Add the price of installation at the dealership or a glass shop—it's definitely not covered by insurance.

No Heat at All

Suppose your defroster grid doesn't work at all. First, check the obvious: Is the fuse okay? Defroster grids draw a lot of current (10 to 20 amps), and if the fuse is undersize, it won't last. If the fuse doesn't look blown, check with your voltmeter—with the key on and the defroster on, you should see 12 volts at both grid terminals (**Fig. 1**).

If the voltage is fine, the problem is somewhere in the wiring or at the grid. Check the connections from the wiring harness to the grid. It's easy for the terminals at the grid to become damaged. Generally, the tab that's attached to the glass breaks off, leaving you with a dangling wire and no way to reattach it. You have two repair options here: soldering and gluing.

If you know how to solder and have a high-capacity soldering iron or gun, solder the tab back on (**Fig. 2**). It may take a third hand to hold the tab against the grid while you solder it. There's usually a metal strip laid on the glass under the silk-screening. Clean the surfaces with alcohol and use 60-40 rosin-core solder. Work fast, because excess heat may crack the glass.

If you aren't confident about your soldering skills, or aren't ready to take a chance on cracking an expensive piece of glass, there's another way. The dealership and most auto parts stores can sell you a special electrically conductive epoxy to bond the tab back on (**Fig. 3**). If it's wintertime, you'll need to work in a heated garage, and have the vehicle inside long enough for it to warm up to at least 65° F. Again, clean the area with alcohol. Mask the glass with tape to keep from getting epoxy smeared on it. Mix up a sparing

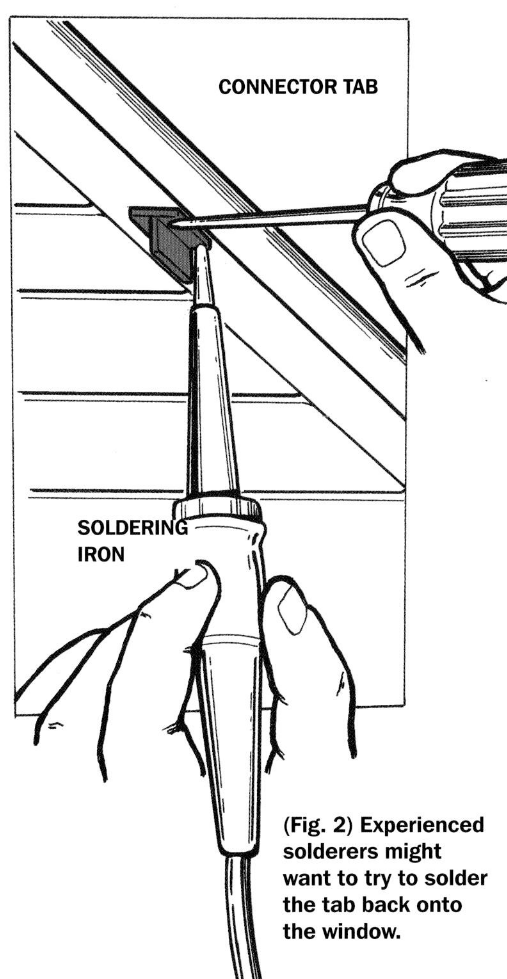

(Fig. 2) Experienced solderers might want to try to solder the tab back onto the window.

amount of epoxy and hardener. Put some epoxy on the tab, and use an ice pick to hold it in place for the 10 minutes or so it will take for the epoxy to harden. You can use a wooden stick or the end of your dampened finger to smear the epoxy within a minute or two of application to improve the cosmetics of the repair. Although the epoxy will set up rapidly, don't attempt to reattach the wiring until it's had 24 hours at 65° F or more to cure and achieve its full strength. The repair will never be as strong as the original wire, so you'll need to be particularly careful not to damage it in the future.

Deeper Problems

Fuse okay? Grid attached to the glass everywhere, but simply no defrosting action at all? Look for a bad switch, relay or timer. For this you'll need a schematic diagram, or considerable experience in troubleshooting wiring problems. Start at the fuse and trace the wiring. If the switch is bad, you'll be able to jumper the switch and get 12 volts beyond there for diagnosis. But you may need to replace the timer—which may be integrated into a larger box of electrical controls buried under the dash. Consult the factory shop manual for your car for a detailed diagnostic procedure. If that's not available to you, you'll have to find the problem the old-fashioned way. Trace the current path from the fuse, to the switch, to the timer, and on back to the window. Remember, the timer will turn off the current within 5 to 10 minutes, so you'll need to keep track of the timer's time window or you'll be looking for current that's not supposed to be there.

Somewhere in the circuit there will be a relay to switch the high current necessary for the grid's operation. This may or may not be integral with the timer. A diagnostic procedure would be to jumper the relay's terminals to see if the relay is bad. You can either jump 12 volts to the relay's coil to make it pull in, or bypass the relay with a large-gauge jumper to see if the grid's wiring is intact between the relay and the window. A separate relay should be inexpensive and available at any auto parts store, but if it's in the same package with the timer you'll pay as much as a hundred bucks.

Don't try to bypass the timer. Rear-window defrosters draw a substantial amount of current—10 to 20 amps depending on the application. Most modern cars use a timer circuit to turn the grid off after a reasonable length of time. There are two reasons for this. The first is to reduce the electrical load on the alternator, which (especially during the wintertime) also supplies electricity for the headlights,

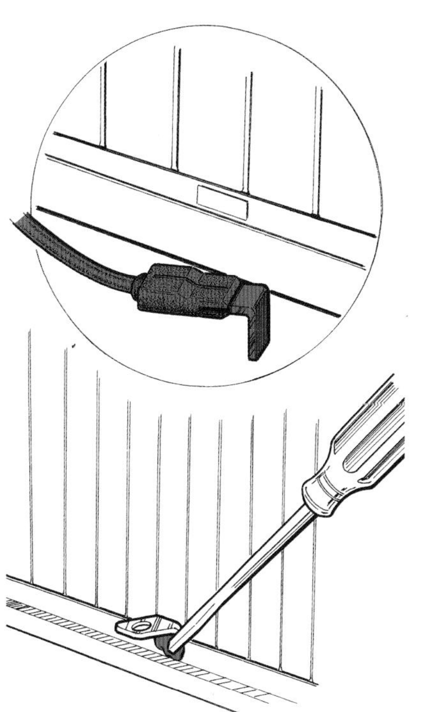

(Fig. 3) Broken-off defroster-grid terminals can be repaired with conductive epoxy adhesive.

heater fan and windshield wipers. Couple that with the extra demands on the battery for starting in cold weather, and there may simply not be enough alternator capacity to keep the battery charged adequately.

The second reason is simpler—the grid may overheat if it's left on too long. Imagine accidentally leaving it on during a long trip on a summer day. The heat from the grid added to the heat of the sun may crack the glass or contribute to deterioration of the window's rubber gaskets.

If you need to replace the timer or switch, you'll probably have to go to the car dealer for the parts.

Easy Fixes

Suppose your grid has several lines that don't heat. You may be able to find the break by simply inspecting the silk-screened grid along its length. This will be easier on hatchbacks, minivans and SUVs because you can open the back up and look at the lines against the sky. Sedans will require you to crawl into the back and poke your head into the area above the rear

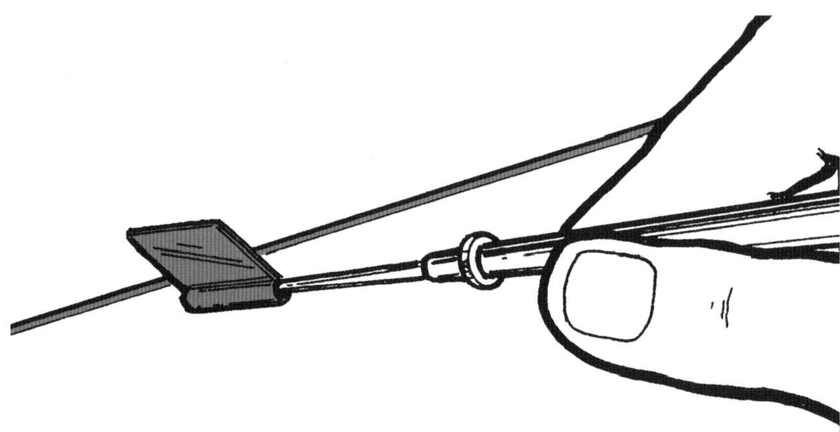

(Fig. 4) Small flags of aluminum foil on your probes will prevent further damage.

deck. Otherwise, you'll need to drag out the trusty DC voltmeter and hunt for it electrically.

Set your voltmeter for the 20-volt scale, and attach a couple of postage-stamp-size pieces of aluminum foil to the leads **(Fig. 4)**. This will prevent the probes from scratching the grid. You can simply lay the aluminum-foil tabs on the glass and press lightly with one finger to make connection with the grid. If the window is large, it may help to have another pair of hands.

Start by measuring the voltage across the entire length of the grid. With the key on and the defroster turned on you should see 12 volts on the meter with one tab at either end of the grid. Now move one tab to the center of the grid and measure again. The voltage should read 12 volts if the break is between the tabs, less if the break is outside of the tabs. Similarly, measure the voltage on a grid line that is working properly, and you should see approximately 6 volts at the center, because you've just turned your defroster grid into a giant rheostat. By moving the tab along the damaged line, you'll see 12 volts on the meter until you reach the break, where the voltage will drop considerably all at once. This should allow you to pinpoint the break.

Repairing the grid is simple. Many auto departments in large stores, and almost any dedicated auto parts store, can sell you a repair kit. Clean the area of the break with alcohol and a fresh, untinted paper towel. Don't use window cleaner, as it may leave a residue of wax or silicone.

The kit will have an adhesive template to stick over the break, but you can use ordinary masking tape just as easily. The masking tape can be used to make a new line that exactly matches the width of your old grid, if the mask in the kit is too wide or narrow. Paint a stripe of the kit's conductive paint across the break **(Fig. 5)**. Allow it to dry for 10 to 15 minutes and remove the mask.

If you have several grid lines that are damaged, simply repeat the process. If the lines are damaged in more than one place along their length, you'll have to go back to step one and find the next break.

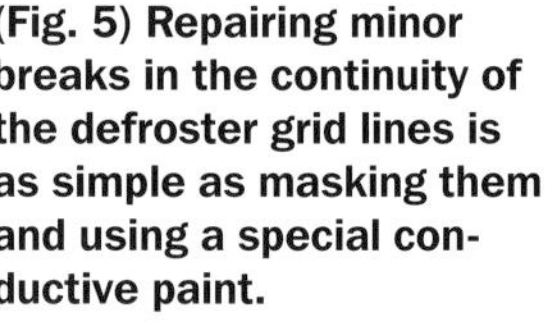

(Fig. 5) Repairing minor breaks in the continuity of the defroster grid lines is as simple as masking them and using a special conductive paint.

EASY

Keeping Your Windshield Clear

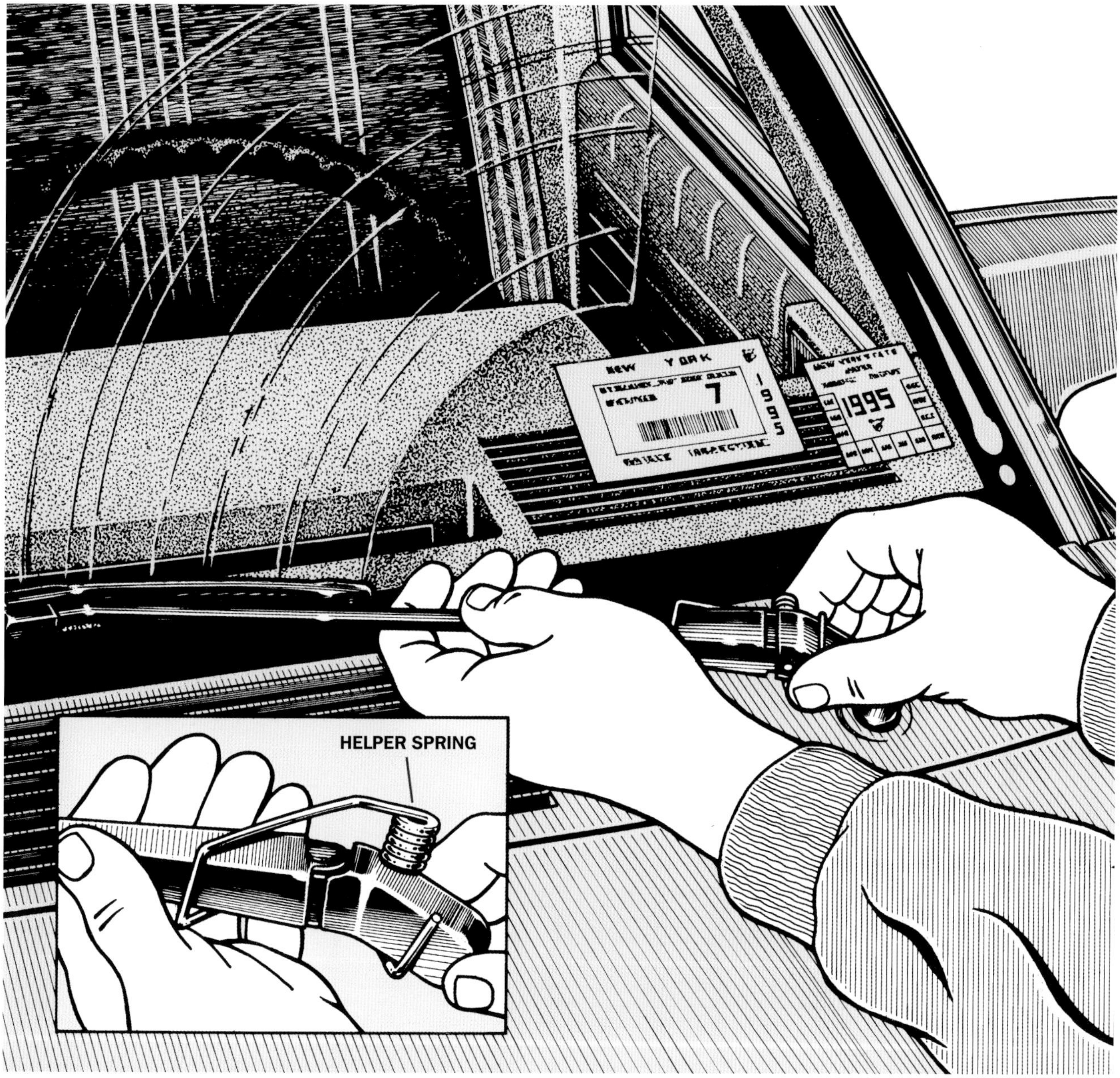

It's a dark and stormy night, Part II. Every drop of rain that splatters on your windshield seems to hide another vehicle, camouflaged by the smear of light and haze coating the glass. Even with your windshield wipers set on high, you can't see more than a few feet ahead. Every few blocks you have to stop and wipe the condensation from the inside of the windshield with your hand. It's a dangerous situation.

Your car has several systems that are specifically designed to keep a clear piece of glass—and nothing else—between your eyes and the road. Outside the glass are the wiper arms, run by an electric motor. Inside is a defogging blower/heater, integral with the heating/air-conditioning system. Keep them at peak effectiveness.

(Fig. 1) Wimpy wiper-arm springs can be fixed by adding helper springs at the arm joint.

Slimed

If you get your vehicle washed and waxed regularly, there may be a buildup of silicones on the windshield, layered with the airborne dirt and dust from industrial plants. Even

(Fig. 2) Replace the rubber squeegee in the blade if it's taken a set to one side or the other.

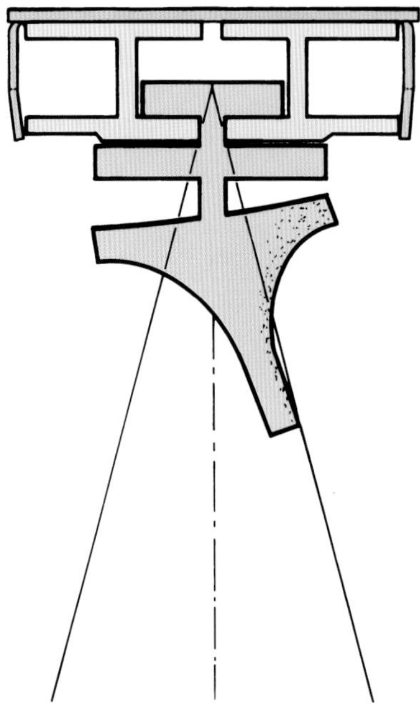

good wipers won't remove this kind of mess. It takes a cleaner with a super-fine abrasive that won't scratch the glass, and, although there are household cleaners in that category, auto parts stores now carry ones made specifically for windshields. When a windshield is clean, water from a garden hose should "sheet"—flow across it, not bead up.

For winter-freeze protection, fill the washer reservoir with a cleaning solution with washer antifreeze, not just a mixture of water and alcohol or ordinary antifreeze. And never use an abrasive windshield cleaner in the washer reservoir.

Check the spray pattern of the washer nozzle. Although some are nonadjustable, individual tube-type nozzles can be bent slightly to improve the spray position, and the base of the nontubular type may be shimmed. The common ball-in-socket variety can be re-aimed, using a straight pin carefully placed in the ball's orifice and used as a lever.

If the wipers chatter and the windshield is really clean, inspect the pivots of the blades. If they're corroded or bent, the blade won't conform properly to the glass. Replace it.

Still chattering? Open the hood and examine the windshield-wiper linkage and mounting. If the motor rocks in its mountings, the blades may chatter. The wiper motor is generally mounted in rubber bushings to reduce noise. Look for broken or deteriorated bushings. Next, check the linkage. Worn bushings and pins can also set up a chatter. If there's anything that can't be tightened, you'll have to begin replacing some parts.

Now check the bushings in the fittings where the wiper arms pivot as they pass through the cowl. Some of these bushings are mounted in rubber, and sometimes it's possible to snug them up. Look for a large-diameter nut below the cowl. The pivot pins

(Fig. 3) A small dab of wiper-blade lubricant can help to keep smearing down and also extend squeegee life.

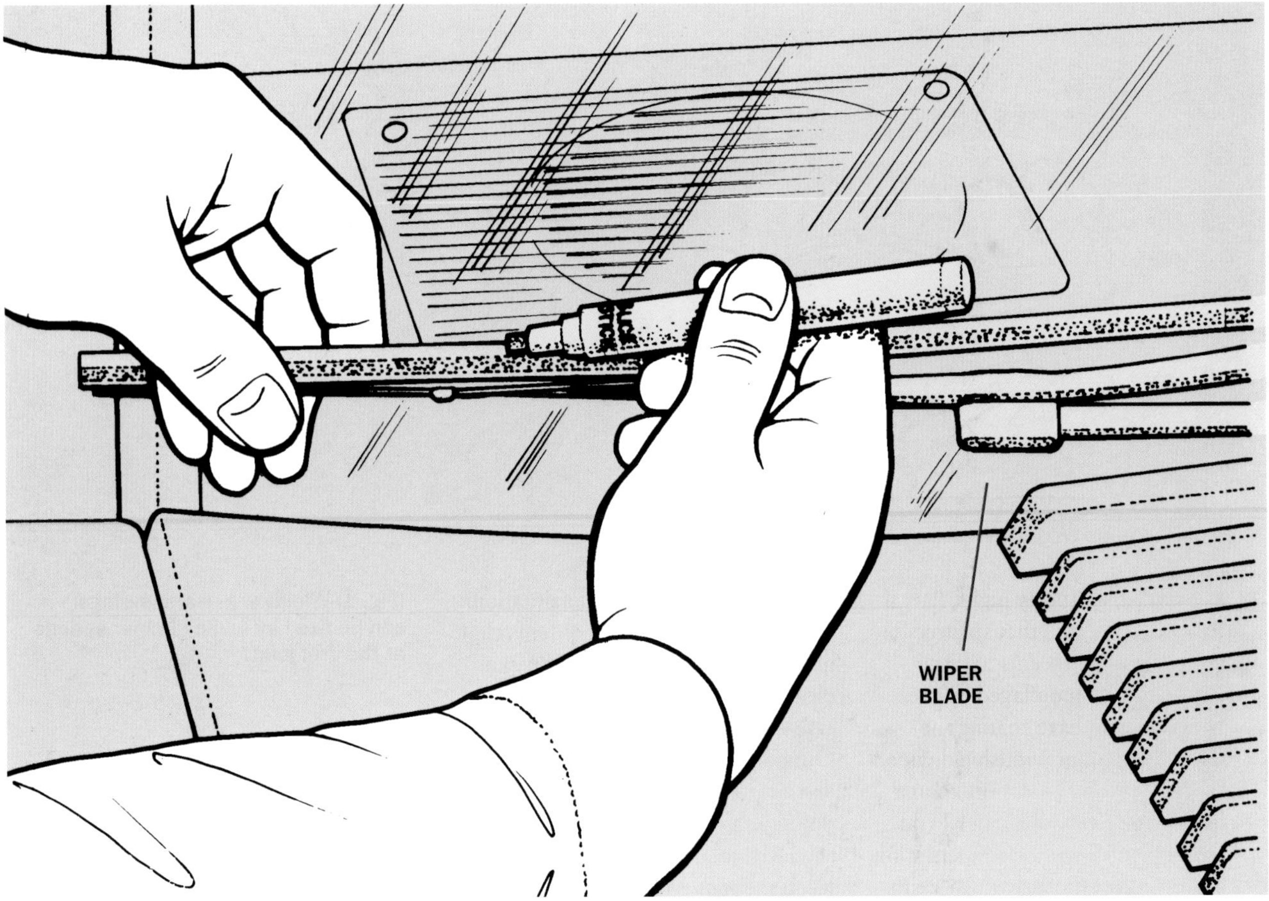

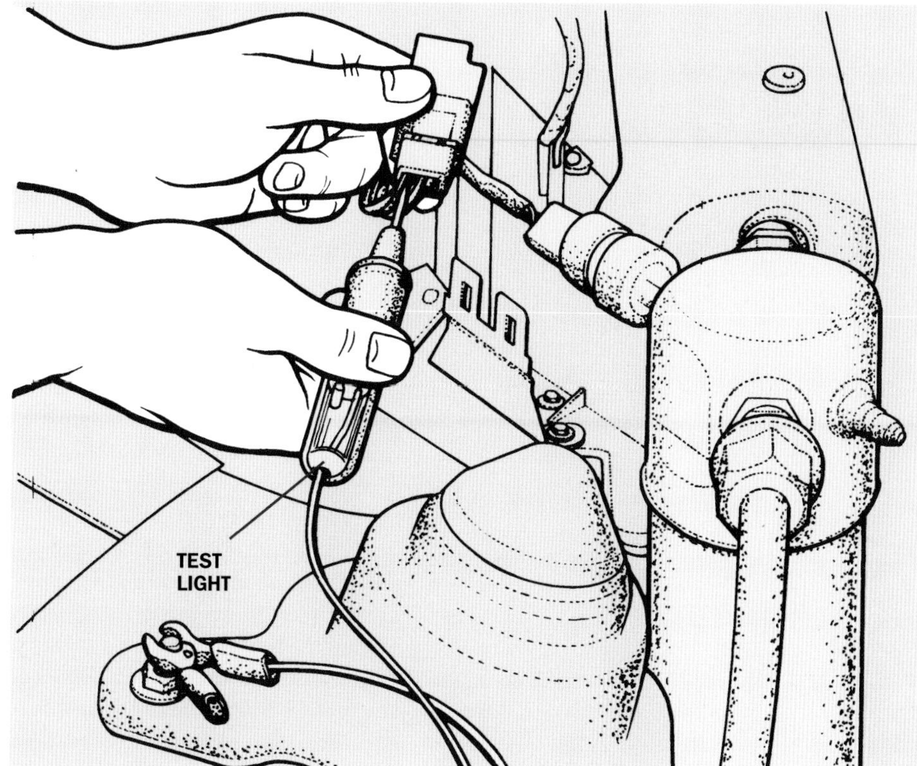

(Fig. 4) If the blower isn't up to speed, probe the blower-motor relay wiring with a test light.

themselves can wear, which can also permit chatter to get started. Parts replacement is in order here.

Lift the arm. If it feels weak, compare it with another car, or measure it on a fish scale. The typical arm, lifted from the blade end, should take about 30 ounces. (Note, however, that fish scales aren't much more accurate than a fisherman's estimate of the length of the big one that got away.) If the arm spring is weak, replacements could set you back more than $70. Instead, install helper springs—they're sold in auto parts stores for just a few dollars **(Fig. 1)**.

Inspect the wiper blades' rubber inserts (the squeegees) for cracks or other deterioration. It's best to remove the blade, hold it in front of you and see if the rubber squeegee tip is absolutely straight down the center of the blade. If it's wavy or tilted noticeably to one side, replace it **(Fig. 2)**. If the blade is good, only the squeegee need be replaced. If the squeegee itself is good, apply a lubricant made for natural rubber to both sides. A quick smear of lube once every week or two should not only extend the squeegee's life, but improve its everyday performance **(Fig. 3)**. Again, look in the auto parts store for rubber lubricant. Don't use silicone.

Fogged In

If the inside of the windshield has a permanent "fog," it may be caused by interior air pollution, including tobacco smoke and fumes from plastic trim. Vinegar does a good job of removing it, but be sure to wash the glass to help clear away the odor. Another option is to clean the glass with an antifog formula, which leaves an invisible coating that retards interior fogging. Unfortunately, the formulas we've seen are not recommended for tinted windows, so watch where you apply it, or simply stick with vinegar.

When you use the defroster, many cars' ventilation systems automatically turn on the a/c compressor, even in winter (temperatures above 50° F), to condense the interior moisture. If your system has a separate a/c compressor control, you may have to push the a/c button to get the desired effect. And if your control panel has a separate button or lever for outside air versus recirculated air, choose outside air—it'll help purge the interior moisture that you and your passengers release, which is a major cause of the fog that mars a normally clean windshield. This probably sounds counterintuitive—isn't there plenty of moisture coming in with the fresh air from the cowl vent? Trust us. Fresh air will evaporate more mist.

Just because you hear the blower fan doesn't mean the air is blowing against the windshield, so put your hand over the defroster outlets. If the airflow is weak, either the ventilation-control system is misbehaving, a cabin air filter is plugged, or there's a dashboard duct unplugged, causing the airflow to leak out before it gets to the windshield. If there's strong airflow from another duct when you select defrost, the control panel is probably at fault.

If the blower doesn't seem to come up to speed but is turning, there's a fair chance that the high-blower relay used on many cars is faulty. Inspect the area around the blower motor, and if there's a relay wired to it, check the connection **(Fig. 4)**. And look around for an inline fuse—wired to the relay—to inspect. It could be blown.

Still have trouble seeing what's ahead on the road? Next time, don't forget your eyeglasses.

EASY

Detailing Your Car

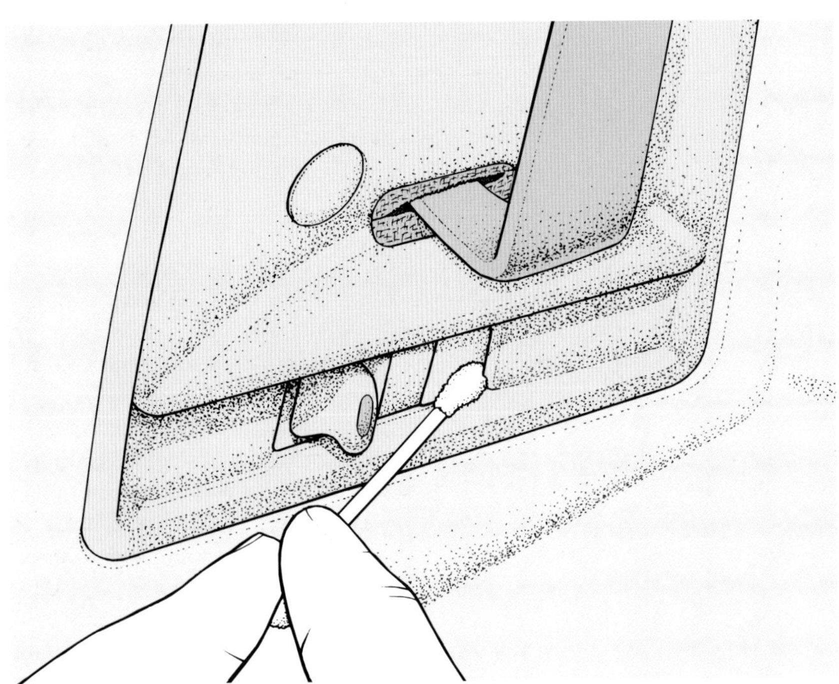

(Fig. 1) Use a Q-tip to scour interior recesses that have collected dust.

It's a Great American Ritual—washing the car. You get your bucket of soapy water and a sponge, fire up the garden hose and go to work. Your neighbor in the adjoining driveway does the same. But he's assembled a whole array of car care implements, including brushes, cotton swabs, a toothbrush and a plethora of cleaning, conditioning and dressing products. By the time you've dried off the body, slapped a coat of wax on the finish and buffed it out, your neighbor is only up to square two. So you move on to the other Great American Ritual—the backyard barbecue, leaving your neighbor elbow-deep in his bucket of soapsuds.

Later, after scarfing down your fifth hot dog and third ear of corn, you saunter over to your neighbor on the pretext of offering him a barbecued chicken thigh. But you really want to see the kind of job he's doing. His vehicle is about the same vintage and in the same condition as yours, but his car gleams like a jewel. Yours just looks clean.

What's your neighbor's secret? He went the detailing route—a process that goes beyond the ordinary wash-and-wax job. Detailing is just that—paying close attention to small details. Sure, it takes a lot more time and effort, but the results can be nothing short of eye popping.

Professional detailers have developed their own tricks of the trade for everything from vehicle washing to cleaning windows to getting ventilation grilles looking supercrisp. To get their results, use products designed for specific areas—wheels, trim, windows, etc. Name-brand products are a safe bet. Be sure to read labels to get the best finish.

Where to Start

The interior is a good starting point, so the dust and dirt you brush out won't settle on a pristine exterior. Remove any floor mats and give the carpeting and upholstery a good vacuuming. Also vacuum the dash and rear parcel shelf. Move the front seats full fore and aft to get to all the accumulated dirt and loose change. If the carpets are clean except for a minor stain or two, use a foaming cleaner to get them out. Saturate the stain with cleaner, working it in with a damp sponge. Let it sit awhile and then blot it out with paper towels or a dry cotton cloth. Repeat if necessary, and then go over the area with a damp sponge before final blotting. Don't oversaturate the carpet and risk getting mildew.

You can repair burns and holes in your carpet by cutting out the offending area with a razor blade or scissors. Then cut a similar-size piece from a hidden spot, such as underneath the seat, and cement it in place using a water-resistant adhesive. Blend in the repair by brushing the nap.

Wash the floor mats, if they're rubber, and apply a dressing that does not leave a slippery finish, for obvious reasons.

Clean interior hard surfaces with a damp cloth and a mild all-purpose cleaner such as Simple Green, diluted about 10:1. If you have vinyl-covered seats, use a conditioner made for that material. Avoid products that give a high-gloss, slippery surface, so passengers won't feel like they're on a roller coaster. If you have leather upholstery, dress the surfaces with a leather conditioner. Never use a vinyl product on leather.

Worn or torn areas of vinyl can be repaired using kits made for this purpose that are available at auto supply stores. Repairs are made with a patch that lets you match the color and grain of your upholstery. Worn areas of leather can be touched up with dyes or a high-grade shoe polish. Just make sure you match the color as closely as possible.

The dash presents a special challenge, with buttons, crevices and bezels that you can't get to with a cleaning rag. You can blast dust and dirt from these areas by using small cans of compressed air made for cleaning camera and computer equipment. Cotton swabs also work well here **(Fig. 1)**. Pay attention to the cleaning products you use on your dash. If your dash has a flat finish, don't use a product on it that will leave you facing a shiny gloss.

Clean air vent grilles with cotton swabs and brighten them up by misting on some spray-on vinyl/rubber dressing or accent spray—just a touch. You can also use these products to cover up light scuff marks on wood trim. Spray the stuff on a soft towel and then apply it to the wood.

Clean glass or plastic gauge lenses with a glass or plastic cleaner, not wax. Pull off any removable knobs to clean the bezels underneath. Ever wonder where the haze on the inside of your windshield comes from, since you don't smoke? It consists of plastisols given off as the plastics used in many new cars slowly cure. Not to worry—a good glass cleaner or vinegar should remove it. If your windows are really cruddy, you may have to resort to stronger measures, such as scrubbing with 4-ought steel wool.

MINOR SCRATCHES can be polished off with clearer waxes or mild polish.

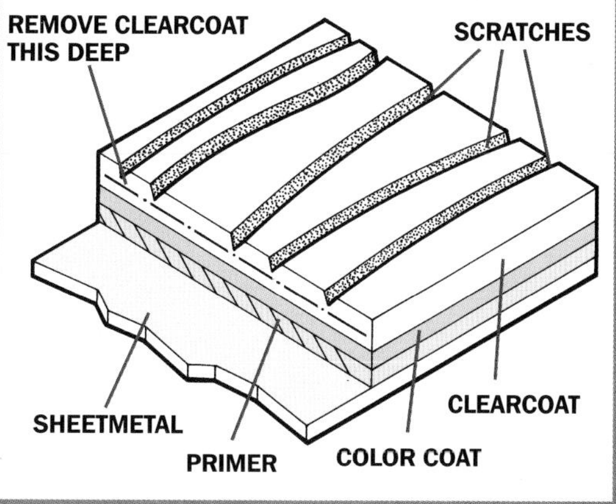

SCRATCHES THAT GO THROUGH the clearcoat into the pigment must be repaired professionally.

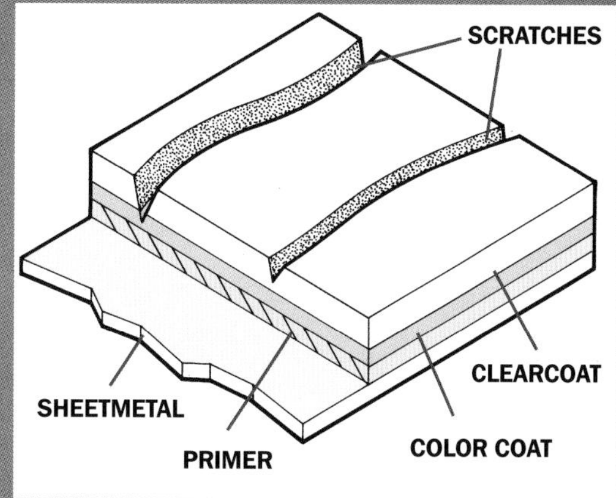

A Word of Caution

If you have aftermarket window tint film, it may be degraded by cleaners that contain ammonia or vinegar. Factory tinting is in the glass and is not affected by these cleaners. One trick used by some detailers for the final touch on window glass is to rinse it down with seltzer and do a final wipe with a ball of crumpled newspaper.

When it comes to first impressions, nothing makes a hit like a jewel finish. But this is possible only after any paint problems are corrected. Just about all finishes today are a 2-step (color) basecoat and a protective clearcoat. The top clearcoat is only about 2-3 mils thick, and when it gets scratched or abraded it refracts light and the color coat underneath doesn't shine through clearly. It's like looking through a scratched or foggy lens.

To evaluate your paint, first wash your vehicle. Work in the shade and make sure the surface is cool. Use a carwash soap, not a household detergent, and work in sections, from the top down. The lower panels tend to accumulate more abrasive dirt. To do a final rinse, remove the spray head from the hose and flood the finish. The water will

HOW IT WORKS

Clearcoat Paint

Most modern cars use a clearcoat paint system. The pigmented layer of paint, whether a solid color, metallic or pearlescent, is covered with a layer of clear paint to provide a higher gloss and a "deeper" look. So far so good.

But the surface of any paint, even clearcoat, is vulnerable to scratches and oxidation. In the past, abrasive rubbing compound could be used to polish out these imperfections. Clearcoat is thinner, and using abrasives is trickier. Removing too much paint will leave the pigment layer exposed, necessitating a respray with more clearcoat. The recommended procedure for oxidation and haze is to use a chemical cleaner or cleaner wax. Look for products that specifically say they are appropriate for clearcoat paint on the label. Light scratches can be buffed out with very mild polishing compound. Do not use rubbing compound on a clearcoat finish. Scratches that go through the clearcoat layer cannot be polished out, although some "color in polish" products or pen-type touchups may provide a visually acceptable fix.

(Fig. 2) Wax your car in the shade, in small sections. A small buffer will help, but hand application will get the job done, too.

tend to run off in sheets, minimizing spotting. Dry with a good-quality chamois or a soft thick-nap terry cloth towel.

Don't forget the wheel wells. Get the crud out with an all-purpose cleaner and a good high-pressure dousing. After you've finished washing your car, apply a vinyl dressing to add some snap to the wells.

Wash the wheels (make sure they're cool) with a brush made for this purpose, but do not use acid-based cleaners on polished alloy wheels or wheels that are clearcoated. You can use these cleaners on rough-textured alloy wheels. Chrome wheels can be gleamed up with metal polish or glass cleaner.

After washing the car, inspect the paint. Stains and scratches can be attacked with a good clearcoat-safe cleaner. The worse the problem, the more aggressive the cleaner needed. Start off with the least abrasive product and gradually move to coarser cleaners as required. Then machine buff (**Fig. 2**).

Polishing and/or waxing is next. Be sure to include doorjambs, and the areas beneath door hinges and behind bumpers. Minor blemishes may be neutralized by wrapping a cotton cloth around your index finger and burnishing the polish into the finish. Polish not only gives the finish its gloss, but it feeds the paint with oils to prevent it from drying out. Polymers in the polish fill in minute scratches in the clearcoat layer, restoring its clarity. If you machine-buff the polish/wax to a high luster, go with an orbital rather than a rotary model, which would be more likely to burn the paint. Treat the plastic chrome on today's cars as if it were a painted surface and protect it with a light coat of wax.

(Fig. 3) A dampened toothbrush can remove wax deposits from exterior trim.

Avoid getting wax or polish on rubber and flat black plastic areas (clean them with a nongloss product), door handles and emblems. If you do get a wax stain on rubber trim, spray it with a mist-and-wipe product and wipe it down with a terry cloth towel. If that doesn't do the trick, this usually works: Microwave some peanut butter and apply it to the stain with a soft toothbrush. Peanut butter's oils dissolve the wax and it's abrasive enough to lift the stain (but it can stick to the roof of your car).

If you get a polish/wax residue around emblems or in crevices, break out the cotton swabs and toothbrushes (**Fig. 3**). It's important that you first wet the area with a mist-and-wipe product such as Meguiar's Quick Detailer. Never brush on a dry surface.

Moving underhood, protect electronic components by wrapping them in plastic. Then spray on a diluted all-purpose cleaner, hosing it off with light water pressure. Vinyl/rubber protectant will dress up nonmetal areas. Let it soak in if you like the glossy look, or wipe it on and off for a more matte finish.

All that's left now are the tires. Clean them first—whitewall tire cleaner works even on blackwalls—and then apply tire dressing. Here again, to get a gloss finish let the product soak in, or for a matte look wipe it on and off with a cotton cloth. Be sure the tires are dry before driving off, or you'll spatter your nice shiny finish. And maybe even your neighbor.

Aligning Body Panels

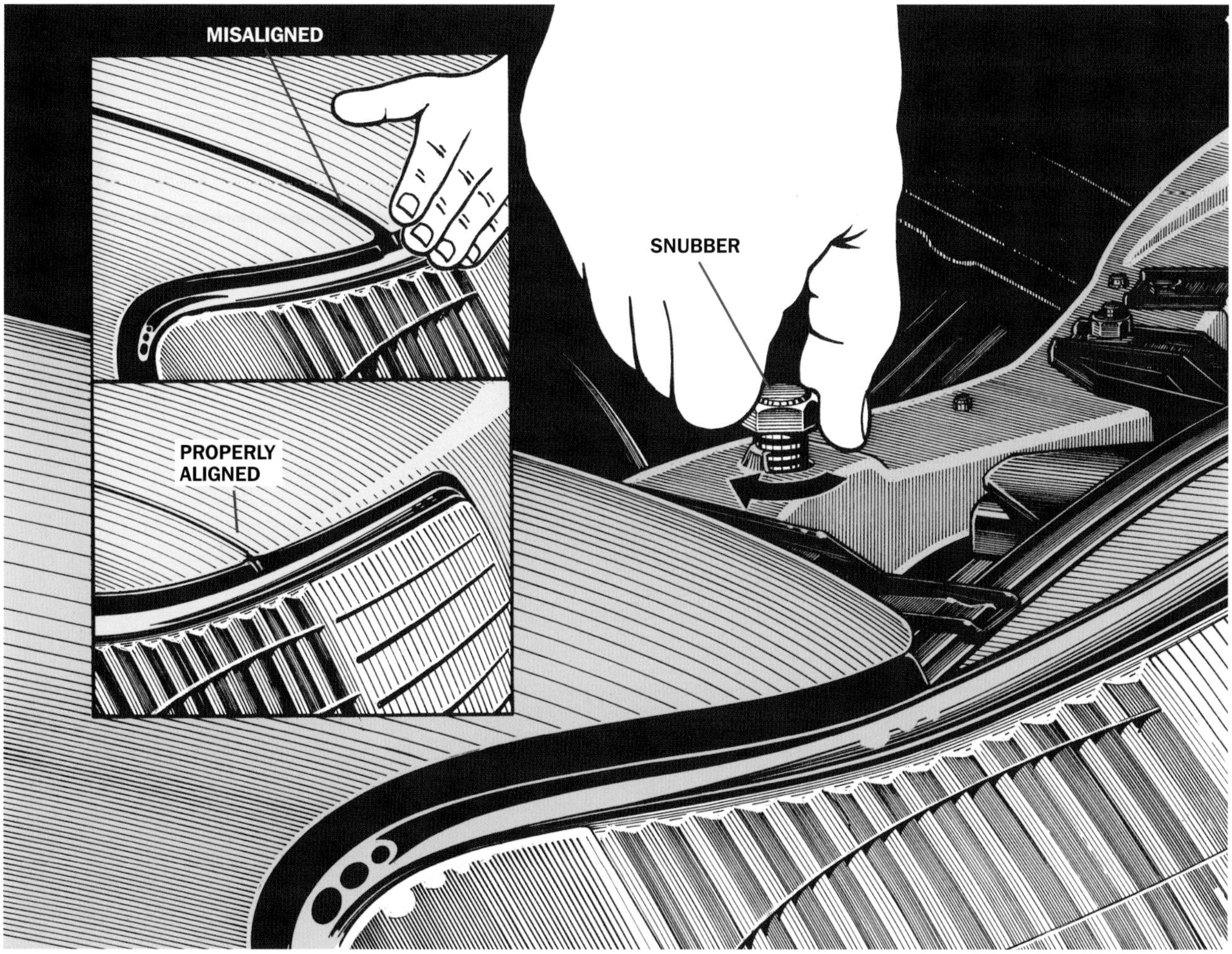

(Fig. 1) Raising or lowering the rubber snubber will raise or lower the corner of a misaligned hood to produce a better fit.

Unpacking the car after a vacation weekend is never fun. Less fun, even, than cramming the family's idea of "just enough clothes for a summer's weekend at the lake" into a modern compact car's diminutive trunk. Were those ski parkas really necessary?

At long last, you head cheerily to the office on Monday morning, glad to be back to the grindstone. At least until you notice, by the cold light of day, the trunklid of your car sitting a good half-inch askew. Must be something still left in the trunk, preventing the lid from closing fully, you say. The trunk, however, is as empty as your wallet. The trunklid is sprung.

Nothing Is Forever

Body panels on cars are made of relatively thin sheetmetal. In the aggregate, they are immensely strong. The panels are particularly strong in protecting the occupants against frontal crashes, telescoping progressively while absorbing energy during impacts. But forcing a trunklid closed against resistance, or slamming the hinge side of a car door on the tail of a ski or even the corner of a duffel bag, can distort the hinges and latches in seconds. Years of driving on pothole-filled streets and countless open-close cycles can make a door that sounded like a bank vault when the car was new now sound like a Cheez Whiz can rolling down a cobblestone hill. Just as the Leaning Tower of Pisa continues its slide toward the courtyard surrounding it, a car's doors, hood and trunk panels can gradually change position, and may need periodic adjustments.

Fortunately, most panel misalignments aren't the result of a serious fender bender. Those usually require the services of a trained body technician and a large hydraulic frame-straightening jig. Simple mis-

(Fig. 2) Hoods and trunks may need to have their latch pins moved up or down to make them close properly.

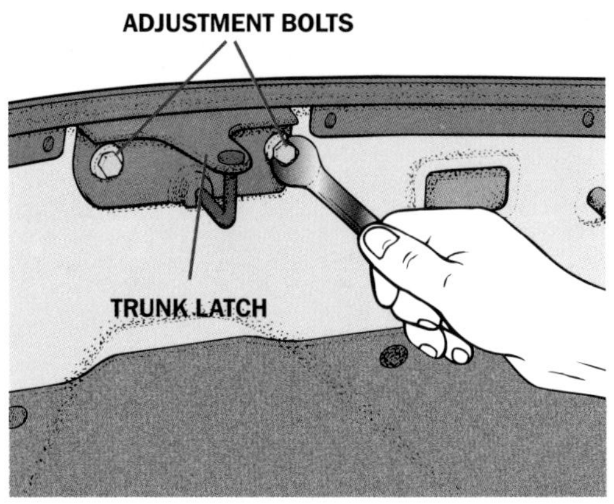

alignments, however, often can be minimized with little more than simple hand tools and a careful eye.

Hoods and Trunks

The simplest misalignment, and the one most often seen while cruising parking lots, is a vertical misalignment of the corner of a hood or trunk. The corner of these opening panels is normally held at the correct height, even with the lip of the fender that abuts it, by a simple rubber snubber. This snubber is usually threaded into a hole in a corner of the panel. Rudimentary threads in the sheetmetal allow the snubber to be screwed in and out by hand. On some vehicles, the snubber is in the hood or trunk panel, sometimes in the bodywork below the panel. Simply screw the snubber in or out until the offending panel is flush **(Fig. 1)**. Some older cars may use a snubber with a threaded rod and jam nut on a steel stud. You'll need to loosen the jam nut, adjust the snubber, and then tighten the jam nut with a wrench to keep it from shifting. Generally, a half-turn or so is sufficient.

More severe misalignment may make the panel's latch either too loose or too tight to open and close properly. Loose latches will rattle. Latches that are too tight will break fingernails, and will eventually break the cable to the interior handle. Fortunately, most hood and trunk latches are adjustable. You may need nothing more than an open-end wrench, or perhaps an Allen wrench **(Fig. 2)**. Sometimes the latch assembly itself is adjustable. Occasionally, the catch on the mating panel can be adjusted instead of the latch assembly. Loosen the appropriate hardware slightly, and tap the assembly just enough to move it almost as far as you moved the snubber. Tighten the hardware, and try closing the hood or trunk. The latch release should pop easily, and the latch shouldn't rattle. Try for about ¼ in. of compression in the snubber on a hood. On a trunk you are likely to find rubber gaskets to compress, and there may be more resistance before the latch pawl snaps home.

If you have an electrically tripped latch, tighten things up slowly. If the latch is too tight, the solenoid may not have the strength to pop the latch open. If you've painted yourself into a corner and can't open the trunk, try having someone else hit the trunk release while you push down on the trunklid. This should release enough pressure on the pawl to let it move.

Fore and Aft

Maybe the hood or trunklid is aligned vertically, but the panel is sitting crooked, or is just too close to the window glass. You'll need to adjust the hinges. Use a felt-tip pen or a pencil to mark the location of the hinges on the inside of the panel. Loosen the attaching hardware just enough to be able to slide the panel to a new position. Do only one side at a time **(Fig. 3)**. Tighten a little, then close the panel and check its alignment. It'll probably take a few iterations, but you should be able to get the panel to center in its intended

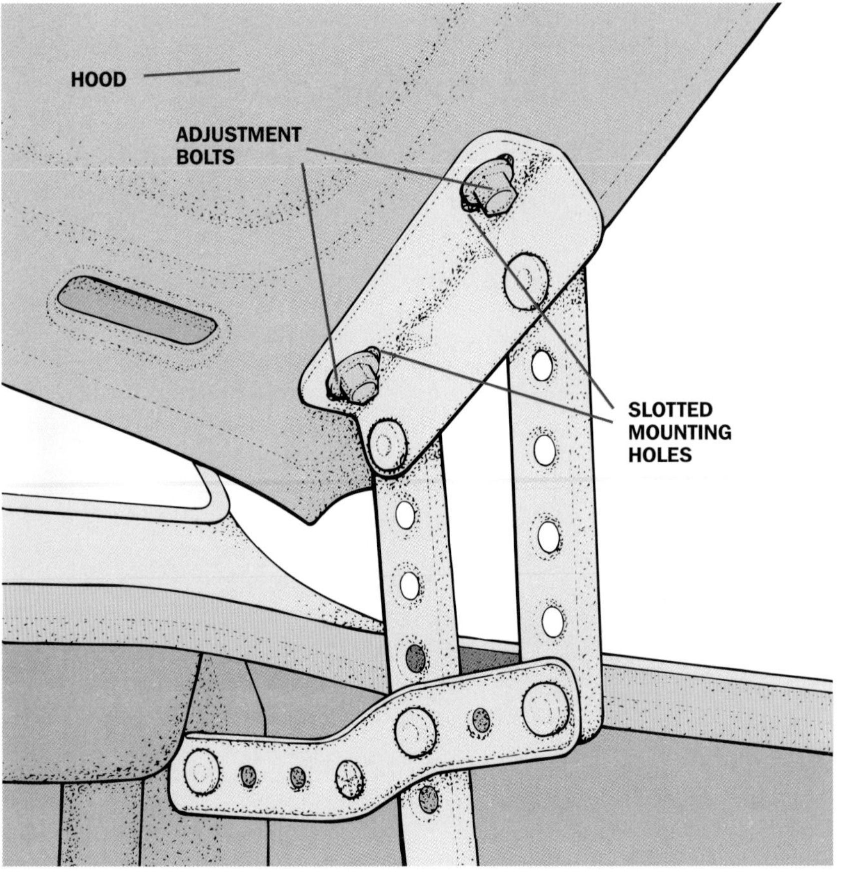

(Fig. 3) Adjust the hood or trunk one side at a time by loosening the attachment bolts and sliding the panel back and forth.

space. After all is said and done, it may not be possible to get the gaps in the panel to be symmetrical. It's not unusual for the gaps to change their width from the front to the rear of the panel. You may need to strike a compromise between getting the panel to sit square in its intended recess both fore and aft, and making all the gaps symmetrical.

If the gaps are square and the panel is sitting so that it's symmetrical, but the gap is wider on one side than the other, there is a fix. With the adjusting hardware good and tight and the panel adjusted correctly fore and aft, open the hood or trunk fully. With both hands, give it a sharp shove in the correct direction. Close the panel and check. If it still sits in exactly the same position, repeat and shove harder. If it has moved partway back to the correct alignment, shove again. Repeat until done. If you shove too hard, just shove back in the other direction. The first time you try this, close the panel carefully, so you don't scratch the paint if you've moved the panel too far.

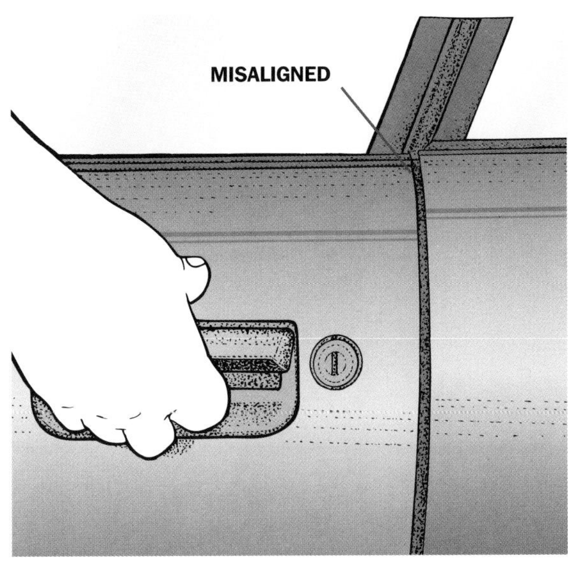

(Fig. 4) If the rear of your car's door sags, the cause may be a door latch that needs to be repositioned, or worn hinge pins.

That Swinging Door

Fitting a door is more complex. If it's out of alignment when closed and latched, you need to adjust the latch **(Fig. 4)**. Sometimes the latch mechanism on the door is the adjustable piece, sometimes you need to adjust the latch pin on the door pillar that the latch engages. It's a simple matter of slightly loosening the attachment hardware, lightly tapping the latch or pin to an approximation of the correct position, tightening, and trying again **(Fig. 5)**. You can move the door's rear edge in or out and up and down with this procedure.

Older cars can have hardware that's difficult to budge. Hardware that uses hexhead bolts or Torx bolts usually yields to penetrating oil, some moderate tapping with a hammer and the prerequisite profanity. Phillips-head attachment bolts require more finesse. Before you round off the heads be sure you're using a proper-size (usually No. 1 or No. 0) Phillips screwdriver. Some screwdrivers have a flat shank or hex-shaped section on which you can put a wrench. Then you can use one hand to push, hard, in on the handle to seat the screwdriver blade while you gingerly rotate it with your other hand on the wrench. As a last resort, use a handheld hammer-driven impact driver. Just remember you're hammering on sheetmetal parts and excess force can bend something in an unfortunate direction.

(Fig. 5) Adjust the door latch mechanism or latch pin to raise or lower the door, or to move it in or out, for a correct fit to the fender.

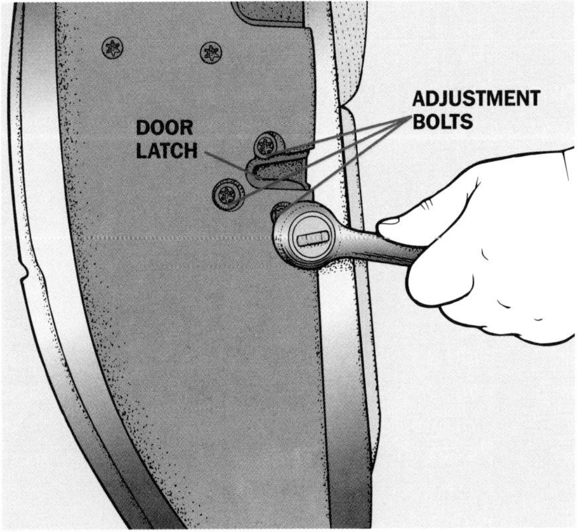

Occasionally, the hinges will fail to keep the front edge of a door in the correct alignment, sometimes because a 9-year-old has been playing at opening and closing the door while sitting in the window frame. Maybe you've managed to close the door on the wooden handle of a leaf rake. Or the hinges could simply be worn.

If the leading edge of the door is too far in or out, you can loosen the hinge bolts and move the hinges in or out one at a time. Don't loosen both hinges together unless the front of the door is too high or low. Generally, this is caused by worn hinges. You can compensate for a small amount of wear by raising the hinges on the pillar. You'll need a helper to hold the door vertically while you tighten the hinge bolts.

Serious wear calls for new hinges. If the hinges are welded to the door, your options are to replace the door or try to find an extremely competent body shop to weld in new hinges.

Another potential problem is a door that sags so badly while it's open that it has to be lifted to engage the latch—which then holds it correctly shut. This is probably caused by a rusted-out A-pillar or very worn hinge pins. A quick short-term fix is to wad up a shop towel and stuff it into the lower hinge. Slowly close the door on the rag until you meet some resistance. This will spread the hinge apart, raising the door's rear edge. Go slowly, and sneak up on the correct adjustment. Seriously worn hinge pins should be replaced.

Prepping Your Car For Paint

Junior has asked to borrow the keys for his big date on Friday. So you reach into your pocket for the keys to your pickup, traditionally his weapon of choice for cruising with the big guys. But this time he demurs—Betty Sue thinks the truck is too nasty-looking, and he'd prefer to use Mom's car.

After the shock of rejection wears off, you stroll out and examine the pickup. After all, when a teenager thinks your truck needs cosmetic improvement, it's time to pull off the blinders and think about a little bodywork.

Painting Is For Pros

Prep work aside, automotive painting couldn't be easier. With a little experience, spraying an entire car should only take about 20 minutes.

All you need is an air compressor and a spray gun. Oh yeah, you'll also need a $30,000 downdraft spray booth (with baking cycle), a supplied-air respirator and a real knack for smoothly flowing on paint without runs, sags or orange peel.

There's the rub. You may have a compressor and spray gun, but even large body shops can barely afford the other stuff. And when you consider that chain refinishers such as Earl Scheib and Maaco can do an adequate job of painting your current ride for $150 to $300, it makes sense to leave paint work to the pros.

Besides, for absolutely optimum results, 90% of a good paint job is not in the painting anyway, it's in the pre-painting preparation. And you can do that yourself.

As you might guess, budget paint jobs don't include a whole lot of prep work. For $149.95, Earl Scheib's preparation includes machine sanding, chemically cleaning the body, spot priming areas that need it and masking over things that aren't supposed to be painted—basically the windows. At some cut-rate shops, chrome and badges are negotiable. Any necessary bodywork costs extra.

Doing your own light bodywork such as fixing small dents and door dings or repairing rusty areas can save you a lot of money and help ensure the quality of the finished job. You can also greatly improve the quality of a budget paint job by removing and sanding under items that the painters would normally mask over, such as badges and assorted trim **(Fig. 1)**. But don't start sanding and dismantling your car first. A body shop will be much more receptive to your plan if you let them know what you're going to do ahead of time.

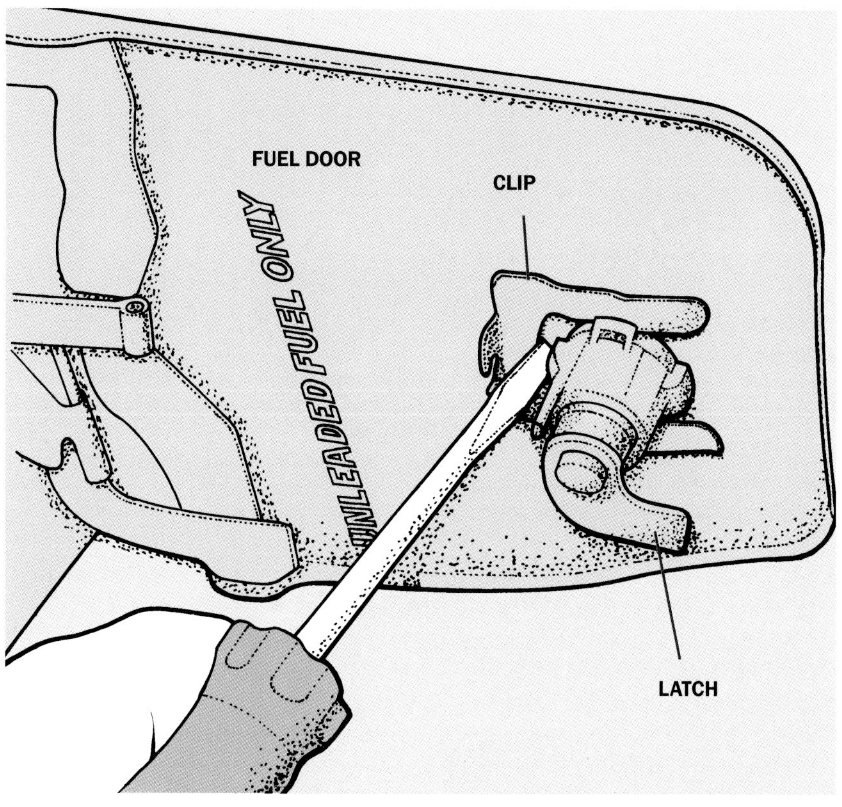

(Fig. 1) Remove as much of the hardware and trim as you can, instead of masking.

Paint Prep Primer

Unless you really hate the color of your vehicle, you'll save yourself work and aggravation if you plan to keep it the same color. Among other things, you can avoid the hours of prep work and extra expense of painting doorjambs and the underside of the trunklid and hood.You also avoid the chance of unpainted spots rearing themselves unexpectedly. A paint match costs extra over the few standard colors of the "basic bargain" price. It's worth the investment.

Start your paint prep by taking your vehicle to a do-it-yourself car wash. Pressure washing the engine, doorjambs, wheel wells and other under-body areas will help to ensure a dust-free paint job later. Cleaning the vehicle's outside will prevent you from sanding in paint-finish-ruining dirt and grime.

Nothing makes paint stick better or

(Fig. 2) The most important thing you can do to make sure the paint shop's paint will adhere is to wet-sand 100% of the existing finish with 400- or 600-grit waterproof sandpaper. Wash the car first, and mask off or remove any chrome or trim.

last longer than a thorough sanding **(Fig. 2)**. Paint needs a microscopically rough, craggy surface to latch on to—professional painters call this effect "tooth"—or the new paint will eventually loosen and fall off the old paint. Sanding large painted surfaces is easy. Problems crop up around areas like badges, antennas, bumpers and door mirrors. That's because no matter how careful you are, it's impossible to remove all traces of shine where the part meets the body. And paint that is applied next to a part instead of underneath causes a paint ledge to form, where dirt, water and ice start prying away. Sooner or later, the paint comes loose. After that, paint-peel is just a car wash away.

The only effective way to keep paint from peeling is to remove each part and sand under it. To have a body shop remove all these pieces can cost hundreds of dollars in labor—which is why the discount shops mask off all those parts (maybe). You can remove them yourself, however, and make a discount paint job look like a top-dollar custom paint job and have the paint finish last years longer. It's not practical to remove the windshield, rear window and door glass. But you can remove items that are common starting points for peeling problems, such as lock cylinders, door handles, luggage racks, radio antennas and side mirrors.

Take It All Off

To remove these parts, it's best to consult your vehicle's factory shop manual, but here are some general procedures. Make sure the window is rolled up, then remove interior door hardware such as the armrest, window crank and inner handle, then pry (or unscrew) the inner panel off the door. Lock cylinders are usually held in place with a spring clip. Door handles and mirrors are usually held by small bolts. The radio antenna, hood emblems and body badges are other places where paint can peel. Usually, it's not necessary to completely remove the antenna. Simply loosen the top retaining nut that holds the antenna in the body, mask the antenna shaft and lower the antenna into the fender or quarter panel. Hood emblems unbolt from under the hood. On older vehicles, badges and letters are mounted through holes in the body and fastened with spring nuts. On newer vehicles, these parts are often fastened with double-sided

(Fig. 3) Use a body hammer and dolly to smooth out minor dents. Take your time.

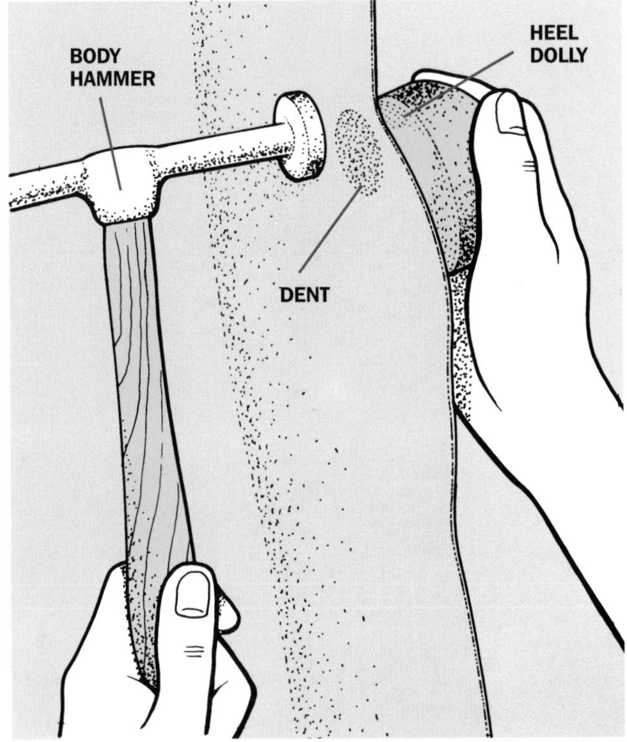

foam tape and are easily pried off with a 1-in. putty knife. If necessary, some time under a heat gun will help convince the adhesive to let go.

Of course, you'll also want to remove all large brightwork, such as chrome bumpers, the grille, headlight doors and taillight bezels. Once everything is removed, dents and dings can be repaired.

But before you start, make an honest assessment of your abilities. Your vehicle is going to end up at a body shop, right? It might make sense to leave those big dents and rust holes for the pros.

Smooth 'n' Fill

For smaller dents that you can reach from behind, use a body hammer and dolly to tap the dent out (**Fig. 3**). To avoid over-stretching the metal, start at the outer edges first and work to the center. Pound down any high spots in the dent, then use a 36-grit sanding disc in a portable drill to remove all traces of paint and primer, and to also help prepare the surface for plastic filler (**Fig. 4**).

Mix the filler and hardener according to the instructions on the can, then, working in one direction, apply the filler to low areas using a plastic squeegee. Plastic filler hardens in two stages. First, it hardens to a consistency approximating that of cheddar cheese and remains that way for a few minutes—exactly how long depends on how much hardener you've added and the ambient temperature and humidity. During this critical time, you can use a perforated Surform file—commonly called a "cheese grater" by the pros—to file away large portions of the filler until it's level with the surrounding area.

After filing, the filler will cure to its full hardness and it can be machine sanded smooth with 100-grit paper. Check the contour of the repaired area with your hand. Gently tap down high spots in the filler with the hammer and then refill these areas, file and sand again. Now the area is ready for primer. In addition to providing a surface for paint to adhere to, primer allows you to build up the area so it can be finish-sanded smooth.

Don't waste your time using lacquer primer from a spray can. These primers are very heavily thinned so the paint can easily pass through the can's miniature nozzles. The result is that primer buildup is minimal. Two-part polyester primer-surfacers, such as Marson's Poly-Fill, are by far the easiest to

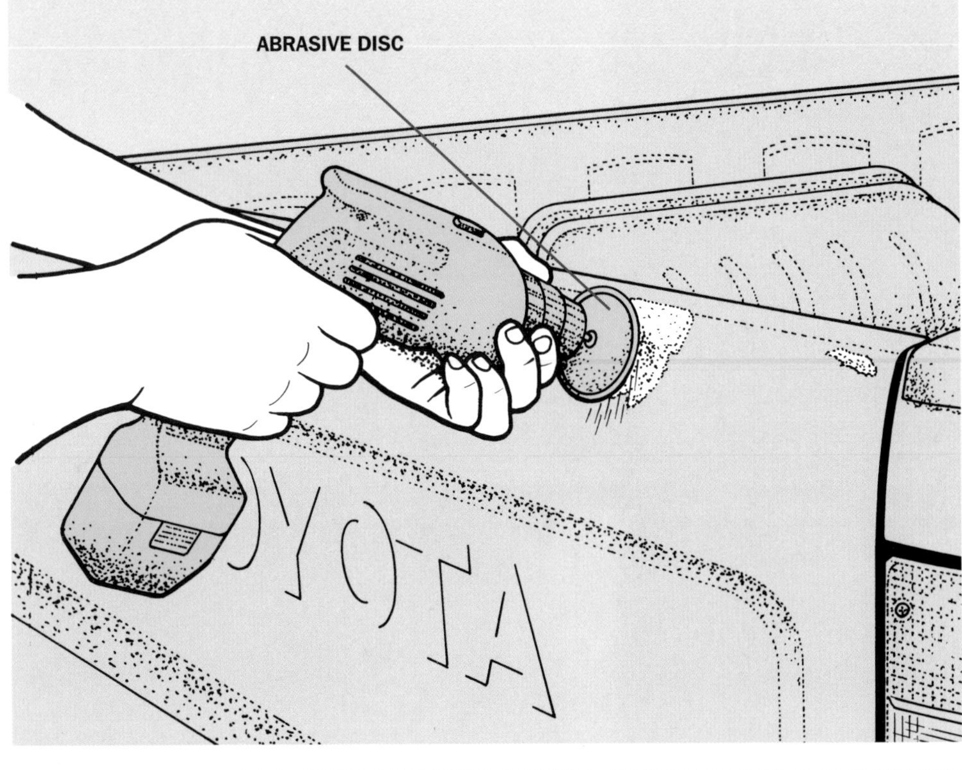

(Fig. 4) Grind all the paint and rust out of dents and creases before applying body filler.

(Fig.5) **Prime and resand the areas you've worked on, then sand again before painting.**

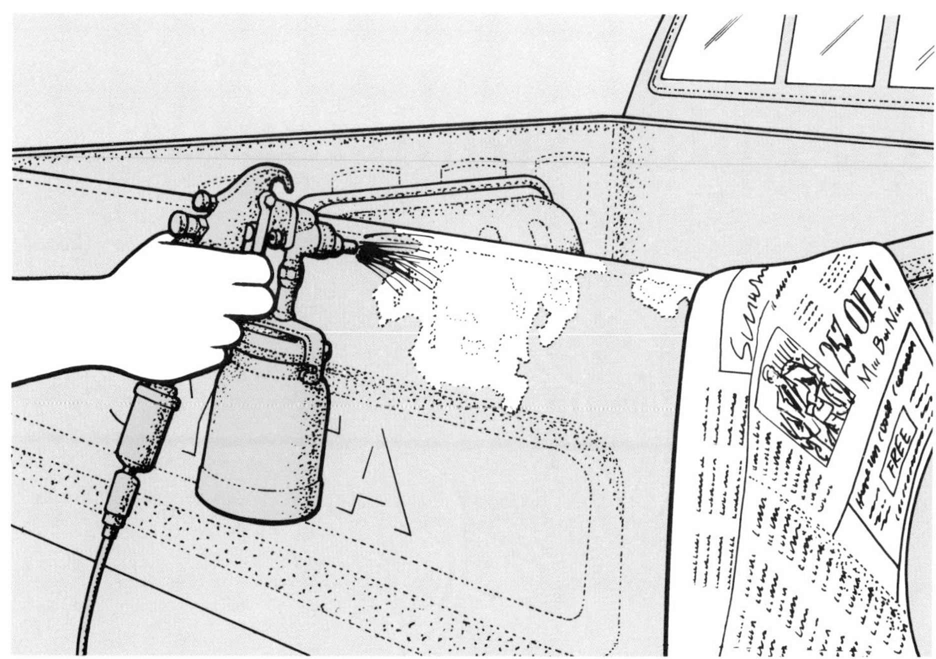

use and give the best surface buildup. Mix the hardener and primer according to the directions, then spray on two or three coats (**Fig. 5**). Once the primer hardens, machine-sand the primer with 180-grit sandpaper to remove heavy scratches and small waves in the body. Then wet-sand the repair with 400-grit paper.

Sand, Sand, Sand

After all dents and dings are repaired, the whole body should be sanded. The object here is exactly the opposite of what you normally try to do to your car's finish—you want to remove every trace of shine from the body. To do that, wet-sand the entire vehicle using 400-grit waterproof sandpaper. Flood the area with plenty of water while you sand, and don't forget to sand all the areas from where you removed parts. Feather-edge nicks and scratches, paying particular attention to chipped areas around door edges and rocker panels.

Once there's no more shine on the body, wash the vehicle with warm soapy water, rinse it and let it dry. You'll be amazed at how much shine there still is.

Before you hit these areas with the sandpaper again, spot prime any feather-edged areas as well as any areas where you've sanded through to the metal. After the primer has hardened, wet-sand these areas and the leftover shiny areas with 400-grit paper, then repeat the wash and rinse.

Still have some shiny spots? Guess what? Do it again!

Getting to the Shop

While the body shop can mask the large areas that shouldn't be painted, like the windshield and the rear window, it pays to run the first layer of masking tape yourself around areas that are immediately adjacent to the body, like the trim around the windshield and rear window, since you can take the time to be extra careful (**Fig. 6**).

Since a well-prepped car is devoid of just about everything that makes it legal for driving on the street, such as mirrors, headlights and taillights, you should seriously consider having your car towed to the shop.

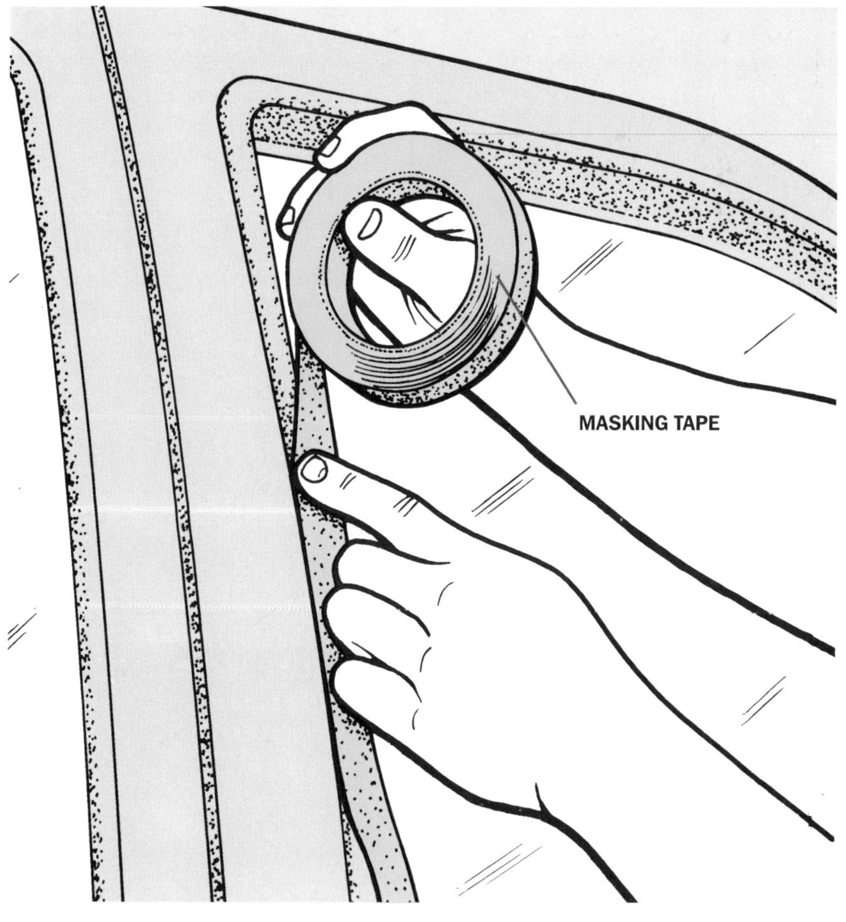

(Fig. 6) **Use fresh masking tape to carefully mask all the body trim on the entire car.**

EASY

Repairing Windshields

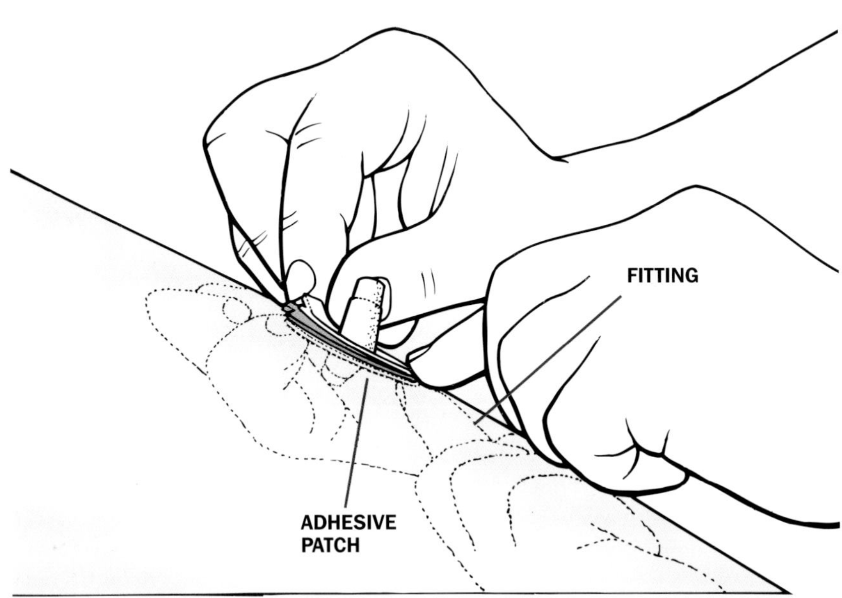

(Fig. 2) Take care to burnish the adhesive patch to a perfectly clean windshield and adapter, or you'll make a mess later.

It's a fine day. The sun is shining, traffic is moving along smartly and you haven't a care in the world. Whack! Until now, that is. Now there's a rosebud the size of a quarter in the windshield. What's worse, it's directly in your line of sight. It must have been a hypervelocity railgun pellet fired at you by an Imperial Stormtrooper, because you didn't see it coming or going. And as your heartbeat returns to normal, the awful truth sinks in: You're going to have to have the windshield replaced. This means dealing with the glass shop, being without your car for a day or two, having a potentially leaky windshield and, worst of all, higher insurance premiums.

Actually, it's worse. Some insurance policies won't even cover chipped glass. Maybe if you just raised or lowered your seat an inch so you didn't have to look right through the chip....

Better Living through Chemistry

Before you panic, drive home and get out your magnifying glass. Take a really close look at your new chip. It just might be possible to repair the chip instead of replacing the entire windshield (**Fig. 1**). The technique is to inject an epoxy or acrylic adhesive or filler into the chip.

TYPICAL STONE DAMAGE REPAIR KIT IS RECOMMENDED FOR

STARS — FLOWERS — B.B. CHIPS — BULL'S-EYES

NOT RECOMMENDED FOR THE FOLLOWING TYPES OF DAMAGE

SPIDER CRACKS (Without Air Pocket) — CRACKS — SURFACE DAMAGE

(Fig. 1) Many chips will be repaired almost completely by adhesive injection kits. But some damage requires complete windshield replacement.

Even if your chip isn't in your direct line of sight, it's a good idea to try and repair it. Water will find its way into the chip, pulled in by surface tension. If the chip goes all the way through the top lamination, any moisture that gets that deep can delaminate the glass from the center membrane. Eventually, the membrane will fog, causing a larger blemish. Water also can freeze in the chip, causing a larger flaw or even a crack. Also, water can carry dirt into the crack—and there's no way to flush it out.

As you can surmise, it's best to do the repair as soon as possible, assuming that it's repairable. Remember that not all chips can be fixed. The best you can hope for is to fill most of the chip. It may still leave a visible flaw. But the improvement on most chips will be dramatic, and at least you've sealed the chip from the atmosphere and probably eliminated the possibility of it growing larger or discoloring in the future.

You can't fix long cracks. So it's critical that you fill chips before they turn into cracks. Basically, any chip that goes into the surface of the glass perpendicular to the surface or at a shallow angle can be repaired. That includes cone-shaped chips, leaf-shaped chips or almost any chip that hasn't flaked a big piece of glass off onto the road.

Let's Go Shopping

Windshield crack repair kits can be found in the auto parts department of many mass merchandisers like Kmart, Sears and Wal-Mart, as well as more traditional auto parts stores like Pep Boys and AutoZone. Failing that, the warehouse-distributor auto parts stores that cater to professional mechanics can supply you.

In the New York area, we found two different types of repair kits and there may be others. Expect to pay around 12 bucks. Procedures differ marginally, but the principle is the same. We fixed a couple of windshields, and the results were excellent.

How Dry I Am

Start with an absolutely dry windshield that's somewhere near room temperature. Tough on a rainy or wintery day, so you may need to park your car indoors for a while to equilibrate. Dry is really essential—you don't want to trap any water in the repair. Use a hair dryer if the window is wet. If the surface is dirty, don't use any detergents or window cleaner. Lighter fluid or acetone can help dry and clean the surface, but don't use so much that it dribbles down the glass and peels the paint, or worse.

Chips Ahoy

We first used a simple kit from Loctite with a one-part adhesive and an uncomplicated syringe to apply it. Start by peeling off the backing film on one side of the precut adhesive strip and applying it to the precleaned glass, centered over the chip. Burnish with the back of your thumbnail or a blunt object (**Fig. 2**). Now peel the remaining film. Orient the plastic adapter so that the fitting is as close to vertical as possible and stick it to the film. Burnish again.

Pull the cap off the syringe, keeping it pointy-end up so the adhesive doesn't wind up on the fender. Attach the syringe to the adapter. Now here's the tricky part—lay your watch down somewhere so you can see the second hand. Grasp the syringe body with one hand to stabilize it, and pull the handle of the syringe out as far as it will go. Because you've taken your watch off, you can hold the handle in this position for a full minute. This pulls a partial vacuum in the syringe—and in the crack. While you're holding this vacuum, the air in the crack bubbles up through the adhesive in the syringe, while adhesive creeps down toward the glass and chip.

Now let go of the handle. Don't follow the handle, let it go abruptly. The pressure wave from the handle slamming down will force adhesive into the crack. Repeat this suck-and-slam operation a half-dozen times or so, forcing the crack virtually full of adhesive (**Fig. 3**).

Now remove the syringe, adapter and adhesive sheet. There will be a film of adhesive on the surface of the glass. You can chase that back with an alcohol-dampened paper towel, but leave the pimple of adhesive right above the crack undisturbed until it cures for a few hours.

With the pimple hardened, simply take a single-edge razor blade and shave the protruding adhesive off. Use a sharp blade, and you'll be able to do this in a single pass.

The Other Path

We tried a different crack repair kit as well. This differed in that it used a two-part adhesive. This required us to mix two small vials of adhesive and hardener in the syringe before starting, which was simple. The adhesive disc and syringe adapter were similar (if not identical) to the simpler kit's, and were applied in an identical fashion. The syringe, however, was more complex. It used a wire latch arrange-

HOW IT WORKS

Laminated Safety Glass

Ordinary window glass, like you have around the house, is pretty amazing stuff. It's clear, strong and cheap. But it's also brittle, shattering into long, dangerous, wickedly sharp shards when overstressed. Plastics would be as strong, but not nearly hard enough to resist scratching and remain clear enough for a car window—just look at any plastic-glazed outdoor bus stop or phone booth, with its patina of fine scratches. For the side windows of cars, automakers have come up with a good compromise: tempered glass. It's stronger than standard, but more importantly, when it does shatter it breaks up into small granules. These granules are still sharp, but should do less damage than the long shards of untempered glass. However, for a windshield, constantly bombarded by pebbles, tempered glass would have a short life span.

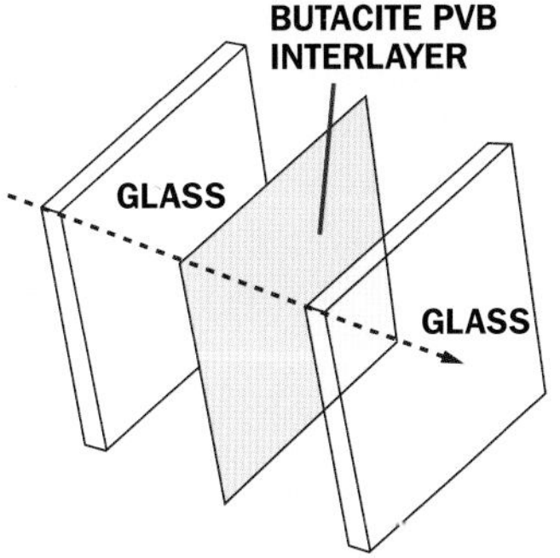

So, many years back, the car manufacturers switched to a laminated glass sandwich for the windshield. It's a simple process. Two thinner sheets of glass are fused to a rubber inner layer. The tempered-glass outer layers are then independent of each other. The rubbery center sheet provides damping to any shock waves from errant stones, reducing the probability of breakage. And if the glass is hit by an object smartly enough, odds are that only the outer sheet will break, as is the case with most stone chips. If a really big piece of debris hits the glass hard enough to break both inner and outer layers, the tough membrane prevents it from winding up in your lap. Even better, the shards of glass from the inner lamination wind up stuck to the membrane, keeping them from spalling away from the windshield at a high velocity, causing great havoc.

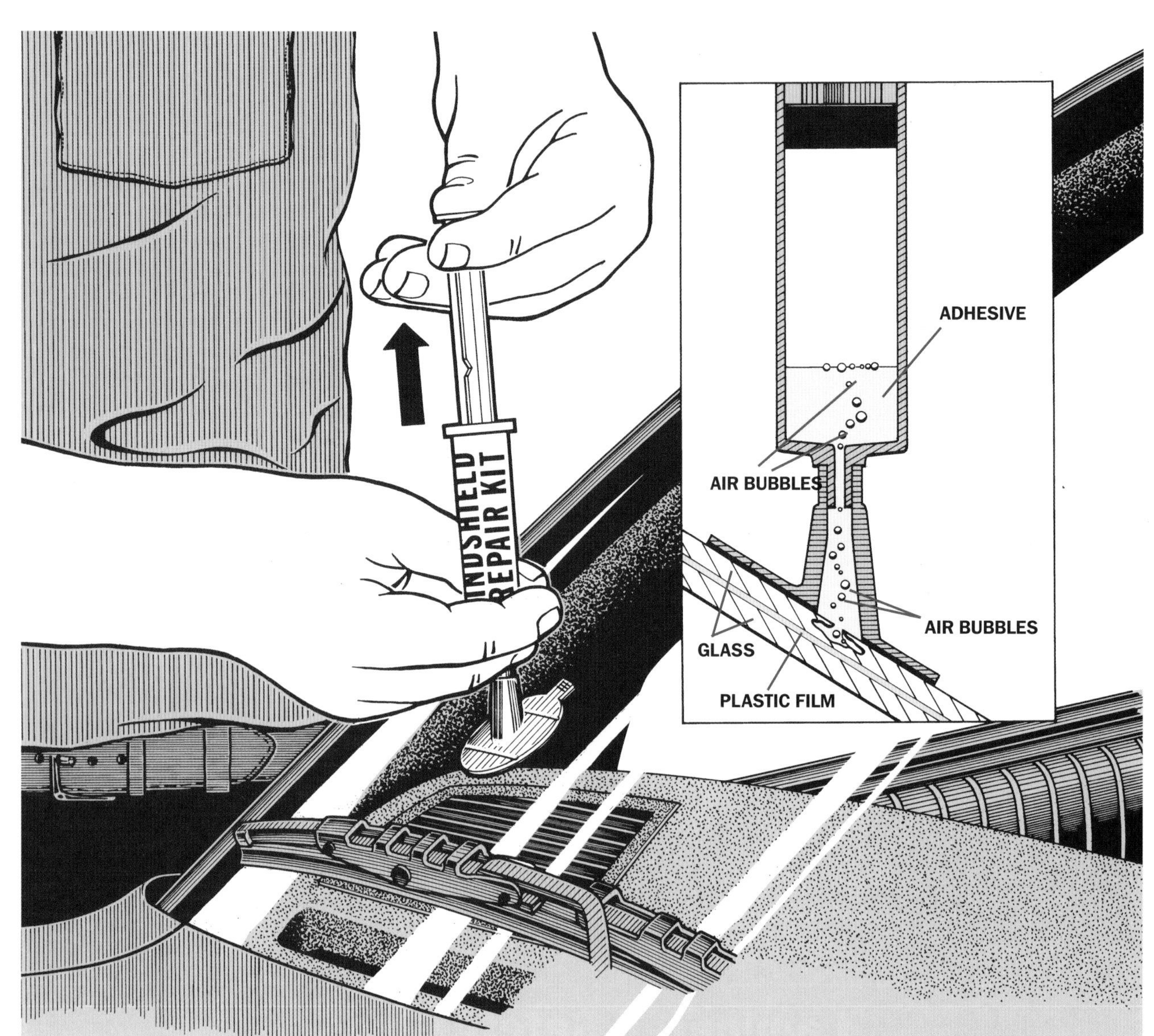

ment on the body that dropped into two notches on the handle when necessary. A simple pushpin stuck into the body was used as a very crude valve to let air in and out of the body. Once the syringe is attached to the adapter (the adapter already being stuck airtight to the glass), the pushpin is removed. Now bottom the syringe plunger, pushing the air out. Insert the pin, and pull the handle out until the clip clicks into the slot. This will hold the plunger out, and the partial vacuum under it for the designated time.

Now, rather than rapidly releasing the pressure like we did with the earlier kit, remove the pin, admitting air into the syringe barrel. Now replace the pin, sealing the hole. Release the clip, and push the handle in, lightly pressurizing the barrel and forcing adhesive into the chip for a minute or so. The second slot will trap the clip as soon as you've pushed in far enough. Repeat this "vent, suck, vent, squeeze" operation several times to force adhesive into the crack.

While the ingenious clip-and-slot and vent business relieves you of the necessity of constantly grasping the syringe barrel like it's the last beer at the picnic, there are caveats. The vacuum pulled isn't as good, purging less air on every iteration. And the simpler kit seemed to force the adhesive deeper into the crack faster by using the plunger as a piston to rapidly pressurize the system.

(Fig. 3) Alternating cycles of vacuum and pressure will push adhesive into the chip, and evacuate air from the bottom of the chip.

Having said that, both kits did a bang-up job. After shaving the excess adhesive off, both cracks are barely visible. The adhesive is clear, and has the same refractive index as the glass so that it renders the crack invisible from almost any angle.

One warning: Don't get cute and try to depress the plunger by hand and squeeze the adhesive deeper into the glass with either kit. The adhesive patch might become unglued and squirt adhesive all over your windshield and fender and shirt. Don't ask how we know this.

EASY

Finding and Fixing Water and Air Leaks

As you finish your morning coffee, you wait for the weather forecast. And it's what you've been dreading: rain. For most people, rain during rush hour means little more than annoyance and perhaps increased driving stress and travel time. But for you, driving in the rain means a miserably wet ride, a ruined suit and possibly ruined shoes as well, unless you take precautions and change into your wet-weather driving clothes. You, like many other folks on the road, have a car that suffers from a water leak.

You're all too familiar with that cold rainwater steadily dripping from under the dash and flowing down your left leg. Your discomfort is exacerbated by the piercing whistle originating at the source of the leak.

You contemplate simply phoning in sick, but then you gird your resolve. Before heading out to the garage, you decide that you're going to find the source of those leaks and squelch them once and for all—even if you have to tear the entire car apart.

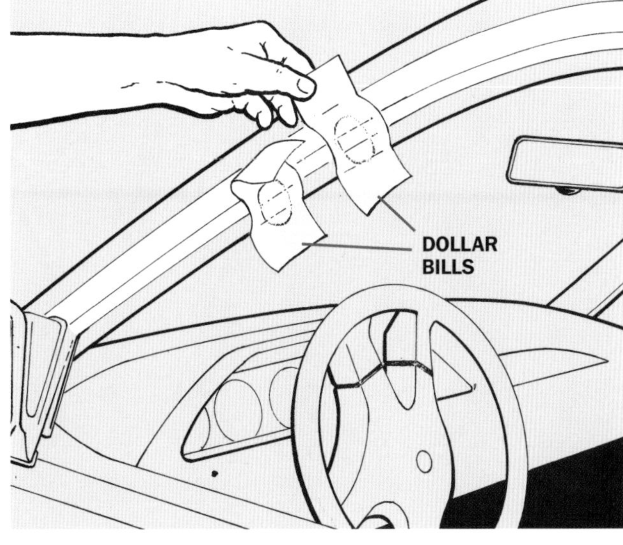

(Fig. 1) A gasket loose enough to let a dollar slide easily might leak air at speed. Tug firmly, but don't tear the bill.

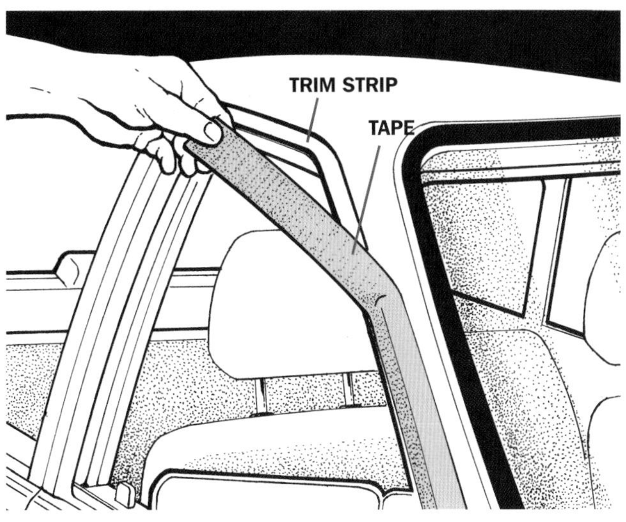

(Fig. 2) Wind can slide under trim pieces and whistle. Use tape to find the culprit, then seal the leak with trim adhesive or silicone seal.

Wind Noise

As you drive, air surrounding the car creates large pressure differentials between the inside and outside of the body. The greatest differential occurs along the sides of the car between the roof and belt line where outside pressure is much lower than the pressure in the passenger compartment.

Weatherstripping and window seals are supposed to keep passenger-compartment air in and outside air out. When they are damaged, however, whistles, hissing and other annoying noises occur.

Therefore, the place to start looking for air leaks is the weatherstripping. Torn, missing or distorted sections are likely sources of leaks that result in wind noise. You should also inspect the door's weatherstrip sealing surface for bumps, lumps or other imperfections that could prevent an otherwise healthy weatherstrip from fully seating.

Replace torn or missing weatherstrips, but do not use a generic weatherstrip intended for storm doors to replace the carefully engineered rubber seal—unless you're desperate. The dealership should be able to order the correct part for you, or you may be able to find what you need on a similar car in a junkyard. It's also possible to repair torn sections of weatherstrip with silicone seal or strong, quick-drying glue. But first clean the pieces with alcohol or lacquer thinner. Don't be afraid to piece short lengths together.

In addition, many firms make replacement gaskets for older cars at very reasonable prices—although you may need to buy an entire kit. J.C. Whitney and other companies also sell weatherstrip by the yard in an array of different profiles.

Distorted sections often can be repaired simply by heating them with a heat gun or a hair dryer and then reforming them by hand.

A quick way to check for air leaks is to rub chalk on the surface of the weatherstrip. When you shut the door, chalk dust will transfer from the

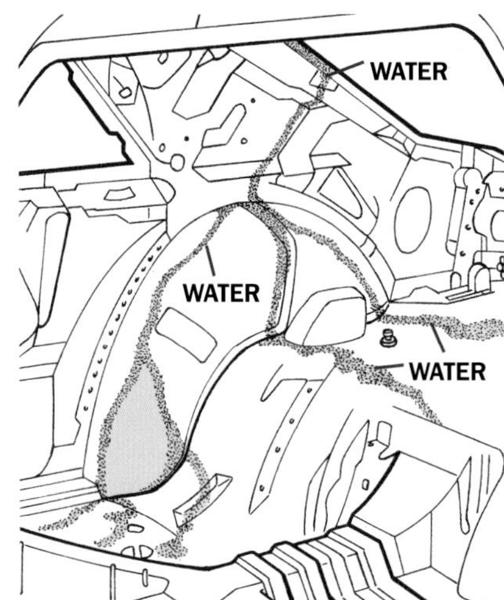

(Fig. 3) Body water leaks are tough to find because the water runs down to a low spot far from the source of the leak.

(Fig. 4) Use a helper and a garden hose to follow water leaks back to their source. You may need to remove some trim to find the spot.

strip to the door on areas that seal properly. You can also check for leaks in small areas by placing a dollar bill between the weatherstrip and the door (**Fig. 1**). After closing the door, pull the dollar bill. If it moves too easily, you've found a gap.

Air leaks can also be caused by a misadjusted door or worn door hinges that allow the door to sag. To check door alignment, make sure there are even gaps between the closed door and the body. The outer surface of the door should also be flush with the surrounding sheetmetal. To check for worn hinges, open the door and lift it up and down to see if the hinges allow movement. If they do, they'll have to be replaced.

Pressure Me

You can simulate inside/outside pressure differentials in a parked vehicle using the heater or air-conditioning blower to pressurize the passenger compartment while you look for leaks.

To do this, begin by blocking all interior exhaust vents (they're usually found on the C pillars) with duct tape. Also make sure that any dash-mounted fresh-air vents are closed. Next, start the engine so the vacuum-operated vent controls will operate, then set the HVAC controls to draw in outside air on the highest blower setting. Shut off the engine and turn the key to the accessory position so the blower still operates, and then close the doors.

In a short while, pressure will build in the passenger compartment. Check for air leaks by moving your hand slowly around window glass and weatherstripping to feel for air leaks. Mark suspect areas with tape so you can correct them later.

Instead of feeling for leaks, you can listen for them by using a stethoscope or by placing one end of a piece of small-diameter tubing at the seal and listening at the other end.

Repair small gaps between the body and the weatherstripping by shimming it with vinyl foam tape. On doors with frames, leaks can also occur around window seals. If the seals are not torn or missing, you can often adjust the window track behind the door panel so the window rides more tightly against the seal.

Wind noise can also be caused by loose driprail covers, molding, the grille and external accessories. If you suspect a noise is coming from one of these areas, cover it or modify its shape with tape to see if the noise disappears (**Fig. 2**). If it does, you've found the problem.

Water Leaks

You may not realize it, but when it rains, water may flow all over the inside of a car body. Depending on the car's design, water can run down the insides of C pillars, the insides of doors and through the cowl. Fortunately, cars also have systems that channel the water to places that serve as drains. If the drain holes are plugged, water backs up and, before you know it, water is inside the car. To keep this from happening, make sure cowling shields and trunk and hood weatherstripping are in place and in good shape. You should also periodically inspect door- and rocker-panel drainage holes to make sure they are clear of debris that would prevent them from draining freely.

In addition to leaking through weatherstripping and window seals, water can drip through body welds, seams, pinholes, plugs and other areas where gaps or holes exist.

Unlike air, water is affected by gravity, so no matter where the leak originates, the water will eventually wind up in a lower part of the vehicle (**Fig. 3**). Water can also travel far from its original entry point. For example, it's not unusual for water to enter near the roofline and travel down the inside of the passenger compartment between the trim and body. Whether it becomes visible before it gets to the floor depends on its course.

How do you tell if a water leak starts at a floor-pan seam or the moonroof? Start with common sense: If the floor pan gets wet only when you drive through deep puddles, assume the water is coming from a rust hole, a missing body plug, body-seam leak or other opening down low. The floor pan, fender wells and the lower portion of the engine bulkhead are prime leak areas. If the floor is wet when it rains, but you haven't driven the car, assume that the water is entering at a higher point, such as a moonroof, roof pillar or the window sealing areas. A drip from under the dash might be traced to the cowling below the windshield.

Fight Water with Water

Not surprisingly, you can use water to find water leaks. The best way to spot leaks is to have an assistant inside the car look for leaks while you spray suspect areas with low-pressure spray from a garden hose (**Fig. 4**).

To accurately pinpoint leaks, you may have to remove interior trim components from the door, roof pillars or even the floor. As you move the water spray from lower to higher points on the vehicle, have your assistant shine a flashlight on areas that correspond to the area that you're spraying.

Leak Repair Products

- **Permatex 65AR: Windshield and glass sealer.**
- **3M 08655: Brushable seam sealer.**
- **3M 08011: Weatherstrip adhesive.**
- **3M 08578: Strip caulk that can be molded by hand to fill gaps, seams and other large areas.**
- **3M 08551: Clear sealer for small leaks around windshield, rear windows, reveal moldings and small seams.**

Leaks in the urethane seal around the windshield or rear window can be especially troublesome to spot. If you suspect an area, wipe the outside down with soapy water, then have your assistant blow compressed air on the area. If the water bubbles on the outside, you've found the leak.

Keep in mind that late-model cars have windshields and rear windows that are installed with urethane sealers. Because they affect the structural integrity of the roof, only glass- or body-repair professionals should attempt to repair these leaks.

Repairs

You'll want to replace or repair all defective seals, weatherstrips and guards (**Fig. 5**). There are many types of material for filling and sealing body leaks. Consult the box to the left to determine the best material for repairing a leak.

If you want to have a leak repaired by a professional, take your car to a technician who is certified by the inter-industry conference on collision auto repair (I-CAR). I-CAR technicians have been trained in the proper methods of sealing bodies.

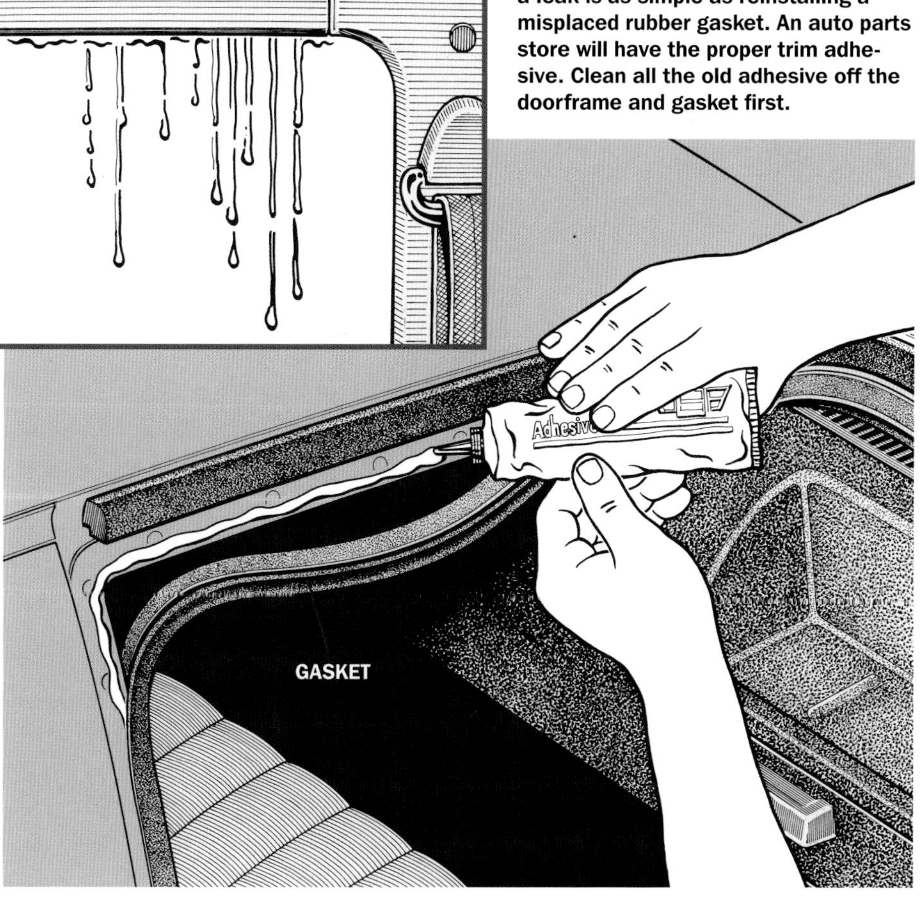

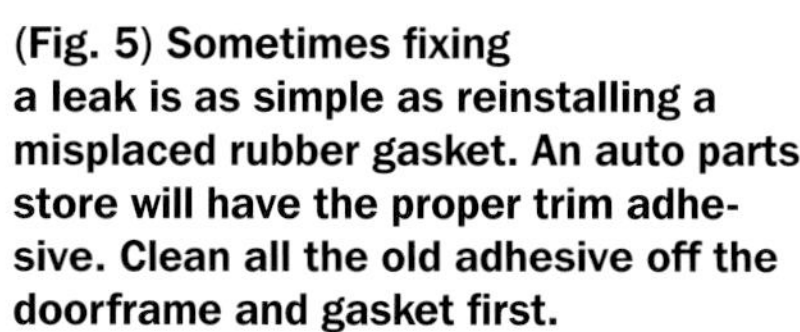

(Fig. 5) Sometimes fixing a leak is as simple as reinstalling a misplaced rubber gasket. An auto parts store will have the proper trim adhesive. Clean all the old adhesive off the doorframe and gasket first.

EASY

Storing Your Car

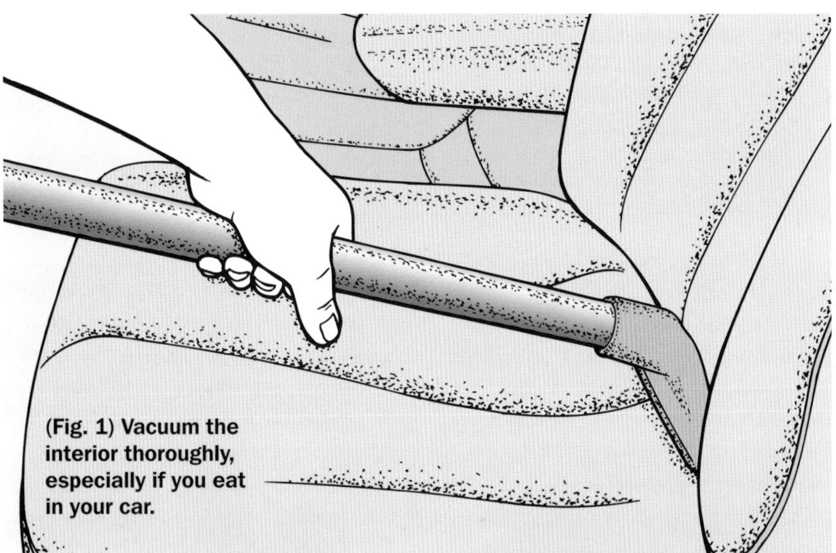

(Fig. 1) Vacuum the interior thoroughly, especially if you eat in your car.

You pull into your driveway, take a loving look at the new convertible and realize: Buying it was the fulfillment of a dream. It's been great fun driving it this summer and fall, but winter is approaching and there's no way you're going to drive it on snow and subject it to corrosive road salt—so you face the problem of storing it until late next spring.

A 2- to 4-month driving season followed by eight to 10 months of storage is something many car enthusiasts

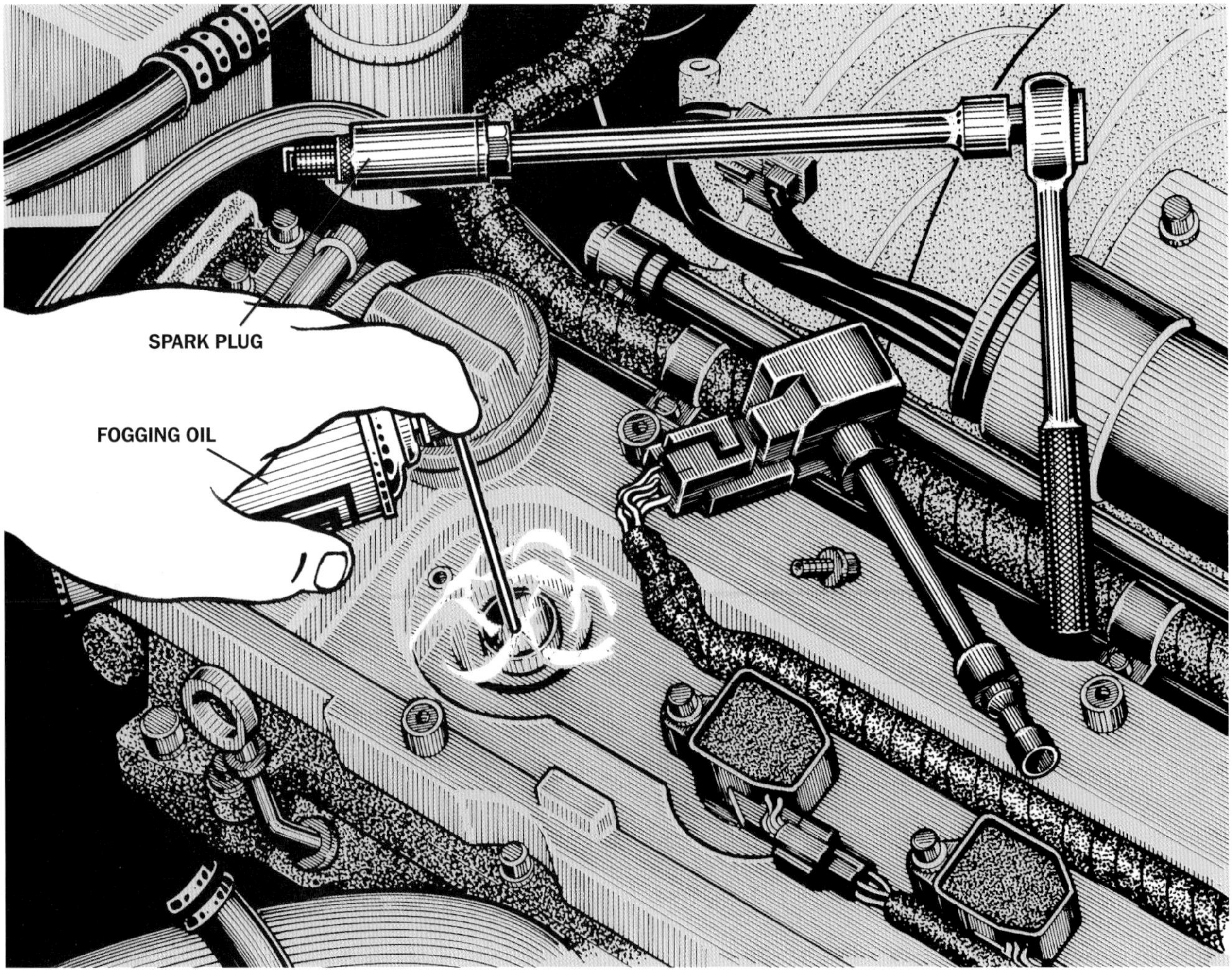

(Fig. 2) To prevent rusting inside the cylinders, spray fogging oil down the plug holes.

SPARK PLUG

FOGGING OIL

go through every year. Maybe you're a snowbird with a pair of vehicles that go into 6-month storage at both your warm- and cold-weather locations during the away season.

Even more traumatic: You've got a work assignment or a military posting far from home and can't bring the car. Whatever the vehicle, the reason and the season, you want to be able to store the vehicle without big expense, yet with minimum deterioration and an easy return to operation.

The Basics

Indoors is always better, particularly for an older vehicle, even if the storage period is summer in the South. If you're going to be away for up to a couple of years, it definitely has to be kept inside. If you don't have the place, find an indoor storage facility—it will be money well spent. In fact, you also should get someone to take out the car periodically for an "exercising" drive. If you can't afford to do long-term storage right, you might have to pay a lot for restoration when you return.

If outdoor "storage" is your only choice, don't give up. There's still a lot you can do to minimize the damage, particularly for seasonal storage.

Prepping the Vehicle

The cleaner the vehicle the better, and that goes beyond wash, wax and shine. Pick a warm, dry day to do the cleaning. Fill the gas tank, then add an adequate amount of gasoline stabilizer (also made for lawnmowers, snowblowers, etc.) to prevent gum and varnish formation. Drive the car long enough to really warm up the engine and mix the stabilizer with the fuel—at least 30 to 40 miles. Remove dirt from the underbody, particularly from the wheel wells. Dirt holds moisture, and the combination of moisture and air causes iron and steel to rust.

Really, really clean the interior and trunk of the vehicle with a household vacuum cleaner, using those little attachments that reach into nooks and crannies (**Fig. 1**). The battery-powered car vacuum just doesn't have the suction. The object is to remove all pizza crusts, jellybeans, dog biscuits—anything that could nourish a critter.

Indoor Storage

Allow the car to air-dry. If the garage or shed has a concrete or earth floor, create a floor vapor barrier with plastic sheeting or tarps. With an earth floor, make a drive-along "path" from strips cut from a sheet of plywood and place them over the vapor barrier.

Remove the spark plugs and spray some oil into the cylinders to prevent rust and corrosion. You can use conventional engine oil with a spray-type squirt can or aerosol fogging oil designed for boat storage (**Fig. 2**). Turn the crankshaft (with a socket and ratchet wrench on the crank pulley bolt) about four to six times to circulate the oil. Reinstall the spark plugs and reconnect the plug wires.

Disconnect the battery cables (ground cable first) and remove the battery. Clean the top and sides of the battery to remove any moisture-retaining, conductive film. Place it on a clean, dry surface such as blocks of wood or a polystyrene spacer (**Fig. 3**). Connect a float charger, one designed to maintain a battery charge for long periods. Removing the battery also gives you the chance to inspect the battery box for any corrosion, and to clean it out.

(Fig. 3) Remove the battery and keep it clear of damp concrete.

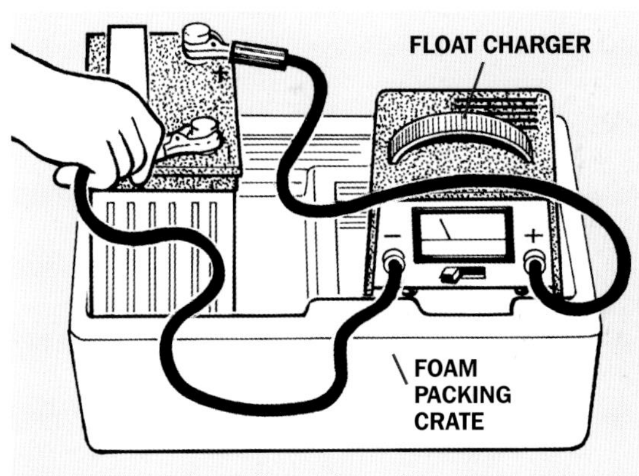

Lubricate the hood release latch, hood and door hinges to protect them from moisture (**Fig. 4**).

Brake fluid absorbs moisture, which can cause rust and corrosion in the brake system. Flush the old fluid with new. Check the freeze point of the engine coolant with a hydrometer to make sure it's low enough for the ambient temperatures.

Protection from rodents and other critters is important. They not only chew on spark plug wires and other wires, but they can crawl into openings and set up residence. Stuff thick, clean rags into the tailpipe, engine air intake and the fresh air intake in front of the windshield, unless it's covered by mesh (or a cabin air filter). If you know you have mice in the area that may enjoy making nesting material out of your cloth rags, use aluminum foil instead (**Fig. 5**). If the vehicle is to be left for six months or longer, the issue of flat-spotting the tires is worth considering. Prevention is straightforward if you have a set of four jackstands. Jack up each end of the vehicle so that it's high enough to slip a jackstand, in the lowest position, under each lower arm. Jackstands will eventually sink into dirt floors—use plywood squares under them.

Stuff clean rags between the wiper arms and windshield to hold the blades off the glass (or remove the blades). This will keep them from sticking to the glass, which could both leave marks and ruin the rubber (**Fig. 6**). Apply a film of rubber lubricant to the squeegees.

Empty a large container of mothballs on the floor all around and under the vehicle to discourage critters.

Outdoor Storage

If you must store outside on an earth surface, the best you can do is park the car on a layer of plywood over a continuous layer of heavy-duty plastic. The combination won't keep all windblown moisture from snow and rain off the underbody. However, to

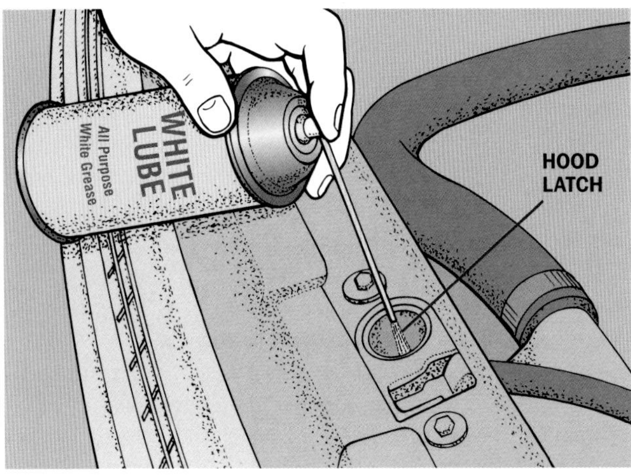

(Fig. 4) Lube all the hinges and latches so you can get them open when you ultimately reanimate your car.

(Fig. 5) Stuff rags or aluminum foil into the tailpipe to keep out rodents and insects.

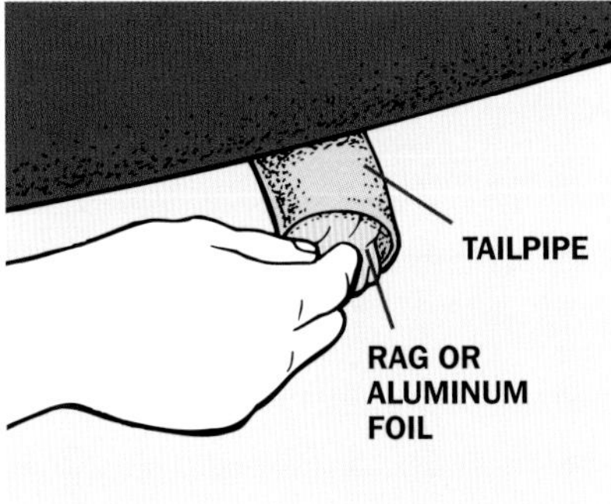

do any better in a windy area you'd have to make the plastic layer oversize. As a final step before placing any cover, lift the ends up and tuck them into the body (trap them in bottom door openings, tape and tie to unpainted trim, etc.) to create a sort of underbody diaper. This is not easy because you don't want plastic sheeting against painted metal body parts, where it could trap moisture and cause rust and paint damage.

Outdoor storage prep, like indoor, starts with a clean, dry vehicle. Put mothballs in the passenger cabin, laying them on sheets of aluminum foil. Leave each window open a half-inch, so the interior can breathe, but cut some strips of fine screening to cover the openings and tape the strips to glass and molding with masking tape. Be careful not to tape to the car body paint surfaces.

Perform all the other indoor prep, including insect- and rodent-proofing and rust and corrosion prevention. Also remove the battery and store it indoors, connected to a trickle charger.

We've saved the toughest topic for last: body covering. The plain fact is that you have to cover the body, and there's no perfect way to do so. That's why we say that indoors is No. 1, and outdoors is No. 2—because it's all that's left.

There are more choices in body covers than we can count, ranging from $20 to more than $300. At the lowest price, you're likely to get just a plastic cover that's made in a few sizes to fit all vehicles in a specific category (car, SUV, truck). It may not fit well and it can trap moisture underneath, damaging the vehicle finish. It's intended as a dust and rain cover for a day or two—at best.

Fit is very important, even if the cover is a "breather" (just porous enough to allow air to pass through, but able to restrict moisture). Wind can whip the inner surface of a loose-fitting cover against the paint and when you peel off the cover, the body may look as if the paint had been sanded. As the prices go up, so does the quality of the fit of the covers—and the materials will be more body-friendly.

(Fig. 6) Prop the wiper arms off the windshield (or backlight) with rags, so they don't stick to the glass.

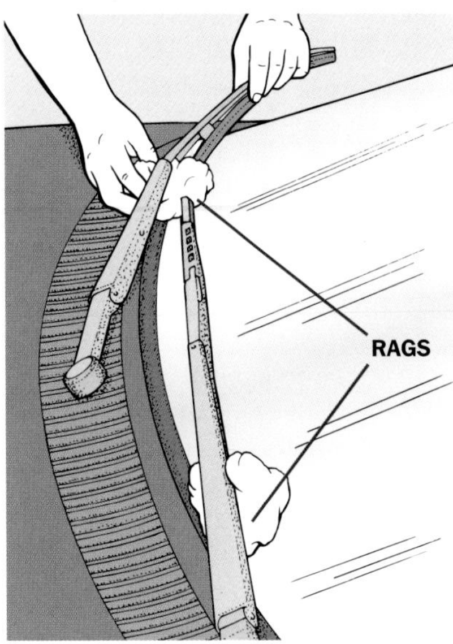

For sunny areas, pick a cover material that keeps out ultraviolet rays to protect the car's finish. But also prep the interior surfaces with suitable protectants such as leather conditioner and plastic treatment.

If you're in a wet 'n' windy area, you can get extra protection by first covering the body paint with soft blankets, tied down with bungee cords. The blankets not only will wick up moisture that gets through, but also provide a protective layer under the vehicle cover.

A premium, breathable custom-fit cover that extends down to cover the wheel wells, and is secured with straps, is your best bet for outside.

Getting Ready to Drive

It's driving season, you've opened the garage door and you're eyeing the car. In addition to unpacking, refitting the battery and so forth, sand most of the rust off the brake rotors with some 100-grit sandpaper on a rubber block, and change the engine oil and filter. You should be ready to roll.

Exercising the Car

Back after an away-from-home work assignment? If you did not opt for the "exercise program," you'll need to take your beloved for a serious drive. Just starting the engine and letting it reach operating temperature is not what we mean. That actually can be harmful, allowing oil dilution by fuel and moisture. A 30-mile drive every 60 days, with brakes, transmission, steering and air conditioning all operating, is what the car really needs. If you don't stint on this, the car will feel every bit as good as you remember.

Drying Out Your Flooded Car

We've all seen it on TV: rainstorms of biblical proportions sweeping entire villages into the sea, and damp, devastated flood victims being interviewed in front of a pile of sodden furnishings and clothing. But then it happens closer to home—only this time it's your car, not the entire village. There's a high-water line halfway up the windshield, and several inches of mud in the interior and the trunk. It smells like a swamp, and it's only getting worse in the hot sun. And the insurance adjuster says he'll be by in a few days.

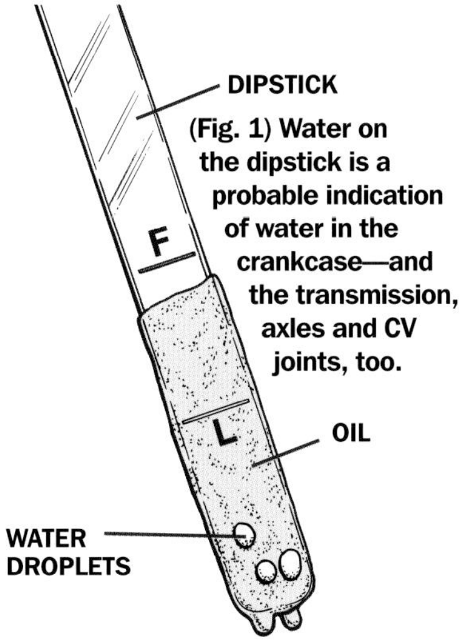

(Fig. 1) Water on the dipstick is a probable indication of water in the crankcase—and the transmission, axles and CV joints, too.

How Dry I Am

Don't wait for the adjuster to arrive. Mold and corrosion are setting in now. You need to clean out as much liquid and mud as you can and dry out your car as soon as possible. Don't try to start the car. If there's water in the engine, transmission or fuel system, you'll just compound the damage.

Disconnect the battery ground strap first—you must do this, otherwise you'll fry something.

Next, begin assessing just how deep the water got. Frankly, if the waterline is as high as the dashboard, you will probably be better off talking the adjuster into totaling the car and getting another. Double that for salt water. The mechanical systems and the interior can be dried out or cleaned with a lot of labor, but the electrical systems on modern cars are extremely complex. These systems rely on a lot of low-voltage signals from sensors in the engine management system and ABS. These low-voltage signals are extremely sensitive to corrosion on connectors, and problems can crop up for years.

Look for a high-water mark. That can be easy—if the water was muddy or there was a lot of floating grass and leaves. But clean water may leave no residue. Look for water inside the doors and the taillights, and dampness in the carpets and interior trim. This will allow you to eliminate cleaning some areas or systems on the car unnecessarily. Let's go through those systems.

Drivetrain

Check the dipsticks for the engine and transmission. If there are water droplets clinging to the end of either dipstick, you absolutely, positively need to change the oil and filter before even thinking about starting the engine (**Fig. 1**). If the water was muddy, it's probably wisest to remove the oil pan from the engine and wash the mud out. Change the oil and filter again in a few hundred miles, too.

Late-model cars have sealed fuel systems, and probably won't get any water in them. But that classic '55 T-Bird probably ingested some water if it was deep enough and lingered long enough. Siphon the fuel out into a container and look for water. If you find any, it's probably best to drop the tank and get it cleaned professionally. Blow out the fuel line, and you may need to get water out of the carburetor float bowls as well. If you find evidence of water in a fuel-injected car or truck's tank, replace the fuel filter as well. That paper element may deteriorate if it gets waterlogged. It's not that a few drops of clean water are bad, but floodwater is usually pretty foul with silt and sludge.

Muddy water can infiltrate its way past engine seals within a few hours (**Fig. 2**). Crankshaft seals, transmission seals and axle and CV joint seals are adequate to keep lubricants in, but they are not designed to keep standing

(Fig. 2) Engine seals are better at keeping oil inside than in keeping water and mud outside.

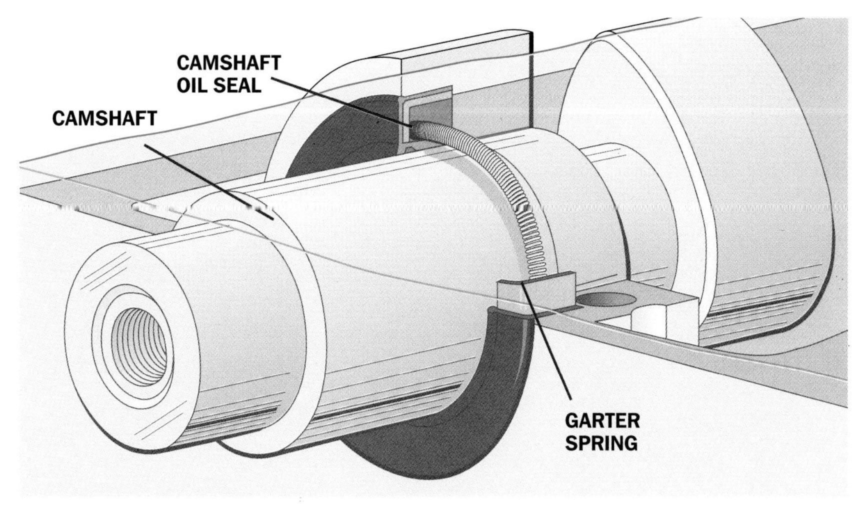

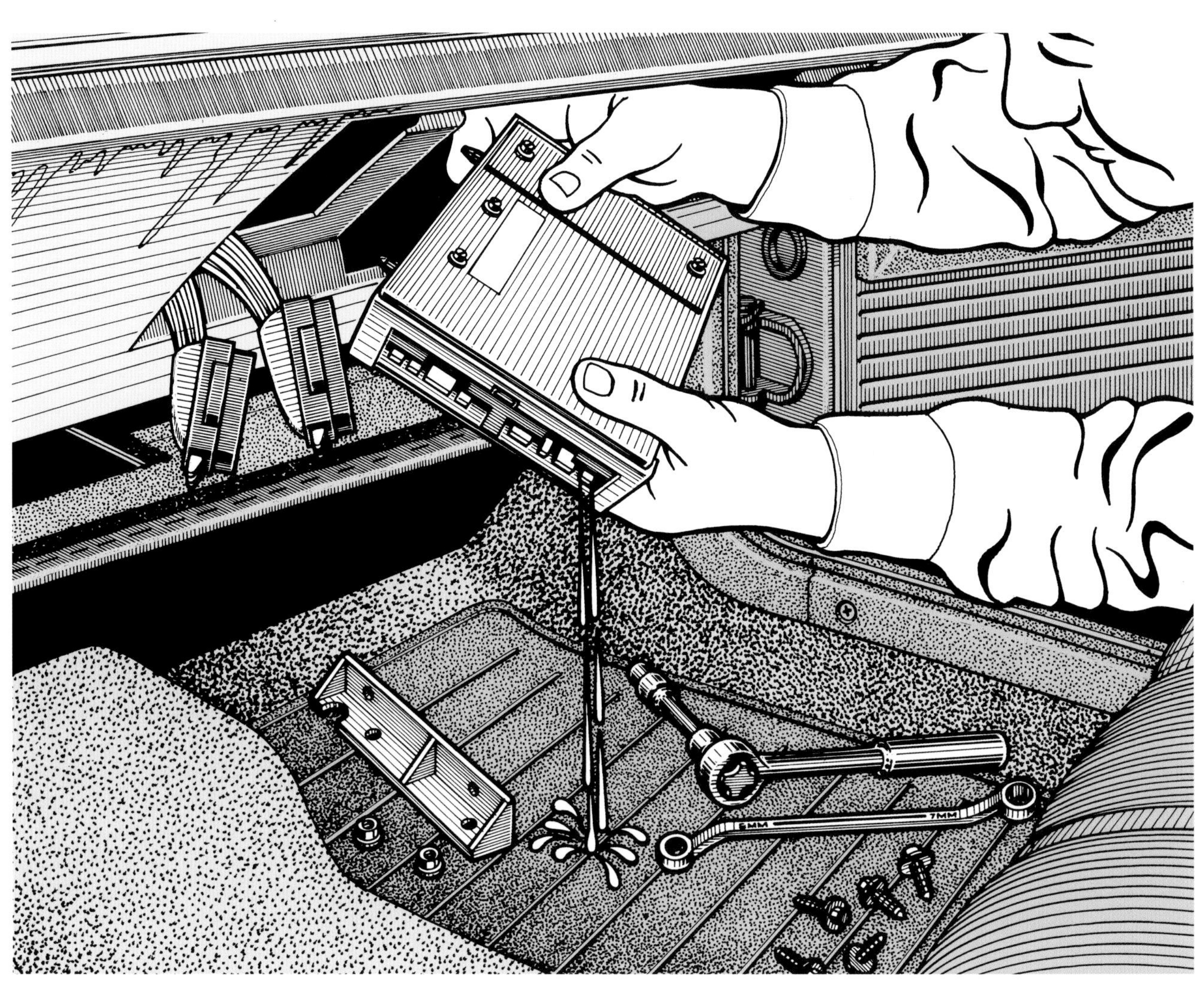

(Fig. 3) Generally mounted in the passenger kickwell, the engine management computer is highly likely to be wet if water rises above the floorboards of your car. Rinse with demineralized water, and dry with a hair dryer. You may be lucky, but more likely, you'll need a replacement.

water from creeping in. Before you start the engine, or tow a car with the wheels on the ground, drain and change the oil, transmission fluid and final-drive lube. Check the dipstick for water droplets. And then change those fluids again in a thousand miles or so if there was evidence of muddy water. And don't forget wheel bearings and constant velocity joints, which will need to be cleaned and repacked. Some front-drive cars have sealed-for-life front axle bearings, and you'll simply have to wait for those to fail, because it's nearly impossible to clean and relube them.

Down Under and In

If the water came up only to the doorsills, you may be in luck. Aside from mud or salt water on the brakes, there's little to damage on the underside of the car. Use fresh water to hose everything down. If the calipers or brake drum cylinders were submerged for more than an hour or two, flush and bleed the brake fluid, in case water seeped backward past the seals.

If the exhaust system was submerged and is full of water, just start the engine after you've determined there's no water in the oil.

Water get high enough to get the interior wet? If the water was clear, fresh rainwater, just vacuum the carpets and let everything air-dry with the windows open in the sun. Odds are that the water was muddy, and that the seats are wet, too. You may not be able to rescue the sponge rubber seat cushions, but it's worth trying. If the seat cushions are wet, rinse with fresh water, and wet-vacuum as much water out as possible. Leave them in the sun to dry. If mildew or mold starts to get a foothold before things dry, use a commercial disinfectant spray to knock it down. Remove as much of the interior as you can, rinse it in fresh water and hang it up to dry. That includes the door panels, and stuff like the interior panels and fiberboard glovebox.

Rinse the inside of the car with clean water and dry it out. This includes the inside of the doors and fenders. Don't forget the trunk.

There's one critical piece of gear you need to deal with immediately if the interior was flooded: the computer. The engine management computer is often mounted behind the passenger kick panel or under the seat, and it's not weatherproofed at all **(Fig. 3)**. Pull the kick panel, remove the computer

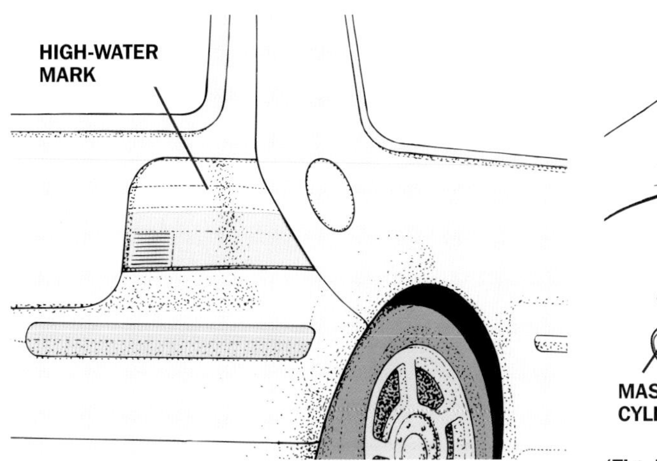

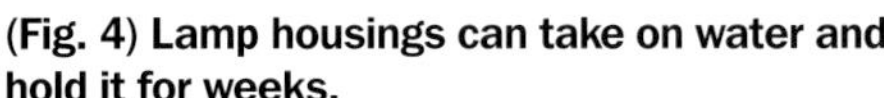
(Fig. 4) Lamp housings can take on water and hold it for weeks.

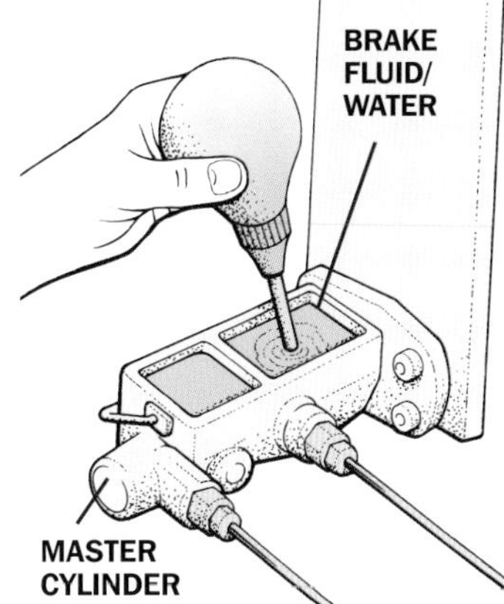

(Fig. 5) Suck most of the brake fluid out and flush the system thoroughly with fresh fluid.

from its harness and get it out. If there's evidence of moisture, rinse in clean water. Then rinse again in demineralized water. Dry with a hair dryer, sunshine or an oven set to 175° F. Clean the electrical contacts on the wiring harness, and lubricate with electrical contact grease. Don't reinstall it until everything is dry.

It's not uncommon to see a high-water mark inside the light housings (**Fig. 4**), especially if the flood lasted for more than an hour or two. Dampness or water/mud inside the head- and taillight fixtures needs to be dried. Remove the wet assembly, pull the bulb and rinse the light housing thoroughly so the chrome-plated reflector doesn't discolor. Dry in the sun. Remember, if you have quartz-halogen bulbs in your headlights, clean the quartz glass with alcohol and don't touch the bulb while reinstalling it or it'll burn out within a few hours.

Brake fluid is soluble in water, so you won't find any wet evidence of contamination. Water can backtrack past caliper and wheel cylinder seals, so prompt flushing is called for. Suck most of the old fluid/water out of the master cylinder reservoir, and refill with fresh fluid (**Fig. 5**). Flush one corner of the brake system until you see fresh fluid at the bleeder by pushing down on the pedal while a helper cracks the bleeder, and then hold the pedal down while he closes it. Repeat. Don't allow any air to enter the system at either end. Run the entire quart of brake fluid through to make sure you've gotten it all. Does the car have ABS? Rinse and dry out the ABS computer, although it may be more difficult to find and remove than the engine computer. Check a repair manual to find it, if necessary. Rinse and lubricate the harness connections to the wheel speed sensors. ABS relies on precision metering valves, lots of electrical solenoids and low-voltage sensors, so you can expect problems down the line, especially if your car was immersed in salt water.

Electrical

As mentioned earlier, modern cars have lots of critical, low-voltage, low-current circuits—the kind that are most sensitive to resistance caused by corrosion in the connectors. Fortunately, these connections are pretty well weatherproofed. But it will still pay to dry them out. Systematically disconnect every electrical connector you can find. Do this one at time so you don't wind up reconnecting them to the wrong place, of course. If you find water or contamination, clean with demineralized water to remove salt or mud, and air-dry. Some connections should be lubed with silicone spray or dielectric grease, while others, usually ones with sealed connectors, should be air dried and reassembled dry and clean. Be sure this type is really dry, as any leftover moisture will be trapped inside the connector forever.

On the Road Again

Finally, after everything has been dried out and lubed, put it all back together and give 'er the smoke test—hook up the battery and fire it up. Won't crank? Guess what—the raging floodwaters may have diluted your battery electrolyte. The only fix is a new battery.

HOW IT WORKS

Salvage Titles

As incredible as it may seem, it's possible for a dealer or an individual to acquire, legally, a title for a car that's been flood-damaged and totaled that doesn't reflect the damage. In most states, totaled cars' titles bear a salvage tag on the title. But a dealer can wholesale the car out to a state that issues the fresh title without tagging the car as salvage. Which states? It doesn't matter because once the title has been laundered, it can be retitled in any state, clean as a whistle. And I'd rather not say, so nobody gets any ideas about laundering the title to a damaged car.

So caveat emptor (let the buyer beware). Always examine any potential used car or truck purchases with a jaundiced eye. Look carefully for evidence that the vehicle has been wet: i.e., mud in unusual places in the trunk, water marks inside the instruments, an owner's manual that looks like it's been wet, warped fiberboard door panels or glovebox interiors.

Repairing Paint Chips

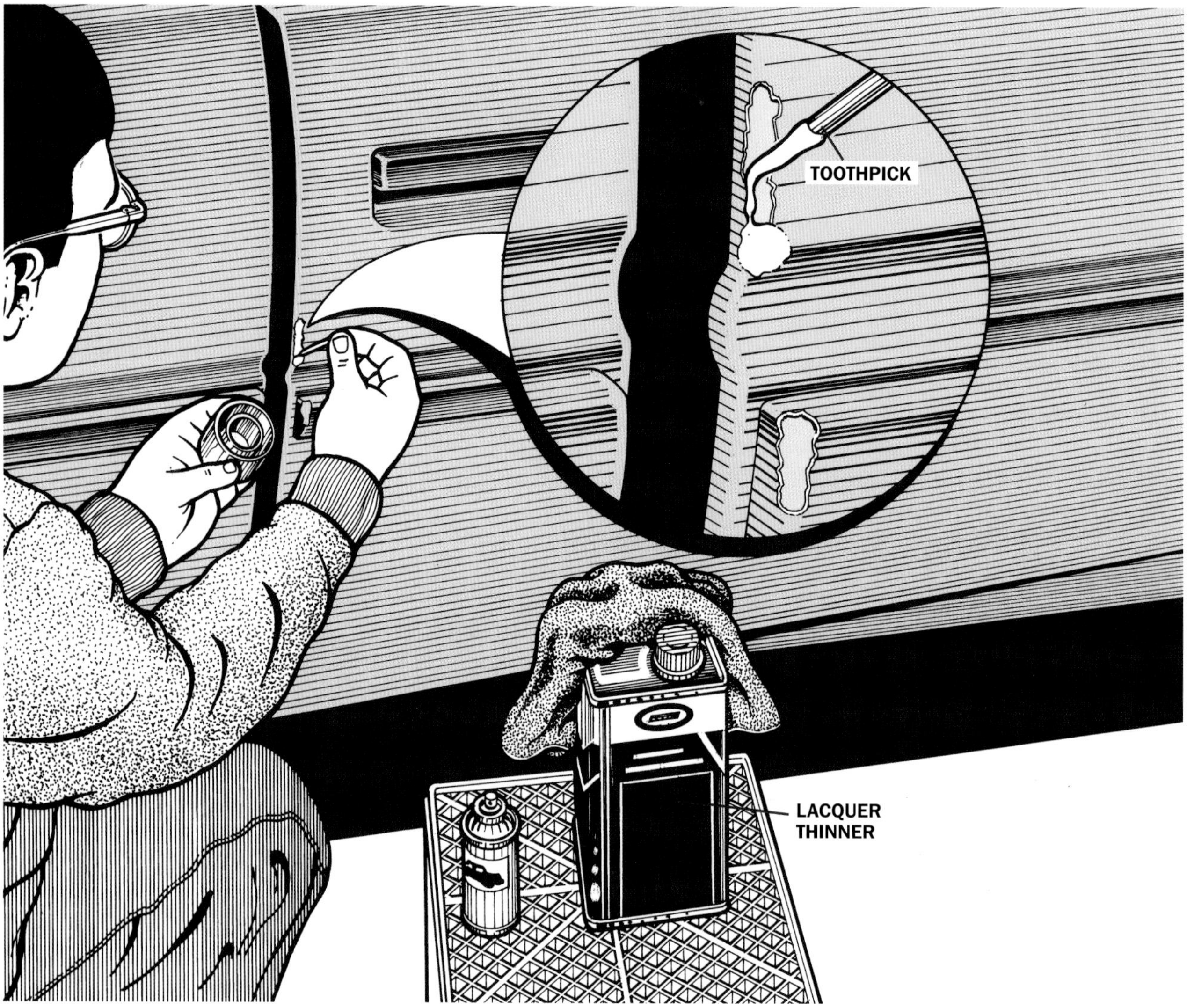

(Fig. 1) **Carefully apply touchup paint to fill chips and cracks. Degrease, sand and prime bare metal before applying color.**

As always, you've parked your new, expensive, shiny car at the far end of the parking lot, several rows away from the nearest vehicle of any sort. You've even been careful to park at the top of the lot's drainage pitch so any errant shopping carts will roll away from, not toward, your car.

But nobody said life was fair. Returning to your car 3 minutes later with a $50 bag of chocolate Napoleons, sushi and okra for your pregnant wife, you find that the unthinkable has happened—there's a rusted, sagging minivan parked only inches from your car. And, yes, the careless driver has managed to chip the paint on your wheel well arch in two places.

Getting It Fixed

The body shop wants $250 to begin repairing it. And the shop foreman says something about clearcoat and not guaranteeing an exact match for your pearlescent mica paint.

Unfortunately, that's about the size of it. It's frustratingly difficult to match many of today's high-tech finishes if you respray an entire panel. If the nick is small, but large enough to go through the clearcoat and into the pigmented paint, your best bet may be a simple touchup, which you can do in the driveway. It won't be perfect, but it may be far less noticeable.

Paint by Number

This method is best for small scratches or the chips that flake off

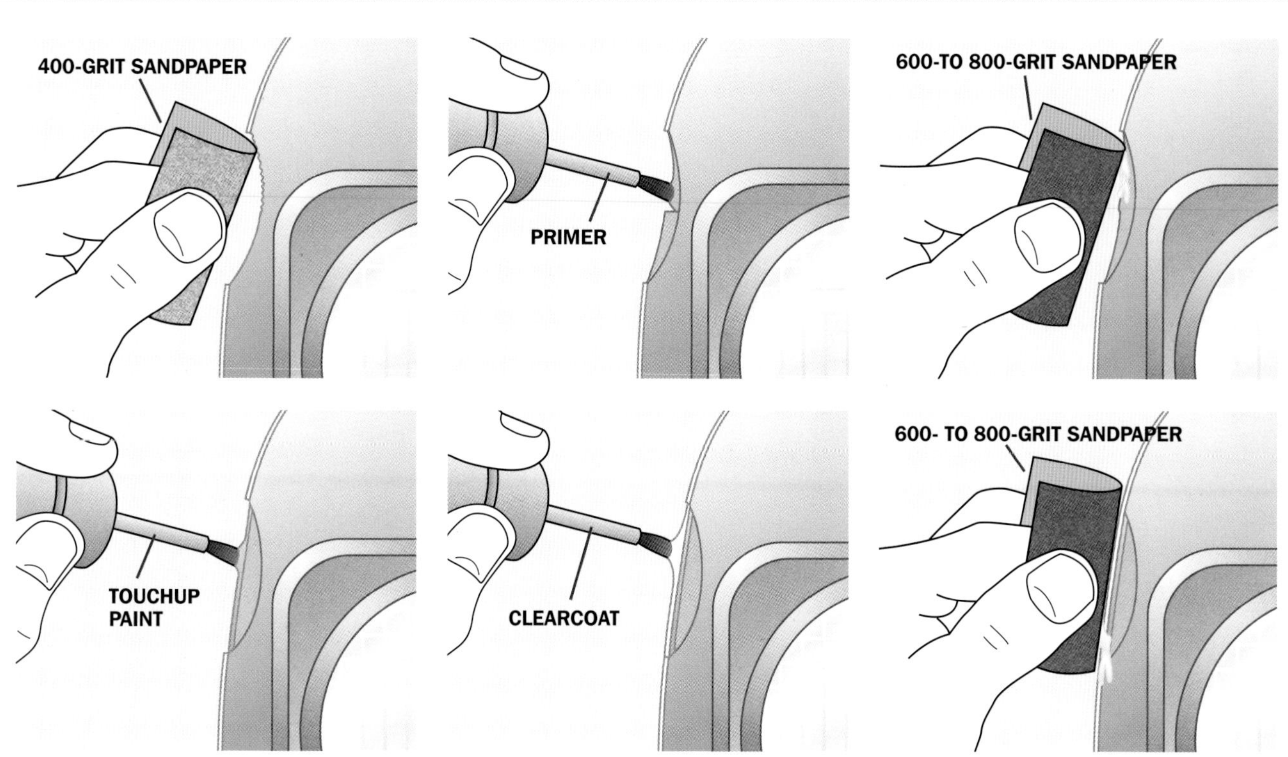

(Fig. 2) Apply primer, color and clearcoat in layers over chipped areas. Sand the area you're working on between layers to keep it smooth.

edges—for example, near trunk and door openings. Work indoors in a heated garage during the cooler months, or outdoors out of the wind and sun. If you live in Truth or Consequences, N.M., or Las Vegas, you may want to work early in the day, before the heat builds up, to keep the paint fluid enough to flow properly.

Go to the car dealership or auto parts store and acquire touchup paint in the appropriate color, clearcoat and, if you've got bare metal showing, primer. Do not use primer intended for lawn furniture or naval vessels—it should be automotive primer, preferably of the same brand as the touchup paint.

Start by using masking tape to isolate the area around the chip, to prevent you from damaging other parts of the finish. Allow about ¼ in. around the damaged spot. Next, clean road grime and wax away from the inside of the chipped area with a cloth moistened with lacquer thinner. (If your car is painted with a lacquer-based paint—which is possible if it dates to the '70s or earlier, or has been repainted—the paint will dissolve in lacquer thinner. Use denatured alcohol instead.) If the paint is chipped down to the metal, use a sharp knife point or some 40-grit sandpaper to rough up the surface, particularly if there's any rust. With the applicator brush in the bottle or with a toothpick, prime any bare metal. Flow primer in a thin coat, but be careful not to lap any primer onto the paint surrounding the chip. Your job at this point is to lay a smooth layer of primer down without any lumps or bumps—just enough to cover the bare metal. Let this dry for at least 24 hours.

Now comes the tricky part. Using the brush or toothpick, fill the chip with paint in a nice, even layer (**Fig. 1**). Don't try to fill it up, just be sure you get to all the corners. Don't let it sag or bulge. If you get a little overlap, use a cotton swab lightly moistened with lacquer thinner to mop up any excess paint. If the paint is too thin, leave the applicator brush out in the open for a minute or two and the paint will thicken. If it's too gooey, a few drops of lacquer thinner will fix that. Thin sparingly, if you must.

Allow the layer of paint to dry for 24 hours. It will shrink substantially as it dries, and you don't want too much paint. If it gets lumpy, you can try sanding it with 600-grit or 800-grit waterproof sandpaper and water (**Fig. 2**). Don't sand the paint surrounding the chip—you want that to remain undisturbed.

Build up the color touchup paint until it's nearly flush with the surrounding surface, but definitely recessed. If your car is still wearing its factory coat, that may be only one or two coats of color. Resprayed cars with a thicker layer of chip-prone paint may require four to six coats. Keep chasing the overlap back with cotton swabs and thinner.

After a week's drying time (longer in cool weather) you can coat the repair with clearcoat. If you've had good luck filling the chip, you may simply be able to continue with the process of flowing touchup paint right up to the original paint without overlap, and achieve a nearly invisible repair.

If not, you'll need to blend the repaired area with the surrounding paint. Overlap the chip by ¼ in. or so. Add enough coats, a few days apart, to allow for the inevitable shrinkage, to make the repair stand a few thou-

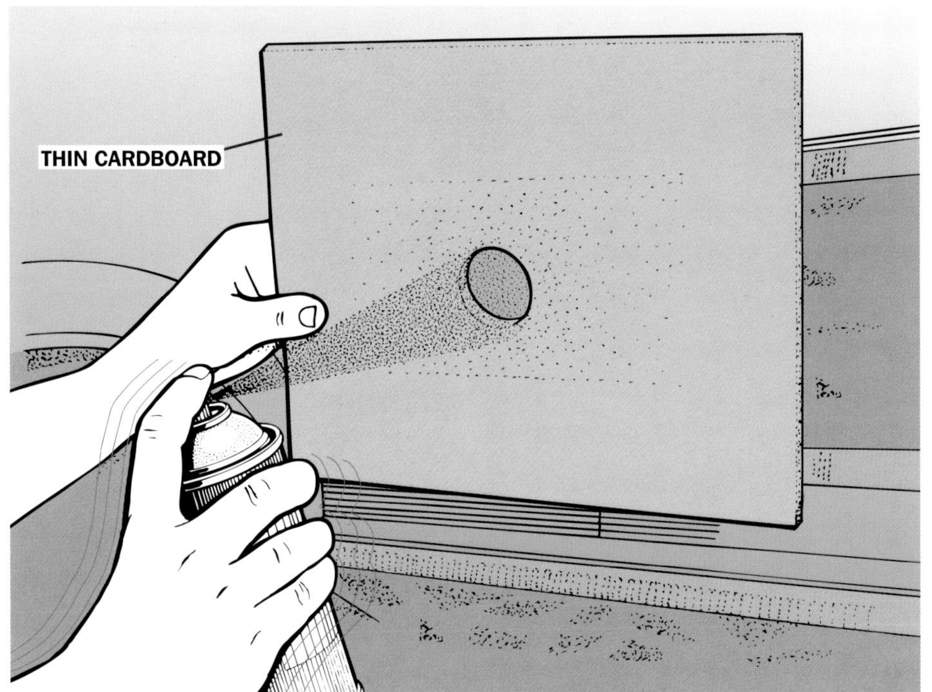

(Fig. 3) Use a cardboard mask to keep overspray to a minimum when spraying.

Wait an hour and repeat. Remove the masking, and use 800-grit paper to remove most of the primer from the paint, leaving the primer in the chip to backfill. Now use rubbing compound on a soft cloth to remove the overspray surrounding the area (Fig. 4).

Be aware that primer and glazing putty will shrink in a few days.

Now that the repair is filled nearly level, mask the area again and spray touchup paint in your matching color through the hole in your cardboard mask. Give it about three coats, roughly a half-hour apart. Remove the masking, and let dry at least overnight. Use rubbing compound on the overspray again. Repeat this process with spray-can clearcoat.

You may wish to lightly sand the clearcoat with 800-grit paper, but rubbing compound should bring up the shine and blend the overspray into the panel's original clearcoat. The repair may still be visible, but it should be far less noticeable.

sandths of an inch—say, the thickness of a sheet of paper—higher than the surrounding paint. Allow the repair to dry and shrink in the sun for a week or so. Now you can gingerly sand with 600- or 800-grit waterproof sandpaper to blend in the color. This will feather the repair into the surrounding clearcoat and smooth the work, but will also leave it with an unattractive matte finish. Use a soft cloth and some rubbing compound to turn the sanded area shiny.

Chipped Off

Got a chip in the middle of a flat panel? If you've tried the above repair and weren't happy with the results, you might get a better, less visible repair with spray paint. Again, you'll need to degrease, derust and sand the area for good adhesion. Cut a 1½-in. hole in a file folder or piece of thin cardboard (Fig. 3). Gently warm a spray can of automotive primer to 100°F with warm water to increase the pressure for a more even spray. Take the spray can in one hand and with your other hold the cardboard with the hole centered over the chip, 2 in. away from the panel. Sweep the spray can back and forth over the hole while spraying three or four passes over the chip. Don't put enough paint on the panel to sag, or even get shiny.

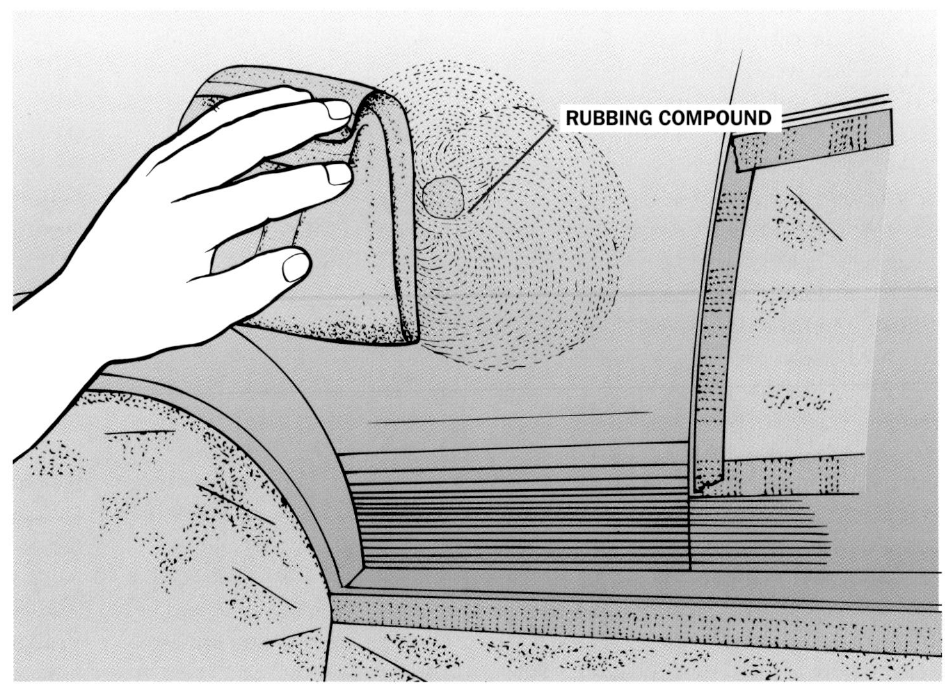

(Fig. 4) Use rubbing compound around the edge of the repair to clean up overspray before spraying the next coat of primer or paint.

Polishing Your Car

In most parts of the country, the winter brings with it some road salt or sand and all types of precipitation. All of the above are less than good for your car's or truck's finish. So spring cleaning not only makes your vehicle look sharper, but it also helps restore and preserve the quality of its finish. Your car will be worth more at trade-in or resale time if it looks good.

You can help ensure that it looks good by regularly shining it up after you've washed it. Before you shine, though, be sure to match the type of polish or wax you use with your car's or truck's paint finish.

Polishing your clean car entails more than simply laying down a thin layer of wax or polish over the paint. The process also involves removing the very fine layer of dull, oxidized and weathered finish on the surface. This dull layer can either be removed chemically or with a fine polishing abrasive. With the oxidized layer removed, the fresh finish beneath it will shine. The wax or silicone in the polish then adds luster and protection to that clean paint.

If your car or truck has a clearcoat/basecoat finish, you must use a wax or polish that's specially designed for it. The wrong product may actually dull rather than shine the finish. If you use a nonabrasive product made for a clearcoat finish on an acrylic nonclearcoat finish, the results will be disappointing at best. Be sure to use a product designed for a nonclearcoat paint.

If you opt to shine your car with a wax, use a quality one that lists carnuba wax among its active ingredients. Or use a synthetic that contains silicone resins or amino-active silicones. (Most products have silicone fluids or oils that will make them easier to apply.)

Regardless of the type of finish your vehicle has and the finish-care product you use, the actual task of shining up the car is pretty much the same. Work in the shade, but not beneath the birds' favorite sap-bearing tree. Begin polishing early enough to avoid having to work in the heat of day, and finish the job early enough to let the wax cure before the dew begins to settle.

Start on the roof and work your way down. Apply the wax or polish to a small section no larger than about one-quarter the area of the roof. Use a soft, damp applicator to put down a layer of wax. Small household sponges make excellent, disposable wax applicators. Don't be alarmed if your applicator removes some paint along with the polish on a nonclearcoat finish. This is the dull, oxidized layer coming up. Avoid getting wax or polish on any matte black plastic parts, rubber trim or molding, or on a vinyl roof. Allow the wax to dry to a haze according to the product's instructions.

To get a show-car shine, buff off the wax or polish in a linear rather than a circular motion. This takes more time but it leaves the car's finish with a uniform-looking luster.

If you're using a totally nonabrasive wax or polish and don't mind swirl marks, you can finish the job using a power buffer. Make sure that the power buffer's lamb's-wool bonnet is clean. Change or rinse the bonnet frequently to avoid scratching the finish. Use the bonnet as a mitten to buff in the crevices and other areas that the power buffer can't reach.

To help maintain the shine on your car after you've restored it, try to keep your parked car covered—in the garage or carport or beneath a cover. Also, periodically hose grit and dust off the finish, but avoid the temptation to wipe down the car after a rain—there's all manner of grit in those standing raindrops.

When the finish no longer beads water the way it did after you polished, it's time to wax again—even if it still looks good.

EASY

Repairing Plastic Bumpers

After you drove into the mall parking lot and saw how packed it was, you couldn't believe your luck when you spotted a space right next to the building. So you hurried into the space without noticing the extra-high concrete curb—until you heard your flexible plastic bumper strike it. To make matters worse, backing up in a panic put a nice tear in the bumper.

Oh well, there's no use crying over spilled milk. Thankfully, you don't have to cry over a split bumper, either. The 3M Co. makes a repair system designed to fix cuts, tears and abrasions in flexible bumpers. Once repaired, the bumper can then be painted its original color with an automotive paint that has a flexible agent so it won't crack when the bumper flexes.

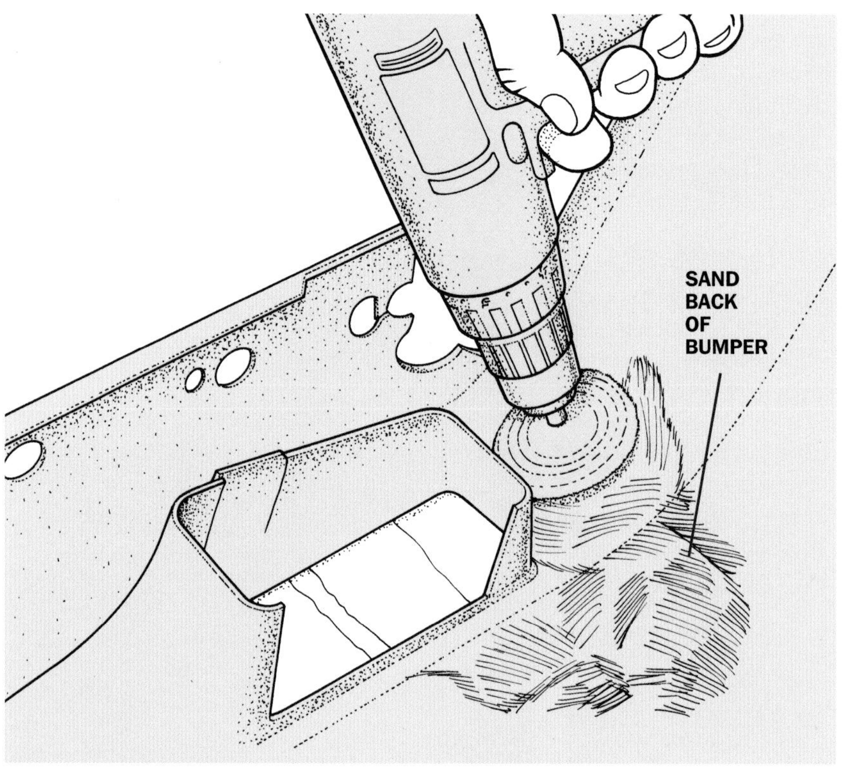

(Fig. 1) Begin the repair by thoroughly cleaning and then sanding the broken part. Then, clamp it in its normal shape.

Velvet Glove

All right, technically it's not really the bumper—it's the bumper's cosmetic cover. The true bumper/impact absorbing system is probably a metal beam that is intended to do the real work. And if *it's* damaged, you'll need to replace the components with new ones to provide your vehicle with the correct crash protection. And don't skimp there. However, the plastic skin isn't structural, despite the fact that it's the most expensive part of both the front and rear bumpers. Odds are that most low-speed mishaps affect only the cover, and those can be repaired if you follow our directions.

The 3M P.R.O. flexible-parts repair system consists of a 2-part flexible filler that is mixed together (like epoxy), a flexible putty and a flexible coating that covers and seals the repair before painting. There's also an adhesion promoter that must be used on plastic parts made with polyolefins. Other items you'll need to make the repair include an electric drill, a 3-in. sanding disc with 36-grit discs, a random-orbit sander with 180-, 240- and 320-grit discs, a rubber sanding block, 240- and 400-grit wet/dry sandpaper, 80- and 120-grit sandpaper, a couple of body-filler spreaders and some method of spraying the coating. While a compressed-air spray gun is ideal, we've illustrated a small aerosol sprayer you can fill with liquid yourself. Pre-Val is one popular brand.

Stocking up

If you've done bodywork in the past, you'll be in good shape to repair these plastic parts. Most of the tools and the style of work is the same, but don't try to use the same materials to repair these flexible parts. The plastic is quite different in its adhesion characteristics from steel or fiberglass. Unless the part is prepped carefully, the repair materials will peel off within a few months, if not sooner. Because the plastic is quite flexible, ordinary body fiberglass resins, plastic body fillers and glazing putty will crack. Permatex and 3M are the major manufacturers who sell appropriate repair materials. The car companies all recommend these products for their warranty repairs.

To find a place that sells them, look in the Yellow Pages for an auto parts store that caters to the body-shop trade. It'll have paint and painting supplies. Sometimes you can find a paint store that also sells automotive paint and supplies. This type of establishment is used to dealing with professional body shop staff, not do-

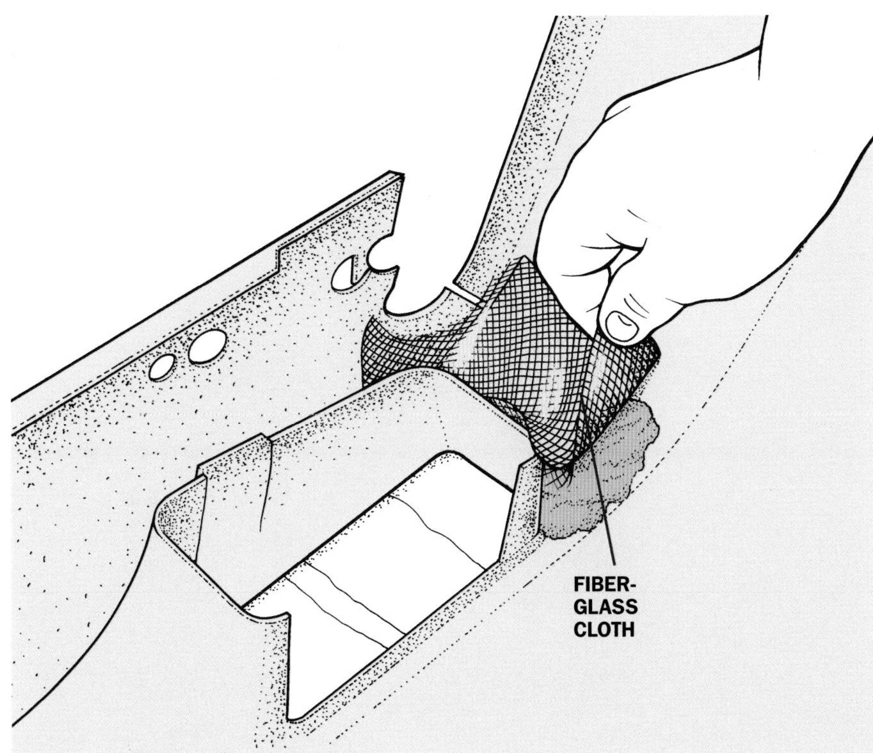

(Fig. 2) Use fiberglass cloth and the special epoxy to reinforce the broken areas. Use your squeegee to work the resin into the cloth.

it-yourselfers, so if you have to ask a lot of questions, be patient and polite.

Most body-working materials are marked "For Professional Use Only." Not to worry, they're not Kryptonite. Use common sense and the same care you would with any epoxy resin or paint with volatile solvents and fine particulates. Avoid skin contact with the uncured resins. Work in a well-ventilated area or use an activated-charcoal painter's respirator to avoid inhaling fumes from the spray gun. Disposable respirators are priced very reasonably. If you plan on doing a lot of bodywork in the future, spring for a better one that uses replaceable activated-charcoal cartridges—it'll be cheaper in the long run. If you're sanding, wear a particle mask. The store that sells you supplies should have all of this equipment.

Plastic Primer

It's possible to repair small cuts, holes, abrasions and other light damage without removing the bumper from the vehicle. However, if the cut is longer than an inch, or it extends to the edge of the part, you'll have to remove the damaged component so you can reinforce the back side of the repair with fiberglass cloth.

As noted earlier, most flexible bumpers are nothing more than bumper covers backed up by other plastic components, a steel structure and collapsible bumper mounts. If you are unsure how to remove the bumper or how to remove the flexible cover from the bumper structure, consult a service manual.

A special adhesion promoter must be used between all the sanding steps on parts made with polyolefin. Therefore, you'll have to determine if the part you're working with is a polyolefin plastic before you begin. In many cases, the letter symbols TPO, PP, E/P or EPDM will be clearly marked on the inside surface of the plastic. Any of these indicate that it is a polyolefin plastic. If you can't find letter symbols on the part, sand the plastic with a 36-grit, 3-in. disc using a drill motor. If the plastic melts or smears, it's a polyolefin plastic. If it sands cleanly, it isn't.

Don't confuse pliable plastic body parts on or around the bumper

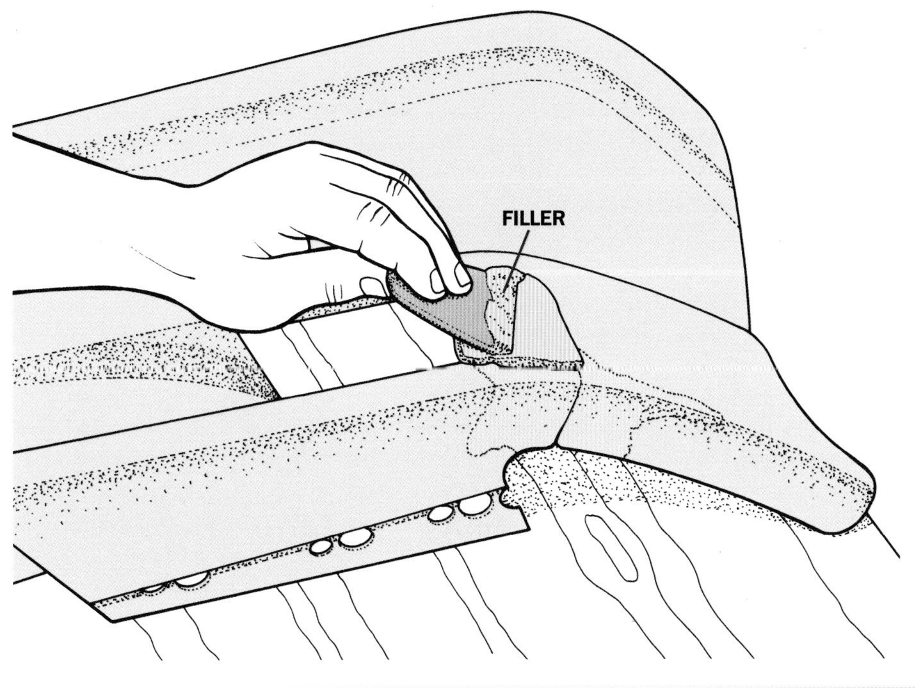

(Fig. 3) Sand a "V" shape into the bottom of the crack. The repair epoxy can then be used to fill in the area. Wait for the resin to cure, then sand.

(Fig. 4) An adhesion promoter should be used to make sure the repair materials and paint will adhere. This is necessary with most plastics used to make bumpers.

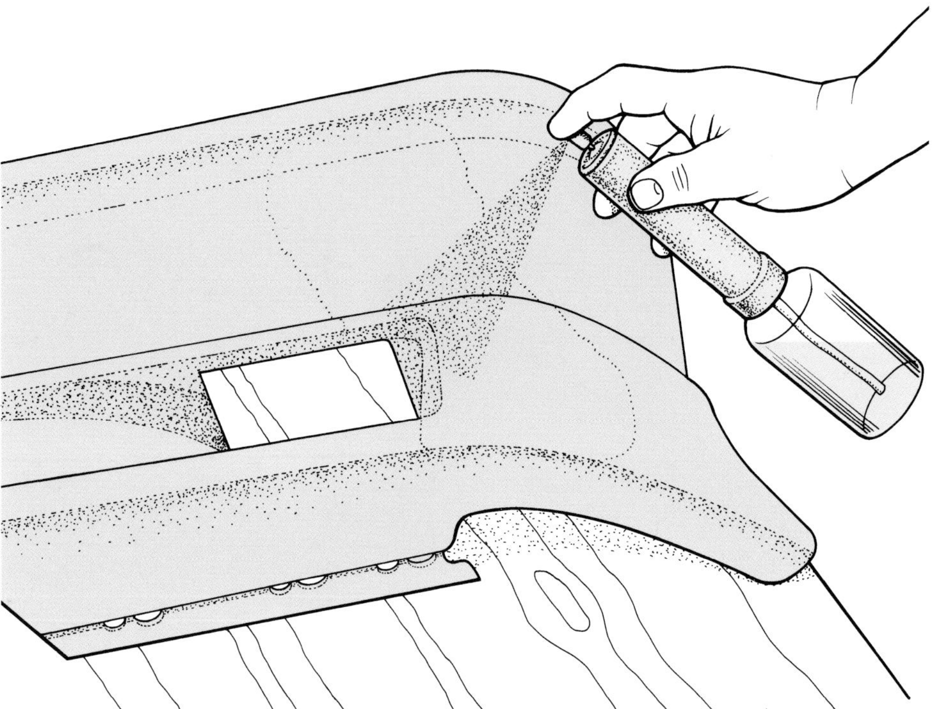

with the sheet-molding compound (SMC) or fiberglass-reinforced polyester (FRP) parts commonly used on fenders and doors. These rigid, composite materials are identifiable by the fiberglass strands visible at tears or holes, and they require a different repair method.

Getting Started

Once you've determined the type of plastic you're working on, wash all the dirt and grime from the inside and outside of the part with soap and water. After the part dries, clean the area to be repaired with a specially formulated adhesive-cleaning solvent to remove any grease or tar. Be absolutely certain the area is completely clean—don't even touch the area with your fingers after it's cleaned. Use clean white paper towels, without any printed pattern, to apply the cleaner and to dry it off. Greasy shop towels, or any other source of contamination or oil, will prevent adhesion between the repair materials and the base plastic of the bumper, giving you at best a short-lived, sloppy-looking repair.

To reinforce the back side of rips, cuts, holes and tears, grind the back side of the area surrounding the damage with a 36-grit disc, making sure to leave a rough area of at least 1½ in. surrounding the damage. Don't grind all the way through the part. Just rough up the surface **(Fig. 1)**. Next, cut a piece of fiberglass cloth tape to fit over the area. Again, keep the area and your hands squeaky clean. Leave the fiberglass cloth in its original packaging until you need it. Cut the cloth with clean scissors on a clean, grease-free countertop. Then, thoroughly mix together equal amounts of the 2-part repair filler. (If you're working with polyolefin plastic, spray the repair area with adhesion promoter and let it dry.) Next, use a plastic spreader to apply the filler to the area before applying the fiberglass tape. Once the tape is pressed down, apply filler to the top of the tape, using the spreader to force filler into the cloth **(Fig. 2)**.

It takes about 30 minutes for the filler to set thoroughly at 70°F, but temperature and humidity affect setup time considerably. If you need to work in the winter, take the parts and repair materials into a heated area hours ahead of time to let them warm up. If you're forced to work outside, the temperature should be at least 65°F. At lower temperatures, the resins will take longer to harden, and they may never develop their full strength. If the part is badly damaged—say you're reassembling a bumper cover that's been broken into two or more pieces—it may be necessary to repeat the grinding/ squeegeeing/cloth routine several times to achieve adequate strength. You may need to fasten the bumper cover down to something to hold the correct shape and alignment while the resins cure. Once they're set, there's no chance of realigning them—so work carefully. Because you're working on the back of the part, be thorough. You also need to take care while working around the areas where the bumper is bolted to the mounting to be sure it fits properly when you're finished.

Once the reinforced area has set completely, check the stiffness of all the repaired areas and make sure the cover fits over the bumper. It may be necessary to repeat the preceding steps, adding one or more additional layers of fiberglass cloth to build up sufficient strength. Just be sure to roughen the surface with sandpaper to get good grip. Allow adequate time for each layer to cure before adding the next. Flip the part over, and use the 36-grit disc to grind about 1½ in. around the damaged area to remove paint and create a rough, tapered low area for the filler to adhere to **(Fig. 3)**. After grinding, featheredge the paint around the damage using the random-orbit sander and a 180-grit disc or a rubber-block sander. Featheredge for several inches surrounding the repair. Blow dust and debris away with an air hose. Squeeze out equal parts of the filler and mix it thoroughly. Use adhesion promoter **(Fig. 4)** on the poly-

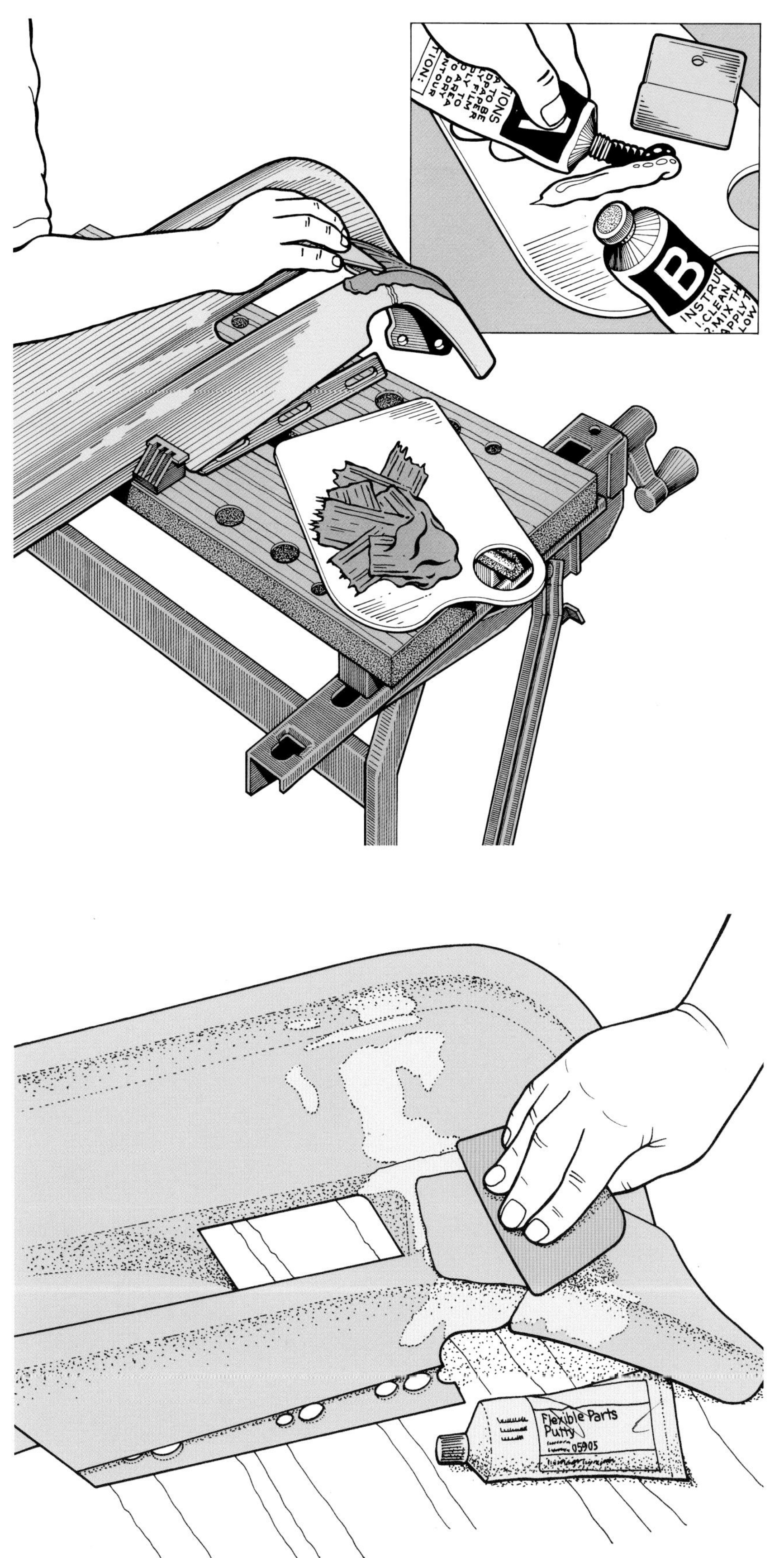

(Fig. 5) Once your bumper cover has been repaired structurally, it's time to begin the cosmetic fix. First, sand the surface. Then, mix equal amounts of the 2-part filler material and use a plastic squeegee to spread it over the repair area.

olefin parts and then spread the filler on the repair, taking care to leave it slightly higher than the surrounding area. If you've ever applied polyester body filler or glazing putty to a repaired steel body panel, you'll feel right at home (**Fig. 5**).

Going for the finish

After the filler has cured, use 240-grit discs to sand the filler flush with the undamaged surface. Fill any pinholes or other imperfections by applying putty with a plastic spreader (**Fig. 6**). After waiting at least 15 minutes for the putty to cure, sand the surface with your rubber block and 80-grit paper to achieve a smooth contour. Sand out the 80-grit scratches with 120-grit paper. Then, apply a double wet coat of the coating material, and wait 10 minutes for the coating to "flash" dry. Then, apply a second coat. After 45 minutes of drying time, lightly scuff sand the area by hand with 320-grit paper, being careful not to break through the coating. The bumper is then ready to paint using color coats recommended for plastic body parts.

The painting operation will probably have to be done at a body shop, but you can prep the part by sanding its entire paintable surface with 400-grit wet sandpaper. Minor imperfections can be filled with more repair putty. The body shop will then have to prime it and spray it with a paint that has a special additive to make it slightly flexible.

If you're tempted to just touch up the panel in the affected areas with a spray can of aerosol touchup paint from the auto parts store, fine. Just remember that the panel is flexible, and the touchup paint won't last. In addition, it will be very difficult to feather into the existing flexible paint without leaving an ugly, low-gloss edge.

(Fig. 6) The spot repair putty can then be used to fill in scratches, pinholes and small imperfections. It's easier to sand than the repair epoxy.

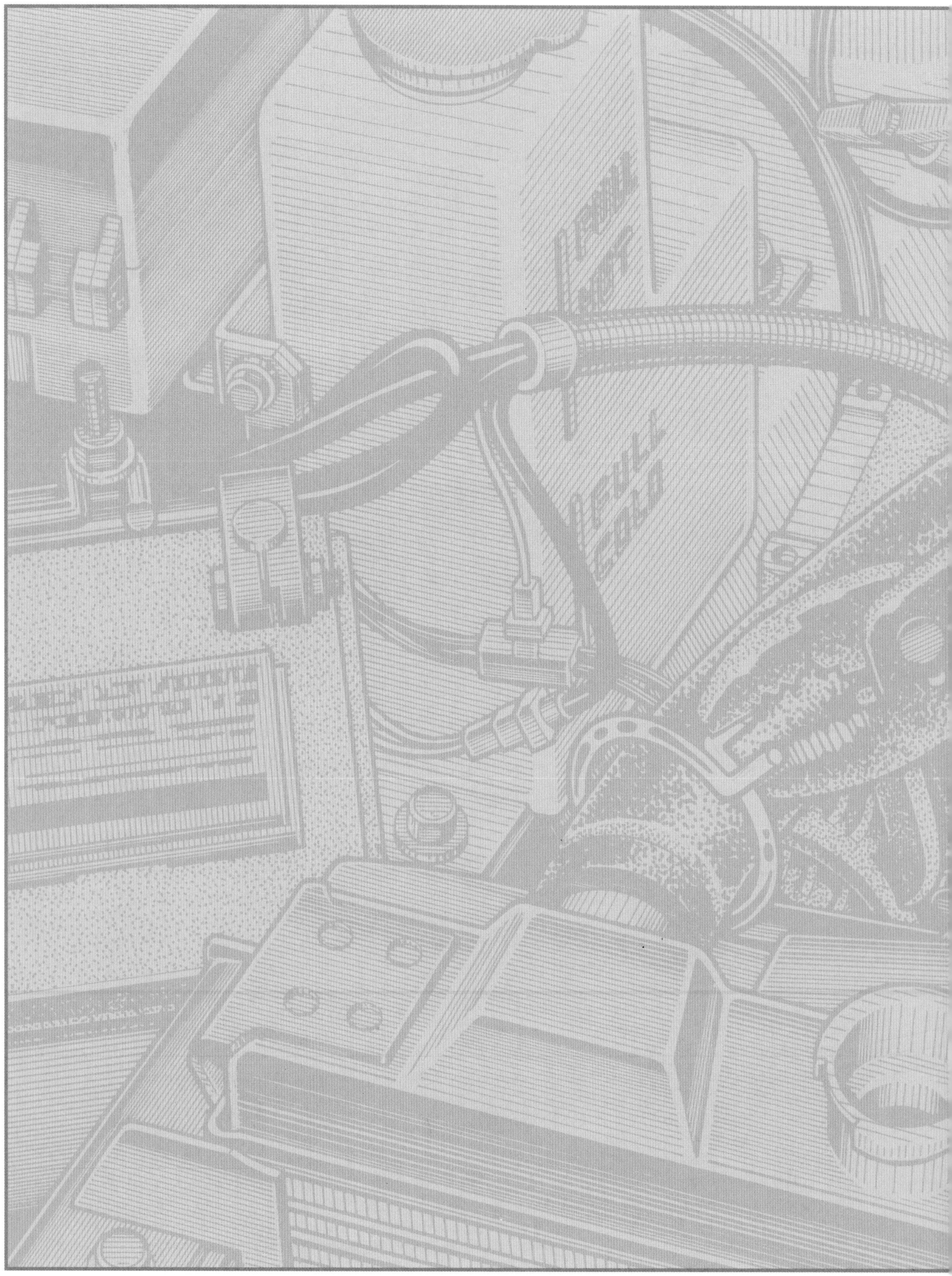

Appendix

Tools of the Trade

To a mechanic, "tools" fall into two important categories: "hardware" tools, the implements that actually do the job, and "software" tools, the books and other publications that provide the information necessary to do the job. To work on your own car with any measure of success, you'll have to stock your garage with some of both.

STRATEGIES AND INSTRUCTIONS

There's no good excuse for a driveway mechanic to be without the factory service manual for his automobile. General auto repair manuals that cover a variety of makes are less expensive than several factory manuals if you have more than one car to work on. You can usually buy the factory manual through your car dealer's parts counter. For some cars, more than one instruction book is necessary to fully cover drivetrain as well as body and electronics.The service manuals for all late-models (since 1996) are on websites maintained by the vehicle makers. So instead of a paper manual, you can gain access when you want, typically for about $15 a day. Manuals for older cars are sold by specialty distributors with toll-free numbers.

THE SERVICE MANUAL

Most factory service manuals begin with a general information section, usually with charts that tell you how to interpret your car's VIN number. You'll be able to pinpoint the specs of the engine installed, the plant at which the car was built, and similar data. Other charts interpret body ID plates with paint and interior color codes as well as trim levels. Other general information will include overall specs, fluid capacities of the various systems, and even data on bolt ID and torque. This chapter should also show the correct jack and lift points for raising and supporting your car.

The general information section is often followed by a maintenance and lube chapter. Use this material in conjunction with our car care plans to tailor the maintenance routines to your specific vehicle.

The rest of your service manual is divided into chapters, each of which covers one specific system, such as heating and ventilation, or a group of systems, such as emissions controls.

Most manual chapters include three types of information. First, where applicable, many chapters begin with a short explanation on how a particular system operates. This information can help when it comes to making logical decisions about the possible causes of a given problem.

Next comes diagnostic information. This troubleshooting material can be very general and somewhat brief or it can be incredibly specific and detailed. Typical of the first kind of diagnostic directions are those for engine mechanical diagnosis. Here you'll find lists of possible causes that relate to a symptom. For example, in the 1985 Celebrity manual there are eight potential problem areas listed under the heading "Excessive Oil Loss."

Much more complicated are the diagnostic procedures for driveability problems. Some makers, such as GM, instruct you to begin the diagnosis of a driveability problem by triggering the diagnostic mode of the computer system. You progress from there to troubleshooting individual systems with test lights, ohmmeters, and the like, and sometimes finish up by checking symptom-organized lists of possible causes.

Other manufacturers, notably Chrysler, begin diagnosis of computer-controlled engine driveability problems with visual checks. In either case, you have to read the manual material carefully and do things in the right order. The procedures work on a process-of-elimination basis. If you don't begin at the beginning, you throw the whole diagnostic plan out of whack.

At some point, the troubleshooting of complex systems is sure to include a diagnostic "tree diagram." You begin by performing the test in the box at top, then depending on the results of that first test, you will be led through a series of steps to diagnose your problem. You'll notice that every path eventually concludes with a repair or with a "system OK."

The third type of information, usually at the end of a service manual chapter, is on repairs. It often doesn't include tasks considered simple by professional mechanics.

THE TOOLBOX

How many tools do you need to service your car? Frankly, as many as you can afford. But you can get by with a fairly basic set if you intend to do only maintenance jobs. But if you're going to perform complicated repairs you'll need a lot of special tools, many of them designed to do just one specific job. Check auto parts stores in your area for tool rental peograms.

Plier Tools

From among the vast number of plier tools, you'll need at least three basic types: a conventional slipjoint plier, a pair of side-cutters for cutting and stripping wire and—among many other uses—prying out cotter pins, and a pair of long-nose or needle-nose pliers.

Once you have the basic three you'll eventually want to expand your plier drawer. You might first add a locking plier; the most common type is sold under the Vise-Grip trademark. Among many other possible uses, this tool can be clamped tightly around a stripped bolt for removal or it can be used to hold parts in place for welding. Lineman's pliers with insulated handles are useful for various electrical-system chores. Water-pump pliers offer nearly parallel jaws and lots of leverage. A second pair of long-nose pliers can be sharpened for service on snap rings, or special snap-ring pliers are available as well. Small side-cutters can be of use when working with delicate components. Hose-clamp pliers are grooved to grab the spring-type hose clamps that are standard equipment on many cars. Wire strippers/terminal crimpers are very useful pliers with a row of split circles on the jaws for stripping wires of various gauges and a special crimping area behind the jaws for attaching solderless wire terminals. Tin snips, available for cutting left-hand curves, righthand curves, and straight cuts, are a necessity if you're going to do serious bodywork.

Screwdrivers

For servicing today's cars, you'll need an assortment of flat-blade and Phillips screwdrivers in various sizes. You'll ruin a lot of screwheads if you use the wrong-size driver. In addition to various-sized tips, you'll need some variety in handle lengths. Cheap screwdrivers are not well suited to driving screws, so buy high-quality tools that will not distort the screwheads.

For most cars you'll also need a couple of Torx-style screwdrivers, distinguished by their six-point drives. On some cars, you'll need this type of screwdriver to replace a headlight bulb or seatbelt housing.

Our favorite screwdriver is a high-quality, flexible-shaft ratchet job with interchangeable bits of tool steel. The extra bits fit in the handle, and are available in every size and style you might need. Angle screwdrivers, with a tip mounted perpendicular to the shaft, are useful for screws that can't be reached with anything else.

Socket Tools

Square-drive tools are probably the most important for someone who intends to service automobiles. To begin, you'll need both 3/8-in.-drive and 1/2-in.-drive ratchets and breaker bars, at least one short and one long extension for each drive, and a complete set of standard sockets for each. If your car is fully metric, you may want to purchase only metric sockets at first. If your car includes both metric and inch sizes, you'll need a set of each.

You'll need a spark-plug socket of either 13/16-in. or 5/8-in. size. Don't just use a deep socket for this purpose. Spark plug sockets have a special rubber insert to hold the insulator, helping prevent breakage while giving you a means to lift the plug away from the engine without dropping it.

A torque wrench is also a necessity, as it should be used for everything from installing wheels to tightening cylinder head or manifold bolts. The most common and least expensive type has a pointer attached to the drive head that rests against a scale near the handle. More expensive types replace the scale and pointer with a dial. A style used by many mechanics has a rotating handle with a scale of torque figures on the tool. You dial in the torque figure you want by turning the handle. Then, when you tighten the bolt, the wrench will click to signal you when you reach the specified figure.

Eventually, you'll want to add universal joints, which can be fitted at the end of an extension; speed handles; T-handles; additional extensions; and a 1/4-in. ratchet, extension, and screwdriver handle for smaller capscrews. Adapters that allow the use of 3/8-in.-drive sockets on 1/2-in.-drive ratchets (or various other combinations) can also be handy at times. You'll want to expand your socket set to include hex or Allen drive sockets, sockets for large slotted screws, deep-well sockets, universal-joint "swivel" sockets, and 1/4-in.-drive sockets, all in both inch and metric sizes.

You'll also want to supplement your standard twelve-point sockets with some eight-, six-, and fourpoint sockets (Fig. 4). Six-point sockets are needed when you have to loosen a bolt with rounded corners where the twelve-point might slip. Our 3/8-in.-drive deep-well sockets are of the six-point type. Thickwall six-point sockets (usually black for identification) are available for use with impact wrenches. Eight- and four-point sockets are for removal of square plugs. If you have the eight-pointers, you really don't need the fours.

If you can't reach the spark plugs on your engine with a conventional plug socket, extension, and ratchet, you may need either a swivel-head plug socket or a 3/8-in.-drive ratchet with a jointed hand that can be rotated to a different angle in respect to its handle.

Wrenches

A basic set of combination wrenches—box at one end and open end on the other—will get you started in this department. Use a box wrench when you don't have clearance for a socket. Open-end wrenches are really only suited to running down a bolt or backing it out, as they slip quite easily, ruining both the bolthead and your knuckles.

An open-end wrench should be used with the handle angled away from the direction of rotation. Once the bolt is rotated, the wrench is slipped off, slid around in a counterclockwise direction and reinserted. Once you've practiced this technique, an open-end can be used to turn a bolt very quickly. When loosening a fastener with a combination wrench, break it loose with the box end, then flip the wrench around and run out the bolt with the open end.

Once you have a basic wrench set, you'll want to expand with some other types. Those that have a box on both ends generally have a greater offset than the combos, making them useful for certain problem areas. Both box and open-end wrenches are available in a variety of lengths. You'll also find box wrenches shaped like a crescent for inaccessible bolts, box wrenches that ratchet, and sockets attached to a handle with an open-end opposite. We frequently use a very thin open-end "tappet" wrench for any double-nutted bolt or stud or in tight spots.

You'll also want tubing wrenches, which are like a six-point open-end with one side missing. Once slipped over a tube, the five remaining points of the wrench can loosen the soft nut on the end of the tube without rounding it off. Special L-shaped box wrenches that can be driven with a ratchet are available for loosening hard-to-reach distributor clamp bolts.

You might be better off without adjustable crescent wrenches, as these tools are most likely to round off a hexhead. But it's good to have a couple of them around in different sizes for those times when you have to turn a simple-to-reach, not-very-tight bolt, the size of which you are not sure.

Hammers

Hammers must be used with great restraint when working on a complicated machine like an automobile. But you will need one from time to time. Begin with a ball-peen for tapping your drift or making a center-punch mark, and supplement it with a rubber mallet for driving things into position. Eventually, you'll want to add a brass hammer for driving lugs into hubs and similar tasks. A plastic-head hammer is useful for dislodging somewhat delicate parts. Finally, you'll want a good hand sledge to drive a large chisel into a large rusty nut.

You'll want to have some chisels, punches, and drifts that you can hit with your hammers. If you work on cars regularly, you'll undoubtedly have to chisel off a rusted nut or bolt before long, probably on a shock absorber. Drifts are used for removing pins from shafts, studs, or hubs. A center punch is necessary to provide a spot to start a drill bit in steel or aluminum.

You'll need only a couple of files at first. A small ignition-point file is good for cleaning up spark plugs or even repairing the threads on a small screw. One medium-size flat file will also come in handy for smoothing rough edges or flattening slightly distorted surfaces. Later, you'll want to add a rattail for smoothing out holes and a threesided file for getting into corners. A hacksaw and a couple of high quality, fine-tooth blades will come in handy if you have to shorten a bolt or fabricate a bracket.

An assortment of tool-steel high quality drill bits and a 1/2-in. or 3/8-in. chuck electric drill is also necessary.

Pullers and Pluckers

Hub pullers, nut splitters, gear pullers, pickle forks, and other devices of this ilk probably won't be purchased until you need them. Sooner or later you will undoubtedly want them, however.

A good three-pronged gear puller can be used for removing a variety of hubs and gears. This tool is available in several sizes to suit various applications. A puller with slots through which bolts can be inserted is useful for removing any type of hub with threaded holes, such as a steering wheel hub or engine damper pulley. Various other pullers, including slide-hammer devices for removal of rear-drive axles, are also available. Some of them can be rented for one-time use.

A nut splitter is a good substitute for a chisel when you have to remove a rusted nut. A ball-joint spreader and rod-end separator, commonly known as pickle forks, are necessary for suspension-system work. The ball-joint spreader has the wider slot between its prongs.

Oil Change and Lube Tools

An oil filter wrench is, of course, an absolute necessity for any driveway mechanic. Before you buy, make sure you get one that will work on your car, as there are numerous types available.

Most of the long-handled metal-band jobs work great where there's room for them, but on most cars there isn't. The best of these are adjustable for different type filters.

A handy oil filter wrench is the type that has a sturdy nylon strap attached to a piece of square tubing with a 1/2-in. hole down the center. The strap is placed over the filter and the tubing is rotated counterclockwise until the strap snugs up. Then a 1/2-in. square drive extension and ratchet are used to continue rotating the tubing until the filter is loosened.

Precision Tools

Every home mechanic should have at least a good pair of vernier calipers for determining the size of pins, bolts, and other similar items as well as a set of feeler gauges and a wire gauge for checking spark plugs. If you're going to rebuild engines, you'll need much more, including micrometers, snap gauges, a dial indicator and magnetic base, a depth micrometer, and—ideally—a dial-bore gauge. A good ring compressor will also be needed for engine work. The best type is a tapered sleeve for each bore size. If you plan on assembling cylinder heads, you'll need a valve-spring compressor that will work on your engine. Those for pushrod engines won't work on overhead cam engines, some of which require specific adapters.

The dial indicator and magnetic base are probably worth having even if you never touch the inside of an engine as they are useful for gauging a lot of different things, such as ball-joint wear and even wheel-bearing adjustment.

OTHER GOOD STUFF

Sooner or later you'll want to invest in a battery charger. A small, 10-amp job can bring a partially discharged battery to full charge in a few hours. You'll need at least a 6-amp model for decent performance. In addition, you'll need a battery post and terminal cleaning tool. You can use a knife for this job, but the special cleaning tool is inexpensive and does a better job. You'll need a timing light to perform tuneups, but be aware many late-models do not require it (no timing marks). If you're willing to suffer, you can use the cheap kind that attaches only to the plug wire. A power timing light, which provides much more illumination and is immeasurably easier to use, costs about three times as much.

And you can't get by without a miniature analyzer, which includes a tachometer, ohmmeter, voltmeter, ammeter, and dwell meter on older cars. Use it for tuneups, charging-system troubleshooting, general electrical-system troubleshooting, and a wide variety of other jobs. On late-models, a scan tool is essential to read trouble codes and engine operating data, including much of the information provided by the tachometer. A volt-ohmmeter, or volt-ohm-ammeter, continues to be useful.

A good set of taps and dies is expensive but necessary when you have to straighten out the threads on a mangled bolt or clean the threads in a rusty cylinder block. Finally, don't forget to be nice to your tools. You don't have to get into public displays of affection, but you should wipe off the grease each time you use one. And you should have an organizational plan for keeping everything in its place, whether you have a twelve-drawer top-and-bottom tool chest or a two-drawer mini toolbox. Knowing where something is when you need it can cut your creeper time in half. It also makes it easier to tell when something is missing.

ABS: see **ANTILOCK BRAKES.**

ACCELERATOR PUMP: a small pump in the carburetor that is activated to spray extra fuel through specific nozzle(s) when the accelerator pedal is suddenly and quickly pressed to the floor on sharp acceleration.

ACTIVE SUSPENSION: a suspension system in which a double-acting hydraulic actuator is present at each wheel. The system is powered by a variable-rate hydraulic pump and controlled by an ECU, which keeps track of body attitude, wheel/hub velocity, forward speed, lateral-versus-longitudinal velocity when cornering, load, and angular displacement. See **SUSPENSION.**

ADJUSTABLE SHOCK: a shock absorber whose road-handling traits can be altered to create a stiffer or softer ride and to adjust for rough roads, heavy loads, etc. While many are adjusted manually, some more recent cars include a switch inside the car that adjusts the shocks electromechanically.

AIR ASPIRATOR VALVE: a device that uses a diaphragm to draw air into the exhaust system to reduce emissions. If a large volume of air is needed, an air pump is used instead.

AIR CLEANER: a housing that holds a filter element that removes dirt from the air flowing into the throttle body, before it is mixed with fuel to form the air-fuel mixture that is burned in the cylinders.

AIR CLEANER INTAKE: the neck, called a snorkel, into which air flows en route to the throttle body.

AIRFLOW SENSOR: see **MASS AIRFLOW SENSOR.**

AIR-FUEL MIXTURE: the mixture of air and fuel necessary to produce power when ignited by a spark plug and burned in a cylinder. The normal mixture is 14.7 parts of air for each part of gasoline.

AIR PUMP: a belt-driven or electrical pump that delivers compressed air to the exhaust system to reduce emissions. Also called **SECONDARY AIR INJECTION** and **THERMACTOR.**

ALL-WHEEL DRIVE (AWD): a drive system in which the driving axle(s) connects the transmission to both the front and the rear wheels. Also called four-wheel-drive, particularly when referring to an SUV or other off-road vehicle.

ALTERNATOR: see **GENERATOR.**

AMMETER: a test meter that reads amps in a circuit.

AMPS (OR AMPERES): the measurement of the energy content of the electricity in a circuit. Also see **VOLTS** and **OHMS**.

ANTIFREEZE AND SUMMER COOLANT: a fluid of ethylene glycol and special additives that when mixed with water lowers its freezing point in winter and raises its boiling point in summer.

ANTILOCK BRAKES: a braking system with electronic and electromechanical components that prevents the wheels from locking up and causing the car to skid when traction at the wheels is uneven.

ANTISEIZE COMPOUND: a paste that is applied to metal parts to keep them from sticking to other metal parts, particularly threaded surfaces such as spark plug threads and wheel studs and bolts.

AUTOMATIC CHOKE: a carburetor choke that operates automatically, according to engine temperature.

AXLE, AXLE HOUSING: a power transfer component with a ball-shaped center section and often two tubes at a 180° angle to each other. In the center section is a gearbox called a differential, with joints for a shaft that goes through each tube. In an automobile, each shaft goes (through a tube, if used) to a wheel to power the car. Or more simply, there is just a suspension assembly that supports the front or rear wheels.

BACKFIRE: an abnormal form of combustion of the air-fuel mixture. The flame may shoot back from the cylinder into the intake manifold and possibly the throttle body. Or it may be delayed until the fuel reaches the exhaust system, in which case it causes a popping sound.

BALL JOINT: a pivot joint, typically used in an automobile's suspension system.

BARREL: the air passage in the carburetor where the throttle is located.

BATTERY: a component that stores electrical energy in the form of chemical energy.

BATTERY TERMINALS: a battery has two terminals, one labeled positive, the other negative, to which thick wires called cables are attached. These cables are the wires for the battery's paths into the electrical system of the car.

BEAM AXLE: an axle that acts as a support for associated wheels, but does not drive them.

BEARING: a smoothly finished round metal sleeve, or a sleeve with smoothly finished metal balls or rollers, to reduce the friction between two parts. In an engine and other components a simple sleeve may be split in two half-circle sections for ease of installation. Also see **BUSHING.**

BEARING CAP: a bolt-down cap used to hold a crankshaft and bearing in position.

BELLHOUSING: the area behind the engine, covered by the front of the transmission, that holds the manual clutch assembly or the torque converter of an automatic transmission.

BLOCK: see **ENGINE BLOCK.**

BEVEL GEARS: a group of gears shaped like slices of a cone, which makes it possible for the axes of the gears to be nonparallel. Bevel gears are used to transmit motion through an angle.

BLEEDING: the process of eliminating air, which can form in bubbles or pockets, from a brake or clutch line by draining the fluid containing the air.

BOTTOM DEAD CENTER (BDC): The position of a piston when it reaches its lowest point in the cylinder.

BORE: the diameter of a cylinder, such as the engine's cylinders or the brake cylinders.

BRAKE BLEEDER: a valve that can be opened as part of a procedure ("bleeding") to expel air from the hydraulic braking system, so the action of the brake pedal is free of sponginess.

BRAKE CALIPER: a C-clamp-like hydraulic device with a piston or pistons to press the brake shoes against a disc to stop the wheel when the driver steps on the brake pedal.

BRAKE DRAG: failure of the brakes to release completely when the driver's foot is removed from the pedal.

BRAKE DYNAMOMETER: a device that measures the power and torque of an engine by restricting its speed (braking) so as to gauge its output.

BRAKE FADE: A deterioration in the brake system, as a result of repeated and protracted use of the brakes, which produces reduced braking efficiency or fade; it is exacerbated by heat.

BRAKE FLUID: a special fluid used in the hydraulic braking system. For automobiles, only a fluid labeled DOT 3 or DOT 4 should be used.

BRAKE LINING WEAR SENSOR: a device on a brake shoe that signals the driver when the lining of friction material on the brake shoe or pad is worn.

BRAKE MASTER CYLINDER: the source of the hydraulic pressure transmitted to the brake system at each wheel. The pressure is developed in this component by the driver stepping on the brake pedal.

BRAKE PAD: The stiff backing plate and friction material which makes contact with the rotating disc on a disc brake when the brake pedal is depressed; it is routinely replaced when excessive wear limits its effectiveness. It also may be called a brake shoe.

BRAKE SHOES: steel plates, either curved or straight, depending on the system, to which friction material called brake lining is bonded or riveted. Also see **DRUM BRAKE, DISC BRAKE,** and **BRAKE PAD.**

BREAKER POINTS: see **POINTS** and **CONDENSOR.**

BULKHEAD: A dividing panel that separates the passenger compartment from the engine (front bulkhead or cowl) and the trunk (rear bulkhead).

BUSHING: a cylindrical sleeve of metal, plastic, or rubber placed between two parts to isolate them from each other. The bushing may absorb shock or help locate the parts.

CAM: a lobe on a camshaft.

CAMBER: a mounting angle of the wheel relative to the road.

CAMSHAFT: a rotating shaft with eccentric lobes that push open the valves for each cylinder. The lobes operate against cylindrical parts called lifters, or other actuating devices called rockers.

CAMSHAFT SENSOR: a sensor that signals to the engine control module the rotational position of the camshaft. This enables the computer to more precisely time the fuel injection and ignition systems for faster starting of the engine.

CAMSHAFT TIMING BELT (OR CHAIN): the rubber belt or metal chain that transfers power from the crankshaft to the camshaft to operate it. The chain or belt must be installed so it maintains the relationship between the camshaft and crankshaft so the valves for each cylinder open and close at the right time for proper engine operation, a factor called camshaft timing.

CARBON CANISTER: a canister filled with activated charcoal. When the engine is off, it absorbs vapors from the fuel system that would otherwise cause air pollution. These vapors are drawn into the engine and burned when the engine is running.

CARBON DEPOSITS: the residue of carbon from burning fuel, which can clog grooves in pistons, combustion chambers, and valves, and cause engine hesitation and other operational maladies.

CARBON TRACKS: fine lines from burned carbon (such as from oil film) that may be found in a distributor cap. Carbon tracks may cause engine misfire.

CARBURETOR: a device that atomizes fuel in air, and meters the resulting air-fuel mixture into the intake manifold. It also includes a throttle body. The carburetor is not used today on other than some racing cars.

CARBURETOR-AIR HORN: the top part of the carburetor, in which the choke is located.

CARBURETOR BASE: the lower part of the carburetor, in which the throttle plate is located.

CARBURETOR CHOKE: see **CHOKE.**

CARBURETOR CLEANER: a petroleum solvent for cleaning the carburetor.

CARBURETOR FLOAT: a device much like the float in a household toilet tank that regulates the amount of fuel in the carburetor fuel bowl.

CARBURETOR FUEL BOWL: a small fuel storage area in the carburetor, at the carburetor fuel inlet. Also called the float bowl because it contains the carburetor float.

CARBURETOR FUEL BOWL VENT: a vent on the bowl. It typically is connected to a carbon canister, which absorbs vapors when the engine is off, and it also may be vented to the atmosphere when the engine is running.

CARBURETOR FUEL INLET: the threaded fitting on the side of the carburetor, to which tubing from the fuel pump is connected. Fuel enters the carburetor at this point.

CARBURETOR NEEDLE AND SEAT VALVE: a valve at the carburetor fuel inlet that is controlled by the up-and-down movement of the carburetor float. When open, it allows fuel to enter the carburetor fuel bowl. When closed, it stops the flow of fuel.

CASTER: an angular relationship between a wheel and its suspension.

CATALYTIC CONVERTER: a component in the exhaust system in which harmful emissions are converted to water and carbon dioxide.

CAVITATION: A condition found in fuel and water pumps as well as fluid couplings in which a partial vacuum forms around the wheels or blades of a pump, lowering the pump's output due to the loss of contact between the blade and the fluid it is pumping.

CHASSIS: the frame or floor pan, suspension, brakes, and steering of a car.

CHECK ENGINE LIGHT (ALSO CALLED MALFUNCTION INDICATOR LAMP): a dashboard light that goes on when the engine control module indicates a failure. It may also be capable of indicating diagnostic trouble codes.

CHLOROFLUOROCARBONS (CFC): The best known of this class of chemicals was R-12 (a popular brand was Freon), which had been used as a refrigerant in a car's air conditioning system but which was phased out due to its negative impact on the earth's ozone layer. It was replaced by R-134a.

CHOKE: a thermostatically controlled plate/flap that pivots to restrict the flow of air through the carburetor when the engine is cold, to improve driveability by temporarily providing a rich fuel mixture. In a radio, a noise suppression device.

CIRCUIT: a complete path for the flow of electricity, such as from a battery, through wiring to a lamp motor, etc., and then back to the battery.

CLEAR FLOOD MODE: a situation in which a carburetor or fuel injection system increases the amount of air or reduces the amount of fuel when necessary to correct a problem called flooding.

CLUTCH: a device used to join moving parts together and disengage them when desired. In a car, a manual clutch, operated by a driver pedal, disengages the engine from the transmission. It consists of a disc coated with friction material, and held in place by a spring-loaded metal plate.

COIL: a winding of wire. See **IGNITION COIL**, for example.

COLD CRANKING AMPS: a measure of the electrical energy a battery can deliver to start ("crank") the engine when it is cold.

COMBUSTION CHAMBER: the area in the cylinder above the piston, where ignition of the air-fuel mixture occurs.

COMPOSITE HEADLIGHT: A non-sealed-beam headlight used in the United States since 1984, which features a separate lens and bulb, each of which can be replaced individually.

COMPRESSION (COMPRESSION STROKE): the squeezing of the air-fuel mixture by the upward movement of the piston into a small space, with the valves closed. It is one of the strokes of the engine. The greater the compression pressure (within limits), the greater is the power produced by the engine when the compressed mixture is burned on its power stroke.

COMPRESSION RATIO: the volume of the combustion chamber with the piston on its compression stroke versus the volume of the cylinder with the piston at the bottom of its stroke.

CONNECTING ROD: a rod that connects the piston to the crankshaft.

COMPRESSOR (A/C): a mechanism in an air conditioning system which draws vaporized refrigerant out of the evaporator, then pressurizes it before sending it to the condenser.

CONDENSER (A/C): a mechanism which converts the vapor in an air conditioning system into the liquid that later vaporizes to cool the air.

CONSTANT VELOCITY (CV) JOINT: a universal joint usually employed to connect the half-shafts to the hubs of front-wheel-drive cars; in a CV joint, the driving and driven portions of the joint rotate at the same (hence "constant") speed.

CONTACT: in an electric switch, the terminals that are bridged or brought together to close the switch.

COOLANT: a mixture of water and antifreeze that absorbs excess heat from the engine and dissipates it into the atmosphere.

COOLING SYSTEM: a system for circulating coolant through the engine, a radiator, and the heater using a water pump to keep the engine from running too hot, and to provide heat for the passenger compartment.

CRANK, CRANKING: the act of starting the engine, in which the starting motor turns a gear on the crankshaft to turn the flywheel fast enough for fuel and ignition systems to quickly go to work and enable the engine to continue running on its own.

CRANKCASE: The portion of the engine which contains and supports the crankshaft; it usually includes the oil pan and the lower part of the cylinder block.

CRANKSHAFT: a rotating shaft that moves the pistons up and down in the cylinders. When it is rotated by the downward force of burning air-fuel mixture oil the pistons, it provides the power that is eventually transferred through the transmission to the wheels to propel the car.

CRANKSHAFT BALANCER (ALSO CALLED HARMONIC BALANCER): a circular device in the front end of the crankshaft, designed to dampen some of the impulses from the combustion events in the cylinders.

CRANKSHAFT JOURNALS: smoothly finished circular surfaces on the crankshaft, some of which are used with bearings to mate the crankshaft to the engine block. These are called main bearing journals. Others, also with bearings, mate to the connecting rods and are called rod journals.

CRANKSHAFT SENSOR: A sensor that determines the rotational position of the crankshaft, and transmits the data to the engine control module.

CYLINDER HEAD: the top part of the engine that contains the cylinder ports, the intake and exhaust valves, on most engines the combustion chamber and on many engines, the camshaft (or two camshafts).

CYLINDER HEAD GASKET: a gasket between the cylinder head and the engine block.

CYLINDER PORTS: passages in the cylinder head, two for each cylinder—one to bring the air-fuel mixture into the cylinder, the other to carry out burned exhaust gases.

DIAGNOSTIC TROUBLE CODE (ALSO TROUBLE CODE): a number stored by the engine control module when it detects a failure in a particular electrical circuit or mechanical system it is capable of monitoring. This number is a useful guide to diagnosis.

DIELECTRIC GREASE (ALSO CALLED SILICONE DIELECTRIC GREASE): a lubricant that repels moisture and has the property of adhering very well to surfaces.

DIESELING (ALSO CALLED RUN-ON): a condition in which a gasoline engine continues to fire after the ignition has been turned off; it is usually the result of excess heat and unusually high manifold pressure.

DIFFERENTIAL: a set of gears that accepts power from the transmission and transfers it to the wheels to drive the car.

DISC BRAKE: a hydraulic braking system in which flat steel plates coated with a lining of friction material (called brake shoes or pads) are pressed by a brake caliper against the sides of a metal disc to which the wheel is attached. The friction material rubs against the sides of the disc to stop the wheel when the brakes are applied.

DISTRIBUTOR: in an ignition system, an electromechanical device that contains a sensor to signal an electronic ignition unit to activate the ignition system, and a rotor to distribute high-voltage electricity to the appropriate spark plug wire, through a cap into which the spark plug wires are fitted. The distributor has been replaced on most engines by electronic devices.

DISTRIBUTOR ADVANCE (WEIGHTS): a pair of spring-loaded centrifugal weights that cause a change in ignition timing at higher engine speeds by pivoting a plate within the distributor; on older cars only.

DISTRIBUTOR CAP: a plastic cover over the distributor. It holds the wires from the spark plugs and the ignition coil.

DISTRIBUTOR DRIVE GEAR: a gear on the distributor that meshes with a gear on the camshaft to cause a shaft in the distributor to turn. The gear is held to the shaft by a pin.

DISTRIBUTORLESS IGNITION: a form of electronic ignition in which the distributor is replaced by an electronic module and a special sensor in the engine.

DRIVEBELT: a rubber belt that transfers power from a pulley on the engine to a pulley on an accessory to operate the accessory. Also see **V-BELT.**

DRIVESHAFT: a shaft from a transmission, either to a wheel or to an axle housing, to transfer power. When used to transfer power to a rear axle housing, it also is called a propeller shaft.

DRIVETRAIN: a collection of components, including the transmission, driveshaft, differential—and any associated shafts, gears, clutches, and joints—which transmits power to the wheels.

DRUM BRAKE: a hydraulic braking system in which half-moon-shaped brake shoes are pushed by pistons in a wheel cylinder against the inside cylindrical surface of a part called the drum, to which the wheel is attached. The brake shoes are coated with a lining of friction material that rubs against the drum surface to stop the wheel when the brakes are applied.

DUAL BRAKING SYSTEM: a braking system which features independent hydraulic circuits for each pair of wheels (divided into front/back or diagonal front/back pairs).

DYNAMIC BALANCING: the process whereby an automotive part, usually a wheel or crankshaft, is balanced so as to correct the tendency of an out-of-balance part to rock or vibrate. The dynamic balancing solution to such rotational problems—as opposed to the method of "static balancing"—is to introduce a counterweight to offset the irregularities.

DYNAMOMETER: A device used to measure horsepower and torque. When applied to an engine it measures the power transmitted to the flywheel; when applied to a chassis, it measures the power transmitted to the wheels.

ECM: see **ENGINE CONTROL MODULE.**

ECU: electronic control unit. It is the "brain" for an electronically-controlled system. One for an engine is called an **ECM**.

EGR: see **EXHAUST GAS RECIRCULATION.**

ELECTROLYTE: A solution used in automobile batteries to conduct electricity; voltage and current are generated when the solution comes into contact with the material on the battery plates. The electrolyte used in batteries is composed of distilled water and sulfuric acid.

ELECTROMAGNETIC PICKUP: see **PICKUP.**

ELECTRONIC IGNITION: the modern type of ignition system, in which electronic components replace some of the electromechanical switches previously used. On newer cars it refers to **DISTRIBUTORLESS IGNITION**.

ELECTRONIC IGNITION MODULE: see **IGNITION CONTROL MODULE.**

EMERGENCY BRAKE (ALSO CALLED PARKING BRAKE): A separate and independent braking system to be used as a backup system in the event of a failure in the primary braking system or to assist in holding the car stationary when parked. A pedal or hand lever is the normal mode of engaging the emergency brake, which is connected mechanically to either the front or rear brakes, although an electric motor and ECU applies the parking brake on some new cars.

EMISSIONS (EXHAUST): those compounds in the exhaust gases that are harmful to air quality. Typically measured are carbon monoxide and and unburned hydrocarbons (gasoline particles), and even oxides of nitrogen, which is a component of groundlevel "smog."

ENGINE BLOCK: the lower part, of the engine, in which the cylinders, pistons, and crankshaft are located.

ENGINE CONTROL MODULE (ECM): the electronic computer that takes readings from various electronic sensors on the engine and possibly the transmission, and performs such functions as controlling idle speed, turning on the air conditioning, regulating fuel mixture and ignition timing and triggering various emission control devices, such as exhaust gas recirculation and the fuel vapor control system.

ENGINE IDLE SPEED: the rotational speed at which the engine runs when the driver's foot is off the gas pedal. The speed is regulated by the engine control module on late-model cars.

ENGINE MOUNTS: The supports that connect the transmission and engine to the car's chassis. Composed of rubber and steel, the engine mounts absorb the motion (twisting, vibrating, etc.) produced by the operation of the engine and transmission; they also assist in reducing the noise and motion transmitted to the passenger compartment. The most efficient recently developed mounts are hydraulic, in some cases electronically-controlled.

ENGINE OIL GALLERY: a series of passages, usually drilled, through which oil circulates to key sections of the engine and to the crankshaft.

ENGINE OVERHEATING: occurs when the coolant in the cooling system is so hot the metals in the engine are at a temperature that may cause damage to them. In addition, the engine runs poorly and usually stalls.

EVAPORATIVE EMISSIONS CANISTER: See **CARBON CANISTER**.

EXHAUST GAS RECIRCULATION (EGR): a system featuring the EGR valve, that controls a portion of the exhaust gas flow. It meters a small amount of burned gases from the exhaust system back into the cylinders to combine with the air-fuel mixture, diluting it. This reduces the fuel mixture combustion temperatures, to reduce formation of oxides of nitrogen.

EXHAUST MANIFOLD: a component with chambers that carry burned exhaust gases from the cylinders into pipes that allow them to flow to the catalytic converter and through that to the muffler and tailpipe.

EXHAUST STROKE: when the piston is moving up in the cylinder, the exhaust valve is open and burned gases are being pushed out into the exhaust system.

EXHAUST SYSTEM: the series of parts that carries burned gases from the cylinder head of the engine out into the atmosphere. It includes one or two exhaust manifolds, on recent-model cars typically one or two catalytic converters, interconnecting pipes, a muffler, and a final pipe called the tailpipe.

EXHAUST VALVE: a valve that when open allows the flow of burned gases from the air-fuel mixture to travel into the exhaust system

FAN BELT: a rubber band used to transmit power from a crankcase-driven pulley to the pulleys driving the fan, alternator, power steering pump, air conditioning pump, etc. It is usually composed of rubber reinforced by steel or cord to minimize the risk of stretching. It may have a V-shaped cross-section or a multi-V shape across the underside (a design called a ribbed belt).

FEELER GAUGE: a blade or piece of wire of predetermined and carefully calibrated thickness, used to measure the gap between two parts. It is most often used as the tool to determine the clearance between a spark plug's inner and outer electrodes.

FIRING ORDER: the sequence in which spark is delivered to the cylinders, which are numbered according to position in the engine. The sequence is determined by what is necessary to provide a smooth flow of power to the crankshaft. A firing order for a six-cylinder engine might be 1-5-3-6-2-4.

FLOODING: a condition in which there is excess fuel flowing from the carburetor or fuel injectors. It may cause the engine to stall or run poorly.

FLUSHING TEE: a device with three hose necks laid out in the shape of the letter T that is spliced into a heater hose, secured with hose clamps. The neck on the stem is covered with a threaded cap, which is removed and a household water hose is attached (with a special adapter) to run water through the cooling system to flush out dirt, rust, etc.

FLYWHEEL: a heavy wheel at the rear of the crankshaft that smooths out its transfer of power to the transmission. It has a gear around its circumference, which meshes with a gear on the starter so the turning of the starter cranks the engine. On automatic transmission cars, it is a thin steel plate, to which the torque converter is attached.

FOUR-STROKE ENGINE: the typical auto engine, with intake, compression, power, and exhaust strokes to form one complete cycle in two complete revolutions of the engine.

FUEL-AIR MIXTURE: see **AIR-FUEL MIXTURE.**

FUEL FILTER: a filter to remove dirt and some water from the fuel. If the filter is installed in the line between the fuel pump and the carburetor or fuel injection system, it is called an in-line filter.

FUEL INJECTION: a system that uses fuel injectors to deliver fuel to the cylinders. Also see **MULTIPORT FUEL INJECTION** and **THROTTLE-BODY FUEL INJECTION**.

FUEL INJECTOR: a device that sprays fuel into a cylinder port or a throttle body. Although most injectors are electromechanical devices, some are purely mechanical.

FUEL PRESSURE: the pressure, measured in pounds per square inch or kilopascals, of the fuel in the line from the fuel pump to the carburetor or fuel injection system. It is measured with a special gauge.

FUEL PUMP: a pump that draws fuel from the tank and delivers it under pressure to the carburetor or fuel injection system. It may be mechanical, operated by the engine, or electrical.

FUEL RAIL: in a multiport fuel injection system, a line of tubing at the engine to which the fuel injectors are attached and from which they receive the fuel they inject into the cylinder ports.

GASKET: a flat material designed to compensate for irregularities and therefore prevent leaks between mating surfaces.

GEARBOX: a housing with gears, such as a transmission.

GENERATOR: a device powered by a drivebelt that converts the mechanical energy of the engine into electrical energy for electrical devices and to recharge the car battery.

GOVERNOR: a mechanical, electrical, or hydraulic device used to restrict the maximum speed of a vehicle in order to reduce wear and tear on the engine and drivetrain and make the operation of the vehicle safer.

GREASE FITTING: a small nipple containing a spring-loaded valve, threaded into a part that needs periodic lubrication with grease. The nipple is shaped to accept the tip of the grease gun.

GREASE GUN: a service tool that injects grease, usually into a grease fitting, but also into hinge joints.

GROUNDING (SUCH AS GROUNDING A TESTER): attaching a wire (such as from a tester) to a ground, a metal part of the engine or car body, or the negative terminal of the car battery.

GROUNDS: the negative terminals of modern automotive circuits. Typically, the engine and metal car body serve this purpose. They provide a complete circuit back to the battery without the need to run many wires to the battery itself.

HALF SHAFT: either of two rotating shafts that connect the transaxle to the wheels in a front-wheel drive car. Half shafts may be either solid or tubular in construction.

HALL (EFFECT) SWITCH: an electronic switch often used as a sensor, such as a type of pickup.

HARNESS: see **WIRING HARNESS.**

HEAD GASKET: see **CYLINDER HEAD GASKET.**

HESITATION: a condition in which the car's engine fails to respond promptly during acceleration.

HYDRAULIC BRAKING SYSTEM: this is the braking system on every modern car. When the driver steps on the pedal, he/she pushes on a piston inside a brake master cylinder filled with fluid. This motion is transferred through the fluid in lines to each wheel, where a disc or drum brake stops the wheel. Use of fluid under pressure to perform work is called hydraulics. On some new cars, an electronic system controls the hydraulic system.

HYDROMETER: a tester for measuring the freeze protection of the engine coolant as well as the specific gravity of battery electrolyte.

IDLE SPEED: see **ENGINE IDLE SPEED.**

IGNITION COIL: a voltage transformer for the ignition system. It converts the 12-volt current from the battery into the high voltage necessary to fire across the spark plugs. The voltage needed typically ranges from under 10,000 to as much as 50,000 volts.

IGNITION CONTROL MODULE: an electronic module that controls the ignition system, perhaps in conjunction with the engine control module.

IGNITION PICKUP: see **PICKUP.**

IGNITION PRIMARY: the low-voltage part of the ignition circuit, such as part of the ignition coil wiring, the pickup, electronic ignition module, and engine control module.

IGNITION SECONDARY: the high-voltage part of the ignition circuit, such as part of the ignition coil wiring, spark plugs, spark plug wires, distributor cap, and rotor.

IGNITION SYSTEM: a group of components in a circuit that transforms the 12-volt battery electricity to approximately 10,000-50,000 volts, and delivers that electricity to each cylinder at the correct instant to ignite the air-fuel mixture.

IGNITION TIMING: See **TIMING.**

INLET SOCK: a coarse fuel filter in an older fuel tank, designed to remove only very large dirt particles; it can last the life of the car.

INTAKE MANIFOLD: a component with passages that lead from the throttle body to the combustion chamber intake port for each cylinder. It carries the air-fuel mixture on engines with carburetors or throttle-body fuel injection, or just the air on engines with a fuel injector at each cylinder (multiport fuel injection).

INTAKE STROKE: when the piston is going down in the cylinder, and the intake valve is open, so the downward movement creates a vacuum that draws in air-fuel mixture.

INTAKE VALVE: a valve that when open allows the flow of air-fuel mixture through the cylinder port into the cylinder.

JUMPED TIME: a situation in which ignition or camshaft timing is incorrect because of a mechanical malfunction.

JUMPER: a wire with a clip at each end. It is used to make a temporary electrical connection.

KNOCK: a knocking sound. It may be produced by worn engine parts, by an ignition system with excessive spark advance, or by low-octane gasoline.

KNOCK SENSOR: a device that senses knock and reports this to the engine control module, which adjusts ignition timing to eliminate it.

LAMINATED WINDSHIELD: a windshield, standard on all American cars, composed of two sheets of glass with a thin layer of plastic between them to keep the windshield from splintering.

LATERAL RUNOUT: a condition in which a wheel wobbles from side to side as it rotates.

LEAF SPRING: a type of spring composed of a flat strip or several long, slightly curved flexible steel or fiberglass leaves (plates). Leaf springs are commonly used in conjunction with the rear axle of trucks.

LEAN FUEL MIXTURE: an air-fuel mixture that contains an excessive amount of air, and thus affects combustion of the mixture in the cylinders.

MALFUNCTION INDICATOR LAMP: See **CHECK ENGINE LIGHT.**

MACPHERSON STRUT: an oversized shock absorber first developed by Earle MacPherson at Ford. It replaces the upper control and ball joint when used on the front suspension; some have removable internal components that can be easily replaced.

MANIFOLD HEAT CONTROL VALVE: a thermostatic valve that controls the flow of exhaust gases so they heat the air-fuel mixture for better driveability when the engine is cold. It was used on engines with carburetors.

MAP SENSOR: a variable resistor used to monitor engine load and accordingly adjust spark timing and fuel mixture.

MASS AIRFLOW SENSOR: a sensor that measures the amount of air flowing to the throttle body in a fuel injection system and reports this information to the engine control module.

MICROMETER: a precision measuring instrument.

MICROPROCESSOR: a small computer.

MID-ENGINE: an engine whose location is wholly or in part within the wheelbase. Due to the more even distribution of weight that it produces, the mid-engine is frequently used in racing and high-performance vehicles.

MISFIRE: erratic operation of an engine caused by failure of one or more cylinders to contribute power. The problem could be in a mechanical system, in the air-fuel delivery, or in the ignition system.

MISS: see **MISFIRE.**

MUFFLER: a part of the exhaust system that contains baffles or special materials to muffle the sound of exhaust gases moving out of the engine.

MULTIPORT FUEL INJECTION (ALSO CALLED MULTIPOINT FUEL INJECTION): a gasoline delivery system in which there is one injector for each cylinder, and that injector is located at the cylinder port.

OHM: the measurement of resistance in an electrical circuit. See **RESISTANCE**; also **AMPS** and **VOLTS.**

OHMMETER: a meter that reads resistance, measured in ohms, in an electrical circuit or wire.

OIL PAN: a removable receptacle that is located at the bottom of the cylinder block and contains the engine's oil.

OIL PUMP: the pump that circulates oil to all the moving parts of an engine. Usually driven from the crankcase by gears or cams, the oil pump is also fitted with an inlet screen to filter the oil before it enters the pump.

OPEN CIRCUIT: a wiring circuit that is interrupted, such as by an open switch, a bad wiring connection, or an internal break in the wiring.

ORIGINAL EQUIPMENT MANUFACTURER (OEM): a generic term that refers to an automobile company or supplier which manufactures the parts used in the original assembly of a car.

O-RING: a type of sealing ring with a cross-section shaped like the letter O, often made of rubber.

OUT OF ROUND: a condition in which a brake drum has lost its original shape due to inconsistent wearing, warping, etc.; a drum that is out of round will produce pulsing, grabby brakes.

OVERHEAD-CAMSHAFT: a type of engine in which the camshaft is mounted in the cylinder head. This design eliminates the use of pushrods.

OVERHEAD VALVE: a type of engine with a camshaft mounted in the engine block, operating valves in the cylinder head through a "train" of valve lifters resting on camshaft lobes, pushrods transmitting the lifting force from the camshaft to rocker arms that pivot to open the overhead valves. Also called "valve in head."

OXIDES OF NITROGEN: an exhaust emission formed by nitrogen in the air at very high fuel mixture combustion temperatures in the combustion chamber.

OXYGEN SENSOR: an electronic device threaded into the exhaust system to measure oxygen content in the exhaust gases. High content usually indicates a lean fuel mixture was burned in the combustion chamber; low content usually indicates a rich fuel mixture.

PASSIVE RESTRAINT: any safety device which restrains the movement of passengers inside a car but which requires no action on the part of the passenger to do so; the most common examples are seat belts and airbags.

PCV: see **POSITIVE CRANKCASE VENTILATION.**

PICKUP: the sensor in the ignition system's distributor. Also a term that may be applied to any sensor or sending unit.

PINTLE: the tip of some types of valves.

PISTON: a cylindrical cap-shaped part that moves from one end to the other in a cylinder, such as in an engine to compress the air-fuel mixture. When the piston moves down under pressure from the burning, expanding mixture, it turns the crankshaft. A piston may also be used to transfer hydraulic force, as in the hydraulic braking system

PISTON SLAP: a slapping noise in the engine caused by piston wear.

PISTON RING: a thin open-ended ring that is installed in a groove on the outer diameter of a piston in order to create a seal between the piston and the associated cylinder and prevent any oil from entering the combustion chamber. Most pistons have three rings, two for compression sealing and one for oil control.

PLASTIGAGE: a plastic material that compresses to the thickness of the clearance between a crankshaft journal and a bearing when the bearing retaining cap is installed, so the clearance can be checked against specifications.

POINTS AND CONDENSER: a simple electromechanical system in which a distributor-controlled switch (the points) and an electrical charge storage device (the condenser) were the control parts for an automobile ignition system. They were replaced by electronic components beginning in the 1960s, although some cars had points and condenser in the early 1980s.

POSITIVE CRANKCASE VENTILATION (PCV): an emissions control system for unburned gasoline droplets that slip past the piston rings and go into the engine crankcase. A PCV valve controls the flow of the unburned fuel back into the cylinders for burning, so that the flow increases with engine speed. If the valve is stuck open, it can upset the engine idle speed.

POWER BRAKE: a device that provides an assist to the driver when the brake pedal is depressed. Although most power brake units are vacuum operated, some use hydraulic pressure.

POWER STROKE: occurs when the piston is pushed down by the expansion of the burning air-fuel mixture in the cylinder.

POWERTRAIN CONTROL MODULE: an engine control module that also controls the automatic transmission.

PREIGNITION: ignition of the air-fuel mixture in the cylinders that occurs prior to the arrival of the spark. It may be caused by a hot spot in the combustion chamber.

PUSHROD: a part of the engine valve system in a "pushrod valve" arrangement. In this system (see **CAMSHAFT**) the camshaft is in the middle of the engine and the pushrod rests in the lifter. The opposite end of the pushrod pushes against a device in the cylinder head called a rocker, which pivots to push open a valve.

RADIATOR: a heat exchanger that dissipates into the atmosphere the heat absorbed by the coolant as it circulates through the engine.

RAM TUBES: tubes of a specific length and shape in the intake manifold that promote performance at certain engine speeds by "ramming" air into the cylinders.

RECHARGE: as in to recharge a battery, which means to restore the electrical energy dissipated in starting the engine and other uses.

REFRIGERANT: the substance used in an air conditioning system that absorbs, carries, and releases heat as it changes from a liquid to a gas and back to a liquid again. The most commonly used refrigerant currently in use is R134a, although older vehicles still may have R-12.

RELAY: an electrical switching device that allows a small amount of current in one circuit to control a much larger flow of current in another circuit.

RESISTANCE: a measurement, in a unit called ohms, of the resistance of electricity to flow in a circuit. It equals the voltage in that circuit divided by the amperes.

RESISTOR: a device that restricts the flow of current in a circuit.

RICH FUEL MIXTURE: an air-fuel mixture that contains more fuel than is necessary for efficient combustion in the cylinders, and so reduces gas mileage. A rich mixture, however, may be necessary for easier cold starting.

ROCKER (ALSO CALLED ROCKER ARM): a pivot installed in the cylinder head. When one end is pushed, the rocker pivots to push open a valve.

ROTOR: another name for the disc in a braking system. See **DISC BRAKE**. Also the term for a rotating part inside the ignition distributor, which serves to distribute high-voltage electricity to the spark plug wires.

RPM: revolutions per minute, the measurement of engine speed.

RUN-ON: the tendency of an engine to run for a brief period after the ignition key is turned off. Also called dieseling and after-run. It may be caused by an engine malfunction or low-octane gasoline.

SAFETY STAND (ALSO CALLED JACK STAND): a device that can be securely locked at a choice of heights, so it can be placed under specific parts of the car underbody to support the weight of the car that has been raised with a jack, and keep the car safely in place.

SCHRADER-TYPE VALVE: a valve with a spring-loaded pin, in which the pin is depressed to open the valve. A Schrader-type valve is used at each tire, on most air-conditioning systems, and on some fuel injection systems. Schrader is a manufacturer of this type of valve.

SENDING UNIT: a device that senses something. On the car it may sense oil pressure in the engine, coolant temperature, air temperature, transmission oil temperature, and fuel level.

SENSOR: a sending unit. Also an electronic device that senses something and reports its reading to an electronic control unit, such as an engine control module. See **OXYGEN SENSOR, THROTTLE POSITION SENSOR, MASS AIRFLOW SENSOR.**

SHOCK ABSORBER: a device that forces fluid through narrow openings to dissipate the energy absorbed by the car's springs when the wheels ride over bumps in the road.

SHOES: see **BRAKE SHOES.**

SHORT CIRCUIT (OR SHORTED CIRCUIT): a wiring circuit that ends short of its completed path because of a wiring fault.

SOLENOID: an electromagnetic switch with an arm or a shaft that can perform a mechanical function when electricity is applied. Most fuel injectors contain a solenoid.

SPARK: in an engine, the high-voltage electricity that jumps an air gap in a spark plug. A check of the delivery of this spark from the end of the spark plug wire is called a **CHECK FOR SPARK** and is a basic automotive test when an engine fails to start.

SPARK ADVANCE: a change in ignition timing, so it occurs earlier than it did, for better performance. Timing may be set back ("retarded") to prevent knock. See **SPARK RETARD.**

SPARK KNOCK: see **KNOCK.**

SPARK PLUG: a part with two electrodes, with a ceramic between them as an insulator, and the electrode tips separated by an air gap, threaded into each cylinder. When high-voltage electricity is applied, it jumps through the air gap between the electrode tips and ignites the air-fuel mixture.

SPARK PLUG BOOT: the nipple end of the plug wire jacket. It covers the terminal on the end of the plug itself.

SPARK PLUG CABLE: another common name for spark plug wire.

SPARK PLUG ELECTRODE: one of two electrical contacts at the tip of a conventional spark plug. The spark is the high-voltage arc that bridges the air gap between them.

SPARK PLUG HEAT RANGE: a spark plug design factor. It refers to the spark plug's ability to dissipate heat.

SPARK PLUG WIRE (ALSO CALLED IGNITION WIRE): a wire with thick rubber insulation that carries the high-voltage spark from the ignition coil to the spark plug.

SPARK RETARD: a change in ignition timing so it occurs later than it previously did, either because of a malfunction or intentionally to stop engine knock caused by the ignition system.

SPEC, SPECIFICATION: a number that is a standard of performance or service adjustment.

STARTER, STARTING MOTOR: the motor that is activated by battery current to start the engine.

STARTER RELAY: a relay used in the starting system.

STARTER SOLENOID: a solenoid used in the starting system, typically built onto the starting motor.

STEERING BOX: a gearbox which converts the circular motion of a steering wheel into the motion of the steering arms, knuckles, and wheels. It is located near the bottom of the steering shaft.

STROKE: the distance a piston travels from bottom dead center to top dead center.

SUSPENSION: a system of bars, springs, and shock absorbers to which the wheels are attached, and which supports the car body and the underbody frame on which it may sit.

TACHOMETER: an instrument for measuring rpm.

TAILPIPE: a pipe that follows the muffler and is the end of the exhaust system.

TEMPERATURE-SENSITIVE BIMETAL COIL: a part made of dissimilar metals that cause the coil to flex with changes in temperature. The flexing bimetal can operate a temperature-sensitive device, such as a carburetor choke, or the hydraulic circuit in most non-electric radiator fans.

TEST LIGHT: a device used to test electrical circuits. It contains a bulb or electronic equivalent, such as a light-emitting diode (LED), that goes on when a circuit is complete and carrying electricity.

THERMODYNAMICS: the science that deals with heat and heat transfer.

THERMOSTAT: a temperature-sensitive valve that regulates the flow of coolant between radiator and engine.

THERMOSTATIC AIR CLEANER: an air cleaner housing with a flap valve that is controlled by a thermostatic device. In one position, it ducts hot air from the area of the exhaust system into the engine for smooth operation when the engine is cold. In the other position, it ducts cool, more dense air from the front of the car into the engine when it is warm for more power. It was used on engines with carburetors.

THERMOSTATIC SWITCH: a switch that opens or closes at a certain temperature.

THROTTLE BODY: the part of the fuel system that holds a flat, generally round plate (the throttle valve) that regulates the flow of air into the cylinders in response to how much the driver steps down on the accelerator. The throttle body may be part of a fuel injection or carburetor fuel system. Regulating the air flow controls the speed of the engine and therefore the amount of power it produces.

THROTTLE-BODY FUEL INJECTION: a simplified fuel injection system with one or two fuel injectors positioned above the throttle valve.

THROTTLE POSITION SENSOR: a sensor that determines how far the gas pedal has been depressed, and delivers that information to the engine control module.

THRUST ANGLE: a locational relationship between the front and rear sets of wheels.

TIE ROD: a rod which is part of the steering system and links the steering knuckles to the steering rack or a center link.

TIME: the state of timing. See **JUMPED TIME.**

TIMING: the regulation of the ignition system such that it produces a spark at the spark plug at the correct instant for combustion; the regulation of the camshaft such that it opens and closes the valves to admit air-fuel mixture and allow exhaust gases to exit the cylinder.

TIMING GUN: see **TIMING LIGHT.**

TIMING LIGHT: a special type of light that when aimed at a mark on a rotating part lights only when a spark plug is triggered, so the mark seems to stand still. The instantaneous alignment of this mark with a fixed mark on the engine permits a check of ignition timing, and adjustment if necessary. See **TIMING MARKS.**

TIMING MARKS: a fixed mark on the engine and a second mark on a part that turns with the crankshaft (such as a belt pulley in front or the engine flywheel in the rear). When these marks align (as checked with a timing light) is an indication of the adjustment of the ignition system. Many late-model vehicles, with computer controls of timing, do not have these marks.

TOE: a measurement of whether the wheels at front or rear point toward each other (called toe-in) or away (called toe-out).

TOP DEAD CENTER (TDC): when the piston is at the very top of its upward movement.

TORQUE CONVERTER: a fluid-filled device with fanlike members that couples an engine to an automatic transmission.

TORQUE WRENCH: a wrench with a dial that reads in a measurement of twisting force, such as pound-feet or ounce-inches, or their metric equivalent, such as Newton-meter, abbreviated N-m.

TORSION BAR: a spring in the shape of a bar. It has been used in the suspensions of many cars.

TORX: a type of screwhead that requires a specific size Torx wrench to be loosened or tightened.

TRANSAXLE: a transmission/axle combination, most often found in front-wheel drive cars, in which the clutch, gearbox, and differential are all housed in a single unit.

TRANSMISSION: a component with gears and shafts that takes the power of the engine and transmits it, through external shafts, to the wheels to move the car. The gears have different ratios to move the car at different speeds.

TRIGGER WHEEL: in the ignition system, a wheel with flat, square "teeth," operated by a shaft in the distributor. It often is used to trigger a Hall-effect pickup to produce a signal to the engine control module.

TROUBLE CODE: see **DIAGNOSTIC TROUBLE CODE.**

TVRS WIRE: a type of resistance wire used for spark plug wires. It minimizes ignition system interference with the radio and other electronic components on the car.

UNIVERSAL JOINT (U-JOINT, ALSO CALLED CARDAN JOINT): a flexible coupling using a double yoke and a four-point cross. It is used most commonly to connect the driveshaft to the transmission and the differential in a front-engine rear-drive car.

VACUUM: pressure that is lower than atmospheric, produced by the engine or a pumping device, measured in inches or millimeters (mm) of mercury. The engine produces about 17-22 inches (approximately 430-560 mm) at engine idle speed. Engine vacuum normally is measured at a hose neck on the intake manifold.

VACUUM GAUGE: a gauge that measures vacuum, such as that produced by an engine.

VACUUM HOSE: a hose that connects a source of vacuum, such as on the engine's intake manifold, to a device that uses it, such as a power brake unit.

VACUUM LEAK: a loss of vacuum from a leaking hose or defective gasket.

VALVE CLEARANCE: an air gap that exists between the tip of a valve and the part that opens it when the valve is fully closed. In some engines this gap is adjustable and must be set to specifications.

VALVE LIFTER: a valve train component. In OHV (overhead valve) engines, the lifter is positioned between the cam lobe and the pushrod. In some overhead camshaft engines, the lifter is positioned between the cam lobe and the valve stem.

VALVE SEAT: a surface in the combustion chamber, against which a valve seats when closed.

VALVE SPRING: a spring that keeps an engine valve closed until pushed open by a rocker or by the valve lifter.

VALVE TRAIN: the system of parts that operates (and includes) the intake and exhaust valves.

V-BELT: a drivebelt with the cross-sectional shape of the letter V that rides in a similarly shaped pulley. Also see **DRIVEBELT.**

VOLTS (OR VOLTAGE): a measurement of electrical pressure. The automobile today uses an electrical system that operates on approximately 12 volts. Most engine control modules and their associated parts contain both 5-volt and 12-volt circuits. A car's ignition system typically develops about 10,000-50,000 volts. Also see **AMPS** and **OHMS.**

VOLTMETER: a test meter that measures volts.

V-TYPE ENGINE: an engine with two banks of cylinders set at an angle, such as a V4, V6, V8, V10, V12, and V16. The number following the V is the total number of cylinders, such as two banks of two cylinders in a V4.

WATER JACKET: passages in an engine through which coolant is circulated.

WATER PUMP: a small pump, driven by a pulley, which circulates coolant through the cooling system; it can be driven by the fan belt, alternator belt, or overhead cam timing belt or chain.

WHEEL ALIGNMENT: adjustment of the suspension and steering of a car so it rides straight down the road and responds predictably in turns. The measurements adjusted or checked include **TOE, CASTER, CAMBER,** and **THRUST ANGLE.**

WHEEL BEARING: a ball or roller bearing assembly that supports whatever part to which the wheel is mounted, so the wheel can spin freely as the car rolls down the road. See **BEARING.**

WHEEL CHOCK: a triangular piece of metal or wood that can be wedged between a tire and the ground to keep the car from rolling.

WHEEL SPINDLE: a flange that holds the wheel bearing assembly. It may be the end of a driveshaft.

WIRING DIAGRAM: a diagram that shows how the wires in the car, or an individual circuit, are connected to components and to one another.

WIRING HARNESS: a group of wires bundled together and covered by a protective jacket.

WIRING HARNESS CONNECTOR: a single connector with many terminals for electrical wiring connections.

INDEX

E

F

G

H